PRAISE FROM AROUND THE WORLD FOR *MARKET MASTERS*

"The words of wisdom from the Market Masters are priceless. They offer guiding principles and lessons for anyone who is interested in the stock market. Whether you are a long-term investor or a short-term trader, this book is an essential read."

— RONALD W. CHAN, FOUNDER AND CIO OF CHARTWELL CAPITAL LTD., AND AUTHOR OF *THE VALUE INVESTORS: LESSONS FROM THE WORLD'S TOP FUND MANAGERS*

"I have found that the best path to stock market success for individuals is to follow the written strategies of legendary investors with a proven track record. Robin Speziale has identified 28 legendary investors in the Canadian stock market and captured in writing the essence of their strategies in his tour de force, Market Masters."

— JOHN REESE, CEO OF VALIDEA CAPITAL MANAGEMENT AND *GLOBE AND MAIL* COLUMNIST

"Robin Speziale has written a fascinating book. The interview with the elusive Francis Chou alone makes it worth it to buy the book."

— MOHNISH PABRAI, FOUNDER AND MANAGING PARTNER OF PABRAI INVESTMENT FUNDS, AND AUTHOR OF *THE DHANDHO INVESTOR*

"A wonderful resource for anyone who wants to study some of Canada's world-class investors."

— GUY SPIER, MANAGING PARTNER OF AQUAMARINE CAPITAL, AND AUTHOR OF *THE EDUCATION OF A VALUE INVESTOR*

"Robin Speziale's new book, Market Masters, provides a wealth of insight into what it takes to succeed as an investor from a group of renowned Canadian investors. I think every investor would benefit from reading the book. Find out what group of 'Master Keys' fits your investment personality and then, if you can, rigorously implement them in a systematic, unemotional way. If you manage to conquer your emotions and use some of the plethora of ideas from this book, you'll be well ahead of the majority of investors."

— JAMES P. O'SHAUGHNESSY, AUTHOR OF *WHAT WORKS ON WALL STREET*

"Only a few investors become great, and they take different paths to get there. For an investor who wants to be successful, this book provides not just the recipe that these investors used to get to success, but also insight into their beliefs, blind

spots, and investment philosophies. I recommend it to those who want to get past cookbook models and to develop their own ways of thinking about markets and investing."

— ASWATH DAMODARAN, PROFESSOR OF CORPORATE FINANCE AND VALUATION AT THE STERN SCHOOL OF BUSINESS AT NEW YORK UNIVERSITY, AND AUTHOR OF *DAMODARAN ON VALUATION*

"One of the most effective ways to improve as an investor is to focus on process through understanding the processes of better investors. In Market Masters, *Speziale has collected Canada's best, and provided a rare glimpse into their methods. The invaluable insights available here will help any investor get better."*

— TOBIAS CARLISLE, FOUNDER AND MANAGING PARTNER, CARBON BEACH ASSET MANAGEMENT, AND AUTHOR OF *DEEP VALUE* AND *QUANTITATIVE VALUE*

"I have been in the investment business for more than three decades, and there is still much one can learn from Market Masters. *This book should be part of your personal investment library."*

— CHUCK CARLSON, CFA, AUTHOR OF *THE LITTLE BOOK OF BIG DIVIDENDS*

"This book is full of useful nuggets."

— VITALIY KATSENELSON, CIO OF INVESTMENT MANAGEMENT ASSOCIATES INC., AND AUTHOR OF *THE LITTLE BOOK OF SIDEWAYS MARKETS*

"You excel by learning from people who are better than you. Robin Speziale's book gives you the insight on how some of the best investors think. Improve your success rate by reading this book and learning how the pros think and act."

— JOHN SCHWINGHAMER, AUTHOR OF *PURPLE CHIPS: WINNING IN THE STOCK MARKET WITH THE VERY BEST OF THE BLUE CHIP STOCKS*

*"*Market Masters *by Speziale is an excellent book and belongs on any serious investor's bookshelf. Investors are often trained in a specific discipline which is learned through apprenticeship. This readily accessible book provides insight into multiple investment disciplines through interviews with experienced practitioners. The breadth of knowledge conveyed by* Market Masters *is both unique and extraordinary."*

— MITCH ZACKS, PORTFOLIO MANAGER AT ZACKS INVESTMENT MANAGEMENT

MARKET MASTERS

PROVEN INVESTING STRATEGIES YOU CAN APPLY

INTERVIEWS WITH
CANADA'S TOP INVESTORS

ROBIN R. SPEZIALE

Public Library

Published by ECW Press
665 Gerrard Street East
Toronto, Ontario, Canada, M4M 1Y2
416-694-3348 / info@ecwpress.com

To the best of his abilities, the author has related experiences, places, people, and organizations from his memories of them.

LIBRARY AND ARCHIVES CANADA
CATALOGUING IN PUBLICATION

Speziale, Robin, 1987–, author
Market masters : interviews with Canada's top investors—proven investing strategies you can apply /
Robin R. Speziale.

Includes index.
Issued in print and electronic formats.
ISBN 978-1-77041-343-6
also issued as: 978-1-77090-887-1 (pdf);
978-1-77090-888-8 (epub)

1. Investments—Canada. 2. Capital market—Canada.
3. Finance, Personal—Canada. 4. Capitalists and financiers—Canada—Interviews.
I. Title.

HG4521.S64 2016   332.6   C2015-907794-X
C2015-907795-8

The publication of Market Masters has been generously supported by the Government of Canada through the Canada Book Fund. We also acknowledge the contribution of the Government of Ontario through the Ontario Book Publishing Tax Credit and the Ontario Media Development Corporation.

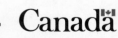

MIX
Paper from responsible sources
FSC® C016245

PRINTED AND BOUND IN CANADA   PRINTING: FRIESENS   5   4   3   2   1

TO . . .
FAMILY: MOM, DAD, AND SISTER.
GRANDPARENTS: REST IN PEACE.
ALL OF MY RELATIVES: IN CANADA,
USA, SWEDEN, AND ITALY.
FRIENDS. TEACHERS.

One percent (1%) of the proceeds from the sale of
this book will be donated to SickKids Foundation

If I have seen further than others, it is by standing upon the shoulders of giants.
— ISAAC NEWTON

It is not a case of choosing those [faces] that, to the best of one's judgment, are really the prettiest, nor even those that average opinion genuinely thinks the prettiest. We have reached the third degree, where we devote our intelligences to anticipating what average opinion expects the average opinion to be. And there are some, I believe, who practice the fourth, fifth, and higher degrees.
— JOHN MAYNARD KEYNES,
"THE KEYNESIAN BEAUTY CONTEST"

One thing I can predict: it is almost axiomatic that the wild enthusiasm of today will be met with the equally unwarranted pessimism of tomorrow.
— DAVID DREMAN

MAXIMIZE YOUR ROI FROM *MARKET MASTERS*
HOW TO GET THE MOST OUT OF THIS BOOK

- Let your mind be open. Remove any biases or preconceived notions, no matter what your level of skill, before you start to read *Market Masters*.
- Get ready. Accept that you will learn new investment ideas and refine old concepts.
- Want it. Continuously foster a desire to master the strategies that will be revealed to you by all 28 Market Masters.
- Make it yours. Highlight the most important things that you learn throughout. Dog-ear this book. Jot crucial points into a notepad. Use all the tools at your disposal so that you can quickly and easily come back to concepts later.
- Key in. After you read each chapter, hone in on the "Master Keys." These keys will ultimately help you unlock the market.
- Take breaks. Stop throughout and think: how can *this* or *that* make me money in the market? When will I apply it? What should I expect?
- Have fun. Imagine that you are there with the Market Masters. Don't rush the journey. Perhaps read one interview at a time. Soak it in, and then come back for more.
- Make connections. The Market Masters share common concepts about the market that have made them successful. Emulate them.
- Go back. After you've read *Market Masters* once, read it a second time, and then a third whenever you feel the need for guidance in a volatile market or when your portfolio seems to be in disrepair.
- Pay it forward. Recommend *Market Masters* to a relative, friend, or colleague.

FOREWORD

Knowing how to invest is an essential life skill. While the education system gives you the tools to earn an income, it rarely tells you how to make your money last and keep it from running out before you do.

I learned about investing only when I started covering mutual funds at the *Globe and Mail* and took the Canadian Securities Course (CSC). I interviewed so many money managers during my 10-year stint at the *Globe* that I finally started to understand how they valued companies and picked securities.

Robin Speziale has interviewed Canada's top money managers in depth. But instead of asking what stocks they like — "the flavour of the month" — he talked to them about the processes they use to find invest-able securities.

At the beginning of his book, Robin talks about his copious legwork. He had to pin down 28 strangers and encourage them to open up about their proprietary ideas and techniques.

Would they return his calls and emails? Would they agree to meet him?

The book you are about to read almost didn't come together. Other authors might have given up. Robin kept pushing and he pulled it off.

I said yes to Robin in 2010 when he pitched me about his self-published book, *Lessons from the Successful Investor*. By then, I had moved to the *Toronto Star* and started teaching an evening course, Investing for Beginners, at the University of Toronto's continuing studies department.

"Why don't you come talk to my students?" I said.

I wanted to see if he could think on his feet in a classroom setting.

Robin aced the audition. Still in his twenties, he had the confidence of someone much older. He paid tribute to his idol, Warren Buffett, and stayed within my time limit. That rarely happens.

I invited Robin to my class again the next year. He also gave a presentation to my investment club, Ellen's Degenerates.

Earlier this year, he asked me to do a foreword for a new book. I didn't know the scope of the project until he sent me the manuscript.

My first thought: What a great resource this is for students, instructors, and do-it-yourself investors.

My second thought: Canada has so many smart money managers. They deserve to be highlighted in something that lasts longer than a daily newspaper article or a *Market Call* show on the Business News Network.

I've interviewed some of these Market Masters (Francis Chou, Kiki Delaney, Paul Harris, Som Seif) and invited some to speak to my classes or club (Gaelan Morphet, Peter Hodson, Randy Cass, Bill Carrigan). There are also a few people I know (Derek Foster, Ross Grant, Benj Gallander) who are compelling communicators about investing, though they don't actually work in the industry.

Good job, Robin. Yours is the first Canadian book I've seen that spotlights such a wide variety of investing styles. You even included low-cost passive or index investing.

Readers, you will find this book useful and lively. Instead of going straight through until the end, you can dip in and out of the chapters as you like, learning as you go.

ELLEN ROSEMAN
PERSONAL FINANCE EXPERT AND
TORONTO STAR COLUMNIST

▲

PREFACE

▼

We in the Great White North have a lot to offer the world. And yet we usually take a back seat to our American brethren, whether in movies or politics or music. The same is true of the investment industry. While Canada is flush with experts on the markets, not much is written or said or thought about them. Why is that? Do we lack able investors? Are they all too timid? Have the best of them moved to the U.S.? In my opinion . . . none of the above. Rather, there's a lack of strong platforms to show-case the investment talent that exists in Canada. "Out of sight, out of mind," as the popular saying goes. I can't remember ever seeing a worthy made-in-Canada investment compilation on any bookshelf, whether that be in a store, house, or school. My mission in writing *Market Masters: Interviews with Canada's Top Investors* is to create a strong platform (but not *the* platform, as that would be much too grandiose), to grow awareness of Canada's Market Masters, and to share their timeless market wisdom with you, the reader. Some are well known; others not so much. Some are top-down, others bottom-up. Some are growth-oriented, others value-focused. Some are active, others passive. You get the point — these Market Masters differ in their approach. Although the 28 Market Masters featured in this book span different areas on the market paradigm, their objective (with exception of the passive investors) is all the same: to beat the market. All of the Market Masters seek to compound wealth over time, which, collectively, amounts to tens of billions of dollars.

But then the question becomes, so what; why should I care? I am aware of the common perception of the Canadian stock market, specifically the Toronto Stock Exchange (TSX), as a "primitive resource-based market." Through this book, I hope to not only debunk that misconception but also to establish why the Canadian market is essential not only to Canadian investors but to international investors, too. While some may discount the Canadian market, others capitalize on its breadth, depth, and activity to further their investment winnings. A striking example came up in my conversation with American-born Bill Ackman. "We've had a very favourable experience in Canada in pretty much everything we've done," said Bill. In another conversation, Kiki Delaney explained, "[On the TSX], there's a lot of world-class international companies."

In most people's eyes, though, the Canadian market remains "chock-full of resource stocks." As you will learn throughout this book, and as echoed by many of the Market Masters, there are many strong multinational Canadian companies on the Toronto Stock Exchange. And the exchange, in and of itself, has a storied history, and during my research I discovered facts that surprised even me.

The Canadian market is strong, resilient, and progressive.

Strong: The TSX, which is more than 150 years old, contains roughly 1,500 listings that together make up $2.575 trillion in market capitalization, with 39.7 billion shares trading hands on an annual basis. That makes the TSX the ninth-largest exchange in the world, just behind China's Shenzhen Exchange, but ahead of the German, Indian, Swiss, Australian, South Korean, Spanish, Taiwanese, and Brazilian stock exchanges. The TSX boasts the greatest number of listings of any exchange in North America and has the second-most listings worldwide.

Resilient: The Great Depression of 1929 did not have as significant an effect on Canadian trading activity, or on the brokerage business, as it did on the U.S. and its stock exchanges. Also, the TSX was not as hard hit after Bloody Monday (1987), posting a one-day loss that was half that of the U.S.'s New York Stock Exchange.

Progressive: In the late nineties, the TSX was the world's first exchange to introduce decimal trading and to install a female president, Barbara G. Stymiest, and was North America's first large exchange to move to a completely electronic trading environment. Recently, there's been a push, most likely perpetuated by investment bankers in light of a commodities bear market, to further diversify the TSX, which may be deemed a renaissance of sorts if the trend continues. For example, many significant non-resource IPOs have sprouted on the TSX: Cara Operations, Spin Master Toys, Hydro One, Sleep Country Canada, and Shopify, to name but a few.

The Canadian stock market is essential. And there's no better authorities to teach you how to capitalize on its treasures than the Market Masters I have interviewed for this book. Ignore this "dark horse," the Canadian market, at your own peril. Little may still be known about the Canadian market by the world's investors, but it will continue to succeed, whether expectedly or unexpectedly, recognized or unrecognized. Canadian stocks have exceeded the returns of international stocks (8.3%), bonds (6.2%), and T-Bills (4.6%), from 1934 to 2014. And we're not very far behind the U.S. market's compound annual return of 11.1% versus Canada's 9.8% over that same 80-year period.

The market is like a cherished childhood videogame of mine, *Pokémon*. At the start of *Pokémon*, Ash, the protagonist, is tasked by Professor Oak with choosing one of three Pokémon before starting on his epic journey: Bulbasaur or Squirtle or Charmander. For a naïve young gamer, picking just one Pokémon was quite the dilemma: which Pokémon was strong enough to actually beat the game? What I found upon playing *Pokémon* three separate times, once with each of the three characters, is that I could beat the game with *any* Pokémon. Any of the three cute characters a player chooses will achieve his or her objective, just as one can beat the market by employing any set of strategies on any part of the market paradigm. With this book at your fingertips, you can pick your favourite Market Master, or even a couple of them, to invest alongside with and beat the market. It comes down to identifying which Market Masters' strategies appeal the most to you and which of those strategies you are most comfortable using in the market. For instance, if you're a conservative person, the risks involved in growth investing most likely aren't for you. Conversely, if you thrive on risk, you may very well find value investing boring. You can be certain that at least one of the Canadian

Markets Masters featured in this book will be suitable for you. The only question is which one.

I finally started writing *Market Masters: Interviews with Canada's Top Investors* in January of 2015. The motivation was ever present as the oil crash of 2014 continued to rattle the markets, most notably Canada's market. At that time, market support levels were tested, and then broken, sending investors into a panic. While "a rising tide lifts all boats" such as when a broad bull run — a prolonged inclining market — pushes all stocks higher, there's a heightened level of skill required to navigate the markets through volatility. Luckily for me, the Canadian investors I had followed since the age of 18 taught me not only how to invest through an upward period but also through an uncertain downward period. It finally seemed the right time to start on the Market Masters journey, to capture Canada's top investors' stories and the strategies they use to beat the market.

It was soon after that glimmer of inspiration, though, that I hit a brick wall.

While I was eager to meet with and interview the chosen Market Masters for my book, only a small fraction of them actually replied to my initial letter in the mail and accepted the request for an interview. If I wanted to make this work, I thought, I would have to remain persistent. I sent another round of requests, this time via email. Only another small fraction of the Market Masters actually responded to me and agreed to the interview. For weeks to come, I would send follow-up emails, and then actually call the remaining Market Masters, to finally schedule all of the interviews. But then reality sank in once again, and my heart sank with it. I'd never interviewed anyone before.

So I researched and then practised various interview formats. I meticulously studied each and every Market Master, above and beyond what I already knew about them. I oriented the interview questions such that the actual conversations with each interviewee would be timeless, regardless of when the reader came across them, but also tailored the questions to highlight the areas that made each particular Market Master unique. I strived to elicit as many investing market strategies as I could from each of the Market Masters, to be certain that readers would actually be able to apply these strategies to make money in the markets. Also, I wanted to make sure that all of the interviews were entertaining and fun to read.

I don't want you to fall asleep, but rather to stay excitably awake in antici-pation of what you'll learn or which Market Master you'll hear from next. I want you to feel that you are actually *there* in the room with each and every Market Master, talking to him or her yourself.

Happily, all of the interviews flowed smoothly, for which I thank all of the Market Masters for being so accommodating, and my assistant, Elena Toukan, for being so thorough in transcribing. The interviews took place over a five-month period, after which point Elena transcribed and then consolidated all of the interviews into book format. Though the pile of interviews was a mess at first, the gradual finessing of the interviews and information over the next couple of months would evolve into the book you're holding now, *Market Masters*.

When you embark on the journey that is *Market Masters: Interviews with Canada's Top Investors*, you will be whisked away into a world and into the minds of Canada's incredible investors. They will share with you their own unique and intriguing stories. They'll divulge their investing philosophies, strategies, processes, successes, challenges, and outlooks. They will open your eyes to a market that you've never quite seen or experienced before. Your perspective will surely change and, in turn, your winnings in the markets will become more plentiful, predictable, and profitable. Whether you are a novice, intermediate, or advanced investor, I can guarantee that you will learn at least one new concept in this book that you can apply to the market to advance your portfolio. And if you've just started out in the market, then this book will be a treasure trove for you in that your investment journey will commence with an enviously advantageous foundation.

I hope you enjoy these exclusive conversations with Canada's Market Masters. I certainly enjoyed meeting, interviewing, and learning from all of them. To complement the interviews I've provided pre-interview les-sons that establish key concepts a reader should understand before they read through each conversation. This is especially important if you con-sider yourself a beginner investor. Also, these lessons are cumulative, so that as you progress through the book, your knowledge of these core concepts will grow, and each interview down the line will flow more easily than the one before. That is why I suggest that you read through *Market Masters* a second time to fully absorb all of the complex strategies that build on the core knowledge foundation developed on the first read-through. You can also consult the glossary at the end of the book if you come upon a term you're not sure about.

Finally, make sure to read all of the bonus material that I include at the end of the book. Especially the Collection of Master Keys section, which is a compilation of the most important things that I learned from each of the Market Masters. These Master Keys can help you unlock the market and open your world to tremendous money-making opportunities.

Health, happiness, and prosperity.

HAPPY INVESTING,
ROBIN SPEZIALE
AUGUST 6, 2015

INTRODUCTION
MEET THE MARKET MASTERS: A-Z

These are the incredible Market Masters who share their unique and intriguing stories about the market and investing.

- **BILL ACKMAN.** A prominent activist investor who isn't a Canadian but seems to have a Canadian love affair. Some of his best investment plays have involved Canadian companies — Tim Hortons, Canadian Pacific Railway, and Valeant Pharmaceuticals — that have enriched his hedge fund's results since inception: 23% annual compound return versus the S&P 500's measly 8%.

- **MARTIN BRAUN.** After years of watching the market rally as he held onto dog stocks, this former value investor turned growth investor runs a high-conviction hedge fund that has skyrocketed up 875% since inception. In its best year, his portfolio was up 57%, and if you'd invested $100,000 with him in 2000, you'd be a millionaire just 15 years later.

- **PETER BRIEGER.** An old-school money manager close to the end of his career who stresses that "time in the market and not market timing" is the key to investing success. With a career in the market spanning 50 years, he's seen the Toronto Stock Exchange go from $800 to $15,000.

- **DAVID BURROWS.** This macro top-down money manager teaches that "the trend is your friend." By astutely following shifts of capital in the market, he participates in breadth expansion, and then run-ups through multiple expansion.
- **BILL CARRIGAN.** A straight-shooting technical investor whose Twitter bio states, "With 30 years' experience in the investment industry I have learned to never get sucked into a compelling story." Bill often makes technical selections that are eventually subject to takeover bids.
- **RANDY CASS.** This former BNN *Market Sense* anchor, now a founder of a robo-advisor firm, promotes the Efficient Market Theory (EMT), and thus doesn't try to beat the market, but rather *be* the market. He explains that "nearly 80% of actively managed Canadian Equity Funds failed to perform as well as the S&P/TSX Composite." Now that's a bummer.
- **FRANCIS CHOU.** An actual early investor with this former Bell repairmen saw his $80,000 grow to $5 million and, at the age of 80, will be worth close to $60 million if compound rates stay constant. Now, this deep-value portfolio manager who likes to pay 50 cents on the dollar runs over $1 billion for his multitude of investors.
- **KIKI DELANEY.** She defied the odds early on in a largely "old boys' club" to become one of the first women in Canada to launch her own money management firm, which now boasts $2 billion in assets under management, and a consistent 20-year track record.
- **JASON DONVILLE.** An ex–navy officer whose aptitude in writing launched him into the investment industry. Today, the athletic, broad-shouldered hedge fund manager employs his strict ROE policy to crush the market — so effectively that he's closed his fund after a continuous influx of investors' money. "Don't fuck with Donville," as one raging fan says.
- **MARTIN FERGUSON.** This small-cap king has picked companies that have gone from good to great by sticking to a simple ROIC formula. It seems that all of the stocks he touches turn to gold.

The same can also be said of his analysts, who've all worked under him and then made it to the top.

- **DEREK FOSTER.** Self-proclaimed "Idiot Millionaire" who reached the $1 million mark by age 34 and retired early into a life of financial freedom and frequent vacations with his family.
- **BENJ GALLANDER.** This cool-as-a-cat, never-follow-the-herd contrarian has been beating the market since 2000, with 19% annualized returns over a 15-year period.
- **ROSS GRANT.** This early retiree was just passed the torch to run the famous Beat the TSX (BTSX) model, which has been used to beat the TSX for 28 years in a row. It's easy to implement, too.
- **PAUL HARRIS, PAUL GARDNER, BILL HARRIS.** These three amigos run a fun, hip, startup-esque money management firm. They aim to double investors' money every 10 years. Plus, they've got an obsession with risk management that saved their firm from ruin at the start of the financial crisis.
- **PETER HODSON.** The owner of *Canadian MoneySaver* was once the growth manager at Sprott Asset Management, the high-flying firm in Toronto. He likened the experience to being in the Wild West, hunting for 200% to 300% returns on individual stocks. While this cowboy's long hung up his hat from money management, he's got some insight you can use to gunsling your way to some of your biggest winners ever.
- **NORMAN LEVINE.** An opportunistic money manager who's got a knack for buying when others are selling or just not looking. He profits from both irrationality and uncertainty in the markets. And to think — he got fired from his first job.
- **JASON MANN.** With 400 highly liquid positions, half long and half short, this hedge fund manager with a bias for momentum beats the market on both sides of the trade by buying under-valued, rising, stable stocks and shorting overvalued, declining, volatile stocks.
- **CHARLES MARLEAU.** This hedge fund manager was groomed by his father to be an investment whiz kid. He's gone on to beat the market by allocating capital to stocks within industries that are leading beneficiaries to shifts in the economy.

- **GAELEN MORPHET.** A value-based money manager who uses her proprietary margin of safety model to buy stocks on the cheap and to gauge the market to make bang-on calls. In 2012, after mass volatility, she predicted a major run-up in both the TSX and S&P 500.
- **BARRY SCHWARTZ.** A money manager whose mantra is to buy competitively advantaged companies that generate "explosive" free cash flow. "I've never made a bad decision by buying into a company paying 8% or 9% free cash flow yield or higher."
- **SOM SEIF.** An engineering grad who at the tender of 27 built Claymore Investments Canada from scratch and quickly captured 15% of the exchange-traded fund (ETF) market before getting bought out by BlackRock. Today, he's created a new company with ETF strategies that strive to *be* the market.
- **RYAZ SHARIFF.** After a complete collapse in the commodities sector, following a long and glorious bull run that spawned many millionaires, multi-millionaires, and billionaires, this commodity manager is one of the last men standing. However, he's still optimistic that the next up-cycle will return with a vengeance.
- **MICHAEL SPRUNG.** A money manager who learned from some of the most prominent value investors in Canada: Prem Watsa, John Watson, Tony Hamblin, and Tony Gage.
- **JEFF STACEY.** A value money manager who employs conservative and repeatable event-driven investing strategies to supplement his long positions. He shares how to capture practically guaranteed spreads through takeovers, for example, Starbucks' takeover of Teavana.
- **CAMERON WINSER.** A multidisciplinary Head of Equities who against all odds broke into the industry with a degree in psychology. His investing approach is akin to peeling back the layers on an onion to reveal ideal stocks.
- **LORNE ZEILER.** An associate portfolio manager who travels the country in the hopes of curing stock market addicts of their seemingly drug-induced antics in the market. A daily dose of logic in their investment decisions is the cure.

PART I

VALUE
(AND SOMETIMES
CONTRARIAN)

Value investors seek out and invest in undervalued stocks in the market. "Undervalued" simply means that those "value stocks" trade below their intrinsic value — the actual worth of a business. That mispricing — a stock's price trading below its intrinsic value — can occur for a variety of reasons, namely sentiment, perception, unusual or short-term events, and broad market declines. Intrinsic value is a culmination of a company's brands, tangibles, intangibles, future earnings, and competitive advantage, among other things. Intrinsic value is seen as a better gauge of a company's worth than merely its book value (assets less liabilities), which doesn't adequately account for the true worth of a company.

Value investors invest in these undervalued, or mispriced, value stocks, in the anticipation that their market prices will revert to their mean or go back to their intrinsic value. But inherent in value investing is the risk that reversion to the mean does not occur in a short time frame and the stock's market price may continue to decline or be volatile. The biggest risk, though, is what is referred to as a value trap, in which a value investor misjudges a stock's intrinsic value, such that the company's fundamentals completely deteriorate and, in effect, validate the stock's lower price. For this reason, value investors must identify a catalyst (for example, a change in management) or a set of catalysts in each value stock to determine whether they will actually revert back to their intrinsic value.

BENJ GALLANDER
THE CONTRARIAN

At first glance, you might not classify Benj Gallander as the investor type. His demeanour is too relaxed — in fact, he's calm, glowing, and happy. He's got a slight surfer-dude slur, and on the day of our interview he looked a lot like a Toronto hipster, with his ruffled hair, open sandals, and unbuttoned shirt. Perhaps Benj hasn't changed a whole lot from his university days, during which he claims to have "majored in pinball, race-track, intramural sports, and cards." Not, he admits, a model student.

Arguably, that freewheeling nature is what makes Benj unique and has perhaps helped him be so successful in the market. It's his youthful way of questioning — constantly asking "Why?" — that helps Benj uncover truths and capitalize on inefficiencies in the market. Throughout the interview, you'll notice that Benj will sometimes ask questions aloud — "Is it a sector that's potentially dying for some reason, or is it a sector that's a necessity and will come back?" This is his mind at work. Unlike most of us, Benj's brain hasn't settled into a mature, biased, deep grey-matter state. Benj continues to question not only his own beliefs and actions, but those of the market, and the participants in it.

Benj is a contrarian. Contrarians *often* go against the herd, or against the majority. I say "often" because contrarians who actually beat the market cannot always indiscriminately buy when others sell and sell when others buy. They'd quickly go bust. Successful contrarians such as Benj make moves in the market based on logic rather than sentiment, and are usually proven right more often than they are proven wrong. Benj describes this contrarian approach as "buying good companies that have been beaten up but have the ability to make big gains at a reasonably fast pace." By investing through a discriminate contrarian framework, Benj can buy low and sell high, and as a result enjoy consistently high returns at *Contra the Heard*.

It was in 1995 that Benj Gallander co-founded the *Contra the Heard* investment letter with his friend Ben Stadelmann. Finally, after coasting erratically through university (Western for his BA and Dalhousie for his MBA), globetrotting freely around the world, and working odd jobs here and there, it seemed that Benj had settled into a groove. Thankfully, Benj has stuck it out at his current job as president of *Contra the Heard*. He's amazing at it. And he seems to be having so much fun. Through *Contra the Heard*'s President Portfolio, Benj has achieved a 19% annualized return since 2000, clearly overshooting the market. Benj's five-year annualized return since 2010 is 28.9%. If in 2000 you had invested $100,000 alongside Benj, and bought all of his stock recommendations, your capital would have grown to $1,358,952.95 over a 15-year period. It should be no surprise that today *Contra the Heard* investment letter counts some of the most successful businesspeople in Canada among its most loyal readers.

I first came to know of Benj through the television show *Market Call* on Business News Network, BNN. This was also at the time when I still practised value investing, as derived directly from the concepts that both Benjamin Graham and David Dodd taught, and so I found parallels in Benj's contrarian framework to that of value investing. I was so intrigued by Benj that I started to email him questions about particular stocks — RIM, Sears Canada, Manulife — to elicit his unique contrarian perspective before making my own moves in the market. Benj was approachable and responded back to me with advice that was bang-on each time.

When I emailed Benj in September of 2011 to ask if he would invest in RIM and if such an investment would fit his contrarian model, Benj replied the next day: "I wouldn't make that bet. And not at that price,

Robin. I don't buy stocks over $25. There is a better chance for a stock to go from $2.50 to $5 than a stock to go from $25 to $50."

Benj was so right. RIM, now BlackBerry, would soon crater to around $5. His advice, generously given, saved me money and heartache.

That back and forth on various securities lasted for years until just recently I asked Benj to be part of my book. He replied in his usual care-free way: "Sure, happy to do it. Let me know what time, Robin. Maybe I can even make us some bacon and eggs." Regrettably, I didn't take Benj up on his offer for breakfast, as I have no doubt that he's as great a cook as he is an investor. And so, it was on a bitterly cold winter day inside Benj's warm and welcoming Etobicoke home that I conducted my first interview for *Market Masters*.

PRE-INTERVIEW LESSONS

BALANCE SHEET: a component of the financial statement that shows a company's financials at a point in time (e.g., Q2 F2015). Main sections are Assets, Liabilities, and Shareholders' Equity.

BLACK SWAN: an occurrence that is extremely hard to predict. Term coined by Nassim Taleb.

CONTRARIAN: an investor who usually bets against the market or "the herd."

DEBT: an obligation to repay principal, plus interest, to a lender (for example a bank).

DIVIDENDS: money distribution paid to company shareholders, usually on a quarterly basis (every three months).

EFFICIENT MARKET THEORY (EMT): the belief that markets constantly incorporate all available information into the prices in the market, and that the markets are therefore efficient.

EXCHANGE-TRADED FUND (ETF): an investment fund that holds a basket of stocks, bonds, or other securities. ETFs trade on the stock market.

HEDGE FUND: a fund that is not restricted by the same limitations placed on mutual funds. Usually employs a wide range of investing strategies (for example, long/short and risk arbitrage).

INFLATION: increase in the general price of goods and services in an economy.

INITIAL PUBLIC OFFERING (IPO): the first sale of a company's shares to the market.

INTEREST RATES: the overnight rate, which is determined and controlled by a central bank. Overnight rates influence the prime rates at banks, which are applied to any loans or lines of credit.

MARGIN ACCOUNT: an investment account that allows investors to buy stocks on loan, with the obligation to pay back, or with the possibility to receive a "margin call" to cover lost credit if the investments decline past a point determined by the brokerage.

MEAN REVERSION: when market asset prices, which fluctuate around an intrinsic value or price, come back to that intrinsic value.

MUTUAL FUND: a pool of money from a group of investors that is managed by a mutual fund manager. The manager makes investments in a mutual fund to grow that initial and subsequent capital.

STOCK: an actual stake in a company. Can be purchased at any point in time during market hours on an exchange at the current bid/ask price.

TAKEOVER: when a company acquires the controlling interest in another company.

Where did you grow up in Canada?

Toronto.

Have you lived in Toronto your entire life?

Yeah, but I've lived in a lot of other places. I attended the University of Western Ontario. I went to Dalhousie for my MBA. I've travelled to over 30 countries. I've worked in France, Nepal, in what was Czechoslovakia, and the Middle East. However, I always come back here to Toronto.

Do you find that it's important to travel?

Yes, I think travelling is important. It broadens your perspective a lot. You gain a lot of experience, you have a lot of fun, and it's great to do when you're young and footloose and fancy-free, because you can do it in a whole other way. Once you have kids it all changes. So it's harder to do. But travelling really appealed to me and I did a lot of it in kind of a rough and tumble way. Also, another great thing you experience when you work in other countries is that you *really* meet people.

It seems that you travelled more than you studied in school. You must have not been a model student.

I was not a model student. Did you ever see the article that the University of Western Ontario wrote on me a year and a half ago? It said my majors were "pinball and cards and sports and the racetrack." So at Western, I wasn't a very good student at all. I got through, and evidently between that and the GMAT I wrote, which scored pretty good, I got into Dalhousie. But I'd taken three years off in between. And that was pretty critical because when I finished university the first time I was 20 years old, and I had a whole bunch of maturing to do, so when I went back three years later, I wasn't old by student standards, but I was older. Here's an inside story: my parents paid for my undergrad tuition at Western and they were ready to pay for me at Dalhousie, but I told them, "You didn't get your money's worth at Western, so I'll pay for Dalhousie myself." At Dalhousie, I did better. Again, I was just more mature; that was key. Because I was footing the bill there, I had to do a bit better.

So how did you first get interested in the markets?

I think part of it was that I was always interested in money. When I was a teenager, a friend of mine became a stockbroker, and I used to go down to where he worked once every few months. I started investing once I was in my late teens and figured this could be a good way for me to make money. Going back further, when I was in grade 11, my geography teacher had us go through all the companies on the Toronto Stock Exchange. Mr. Richards would ask, "Okay, *this* company; what company is it?" He'd just give us the symbol. I already knew a lot about the market because of my dad. He didn't invest in the stock market. He was in the lumber business. But I got positive feedback from my dad. Maybe that was encouraging for me [*laughs*].

Did you pick up any lumber stocks early on, based on your dad's influence?

Not early on, but later on I bought Abitibi and that might have been partially my dad's influence. I got absolutely hammered on it, but part of that was because I was stupid and made mistakes and I should have sold out when there were definite signs to sell out. Unfortunately I didn't sell out on time. That goes down as one of my big mistakes.

What went wrong with Abitibi?

Abitibi had a high debt load. I'm very anti-debt now.

Did you read books on investing in your early years?

Yeah, there were a lot of books — *Security Analysis* by Benjamin Graham was a big one. Another good read was *Where Are All the Customers' Yachts?* Also, Peter Lynch's *One Up on Wall Street*.

Any more notable books?

James O'Shaughnessy has a good book, *What Works on Wall Street*. There's a lot of books that I've read, and that I continue to read. But I don't focus on investment or business books now. I still do occasionally read them though, in order to keep *au courant* about what's going on.

You've published three books, is that right?

Yes: *The Uncommon Investor*, *The Contrarian Investor's 13*, and *The Canadian Small Business Survival Guide*. All of those became bestsellers. And otherwise just small stuff.

Jumping back to your comment about money, just how interested were you in money?

[*Laughs*] In the yearbook for grade 13 I wrote, "Billionaire! No, let's be realistic. Millionaire" in the future ambitions section. Now, though, I'm less interested in money. At that point in my life I was very focused on money. It's important to have a nice place to live and, in my case now, provide for my kids and my better half. So money remains important but I'm not fixated on it.

What were the first couple of stocks you remember buying in your early years?

Inco. And the major reason was that Inco's miners went on strike. I just thought, well, the strike's going to end, and if the strike ends, the stock will probably do better. Another early one was Liberian Iron Ore. Right off the bat I had a contrarian view. I figured if stocks were beaten up, you had a better chance for bigger gains. And Liberian Iron Ore had been really beaten up.

Did your position in Inco work out as planned; when the strike ended, did the stock pop?

I don't remember Inco popping right away. However, I remember doing well on it. It's in a field that was necessary. I doubt that I did much of the analysis that I do now in terms of actual ratios, debt, and so on. But there's also a point where simplicity can work really well. For example, six years ago, I was buying all of these U.S. financials. My basic premise then, after the financial crisis, was that the U.S. financial system was going to continue. And the question then was, which companies would survive? Something similar happened when I went to work in Czechoslovakia in '92. The U.S. banks had taken a huge beating. So back then I bought into Bank of America, Continental Illinois, and did *very, very* well on them after they'd been beaten up. This philosophy was very much the same again in 2008, 2009, 2010. Buying into them. So that was simplistic, but then I started looking more deeply at the ratios and the debt and that kind of thing.

You were buying into U.S. financial institutions in the aftermath of the financial crisis, when the majority of the market was thinking, "It's all over." Is that the best time to acquire stocks — when there's fear in the market?

Yeah, Bernard Baruch said it well: buy when there's blood in the streets. So, if everything or virtually everything has been beaten up, you've then got a much better chance in the market. If there's a sector that's beaten up, that gives it a point in the system that I use. However, the next question would be, is it a sector that's potentially dying for some reason? You know, like horses and buggies, or newspapers, to some degree? Or is it a sector that's a necessity and will come back?

If one deems that it's a necessity, then the question becomes, which companies do you choose from in that sector? For example, after 9/11 all the airline stocks got killed. So that's when we bought into KLM. The simplistic thought was that people were going to start travelling again. Also, people in Third World countries were going to become richer and as a result would be wanting to travel. So at that point we bought into KLM, which had among, if not the best, balance sheet in the industry. We paid $8 and change, and sold out at $32 and change, which was where it had been before. Now, after simplistic analysis, you do the more in-depth analysis, but when I first started doing this I'm not so sure that I did the in-depth analysis.

You alluded to an investment point or grading system — can you elaborate?
If a company gets 10 points and over, based on my defined metrics, then it's of interest. I don't recall a company that's ever gotten more than 16, 17, 18 points. I go through that point system as it's a good starting point in many ways. For example, in the system, if I think there's a takeover possibility, and there has to be a rumour about it, the stock gets a point for that.

BENJ GALLANDER'S POINT TALLY SYSTEM

RECENT DOWNWARD SHARE PRICE SPIRAL	−1
SINGLE, DOUBLE, TRIPLE, QUADRUPLE PRICE UPSIDE	+1 TO +4
NEGATIVE MARGIN OF SAFETY	−1
STOCK IS LIKELY TO UNDERGO A SHARE CONSOLIDATION	−1
GOOD OR EXCELLENT MANAGEMENT	+1 OR +2
MANAGEMENT OWNERSHIP POSITION	+1 OR +2
INSIDER TRADING	−1 TO +1
EXCESSIVE VERSUS EQUITABLE EXECUTIVE COMPENSATION	−1
HIGH RESEARCH AND DEVELOPMENT EXPENDITURES	+1
FAVOURABLE DEMOGRAPHICS	+1
EXCESSIVE OR REASONABLE DEBT	−2 TO +2
DIVIDEND PAYOUT	+1
POSITIVE FINANCIAL CONDITION	+1 OR +2
AMOUNT OF TIME FOLLOWED	+1 TO +4
BOOK VALUE	+1 OR +2
REASONABLE PRICE/EARNINGS	+1
DOWNTRODDEN INDUSTRY	+1

READABLE ANNUAL REPORT	+1
PUBLIC AWARENESS	+1
EXCELLENT CASH FLOW	+1
OUR UNDERSTANDING OF THE BUSINESS	+1
POSSIBILITY OF A TAKEOVER	+1
INTANGIBLES	+1

Source: *The Contrarian Investor's 13*, the Point Tally System, page 15.

Aside from your Point Tally System, can you expand on your stock screening process?

I just did a screen this week. I do it every three to four months on every company in the Toronto Stock Exchange, New York Stock Exchange, NASDAQ, AMX, and over the counter stock that has gone down in value at least 33% over the past year. That's the first filter that I start with in my system. Then I look at the chart for the past 10 years, and then more closely at its debt, among other things.

Clearly, you capitalize on beaten-up stocks, but only those stocks that you foresee will rebound. What are the origins of your contrarian approach?

Early on it was a natural way for me to go. The question then was, how do I define and refine my contrarian system so that it would work and so that I would cut my losses and hopefully have good gains? And everything's moot from there. Earlier on I would bind to initial public offerings but found that that didn't work out very well, except maybe for the stockbrokers. So I stopped doing that. Similarly, when I would invest in some younger companies that were having difficulties, I often found that didn't work out so well. So that's why I went to the 10-year rule. There's lots of ways to make money in the market. And people do it in many different ways. The contrarian system that I use combines a lot of different systems. It combines things like momentum, technical analysis, and fundamental analysis. But whereas a lot of institutions will push a stock that's $30 and sell it for $33, that never made a lot of sense to me. Maybe I'll be lucky to buy a stock at $5 or $8 that will get up over $20 and the institutions will then take an interest. And then they'll get their people into it, and then I get to profit from the momentum that they create. That happens a certain number of times.

Sometimes you score a double whammy: you enter a position, see a gain, but then once the institutions come in, you get another round of gains.

Yeah. If I'm buying a stock under $5, there's a lot of institutions and funds that won't even buy it under $10. It's only once it hits those higher levels that they can buy in. In simple economics of supply and demand, all of a sudden there's more demand but supply doesn't change; it's constant. And that pushes the stock up further. So then the question becomes, when do I get out? When we buy I set an initial sell target, which is something I don't believe I did in the early days. That grounds me now. I pretty much only sell some of a position at or near the target. There's some variances like if the price hits the target in November or December, odds are I won't sell, because at the end of the year I get to defer taxes for another year, which is a great way to keep more money in the kitty. And if I think a stock has tremendous momentum I may hold on longer. Say it's March and I notice that in eight or nine out of the past ten years in April and May the stock price has gone up, well then I'll get into market timing. Some people eschew market timing and say that it's an awful system, but to me market timing is really important, in relation to both the stock market itself, and to individual companies. That way, I can get more of a kick. If you can make an extra 2, 3, 5%, well, it adds up.

I assume that, naturally, some contrarian bets didn't work out for you over the years.

The first investment that I really screwed up on was Northland Bank. If you want to come up to my office afterwards I'll show you a stock certificate for Northland Bank, which is all I have left. Part of the thinking behind buying into Northland Bank was that a Canadian bank had never gone bankrupt since, I believe, 1928. And so I bought in, and I think I averaged down maybe four times, which is something I would not do now. But back then I thought that I was going to be right. Then the Canadian finance minister at the time stepped in and closed it down. Northland Bank was then de-listed from the market. I lost every penny I put in it. I put in too much money relative to the limited amount of money that I had at the time, but it was a really good learning experience. However, I wish that the stock had doubled or tripled. Now I only average down once on any stock because of that experience. Also,

Northland Bank hadn't been around for 10 years. Now I only invest in companies that have been around for 10 years.

You learn the most, in my opinion, from your mistakes. But sometimes you listen to some of those people out there and it sounds like they never make mistakes. I get told by people who watch me on BNN that they respect that I'm willing to admit my errors. That's the nature of the beast. The question is then, what do you learn from your mistakes; what do you do with them? Sometimes you make a mistake, but then the question is, how do you extradite yourself from the position? How do you do it in the best manner possible? Sometimes you do make a mistake and invest too early, but then perhaps you stay with the position and end up doing really well. Other times you invest and it's just a bad decision, so you take the tax loss and get out. And I'm better now. Early in my investment career it was harder for me to admit when I was wrong, and to me that's an error. It's a fatal flaw for many people, and it's important to say, "Okay, maybe I was wrong," and "I have to get out of this position, take my loss, and move on." If you can lose 20% instead of 50 or 100, that's huge.

So what about risk management? Do you diversify as a way to limit the impact from your mistakes?

To my way of thinking, if you're buying 60, or 100, or 200 stocks through funds, you're overly diversifying. If you overly diversify, you cut your returns automatically. It's like picking a hockey team. You want to pick 22 guys who would be anybody's best choice. A lot of people would come up with a lot of the same players. Now, what's the minimum number for diversification? You can look at different research, but I'll say maybe a dozen stocks. On average, in my portfolio, I've usually held 15 to 25 stocks. I don't want to exceed 25 stocks. Though I do buy some other stuff outside of *Contra the Heard*'s President's Portfolio. For example, I buy a few other U.S. financials. But if I put them in the President's Portfolio it would be too heavily weighted in financials. So we have to find that balance. But way too many people over-diversify. They invest in all these funds in their portfolio and they work against each other. So the question is, if you're buying the funds, which funds do you buy into, and when do you get out? Because odds are your brokers are going to tell you to get out and your fund manager isn't, because they want their 2.2% management fee or whatever it is. The game is changing because people are going more into exchange-traded funds (ETFs) where one can pay like half a percent or three-quarters of a percent, so you'd be way ahead. But it still makes more sense to me to cherry-pick stocks.

What have been some of your best "cherry-picks"?

Over the years I've owned so many stocks. However, I do remember some that have had tremendous moves. Alpha Pro Tech was one I bought three years ago at $1.17, and it didn't do anything for a long time. Then, last August, within a two-month period, it went from $2 to over $10. That was insane. Its huge pop stemmed from the Ebola scare. So that was completely abnormal. However, I didn't play it all that well. I sold 58% of the position at the initial sell target of $3.34, and then 21% at six and change. I'm still holding a 21% position at about $2.60. So I look at how I played it, and the first part was good; selling at the target price. The second part, I could have held on. The third part, I was thinking about selling at $10.24, and if I'd done that it would have been amazing. Instead I thought, I'll go $11.24. I shouldn't have done that.

Regardless, those gains were *really, really* big. And our subscribers did *really, really* well. And we did *really, really* well. But I look at it and say, "You know, if only I had played Alpha Pro Tech smarter . . ." Anyway, it was a complete aberration of the stock in terms of the way it moved. There's nothing linear about stocks. Two stocks that I did really well on were Service and Stewart Enterprises. Both were in the funeral industry, and that whole industry got killed, because they did what many industries do: things were really good, people were dying, but then they started doing takeovers. They just kept on taking over and consolidating businesses, and they took on huge debt loads in the process. I bought into both; they subsequently went down, and so I held both stocks over 10 years. But finally they both started really flying as they took care of their debt load. Stewart Enterprises started acting really strange. It hit the sell target but I didn't sell because there was so much volume and four or five days later Service came in with the takeover offer for Stewart Services. They're the two biggest funeral homes in the U.S., so the gains were three, four, five hundred percent, and both companies were paying dividends. So that was on top of it.

It took a long time, but if you hold a company for 10 years, and it doubles, that's a 7% annual gain. If you're holding for three, four, five years, or if you're holding ten-plus years and your gain is three, four, five hundred percent plus dividends, your gains are huge, absolutely huge. But you know most people aren't going to do that. They aren't going to wait that long. Things have changed. You've probably heard me talking about the way things have changed because of technology. Everything moves more quickly and, as a result, people react more quickly in the markets. I think it's a major mistake, and that's something I've had to control, to not be too tuned into the computer. Too many people wave with the noise, and that really hurts returns. Anyway, it's rare that I have a stock that I sell within a year. If it happens, normally that's on a takeover.

Any more big winners?

Indirectly, by staying out of the tech frenzy. I remember being up north where we rented a little cabin and had a bunch of people over. And on the day, I think the NASDAQ went up five hundred points, and then hit five thousand. I was actually watching the run-up on TV, and was basically saying aloud, "What the fuck?" I just thought, "This is insane." Complete insanity. I remember I was on the CBC, this morning radio show debating with a fund manager who was saying that "We're in a new technology paradigm." I was just saying, "I don't buy this at all." I didn't believe we were in a new paradigm. It made no sense to me. So, ultimately, I was proven correct. A number of years later, after the crash, I bought a number of technology stocks and did quite well on them. Some of them, as usual, took time.

Given that the oil sector has recently been clobbered by supply-driven crash in 2014 and 2015, will oil stocks be your future big winners, just like tech stocks were after the fallout?

I pulled the trigger on two energy stocks. I was early and I was over-anxious, which I shouldn't be at this age. I should have waited about two more weeks, until mid-December. But they seemed really cheap. I bought two on my own and two in the portfolio. One's actually up and three are down. Honestly, I'm surprised I did that. But I continue to live and learn. I like to think this is the last time I'll make that mistake. Now, this is again a good question: now that I've made those mistakes, what do I do? I'm not just going to turn around and take a tax loss right away unless I think that the fundamentals of the corporations are worse, and that the sector has changed. But you know, retrospectively, two and a half months later, I'm thinking, "Why did I do that?" I could have bought the same companies but paid less after the crash had completely decapitated. I would have been in better shape because I wouldn't have lost that much. I'm still learning, but the key is to avoid being overanxious. We'll see how it turns out.

Hindsight is 20/20. If someone had handed you $100,000 when you first started out in the markets, what would you have invested in?

Perhaps more oil and gas, perhaps more low-priced stocks, perhaps gold. I'd have to look exactly at the market back then. I would have followed the Point Tally system I have now. So I guess that's key. In the early eighties when the oil and gas sector got beaten up, the objective would be like it is today: find companies that are beaten up and still have good balance sheets. When I look at the screen now, there's a ton of oil and gas companies that come up but their debt loads are much too heavy. So it would be pretty much the same scenario as we have today. Suddenly, we've got the risk/reward issue.

Interesting. You mentioned gold. Was the rapid gain in the price of gold during the seventies due to rampant inflation?

I think that was the height, 1980. A lot of that run-up was based on inflation concerns. As a result, there was a gold mania. And of course, the U.S. government eliminated direct convertibility of the U.S. dollar to gold a number of years before the freeze on the price of gold, so that allowed it to go up further. Bre-X was a major excitement during that period, too. Many people saw Bre-X going up, so gold was perceived as the place to be. But then Bre-X crashed, along with gold, and people got scared. It was a good time again to invest. It took a long time for gold to come back, but then it had the major run after the financial crisis and now it's still hanging by about a third of that extension.

Gold companies are a lot like oil and gas companies. There's a certain mindset in people who run those sectors, to some degree. They just started doing takeovers and taking on debt, but guess what? The gold price doesn't keep going up forever. To me, there's nothing surprising about that mindset. During the recent gold euphoria there were no gold companies, or very few, coming up on my filter. Now, there's quite a lot. Just over a year ago I bought into Harmony Gold, a big South African producer, and then in December I bought into three small gold companies, which was the first time I made a major step back into gold. These companies seem to have done certain things to turn themselves around. The gold price could keep going down, but it can't go down as much as it could have gone down two years ago, as it's not as high now. I don't know where the price of gold is going to go, but I recently looked at these gold companies on the market; two have no debt and the other ones seem to have pretty good potential. Anyway, this is a great chance to buy heavily into an out-of-favour sector. It's closer to turning around than it would have been a year ago. But a lot of people still don't want to invest in commodities; they won't touch the sector.

Let's talk about your investment letter, Contra the Heard.

So in '94 we started the *Contra the Heard* investment letter. And of course it's expanded and continues to expand over the years. You know, I'm amazed that we're in our twenty-first year. I'd say that's a pretty good success story. The returns have been great and we've had a lot of long-term subscribers. It's fun for the most part but, like any business, it's not fun all the time. Mark, who works with us, has been here for 14 years. Phil, who worked first part-time for a while, came out here from Victoria to work with me. So we've got a nice little group. The simple fact that everybody, including Lloyd, but except for Phil, has been with us over 10 years, says something. Everybody seems happy. Over the years we've gone through the good times and the bad. In 2008 we lost 36.4% in the market. That wasn't a fun or happy time at all. Though we have a pretty good idea now about all our strengths and weaknesses, and we get along. So it's great.

During that tough time, 2008 to 2009, did you experience subscriber attrition?

Oh, huge. We went from a thousand down to about four hundred subscribers. So we got killed. I don't know what we charged exactly at the time, it might have been about $500 then, but a lot of people, whatever we were charging, thought, "Well I can lose the money myself and not pay you guys to do it." We lost money in 2007, and then in 2008 we suffered a big loss, too. But then in January 2009 I wrote to subscribers, and said, "I think we've got the best portfolio we've had in years, because they are almost all beaten up. And sure enough, the returns from 2009 until now have been phenomenal. In the past five years, our returns have been 28.9% annual. I mean huge. But during tough times, people get scared, and, well, that's the wrong time to run out of the market. I'm hopeful that this year will be a good year for markets.

The biggest holding in your portfolio right now is Fidelity Southern.

Yes. Fidelity Southern. I think the other one's ATS Automation.

Fidelity Southern has gone up five times.

Yes. But if that doesn't have all that much more to go up, there's another one — Integrated Silicon. I don't know what percentage of the portfolio that is —

. . . 8.7%.

So that's high, because I think we paid five dollars and change. Currently, it's sitting at about $17.

Integrated Silicon has more than tripled then.

Yeah. We've had it for a number of years. They have paid a special dividend over time, and now they actually pay a regular dividend, too, which is great because I love dividend-paying stocks. One of the things I've said on air and in the book is that "dividends allow me to be stupid longer." So about half the stocks I own pay dividends. In the system I use there's a point for dividends. If I go to a bank now it's hard to get 2% on savings. So it's really good now if I can get 2% on stocks through their dividends and hope for capital appreciation. So much the better.

Do you ever keep cash on the sidelines, or are you always fully invested in stocks?

I always have cash on the sidelines. It's good to have for rainy days. Recently I invested more in the U.S. so I have less USD, but still a fair bit. I think cash is a good thing to have; however, the question is, when do I deploy it? Before you invest in stocks it's really good if you pay down your debts, or pay off your debts. Because that's a guaranteed return. Even now if you'd gone and mortgaged at 3 to 4%, and you're in the 50% tax bracket, for example, you've got to get about a 6% return to offset that. We've done way better than that, but it's not so easy. Further, one thing I've been saying for a few years — maybe it won't happen anytime soon — is that interest rates are going to go up. They could go down further but interest rates will eventually go up. And it wouldn't surprise me if when they start going up that they start going up fairly quickly because governments and central banks tend to overshoot. And when they go up there's going to be a lot of difficulties, because a lot of Canadians are more indebted than they've ever been before.

Higher interest rates can squeeze people out of the stock market, if they'd been using money on margin.

Margin is a major danger. You can make a lot more money in the markets; I've heard people say, "Margining would have made you way more money," and they're probably right. But I want to sleep well at night. I tried shorting stocks and found it wasn't for me, because I didn't know how much I was going to lose. If I buy a company and it goes bankrupt, okay, I can lose *that* much money. I'm not happy about it. But if I short a stock, I don't know my potential losses. Shorting is very time-sensitive. As an investor, I think it's important to do what works for you psychologically.

You mentioned that you're more invested now in the U.S. market. What are the opportunities there?

I bought Magic Software. It's on a U.S. exchange but it's an Israeli company. There's a number of Israeli companies that sometimes come up on my watch list.

Have you ever looked to Asia for opportunities?

Years ago. Some of them come up again through U.S. markets. Going back to the mid-nineties, I actually bought into mutual funds. So I bought into an Asian mutual fund and a few others, and I actually did very well on them. But then I realized the last one I bought was a Japanese equity fund, which I did well on, too, but they take too big a management fee. And they take it win, lose, or draw. Right now I just stick to North American markets, and what I can buy via North American markets overseas. Are you going to talk to Francis Chou?

Yes I am.

Francis lost a lot of money, too, in 2008, and so he decided not take a fee from people. I had so much respect for him doing that. I've never been to his office but I understand it's a really small office — nothing really fancy. Whereas Sprott's office is big and beautiful. I was there. About half an hour before we sat down and talked I was just mesmerized by

Sprott's money room, sword room, view over the lake, paintings, and sculptures. It was all fantastic. But of course it was all bought with money that came from his investors.

Good segue to my next question. Do you attribute being a successful investor — people like you, Chou, or Sprott — to experience or talent?

I think we all have an envelope in which we can work. I could never have been an NHL hockey player, because even if I played and played and played and put in my ten thousand hours like Malcolm Gladwell argued in the book *Outliers*, I wouldn't get there because I can't skate well. I would just get a little better. Conversely, I had a certain affinity for the market. I'm a great believer in both genetics and environment. Genetically we're all predisposed to certain things. And then it's how you work within that and then stick to it, which you have to do often through the bad times. There's also a psychological component. Fourteen years ago when I did the tour for my book *The Contrarian Investor's 13*, an interviewer at a TV station asked, "How can you buy into an airline stock and how can you buy into Japan?" At the time, the 9/11 attacks had recently happened, and Japan's economy was suffering. I responded, "Well, the Japanese people, and I'm not stereotyping, are *really* smart, and they're industrious; I think Japan is going to come back." I used the same argument here as I did for airlines in 2001, which we previously talked about. Regardless, he really wanted to come after me. So you have to have a certain willingness to just go against the flow. That's easier now because my track record's been good. People have given me more poetic licence. Though I still say to my subscribers, "Look at what we buy, don't just buy it, that's just stupid." But it's a combination: part environment, part affinity, and part owning up to mistakes and learning from them.

That point you make to your subscribers — "Don't just buy it" — runs counter to the herd mentality. Nortel comes to mind.

Nortel was a major catastrophe. A lot of people got wiped out. I remember I ran into a friend on the golf course, and we started talking about the markets. His grandfather had left him shares of Nortel in his will. At that time, Nortel was well over a hundred dollars per share, and I said, "You know, you might want to sell some of it." And he said, "No, no, it's going up." Anyway, the next time I ran into him, Nortel was like three bucks or whatever. I felt for the guy, but nothing goes up forever. There's no stock that does that. These stocks that go up for a long time, like Apple, are a complete exception. I've been on about Apple for years. I thought it would get killed. I thought it would get killed after Jobs died, but it didn't. It went down a little. But at some point they're not going to be the technological leaders. I don't know when that will happen. And, again, I've been wrong. But being wrong in this case hasn't cost me any money. I have a number of friends who talked about investing in Apple when it was under $10. But they didn't do it.

Was that the nineties when Apple reached its nadir?

Yes, right about the time when Steve Jobs came back.

Did you consider investing in Apple then?

I don't remember looking at Apple then, but I had a couple of friends who were far more computer savvy than me and they loved Apple. They said, "Apple's a great product." But Apple was more of a niche product at that point. Great for graphics, but not so great for everything else. If I'd listened to them then I would've made a lot of money. But I would have probably sold Apple after a run-up at $12 or $15.

It's a "black swan." Who could've predicted then that Apple would rebound and transform itself into the biggest technology company in the world today?

The question is, who would have held Apple for that long? Because very few people actually do hold through all the gains. And I'm not a believer in "buy and hold," because all things do not go up forever.

Speaking of these "special situations," are takeovers more predictable than rebounds, such as Apple's rebound?

Often, yes. Sometimes you can catch takeovers, just because of a rumour. We did really well on Hudson's Bay. But people thought we were crazy buying retail and buying up when we did. There were already rumours on a Hudson's Bay takeover but it took a number of years before it actually got bought out. I think on that play we might have made about 100% return. And with new management-driven rebounds, what often happens is that the stock price immediately goes up, because of the new CEO's introduction. But then the euphoria turns, because often the CEO starts cost-cutting and then some of the numbers don't look so good even though the company may be getting better. We just have to be really aware and confident of new management in a rebounding company.

Do you believe that the stock market is efficient?

No. If I believed it was efficient there would be no point for me to invest. One of my professors, Alan Rugman, and I had this debate in MBA school when I'd already been investing in the market for a few years. He believed it was efficient. And a lot of universities taught that back in the day; I'm sure there's people who still believe in the Efficient Market Theory. But I don't believe in it. How can a market be perfectly efficient when it drops 22.4% in a day? It's impossible. All the information is out there. It makes no sense. Now somebody could say, "Well that just proves that it's perfectly efficient." But the question is, how will people react to the same information? Some people will view it as positive. Some people will view it as negative. For example, there's a car accident: one person will say it's *this* person's fault, and one person will say it's *that* person's fault. People look at things differently. So looking at stocks, how can anything be perfectly efficient? Also, people don't have equal access to information. If we went on the assumption that everybody deciphered information in the same way, then when did they get that information? I'm not out there with my iPhone or iPod. I look at information when I get home. A lot of the information that comes out during the day people have before me, so I effectively create an inefficiency. So no, I think the Efficient Market Theory is bogus. However, it's fascinating how many theories are believed and are taught and then they're just proved to be wrong.

So because the markets are driven by humans, they're always going to be inefficient?

Human psychology is a major driver of how people react. And that's what creates so much of the pendulum effect that goes too far, which allows me to make money, both in the times of euphoria and the times of depression. People do not react in many cases rationally.

What is your outlook for the markets?

Right now the U.S. job data is interesting, in that the U.S. seems to definitely be in a recovery stage. And that makes people more prone to invest in the American economy and in the U.S. dollar. Gold has held up pretty well during a time of power for the American dollar, because if the American dollar's powerful, gold should come down. The American dollar is currently the reserve currency. But at some point that's going to change. Maybe it'll be the renminbi. I don't think it'll be the rupee so fast. I would love that but it hasn't been too stable lately. So it's going to shift from the U.S. dollar to maybe another currency or maybe a basket of currencies. That means there's going to be less demand for the American dollar. That's going to lower the American dollar, plus the American economy at some point will go down again. That'll make gold more in demand, so to speak. And gold will then go up. I wouldn't be surprised if all that happens in the next 10 years.

Jim Rogers has the same argument about the trajectory of America. He moved his family to China, so that his kids would be ready for the economic shift.

Rogers is a really smart guy. He has done really well and has made some really good calls. I read one of his books. The fact that he took his kids to China so that they could learn Chinese is forward thinking. Chinese is the language of the future in many ways. It's a great move. And great for his kids. You get command of it much more quickly at that age. There are kids who are bilingual here, and that's great for the brain; it opens up all these passages.

Speaking of Rogers, do you validate any of your ideas with publicly available hedge fund holdings?

When I'm bored I'll go and look at their websites and see what they're holding and what they're doing. Even though some of them might be contrarian, most of the stuff they buy isn't what I would buy, and a lot of it's at much higher price points.

Any last words for the readers?

You have to learn from your mistakes. I've learned that debt is a killer in many situations, so if you can invest in companies that have very nominal or no debt, that helps companies survive during the hard times. Also, look in the out-of-favour areas of the market. You've got a better chance there. Also, try to avoid a lot of the noise, because there's more noise now in the market because of the internet than there's ever been. For example, we bought into BlackBerry, and every day, we could shift your opinion of BlackBerry based on the news. You have to just say, "Okay, I bought this stock for this reason, but does the thesis still hold?" That doesn't mean that you should just hold by being stubborn. You need to continue to evaluate whether it still makes sense.

The key lesson to take from Benj is that you should constantly question yourself and the broader market. Do not be swayed by heuristics, preconceived notions, or sentiment. Logic should pierce through every investment decision that you make. There's no doubt, though, that it's tough to go against the herd. As Benj says in his book *The Contrarian Investor's 13*, "Being a contrarian, at heart, is a matter of character. It is by no means for everyone, but for the person who is willing to be disciplined when the common view says, 'You're wrong, buddy; don't you think the time has arrived to see reality?'"

While I do greatly respect Benj's contrarian approach to investing and have seen how well it works for him, those kinds of stocks do not make up the core of my own investment portfolio. Only about 10% of my portfolio is comprised of contrarian stocks, as I found that over time I was being burned by "dog" stocks — those stocks that got beaten up but then never turned around or got taken over. Clearly, I am not as good a contrarian as Benj.

Ultimately, you must be the judge as to whether being a contrarian investor works for you. Benj does admit that it can be tedious. "The valuation cycle — from an undervalued, out-of-favour stock at the time of purchase, through the period of recovery to full value and our sale — is irregular. Quite often, the market is slow to appreciate the improvements in a company's fundamentals — but when sentiment shifts, it often does so dramatically, as institutions and brokers gravitate towards strong performers and propel them even higher. For this reason, turnaround situations often more closely resemble the so-called J-curve of successful venture capital funds than the more linear progression of their big-cap, 'growth' brethren." Even when the contrarian approach is working itself out, one must be patient and wait for pops in stocks or erratic upward price movements. Contrarian investing can be frustrating and unrewarding for those who do not share Benj's cool temperament.

Interestingly, Benj tells me that some of his biggest profits have come from takeovers. "At any point in time, the companies in our portfolio will be at different points in this valuation cycle. When it happens that a large proportion of these stocks are toward the end of this process and are appreciating rapidly, we end up with another of those banner years. This natural variability is amplified by the effect of takeovers. Often these occur at substantial premiums and they are responsible for some of our best profits." Perhaps you can focus more on takeover opportunities than on "undervalued" turnaround opportunities in your own portfolio.

Throughout my interview with Benj I could sense that while he was happy to talk about his achievements in the market, perhaps his heart had shifted to a different place over the years — his wife, two kids, and other endeavours such as being a playwright. But make no mistake, this has not hindered Benj's performance in the market.

The following is an excerpt from *Contra the Heard*'s investment philosophy:
- Concentrate on turnaround situations and stocks which are currently unpopular but are likely to regain their lustre
- Focus on stocks that have the ability to increase in value by a minimum of 50%
- Carefully analyze corporations' financial statements, concentrating on debt ratios and book values
- Analyze management's ability to achieve stated goals
- Invest only in organizations that have existed for at least 10 years
- Pick takeover candidates well before takeovers occur, for near-optimal returns
- Normally sell a minimum of 50% of a stock upon achievement of our target, while "market timing" the remainder
- Practice patient investing while ignoring the daily pulse of the market
- Advocate diversification
- Remain independent of any broker, corporation, or financial institution
- Put our money where our mouth is by notifying readers of the *Contra the Heard* investment letter only of stocks that we actually buy
- Appreciate stocks that pay regular dividends

1) "'Buy when there's blood in the streets.' If everything or virtually everything has been beaten up, you've then got a much better chance in the market. During tough times, people get scared, and, well, that's the wrong time to run out of the market."

2) "If I'm buying a stock under $5, there's a lot of institutions and funds that won't even buy it under $10. It's only once it hits those higher levels that they can buy in. In simple economics of supply and demand, all of a sudden there's more demand but supply doesn't change; it's constant. And that pushes the stock up further."

3) "When we buy I set an initial sell target, which is something I don't believe I did in the early days. That grounds me now. I pretty much only sell some of a position at or near the target."

4) "I only average down once on any stock."

5) "I only invest in companies that have been around for 10 years."

6) "It's important to say, 'Okay, maybe I was wrong,' and 'I have to get out of this position, take my loss, and move on.' If you can lose 20% instead of 50% or 100%, that's huge."

7) "If you're buying 60, or 100, or 200 stocks through funds, you're overly diversifying. If you overly diversify, you cut your returns automatically. I've usually held 15 to 25 stocks. I don't want to exceed 25 stocks."

8) "Things have changed because of technology. Everything moves more quickly and, as a result, people react more quickly in the markets. Too many people wave with the noise, and that really hurts returns."

9) "Dividends allow me to be stupid longer. About half the stocks I own pay dividends."

10) "I always have cash on the sidelines. It's good to have for rainy days."

11) "I've heard people say, 'Margining would have made you way more money,' and they're probably right. But I want to sleep well at night."

12) "Nothing goes up forever. There's no stock that does that. These stocks that go up for a long time, like Apple, are a complete exception. I'm not a believer in 'buy and hold.'"

13) "Sometimes you can catch takeovers, just because of a rumour."

14) "There's people who still believe in the Efficient Market Theory. But I don't believe in it. How can a market be perfectly efficient when it drops 22.4% in a day? It's impossible. Human psychology is a major driver of how people react. And that's what creates so much of the pendulum effect that goes too far, which allows me to make money, both in the times of euphoria and the times of depression. People do not react in many cases rationally."

15) "I've learned that debt is a killer in many situations, so if you can invest in companies that have very nominal or no debt, that helps companies survive during the hard times."

BARRY SCHWARTZ
MONEY FOR SOMETHIN'
AND YOUR CASH IS FREE

Should Barry Schwartz be smiling? An 18-year compound return of 8.7% doesn't put him at the front of the pack. Though his clients, who must invest a minimum of $1 million with Barry, sleep well at night knowing that their hard-earned money isn't wildly gyrating year after year, but growing at a safe and steady pace, albeit above market returns. That's why Barry is smiling.

Barry Schwartz tells it like it is. He's direct and quick to answer, in such a succinct way that you'd swear he practised his answers days before the interview. To think that Barry pretty much stumbled into the investing world is unusual. Investing wasn't his original game plan. David Baskin invited Barry into his firm, took him under his wing, and groomed him to be a prudent investor. Barry joined Baskin Wealth Management in 2000 and became a partner in 2005. Today, Barry is completely focused on strong large-cap franchise businesses with explosive free cash flow and an enduring competitive advantage. Throughout the interview, Barry repeats "free cash flow" over and over again to exemplify its importance. Seriously, as you read through the interview, count how many times Barry says "free cash flow." In Barry Schwartz's court, cash is king.

While Barry publicly describes himself as a value investor, it isn't in the Graham and Dodd sense of the term — buying deep value stocks at below their intrinsic value. Rather, Barry invests in businesses for the long term. Businesses that will not lose their value in 10 years' time. In fact, Barry invests based on Warren Buffett's ideologies, ideologies that in my opinion are derived more from Philip Fisher than they are from Benjamin Graham, even though Buffett himself would say otherwise: he claims, "I'm 15% Fisher and 85% Benjamin Graham."

Before heading up to interview Barry in his office, I grabbed a quick sandwich and drink at Starbucks on the ground floor of his building. It was only until after the interview that I realized Starbucks would fit perfectly into Barry's ideal portfolio. Upon reaching Barry's office floor, I was greeted by his assistant, who asked me to take a seat before seeing Barry. When he arrived, it was with a huge smile. Barry struck me as a man who was doing exactly what he wanted to be doing with his life.

PRE-INTERVIEW LESSONS

ASSETS: what a firm or individual owns (e.g., buildings, inventory, and brands).

ASSET ALLOCATION: the percentage of capital that you invest into various asset classes (stocks, bonds, etc.). Your asset allocation is based on a variety of factors such as return objectives, risk tolerance, and income needs.

BOND: a debt instrument with the promise to pay interest and to return the principal amount on a specified maturity date.

BULL MARKET: a prolonged inclining market.

BUY-BACK: when a company buys its own shares to then terminate or cancel them. This action reduces the amount of common shares outstanding.

CAPITAL EXPENDITURE (CAPEX): improvements, projects, or new investments undertaken by management.

COMPETITIVE ADVANTAGE: a market advantage. Usually refers to companies that have such a powerful brand that customers buy their product on brand alone (e.g., Disney). Can also include companies that enjoy, for example, unusual pricing, service, or regulatory advantages.

DAY-TRADERS: people who make it their daily business to trade stocks.

FREE CASH FLOW: the money left over in a company on a regular reporting basis (quarterly, semi-annually, and annually), calculated by subtracting capital expenditures from operating cash flow.

INDEX FUND: a mutual fund or ETF that strives to match the movements and returns of an index.

INTRINSIC VALUE: the actual worth of a business, which may or may not be different than its book value or market capitalization. Can be a highly subjective figure.

MARGIN OF SAFETY: the difference between a stock's market price and its intrinsic value.

MISPRICING: when investors, usually value investors, deem that a stock is being priced inaccurately on the market based on its underlying business fundamentals, or because of sentiment, or unusual events.

P/E: price to earnings ratio. Measures the price that investors will pay for a company's earnings per share. Current stock price divided by its current earnings per share.

RETURN ON EQUITY (ROE): a company's ability to generate profits from their shareholders' equity (not including long-term debt).

STOP-LOSS ORDER: an automated order to sell a stock at a designated price below the purchase price. Used to limit downside risk should a stock decline in price.

VALUE INVESTOR: an investor who buys "undervalued" stocks.

VALUE TRAP: a value stock that continues to get cheaper and fails to rebound.

Where did you grow up in Canada?

Toronto.

When did you first get interested in the markets?

My father was always interested in numbers and investing. Numbers are in my blood, too. As a young kid, I was fascinated by baseball, baseball statistics, and baseball scores. I would play fantasy baseball, make my own lists, look at the batting averages, runs batted in (RBIs), and the percentages. As for following investing, there's nothing I can pinpoint that would say I was interested as a young kid or growing up or even in university. To be honest, in university I was actually interested more in humanities and religious studies.

I submitted an application for the Schulich School of Business in my second year of university because I wasn't finding myself in first year, and got accepted. Later, I managed to get a stint at CI Mutual Funds and worked in the trust accounting department — more of a back-office type role. I didn't obviously love that. However, when I started in the mid- to late nineties at CI, this was the beginning of a stock market boom, and everybody and their brother was making money investing. You could pick dum-dum-dot-com and you'd make a fortune. I got caught up in that.

I like to say that investing in AOL helped my wife and me buy our first house. I remember putting $20,000 into AOL. But I still didn't really know anything about investing. A year later it was worth about $100,000. Those were the crazy days. That got me interested and fascinated by the markets. I can't say that I read any books about investing. I was lucky enough to meet David Baskin at the time, in the summer of 2000. I had graduated from my MBA and Baskin Wealth Management was a very small firm, only managing money for about 20 families, with about 20 million dollars in assets under management. Teeny-tiny. But it mushroomed from there. In the early 2000s there wasn't a lot of options for Canadians to get access to independent money managers.

Aside from AOL, did you buy any other stocks during those boom times?

Oh, I treated the stock market like most naïve investors treat it: like a casino. "I'm going to buy this stock and sell it two days later."

I remember there was a stock called On Sale. It was like a Bid-dot-com — Canadians may remember that name. People made a lot of money, but lost a lot more on Bid-dot-com. I remember buying On Sale in the morning at CI Mutual Funds, while working there. You know, CI probably won't be happy to hear this, but I was focused more on trading my own portfolio at work than doing actual work *[laughs]*. I remember building a $2,000 position in On Sale — I think the ticker was ONSL at the time — and selling it after lunch for $5,000 and thinking, "I'm a genius." I remember telling my fiancée at the time, "Oh I'm going to quit work and become a day-trader." This was the height of the day-trading insanity. There were places you could go and day-trade for a living. Only later did I figure out that everybody was completely foolish during that euphoric time *[laughs]*.

The party can't last forever.

That's right. Do you know the famous story about Joseph Kennedy? When he heard the shoe-shine boy or the cabbie give him investment advice, he knew that it was time to sell or short everything. And the nineties was really the day and age when everybody could start to day-trade. The stock market went in only one direction. It didn't matter what you picked — as long as it had "dot-com" next to it, it would be up the next minute.

From boom to bust. Did you immediately change course once the tech bubble popped?

I got lucky. I cashed out to buy a house *[laughs]*. I had no more investments. I was a young guy just getting married and needing a job. Plus, I had a brand new, shiny MBA. I didn't know anything about portfolio management or money management, and so David hired me as a warm body to help do the more menial tasks at Baskin Wealth Management. So here I was, an MBA, thinking I'm the cat's meow. My first tasks were data entry, answering the phones, photocopying, and filing. I did not meet any clients for a couple of years. I was just a warm body. But I was also like a sponge, soaking up what David knew.

I think that over time David started to give me more autonomy in providing investment advice. But I don't think we clicked as a team until probably 2004 or 2005, when I finally understood what real portfolio management is all about. Portfolio management is more than just buying good stocks. There's relationship management, asset allocation, knowing the ins and outs of the paperwork and different kinds of accounts, and the benefits of *this* security over *that* security in which account. That all just takes time and learning.

What were the key investing principles that Mr. Baskin imparted to you early on?

I remember it quite clearly; in 2002–2003, we were starting to gain momentum but then we ran into a rough market. 2001–2002 were not good years for the TSX because if you remember there was the Nortel debacle. I remember being on my honeymoon in October 2000 in Jamaica and turning on the TV and seeing the Toronto stock market down seven hundred points and then calling into the office and it was down another three hundred points to a [total of a] thousand points. Everything got obliterated with Nortel. David said, "We don't buy Nortel for our clients because it's not profitable. We stick to profitable companies." That stuck with me.

I remember David also diversified clients' portfolios, only put maximum 5 or 6% in any one stock, and only stuck with companies that paid dividends. Nortel never paid a dividend. But I remember in 2002 going into his office during a bad stretch, and asking, "David, why don't we do stop-losses? Won't that protect our clients' money?" And then he gave me a whole argument as to why stop-losses don't make sense. For example, you can wake up the next day and find your great stock down 10% for no reason, and you're cashed out. You're really giving up all your control in the stock market to nervous people. Lots of stocks are volatile. Even the great ones can go up or down 50% in a year. And that's not how we invest. We don't let the stock market drive our investment decisions. We research companies, we think about their fundamentals, and we buy them with an eye that they'll be worth a lot more in the future. We don't sell them two seconds after they go down.

You've taken a sizeable position in GM. Today I learned that both George Soros and Warren Buffett increased their positions in GM. What's your conviction in GM? It's been very volatile.

To really make a lot of money with an investment, you need to have conviction and an egotistical attitude to say, "The stock market is wrong, and investors are misinformed." You should use the volatility and the headlines to your advantage. Your greatest weapon is your ability to pull out a calculator and crunch the numbers and say, "Wait a minute, guys, something doesn't make sense here." With GM, the addressable market is growing, the valuation is reasonable, the balance sheet is improving, and they just started a dividend. Also, the economy's improving, which has got to be good for the car business. Bad stuff happens to companies all the time, but if they're profitable companies, they can get through it, and sentiment may revert. And that was my thesis for GM. It will mean-revert out of this pattern. It's too cheap now.

I always go back to one of my favourite books, *The Most Important Thing*, by Howard Marks, where he hammers home the point, "Who doesn't know that?" What he means is that *most* of the time news is reflected in the price of a stock and in its valuation. Sure, GM is responsible for a lot of bad stuff in the past couple years, but isn't that already reflected in the fact that it's sitting at only seven times future earnings? Isn't that reflected in its valuation? Who doesn't know that? And this is strange to say, but I get a lot of comfort when I get push-back from clients on stocks that are in the headlines or have under-performed. Because if you have a situation where every regular joe on the street who's not paying attention is now attuned, then that means they're telling their brokers to sell the stock and pushing it below what it's actually worth. There's no science to this, and I always laugh when I hear guys say, "Well, the number's telling me this, and I'm going to buy something that does this, and I have a target price of *this*."

A lot of my success has come from experience, but there is some gut feel to it as well. GM's recall scandal is not new. Similar scandals have happened to *many* companies over and over again. A perfect example and a stock that we researched but didn't buy was Moody's. Moody's is one of the greatest businesses in the world. Asset-light. Fantastically high ROE. Consistent stock buy-backs. It's a remarkable business. What happened was they got slapped with a lawsuit, and investigations started into their crappy rating services during the financial crisis in 2008, 2009. Are they responsible? Maybe, maybe not, who knows. But the stock just cratered. And at that time, Moody's was the most wonderful buying opportunity. But we got scared away from it. We want to learn from those experiences. Bad things happen to good companies, but that provides you with opportunities.

What are some other examples where you bought into a hard-hit stock, people told you it was the wrong move, but in the long term you were proven right?

There's just so many examples. Most recently with Shoppers Drug Mart, where the company was getting hit on all fronts — heightened competition and new generic pricing regulations by the government. The government said, "Shoppers Drug Mart, you can't charge this much for generic drugs," and the market got all scared and analysts said, "It's all over, the hyper-growth is done; the valuation is too expensive; the earnings are going to be squeezed." Well, what the market missed and what they always miss is that when companies generate free cash flow, and a high amount of free cash flow, good things happen. If you shoot a bazooka, you're going to blow something up. It's the same effect with free cash flow. If you're shooting out all that cash, something explosive is going to happen. Either the company's going to buy back its stock or make an acquisition or reduce debt or somebody's going to take notice and snap it up. That's exactly what happened to Shoppers Drug Mart. Loblaws took notice and essentially said, "We want the free cash flow." Earnings are one thing, margins are another thing, and balance sheets are important, but I've never made a bad decision by buying into a company paying 8% or 9% free cash flow yield or higher.

Are there certain industries that have inherently strong free cash flow?

Companies that are asset-light. Companies that don't require a lot of maintenance and capital expenditures to keep their lights on. So think about my business: my main investments are people. I don't need to spend fortunes on computers, on new equipment, or to renovate my office every year. All I need to spend money on is people, which is already included in the income statement. Maintenance expenditures to keep the lights on are not very high. So I can generate a lot of free cash flow with my asset-light business and wonderful things happen; my business continues to grow and I keep my costs under control. Think about the financial services sector. You can generate a lot of free cash flow. Companies that have very good control over their costs are the ones that shoot out the most free cash flow. Tim

Hortons was a perfect example, and there's Burger King now, too, through Restaurant Brands International. With the royalty structure, Tim Hortons virtually doesn't even need to spend any money. They're getting the money flowing back to them without spending a lot on capital. So we look for those ideas and opportunities.

What about on the revenue side?

Companies that have pricing power generate high free cash flow. If you have control over your pricing, too, then you can either benefit when input costs go down or when prices go up. Warren Buffett said something along the lines of, "If you have to have a meeting before you go out and raise your prices 10%, that's not the type of business I want to be in." Starbucks doesn't have to have a meeting before they raise their prices. They just do it. Tim Hortons? They just do it. And that feeds into the free cash flow. That's why we really like to avoid commodity stocks. They have no pricing power.

Do you have any commodity stocks in the portfolio?

The only oil company we own now is Suncor. If you're going to own a company that has no pricing power, own the one that either has the lowest cost or the one that doesn't need to go out and find the supply. Suncor isn't necessarily the lowest cost operator even though they're very good cost operators. But all the oil they need to drill is sitting out in front of them. They don't worry about replacing their reserves as quickly as Exxon or BP. Suncor has about 40 or 50 years' reserve sitting out their front door at their headquarters in Fort McMurray or wherever it is.

So that's an interesting business. However, we sold out of Suncor in March. While we like the management and the assets, we couldn't justify the valuation at current energy prices. The other commodity stock that we own that we bought a few years ago is Acadian Timber. That was on a thesis that the U.S. housing market was going to recover and that the price for hardwood logs and softwood would improve over time.

Has that thesis played out? That the U.S. housing recovery would push up Acadian Timber?

It has played out but with investing it's always so interesting in that things happen that you never would have thought about, which is the Canadian dollar dropping to 80 cents. Obviously, that's wonderful for a business that has all its costs in Canadian dollars, and all of its products priced in U.S. dollars. As a result, Acadian Timber has had a 25 to 30% lift in margins. That thesis played out, but the way it did — the Canadian dollar dropping in value — wasn't entirely built into our thesis.

Clearly your portfolios have very little exposure to commodities. Is that a part of your risk management strategy?

I think we've gotten smarter over time. When you stick your fingers in the tiger's cage, you get bit. So you don't do it again. You know, the cat doesn't go sit on the hot stove. It learns its lesson and moves on. 2007–2008 was an eye-opening experience for us and has shaped our investment strategy today.

What was the office like during the financial crisis?

We were constantly on the phone, constantly with clients. I couldn't breathe. Clients needed hand-holding, a shoulder to cry on, and an ear to yell at.

If you were to summarize your message to the client on the other end of the line, what did you tell them? How did you comfort them?

Flat-out say, "You own good stocks. Here are the steps that we're taking to protect your capital, but we're not going to sell." In 2008, many stocks were trading at science fiction levels, and science fiction is fake. Ignore it, and it will come back. Of course, we didn't know that the markets would come back, but we felt that the prices that the market was offering for some of these stocks was below their replacement value, and in some cases, cash on their balance sheet.

What were some of the bargain stocks you picked up throughout the financial crisis?

I wish I could tell you that we were 100% in cash in October 2008 to pick up bargains, but we weren't. We were fully invested. Prior to 2008, we said, "Oh my god, a recession is coming in the U.S." Anybody could figure it out. The warning signs were there. So we sold all of our U.S. stocks and bought Canadian stocks. But we didn't understand the magnitude of the coming recession, that it wasn't only the recession but a full-blown credit crisis. Anyway, we didn't have a lot of cash to deploy because we were fully invested. So we kind of just had to suffer through the financial crisis but not sell.

Okay, so moving on to greener pastures, what have been some of your biggest winners?

I would say the best stocks have been the ones that we have held for the longest time. Companies like Saputo Cheese, Home Capital, Bank of Nova Scotia, and TransCanada. If I look at my top 20 stocks today, about 50% of them we've held for 10-plus years. Those stocks all have something in common: they're quality businesses that raise dividends almost every year, that generate a lot of free cash flow, that are in businesses that sell products and services that people use every day, and that have potential for growth. Also, in most cases, there's smart family ownership in those stocks.

Others are a result of smart management. Recently we've added U.S. stocks, but for the bulk of the portfolios we own rock-solid Canadian blue chips: the banks, the utilities, the telecoms, the pipelines. Some of the stocks that come to mind that have been huge gainers for us are companies like Keyera, which we started buying at about $13 a share when it was an income trust and paying a 10% yield at that time. Keyera is now over $80 a share. It's increased its dividend every year since we've owned it. I remember buying Home Capital at $4, which is now a 10-bagger at $44. I remember buying Saputo Cheese probably in the $7 to $8 range, and now it's $30, maybe more because it's split so many times. We have some clients with Bank of Nova Scotia shares originally purchased in the teens, as well as TransCanada purchased in the $20 range. Don't forget clients have gotten a steady stream of rising dividends from all those stocks.

So why Saputo Cheese? Back then, it wasn't as well known a franchise as it is now.

I would say it had everything that we were looking for. It was an easy-to-understand business. Plus, people like cheese *[laughs]*. It has generated a lot of free cash flow, and they started doing smart things with that cash flow. They started making acquisitions and diversifying their business out of cheese and milk into different countries, while sticking with their core business.

Do you follow the moves of any other prominent investors?

Obviously Buffett. There's no one else you should be paying attention to, and every stock pick that he and his team come up with you should study, identify, figure out, and then probably buy it. I respect him. However, over the years I've been paying attention to a lot of 13Fs, which as you know are quarterly reports filed to the U.S. Securities and Exchange Commission of other money managers who have been in business for a long time. I gravitate to the long-term investors, not the traders. Wally Weitz — I like what he's done with his fund. Chuck Akre — he's been in business for a long time managing money. Also, the guy managing the portfolio for Bill Gates and his family foundation. Lou Simpson, who is the protégé of Buffett, who used to run the money at Geico, but then started his own fund — lots of great stuff there.

That's where I get my ideas. The Einhorns, the Ackmans, the Teppers of the world are all too "tradey" for me. They may be brilliant guys but they don't fit with my style. I like value investors who have long-term track records, are patient investors, and are long-term holders of stocks. I think our style has gravitated over the years from just looking for basic 10-times-earning or less companies to companies at 20 times earnings, if they fit with our core investment principles and we can get margin of safety.

So you're willing to pay a higher price for quality businesses?

We've started to do that and have had great success with that. You can only get smarter in this business by taking on and learning more about different styles and improving your game. You can't be dogmatic and say, "I only buy companies with 10-times earnings, and if I don't find them, I don't buy them." Well then, of course, if you did that you would never find anything to buy over the last four years.

Have you done the opposite — paid a lower price for a bad business? In other words, got caught in a value trap?

Oh yeah.

Can you give some examples?

"Value trap" is just a term used for a stock that hasn't worked out in the short term. And we've made the mistake of having too short a time horizon for some of these stocks and just not being patient enough. A stock that comes to mind that I think we really screwed up on was Staples. When we bought Staples in 2011, the thesis was, "Staples is trading at 10 or 11 times earnings. And yeah, Amazon was a gorilla, but we know from our business for example that we want all of our office products delivered the next day by one company, and not come piecemeal from Amazon." But we didn't think about the fact that Staples' store business was doing horribly and no one was going into their stores to buy stuff. So here's a company with a wonderful business, the next-day delivery business, but also stuck with a terrible core business, its retail stores.

What happened was the stock price cratered on us, the store business kept doing worse and worse and worse, and even though overall Staples was generating a lot of free cash flow, buying back stock, and raising dividends, the B2B [business-to-business] office products delivery service wasn't offsetting those declines. And so, the earnings never grew, and we pulled the trigger at a really bad price without thinking about the positives that could occur at some point, whether merging with Office Depot or slicing off the retail division. We weren't patient enough. We forgot the core principle about free cash flow, and that good things happen to companies that generate a lot of free cash flow, and if a company doesn't turn it around, someone else is going to turn it around for them.

So your Staples thesis was eventually proven to be valid. It was just a matter of holding it for the longer term through the eventual merger.

We got disenchanted with the company. It was always missing its earnings. And with the lack of aggressiveness from management, we voted with our feet. But that would be an example of a value trap that we gave up value for in the short term. I don't know if there is a true value trap out there. I think that you just have to watch companies like a hawk and pay attention for obsolescence, whether management is doing the right things with capital allocation. Value will often be recognized in the market. That's why you buy and diversify, because you're never going to be right on every stock.

Can you describe your investing process? There's thousands of stocks out there. How do you start and how do you whittle down your stock list?

We do three things here. We do reading, cloning, and screening. First, there's reading. Reading involves reading a lot of analyst reports. We subscribe to a service that gets us access to analyst reports so we can look at a lot of different companies that way and whittle it down. We do a lot of reading of value investing blogs and other blogs, annual reports, and newspapers. Anything where we can generate an idea. Sometimes we make the micro fit the macro. "The housing market in the U.S. is getting better. The U.S. banks are stabilizing. The U.S. consumer is stabilizing." I do a lot of reading. My whole weekend is spent reading about investing. I hope my kids don't hate me for that, but they're now old enough where they don't need me to watch them 24/7.

Second, there's cloning. When I say cloning, that's cloning the 13Fs of other investors. I'm happy to be a shameless copycat. I'm presuming that Warren Buffett and Lou Simpson and the like have done a lot of homework and research on their investment ideas. They're also managing multiple billions of dollars and they don't want to look dumb. That doesn't mean I buy it willy-nilly, but I look at it and do my own research and have the rest of the team here come up with research, to see if it fits our basket of principles. Sometimes their stocks do and sometimes they don't. Cloning gives us a starting point; we're always looking for new investment ideas.

Third, there's screening. We screen for high free cash flow yield, return on equity, return on invested capital, good balance sheets, and dividend aristocrats — companies that have long track records of dividend increases. We also screen for low P/E just to grab ideas. One of the stocks that came out of that screening process for us was Dr Pepper Snapple. We bought Dr Pepper Snapple in 2012. It was trading at $45, and was supposed to earn about $3 a share, so it was 15 times P/E. We asked ourselves, "Why is this stock trading at a 25% discount to Coke? It's got better growth, they're buying back stock, and it's got a free cash flow yield."

Why was Dr Pepper Snapple trading at a discount to Coca-Cola?
Why was it cheaper than Coke? Well, it's a much smaller company. Coke's been around for a long time, whereas Dr Pepper was relatively new. Even though it's been around for a hundred-plus years, it was spun off in this incarnation from Cadbury, and then put together into two companies, which spawned Dr Pepper Snapple. Sometimes there's mispricing in the market. That usually happens with relatively new companies that don't have a long track record or very much analyst coverage: the neglected stocks. There are always opportunities in companies that don't have analyst coverage or are neglected or are smaller ideas. Anyway, Dr Pepper Snapple fit into our thesis: easy-to-understand

business, growing potential, an addressable market, and high free cash flow. Although carbonated soft drinks aren't having so much growth in North America, there's potential outside of our borders.

How often do you screen stocks?

There's no rhyme or reason, just when we have time. We do screens, but we don't love to buy just any old stock. We want to stick to 25 to 30 stocks per family, per client. So if we come up with a new idea, there has to be rationale to kick one out.

With a bull run from 2012 to 2015, has there been a change in the stocks that you see through your screen?

Stocks are clearly not as cheap as they were back then. You can't find as many stocks for 15 times earnings or less. But I always keep in the back of my mind that stock prices are a function of interest rates and inflation as well. The lower interest rates go, the more attractive the cash flows that a company generates. Most people use a 10% discount rate. I don't know if we're ever going to see 10%. The dividends that these companies generate and the growth of the dividends should be worth more than the bond yields of their companies. If you flip back the bond yield of the tenure, and it's getting you 2%, you're paying 50 times earnings for bonds. So bonds are much more expensive.

Professor Schiller publicized that the focus of his next edition of the book Irrational Exuberance **will be the looming bond bubble.**

You've got to wear a bulletproof vest to buy bonds in this day and age.

Did you foresee a bubble forming anywhere?

Nobody can see a bubble before it pops. Though this is a strange environment. Asset allocation has taught us that if stocks don't do well, then your bonds do okay. However, in the last five years bonds and stocks have both done okay. They're 100% correlated. That's wonky. The whole asset allocation concept has been flipped on its head. I've never experienced it like this. And then rebalancing right now is really tough. I can't fathom buying 2% bonds for my clients who pay me a multiple of that. Because if I did, after tax, after fees, and after inflation, they'd be losing money. I can't put my clients into a product that's guaranteed to lose them money. Conversely, there's no guarantee that I'm going to make them money with stocks, but I can guarantee that I'm going to lose them money now by buying long-term bonds, unless we have deflation.

Do the "little guys" have any advantages in the market over you?

Absolutely. It is easier to buy some smaller-cap companies. The billion-dollar or less stocks that a company like ours can't get access to any-more because we have gotten too big and would own too much of the stock, putting our clients into an illiquid situation. There's some statistical bargains that you could find for a billion dollars or less of good-quality companies that have been around for a long time with good balance sheets. However, I truly believe that this is something that you need to spend 50 to 60 hours a week on. You need to be reading all the time and you need, as Buffett said, to read thousands of pages a month. You need to be on top of it.

Buffett would recommend that the average retail investor simply go into an index fund.

Yes, that's your best bet. But not all index funds are created alike. Take the TSX. It's a stupid index, a *terrible* index. It's too small and poorly diversified. For example, one or two companies can get too big and have a detrimental impact on the index when they flop. Remember Nortel or BlackBerry? Yet if we compare ourselves to the TSX [Toronto Stock Exchange] we look like geniuses over the past few years. The best would be to buy a U.S. index fund and maybe hedge part of that in Canadian dollars. Because if you're a Canadian your expenses are in Canadian dollars, and you probably want to match your lia-bilities to your assets, so to speak. What we like about the S&P 500 [Standard and Poor's 500] is that it's broad diversification. It's only 9% oil. It has one commodity base metal company, whereas the Canadian market is oversaturated with commodity companies.

Index funds are no fun though. What if the common investor wants to be active and beat the market?

I always get a laugh when my clients who have been investing a long time, but haven't paid attention, tell me that they own the banks and the utilities and they've just done phenomenal. So if you're really going to be an active investor in the market, stick to dividend payers that have a track record of raising dividends. Ten years from now, you'll probably outperform most mutual funds and money managers.

Did you count how many times Barry mentioned "free cash flow"? (The answer is in the Collection of Master Keys at the end of the book.) I'm sure that you can now fully appreciate the value in free cash flow, maybe as much as Barry. I've included some key lessons straight from Barry's blog based on his experiences in the market.

BARRY SCHWARTZ'S LESSONS LEARNED FROM THE MARKET

Over the past 15 years I've learned a few things about investing and managing money. No two investors are alike. But here's what works for me.

1. I am not a better investor because of my university and investment degrees. All that I have learned about investing and managing money has come from my time in the market, reading about investing, and listening to my partner, David Baskin.

2. If I've done my homework and properly valued a company, the only person I should listen to is me.

3. The internet is a great resource to find investment ideas. In an instant, I can look at the holdings of great investors, read terrific analysis from various blogs, and get all the data I want. It can be overwhelming so you have to focus your time.

4. I have never regretted buying a stock with a low valuation and a reasonable balance sheet that either raises its dividend or buys back a lot of stock.

5. Companies that grow their dividends even with low yields will outperform those with high yields but that offer no dividend growth.

6. I am happy to listen to others' opinions, but I will never make an investment decision based on what someone has told me until I've done the valuation work myself.

7. Nobody, and I can't stress this enough, nobody can time the market or can predict what will happen with the economy, interest rates, or currencies with any accuracy over the long run.

8. Buy and hold works for us and our clients. Our best investments are ones that we have held but constantly monitored over the long run. Companies like Cineplex, Saputo Cheese, Bank of Nova Scotia, TransCanada Pipelines, Keyera, and Home Capital, to name just a few, have been holdings for us for over 10 years and have created a lot of value for our clients.

9. Free cash flow yield is our best friend. Good things happen to companies that generate a lot of free cash flow.

10. When the market goes down there is no shortage of people telling you that it will get worse or that they knew the market was overvalued. Those same people never tell you when to buy or when the market is undervalued.

11. Commodities are our worst enemies. No company has the ability to control its destiny, but companies that have pricing power at least have a fighting chance. Commodity producers are price takers, and in our experience they take their fair share of punishment.

12. Whenever someone tells me to sell something because it hasn't done anything lately, I get super excited. I don't care what a stock has done, I'm only interested in its future potential.

13. Whenever someone says a business or industry is in structural decline, I also get super excited. We've made a lot of money buying companies that supposedly were selling a product or service that people aren't going to use anymore. Things don't change that fast.

14. Charlie Munger has served me well by revealing the three Cs of investing: cannibals, compounders, and cloning. Cannibals are companies that buy back a lot of stock. Compounders are companies that generate high return on equity and return on invested capital. Cloning is looking at what great investors, such as Charlie Munger's partner, Warren Buffett, are buying or selling and figuring out why.

15. Every single dip in the market has been a buying opportunity since the beginning of time. You can be miserable during a bear market [a prolonged declining market] or correction but don't panic. Every day the market is open is a chance to learn something new. Keep on learning.

1) "Do you know the famous story about Joseph Kennedy? When he heard the shoe-shine boy or the cabbie give him investment advice, he knew that it was time to sell or short everything."

2) "We don't buy Nortel for our clients because it's not profitable. We stick to profitable companies." (As recounted by Barry Schwartz)

3) "I only put maximum 5 or 6% in any one stock."

4) "Stop-losses don't make sense. For example, you can wake up the next day and find your great stock down 10% for no reason, and you're cashed out. You're really giving up all your control in the stock market to nervous people. Lots of stocks are volatile. Even the great ones can go up or down 50% in a year."

5) "We don't let the stock market drive our investment decisions. We research companies, we think about their fundamentals, and we buy them with an eye that they'll be worth a lot more in the future."

6) "To really make a lot of money with an investment, you need to have conviction and an egotistical attitude to say, 'The stock market is wrong, and investors are misinformed.'"

7) "Bad things happen to good companies, but that provides you with opportunities. If they're profitable companies, they can get through it, and sentiment may revert."

8) "When companies generate free cash flow, and a high amount of free cash flow, good things happen. If you shoot a bazooka, you're going to blow something up. It's the same effect with free cash flow. I've never made a bad decision by buying into a company paying 8% or 9% free cash flow yield or higher."

9) "Warren Buffett said something along the lines of, 'If you have to have a meeting before you go out and raise your prices 10%, that's not the type of business I want to be in.'"

10) "We've gotten smarter over time. When you stick your fingers in the tiger's cage, you get bit. So you don't do it again. You know, the cat doesn't go sit on the hot stove. It learns its lesson and moves on."

11) "[Great] stocks all have something in common: they're quality businesses that raise dividends almost every year, that generate a lot of free cash flow, that are in businesses that sell products and services that people use every day, and that have potential for growth."

12) "You can't be dogmatic and say, 'I only buy companies with 10-times earnings, and if I don't find them, I don't buy them.' Well then, of course, if you did that you would never find anything to buy over the last four years."

13) "Value will often be recognized in the market. That's why you buy and diversify, because you're never going to be right on every stock."

14) "There are always opportunities in companies that don't have analyst coverage or are neglected or are smaller ideas."

15) "It is easier [for retail investors] to buy some smaller-cap companies. The billion-dollar or less stocks that a company like ours can't get access to anymore because we have gotten too big and would own too much of the stock."

MICHAEL SPRUNG
THE SCIENTIST

Michael Sprung must have been both the shyest and smartest kid in class. You know, the kid who coasted through school with A-pluses without much effort. Well, Michael would go on to study actuarial science, which — based on what it takes to grasp and fulfill the curriculum — is right up there with rocket science as far as I'm concerned. After that he obtained an MBA and then qualified as a CFA. Today, Michael is still relatively shy. He looks exactly how you might expect an actuary to look: white shirt, black slacks, black shoes, and tidy white hair. The thick lenses of his glasses enlarge his eyes. He is soft-spoken. Our interview starts slowly, but Michael opens up as he gets more comfortable with me and the format. The more he talks about investing, the more he comes to life.

Investing happened to be Michael's calling. He could have very well become a salaried actuary employee at an insurance company, tucked away into a neat little cubicle. Instead, he founded Sprung Asset Management, and as Sprung's president, Michael's got lots of interesting stories, insights, and forecasts on investing in the market. Reading the transcript of our interview later, I realized that of all the interviews I had conducted, his transcript was the most cohesive and succinct in its raw form. Michael is a man who thinks clearly and articulately, and who speaks the same way.

Michael Sprung is a student of value investing. Michael's "school" was his first employer, Confederation Life, where he learned value investing and worked under value managers who would go on to storied careers of their own. "Anyone who went to Confederation Life would consider themselves value investors today," said Michael during our meeting. Michael and I met in a small, spare meeting room. We pulled our chairs up close and then began with the click of the red button on my recorder.

PRE-INTERVIEW LESSONS

CFA: Chartered Financial Analyst (an official accreditation).

CONGLOMERATE: a large company that contains an expansive and diverse set of businesses (e.g., Berkshire Hathaway).

CONSERVATIVE INVESTING: an approach in which investors make safe investments in the market.

LARGE-CAP STOCK: a public company that usually has a market capitalization over $10 billion.

MID-CAP STOCK: a public company that usually has a market capitalization of between $2 billion and $10 billion.

RISK MANAGEMENT: when an investor implements controls in his or her trading or investing practice that protect the downside in order to preserve capital.

SMALL-CAP STOCK: a public company that usually has a market capitalization of between $50 million and $2 billion.

WATCH LIST: a list of stocks that an investor creates to monitor, and possibly invest in, in the future.

WEIGHTING: the percentage of capital that you allocate to each of your investments (stocks, bonds, etc.).

Where did you grow up in Canada?

I grew up in Waterloo, Ontario.

How did you first get interested in the markets?

I got my undergraduate degree at the University of Waterloo studying actuarial science. My father was an actuary and I thought that was the way I might head. However, by the time I finished my undergraduate degree, I decided that I wanted to do something different, but something that would still use my mathematical skills. So I went from Waterloo to the business school at the University of Western Ontario (now called the Ivey School of Business), and it was in my first year there that I really began to focus on investments. I had just heard about the CFA designation, so I began to take the courses that would lead me in that direction: corporate finance, investment management, international finance, financial accounting, and so on.

When I finished my MBA, I stayed on at the University of Western Ontario for years as a research assistant with a professor who had taught us quantitative methods. I researched with him and we published a couple of papers together. I audited and enrolled in a few more courses in this period. As it turned out, a couple of my classmates had gone on to work for Confederation Life in the investment research department. I heard from them that Confederation Life was looking for another investment analyst. In those days the LifeCos [Life Insurance Companies] had huge research departments. At Confederation Life there were 13 to 16 analysts who were reporting to half a dozen or more portfolio managers. They were big departments, so it was a good place to go for early training, and that's the genesis of my beginnings in the industry.

What were the first couple of stocks you were asked to cover at Confederation Life?

Well, the first stock I covered was Thomson Newspapers, which is now Thomson Reuters. And then from there I went to look at the broader communication sector: Bell, Rogers, and so on. Within a short period they wanted to broaden you so that you weren't just coherent in one industry, so the second industry I tackled was forest products. Back in that day I began to cover photography: Kodak and Polaroid in the U.S. When I left Confederation Life, I had had exposure to at least five or six industry groups.

Where did you learn value investing?

Confederation Life was a school of value investing. That basically fit in with my philosophy and temperament anyway. Anyone who went to Confederation Life would consider themselves value investors today. There are different degrees of value investing, though. There is deep value, which Foyston and Gordon practised there. And then there is relative value, which became popular once people started to follow Berkshire Hathaway's Warren Buffett. Warren Buffett was as big then as he is now. Also, some of the portfolio managers we reported to were Prem Watsa, John Watson, Tony Hamblin, and Tony Gage, who all subsequently had great careers in the business. So it was quite a school of value investing.

Did you read **The Intelligent Investor** *prior to joining the company?*

No, but I certainly had to read it during my time there [laughs].

Did you have a mentor who instilled value investing in you?

I would say to some degree it would have been Prem Watsa or Tony Gage, who was actually a fixed-income guy. Whenever you had trouble or you were trying to sort out a problem, they were very enthusiastic, very mentor-like, and they would give you different ideas of how to look at the company maybe a little bit different or how to tear the numbers apart.

In those early days, did you personally invest?

I didn't have a lot of extra change but, you know, I managed to finish school without any debt, so, yeah, I began to tinker in the markets a little bit.

Do you recall your first big win from those early days?

No, because in those early days I was initially investing in safety. So banks and so on.

Where did you go after Confederation Life?

I went to a firm that technically would be considered on the sell side of the street: Cassels Blaikie and Company Limited. I was a partner there for about eight years. And at the time, that firm was probably the oldest surviving member of the Toronto Stock Exchange. I can't remember when they got their original seat but it was in the 1800s. So a lot of the clients in the firm were fourth generation. It had a lot of discretionary management, but it hadn't yet congealed into what I would call a formal counselling environment.

They hired me as the first person to establish a fundamental research department and work with the fellows who managed the discretionary accounts in order to streamline the portfolio management process. The discretionary management side of the firm operated quite independently from the brokerage side. We did have clients in those days that were penny stock investors, as well as more serious investors, and then we had the discretionary management side, where we managed some family foundations and individual accounts for some fairly well-known Canadian families. That was a really good period.

Can you name some of those well-known Canadian families?

I don't think I really should.

Elaborate on how you streamlined the portfolio management process at Cassels Blaikie and Company Limited.

Well, not only picking stocks but trying to look at things as a cohesive whole. For example, portfolio structure, industry exposure, alternative strategies, and things like that. I worked closely with other members of the board. One person I worked most closely with in that period was Peter Harris. Peter Harris had been the former chairman of A.E. Ames, which in its day was a leading brokerage firm in Canada. A.E. Ames eventually got purchased by Dominion Securities, which eventually rolled into Royal Bank. In their day they were one of the biggest, oldest firms in Canada. They would have competed with Wood Gundy and so on. And so I worked a lot with him.

One exciting part of that was that in addition to just looking at the large-caps from an overall perspective, we got involved in looking at a number of small-caps. For instance, I think we were among the first people to go down and talk to Frank Hasenfratz at Linamar. We were probably very early in going to visit Michael DeGroote at Laidlaw. There were a number of companies like that that we got in at the ground level. And eventually one or two of those companies would be sold to larger entities and the senior management of those entities became clients. So that was really neat.

Clearly, Linamar became a great success. But what ended up happening to Laidlaw?

At that time they were pretty much strictly in garbage collection. Then they branched out into school busing. And then in the late eighties they sold out to Canadian Pacific Railway [CP]. After that they incurred a lot of liability associated with running school buses. CP eventually sold off the business. One thing I'd say I've observed over the years is a lot of the large Canadian companies, whether it be CP or Bell Canada or whoever, at various times have diversified and transformed into conglomerate companies. But then later they decide to go back their core business model again.

Investing into non-core assets diluted their returns for shareholders.

Yes. There was Imasco, which was in a lot of industries. All of a sudden they made the bid for Canadian Tire. Imasco put a huge premium on the voting stock. So you had companies that were going into entirely different industries. TransCanada Pipelines got involved with so many different assets that eventually they had to just go back to their core business.

Let's fast forward. When did you start up your own firm?

It would have been towards the end of 2005.

What is your core investment philosophy at Sprung Asset Management?

We mainly manage money for families. A lot of the money that we manage is actually in family trusts. So it tends to be *very* conservative management for the most part. We've got a few clients who would be a little more risk-tolerant, but those would be exceptions rather than the rule. We're still in what I would call the building phase of this company. Hopefully we will be for some time. Our core philosophy is trying to minimize downside risk. A lot of our clients are survivors of what I would call the "chasing the performance" game. Particularly after 2008, we had a number of new clients come who had been very happy when they'd been with very hot managers when times were good, but when things went bad they realized that risk is a two-edged sword.

How do you limit downside risk?

As value investors, we invest with what is commonly called a margin of safety. Most of the accounts that we manage are balanced accounts, so they have a mixture of fixed income and equity. More recently, on the fixed-income side, given interest rates as low as they are, we've gone to a short duration, which tends to stabilize that part of the portfolio, which in turn counteracts some of the volatility we've seen on the equity side.

You must avoid the technology sector then. That can be extremely volatile.

As a value investor, and as a general principle, we have not invested a whole lot in technology. Valuations look out of line. We tend to look for real earnings multiples, price to book, return on capital employed, and so on. As a result, the technology sector has never been an area where I've had a lot of exposure. Over the years I've had some, but it's been rare.

You mentioned that some clients invest with you because they were burned dearly in the past; for example, in the tech boom/bust. I'm sure you've experienced many bubbles.

Yes, I've been doing this now since 1979 when I started at Confederation Life, so I've seen many bubbles. I think the first bubble I saw burst was gold, which would have been in the very late seventies. One of the fellows who was covering the gold sector was on holiday; he phoned from the Eaton Centre and said, "Sell our gold stocks, people are lining up to buy gold."

Was that an indication of the peak of the gold bull cycle — insatiable demand for gold?

When you see that retail investors are all rushing in and that people are lining up to buy something, that's usually a good time to sell out. And then over the years we saw the Mexican debt crisis and the emerging world debt crisis. In the early nineties we saw the real estate crisis; there were a lot of very large real estate companies in Canada then that all went bust in that period.

Do booms and busts change you or what you invest in?

No, it evolves over time. Hopefully when something like either real estate or technology or any industry becomes *really* popular you're selling *[laughs]*. The whole key to value investing is to buy often when stocks are unpopular, when people do not recognize the inherent value in those companies.

Are markets and most stocks too popular now?

We're finding it harder to find significant value in a lot of sectors right now. I'd say selective areas in the financial sector offer some good value at the moment. Other than that, a few companies in the industrial sector and even the energy sector. We've seen more of a diversion between the U.S. and the Canadian market in the last few years. The U.S. economy has become much stronger. Our economy has been hurt most recently by its exposure to oil and gas. For the most part, materials and commodities have been in a secular downtrend for the past few years. However, these cycles come and go, and so it becomes a function of *where* you look for opportunities.

I'd say today we are turning our attention more to those depressed areas: companies that have the balance sheet or the financial stability to survive the current climate. And so whenever the next turn in that market comes, you're going to see some fairly significant price appreciation. Now, there's always the question of whether you are too early or too late, but as long as we are fairly convinced that a company has the wherewithal and good management to be a survivor, we don't mind being too early.

Do you see a bottom now in the commodity market?

I don't think anybody knows where the bottom might be. Although, as a value investor, we do look at the macro-economic environment. We just don't spend a lot of time there. We try to concentrate more on the micro-economic studies of the individual companies.

Are you taking on any positions in those depressed sectors?

We've added one or two positions in the material sector. We've added some oil and gas companies, too. So we are beginning to pick away. Our view is that you don't have to buy a full position immediately. But like anything else, you're not always right. So if you buy a stock and all of a sudden it goes down 15% or more, the real question at that point becomes, were you wrong or is this an opportunity to buy more?

How do you determine whether to cut your losses or to stick to your thesis?

We try not to look at the short term very much at all. We look at everything with a three- to five-year time horizon or more. And I'd say more towards the five years than three. What we're always trying to determine within a business cycle is which companies are selling relatively inexpensive today that at some point in that cycle should eventually reflect value.

Which eventually successful stocks did you stick with regardless of others who said you were dead wrong?

There are two examples in recent history. Alliance Grain Traders, which is now called AGT Food and Ingredients, and Progressive Waste, which is a waste management company. Progressive Waste was well managed, but was having some difficulties in the Northeast U.S., where it was operating. It was selling in the mid- to low $20s. More recently, people have begun to see the value in those companies and they've come up quite a bit. Those are always the really nice ones to own [laughs]. Oh, and around 1999, I made a bet with some portfolio managers that over the next four years Manulife would outperform Nortel, and they thought I was a fool. Nortel was trading at 120 times earnings. Anyway, Manulife outperformed in that period. I won the bet.

What about the stocks that kept on declining? Essentially, your critics were right.

Oh yes, we've all had many of those, especially in the last down-cycle.

Can you give an example?

Teck Resources took quite a beating in the last downturn.

How do you avoid value traps?

By looking at how the components of how the company achieves a return on equity. What is its financial leverage? What does its balance sheet look like? Look for those companies that have deteriorating leverage or margins relative to their competitors — that's usually a sign that a value trap is going to develop. Although we've never owned BlackBerry, they were once at the very top of the market with huge market share, which was probably was not sustainable for a long period of time. Ultimately BlackBerry failed to address the consumer side of that market or see the demand for greater functionality. So it's usually a range of dynamics that causes us to cut losses and get out but, like anyone else, we've been known to ride stocks down quite a ways before we give up. I think as Charles Ellis, who's a famous investor, said, "a lot of investing is winning the loser's game." You just try to make fewer mistakes than your competitors. And as long as your winners outweigh your losers, you're doing well [laughs].

What have been some of your biggest winners?

AGT was certainly one of them. Progressive Waste was another. Another stock we bought into quite early was Loblaw. Well, indirectly, through the parent company, Weston. Both of those stocks have turned out to be winners. More recently, Loblaw has turned out to be a bigger winner, and Weston still reflects that to a great extent. Back then, people were saying that Loblaw had lost their competitive edge. "They're losing, they're bound to lose market share, you've got Metro and Sobeys all making moves in the Ontario market, it's a competitive market." Unfortunately, what people started losing sight of was the fact that Loblaw was a market-dominant company with great financial resources behind it.

Would you argue then that the markets are not efficient?

Well, I'll quote Benjamin Graham: "In the short term the market is a voting machine, in the long term it's a weighing machine." I'd say in the long term, Efficient Market Theory has some application. Though in the short term there are anomalies within the system where stocks do get mispriced. Hopefully you're prepared enough to catch those anomalies. As value investors, we can't cover every stock in the world, so we set up mechanisms by which companies come into what I would call our working list or watch list. Companies leave over time but there's a large selection of companies that we're monitoring at any point in time, of which a subset is companies that we're actually interested in investing in.

What criteria do you use for your watch list?

We look at a number of components. But there's two very important ones that we use. First, we utilize what is called a DuPont analysis, which breaks down the return on equity into the sources of that return: pre-tax margins, tax rates, financial leverage, and asset turnover. Second, we prefer companies that have long histories as opposed to short histories so that over time we can look at companies and discern *what* they have been able to earn, and *how* they have been able to earn. This is useful information, because they may not be earning that today, so what are the chances of some reversion to the mean? Or what trends are happening within that company that could cause it to become more profitable than they traditionally have been?

But most of the time it's the former rather than the latter. You're looking for companies that maybe currently are not earning an adequate return on equity, but given the business cycle or a longer time frame, you can see good advantages for that company to get back to where it once was.

Do you also employ the discounted cash flow model?

We do. I'd say depending on the company, or the industry, we look at discounted cash flows, return on capital employed, cash flow analysis, and economic value added. We look at all those factors, and some of them are more applicable to some companies than to others. There's not one valuation technique where we'll say, "Oh that company fits perfectly in that particular peg."

What was it like for you during the financial crisis?

That period was *very* painful. You'd come in to your desk every day and you'd see the market down three hundred, four hundred, five hundred points. It was just like having butterflies in your stomach some days. You'd see valuations deteriorating before your eyes. That was so much different from 1987, when you had a one-day 25% drop, and there — you're done. But even that was a crawl back because I think after any market correction of those kinds of magnitudes, that's where you see the retail investor disappear for a while, sometimes a long while, until they get some confidence and start coming back into the market, hopefully by then as a value investor. By that time many of the institutional investors have picked their spots.

Was that a good time for value investors, once the dust settled?

We certainly bought a lot of financial stocks in that period, and that turned out to be a very good decision. People always talk about asset mix: your balance between equity and bonds. Well, when you hit a market like that it takes care of your asset mix pretty quickly all on its own. All of a sudden you're underweight equity. And you know, that goes back to what I was talking about earlier, that to a great extent the fixed-income side of what we've managed has been somewhat of a tempering influence to the volatility on the stock side. Although we have a wide variance of returns because our clients have different objectives and different risk tolerances, we were down only about 12% in 2008, which wasn't too bad. But a lot of that can be attributed to our exposure to fixed income.

That's incredible risk management. Did you exit any positions during the financial crisis?

We ultimately bailed on one or two, unfortunately close to the bottom *[laughs]*. But for the most part we stayed the course because that's what we're paid to do. The difference between a professional investor and a retail investor is having the fortitude to stick with your knitting. I've always said that the worst mistake that I see retail investors make is to become value investors when that's popular, and then all of a sudden become growth investors when that's popular. You get whipsawed on making changes between macro-economic sector rotation and micro-economic stock selection. That's where most people go wrong. Quite frankly, going from value to growth is a continuum; it's not like they're separate.

Is there ever a sure thing in the market?

A number of bank analysts over the years have always made the argument that if you had just bought bank stocks your whole life, you would have done very well over time. Whereas I think our response as portfolio managers is that diversification is a key to managing risk. You might not have a great deal of diversification, but certainly different industries at different times and in different environments are going to react differently. We saw that in a 2008 — the financial firms were extremely hard hit. So I think that's not a place for people to really hang their hat.

You studied actuarial science and you're a CFA holder. Does math play a part in the markets?

No, not really, because I think, with all due credit to my competitors, there are some extremely competent investors out there that didn't come from a mathematical background or even a science background. Investing success, like any other discipline or profession, is achieved through the rudimentary core knowledge that you need to know. It's in the application — how you think, your discipline, and whether you can stick with that discipline.

What advice do you have for investors starting out in the markets?

Well, if you go to my website, I have a suggested reading list buried somewhere in there. There must be a list of 20 or 30 books or more for beginning investors or novices to more sophisticated investors. I don't think that every investor out there can read *Security Analysis* by Benjamin Graham *[laughs]*.

Is this an opportune era for investors?

Let's face it. We've just come off a 30-year bull market for bonds. I don't think the next 30 years is going to be a bull market for bonds. We're going back to a period where maybe we're going to see more performance in equity markets. One can argue today whether or not equity markets are overvalued or not, but I think if you were to look over the long-time horizon, we're going back into that kind of environment where they have to be.

Please elaborate.

What we're seeing in the bond markets today is very artificial. What I see happening in the world is a race to the bottom. People are trying to devalue their currencies against the strength of the U.S. dollar. That's beginning to affect U.S. manufacturing, and at some point the U.S. is not going to take lightly everyone devaluing their currencies to this extent. The degree to which they can is limited, particularly when you get into negative rates. People will take a negative rate because what they're paying for is liquidity and insurance. But that won't last that long. With the number of countries that are now doing quantitative easing, this is something that the world has never seen before. And I don't know how this experiment's going to end. But usually when governments start out on these experiments, by trying to take the cyclicality out of the business cycle, it doesn't end well.

Michael alluded to economic business cycles. The cycle can flow through four stages: expansion, peak, contraction, trough. An investor can align his or her investments to the stages in the cycle that are most beneficial to the market. For example, the trough stage is usually the ideal period to acquire new stocks because the economy will soon go through an expansion stage, and many securities will experience reversion to the mean.

Michael also said that he uses DuPont analysis, which is an extra layer of fundamental rigour that you can apply to your security selection process. DuPont analysis (also called the DuPont Identity, DuPont Formula, or DuPont Model) provides a greater understanding of a company's current and potential future ROE.

DuPont analysis breaks down ROE into the three components:
- Operating efficiency, measured by profit margin

- Asset use efficiency, measured by total asset turnover
- Financial leverage, measured by the equity multiplier

The formula used to break down these factors is:
ROE = Profit Margin (Profit/Sales) × Total Asset Turnover (Sales/Assets) × Equity Multiplier (Assets/Equity)

Michael also hinted at a great way to identify value traps early on: deterioration of margins. BlackBerry's gross margins, for example, suffered a complete deterioration over time. Gross margins started to fall gradually and then rapidly as BlackBerry weakened due to new competition in the smartphone space. BlackBerry's gross margins went from 55% (2006) to 44% (2010) to 35% (2012) to 31% (2013) to −0.6% (2014). BlackBerry's stock may have seemed cheap by standard valuation measures such as P/E, but would turn out to be a value trap due to a collapse in its business.

Further conversation with Michael revealed that his portfolio was only down 12% in 2008. That's remarkable, given that the S&P 500 was down 41% and the TSX down 35%. On his firm's website, Michael eloquently sums up his risk management strategy.

> With over three decades of experience, we have found that our three-part value investing strategy is the best way to reduce risk and volatility and earn consistent returns over time.
> - Appraise the intrinsic value of each company over a business cycle
> - Seek long-term growth of capital by investing in companies that we perceive to be mispriced
> - Utilize a margin of safety to promote return of capital . . . not just return on capital
>
> Value investing shifts our portfolio management focus away from speculative profits, market trends, and the frequently changing opinions of experts, focusing instead on company and market "fundamentals."
>
> Why does our value investing approach work? The prices of well-established, high-quality stocks tend to rise over

time as the companies create value for shareholders. Stocks touted by brokers and the media often rise to extreme highs in expectation that they will meet or exceed their short-term earnings forecasts. However, they can decline dramatically when they fail to meet those forecasts.

In psychological terms, investors put unrealistically high expectations on stocks that are in the broker/media limelight, often missing opportunities in those companies not currently in the limelight. Over time, patient investors are rewarded for focusing on the long-term fundamentals while avoiding the volatility inherent in chasing short-term trends.

MICHAEL SPRUNG'S TOP 15 READING LIST

1. *The Intelligent Investor* by Benjamin Graham
2. *Common Stocks and Uncommon Profits* by Philip Fisher
3. *Extraordinary Popular Delusions and the Madness of Crowds* by Charles Mackay
4. *Investment Policy: How to Win the Loser's Game* by Charles Ellis
5. *Against the Gods: The Remarkable Story of Risk* by Peter Bernstein
6. *Triumph of the Optimists: 101 Years of Global Investment Returns* by Elroy Dimson
7. *Warren Buffett Speaks: Wit and Wisdom from the World's Greatest Investor* by Janet Lowe
8. *Security Analysis* by Benjamin Graham and David Dodd
9. *Handbook of Canadian Securities Analysis: A Guide to Analyzing the Industry Sectors of the Market, from Bay Street's Top Analysts* (Volumes I and II) by Joe Kan
10. *The Mathematics of Investing* by Michael C. Thomsett
11. *The Undercover Economist* by Tim Harford
12. *The Black Swan: The Impact of the Highly Improbable* by Nassim Nicholas Taleb
13. *Poor Charlie's Almanack: The Wit and Wisdom of Charles T. Munger* by Peter D. Kaufman
14. *Guns, Germs, and Steel: The Fates of Human Societies* by Jared Diamond

15. *A Farewell to Alms: A Brief Economic History of the World* by Gregory Clark

---

MASTER KEYS
MICHAEL SPRUNG

1) "Our core philosophy is trying to minimize downside risk. . . . Risk is a two-edged sword."

2) "When you see that retail investors are all rushing in and that people are lining up to buy something, that's usually a good time to sell out."

3) "The whole key to value investing is to buy often when stocks are unpopular, when people do not recognize the inherent value in those companies."

4) "There's always the question of whether you are too early or too late [investing in a value stock], but as long as we are fairly convinced that a company has the wherewithal and good management to be a survivor, we don't mind being too early."

5) "If you buy a stock and all of a sudden it goes down 15% or more, the real question at that point becomes, were you wrong or is this an opportunity to buy more? We try not to look at the short term very much at all. We look at everything with a three- to five-year time horizon or more."

6) "Around 1999, I made a bet with some portfolio managers that over the next four years Manulife would outperform Nortel, and they thought I was a fool. Nortel was trading at 120 times earnings. Anyway, Manulife outperformed in that period. I won the bet."

7) "Look for those companies that have deteriorating leverage or margins relative to their competitors — that's usually a sign that a value trap is going to develop."

8) "'A lot of investing is winning the loser's game.' You just try to make

fewer mistakes than your competitors. And as long as your winners outweigh your losers, you're doing well."

9) "In the long term, Efficient Market Theory has some application. Though in the short term there are anomalies within the system where stocks do get mispriced. Hopefully you're prepared enough to catch those anomalies."

10) "The worst mistake that I see retail investors make is to become value investors when that's popular, and then all of a sudden become growth investors when that's popular. You get whipsawed on making changes between macro-economic sector rotation and micro-economic stock selection."

11) "Investing success, like any other discipline or profession, is achieved through the rudimentary core knowledge that you need to know. It's in the application — how you think, your discipline, and whether you can stick with that discipline."

GAELEN MORPHET
INVESTING WITHIN A MARGIN OF SAFETY

It was through a story in *Canadian Business* that I became aware of Gaelen Morphet. The magazine featured one of Gaelen's largest and most successful holdings: Alimentation Couche-Tard. It's a stock that she continues to hold today. Alimentation Couche-Tard has been such a high-flying stock that Gaelen's been forced to sell portions of it over time, taking profits off the table, and reducing its position size in her portfolio.

In her role as chief investment officer at Empire Life Investments, Gaelen oversees a number of funds. The flagship, Elite Equity Fund, has returned 9.8% since its inception. The other funds comprise Empire Life's "first family of mutual funds." In total, Gaelen is responsible for approximately $9 billion in assets.

On top of having a knack for picking the right stocks, Gaelen has also been known to make superb calls on the direction of the market. One such call in 2012 turned out to be right on the money, so to speak. In a June 2012 article in the *Morningstar Manager Monitor*, Gaelen said, "We're actually in a sweet spot right now. As a value investor, you try and capitalize on the emotionalism of the market to buy names when they're cheap and sell them when they're expensive. Almost every stock out there is a value stock right now."[1] And sure enough, after a broad market decline that started in 2011 and was perpetuated by the Euro Crisis, the TSX finally started to turn up in 2012, and continued to rally all the way into late 2014.

How does Gaelen make such bang-on calls? The answer is that she employs her margin of safety model. Gaelen scans the market on a weekly basis and measures the margin of safety (the difference between intrinsic value and market value) in individual stocks based on Graham and Dodd's teachings about fundamental value investing. Gaelen then invests in stocks that are below their long-term or intrinsic value. She's refined Graham and Dodd's framework and models intrinsic value using a combination of current book value, return on equity, earnings per share for the next two years, projected book value, normalized return on equity, normalized earnings per share, and relative P/E ratio. She uses that information to determine the net present value of a company — in a similar way to the discounted cash flow model. You'll learn more when you read through our conversation.

Gaelen was relaxed, composed, and open to sharing her stories with me. She removed her thick-rimmed glasses when she wanted to emphasize a point. We met in a large room at Empire Life that could probably have accommodated 20 people.

PRE-INTERVIEW LESSONS

CATALYST: an event that positively affects a value stock and sends the stock price higher (for example when a company finally reverses a decline in revenue or a management change).

IRRATIONALITY: a general enthusiasm for a limited period in the markets that inflates asset prices to a level not supported by fundamentals.

LONG-TERM: a holding period for a stock usually greater than one year.

OVERVALUED: assets that are priced considerably over their fair value or intrinsic value.

---

1 © *Morningstar*. All Rights Reserved. Reproduced with permission. "Morningstar Manager Monitor: Gaelen Morphet — Empire Life Investments, Inc." 29/06/2012

PORTFOLIO MANAGER: a finance professional who manages the investments in a portfolio.

SENTIMENT: the common feeling or emotion that participants in the market share.

SHORT-TERM: a holding period for a stock usually less than one year.

Where did you grow up in Canada?

I was born in Hamilton but spent my younger years in Northern Ontario. We lived in Swastika — yes, there is a town with that name — and Porcupine. My father was a doctor and he travelled to smaller towns to provide them with medical help. This is where I got exposure to the mining industry, which would lead me to have an expertise in resources. I used to play in the abandoned mine down the street from my house.

Where did you go for university?

I went to the University of Western Ontario, where I studied psychology. I later completed my CFA. I think it has been a good combination since the markets run on a combination of finance and emotion.

How did you first get interested in the markets?

I'd been interested in the stock market from my university days. So when I moved to Toronto I took a job in the research department at McLeod Young Weir. My job was to clip the company news from the Dow Jones newswire, photocopy it, and give it to the appropriate analyst. I was like a sponge. I read everything that I clipped. I was immersed in the investment world and started to develop a very broad knowledge base on the companies and the markets.

Also at the time, I worked for a research director who inspired me, telling me, "The sky's the limit. If you prove yourself, you can go anywhere you want in this business." This stuck with me. I was so intrigued by the investment world and began to read everything I could get my hands on. I have loved every minute of it and still do.

What were the first couple of stocks that you covered as a research analyst?

I covered a wide variety of stocks as a research analyst. In my early days I was the resource expert. The one the really sticks out in my mind is Bre-X. It was amazing how enthralled people became, how easily convinced of something that was completely fabricated.

How would you describe the markets when you started?

I started in 1984 in an era of high interest rates. The industry had gone through a downsizing following the 1982 recession. A recovery was underway and then came 1987 and Black Monday when the stock market crashed. I sat in front of a terminal and watched the market drop and keep dropping. It was both fascinating and terrifying.

What was it like that day; how did the firm react to the '87 stock crash?

The team was in shock, even many of the investment veterans. We thought the worst of the damage was over on Friday but then Monday came. The Dow was down 508 points, more than 20% in one day. I was fairly new to the industry at the time so I didn't have a lot of context. But I remember that it was *very* quiet in the research department that week. Virtually no one had lived through an experience like that in their career so it was very unsettling and unnerving for a lot of people.

When I met with Norman Levine, he actually had a framed photo taken of a computer monitor, showing the declines from the '87 crash. Such broad declines.

I've kept the newspapers. Occasionally throughout my career I've gone back to read the articles from before and after the crash. It's fascinating because there are a number of people who claim they forecasted it, but in 1987 there was very little indication of what might happen. But upon reflection and even reading into that period, it wasn't an overvalued period. People have to remember that there weren't circuit breakers then. Fear was rampant and that's why markets went down so much.

So circuit breakers would limit the downside today. We won't see another mass crash?

Yes. When I say circuit breakers, there weren't any, so that's why fear just built on itself. Today we have the stop-loss, which acts as the circuit breakers and limits any one-day decline.

Can you walk me through your investment framework?

I am a disciple of Benjamin Graham: a value manager. Most of my research is based on price to book, return on equity, and intrinsic value. I follow the theory that all companies have an intrinsic value, and that stock prices fluctuate around that intrinsic value. Fluctuations can be driven by a financial issue or an operational issue — so they can be fundamentally based. Or even because they are out of favour from a cyclical perspective.

But the reaction is primarily emotional, and a lot of people will extrapolate when these events happen. For example, if an operational problem emerges, investors tend to assume the worst and often move to something that isn't having problems. Value managers often look at this as an opportunity to purchase the stock with the view that the stock will recover when the problem is solved.

Benjamin Graham described those daily fluctuations as "Mr. Market." Mr. Market can be manic, then depressive, and then back to manic.

Because of that behaviour, I am very focused on the true value of a company. So when volatility, fuelled by emotion, comes along, I still know a company's true value. If I know the company really well, I can make a judgment call on whether there's permanent value destruction, or whether it's just a temporary issue. A lot of market movements are emotionally based. A company can have the same earnings, same management team, same strategy, and can have a 10 P/E or a 14 P/E, depending on whether the market wants to invest in that stock or not. However, there's very little difference in the company — it will be all within the context of what's going on in the market.

Let's look at present day. Right now, investors are very concerned about energy stocks and are hesitant to invest in them. Fast forward six months and the sentiment could be entirely different towards these stocks. There may not even be a fundamental change; investors could just decide that energy stocks are cheap relative to the rest of the market so they start picking away at them. Before you know it, everybody's piling in. That is the way the market works. It is dynamic and relative. It is not black and white.

You really need to cut through the emotion and buy rationally in the market.

That is true. You need to know your companies and be prepared to take advantage of the emotion that volleys a stock's prices. I also believe that you need to stay invested to build wealth over time. If you trade in and out of the market, you'll miss the best moves. To cut through the emotion and act rationally, you need to buy high-quality companies and let them appreciate in value over time. Staying invested through periods of emotion is the discipline investors need to make money.

Do you add to your long-term positions when the market gets "emotional"?

Absolutely. I look for companies that build their intrinsic value over time. The opportunity to add to positions comes when sentiment becomes excessively pessimistic.

How do you formulate intrinsic value for the companies that you analyze?

[Gaelen moves a printout of her stock valuation model to the centre of the table. It's a big spreadsheet listing the companies under analysis, along with multiple columns — the valuation metrics — that she goes on to explain in detail.]

Here's the intrinsic value I'm calculating. These are the components of it.

So the main components that form intrinsic value are current book value and return on equity, earnings per share for the next two years, projected book value, normalized return on equity, normalized earnings per share, and relative price to earnings ratio. But what's the analysis process?

I use all these components to calculate the intrinsic value for the stock. I then compare the intrinsic value to the current stock price, and record the difference. I want stocks that are trading below their *long-term* or intrinsic value.

Okay, I see that in your model, you've sorted companies from the highest intrinsic value compared to current stock price to the lowest. So, high differentials would imply larger margins of safety in those companies?

That's exactly what I'm after. Let's take Bank of Nova Scotia as an example. Currently, BNS is one of the cheapest stocks in our universe and is a well-run company. However, investors are concerned about the bank's exposure to the Canadian housing market and to areas of the world that are not doing well, which is reflected in the stock price. BNS is the most internationally diverse bank in Canada. But over the longer term, Canadian bank stocks in general have been superior investments with very strong ROEs and steadily rising dividend payouts.

If you look closely at the numbers, BNS is really inexpensive. It could realize a 42% return, in theory, over the next two years, if the company is able to trade at its 10-year ROE. Following the financial crisis, investors thought the Canadian bank ROEs would come down materially as regulation increased, the savings rate in Canada plummeted, and lending waned. They were wrong. Canadian banks have been able to maintain their ROE levels. They are very diverse, well-run institutions with many levers to pull to maintain and grow their earnings. A consistently strong ROE gives me confidence in my investments. When the market becomes more pessimistic I take advantage of that pessimism and add to my positions. Likewise, when markets become overly optimistic, I will pare back.

You place a very large focus on the ROE metric. Can you explain what return on equity means for a company?

I look at return on equity as a measure of profitability. It is important to look at ROE on a historical basis because it indicates how well that company has been run and the return it has delivered over time. I am looking for consistency in the ROE over the long term.

How long is "long term"?

I prefer not to invest in companies that have a shorter-term track record. There may be many reasons why the company did well in the short term but that doesn't necessarily mean it is a good investment over the longer term. A longer time period allows you to evaluate the company's performance over different economic periods, giving you a better indication of how the stock will react, regardless of the macro-economic picture. It also gives the company time to stumble and you can observe how the company deals with these challenges. This is really important because you want a high-quality investment that pays a dividend and can withstand whatever is going on at a macro, cyclical, operational, and financial level. Only time can give you that perspective.

What's the frequency at which your stock valuation model is updated?

It's a live document. I can look at it in real time but I produce it once a week. There's not that much change on a daily basis or even on a weekly basis. The real benefit is looking at it over time. As a value investor, I'm very focused on identifying value traps. Those are stocks that look cheap but are going to stay cheap forever. Some of the reasons a stock may be a value trap is because it has too much debt, doesn't have good management, or lacks good corporate governance.

Unfortunately, quantitative analysis doesn't capture corporate governance issues, which tend to be more qualitative. If a company has had some corporate governance issues, I tend to sit on the sidelines. This differentiates me from some other value managers. I believe there's a broad enough universe of stocks to choose from that don't have corporate governance issues. Oftentimes you find out just how deep corporate governance issues are over time.

Value investing then is both art and science. Your model gives you data on cheap stocks, but you must then consider why they're cheap and what it will take for their prices to rise again.

Yes, that is correct. Catalysts are important. Investors need to remember though that there's an opportunity cost of staying invested in a company you think is a takeover target. It becomes a balancing act. As a portfolio manager, you can't have a portfolio comprised of stocks that may have a catalyst someday.

In addition to catalysts, I examine stocks that don't have a lot of coverage or are overlooked. This can happen to stocks if the float isn't large enough, the industry is not well known, or not a lot of analysts are bringing it to your attention. To create a successful portfolio, you need different types of stocks — some that deliver today and some that'll deliver in the future. It has to be a dynamic portfolio — which many investors miss. The portfolio shouldn't be a compilation of 20 of your best ideas that are going to go up over the next two years. Rather, the portfolio should be a combination of stocks that are reaching their intrinsic value, trading below their intrinsic value, and some that are going through their intrinsic value.

Are you a consistent value manager?

Yes. However, I would acknowledge that the definition of "value" has become much broader than it was in the past. I'm often surprised by managers who label themselves as value, as I would refer to them as GARP, growth at a reasonable price.

What version of value investing do you practise?

I refer to myself as a relative value investor. I construct portfolios of high-quality stocks that are less expensive than the market at all times. My goal is to have the portfolio appreciate while always protecting the downside. I do this through diversification and having exposure to many different industries and stocks. And by focusing on stocks that pay dividends. Value investors are different sorts. They're typically patient, very focused, disciplined, and tend not to go with the crowd.

In 2012 you stated that it was a good time to be in the markets. That was an excellent call. Some say that 2012 was the actual start of our bull market and that 2009–2012 was simply a recovery period after the financial crisis.

Staying fully invested in the less expensive areas of the market is the way to build wealth, and not by saying that "the entire market is overpriced." One thing that most long-term investors have recognized is that the market can stay overvalued for quite a long time. If you're always building wealth with a portfolio that's less expensive than the market, when the market rolls over, you'll have that margin of safety that other investors do not have.

What was it like for you in 2008 when the markets rolled over?

Going into 2008 was a very tough period. Lieh Wang and Nessim Mansoor, my long-time value partners, and I were under a lot of pressure. We underperformed in 2007 because we were not willing to invest in energy stocks that were reflecting $150 oil and stocks like Potash Corp., where some investors were forecasting ridiculous potash prices. There comes a point in your career, and if you've been in it long enough, several times in your career, where you aren't willing to follow the market up. And that was one of those periods — it was very stressful. We did not believe the global growth story would go on unabated forever. Stocks were just far too expensive. So, we pulled back significantly on our energy exposure and some of our commodity exposure. And there were many people who thought we just didn't get it.

You were right in the end.

Yes, we were right and our clients were pleased. But it was hard to be happy with the financial world in turmoil. The takeaway is to continually balance the upside and the downside, and over the long term you're going to do better for your clients. To be a good investor you must go through some very difficult times where you really do question your abilities and your resolve. Thank goodness I had great partners in Lieh and Nessim. We reinforced each other and our beliefs and the outcome was what we expected.

You preserve capital through risk management.

I do preserve capital through risk management. However, there is always pressure when the markets are going up and you're not fully participating.

Well, everyone said that Buffett had "lost it" in the nineties by not participating in the tech boom.

Yes, I was also in the same camp at that time and there was a certain level of comfort knowing I shared the same views as Warren Buffett. It paid off for both of us.

Is it more difficult to find value in the market now? Do you keep more cash on the sidelines when markets become overvalued?

I keep cash very low and aim to be fully invested. I mentioned I'm a relative value investor, so I'm always checking my portfolio to make sure it's reflecting that relative value. I do this by making sure my portfolio is less expensive than the market on a price to earnings, price to sales, price to book value, price to cash flow basis and it has a higher yield.

That doesn't mean every stock in the portfolio must have those qualities at a discount to the market. But collectively, if you constantly maintain that discount, then you've got that margin of safety in your portfolio relative to the market. I believe there's too much risk involved in market timing. I believe if you invest in the right stocks, keep your resolve, and stick with them, then over the long term you earn more for your clients than most other investors. That has been my experience over more than 30 years of investing.

But is the use of technical algorithms making the markets more efficient, undermining your relative value concept?

Technical algorithms are not necessarily making the market more efficient. I haven't really felt an impact either way. I actually think it's been more of a stock-picker's market in the past several years, which is wonderful for those of us who are stock-pickers and not momentum-based investors. There have been periods during my career, for example going into 2000, where the momentum players had a real advantage over the stock-pickers, and that was a really tough period to live through. But good stock-picking always wins the day in the long run.

What's been one of your biggest winners?

One of the biggest successes has been Alimentation Couche-Tard. I've been selling it as it has been going up but it is the ideal value stock. The intrinsic value is growing as fast or faster than the stock price. But it has become a very popular stock. There are still many things I like about the stock but market expectations are very high right now. As a value manager, I prefer stocks that have limited downside and plenty of upside. And when everybody's playing the same stocks and the expectations are there, it's difficult for companies to always meet investors' expectations, and that's where the volatility comes from.

I'm less comfortable being highly exposed to stocks like that, even if I think they're great companies and will continue to grow. The market will start building in expectations that are too high and then volatility will build around that stock.

That's an important point. A company can post record earnings, but if they don't beat expectations, the stock can actually go down.

Yes, a company can have a great earnings profile and the stock can actually go down. The investor will think, "I can't believe it. The company just reported a 25% increase in earnings but the market was looking for 28% and it took the stock down." A great deal of investing is about meeting or exceeding expectations.

That seems irrational.

That's the part that makes very little sense to inexperienced investors. These characteristics are typically what growth stocks are all about: meeting expectations. That's why I prefer to invest in higher-quality companies that don't have that variability in stock prices attached to expectations.

Do you also use technical analysis to inform your investment decisions?

I do look at relative strength and technical analysis. I've used the same group of technicians who have a long history of doing this type of work and are well respected. But technical analysis is just one component of the whole stock selection portfolio management process.

So you would never base a final stock selection decision on a chart or technical analysis?

No. But it is amazing how many people do follow technical analysis. That's why I think it's good insight as part of your process.

What tips do you have for investors just starting out?

I would tell them to read the newspaper every day. If you can read the financial section of the *Globe and Mail* or the *Financial Post* daily, you will begin to get an understanding of so many of the factors that impact companies and the capital markets. The *Financial Times of London* is an exceptional international read.

This is the Facebook age, though. The "news" is usually gleaned from a friend's "timeline." What about books?

I recommend *The Intelligent Investor* by Benjamin Graham and *Stocks for the Long Run* by Jeremy Siegel. However, I caution that often the real-life experience is quite different than the academic approach found in many of these books.

You need skin in the game to learn?

You need skin in the game. You actually have to own stocks to really understand the investing experience. It's not good enough to follow that stock in the newspaper every day, because you have no skin in the game. Investing is largely emotional. In order to get really good at it, you need to understand how you feel when your stock goes down 20% and what your reaction will be.

I succumbed to my emotions in the early days of investing.

We've all succumbed to emotions in the early days of investing. One of the most frequently cited mantras we hear is "Buy low, sell high." But what's missing from that mantra is that when things are low, it's usually because something has gone wrong and there is worry about the stock. It is human nature to want to buy a stock when it is on a winning streak, not when it has not been performing. Instead, you want to buy something that's done *really* well, which is when you're supposed to be selling. And it's hard to sell when the stock has made you money because you want to make more. These are the emotions you have to deal with when it comes to investing. You have to learn to be disciplined.

Anything else to add?

Just one thing. You can be a good investor by following the basic principles of investing that you read about in investing books. Investing 101: buy low, sell high, be diversified, stay invested, dollar-cost average, keep it simple, and so on. It sounds easy but it's very hard to put into practice. To help yourself out, put a disciplined framework together and stick to it. Over time you can refine it. Believe me, it will work.

Gaelen's margin of safety model makes a lot of sense. Not only does Gaelen limit the downside, but she also captures the upside. Gaelen sorts companies from highest intrinsic value compared to current stock price to the lowest. High differentials would imply larger margins of safety in those companies, and also greater upside returns. Her disciplined approach of investing into companies with margins of safety has paid off. Recently, she was awarded the FundGrade A+ rating for some of the funds under her oversight. Fundata picks their winners based on an objective score-based calculation that determines the "best of the best" for each calendar year. The prestigious A+ rating is only awarded to less than 4% of funds available in Canada.

MASTER KEYS
GAELEN MORPHET

1) "The markets run on a combination of finance and emotion. [But] investing is largely emotional. In order to get really good at it, you need to understand how you feel when your stock goes down 20% and what your reaction will be."

2) "I follow the theory that all companies have an intrinsic value, and that stock prices fluctuate around that intrinsic value. I look for companies that build their intrinsic value over time. I . . . compare the intrinsic value to the current stock price and record the difference. I want stocks that are trading below their long-term or intrinsic value."

3) "If . . . a problem emerges, investors tend to assume the worst and often move to something that isn't having problems. Value managers often look at this as an opportunity to purchase the stock with the view that the stock will recover when the problem is solved."

4) "If I know the company really well, I can make a judgment call on whether there's permanent value destruction."

5) "Before you know it, everybody's piling in. That is the way the market works. It is dynamic and relative. It is not black and white."

6) "You need to stay invested to build wealth over time. If you trade in

and out of the market, you'll miss the best moves. You need to buy high-quality companies and let them appreciate in value over time."

7) "When the market becomes more pessimistic I take advantage of that pessimism and add to my positions. Likewise, when markets become overly optimistic I will pare back."

8) "I look at return on equity as a measure of profitability. It is important to look at ROE on a historical basis because it indicates how well that company has been run and the return it has delivered over time."

9) "A longer time period allows you to evaluate the company's performance over different economic periods, giving you a better indication of how the stock will react, regardless of the macro-economic picture."

10) "I'm very focused on identifying value traps. Those are stocks that look cheap but are going to stay cheap forever. Some of the reasons a stock may be a value trap is because it has too much debt, doesn't have good management, or lacks good corporate governance."

11) "To create a successful portfolio, you need different types of stocks — some that deliver today and some that'll deliver in the future. The portfolio should be a combination of stocks that are reaching their intrinsic value, trading below their intrinsic value, and some that are going through their intrinsic value."

12) "My goal is have the portfolio appreciate while always protecting the downside. I do this through diversification and having exposure to many different industries and stocks. And by focusing on stocks that pay dividends."

13) "If you're always building wealth with a portfolio that's less expensive than the market, when the market rolls over, you'll have that margin of safety that other investors do not have."

14) "To be a good investor you must go through some very difficult times where you really do question your abilities and your resolve."

15) "As a value manager, I prefer stocks that have limited downside and plenty of upside."

16) "When everybody's playing the same stocks and the expectations are there, it's difficult for companies to always meet investors' expectations, and that's where the volatility comes from. A great deal of investing is about meeting or exceeding expectations."

JEFF STACEY
THE CLASSIC VALUE INVESTOR

Jeff Stacey was waiting for me in the Gold Room at the Royal York Hotel, reading the *Financial Times* and sipping coffee from a white china mug. Nobody else was around him in the classically appointed room that brought to mind images of captains of industry from years past congregating to shape Canada's economy. It's hard to fathom now that the Royal York was once downtown Toronto's tallest building.

It wasn't officially spring just yet, but the sun was piercing the window onto the table at which Jeff and I would sit and chat. It was so bright that I would later draw the blinds. Jeff was visibly eager to talk to me about his passion: value investing. I was eager, too, as Jeff has been successfuly practising value investing since founding Stacey Muirhead Capital Management in 1994, and is a friend of Prem Watsa, a notable value investor. Days after our interview, he would host the question and answer segment of Prem Watsa's Fairfax Financial Value Investing Dinner Gala.

Jeff Stacey has learned value investing from both the experiences and writings of super investors such as Benjamin Graham, Warren Buffett, and Sir John Templeton. Over time, he has identified the following enduring value investing principles, which he judiciously applies to all of his long-term investment efforts:

- Think about stocks as part ownership of a business
- Maintain the proper emotional attitude
- Insist on a margin of safety
- Do not diversify excessively
- Invest for the long term

Jeff looks for companies with outstanding business economics that are run by capable and honest managers and that are available at attractive prices. He describes this concept simply as "Great Business, Great People, Great Price." Jeff also has some great stories on event-driven investments. Specifically, he explained how he profited from Starbucks' acquisition of Teavana amidst the threat that that deal could have blown up.

PRE-INTERVIEW LESSONS

ANNUAL REPORT: a financial account sent on an annual basis to share-holders.

DEFAULT: when a company or person fails to or chooses not to repay their debt obligations and are unable to repay their debt obligations in the future.

EVENT-DRIVEN INVESTMENT: an investment prompted or triggered by unique situations in the market that occur within a certain time frame (example: risk arbitrage).

FORWARD P/E: measures the price that investors will pay today for a company's future earnings per share. Current stock price divided by future earnings per share projection.

RISK ARBITRAGE (MERGER AND ACQUISITION): when an investor purchases stock in a company that is to be acquired, in anticipation of a gain from the spread in the current market price and final purchase price once the deal finally closes.

Where did you grow up in Canada?

I grew up in a small southwestern Ontario farming community: Mitchell, Ontario. It's about 12 miles west of Stratford.

How did you first get interested in the markets?

Through my father. The company that he ran had a pension plan and he would have all these annual reports sitting on the corner of his desk. I would get interested in those reports and he would take me through some of the basics, and then I bought my first stock when I was 16 years old.

Which stock was that?

Ranger Oil. But if I knew then what I know now I probably wouldn't have bought that security. Thankfully, it worked out all right.

Afterwards, did you invest based on the value investing framework?

That actually came later. I was still speculating in those early days — buying stocks without an underlying philosophy or program. I caught a very hot oil and gas market, but of course I didn't recognize that at the time. So it was really more haphazard. I didn't have a plan. The plan came later.

After I got out of business school I went to work for a small Toronto brokerage firm where somebody showed me Warren Buffett's annual report in the mid-eighties. Then I got exposed to Prem Watsa very early after he started Fairfax. So the philosophical part of value really came later. My early purchases as a teenager were wandering in the desert without a plan at all.

In which year did you start your own firm?

The original partnership started in 1994. I had left the brokerage business a couple of years before that trying to get it all up and running.

What was the market like in '94 when you first opened the doors?

You know what, I suppose in many respects it was no different from today. We had come off this bad time in the early nineties. Of course interest rates were *much* higher than they are now. But other than that, not much has changed. We're still looking for all the same attributes — that part of it really hasn't changed for me. And the environment hasn't changed other than I think today things are more expensive and it's harder to find value today.

How did your funds perform in the beginning?

So, early on we had a couple of very good years, and then we had the whole ramp up into the tech bubble. We had no interest in playing in that area. We did okay but you always want to do better.

Your investment strategy contains three subsets: global reach, multi-strategy, and value. Can you expand on those three subsets?

We consider ourselves *classic* value investors. We've got a global focus and we're prepared to go anywhere. The multi-strategy piece may be somewhat different but it's not totally unusual. We've got four main buckets of operation: long-term value investments, event-driven trans-actions, distressed credit investments, and cash. Long-term value is obvious. So we're trying to estimate intrinsic value, we're trying to buy with a margin of safety to that intrinsic value, and we're trying to be rational and patient in all that we do.

Can you elaborate on event-driven transactions?

Event-driven transactions are the pursuit of profits from announced corporate events. So that's liquidations, mergers, acquisitions, recapital-izations, tender offers, anything where you can say, "Okay, if this event happens we're going to make *this* amount of money in *this* amount of time." It was a mainstay of Warren Buffett's playbook, certainly with the Buffett Partnership and during the first 30 years at Berkshire Hathaway. It's only been in the last 15 or 20 years that he hasn't really done a lot of arbitrage or event-driven activity because he's so large now. Unfortunately, this activity doesn't get associated with value investors. I think what we're doing is a definite part of the value craft.

What about distressed credit?

Okay, we will consider bonds that are high-yield because there's a per-ception that the companies aren't going to be able to keep paying, so the analysis is all around why we believe that they'll be able to keep paying. Of course, after a company defaults then the question becomes: what are you going to get after this company gets restructured? Usually that's cash and a package of new securities. You never end up whole to par, but because you bought them right, you can usually make good returns. What we like about distressed credit investments is they tend to have their own cycles separate from what markets are doing. Although in severe wipeouts like 2008 and 2009, of course everything just goes down. So in severe market corrections that probably tends not to hold. But as a general rule, it gives us more than one page in our playbook.

And cash?

Cash, or, jokingly, cash and other stuff *[laughs]*. We're not afraid to let the cash build up when we have more money than good ideas. And again, that's different than some people in the sense that they're always fully invested. We just like to have that ability to go to the sidelines if we're not finding stocks that make sense for us to invest in. Although benchmarks certainly are an important part of performance measurement, we're not slaves to trying to outperform a benchmark. We want to get superior absolute returns over the long run, and hopefully with consistency.

The event-driven strategy makes up about 20% of your portfolio right now.

Yeah, I mean it's been anywhere from zero to 45%. It's fair to say that we would love to have all of our money in long-term investments if we could get it deployed. You get the tax benefits of being long-term. But of course, the investment world's muddier than that.

Can you give an actual example of an event-driven trade that you made?

Right now we're participating in the Talisman takeover by Repsol. We paid $7.65 in U.S. dollars. The spread is good because of course oil prices are coming down — people are fearful. But if you look at the transaction documents you can quickly determine that Repsol has excluded the price of oil as a material-adverse condition.

Can you clarify that trade?

So we bought Talisman stock after the announcement that Repsol would buy it out. We're not trying to guess on which company is going to get taken over. It's a matter of public record. With this Talisman risk arbitrage trade, we're going to get $8 per share when the deal closes. It was trading at $7.65 or whatever, so there's 35 cents plus the 11 cents from one last dividend.

How soon after the takeover announcement did you buy Talisman shares?

Oh, it was several weeks after — there was lots of time. Oftentimes we won't get into a deal right after the announcement. We'll wait for the documents to come out so that we can see the particulars of the transaction. Sometimes we'll buy it on the announcement where we feel we understand what we're getting involved in. You need to monitor these potential transactions along the way. Sometimes a spread will open up for whatever reason. We weren't in Talisman early because our annualized rate of return was going to be unattractive, but then the price dropped such that the annualized rate of return went up above 15%. So you also have to monitor takeover plays along the way.

Can you give another example of another event-driven merger arbitrage play?

A little over two years ago, Starbucks made an offer to buy Teavana, which is a chain of roughly three hundred stores selling loose-leaf tea and tea accessories. Starbucks had spent a lot of time considering how to get into the tea market, so they made an offer to buy Teavana. In this case the original founders and a private equity firm owned about 70% of the stock. There was a 30% float. They entered a support agreement, and there was a no-vote issue. It was a done deal. I think that the Teavana purchase was going to cost roughly $800 million to Starbucks. Starbucks had the cash on hand so there was no financing risk. The strategic fit seems obvious. But right after the deal was announced Teavana traded to within five cents of the buy-out price to I think $16.45. So we decided to pass on that risk arbitrage trade, as the spread was too thin.

However, out comes a short-seller who puts out a piece of research that states, "We've had Teavana teas analyzed by a private lab that we're not disclosing the name of, and they're all laced with pesticides. And furthermore we think that Starbucks is likely not to proceed with the Teavana deal." That hit Teavana stock. So, we think, "Okay, the stock's now down to about $15.75, so now there's a 75-cent spread."

We actually went out to buy some of the teas at the various stores. We didn't drop dead after drinking them. It just seemed wacky to us that a company who knows the coffee and tea space like Starbucks does wouldn't have considered the source of Teavana teas as part of its due diligence process. We bought into Teavana. So, long story short, Harold Schultz leads off the Starbucks investor day announcing, "We are so excited about Teavana, we can't wait to get this transaction closed, we studied this category for years, we think this is one of the great players, we think we can do some great things to help it as a concept; certainly having this tea offering is great." The deal closed exactly as planned, on the timelines that were initially articulated.

How do you come to know of these acquisitions?

We just read the documents and press releases like everybody else.

But is there a central source of information?

We do get some lists sent to us of all the active deals. We get them provided to us by brokerage firms that trade in these securities. But every big merger is widely reported on. From an informational point of view there's certainly more awareness about mergers than anything else. Sometimes maybe the smaller arbitrages can be a little bit less efficient in the sense of, you know, some small deal may not get reported so you have to do a little more digging there. You can Google search "mergers and acquisitions" and have more than enough names come back to work on.

Let's move on to your long-term strategy, which forms the core of your portfolio. You analyze three factors before you buy into a company. It should be a great business. It should be run by great people. And it should be at a great price.

Let me just start by saying that we don't have any magic black box that somebody else doesn't have. We're looking at all the same valuation measurements: price to earnings, price to cash flow, owner-earnings or the true free cash flow after maintenance capital expenditures. I might put a slightly different spin on "It should be at a great price." Great price can be relative. So let's be absurd for a moment. If you knew as a certainty that something could grow 50% a year for a long period of time, of course it's worth more than seven times earnings.

You buy into future earnings then.

Yeah. The deep-value guys will state, "I want to buy something at a discount to book with a dividend yield and a single-digit price earnings multiple." You know, that's probably a great price for a rotten business. But if it's a better business you can pay more. In my absurd example, what you need to do is build in a margin of safety, because nothing grows forever. If we could buy a business at 12 or 13 times its current earnings, that consistently generated 20% returns on shareholder equity without employing a lot of leverage, then that would be an outstanding bargain. We don't need to buy it at seven, or eight, or six times its earnings. The point I'm trying to make is that value depends on the quality of the merchandise.

Do you use the discounted cash flow model to calculate a company's present value?

I agree with the concept of discounted cash flow in theory. The problem of course is what interest rates are you going to use in the model to accurately project present value? Anyway, we don't actually do discounted cash flow analysis. Instead, we spend a lot of time trying to understand the qualitative competitive advantage that a business has because that allows you to say, "Okay, we think it can continue growing, maybe not on some precisely plotted model that discounts it back at 10% annually because of these competitive advantages, and we see nothing that would lead us to the conclusion that these competitive advantages are diminishing."

You're quoted as saying, "Within the value camp, there are deep-value managers who buy into lower-quality companies but they're on the cheap. Others buy quality companies at bargain prices." Were you originally a deep-value manager? You obviously are not anymore.

I think most people start out in that first group — the Graham and Dodd deep-value camp. And many stay in that camp forever and do very well in that camp. It's a perfectly valid way to make money. And then I think some people over time move more to what I'll loosely call the Buffett school, where they'll pay more than those deep-value prices, and get a company that's considerably higher quality. Of course, those are relative statements. The mistake that the good business buyer will make is he'll pay too much for something that he or she thought was a really great business that turned out not to be a really great business.

I believe Charlie Munger said, "Even the world's greatest business is a horrible investment if you pay too much for it." Pick your poison. The trick in what we do is to invest in enduring, high-quality businesses that can last for a long period of time.

Can you give an example of an enduring business?

Usually consumer items that have brand attributes and that are needed by consumers every day.

Do you still employ any of the traditional value criteria from Graham and Dodd, such as a strong focus on the balance sheet? Asset plays and so on.

Oh, sure. But I wouldn't be necessarily so formulaic as to say, "We won't buy a stock unless it's less than one and a half times book value." Where we do think a lot about the balance sheet is in examining the assets a company holds and whether those assets are productive. There could be hidden assets. For example, real estate that is on the books for next to nothing but could be sold to unlock huge value. Or there's what's called asset intensity. For example, this very hotel that we're in — the Fairmont Royal York. The asset-light management company is generating these recurring service fee revenues from this hotel. That's a classic example of a business that from a balance sheet point of view doesn't really have much in the way of assets but it has enormous economic value.

Did you actually own a position in Four Seasons?

Yeah, going back we owned Four Seasons when it was a public company. A lot of these companies need to retain a residual piece in real estate, so maybe they own 10, 15, or 20% of each hotel property, but it's asset-light in the sense that they don't own all of the property, yet they're generating these recurring fee streams.

Are the markets overvalued now? Some say we're in year six of a bull run that started in 2009.

Well, we've found more event-driven things to do recently. But our cash is certainly building up. We've reduced weightings on wonderful businesses that are clearly becoming more stretched than they've been in a *long* time. Again, that ties back to our multi-strategy approach — we like having more than one page in our playbook.

Do you agree or disagree with the Efficient Market Theory?

[*Laughs*] Disagree.

Why do you disagree with EMT?

Let's go to 1987. On Friday the Dow Jones Industrial Average was 2,700. Monday it's 1,700. Well that's not efficient. Period.

Okay, but do you think that with the prevalence of the internet, and information, that the markets have gotten more efficient with time?

There is no question that the playing field has been levelled because of the availability and ubiquity of information. However, information is not the same thing as wisdom or knowledge, and so you still have to interpret that information. Human behaviour has not changed. The human condition is subject to cycles of both greed and excess optimism, or fear and excess pessimism. That was true before the internet, and that is still true today even with the ubiquity of the internet.

On your blog you echoed an argument that Bill Miller had made, that investors still have an edge in the markets — analytical edge, informational edge, and behavioural edge. Can you elaborate?

An informational edge is just the ability to go deep on something. To determine how a product's selling by going out and calling on some retail stores and talking to the people who sell that product out in the field. That's the kind of informational edge that you can get by working hard and doing your homework. To try a consumer product and then determine what's good and bad about it. Also, observing what other people are doing and buying. We're global investors and you can't just do that sitting in your office. You have to get out and you have to travel and you have to see what people are eating, what they are drinking, what they are smoking, what they are wearing, and so on.

Can knowledge of management give you an edge, too?

You need to align yourself with managers of businesses who have high levels of capability but also high levels of integrity. I think we've paid more attention than most to management, but I would say we probably haven't paid enough attention to management over the years. We maybe have put our trust in certain management teams that eventually let us down because they were not good capital allocators or not aligned with our interests. You need to buy a stock at a price that you can live with *[laughs]*.

You've been burned by management.

Whether you can or can't visit management — that's the toughest part of the game. It's the toughest thing to appraise. However, the signs are there in the public record. Read the letter to shareholders in the annual report. Is management talking to you like an owner, or does it seem like it's written by some PR person who really doesn't know what the business is about?

There can be lots of marketing jargon in some annual reports.

Yeah. Also, look at their compensation package. You can get clues from the management compensation package. Google them. My experience is that really great managers make their business their life's work.

Someone like Schultz. Coffee's in his blood.

Or Prem Watsa at Fairfax. It's his life's work. Buffett, too. And there are others as well.

Perhaps Ballsilie vying to buy an NHL team was ample evidence that he was not making BlackBerry his life's work anymore. That would have been a good time to sell.

Yeah, oh, and then the final piece is, does management have their money up on the same basis that you do? Do they own a stake of the company? I get asked all the time, "Well, how much of the company do you want management to own?" I don't think that's the right question. It might be a very small fraction. Regardless, it's not always easy to figure out.

Final closing comments?

You cannot *ever* sell your integrity in this business. You have to look yourself in the mirror in all that you do. We'll make enough mistakes where we think we've got it right, but we're certainly going to pass on some things.

So risk management's very important in order to preserve capital.

Yeah, absolutely. We'd rather lose 50% of our clients than 50% of our clients' capital. I really believe in that; you have to be out in front of the greed. Understanding your behavioural traits is important. You also need to have a philosophy, an approach, and, yes, a basic skill level. But it's as much about understanding your own personal behavioural makeup as being able to control that personal behavioural makeup to do the right thing at the right time.

While Jeff is a classic value investor, he does get creative when it comes to capturing additional low-risk returns in the market. Perhaps "event-driven" investing is what Ben Graham, father of value investing, was doing when he took the last puffs from what he called "cigar butts" for quick short-term returns. Jeff thoroughly explains his event-driven investing strategy on his website; I've excerpted some of his explanation here.

> Event-driven investing involves the pursuit of profit from an announced corporate event such as the sale, merger, recapitalization, reorganization, or liquidation of a company. It can also involve spinoffs and self-tender offers by a company or

other event-specific special situations. Financial results from event-driven investments depend more on a proposed corporate action rather than on overall stock market behaviour. This activity features securities with a timetable where we can predict, within a reasonable probability, when we will get how much and what might prevent that from happening. Essentially, to properly evaluate a potential event-driven investment, we must answer four questions as follows:

- How likely is it that the promised event will indeed occur?
- How long will our capital be locked up?
- What chance is there that something still better will transpire? (An example would be the emergence of a competing takeover bid.)
- What will happen if the event does not take place? (Examples would include anti-trust action or financing glitches.)

We only participate in event-driven investments that have been publicly announced. Also, where possible, we attempt to reduce risk through some sort of hedge. An example of this would occur in the situation where an acquiring company is offering some form of exchange of its shares with a target company. In such a situation, we may sell short the proper ratio of shares to be received from the acquiring company in order to lock in a spread.

The gross profits from most event-driven investments are normally quite small. However, the predictability of the return coupled with a short holding period usually produces acceptable rates of return. Event-driven investments typically produce more consistent profits from year to year than our long-term investments because the returns are to a large extent irrespective of the course of stock market averages.

1) "We're trying to estimate intrinsic value, we're trying to buy with a margin of safety to that intrinsic value, and we're trying to be rational and patient in all that we do."

2) "Event-driven transactions are the pursuit of profits from announced corporate events. So that's liquidations, mergers, acquisitions, recapitalizations, tender offers, anything where you can say, 'Okay, if this event happens we're going to make *this* amount of money in *this* amount of time.'"

3) "We will consider bonds that are high-yield because there's a perception that the companies aren't going to be able to keep paying, so the analysis is all around why we believe that they'll be able to keep paying."

4) "We're not afraid to let the cash build up when we have more money than good ideas."

5) "We're not trying to guess on which company is going to get taken over. It's a matter of public record."

6) "Every big merger is widely reported on. From an informational point of view there's certainly more awareness about mergers than anything else."

7) "If you knew as a certainty that something could grow 50% a year for a long period of time, of course it's worth more than seven times earnings."

8) "The deep-value guys will state, 'I want to buy something at a discount to book with a dividend yield and a single-digit price earnings multiple.' You know, that's probably a great price for a rotten business. But if it's a better business you can pay more."

9) "Value depends on the quality of the merchandise. The trick in what we do is to invest in enduring, high-quality businesses that can last for a long period of time."

10) "We spend a lot of time trying to understand the qualitative competitive advantage that a business has."

11) "The mistake that the good business buyer will make is he'll pay too much for something that he or she thought was a really great business that turned out not to be a really great business."

12) "There could be hidden assets. For example, real estate that is on the books for next to nothing but could be sold to unlock huge value."

13) "The asset-light management company is generating these recurring service fee revenues from this hotel. That's a classic example of a business that from a balance sheet point of view doesn't really have much in the way of assets but it has enormous economic value."

14) "There is no question that the playing field has been levelled because of the availability and ubiquity of information. However, information is not the same thing as wisdom or knowledge, and so you still have to interpret that information."

15) "The human condition is subject to cycles of both greed and excess optimism, or fear and excess pessimism."

16) "You have to get out and you have to travel and you have to see what people are eating, what they are drinking, what they are smoking, what they are wearing, and so on."

17) "Read the letter to shareholders in the annual report. Is management talking to you like an owner, or does it seem like it's written by some PR person who really doesn't know what the business is about?"

FRANCIS CHOU
DEEP "50 CENTS ON THE DOLLAR" VALUE

Francis Chou is arguably the only staunch Graham-and-Dodd value investor in Canada today. I say "staunch" because both the concept and application of value investing have become diluted over the years since Benjamin Graham fathered the philosophy in 1949's *The Intelligent Investor*. Benjamin Graham would seek out and buy a dollar's worth of tangible assets for 50 cents. Value investing has evolved, though, because tangible assets are not as prevalent in companies today as they were in the decades from 1890 to 1980, when industrial, transportation, chemical, steel, textile, and oil and gas companies represented the majority of the stock market.

Today, an investor cannot simply "buy a dollar's worth of assets for 50 cents," since most companies that make up the stock market do not consist entirely of tangible assets, but rather, to a greater extent, intangible assets. Intangible assets include — but are not limited to — trademarks, copyrights, patents, and brands. Notable examples of predominant intangible companies are Google, Apple, or Microsoft. Success as a Graham-style value investor in today's market is limited because intangible assets do not hold the same value nor do they produce the same predictable returns as tangible assets. For example, Graham could quite easily and confidently calculate the liquidation value of a steel manufacturer's machinery and equipment based on readily available market prices, as one key input to determine the worth of that company. From there, he would invest in that steel manufacturer if, say, its price was lower than its net current asset value (current assets less total liabilities). But how do you calculate Microsoft's worth when intangible assets make up the majority of its business? Think about it, the value of intangible assets can be transitory in that they often do not stand the test of time from the effects of innovation or competition. Even Benjamin Graham, late in his career, declared, "I am no longer an advocate of elaborate techniques of security analysis in order to find superior value opportunities. This was a rewarding activity, say, 40 years ago, when our textbook *Graham and Dodd* was first published, but the situation has changed a great deal since then."

Given today's reality, Francis Chou has still been able to successfully apply the same Graham-and-Dodd value investing principle to his security selection in both tangible- and intangible-asset-based companies. Using as an example Warren Buffett, who went from being a staunch Graham value disciple to more of a growth at a reasonable price investor, I asked Francis whether he's ever felt the need to change, to which he replied, "As my knowledge of businesses has grown, I've bought good companies as well as mediocre companies. I'm all over the place — wherever I can find bargains." While deep-value investing represents the core of Francis's philosophy, he's complemented his funds with other securities, ones that do not fit into a "deep value" category.

Francis was a 25-year-old repairman for Bell Canada when he pooled $51,000 from himself and six coworkers to start an investment club. That investment club would eventually blossom into Chou Associates Management Inc., which now has around $1 billion of assets under management. The flagship Chou Associates Fund has boasted a long-running and consistent track record since its inception in 1986. Francis sent me Bloomberg screenshots of the Chou Associates Fund's 15- and 20-year annual compound returns. Fifteen-year compound annual return: 11.69% versus S&P 500's 4.23%. Twenty-year compound annual return: 13.19% versus S&P 500's 9.81%.

Both Bloomberg screens were fascinating. The 20-year chart showed the Chou Associates Fund trailing the S&P 500 from 1995 to 2001, during the technology bubble, then vastly outpacing it from 2001 to 2015. Value investing won. Morningstar has shown that the Chou Associates Fund has achieved the highest return of all Canadian mutual funds between 1986 and 2015. Amazingly, Francis achieved the highest returns over this long period with one of the lowest standard deviations in the industry, meaning that his fund experienced only minor volatility or ups and downs. Therefore, the Chou Associates Fund actually ranks the highest according to the Sharpe ratio of portfolio risk-adjusted returns. Using his fund as an example, Francis will often say that the Modern Portfolio Theory (MPT) is bunk. "MPT says that to get high returns, your standard deviation has to be higher; however a positive correlation between risk and return is not found here [in my funds]."

Francis's was the most challenging interview to secure for this book. It took a letter, multiple phone calls, and multiple emails to both him and his assistant to finally schedule our talk. Francis told me, "You can get all of this information from my annual report" or "Go use what's been written on me online." However, I pleaded with Francis that those resources would not suffice, as I needed to produce an in-depth, informal, and entertaining interview. Finally, I got the interview. And trust me, it was worth it.

Francis's office is located north of Toronto, far removed from Bay Street. It's just him and his assistant, Stephanie, who work in the office, an office so spare that you could probably fit everything in it into one box. Francis is definitely not an accumulator of things, and he is the embodiment of a successful value investor. This tells you that all you really need to invest is a computer, account, and good ideas.

There is a tinge of sarcastic humour to some of what Francis says. At times, you'll need to read between the lines, and his humour may not always come through on the first read. Also, occasionally during our interview, Francis would expect me to answer some of his questions. He asked me, "What's the most important thing to check in the bank?" to which I incorrectly answered, "ROE." He turned me, the interviewer, into the interviewee. To find out what I should have said, and to learn from a value investing master, you will have to read the interview.

BARGAIN: a term usually used by value investors to denote a value stock.

BUSINESS MOAT: the illustration of competitive advantage, which is usually created by strong brands, unique assets, long-term contracts, market position, or some combination of all of these factors.

DOLLAR-COST AVERAGING: when investors continue to put money into a stock while its price on the market declines, either to reduce the average purchase price (and limit their loss), and/or to buy more when it's cheaper, signifying a value stock opportunity.

INTANGIBLES: non-physical assets, such as brand, that cannot be easily or accurately quantified by accountants and can be subject to depreciation-based changes in perception alone in some cases, or write-downs on erroneous acquisitions (i.e., "Goodwill") from the past that did not realize an ample return.

MODERN PORTFOLIO THEORY (MPT): a systematic approach to portfolio diversification based on asset class allocation (e.g., bonds, stocks, etc.), that seeks to maximize return for a given amount of risk in one's portfolio.

QUANTITATIVE EASING (QE): when a central bank (e.g., U.S. Federal Reserve) creates new money to buy financial assets, most commonly bonds, in order to influence higher private sector spending and to meet the designated inflation target during recessions or downturns in the economy.

VALUATION: the worth of a company or asset.

How many clients are currently invested in your funds?

It's hard to say for sure, but I assume in the area of one hundred thousand accounts.

You manage about $1 billion in assets. Is that in total, or just in the Chou Associates Fund?

That's in total, including the Chou America Mutual Funds.

How much assets under management did you start with at your firm?

Back on July 1, 1981, I started with $51,000 when I was at Bell Canada.

That's phenomenal growth. You came to Canada for work. You were actually born and raised in India, is that correct?

Yes, in a city called Allahabad in India. But my parents moved to India from China.

Why did they move to India?

My dad got a job as a university professor, teaching history, philosophy, Chinese history, and Chinese language.

Did your parents influence you early on to invest in the market?

No, my dad died when I was seven years old.

I am sorry to hear that. When did you first become interested in the markets? Was it once you moved to Canada?

I came to Canada in 1976. I became interested in the markets shortly thereafter, probably around 1979.

What was the spark that got you interested in the markets?

Buying bargains, which I was doing all my life while I was in India. After my dad died when I was seven years old I started to do most of the shopping for the family. In India the shopping is very different than it is here. If you go to Loblaws, the price of everything is marked, so you just pick whatever you want, pay at the cashier, and then off you go. In India, you have to haggle for everything. But haggling is not that simple. Before you can haggle, you first have to go to several vendors to determine the quality, and then compare the prices, so that you can buy the best quality at the cheapest price.

I can see the bridge — you buy bargains in the market, too.

That's correct. So, in a way, I was doing the same thing in India. Everything you buy, whether it's milk, meat, vegetables, or whatever else there — it was my job to make sure I was paying the lowest price for the best quality.

And then you were introduced to **The Intelligent Investor,** *and value investing, which solidified your investment strategy.*

Yes, I read something, most probably in the *Financial Post* in 1979, saying that the father of value investing was Benjamin Graham. So one thing led to another, and I found my niche, so to speak.

Were you personally buying stocks early on?

No, I did not buy stocks then — I had no money. I was scrambling for a living.

You got a job at Bell Canada, gained some assets, and then decided to start up that investment club, which I believe included five or six of your coworkers?

Yes, there were six.

Where are those six coworkers now?

Some have died. That was a long time ago — 1981, which was 34 years ago. While some former coworkers have died, others are alive, and worth a lot of money.

The ones who are still alive — how wealthy are they now?

One of them who is around my age gave me $80,000 to invest in 1981 and right now he's worth $5 million. When he gets to the age of 80, if we continue to compound at that same rate, he will be worth close to $60 million.

Wow.

And if he lives to 90 years old, he'll be worth $200 million, just from that original $80,000, assuming that we can maintain the compound rate we have earned in the past. But even if that original $80,000 investment grows to just $100 million, that is a lot of money for a telephone technician. There are tens of thousands of MBA students graduating every year from elite universities in North America. How many of them can boast about developing a net worth close to $10 million in their lifetimes, let alone $100 million?

He's financially independent now.

Yes, he doesn't need anything. There's a few guys like that.

Do you still keep in touch with all of the original investors from your Bell Canada investment club?

Some of them; not all of them.

Did any divest their shares?

Yes. Most probably.

How did you initially turn the club's $51,000 into $1.5 million? What did you invest in?

The returns were compounding fast. Later on some new money came in and the $51,000 grew.

But do you have examples of some of the early investments that you took on?

Those were some of the best times to invest. You could buy anything and you would probably do well.

Businessweek issued a feature article just before that period. It was entitled "The Death of Equities." I believe that it was written in 1980.

1979.

Yes, 1979. Their headliner statement was completely wrong. 1981–1982 was the start of a long-term bull market. Do you attribute your early success to that bull market?

No, not at all. Read my annual letter of 1981. My success has nothing to do with the fact that it was a bull market.

[I did read it. The quote below is from that annual letter.]

Is this the time to invest? Yes, definitely. Stocks, in this doom and gloom environment, are cheap by every historical standard. . . . What I would propose in the future, if the market is more demoralized than what it is now, is that we should open this fund to the public. There is no better time to invest aggressively. Stocks are selling at a substantial discount from book value and even during the Great Depression, the Dow [Dow Jones Industrial Average] did not trade below book value for more than a few months. . . . Companies in the United States are selling at giveaway prices.

Interesting — your foresight was spot on.

So, you cannot say that my success is because of the bull market.

You said the opposite of what the experts said at the time — you said that the stock market was alive, not dead.

That's right. My 2014 annual letter explains the framework of what I was thinking at that time.

I have been managing money since 1981 and one of the benefits of managing money for so long is that you get exposed to many financial and economic scenarios. When I was first thinking about the current market I couldn't help recalling what happened over the 15-year period from 1966 to 1981. The Dow hit a high of approximately one thousand in 1966 and for the next 15 years it would approach that level only to recede back again. Inflation, which was subdued in the 1960s, started to go up in the 1970s, the result of printing money in the 1960s to finance the war in Vietnam.

By 1980, the combination of high inflation and low GDP growth was the story of the day. When Volcker was named Chairman of the Federal Reserve board in 1978, his first mandate was to tame inflation. By June 1981 the federal funds rate rose to 20%. Eventually, in June 1982, a highly important economic measure, the prime interest rate, reached 21.5%. The 30-year bond hit a high of 15.2% yield when Volcker put the brakes on money printing. The Dow tumbled, selling at a severe discount to book value.

At the time, I was wondering how much lower the market could go. This is how I looked at the scenario: the interest rate was so high that I felt it could not remain at the level for any extended period of time without just killing the economy. Volcker's mandate was to break the back of inflation, and when he did that, interest rates were bound to go lower. Even if they didn't, the market was incredibly cheap: approximately six times earnings and roughly 6% dividend yield. The Dow had been earning, for a long time, on average, 13% on its equity and there was nothing to suggest that it was not going to earn the same in the future.

If interest rates went down, the end result would be that the companies would be worth a lot more. The discount rate that used the discount future earning power is somewhat linked to the prevailing long-term interest rate. When companies borrow money, the rate they pay, depending on their credit rating, is benchmarked to the prevailing interest rate plus or minus a few points.

The climate for investing in 1980 was one of extreme fear. For example, pension funds, as a group, invested only 9% of net investible assets into equity. In contrast, in 1971, 122% of net funds available were purchased into equities; in other words, they sold bonds to buy more of the equities. Those who wanted to get into the investment field in the late 1970s and early 1980s were considered pariahs at the times, and were to be avoided at all social gatherings as one would avoid the plague.

At that time I was getting totally immersed in the works of Benjamin Graham. I was hunting for every scrap piece of information I could find on Benjamin Graham and Warren Buffett. Although I was new to the investment scene then, the scenario had a smell of true success for any value investor. Not just success but something that would enable you to cook up a grand career.

Okay, you clearly had the correct foresight, and took the right bet on the stock market.

Yes. It was not a speculative bet but a bet based on reason and logic. You can see how confident I was. I knew my stuff. That's why I can say without hesitation that my success was not because of the bull market.

So, it's about making the right call, and then having the conviction to invest. Are you as confident in the market now? Multiples seem high.

Everything is so high. But I wrote about that too in my 2014 annual report. In the last half I provide a framework where I contrast the current scenario to the scenario in 1981. Everyone is so bullish but I'm really negative. Look particularly at the last sentence in my 2014 annual report.

By contrast, current conditions today make me feel like investors are being set up for a heartbreaking disappointment, especially for the unwary.

Are lofty valuations in the market today the result of quantitative easing programs around the world?

Yes. A lot of people don't understand the dangers, so they can see the bullish side, but not the negative side.

And so, when rates eventually go up, people will cycle out of equities and go into bonds?

Yes, but we don't know for sure. We only know that the rates can change in the future. The same thing happened in 1981. I didn't know the market was going to take off in six months, but I knew you couldn't get stocks any cheaper than their prices at the time, though all the numbers were indicating that everyone was running away from the stock market. Pension funds were running away from equities and you could see that. So, basically, my success in 1981 wasn't because I was just there; it was because I understood what was happening.

You had conviction.

I took a stand.

After running the investment club for many years, you joined GW Asset Management. And that's where you met Prem Watsa.

That's right. After working seven years at Bell Canada, it was time to leave. I had already delivered some great numbers by 1982. From '81 to '82, in a six-month period, do you know how much the TSX dropped?

No.

40%. When I was running the fund, how much do you think my fund dropped?

10%?

5%.

That's great. I've heard that you were the "most talented employee" at GW Asset Management.

No. I don't know about that.

Whether true or not, why would people say that about you?

Could be just hindsight, because I'm successful now.

How did you meet Prem Watsa at GW Asset Management?

Prem was working there. He had been working at Confederation Life, and then Gardiner Watson wanted someone to run an asset management company as a subsidiary of Gardiner Watson, so that was how Prem landed there in late 1983.

You and Prem have been close since. And if we were to compare the portfolio of Fairfax Financial Holdings to your Chou Associates Fund, there are some commonalities. For example, Resolute Forest Products.

Value funds tend to have a 5% overlap. My funds may have commonalities with the funds of a lot of other value guys.

I would understand that for a stock like Google, but not for a smaller stock like Resolute Forest Products.

Resolute has more than a $1 billion market cap.

Okay, moving on then. Do you work best alone?

Yes, I just work on my own. I've been doing it since I started my fund.

It's just you investing in the funds?

Yes. Normally you need 40 to 80 people, when one has seven funds and $1 billion in assets.

What do you do for the most part on a regular day?

Just read.

What do you read?

All the newspapers, and all the publications such as *Newsweek, Forbes*, the *Economist*, as well as trade magazines, politics, scientific journals, and biographies. I read about anything and everything. Nothing is irrelevant. Investing is not done in isolation. When you read about great men and women of the past, it is like having a conversation about world affairs in your living room. It is not only educational but it builds perspective about life and business in general. I have been involved in business and investing for close to 40 years and when you have been doing this for so long you will always encounter situations similar to what these great people have faced in their lives. By reading about them, you know what kind of actions they took and how well it worked for them. You cannot ask for better guidance than that.

Do you take on positions from any of the companies that you read about in the news?

No. My first job is to check whether the company in question meets my investment criteria. It could be a good company, a bad company, or it could be a CRAP. Do you know what CRAP means?

No. Is it an acronym?

It means "cannot realize a profit."

What do you expect from CRAP companies — that they'll eventually turn around and generate a profit?

You examine the capital structure first. In terms of priority, you look at the most senior bonds, down to the most junior bonds, and finally to equities. But sometimes you can buy a senior bond at 40 cents on the dollar and if it goes into bankruptcy you can get 80 cents on a dollar.

Was that why you bought into Sears, which you have a stake in? Was it because of the real estate that may be worth more on the books than what it's trading at on the market?

Yes, the real estate is worth more than what the stock is trading at on the market.

How do you generate your best investment ideas?

I do screens, read a lot, and talk to other talented portfolio managers to see where they are seeing bargains.

So you have a sounding board.

Before you make a purchase, you should look for investors who are negative on the stock.

You want to test your logic?

Disconfirm your own thesis.

Would you consider yourself a deep-value investor?

Most probably. And that's how most would label me. But in some ways it's not really true, because I also buy a lot of good companies.

So, you're a lot like Warren Buffett then. He went from just picking up cheap "cigar butts" and getting a couple more puffs to investing in quality companies for a fair price, too.

I do the same.

How have you evolved?

As my knowledge of businesses has grown, I've bought good companies as well as mediocre companies. I'm all over the place — wherever I can find bargains.

So what's your portfolio allocation? You mentioned that you primarily buy into CRAP. But how many quality companies do you own?

It depends, based on the time period. In the nineties I had a lot more "good" companies than I do now. To purchase good companies right now you need to pay more than 25 times earnings. That is not cheap. So I just go wherever I can find bargains. For instance, in the years 2000 to 2002, I was basically in distressed bonds. I just go wherever I can find something undervalued.

Where are you finding value now?

There is hardly anything to buy.

So there's a lot of cash on the sidelines?

Yes, and I think if you break even over the next five years, you will have some of the best numbers five years down the road.

Do your funds experience higher performance than your peers during bad markets?

By and large, I had better performance than other mutual funds in bad times.

How were you investing right before the financial crisis? Did you foresee the crisis?

You should read my 2006 annual report. In it, I warned investors and explained how I was already planning on going into CDSs [Credit Default Swaps]. Here is what I wrote about the stock market, potential banking crisis, and sub-prime mortgages in that report:

According to the Bank for International Settlements, contracts outstanding worldwide for derivatives at the end of June 30, 2006 rose to $370 trillion. We are alarmed by the exponential rise in the use of derivatives. No one knows how dangerous these instruments can be. They have not been stress-tested. However we cannot remain complacent. We believe the risk embedded in derivative instruments is pervasive and most likely not limited or localized to a particular industry. Financial institutions are most vulnerable when (not if) surprises occur — and when they occur they are almost always negative.

As a result, we have not invested heavily in financial institutions although at times their stock prices have come down to buy levels. Some 30 years ago, when an investor looked at a bank, he or she knew what the items on the balance sheet meant. The investor understood what criteria the bankers used to loan out money, how to interpret the loss reserving history, and how to assess the quality and sustainability of revenue streams and expenses of the bank to generate reasonable earnings. In a nutshell, we were able to appraise how much the bank was worth based on how efficiently its bankers were utilizing the 3-6-3 rule.

The 3-6-3 rule works like this: the bank pays 3% on savings accounts, loans out money to businesses with solid financials at 6%, and then the banker leaves the office at 3 p.m. to play golf.

That was 30 years ago and you can see how easy it was to evaluate a bank.

Now, when an investor examines a bank's financials, he or she is subjected to reams of information and numbers but has no way of ascertaining with a high degree of certainty how solid the assets are, or whether the liabilities are all disclosed, or even known, much less properly priced. As the investor

digs deeper into the footnotes, instead of becoming enlight-
ened, more doubts may surface about the true riskiness of the
bank's liabilities. Those liabilities could be securitized, hidden
in derivative instruments, or morphed into any number of
other instruments that barely resemble the original loans.

We wonder whether bankers are using a rule that is as
difficult to understand as their derivative instruments. We
call it the 1-12-11 rule: namely, the bank pays 1% on checking
accounts, loans out money to businesses with weak financials at 12%, and the banker leaves the office at 11 a.m. to play
golf with hedge fund and private equity managers where
they discuss how to chop and/or bundle the loan portfolios
into different tranches and create, out of thin air, new derivative products that are rated triple A (from products that
originally were B-rated). These products are then sold to
institutions (who may be oblivious of the risk involved) that
are reaching for yields.

The above example is written tongue-in-cheek and it is not meant
to be entirely representative of what bankers do. It is meant to show
just how creative participants have been in producing new derivative
products, with little regard for a sound understanding of their leverage
and true risk characteristics. We may be witnessing a "tragedy of the
commons" where the search for quick individual profits is causing a
system-wide increase in risk and reckless behaviour.

How did the sub-prime mortgage lenders contribute to the problem?

Some of the greatest excesses of easy credit were committed by sub-
prime mortgage lenders. Credit standards were so lax and liberal that
homeowners didn't even need to produce verification of income to
be able to borrow up to 100% or more of the appraised value of their
houses.

What was your conclusion?

My report concluded as follows:

From these examples, it appears obvious that investors are
throwing caution to the wind. Risk is not priced into riskier
securities at all. Whenever the majority of investors are
purchasing securities at prices that implicitly assume that

everything is perfect with the world, an economic dislocation or other shock always seems to appear out of the blue.
And when that happens, investors learn, once again, that
they ignore risk at their peril. We continue to diligently look
for undervalued stocks and will buy them only when they
meet our price criteria — in other words, when they are
priced for *imperfection*.

Interesting. Can you expand on Credit Default Swaps?

This is what I wrote on Credit Default Swaps [CDSes] in 2006:

> In terms of investment ideas in derivatives, we believe that
> CDSes are selling at prices that are compelling. At recent prices,
> they offer the cheapest form of insurance against market dis-
> ruptions. In CDSes, one party sells credit protection and the
> other party buys credit protection. Put another way, one party
> is selling insurance and the counterparty is buying insurance
> against the default of the third party's debt. The Chou Funds
> would be interested in buying this type of insurance.
>
> To give you some sense of perspective, in October 2002,
> the five-year CDS of General Electric Company was quoted
> at an annual price of 110 basis points. Recently, it was quoted
> at an annual price of less than eight basis points.
>
> To make money in CDSes, you don't need a default of
> the third party's debt. If there is any hiccup in the economy,
> the CDS price will rise from these low levels. The negative
> aspect is that, like insurance, the premium paid for the pro-
> tection erodes over time and may expire worthless.
>
> Unfortunately I could not get the approval to purchase
> CDSes for my funds quickly. I was having some problems get-
> ting regulatory approval, getting comfortable with counter-
> party risks, and so on.

Let's focus on your current investment process: do you invest bottom-up?

Yes. Initially I analyze bottom-up and then I go top-down. For example,
let us look at the banks. What's the most important thing to check in
the bank?

ROE?

No. It is the loan portfolio, the book of business. You start with the loan portfolio and then you go from there. But most investors invest in terms of premium or discount to book value. That is a serious mistake. Let's say the year was 2006. You examine the loan portfolio and see all the junk there. As a result, you wouldn't touch a U.S. bank with a barge pole. The question about loan growth becomes irrelevant then.

So you don't systematically scan stocks for low book value?

No. I'm a businessman. I have the benefit of having worked in operations. So I have an understanding of business, and not just book value. I bring another element to my analysis.

It's your wisdom and experience that makes you successful. You don't indiscriminately scan and invest in stocks.

Exactly.

How do your holdings post such strong returns?

I'm trying to buy 80 cents for 40 cents. It does not matter whether they are good companies, bad companies, or distressed companies.

Then how do you evaluate intrinsic value so that you can buy bargains?

The first thing you have to do in this business is to make sure that your valuation is accurate. That's how it starts. If you think a stock is worth $100, you try to buy it at $60. But if your valuation is wrong, and four years down the road it turns out it's worth only $60, then you won't make it in this business.

How do you ascertain that your valuation is accurate?

You're a businessman and you look for these assets. Then you ask, "If I were to buy this company, how much would I pay?"

You also ensure that there's a catalyst, right?

Buy and wait works most of the time, but a catalyst accelerates the process and generates higher returns.

Have you taken on a position that didn't work out right away but worked out in the long run?

Oh, yes.

Can you share an example?

Yes, one instance happened two years ago when I bought a stock called Overstock.com that I thought was worth closer to $25. I bought it for Chou Opportunity Fund around $14 and it promptly went down to $7. I bought some more at that price. A bargain at $14 became a super bargain at $7.

Why did you think that it was worth closer to $25?

That was just my valuation. That's what I thought it was worth based on its inventories, revenues, double-digit percentage growth in revenues, the potential of the business, the website, and a combination of factors that didn't show up in the operating statement. Eventually, it went up a year later to $34.

Once an investment reaches your target price — in Overstock's case, $25 — do you start to sell?

Yes, I would start selling then.

And then allocate that capital in other positions?

Yes.

With Overstock, you practised dollar-cost averaging. It went lower, and you bought more shares.

No, it was not precisely dollar-cost averaging. You don't automatically buy when it goes down. It all depends on your valuation. In this case, it was still worth $25 after reassessing it after the drop, so at $14, I was getting a 44% discount and at $7, I was getting a 72% discount.

Has there been a time though when you sold out of a stock because it dropped?

No, you don't sell because of that. But if my revised valuation is $7, I would sell it. It would mean my original valuation of $25 was wrong.

I see. So, if the business deteriorates along with the stock price, then you would sell?

Yes, if I think the valuation is now not $25, then I've made a mistake. A downward revision to $7 would prompt me to sell. The decision is totally based on valuation.

Normally you don't invest in technology, correct? Overstock is close, but it's e-commerce.

I shy away because of obsolescence and so on. I cannot predict the future of technology, and I don't know what will happen two years from now where there could and probably would be newer technology.

But you invest in BlackBerry — why is that?

Some of my investment choices like BlackBerry are because their patents are worth so much more than their stock price. For example, I bought some BlackBerry when it was around $7 because I valued the patents at about $13.

I'm interested in your thoughts on the Indian market. You were born there.

Indian people are highly intelligent and highly creative.

I agree — they generally are highly educated.

There's no reason why Indians shouldn't flourish in India.

Have you taken on any positions in Indian companies?

At this time, no.

Do you plan to?

We are looking into it.

Which companies would you look at in India?

I would take the same approach as I do here.

But I imagine a lot of them would be startup companies that you'd avoid.

They need to have some history. I am someone who will look at 10-year history, even a 20-year history.

Do you look for consistent earnings?

Yes. I don't mind even if the revenue decreases as long as management is doing the right thing. I don't want to chase businesses where management is making decisions that don't make economic sense.

What about increases in book value. Is that important?

I think increases in intrinsic value are more important than increases in book value.

What's the difference?

Sustainable earning power, business moats, and competitive advantage relate more closely to intrinsic value and therefore are more important than just increases in book value.

So you also need to understand whether or not a company will have competitive advantage for the long term?

Yes, five years, ten years down the road, if you're going to go the route of good companies.

How can you predict that?

Well, with firms such as Sears and BlackBerry, you don't know. Therefore, you look for asset coverage like real estate or patents. With others, like Coca-Cola, you can predict for sure.

Which companies generally don't have enduring competitive advantage?

Technology companies for sure. Mining and commodity companies come to mind, too.

Do you have anything else to add?

It's important to remember that investments are most profitable when the selection process is most businesslike. Therefore, you must have the skill level to evaluate a business. As for assets, evaluate what they are worth, because the accuracy of that valuation will determine how well you perform as an investor. I enjoy doing this. It's very hard to say but I think the best way to describe it is that I've found my calling, which makes it easier and more enjoyable.

Do you have a succession plan in place?

At this time, I don't. I'm still fairly young. One of the benefits of starting young is that one can have a 30-year record, even 35 like I have, and I can still manage the funds for a while. That is one of the benefits of starting so early.

Have you groomed anybody, though?

At this time, no. Eventually, I will have to. That question will get more pressing as I get older.

Are you considering having your kids enter the business?

I'll leave it to them to decide. This business of investing and how I do it is very psychological.

By psychological you mean that when you have a conviction you stick to it, right? You don't sell out based on general market sentiment?

You have to go against the grain. You have to do your own independent work, your own analysis, and you stand on the merits of your own judgments. The stock market will tell you in two years, maybe four years down the road, whether you've been accurate or not.

Have your kids shown an interest in the business?

One is seriously interested at this time.

What struck me most about Francis was his strong sense of confidence. He is very certain of himself, his performance, and his outlook.

His track record shows that his predictions have come to pass, whether they were good or bad for the markets. In the early eighties he predicted that the future would bring higher equity market prices as rates started to decrease. That's precisely what happened. Now he warns that an imminent increase in rates would hamper equity markets. Time will tell.

Francis mentioned to me that he personally started buying Fairfax Financial (FFH) stock at $3.25 early on in his career. FFH is now around $605 per share. You don't have to do the math to fathom that the return on his investment in Fairfax Financial is mouth-watering. While Francis is no longer on the senior management team at Fairfax Financial, he still considers its founder and CEO, Prem Watsa, a close friend and confidant. I will close this section with Francis Chou's investment philosophy, as he describes it on his firm's website:

> The investment process followed in selecting equity investments for the funds is a value-oriented approach to investing. This involves a detailed analysis of the strengths of individual companies, with much less emphasis on short-term market factors. Far greater importance is placed upon an assessment of a company's balance sheet, cash flow characteristics, profitability, industry position, special strengths, future growth potential, and management ability. The level of investments in the company's securities is generally commensurate with the current price of the company's securities in relation to its intrinsic value as determined by the above factors. That approach is designed to provide an extra margin of safety, which in turn serves to reduce overall portfolio risk. The manager may decide to maintain a larger portion of the fund's assets in short-term fixed-income securities during periods of high market valuations and volatility. This temporary departure from the fund's core investment strategy may be undertaken to protect capital while awaiting more favourable market conditions.

Says Francis, "We do nothing fancy. We are just looking for undervalued stocks." Francis provided me with the following information about the three areas on which they focus:

- Good companies
  - › Sustainable earning power (look at owner's earnings) for the last 10 years, generally not in mining, commodities, or IT
  - › Management showing reasonable allocation skill
  - › Companies that are not highly leveraged
  - › Companies selling for less than 10 times earnings
- Mediocre companies
  - › Liquidation value
  - › Potential turnaround situation
  - › Sum of the parts valuation
- CRAP (cannot realize a profit) companies
  - › Look at bonds first
  - › Start with the most senior bonds in the capital structure
  - › Assume it's going bankrupt

Finally, at a value investing conference, Francis presented this closing advice for the audience:

> In conclusion, if you stay patient, buy when it's cheap, and don't chase the stock when it runs away from you, there's no reason for you not to beat the market. The market is there for you to take advantage of, not to let it control you. Have the courage of your conviction, courage of your work, courage of your analysis, and courage of your judgment, and you should beat the market.

MASTER KEYS
FRANCIS CHOU

1) Relating shopping in India to investing: "It was my job to make sure I was paying the lowest price for the best quality."

2) "I contrast the current scenario to the scenario in 1981. Everyone is so bullish but I'm really negative."

3) "I didn't know the market was going to take off in six months [in 1981], but I knew you couldn't get stocks any cheaper than their prices at the time."

4) "When you read about great men and women of the past, it is like having a conversation about world affairs in your living room. It is not only educational but it builds perspective about life and business in general."

5) "My first job is to check whether the company in question meets my investment criteria. It could be a good company, a bad company, or it could be a CRAP [cannot realize a profit]."

6) "I do screens, read a lot, and talk to other talented portfolio managers to see where they are seeing bargains. . . . [And] before you make a purchase, you should look for investors who are negative on the stock."

7) "I just go wherever I can find bargains. For instance, in the years 2000 to 2002, I was basically in distressed bonds. I just go wherever I can find something undervalued."

8) "Whenever the majority of investors are purchasing securities at prices that implicitly assume that everything is perfect with the world, an economic dislocation or other shock always seems to appear out of the blue. And when that happens, investors learn, once again, that they ignore risk at their peril."

9) "We continue to diligently look for undervalued stocks and will buy them only when they meet our price criteria — in other words, when they are priced for *imperfection*."

10) "Initially I analyze bottom-up and then I go top-down."

11) "Most investors invest in terms of premium or discount to book value. That is a serious mistake. Let's say the year was 2006. You examine the loan portfolio [of a bank] and see all the junk there. As a result, you wouldn't touch a U.S. bank with a barge pole."

12) "I'm trying to buy 80 cents for 40 cents. It does not matter whether they are good companies, bad companies, or distressed companies."

13) "The first thing you have to do in this business is to make sure that your valuation is accurate. If your valuation is wrong . . . then you won't make it in this business."

14) "You're a businessman . . . you ask, 'If I were to buy this company, how much would I pay?'"

15) "I don't know what will happen two years from now where there could and probably would be newer technology."

16) "I don't want to chase businesses where management is making decisions that don't make economic sense."

17) "Sustainable earning power, business moats, and competitive advantage relate more closely to intrinsic value and therefore are more important than just increases in book value."

18) "Investments are most profitable when the selection process is most businesslike. Therefore, you must have the skill level to evaluate a business."

19) "You have to go against the grain. You have to do your own independent work, your own analysis, and you stand on the merits of your own judgments."

PART II GROWTH

Growth investors invest in stocks that have higher-than-average return potential compared to other stocks in the market. That means growth investors use criteria such as revenue growth, earnings growth, return on equity, and return on invested capital, among other metrics, to inform their investment decisions. These criteria can be augmented by strong management that is skillful at capital allocation, such that those managers can maintain high growth rates for as long a period as possible.

The law of large numbers often means that growth stocks' compound returns do lower over time, and so the once high-growth achieved by those growth stocks can stall. That is why growth investors tend to allocate their money into new growth stocks that should experience high multiple expansions into the future, at least until they, too, face an abatement in high growth compound returns. The risk inherent in growth investing is that growth investors can "chase hot stocks," effectively buying high and selling low, or simply rack up high commission fees from a higher-than-average turnover in their portfolio.

The risk/reward concept argues that growth investors are rewarded for their assumption of greater risk in the market. Usually, growth stocks exist in the micro-cap, small-cap, and mid-cap segments of the market, because as previously mentioned, growth stalls due to the law of large numbers (that is, compounding returns can't be high forever). Eventually growth stocks can become large "steady" stocks.

MARTIN BRAUN
THE REFORMED VALUE INVESTOR
TURNED GARP INVESTOR

You know that saying, "Don't judge a book by its cover"? I was reminded of that adage when I met Martin Braun for the first time. As I walked into the colourless JC Clark offices, Martin greeted me with a somber hello, wearing jeans and a pressed shirt and sporting a beard. Martin walked me over to the room where we would hold our interview. Before we started our conversation, he opened a can of Dr Pepper and ripped open the wrapper of a granola bar. I don't know many adults who drink Dr Pepper these days. Was this his lunch? Martin was cool as a cat, to the point that it almost seemed as though he had checked out of work. But again, don't judge a book by its cover. Instead, judge Martin by his returns.

The JC Clark Adaly Trust, which Martin runs, has achieved 15.83% compound annual returns since inception in 2000. Clearly, he's beat the TSX by a wide margin. Martin's cumulative return since 2000 is 875%. If you had invested $100,000 with him in 2000, he would have made you a millionaire by 2015. In his best *month*, Martin achieved a 21% return. In his best year, Martin achieved a 57% return. And in 2015, a year that was marred by market volatility, Martin was already up 17% by June. In other words, don't underestimate Martin. It's true that he makes investing look easy. But don't be fooled — the market is a very complex and treacherous place, and Martin has found a method that works for him.

Early in his career, in 1988, Martin joined Gluskin Sheff + Associates, where he spent 10 years being responsible for the analysis and management of the Canadian and U.S. equity portfolios. But Martin struggled. That may seem surprising in light of his current returns, but it's because, as Martin explains it, "I started out as a value investor." It was only when he found himself sitting on the sidelines and not participating in the spectacular gains others generated during the bull market that Martin converted to a GARP (growth at a reasonable price) investor. After his epiphany, Martin decided to leave Gluskin Sheff + Associates and strike out on his own, co-founding the Strategic Advisors Corp.

Over the next seven years, as Strategic Advisors' president and portfolio manager, he managed the Adaly Opportunity Fund (now rebranded the JC Clark Adaly Fund). In those early days, Martin's core strategy was purely risk arbitrage. He explains in the interview that during the early 2000s, merger and acquisition spreads in the market were often overlooked, and so one could capture 20% spreads on a consecutive basis. Once the market became more efficient, though, and squeezed those spreads, Martin shifted to what remains his strategy today: growth at a reasonable price. Martin is a high-conviction investor, so his hedge fund is usually limited to under 20 stocks. Those stocks can be described as high-growth, small- to mid-cap companies that are on the verge of making it to the big leagues. Martin has a knack for finding and then investing in companies before they make rapid price advancements in the market.

PRE-INTERVIEW LESSONS

CONVICTION: when an investor has such a firm belief in a particular stock that he or she allocates more money to it than usual in anticipation that its returns will be more than those of other holdings in the portfolio.

INFLECTION: the turning point in a company or stock price, either up or down, for better or worse.

OPTION: the right or obligation to buy or sell a security at a specific price, at a specific quantity, within a set period of time.

OPTIONALITY: asset returns that are not currently priced (or appreciated) in the market but that can occur in the future, if one or some factors (options) play out.

PROBABILITY: the likelihood that an investment will perform or not perform based on an investor's initial thesis. Probability can be applied at the market, portfolio, and stock level.

SPINOFF: a divesture of a parent company's division or subsidiary to existing shareholders in the form of a new publicly traded company. For example, eBay's spinoff of PayPal in 2015.

Where were you born and where did you grow up in Canada?

I was born and raised in Montreal and I went to McGill University.

And how did you first get interested in the markets?

I got interested in the markets not because I was into business and finance as a kid but because I was in an MBA program at McGill, which I withdrew from halfway through because I didn't like it very much. But in the process I met a guy from Chicago who became my best buddy and he grew up with the stock market. His dad was a broker and so the markets had been a part of his life since he was a little kid. He had the bug and he'd sit there in class reading the stock quotes in the paper. Back in those days that was the best source for stock prices, though the data was always old: closing prices from the day before. While you're sitting there waiting for the class to begin you had no idea what was going on in the stock market, because you didn't have mobile devices back then.

Anyways, I asked him, "What are those tiny little numbers and letters that you're staring at?" Frankly, I could barely even see them. He thought I was an idiot because, after all, I was in business school. How could I not know what the stock pages were? So he patiently explained it to me and I got hooked on the process. It reminded me of when I used to go to the horse races and go through the little letters and numbers on the racing form denoting how the horses had done in their previous races and I thought, "You know, this is very similar to trying to predict which horse is going to win a race." So I got hooked on the markets.

Did you buy stocks in university, the ones that you followed in the paper?

Yeah, but in a very small way because I was just a poor student. Five hundred dollars to me was a lot of money back then. Because I had limited funds I might have bought a hundred dollars' worth of shares but still watched every tick as it went across the bottom of the TV screen, mesmerized by the Sony quote, for example *[laughs]*.

[Laughs] Waiting for Sony to cross.

Yeah, I waited for SNE to cross and if it ticked up by 1/8 I got all excited but if it went back down to $7 I got all depressed.

What investing principles did your friend pass onto you?

It was a long time ago. I think that primarily he was a value investor. He liked to buy stocks with a low P/E. However, I'm not sure how sophisticated he was. At the time he seemed like the most brilliant guy in the world to be able to predict where a stock would go but in retrospect I don't remember taking away very much from him other than he just preferred it if the multiple was low. I don't think he was a chartist. I can't credit him with much more than just introducing me to the market.

It's obvious though that you're not a value investor. You invest in growth stocks. What happened along the way?

That's an interesting observation. When I started to look for stocks to buy I was a value investor. I was a value investor who needed a catalyst. So it was a combination of buying cheap but also looking for evidence that something was going to change. For example, a company that was going to be acquired by a bigger company. Or some kind of corporate development that would surface. I was definitely in the value camp. But then as the years went by, and many years have gone by since, I've learned that being a value investor is very often a bad idea because a lot of value stocks are value traps; they lure you into the position because they're "cheap." But in actual fact they're cheap for a reason.

I'm not suggesting that the market is 100% efficient, but the market's not stupid and most of the time stocks are cheap for a reason and the market knows that. So you're not going to really come out ahead as a value investor if all you are is just a value investor. Clearly, for the longest time now the market has been a growth market. But back then I was never the kind of growth investor who bought tech stocks and biotech stocks and didn't really care about the multiple. I was the complete opposite of that. Anyway, eventually I could see that the trend was against me. I had to make concessions to growth and so I developed a hybrid style of being cognizant of value but looking for growth. At some point many years ago they invented this term: "GARP," growth at a reasonable price. I didn't invent it but I became a GARP investor before the acronym was invented. I think that today most investors would probably fall within the GARP camp. I still feel that value is important. But l think that growth is the key driver in the markets and that you need to look for catalysts. It's the combination or synthesis of all three — growth, value, and catalysts — that create, for me, the investment thesis that I'm looking for.

What was the exact inflection point from being a value investor to becoming a GARP investor?

The mid- to late nineties cured me of my value habits. That was the period leading up to the dot.com mess, when Amazon, Yahoo!, and eBay burst upon the scene. That first wave of internet digital stocks. Prior to the mid-nineties there weren't too many of those stocks. Apple was a beaten-up, crappy little company that had failed to win against the IBM clone world. Microsoft was around but it wasn't a very sexy stock anymore. And of course we'd had a couple of mini-recessions that took a lot out of the market. So by the mid-nineties there wasn't a lot of excitement in that space until all of a sudden the internet market started to heat up and of course you know the rest is history. By the end of that decade — 2000 — it was just crazy; any stock with a dot.com in its name sold.

I was at Gluskin Sheff at that time and had been asked to manage the U.S. portfolio. I hadn't been professionally investing in U.S. equities prior to that so it was new for me. Coming from Canada, where value investing is far more prevalent, I naturally brought that style to the U.S. portfolio. So I wasn't buying the Amazons and eBays — that just wasn't my *thing*. Well, I got my clock cleaned. I didn't get it. I was buying companies that had better balance sheets, better ROEs, better cash flows, lower P/Es, average market caps — call it a billion at most — but I was getting trounced by huge companies. Pharmaceutical companies, big banks, big consumer product companies, all massive mega-cap stocks with single-digit growth rates that were going up at 20% a year. I was only going up 5% to 8% a year. I realized at that point that there was something wrong with the way I was looking at the market and trying to make money.

Ultimately, what was wrong with your approach?

I didn't figure it out right away. I just licked my wounds and sulked a lot and whined and complained how it was not fair. But eventually, over many years, it sort of dawned on me that being a value investor is just not the answer. It's not how you're going to come out ahead in the long run. You have to make some concessions to the fact that the market's much bigger than you and that you need to figure out the market; the market doesn't have to figure out you.

So that was your evolution as an investor. What about your career path?

I was on the sell side. That was the easiest way to get into the business after I did an MBA at the University of Western Ontario. But having gotten into the industry and spending a few years being a sell-side research analyst, I realized that the sooner I transitioned to the buy side the better, because ultimately I wanted to be a money manager.

In 1988 I was approached by one of my better clients, Ira Gluskin at Gluskin Sheff, which had just started a few years earlier, who said that he liked the work I did and asked whether I would leave my sell-side job to come work at GS+A. I jumped at the opportunity. I became a generalist analyst for them, and then when their lead manager on the Canadian side, Kiki Delaney, left I inherited the job. I became the Canadian equity manager and a few years later became the U.S. equity manager. And then in 1997, after nine years with Gluskin Sheff, as a partner with a certain amount of sway, I approached them and asked if we could start a hedge fund. They rejected the idea.

Why did they reject the hedge fund concept?

From one conversation in particular, Gerry Sheff said to me, "Why would we change anything? We must be doing something right." At that time, we had over $1 billion in assets under management. When I joined, the AUM was just $140 million. So we had multiplied that many times and I guess Gerry figured he had the secret sauce. Why complicate things? You see, the hedge fund space in the U.S. had been growing for decades, and in Canada it was just on the cusp. So, eventually I left Gluskin Sheff. Within the year I was gone and ready to start my own hedge fund.

That must have been a tough decision. You were a partner at Gluskin Sheff.

Yeah, but on the other hand I eventually became *persona non grata* [laughs]. I was the golden boy for many years but by the time I left I was not the golden boy anymore.

So, you started to stand out for all the wrong reasons?

It was just a bunch of things. I didn't exactly blow the doors off when I was running U.S. equities, which I mentioned earlier. I was having a hard time figuring out why I was having such a hard time beating the U.S. market. But it doesn't matter because it worked out *really* well in the end for them and it worked out *really* well for me, too. I left in the spring of '98 and registered a money management company with the thought that I would launch a hedge fund. But I also wanted to partner with people; I didn't want to do it alone. I eventually found some people to partner with, and by the fall of '99, we had a deal and the firm I created was renamed Strategic Advisors. Six or seven years later, though, it would be renamed again, to Trapeze Asset Management.

The proposition I had brought to the two guys that I went in with was that we would share the economics of their company. And, that I would also have direct economics and control over the hedge fund. For background, they had struggled with their previous firm, which is what brought them to me, in need of something that would help salvage what was left. My hedge fund launched on January 1, 2000. It was named the Adaly Opportunity Fund, and the overall business was a huge success.

We started with almost nothing because I had a non-compete clause coming out of GS+A, so I couldn't take clients or their assets. Anyway, by September 2006, we had about $1.5 billion under management. My fund was a big success; they were doing really well; everything was just great; but internally there was some friction between us. The friction was because of their style versus my style, my not being a member of their family, and of course the economics of our arrangement. That led to them basically saying, "Martin, it's over between the three of us." So we had a parting of ways.

What happened next?

After I left, they had a notable reversal of fortune. Anyway, part of the deal when I left was that I took the Adaly Fund with me. So I started another company called Adaly Investment Management, to manage the Adaly Fund. The new vehicle was 100% owned by me, and all that happened was that the Adaly Fund, which had been around almost seven years, just got moved across the street.

Then, sometime around 2012, after managing the fund for about five years, I decided I didn't want to do it anymore. I was done with the business. I had a bad year in 2011 and was beaten down, run down, and burned out. I'd made enough money in my life that I didn't need to work for a living, so I just reappraised my priorities and thought, "You know what? I'm done." So I looked to shop the firm around. But I had four employees and I didn't want to put them all out on the street so I tried to find a deal that would preserve as many jobs as possible. The employees that were the most vulnerable were the two analysts. JC Clark was the only firm that was interested in acquiring me, my business, and also willing to take those two analysts. So I did that deal.

That's very thoughtful of you to also look after their interests.

I hired them many years earlier. One had been with me about seven years and the other around nine years. I hired them when they were in their mid-twenties. By now, both were married, and one had two little kids. A lot happens in that period of your life. I was there for them from the beginning so to just put those two guys on the street didn't sit well with me. So we all came on board at JC Clark in November 2012, but ironically 20 months later they left and now run a Canadian equity mutual fund. The other two people got jobs eventually as well. So happily all four of my former people are now working.

It was hard to admit that I didn't want to own a money management business anymore. But I just wanted to kick back and go into a semi-retirement mode. I was potentially putting four people who were not of the same financial means as myself out of work, but sometimes you've just got to do what you've got to do for yourself, and if you're doing it for the right reasons things work out and in this case everybody's happy where they are.

What's it like now? Do you feel like a lone wolf in a big firm?

Just to clarify, this is not a big firm. When I brought the Adaly Fund into JC Clark, the thought was that we would manage the fund, do our own thing, and share the economics much like I shared the economics with the Abramsons, the owners of Trapeze Asset Management. That was fine with me. At this stage of my life, money is not the reason why I do things. So it was perfect for me to just come here, bring my guys, do my thing, with no one telling me what to do, and working at my own pace. I'm in a much better headspace now. In fact, I've been totally re-energized over the period. I've gone from being semi–burnt out in 2011 to feeling like a kid again.

Health and happiness is important.

Yeah. So, through it all, the fund that I started on January 1, 2000, is still around. It still has the word Adaly in it but it's now the "JC Clark Adaly Fund" or the "JC Clark Adaly Trust." Many of the clients who are in it today have been in it for the better part of 15 years so I have a loyal crew. I'm the largest investor in the fund. Collectively, 20% of the whole fund is owned by my immediate family.

What are the assets under management today?

The fund's about $60 million. But at one time Adaly Investment Management managed almost $300 million. The majority of that though was third-party management — managing other people's funds. When I decided to shut my company down, those contracts were terminated.

Let's move on. The year 2000, which was also the fund's inception, was a turning point in the market. The tech boom ended in a big crash . . .

It was in March when it crashed, I believe.

What investment themes did you capture after that turning point in the market?

That was a crazy period in '98 and '99. It got really nuts. As a value investor, you can imagine that I just sat there and watched stocks go crazy. Interestingly, they had no revenues, no earnings, but market caps in the billions. It was bizarre. So I asked myself, "What kind of a fund am I going to start in an environment like this?" The answer was an arbitrage fund. I'm not sure how familiar you are with merger arbitrage but that was the focus.

You capitalized on spreads in the market, which resulted from various mergers or buy-outs.

Yes, that's quite well known and everybody does it, including the bro-kers themselves, but it wasn't that well capitalized back in the nineties. I was shocked at the kinds of spreads you could make: literally 30% returns on announced deals and some of them were double and triple even that.

What were some of the best arbitrage spreads that you capitalized on during that period?

Geez, we're talking about 15 years ago. We had a massive database. Every time a company announced it was being acquired it would go into that database and we'd just go trolling through the database looking for the best spreads with the least risk. I can't really pull one out and say, "This one was the best." However, there was a big deal a few years earlier that blew up. It was UAL. I believe that United Airlines, UAL, was going to be acquired by the union or the union in concert with some institutions. I don't remember exactly. It was a multi-billion-dollar deal and they were going to take UAL private but the whole deal fell apart. Everyone got their clock cleaned. That took a lot of capital out of the market.

As a result, by the time I came along in '98, the spreads were really good. I could just do plain vanilla deals for 12%, or 14%, or 16% annualized. Some of the better deals, which had a financing requirement that wasn't quite confirmed, would have 20 to 30% spreads. But then the little deals that were hard to put on or people thought were very risky would have 40%, or 60%, or 80% annualized spreads. Anyway, I started the Adaly Fund as a merger arbitrage fund. But it didn't take me very long to figure out that I didn't just have to trade on announced deals. I could also trade rumoured deals or theoretical deals.

Can you give an example?

Okay, although this one's actually a spinoff, it still fit into my arbitrage strategy. Very early on, maybe in the first month of the fund's life, I came across something called Teleclone; people from the old days will remember this. It was a play on whether Bell Canada, which owned the *controlling* interest in Northern Telecom, or Nortel, would divest, or dividend out Nortel to its shareholders. The thought being that when you looked at the price of the Bell Canada shares in comparison to the price of Nortel shares, you paid virtually nothing for the actual phone company. The thought was that one day the Bell board of directors would vote to spin off Nortel and then the Bell shares would go up.

Teleclone was a synthetic instrument that had been created out of some investment banker's head and sold into the marketplace on the premise that if you bought it you were effectively buying Bell's phone company for very little and when eventually Nortel got spun out that the Bell value would pop. As a result, you as a Teleclone shareholder would be rewarded. Unfortunately, after it got issued to the public and started to trade, Teleclone went down the toilet. The Bell board met a couple of times, but nothing came of it, and people just started to give up on the idea. Teleclone went so low that investors were being paid to own Bell Canada. To elaborate, the value of Nortel in Bell Canada was more than the price of Bell Canada shares. That made no sense at all.

Before you go on can you explain the structure of Teleclone?

Teleclone was constructed by going to the Bank of Montreal, buying a whack of Bell shares, and then short-selling a whack of Nortel shares and capitalizing that position with the IPO proceeds.

Did you buy into Teleclone at that point of capitulation?

Yeah, Nortel went the wrong way and so there was a massive margin call. I figured that Teleclone would eventually work and so I thought, "Why not get in after all the pain and suffering?" Teleclone was sold to the public at like $28. By the time I stumbled across it, Teleclone was $4. So I started buying it in the low single digits and it ended up being the biggest position in the fund. Eventually the spinoff did happen and Teleclone shares subsequently went up to around $35. Five times return. It didn't take long. It took maybe 90 days. So that was what I would do; not just trade on deals that were already announced but also trade on the possibility of deals. However, after a couple of years, more capital came into the space, and as result, the spreads collapsed. Suddenly the mid-teen spreads were down in the single digits so I lost interest.

Did you completely shift your fund's primary investment strategy, or diversify into others?

I had to really redefine my fund. So I went back to the drawing board, rewrote the O.M., and renamed the fund from Adaly M&A Opportunity to just Adaly Opportunity. By the way, "Adaly" comes from my two kids. My son's name is Adam, and my daughter's name is Alyssa, so I just took the "Ada" and the "Aly" and put them together. Interestingly, Greivis Vasquez, a former Toronto Raptors guard, got his name "Greivis" from the combination of his father's name, Gregorio, and his mother's name, Ivis. Anyway, I evolved the fund into what is now called a multi-strategy fund.

Can you elaborate on your multi-strategies?

Long, short, some bonds, some converts, derivatives like warrants, futures, options, and arbitrage. Mostly North American. One of the things that I like about a hedge fund is that it's flexible. I can do whatever I think is the right thing to do. Whereas when you look at most mutual funds they have names that tell you what they do. So this is the CI Canadian Equity Large-Cap Fund or this is the U.S. Equity Mid-Cap Fund. That's the name of the fund and that's what they do and that's the guy's mandate. He has to stay within X and Y. A good hedge fund manager is not limited by those little boxes where you need to play within a specific sandbox. You can do whatever the spirit moves you to do. Now, if you're a lunatic, that's not good, but if you're skilled, if you're intelligent, and if you're a student of the market, then that flexibility is really good.

And so in the life of my fund — it's in its sixteenth year now — I've had to adjust because the markets don't stand still. Their complexion changes all the time. For example, in the mid- to late nineties and then after the crash, I couldn't just sit there and say, "This is what I do and I can't do anything different." Something works for a while and then it doesn't work. Then it works again, and then it doesn't. We hedge fund managers don't want to just sit there going, "I'll wait three or four years until my style comes back in favour again." We adapt. There are other guys like my buddy Richard Rooney at Burgundy Asset Management who doesn't care as much; he's positioned for the long term as he has been for the last 25 years, and it's worked because his team has built a $30-billion business. That's fine. It suits his temperament. But that's not going to work for me. It doesn't suit my temperament. Hopefully the investors in my fund appreciate that I am a student of the market, and it would be a mistake to put handcuffs on me.

Yeah, you mentioned that as a value investor, you would watch your value stocks return 5 to 10% while the market would return 20%-plus annualized. Since then you've clearly adapted, and surpassed the markets. In 2014 your return was 48% versus roughly 10% for the market.

Well, the actual return was 49%, and it was the lowest of the various classes because Adaly has older and newer classes of units. There's A, B, C, D, and F and the fee structures vary. The fee structure on the Trust classes is a teeny bit more onerous than on the old A or B classes. The A was the most generous to the investor. So that's why you get 49% on the D and 50% on the B and the A is like 51%. The truth is that without all the fees we probably made 65% last year, but who's counting, right?

Can you explain exactly how you generate those high returns in your fund today?

In a way I'm coming back to the most fundamental of fundamentals. You know, Graham and Dodd, and its greatest practitioner, Warren Buffett. I invest in a handful of businesses, not a whole bunch of them, and get to know them *really* well. One guy, I don't know who, said "Just put a few eggs in the basket but watch the basket *very* closely." I've come around to that. I might still take on a little extra risk with smaller positions but what I say to investors is that I'm looking for 20 good stocks. The other day I was at a forum and Jonathan Bloomberg was there — he's a principal of a very good firm called BloombergSen. Anyway, Jonathan said, "Fifteen stocks and that's it." They actually owned 14 stocks and were about to sell one of them. His returns are fantastic. Warren Buffett is the same kind of animal. Not big on the short side.

Just find a great business and learn it upside down and inside out so that nobody knows more about that business than you. Once you've learned so much about that business, don't put just a couple bucks in — put a lot of bucks in. And then find a dozen other stocks just like it and just draw the line there. If one of those stocks goes off the rails then you'll be one of the first ones to realize that it's coming off the rails, and push it out the door before everyone else.

Okay, you run a high-conviction fund. Do you also use technical analysis before you buy into a position? For example, look at relative strength or momentum?

No, I don't. I'm not into momentum very much. I'm really a fundamental-based investor. I want to invest in a company that most people don't appreciate how good it is or how good it's going to be. Sometimes it's already achieved something special but people don't realize how good it *truly* is. I mean, five years from now you're going to be looking at a much bigger multiple because you won't be the only guy who knows it's a great company. And of course earnings will be much higher as well. Then there's other companies which haven't really achieved much, but might be on the cusp of something special. There might be a few small brokers who know the story but most people haven't done a lot of research on it.

Some of the stocks that you own have low coverage, only a couple of analysts.

Yeah, maybe none. It could be that just a few buy-side guys are sticking it in their personal accounts. It's not well known, but you've got to know the company, what they do, and the ultimate potential.

Can you give an example of a small-cap company with very low coverage that went from good to great after you bought into it?

Yeah, I've got a perfect example: Patient Home Monitoring.

PHM is being touted by all the analysts now.

Yeah, we bought into PHM about a year ago. It was 30 cents, and it became our second-largest position. We actually are selling out now . . . I can tell you this because my words won't be in print for a while. Today we sold two million shares in the market at just under $2. At that price we earned six times our original investment. Why did we buy it? It was a tiny little company. Also, we liked what management said to us. They had an opportunity to acquire small businesses in the United States on the cheap that cater to patients who had chronic conditions that could be addressed in a home setting.

Why are you selling PHM shares on the market now?

There's this one guy, Fabrice Taylor, who jumped on the story. He has a strong retail following. So as a result of recommendations like that the stock went up a lot and they were able to issue shares to the public at pretty good prices for the company. Then PHM took the money and made more acquisitions and the acquisitions caused the stock to go up even more so they issued some more shares at favourable pricing and, well, you know how it goes. That kind of behaviour makes me nervous. Anyways, up here it's enough. I've seen this stock go up by almost six times in ten months. We've made so much money that I think the only sane thing to do is to sell. Besides, the valuation is stretched; more and more shares keep getting issued, and there's no longer-term track record I can point to. Truth is, I'm a cynic by nature.

What will be the next hot stock? Which industry?

Health care is a hot area right now. Everyone wants into it. PHM is not the only hot health care stock on the market.

Concordia Healthcare, Valeant . . .

Yeah, we've probably made 12 times our money on Concordia Healthcare in the last 16 months. And again, it's a roll-up company that has somehow convinced the street that they should just go buy the shares every time they acquire a new suite of drugs, and then the stock goes up, they issue more shares, they buy some more drugs, the stock goes up again, they issue more shares, and so on. Concordia Healthcare was originally a shell; a $1 shell. They put Concordia into the shell at $1, and now it's almost $100.

What about the stocks that you bought into that didn't go from good to great?

Generally that's because of mis-execution. You know, management has all kinds of really good ideas in the business world like "I'm going to do this, I'm going to do that," but then sometimes you look back and see that never happened, and go, "What happened?" Well, it takes a certain skill to be able to execute. It's one thing to say, "I'm going to do this," and it's another to actually do it. How many guys say they're going to write a book about money managers and how many actually do it? It's the same in this business. For example, you come into my office and say, "Martin, you should buy my shares, I'm going to do all kinds of wonderful things," and I say, "Hmm, I don't know," and then three years later I ask myself, "What was the name of that company? They were going to do all kinds of wonderful things. Oh, I remember now," and you look them up, and they're at 10 cents a share.

Some people have the ability to execute and some don't. Some people motivate well and can get everyone fired up like they're on a mission. They're great motivators, great team leaders, and great executors. Bay Street loves them. On the other hand, the other guys just fall flat. Usually, the stocks that I didn't make money on or I lost money on was because I misjudged management.

You buy into companies with good executers.

That's the big thing. Running a public company, and getting Bay Street behind you, is crucial.

If you were to take your 20% stake out of the Adaly Fund, which I'm sure you won't do any time soon, where would you put that money? If you were to choose any other money manager.

Well, I'd give some money to Jason Donville. Have you already talked to him?

Yeah. Interestingly, he has recently closed his fund to new money.

Because he had so much money coming in.

He wants to maintain the same level of returns. Anyway, he showed me his office library — there must have been a thousand books on his bookshelf.

Yeah, what a show-off. I mean, my thousand books are at home. I don't bring them to the office to show off.

He's built like a football player, too. Plays lacrosse. I did not expect that.

He's very disciplined. The two guys, John and James, who used to work for me and are now at Sprott, would often praise Jason Donville. We used to sit around and talk about who we wanted to be like, who we wanted to emulate, who best fit in terms of investment style, and the name "Donville" was always at the top of that list. So, Jason's fund might be one of the places I'd go.

Interesting. You were a writer for the Globe *and* Mail's Report *on* Business, *too.*

Yeah, I had a column in the Report on Business [ROB].

Through that role, you also interviewed prominent money managers.

Well, first of all, I must correct you. I was already a semi-prominent money manager myself at the time. I was approached by the editor of the ROB and of the *Globe and Mail*, a guy named Ed Greenspon, who was a childhood acquaintance. So they approached me, knew I could write, because I'd written some op-ed pieces, and they asked, "Will you do this?" I agreed to do it. Now this was a decade ago. But I did commit to doing a column every week for the ROB. They told me, "Write whatever the hell you want, Martin." You probably read some of the stuff . . .

Yeah, I've gone back and looked in the archives.

In the 40 columns I wrote, I don't believe more than two were actually interviews with money managers. One was with Ira Gluskin and the other was with Eric Sprott. However, most of the columns were my ideas. I was the president of Strategic Advisors at the time so I was running my own fund and generating my own ideas and naturally I was going to use the feature as a bit of a tout piece for me. So long as I wasn't contravening any securities rules.

Out of the 40 or so columns, which one became the most popular or most read?

The one comparing hedge fund managers to mutual fund managers.

You compared their performance?

No, it was really funny. It was tongue-in-cheek. I made fun of the stereotypical mutual fund manager and the stereotypical hedge fund manager. I cracked myself up writing that piece. And even now sometimes I'll dig it up, read it, and still get tears in my eyes.

What are the differences between a mutual fund manager and a hedge fund manager?

I'm not going to spoil it for you, you have to check it out.

Okay.

THE DIFFERENCES BETWEEN HEDGIES AND MUTUALS

SATURDAY, JULY 10, 2004

Hedge funds, typically the preserve of the wealthier investor, have more latitude to use aggressive strategies unavailable to mutual funds, such as selling stocks short and hedging.

As the manager of a hedge fund, it is obviously in my best interest to have them viewed in a positive light by the investing public. Whenever one of them messes up, it's inevitable that "hypocrites and ingrates," to use the voluble Lord Black's parlance, will come out of the woodwork to heap obloquy on us all.

The recent travails of the mutual fund industry have taken some heat off the upstart "hedgies," a development that I have thoroughly enjoyed, given my long-standing aversion to these leviathans. But there still remains considerable misunderstanding of hedge funds, and how they differ from the mutuals. And so, this column is an attempt to outline the key differences between the two.

First, I would like to discuss appearance. Hedge fund managers generally don't wear ties. They also tend to have more facial hair, which includes longer sideburns. The exception is female hedge fund managers, of which there are very few.

Mutual fund managers wear suits and ties to work, removing the jackets on their arrival. The suit was purchased on sale, and is worth half those worn by brokers covering the account.

Hedge fund managers don't usually live in the suburbs,

and if they do, would rather not. Mutual fund managers are supposed to live in the suburbs, and if they don't, are in danger of starting hedge funds.

Recently, mutual fund companies got into trouble for allowing certain hedge funds to engage in "late trading" and "market timing." Late trading occurs when orders placed after four p.m. are filled at the same day's price, instead of the following day's. Market timing involves frequent trading by short-term investors hoping to exploit pricing lags. Hedgies are naturally drawn to these tactics, given their predilection for the frequent redemption of other people's paper — as opposed to their own.

Hedge fund managers have a large chunk of their net worth in their own funds. Mutual fund managers have a large chunk of their net worth in their suburban homes, and shares of the mutual fund company. This inspires camaraderie among managers in the company's stable, improving turnout at corporate picnics. I don't do picnics.

If you think of money managers in anthropological terms, mutual funds are asset gatherers and hedge funds are performance fee hunters. Collectively, we are the hunter-gatherers and we do a lot of foraging. Here I quote from my encyclopedia: "Hunter-gatherers are relatively mobile . . . they have fluid boundaries and [move on] as the resources of one region [are] exhausted." Hmm, sound familiar?

With a hedge fund, you always know who your manager is. If he leaves, or more likely dies, the fund is usually wound up. With a mutual fund, "death ends a life, not a relationship," to quote Jack Lemmon. Besides, most people don't know who manages their mutual fund, and when there's a change of manager, it's not enough of a reason to let them out free-of-charge.

Here's another important difference: when a hedge fund manager blows up, he's out of business, usually for good, although he might resurface as a stockbroker. When a mutual fund manager fails, a position opens up in marketing.

Hedge funds come in all shapes and sizes, but few of them actually "hedge." In my fund we do something called "arbitrage," which is similar to hedging but more lucrative and smacks of erudition.

Still, I think hedge funds are appropriately named, given that when asked exactly what kind of investing his fund engages in, the typical manager will hedge his answer.

So much for my brief elucidation of hedge funds and mutual funds. To His Lordship, it might appear anodyne or even otiose, while youse other palookas might have to "Google" Webster's. It's hard to write for all constituencies.

The Globe and Mail *should reprint that article.*

It was so funny. I came up with such great lines. And then the other one that didn't get as much feedback but I thought was literarily my best was when I went to Sri Lanka and was in the capital, Colombo. I dropped in on the Sri Lankan stock exchange, met some guys, and subsequently wrote a column about Sri Lanka, their economy and stock market, and also about a couple of stocks that the broker recommended for me.

What about the investment calls that you made in those other articles?

Well, I recommended that people buy CallNet, which was a telecommunications company in the early days of cell phone and cable companies. It was an alternative long-distance company. It's amazing how far technology has come and it wasn't even that long ago. I thought CallNet, which had been beaten up because they weren't really putting up the numbers, would be bought out within the year, and it was, at a very big premium. I can't remember them all, but they're all there. Once in a while I go Googling to see what's still out there. I've got hard copies sitting in a binder at home. But if you Google me enough you'll find the articles. You probably know your way around the internet better than me.

[Laughs] Do you have any final advice for investors?

Well, I'd say generally for the guy who's not doing this for a living: don't invest on the basis of a tip. Do your own research. Even if someone tells you that you should go buy some shares, don't just go "Okay!" and buy some shares. Check it out. The information is out there. Try to get as close to the business as possible. Maybe it's a consumer-oriented business and as a consumer you can check it out and see if it makes any sense to you as a consumer. Peter Lynch used to talk about that all the time. If you can't really get really close and do that kind of work or if you're just not built that way then at least make sure that the person giving you that information is a good source for that information. That he's not just a talking head who's passing on that bullshit from somebody else. I think that, generally speaking, the research and the commentary from media is very bad. You generally don't want to do what they tell you to do.

Don't follow the media?

In my opinion, the content is worthless. Also, reading the paper thinking you'll find some good stock ideas is very treacherous. By the time those stocks make it to the mainstream media they've probably been largely exploited and there's not much money left for you, the little guy. And frankly, a lot of the sell-side research, the stuff that RBC or Scotiabank or TD or whoever puts out there in print is not particularly actionable. By the time you read it, it's probably stale. So there's no easy way for the average guy to make it in the market. Research and hard work are probably the cure for most things in life. If you want to get good at anything in this world, be it writing or making money in the stock market, you have to practice your craft. You don't just stumble into it. You might get lucky the first time or the second time, but you'll get wiped out by the third time. It's like a guy who goes to Vegas and gets "hot." Day one at the table he cleans up. Day two he breaks even. Day three he gives it all back to the house, plus some. There's no shortcuts, and there's no such thing as a free lunch.

You've got to be a skeptic. As far as the professional side of investing goes, I always think about the risk first. I realize that the returns on my fund have been very good and perhaps it has led you to believe that I'm that kind of guy, that I'm always looking to hit the ball out of the park. But actually, no. I think more about how much risk I'm assuming with each position within my fund. If I can deal with the risk side then I find that the return side tends to take care of itself because there's a lot of optionality in investing.

What's optionality?

Optionality is a buzzword for "pregnant with possibility." It's a fancy way of saying "upside." So there's a lot of cheap optionality embedded in stocks. In other words, you're not paying for *this* happening, and you're not paying for *that* happening; you're paying maybe a little teeny bit for a third thing and maybe a little bit more for a fourth thing happening to the stock. If any of those four things were to happen you'd make good money because the market's not really paying for them. Any one of them. But if all four of them kicked in, oh my god!

That's what I mean by optionality. The optionality is the part of the equation that the market has not paid for. What the market has already paid for is the risk; the disappointment the market might face when it realizes that what it's been paying for isn't going to happen. They were thinking that the company was going to make a dollar a share and it only made 90 cents. They say, "Oh, I'm so disappointed," and the stock goes down. Because the market was paying for a dollar. But if the market was paying for 75 cents and the company makes 90 cents, then, "Oh, the market's happy," and the stock goes up. What you have to worry about is what the market expects and what it is paying for. Will it come short or not? If it does miss, then maybe I lose 10% and if you can live with that, then that's the downside. But what about all the good things that could happen? Other than that possible 10% hit, you're getting it for free.

Speaking of that concept of optionality, Automodular recently popped up on my stock screen. They lost a big Ford contract and so they're just floating around on the market while looking for other contracts or other business activities. They're trading at their cash value. Is that an investment you would buy into because there could be a significant pop if they sign a new deal? Optionality.

Yeah, we used to own it, actually — a few years ago. It's a tiny little company that sells to the auto industry. I would check it out. If you can identify that at this juncture your downside is very low and yet there's this optionality of winning back the Ford contract, getting another contract, developing new expertise, or a new business, or something were to happen that the market's not paying for, then the risk-return is in your favour. Yeah, you could lose another 10%, but you could also make 30%, 50%, 100% and the ratio of what you could make versus what you could lose might be three to one, or five to one, or more. You know, you'll take that every time.

And if you have five or ten of them, or in my case 15 or 20 of them, the odds are in your favour. People always ask me, "What's your favourite stock?" I don't want to answer that question. I don't want to say what my favourite stock is because they're all okay, you know. So I say, "Look, it's a portfolio. I can't tell you. But I can tell you that I invested in 15 or 20 companies and on each and every one of them I have downside but I figure my upside is at least three to one of my downside. And even if my numbers are right, I can't tell you which ones of the 15 or 20 are going to be clunkers, but I can tell you that in the total scheme of things, we'll be okay." That's all you want to do when you put together a portfolio: make sure the ratio of the upside to the downside is in your favour.

So, you accept that win/loss probability in your fund.

You can sit down with a calculator and figure it out. I often do. It's part of what we call attribution analysis — which is dissecting the returns. Let's say that I buy 50 stocks, and I'm wrong on 20 of them. So, 30 right, and 20 wrong. That sounds acceptable. It sounds like I'm going to make money overall. But what if the 20 lost on average 20% and the 30 on average made 12%? Well, that's not very good. You can play with your calculator, and see very quickly what a crappy return that is. But what if the 20 that went down fell an average 10% and the 30 that went up rose on average 25%? Ah, that's a different story. So it's not just, "Okay, I have to be right every time." You're not going to be right every time. But you can try to protect the downside and on the upside let the good ones run. I call it the law of large numbers.

Okay. What are the qualities of a good money manager?

One, they're intelligent . . . duh. Two, they're passionate about it. They'd do this for nothing. Three, experience. And four, discipline. That's the one people don't think of right away. Discipline is huge. There are a lot of *really* smart guys who have very checkered careers in the investment business and at the end of the day, when you ask why, I think it's because of discipline, or lack thereof. I think they just kept straying. And they just got seduced by stuff. Myself included, by the way. In my weaker moments, I've been seduced many times and strayed but I'm still here to tell the story. It requires a lot of discipline to be a good money manager because people are constantly coming at you. "Invest in my company! Buy my deal!" And you've got to have the strength to say no. If you have that strength and that discipline to say no then you're way ahead of the game. I know that Richard Rooney is very disciplined. Jason Donville is very disciplined. BloombergSen is very disciplined.

And then there's talent. You have to have a talent to write, or to speak. Some people can just talk, you know? Words flow out of their mouths and they just captivate their listeners, and some people just write really well and people read them and go "Wow, that's really interesting." So in money management there's a talent to it. It's not just boring, analytical, left-side-of-the-brain stuff. The right side of the brain plays a big part as well. The intuitive side. Now if you meld the right and the left, and this is not original, you get a whole-brained approach going, and you're way ahead. So I actually think the best money managers are quite whole-brained in their approach. They can somehow synthesize the analytics side with the intuitive side of the brain.

Out of all of the Market Masters that I interviewed for the book, Martin resonated the most with me, as I am also a reformed value investor turned GARP investor. I too loathed sitting on the sidelines, watching my portfolio stagnate, waiting for value stocks to finally turn around, while the markets continued to forge ahead. Clearly, value investing, or at least my perceived "value stocks," were not being rewarded in this current market environment. So, like Martin, I switched to investing in stocks that had growth potential, as evidenced by growing revenue, earnings, and a high return on equity, albeit at a reasonable or fair price. I don't want to pay too much for growth and risk a situation where, if growth stalls, my growth stocks drop like a rock.

Honestly, I don't understand why Martin isn't covered more extensively in the financial press. His fund pushes the limits on a daily basis, in a good way. Perhaps, like artists recognized after their lifetimes, Martin will become a legend with investor generations to come. A market-beating, Dr-Pepper-drinking legend.

MASTER KEYS

MARTIN BRAUN

1) "I've learned that being a value investor is very often a bad idea because a lot of value stocks are value traps; they lure you into the position because they're 'cheap.' But in actual fact they're cheap for a reason."

2) "Growth is the key driver in the markets. [But] it's the combination or synthesis of all three — growth, value, and catalysts — that create, for me, the investment thesis that I'm looking for."

3) "You have to make some concessions to the fact that the market's much bigger than you and that you need to figure out the market; the market doesn't have to figure out you."

4) "Every time a company announced it was being acquired it would go into that database and we'd just go trolling through the database looking for the best spreads with the least risk."

5) "It didn't take me very long to figure out that I didn't just have to trade on announced deals. I could also trade rumoured deals or theoretical deals."

6) "A good hedge fund manager is not limited by those little boxes where you need to play within a specific sandbox. You can do whatever the spirit moves you to do."

7) "In the mid- to late nineties and then after the crash, I couldn't just sit there and say, 'This is what I do and I can't do anything different.' Something works for a while and then it doesn't work. Then it works again, and then it doesn't. We adapt."

8) "I invest in a handful of businesses, not a whole bunch of them, and get to know them really well. . . . 'Just put a few eggs in the basket but watch the basket *very* closely.' I'm looking for 20 good stocks."

9) "Once you've learned so much about that business don't put just a couple bucks in — put a *lot of bucks in*. If one of those stocks goes off the rails then you'll be one of the first ones to realize that it's coming off the rails, and push it out the door before everyone else."

10) "I want to invest in a company that most people don't appreciate how good it is or how good it's going to be. Sometimes it's already achieved something special but people don't realize how good it truly is."

11) "It takes a certain skill to be able to execute. It's one thing to say, 'I'm going to do this,' and it's another to actually do it. The stocks that I didn't make money on or I lost money on was because I misjudged management."

12) "Don't invest on the basis of a tip. Do your own research. Even if someone tells you that you should go buy some shares, don't just go, 'Okay!' and buy some shares."

13) "Try to get as close to the business as possible. Maybe it's a consumer-oriented business and as a consumer you can check it out and see if it makes any sense to you as a consumer."

14) "I think that, generally speaking, the research and the commentary from media is very bad. You generally don't want to do what they tell you to do."

15) "Reading the paper thinking you'll find some good stock ideas is very treacherous. By the time those stocks make it to the mainstream media they've probably been largely exploited and there's not much money left for you."

16) "You might get lucky the first time or the second time, but you'll get wiped out by the third time. It's like a guy who goes to Vegas and gets

'hot.' Day One at the table he cleans up. Day Two he breaks even. Day Three he gives it all back to the house, plus some."

17) "I always think about the risk first. If I can deal with the risk side then I find that the return side tends to take care of itself."

18) "There's a lot of cheap optionality embedded in stocks. In other words, you're not paying for *this* happening, and you're not paying for *that* happening; you're paying maybe a little teeny bit for a third thing and maybe a little bit more for a fourth thing happening to the stock. If any of those four things were to happen you'd make good money because the market's not really paying for them."

19) "If the market was paying for 75 cents and the company makes 90 cents, then, 'Oh. The market's happy.' and the stock goes up."

20) "I figure my upside is at least three to one of my downside. That's all you want to do when you put together a portfolio: make sure the ratio of the upside to the downside is in your favour."

21) "The best money managers are quite whole-brained in their approach. They can somehow synthesize the analytics side with the intuitive side of the brain."

JASON DONVILLE
THE HIGH-GROWTH ROE INVESTOR

Don't fuck with Donville. Seriously, there's a fan website by that name that follows Jason's stock picks. The creator of dontfuckwithdonville.blogspot .ca stated the following in his first post in 2014: "Jason Donville is the shit. He made me wealthier and aware of some great companies that I'd never heard of. From what I know, more than 50% of my actual portfolio includes some of his suggestions." Now that I have met Jason in person, the "Don't fuck with Donville" line makes sense. Aside from his phenomenal stock-picking prowess, market-crushing returns, and beaming confidence, Jason is built like a truck, a physical asset that perhaps benefits him on the lacrosse field more than it does in the office at Donville Kent Asset Management (DKAM). An avid field lacrosse player, Jason also personally mentored his two sons in the sport, and currently coaches the Edge Lacrosse elite travel team. With no disrespect, though, I'd wager that Jason scores even higher in his hedge fund than he does on the lacrosse field. To say that Jason's brain trumps his brawn is no small claim, but it is nevertheless true.

DKAM's flagship Capital Ideas Fund has been the envy of Bay Street. Within just seven years, the Capital Ideas Fund has beaten the TSX

Composite Index by 350% in cumulative gains. That's 350% in "alpha," or the amount by which Jason's performance exceeded the benchmark index. From 2008 to 2015, the fund achieved a whopping 525% in cumulative gains. That's a 27.9% annualized return since inception. How did Jason not only beat the index but achieve such high alpha? Straight from the Capital Ideas Fund letter:

> Through the application of our focused investment strategy, we search for companies that possess high levels of return on equity, reasonable valuations, and positive share price momentum. Portfolio companies typically have a track record of achieving high returns on equity, and are capable of generating high returns on equity for many years without the addition of significant amounts of equity capital other than that which is being generated internally. These companies are run by strong management teams that have a significant ownership stake in the business.

The return on equity (ROE) metric is crucial to Jason's hedge fund's success. ROE is not just a figure. It's an initial hurdle that a company must pass, Jason's rigorous test (ROE greater or equal to 20%), in order for any security to progress to future stages of analysis. During our interview we discussed everything from Jason's philosophy, to his process and his strategy, along with the unorthodox way Jason entered the investment world — starting in the navy.

Jason has curly gelled-back silver hair and wears thick, round glasses. On the day we met he was dressed down in jeans and a shirt with rolled-up sleeves. Throughout the interview I noticed that Jason's brain sometimes works faster than his mouth. From time to time he needs to rewind after he speaks, as though he can't vocally articulate his thoughts and ideas at the same rate that his brain produces them. His brain is always working at full speed. If his brain was a car, it'd be a Ferrari. Before starting the interview with Jason, I thought, "Jason would be a great guy to have a beer with. He's a guy's guy, on and off the lacrosse field *and* his hedge fund's trading floor."

PRE-INTERVIEW LESSONS

ALPHA: the amount by which an investor's performance exceeds his or her benchmark index.

BROKER OR BROKERAGE: an agent who handles the public's orders to buy and sell securities, commodities, or other property. A commission is generally charged for this service.

CAPITAL ALLOCATION: when management makes investments in a company to improve operations, revenues, and expand product lines, or to make new acquisitions. Successful capital allocation requires an ample return on that investment (return on invested capital, or ROIC).

FED: the U.S. Federal Reserve, the American central bank that sets monetary and fiscal policy (such as overnight rates and money supply) and motions to control factors such as inflation. Similar to the Central Bank of Canada.

FRONT-RUN: when a broker places a trade based on privileged information before a large client places a trade in order to profit at the outset.

GROWTH: stocks that have higher-than-average return potential or positive financial changes to a company (e.g., revenue growth).

MANAGEMENT: the salaried team of individuals who manage a company. May or may not be the founders or family owners, and may or may not own a stake in the company.

PORTER FIVE FORCES: a framework containing five "micro environment forces" developed by Michael E. Porter to analyze the level of competition that a company faces within an industry. Those forces — threat of new entrants, bargaining power of suppliers, bargaining power of buyers, threat of substitutes, and industry rivalry — can affect a company's ability to make a profit.

TURNAROUND: the outcome by which a fledgling company improves itself to regain and sometimes even surpass its previous success. An example of a turnaround would be Apple in the late nineties to the early 2000s.

Where did you grow up in Canada?

I was born in Scarborough but my parents and I moved to Alberta when I was one. My parents were people stereotypically from Scarborough. Neither had graduated from high school. Both of them dropped out in grade 10. They were the lower-class white working poor. That's what they were and they wanted something better out of life. Alberta was booming, so they went there for opportunity and we ended up staying there. So I actually grew up in Alberta.

My parents struggled for a good chunk of my childhood but my dad eventually became a tradesman and they've done well subsequently. My family was very pro-education. That was one of the good things about my childhood. You didn't want to bring a bad report card home. But nobody in the family had a finance background or worked in a white-collar job. So that's a not-so-typical hedge fund background.

It's not typical at all. How did you get interested in the markets?

I had lots of part-time jobs when I was a kid. I was always fascinated by the stock market. In the mid-1970s the province of Alberta decided to privatize the Alberta Energy Company. Any citizen of the province of Alberta could then subscribe for a hundred shares down at the local bank branch. And my parents did that. Soon we started to receive annual reports in the mail from Alberta Energy. I would track the movement of the share price of Alberta Energy in the paper every day. My parents probably owned $1,000 of stock. So I just found this to be a *really* fascinating process. But even if you told me when I was 15 that I was going to become a hedge fund manager I would probably be skeptical. It was probably more likely that I was going to become a writer.

A writer?

Being a writer is a thread that weaves through my story. I had an uncle who was quite well educated. He introduced the International Baccalaureate program to Canada. He used to teach at Pearson College in British Columbia. Pearson is a private school for grades 11 and 12. Kids come from all over the world to attend Pearson College. Anyway, my uncle got the idea of a "renaissance man" in my head. As you know, a renaissance man is someone who is familiar with literature, mathematics, art, physics, and languages. Additionally, around age 16 a certain ambition kicked in. Not suddenly, but it dawned on me that I was a good student and that if I worked hard I would get great results. And then in grade 12 the Royal Military College came on to my radar as a place to go for my undergrad. For me, coming from a poor background, going to RMC where everything was paid for was great. Plus, you spent your summer at sea or on a flight line. There was an incredible amount of adventure.

So how did writing weave into your story?

So I completed an undergraduate degree at RMC in liberal arts. Most of my course work was essays. After I graduated I enlisted in the navy. But before I left, one of my professors who was a retired infantry officer said, "Don, you're a good writer. You should keep it up because you'll be valuable." You see, when you join your ship or your unit in the navy, junior officers are assigned secondary duties. My professor proceeded to say, "Tell them that you want all the secondary duties that involve writing." So I did that — "Give me anything that involves writing; I'm a good writer," I told my superior. It was a win-win because then the senior officer knew that he got a junior officer who could write well. There's just so much administration work in the navy. You could be writing thank-you letters one day and the next day writing a charge report for some guy who got caught with marijuana in his possession. Every day I was just writing, writing, writing. Eventually it got to the point where I was writing for the navy base newspaper.

And then all of a sudden the admiral's speech writer was going on maternity leave. He called my cabin and asked, "Jason, would you like to come up and work as a speech writer for six to twelve months?" And I said, "Wow, I would love to do that!" I ended up writing one speech that I still have in my possession for the NATO's First Ministers' Conference in 1989. After the navy, I enrolled in my MBA at Western University, where the curriculum was essentially all case study. There's no Q&A. Once again, my writing skills helped me get fairly high grades there because I was a good writer. Two guys can express the same idea but the stronger writer will get the higher grade. After graduation, I bought a one-way ticket to Asia. There, I marketed myself as a good English writer with a good education but no industry background.

Singapore, right?

Yeah, so I got to Singapore in 1992 and just basically started to cold-call firms for a job. At that time, though, a lot of these Singaporean firms had Singapore or Asian analysts but English was either not their first language or wasn't a strong first language. They grew up in a bilingual or trilingual environment. So even if they went to a Singaporean university or they went to a UK university, their English and their writing skills weren't flawless. I would do my own analytical work but I could also help to clean up the other analysts' reports. Once again, writing became a competitive advantage for me. Also, as is the same today, I had a quirky flair, or style, to my material. You'll see it in my DKAM *ROE Reporter* newsletters. They're not your typical newsletters. There's storytelling. It's like a TED talk.

Your newsletters are fun to read.

I've learned to tailor my writing to my audience. Finance can be dry but if you turn it into a story and if it's a bit self-deprecating, but still has a message, people start to bond with you. They see through the analytical work and realize that there's a decent person on the other side. Trust comes from that.

Strong writing skills have helped you throughout your entire life, in pretty much any endeavour.

Yeah, and when you're working as an analyst, you're writing something every day. So you're like a journalist. You're looking for journalistic scoops. You're writing for deadlines all the time; you have time pressures. You don't quite have the same level of fact-checking standards that a journalist has, but nonetheless if you put out something that's factually wrong, within an hour you will receive an email: "Didn't the guy read the annual report?"

You eventually returned to Canada. Did you immediately move to Toronto to start your hedge fund, DKAM?

No, I came back to Calgary. Because that was my hometown. And part of it was because we were coming back for quality of life issues. Particularly on my wife's side. I ended up being there for three years and started a small brokerage firm, Lightyear Capital. The problem was that as a non-oil-and-gas guy it was really hard to do what I liked.

It must have been a challenge to raise capital in Alberta. Everyone there invests in oil and gas for the most part.

Yeah, and it just wasn't the right location for what I was doing. I needed to be in a headquarter town. Even if I was in the U.S., I couldn't do what I do in Kansas City or in Minneapolis. I had to either be in Toronto or in New York City or in Hong Kong or in Tokyo. I couldn't be in a regional city. If I was an oil-and-gas guy I certainly could be in Houston or in Calgary. But for the kind of companies I was interested in, I had to be in a city like Toronto.

So you closed Lightyear Capital?

I sold out to my partners and moved to Toronto, where I got a job with Sprott fairly quickly.

What was it like to work with Eric Sprott?

At that time, there was Sprott Asset Management, fund management, and then there was Cormack, the brokerage. Eric moved over to the asset management business and I was on the brokerage side. However, I would see Eric across the hallway. Eric knew me but this was 2002–2003, which was when I was in the process to become a financial services specialist. However, Eric saw all financial services companies as a house of cards. He was friendly to me but he would say, "I'm really not interested in anything that you're covering, with the only exception being Canadian Western Bank," which is in Edmonton. Because, "when all the banks in the world fail, natural resources go through the roof, and CWB will be the last bank standing."

Do you think he's still sticking with that "the world is going to implode" macro thesis today?

I don't know, because I haven't spoken to Eric much in the last five years, other than just social pleasantries. I feel bad for those guys. First of all, everybody loves Eric Sprott because he treats everybody so well. Secondly, he had so many things right. However, you can get the macro thesis right but still not get the stock picks right. As far as the 2008–2009 crisis goes, he didn't perform any better than anybody else. And then, once the financial crisis was over, he probably stayed on the natural resource trade too long, in my opinion. He became too fixated on gold and natural resources.

And was that the inflection point in the markets — the financial crisis — when you started up your own hedge fund, Donville Kent Asset Management?

Yes.

But why did you ultimately leave Sprott?

I was at that age where having a 25-year-old salesman tell a 40-year-old analyst to put his heels together was getting tedious. That was happening all the time. As an analyst, you were always junior no matter how many years you had been an analyst. The other issue would come up any time I made a PA trade. PA means personal account. I'll give you an idea of the trading floor. There were about 20 traders and 15 salesman. So 30 or 40 guys in the room. Anyway, one day, the head trader got a ticket for somebody's $500,000 purchase of MTY Food Group shares. It said "pro," which meant that it was a staff member's trade. The head trader turned to the sales desk and yelled, "Who the fuck is buying fucking half a million shares in MTY Food Group? I've never even heard of this fucking company before! What do I need to know about this stock?"

All of the salesman were perplexed. "We have no clue what you're talking about," they said. The head trader then looked at the employee number on the trade ticket and shouted, "It's fucking Donville — what the fuck?" He called me out and said, "If you are buying this kind of fucking stock, why the fuck don't our clients have the first kick at it?"

I responded, "I'm a financial services analyst. This is a quick-serve restaurant company." He barked back, "I don't give a flying fuck what it is. If it's good enough for you to buy in this kind of fucking size then I expect that there should be a research report on this —" Blah blah blah. And then he looked me square in the eyes and said, "Do you just sit here and spend all of your fucking time working on your PA and don't write any research?"

That doesn't sound like fun.

Yeah. At that time I was by far the most prolific research analyst there. You've seen all of the awards that I've won as best analyst and stuff like that. They acted on competitive jealousy. When my PA stocks would go up 50% they just got more jealous. So eventually my personal investing got harder to do inside of the brokerage. The expectation was that the analyst would just write research and never actually invest their own money. Which is crazy, because the analysts who become good stock-pickers are actually your most valuable resources. So, for me, it was time to move on. I initially left to go to Home Capital to start their hedge fund. I was there for about five months but then the financial crisis storm clouds started to form and so we just agreed that it wasn't going to work. At that point, there were some legal costs that had been about $140,000. I just wrote Home Capital a cheque for $140,000 to pay for all the costs.

That's great — you stood up for yourself and moved on. It makes sense now that there's a website called . . .

Yeah, dontfuckwithdonville.com. My kids think it's hilarious.

It is hilarious and surprisingly informative.

Yeah, you know, it's funny.

The owner of that website is a raging fan. He tracks your stock recommendations and then actually invests in them — with outsized returns.

But I also haven't endorsed it because I've got to be careful. Though as long as I don't feel like he's distorting anything about me, my fund, or my stock picks, then it's probably fine. Because every now and then he'll have a comment on the site about a stock that I've never researched or invested in before. But he's not saying, "You should buy it." He's just saying, "Here are five companies that Donville likes and I like four out of the five." He's not making any judgment calls.

Interesting. You must have more fans across the country.

I used to be really good at responding to emails. People would email, "Hey, do you still like X stock?" I'd respond, "Yeah, I think it's still a great company." And then that person would post my comment on the Stockhouse message board — "I just talked to Donville and here's what he said . . ."

So now I'm *really* careful with my comments through emails. Because there's people out that are always trying to use it to promote their stocks.

That can damage your reputation. If investors want to follow your actual positions, they should read your ROE Reporter *newsletter, right?*

Yeah, and I'm on TV pretty frequently. I'm always very open about what we own and whenever I go on TV I'm allowed to disclose my top five positions, including their percentage allocation in my fund. I'm pretty good at that. But obviously, on any given day, if I'm adding to a position or subtracting from a position, I don't want the market to know. Because I don't want people to front-run me. So I just disclose stocks that are in a stable position in my hedge fund.

Your fund, Capital Ideas, was up 22.7% in 2014, which was double the index's return. You were heavily exposed to pharmaceuticals, software, and IT. Why those three sectors?

Well, look around. The world is slowing down growth-wise. Most of that is actually explained by demographics. Obviously the leveraging and de-leveraging of individual balance sheets, government balance sheets, and corporate balance sheets has an impact, too. But the bigger impact is a result of demographics. When I look around I think, "Where does growth come from?"

Let me give you an example. Leon's Furniture. We don't own it but it's a great company. They're not going to sell 15% more chesterfields next year. Because there's no demographic surge to generate that growth. Where the growth of the world is coming from is new product development in knowledge-based industries, whether it's a drug or a software system or a piece of technology that nobody owns. Whereas 99% of us already have chesterfields and maybe 1% of us are going to replace our chesterfield.

At one point in the last 15 years none of us had a smartphone. That was a growth industry — we all bought smartphones over a period of 15 years. Indeed, all of the action is in the knowledge-based industries, though the health care sector has the added benefit of a very attractive demographic profile. So while there's no demographic surge right now for chesterfields, there is a demographic surge for the kinds of things that people in their sixties and seventies need for health reasons.

Interesting. And now, going into 2015, you have lowered your exposure to financial institutions.

Yeah.

Why?

Think about the market as a baseball game. Let's say there's nine innings in the game. We're now six years into this bull market. You never know until it's over, but we're probably in the seventh or eighth or ninth inning of the baseball game. That's usually a bad time to own financials. They don't do particularly well late in the cycle and then they typically lead us into the trough. So at this stage in the cycle, I don't want to own a lot of financials.

So weakness in the financial sector can be a leading indicator that the economy is headed for a downturn?

Yeah, markets predict things to the extent that you could get a sense of whether you're in the sixth or seventh inning — that's when you want to lighten up on certain holdings. Generally speaking, the time to buy financials is after the market's been crushed. Now, for really high-quality financial services stocks, we'll just hold on to them for the long term. But we wouldn't be adding to or loading up on financials right now.

Would you put Canadian banks into the high-quality camp?

They don't achieve the ROE that we want. We base decisions on adjusted ROE as opposed to stated ROE because the stated ROE doesn't take into account the difference in the dividend policies of all these different companies. Conservatively, banks are going to make a 12% return per year in the market, year after year. And they're going to realize that return in the form of a 4 to 5% dividend yield and a 7 to 8% capital appreciation. So for the average retail investor who wants to own individual stocks, the banks are actually a great deal. Particularly if you're going to hold them for five or ten or fifteen years because our banks are really strong. Their share prices might come down just because of market sentiment but I'm not worried that they're going to be doing any dividend cuts in the future. Again, though, we look for higher return on equity — 20%.

Your main focus is on ROE. However, you've said that while the companies in the TSX have competitive products and services, their ROEs are usually too low for you.

Not usually too low. They are low. If you start your analysis by looking at the companies that have really competitive products, you'll find that they're not really profitable. Why? Because of the capital structure and the capital allocation skills of the company. Let's say that you and I enter a partnership to make a new smartphone. It has a very nice gross margin and even an attractive net profit margin. But we built up massive overhead, too. And that's where the whole capital allocation game becomes really important.

So first we look for companies with ROE greater or equal to 20%. Second, we look for companies in that high-ROE group that are sustainable based on the competitiveness of their products. Third, we assess management's ability to allocate capital at those companies. Once we validate those three things, we typically find companies that we can invest in.

But how do you determine which companies or products will be sustainable in the future?

I'm continuously looking through my database for high-ROE stocks. So that's any company that has an ROE of 20% or more. Then I look at the source of the ROE. Is it coming from leverage or is it coming from the sale of assets or is it coming from profit margin? Essentially, return on equity can be broken down into three pieces through DuPont analysis. You've got good ROE and bad ROE. We want to make sure that the ROE is good ROE.

Once I've decided that any company is of interest to me, I'll turn them on to my associates and say, "Get me a two-pager." A two-pager is basically a seven-year history of the company's financials. I often say to people, "If you're thinking of investing in two companies and you run the numbers over the last seven years on both companies and you put them side by side, the good company will leap off the page at you." That snapshot is so important in terms of understanding the difference between a good company and an okay or maybe even crappy company. The reason is because you can fake good ROE in one year. But to achieve high ROE seven years in a row is tough. You can show me the numbers and say, "Here, this is the company's seven-year ROE track record," and I'll go, "I don't even know what they do but there's probably a really good company here." Here's a simple way to think about it: let's say there's a company that makes $20 million in profit and has $100 million in equity. Are you following me?

Yeah, that would work out to 20% ROE.

Yeah. At the end of the year, say you make that $20 million. So now the equity goes up to $120 million if management takes that $20 million of incremental profits and just puts it in the bank. If it's in the bank then they're going to make 1% on that. So the following year the return is still at $20 million just about because 1% interest is almost no interest at all. But now, let's do the math, it's 20 over 120. The next year after that it's 20 over 140. See how fast the ROE comes down to 15%?

So when I see a company that has achieved an ROE of 23, 22, 23, 24, 23, 22, over the past seven years, without even knowing what industry they're in, I go, "Wow! There's something in place here. There's something magical going on here." That's the magic that you're looking for in terms of those long-term sustainable companies. We can do that analysis in under an hour and that tells us whether we should spend more time getting to know a company.

Where do your associates get that long-term financial data?

We just pull it off SEDAR [System for Electronic Document Analysis and Retrieval, a mandatory documents system for Canadian public companies] and put those two pages together on each company. Those two-pagers look like the reports that Buffett used to read at the local library. That's what we create in house. Nobody else does it that way. Though if they do it, it's only on the large-cap stocks.

Yeah, Buffett used to peruse all of the Value Line *reports.*

Right, and it's just boom boom boom boom boom. It's just this straight "Give me the financial history of the last seven years."

Okay, that covers how you would determine sustainability. Now what about management? How do you assess the quality of management? You mentioned they must be good capital allocators.

Okay, so there's a whole bunch of stuff. The assessment of management is something that takes place over time. When you meet with management face to face you don't get 10 hours with these guys; you get an hour. For our type of investing we want competitive advantage and then we want capital allocation skills. So most of the questions we ask when we meet face to face with management are focused on those two areas. "What's happening in your environment? Anybody new, or any new upstarts, or anybody thinking of entering your market?" Because the great enemy of a high-ROE company is competition. If management says, "No. We're not aware of anybody who is thinking of entering the market," then that's a great thing.

Then we get a read on their capital allocation skills. Now, capital allocation takes different forms depending on what business or industry the company is in. In a lending environment like Home Capital where they just write mortgages each year, they don't need to acquire anything or buy anything. Through their network they just put out more capital in the form of mortgages. So it's very straightforward for them to lend more money. In the case of a lot of the most attractive industries, though, and the reason why a lot of these software companies are so attractive, is that their client relationships are sticky and they're also high-margin. Once you get clients, you never lose them. Well, that's the same for everybody else in their industry. Therefore, by raising sales and promotional expenses they're actually not going to get much more business because the additional business that they're trying to acquire is actually equally sticky. And then they get to a certain point where the owner wants to move on and then big boys acquire them. Because again, just upping sales and promotion to steal away another client in a sticky business doesn't work.

But often you'll hear analysts say, "There's no organic growth." Well, this is not an organic growth story; this is growth through acquisition. MTY Food Group, which is all about fast foods, does acquisitions but they also open up new locations. So once again we look at MTY Food Group, see that their ROE has never gone below 23%, and determine that they're clearly able to take a year's profits and channel it back into the business to keep their ROE at that level. But so many analysts just talk about the organic growth. That's craziness!

Why is organic growth so crazy?

Think about it. You and I get the rights to buy a McDonald's in downtown Toronto. And after a year we do $3 million in sales. After year two we do $3.3 million in sales and then it just stays at $3.3 million but the profit margin is massive. However, there will be no organic growth anymore. Because once that location is fully up and running it doesn't grow anymore. It just throws off massive cash flow. So saying, "Let's just up the advertising" is just crazy. There's no more growth there. Instead, what we should do is talk McDonald's into giving us a second location. And yet the number of guys that will criticize these quick-serve restaurants for their lack of organic growth is crazy. It doesn't work that way. Just visualize yourself as a guy running a McDonald's franchise. Get those MBA and B-Comm buzzwords out of your head.

Do you exit a position if management's ROE or capital allocation performance declines?

I'll use Solium Capital as an example. When I first moved back to Canada 1999, I met the founders of Solium Capital. There was a guy with the Calgary Flames who was actually working for them as a salesman. Anyway, they were unprofitable but then merged with another company that brought in a whole bunch of really good technology. It has been profitable ever since. We've owned it off and on. I just recently sold out this year because the ROE dipped down to 17%. Regardless, it's a good company. For a lot of guys, 17% ROE is still high enough.

Who are the top capital allocators in Canada? In the past, you've made mention of the CEO from Constellation Software.

Mark Leonard.

Who else?

Gerry Soloway at Home Capital would be another one. I don't own Stantec because the ROE isn't high enough, but I think that the management at Stantec are good capital allocators. Most of the companies we own have people running them that are very good capital allocators. Because if you can keep your ROE over 20% year after year, you almost by definition are a good allocator. But as the company gets larger, capital allocation becomes more a corporate skill, as opposed to an individual skill. For example, one can attribute the capital allocation skills of a small entrepreneurial company like MTY Food Group to the CEO rather than to the management team as a whole.

So I assume that you primarily take on positions in small- and mid-cap companies?

No, we are market cap agnostic. We buy into companies like Valeant and CGI, which have market caps over $15 billion. And then we buy into smaller companies with $100-million market caps in some cases. We don't care about market cap. We care about the ROE.

And you only invest in Canadian companies?

Only in Canada. But this approach works anywhere. This isn't unique to Canada. A few guys in Europe looked at my fund. They were either professors or grad students. I don't remember. They wrote to me and said, "It's hard to find companies in Europe that actually meet your criteria." It's true. The high ROEs are just not there. But in Asia it works. I used to do this in Indonesia, and in Singapore, and it worked in both of those markets.

But what if high ROE comes at a high cost? Currently, the Canadian markets' valuations seem overstretched compared to the growth prospects in the country.

Yeah, valuations are quite rich right now. But we also have a risk-free rate that is somewhere between 1% and 0%. Theoretically, when you work through any of the valuation models, and the risk-free rate goes down to 1%, you can justify virtually any multiple. But a lot of analysts will say, "The historical multiple for the market has been 15 times and currently it's at 18 times." Yeah, but interest rates have never been this low in North America — below 1% or at 1% and probably moving lower.

What risk management mechanisms do you have in place if you're wrong on the direction of the market?

We have always been able to go long and short. We short the market. Our biggest tool for risk mitigation right now though is put options on the TSX. That's an insurance policy. We buy puts out of money so that they are not that expensive. That won't protect me from a 30% correction but it should protect me from a 10% correction. And it doesn't cost me that much.

Regardless, your fund has captured massive upside in the market: 22.7% return in 2014, and 55% return in 2013.

We've done 27.9% annual returns since inception.

So, why would you close off the fund to new money? I just saw the announcement this week.

The reason we're closing the fund is fairly straightforward. If you look at people who manage $200 to $300 million they can put up really good numbers. But when they start to manage billions of dollars then that gets really hard in Canada. The market will force you into the large-caps, which is the most liquid part of the market. I don't mind owning large-caps but I don't want to be in the situation where the small- and mid-caps don't move the market. In Canada, the mid-cap segment is probably the most inefficient part of the market. So it's quite simple: I want to outperform more than I want to manage $3 billion. I don't want to be forced into basically owning the TSX 60.

So you achieve greater returns in the mid-cap segment of the market — it's inefficient. But there must be other reasons that you outperform the market.

I think we have a better methodological mouse trap. I didn't invent this style of investing. This is Buffett's style of investing. Why has Buffett been able to achieve a 20% return over 50 years? Because he focuses on companies that are growing at 20%. I also think though that measuring growth in terms of return on equity and book value per share is a better methodological way than measuring growth in terms of earnings per share. For example, for 50 years you can look at the Berkshire Hathaway annual reports; and what's on the first page?

There's the comparison between the S&P 500's return and Berkshire Hathaway's book value growth. Side by side.

He doesn't spoon-feed you. But what's he telling you right there on page one is "This is how you do it."

Book value growth.

Right, so he said, "Focus on the growth and the book value per share." Book value per share in old accounting terms was referred to as the net worth of the business. If you focus on companies where the net worth of the business is growing at a *very* steady clip, then the share price chart will take care of itself as long as the ROE stays intact.

So, why haven't other money managers done what you've done to achieve the same high returns?

A friend of mine in New York used to say to me that "Everybody talks Buffett but only a few people do Buffett." So that would be one aspect of it. Unlike mutual fund managers who have concentration limits, we can concentrate holdings in our portfolio. They can't put 12% of their money into their best idea. And honest to god, if I could only put up to 3% in any of my best ideas I think I would still outperform the market. But it wouldn't be as easy as if I could instead put 50% of the fund into my five best ideas. Because if you're a good stock-picker, concentration works in your favour, and if you're not, you should own an ETF [exchange-traded fund] instead. Truthfully, though, if you're going to use concentration and you're not a good stock-picker, you're going to be out of this business pretty quickly.

Have you ever met Buffett?

No, I've been to Omaha but I've never met him because I'm not in love with the man. I love his ideas and the way he thinks, but I'm not a rock star kind of guy who's like, "Oh my god, to shake his hand would mean so much to me." That doesn't mean anything to me at all. Obviously, though, if he was around or he walked into my boardroom I would love to hear him speak. But Berkshire Hathaway's annual report is good enough.

However, a lot of the best stuff that he wrote was 15 years ago. I have a printout of all the Berkshire Hathaway annual reports going back for the last 50 years. A lot of the stuff from the last 10 years has been more about praising people rather than offering insight into his investment process. So a lot of the stuff that's the best about Buffett has actually been packaged and distilled by other writers. The same can be said of Benjamin Graham. People talk glowingly about reading *The Intelligent Investor*, which I've read a couple of times, but it's dry.

It is dry. Especially the chapters on bonds.

It's not a great read.

And it's long.

Yeah, exactly. People who tell you that "Oh, yeah, *The Intelligent Investor* is my favourite book" are the same people who tell you that they love jazz but never go to a jazz club. They say it to be hip and cool. But it's not. There's only two chapters in there that I would recommend to our guys to read. But the people who've written about Buffett are fantastic, such as Mary Buffett's *Buffettelogy*.

*I've read **Buffettology**. It is a fantastic book.*

Yeah, so *Buffettology* is great. If you can get through *Snowball*, it's great, too. But also the one by the *Wall Street Journal* guy that was written about a decade earlier: *American Capitalist*. It's only about 275 pages. But I think *Buffettology* is probably the best of all the stuff that's been written on Buffett.

Some would argue that Buffett was an activist investor in his early days. Going back to your point that companies in the TSX have fantastic products but through bloated overhead or poor capital allocation, their ROE is usually below 20%, have you ever considered becoming an activist hedge fund manager? Go on boards and improve capital allocation and ROE?

Not yet. Maybe that's something down the road. But it's not something that's on my radar screen. In part because we don't buy turnarounds. It might be because we don't have the muscle. We wouldn't own enough stock to be able to push for a turnaround. I continue to look for great companies that are a fair price as opposed to cheap stocks. And that's what Buffett evolved into as well in his career.

What's your outlook on the markets?

In terms of just raw P/E, price to book, and price to cash flow, it's expensive in a historical context. However, if you believe that interest rates are going to stay where they are right now, the valuations are completely just and in theory can go higher. Here's a simple way of looking at it. Flip over a 20 times P/E; it's got an earnings yield of 5%. You can invest in that company or get 1% by putting your money on deposit. Now in the past we've been able to get a 10% earnings yield. But we might have also been able to get 7% on deposit at the bank. So you look at that as a ratio and go, "My god! As a ratio, stocks are actually, in relation to the risk-free rate, cheaper than they've been in the past." Even on a spread basis, stocks are cheap.

But here's the part that's tough. If interest rates are going higher then we're going to get into inflation. Where does inflation come from in a world where birth rates are plummeting? Where do we get the surge in aggregate demand that typically is the precursor to inflation? I don't see it. Asia and Europe are both slowing down. There's a whole bunch of countries in the world that have virtually negative birth rates. So where does it come from?

You're obviously not worried about rate increases then.

I think we're going to continue to be *really* nervous nellies about these multiples. But unless inflation goes up, I don't see interest rates going dramatically higher.

The Fed downgraded their inflation projections.

I made hints at that in the January newsletter. Because when you live in Asia where there's so many countries in such a small area, you become a lot more attuned to currency impacts than people realize. I was looking at what was happening to the Canadian dollar versus the U.S. dollar and thought, "Boy, the U.S. is going to slow down. By

June we're going to see the growth numbers in the U.S. come down dramatically because all the exporters are going to get killed."

Yeah, P&G's [Procter & Gamble's] profits dropped dramatically on their last quarter.

Right, and that's what I talked about in January. I don't see interest rates shooting back up.

Any final advice?

Yeah, here's my thesis on life. If you want to be a great doctor, don't go ask a guy who's a counsellor how to become a great doctor. Go ask a great doctor how to become a great doctor. If you want to be a great investor, then study the great investors and pick one who fits your style and then master that style. In terms of the way academics would define it, I'm a growth investor. And, actually, so is Buffett. But Buffett doesn't like that title. While a lot of people call him a value investor based on the way academics look at value versus growth, he's definitely not a value investor. He was before he met Munger, but then he became a growth investor.

Anyway, you must also understand your temperament. And the reason I say temperament is that if you're a value investor then you're investing in turnarounds. Therefore, you need to know how bankruptcy works. You've got to have an ability to know how boards can turn a company around. So when you say you're going to be a really great value investor, there's a bunch of skill sets that have to come with that. You need to be able to know that once a company goes into bankruptcy, how much is left over and how does that process work. There are a few guys who are value investors who don't have that skill set.

I have an undergraduate background in economics and political science. A lot of what I do involves Porter five forces. It's about competitive advantage. So if you want to invest like I do and you enjoy competitive advantage and you enjoy microeconomics and stuff like that, then this is a good style. But your style of investing has to fit your personality type. And I think that there's a lot of more negativity in value investing because you're buying companies that are cheap but are problematic. Whereas I'm buying awesome companies and just hoping that they'll be awesome forever. I get to hang out with the *really* great CEOs all the time as opposed to having argumentative discussions with mediocre CEOs who aren't doing a very good job running their companies.

After the interview, Jason offered to take me on a tour of his office, which looks more like a university student's dorm room than the typical office of a hedge fund manager. Trophies and medals lined the wall and a lacrosse helmet lay on the floor. There must have been five hundred books on his shelf. It was a comfortable place to work or to hang out, and a shrine to Jason's passions in life.

Jason's focus on ROE is the clearest of all the Market Masters. He only invests in companies that show at least seven years of ROE that is 20% or higher. I agree with him that ROE is a fantastic gauge of management's ability to successfully allocate capital. So, after the interview, I ran my own filter of companies with greater or equal to 20% ROE on the TSX and subsequently invested in a handful of those securities that proved to have long-running and sustainable return on equity combined with enduring competitive advantages. I'm excited to see how those high-ROE securities play out in the market over time.

I was surprised just days before my interview with Jason when he issued a press release announcing that the DKAM Capital Ideas Fund was closing to any new money. Jason said in the release, "Many years ago, when the Capital Ideas Fund was quite small, I indicated that when the fund reached the $250-million level, we would close the fund (and trust) to outside investors. That day has arrived. As such, the DKAM Capital Ideas Fund LP and DKAM Capital Ideas Trust will not be accepting new capital as of April 1st, 2015." I do hope that the fund opens again in the future as its returns are phenomenal. As Jason explained in our interview, though, when you start to manage billions of dollars, the market will force you into investing in large-cap companies, which is the most liquid part of the market. Large-caps certainly do not offer the same rate of return on the market as small-cap or mid-cap companies.

Jason's investment philosophy and process are summarized on his website as follows.

INVESTMENT PHILOSOPHY

We believe that superior long-term investment returns can be achieved by focusing on companies that consistently earn high returns on equity (ROE) while possessing some form of competitive advantage that can be sustained on a multi-year basis. A competitive advantage is typically achieved by the existence of 1) a barrier to entry into the industry, 2) a superior product or service that is not easily replicatable, or 3) a superior physical location. Once we have identified a company with an attractive competitive advantage, we then look to acquire shares at a price we deem reasonable in relation to our assessments of the future cash flows of the business. In summary, we attempt to buy outstanding businesses at a reasonable price, rather than inferior businesses with low relative valuations.

INVESTMENT PROCESS

IDEA SCREENING
Our first step is to screen Canadian public markets for stocks that are currently earning high returns on common equity, typically in excess of 20% at a minimum. Basic screens, on-going communication with our global network of industry contacts, industry publications, and financial media are all potential sources of new ideas.

PROPRIETARY DATABASE RANKING
Once we have identified a company that meets our initial criteria, we make several adjustments to company / analyst earnings forecasts in order to take into account non-cash items. Subsequent to the adjustments being made, we enter

the relevant data into our proprietary database where each company's ROE, valuation, and share price momentum are scored in relation to all other stocks in our universe.

ANALYTICS
Those stocks that achieve the highest aggregate scores in our database are then subject to comprehensive quantitative analysis, which includes extensive earnings modelling as well as scenario analysis.

MANAGEMENT EVALUATION
Our final step involves face to face meetings with company management, channel checks, and discussions with industry analysts. If this process is successful, the position is added to the portfolio, constantly monitored, and actively traded.

MASTER KEYS
JASON DONVILLE

1) "You can get the macro thesis right but still not get the stock picks right."

2) "If I'm adding to a position or subtracting from a position, I don't want the market to know. Because I don't want people to front-run me."

3) "Where the growth of the world is coming from is new product development in knowledge-based industries. Whereas 99% of us already have chesterfields and maybe 1% of us are going to replace our chesterfield."

4) "Think about the market as a baseball game. Let's say there's nine innings in the game. We're now six years into this bull market. You never know until it's over, but we're probably in the seventh or eighth or ninth inning of the baseball game. That's usually a bad time to own financials."

5) "The time to buy financials is after the market's been crushed."

6) "We base decisions on adjusted ROE as opposed to stated ROE because the stated ROE doesn't take into account the difference in the dividend policies of all these different companies."

7) "First we look for companies with ROE greater or equal to 20%. Second, we look for companies in that high-ROE group that are sustainable based on the competitiveness of their products. Third, we assess management's ability to allocate capital at those companies. Once we validate those three things, we typically find companies that we can invest in."

8) "Return on equity can be broken down into three pieces through DuPont analysis. You've got good ROE and bad ROE. We want to make sure that the ROE is good ROE."

9) "You can fake good ROE in one year. But to achieve high ROE seven years in a row is tough. . . . So when I see a company that has achieved an ROE of 23, 22, 23, 24, 23, 22, over the past seven years, without even knowing what industry they're in, I go, 'Wow! There's something in place here.'"

10) "If you're thinking of investing in two companies and you run the numbers over the last seven years on both companies and you put them side by side, the good company will leap off the page at you."

11) "The great enemy of a high-ROE company is competition."

12) "Most of the companies we own have people running them that are very good capital allocators. Because if you can keep your ROE over 20% year after year, you almost by definition are a good allocator."

13) "Our biggest tool for risk mitigation right now though is put options on the TSX. That's an insurance policy. That won't protect me from a 30% correction but it should protect me from a 10% correction."

14) "In Canada, the mid-cap segment is probably the most inefficient part of the market."

15) "Measuring growth in terms of return on equity and book value per share is a better methodological way than measuring growth in terms of earnings per share."

16) "If you focus on companies where the net worth of the business is growing at a very steady clip then the share price chart will take care of itself as long as the ROE stays intact."

17) "If you're a good stock-picker, concentration works in your favour, and if you're not, you should own an ETF instead."

18) "We don't buy turnarounds. It might be because we don't have the muscle. We wouldn't own enough stock to be able to push for a turn-around."

19) "I continue to look for great companies that are fair price as opposed to cheap stocks."

20) "If you want to be a great investor, then study the great investors and pick one that fits your style and then master that style."

21) "Your style of investing has to fit your personality type."

22) "I'm buying awesome companies and just hoping that they'll be awe-some forever. I get to hang out with the really great CEOs all the time as opposed to having argumentative discussions with mediocre CEOs who aren't doing a very good job running their companies."

MARTIN FERGUSON
THE SMALL-CAP KING

Martin Ferguson is the small-cap king of Canada. That said, he's surprisingly humble about it. Martin's New Canada Fund has achieved a 13.7% compound annual return over a 10-year period, and an annualized 15-year return of 16.5% compared with the median 10.7% return in the Canadian Small-/Mid-Cap Equity category as tracked by Morningstar. In 2013, the New Canada Fund posted an impressive return net of fees of 49.4%. Assets under Martin's superb management are above $1 billion.

Surprisingly, though, Martin still didn't feel worthy of being interviewed. He assumed Jason Donville recommended him to me to be interviewed, but I had known about Martin's exceptional market performance for years. "I would be pleased to talk to you and answer your questions, if only to determine if I am 'Master' material. I value Jason's opinion on many investment topics but his recommendation [of including me in your book] may be beyond his area of genius," said Martin.

I responded almost immediately with this list of why I had independently, and irrefutably, included Martin in the Market Masters roster:

- Thirty-three years in the investment industry

- Market-beating returns at Mawer New Canada Fund since its inception
- Best Canadian Small-/Mid-Cap Equity Fund at the 2012 Morningstar Canadian Investment Awards
- Analysts' Choice Award as the Best Small-Cap Canadian Equity Fund in 2002, 2003, and 2004
- Morningstar Domestic Equity Fund Manager of the Year

Thankfully, Martin finally agreed to be featured in this book. Although his process for picking small-cap stocks is not necessarily unique, it is rigid and scientific and thus not easy to implement on the first go. For example, we discussed the significance of internal cost of capital. Martin primarily employs the return on invested capital or ROIC metric to valuate stocks, and will favour companies where ROIC is greater than their internal cost of capital. From there he overlays various other models, admittedly more advanced and again increasingly difficult to implement for the beginner investor. The formulas we discussed may seem complex at first. But my recommendation is to work through those formulas with actual stocks (for example, try them with Bell Canada). As the saying goes, practice makes perfect.

During the interview, I asked Martin to compare and contrast his approach to Jason Donville's preferred ROE (return on equity) valuation method. His reply is food for thought. Finally, you'll learn that Martin has a golden touch that transforms not only his small-cap stocks into winners, but also his entry-level employees into top performers.

PRE-INTERVIEW LESSONS

BUBBLE: an unsustainable event that usually occurs at the end of a "boom," marked by an equally huge, but opposite, move (a decline or "bubble burst") in the stock market that can wipe out previous gains (for example the 2000 tech bust).
CONSOLIDATION: companies within a sector (e.g., health care) that merge to create a smaller number of larger companies or volume that builds

at or around a particular price point in a stock and determines its technical support.

DIVERSIFICATION: the allocation of money into unique investments with the intent to reduce risk in your portfolio (e.g., to invest in stocks and bonds so that you are protected if bonds go down but stocks go up).

DIVIDEND DISCOUNT MODEL: the calculation by which investors determine the price of a stock by discounting dividends back to present value.

RETURN ON INVESTED CAPITAL (ROIC): a measure of a company's ability to invest and use its money to generate incremental returns for its shareholders (including long-term debt).

RISK-FREE RATE: the return from a relatively conservative investment, such as a GIC.

RISK PREMIUM: the return over and above the risk-free rate, which an investor can achieve in the equity market.

Where did you grow up in Canada?

I was born in Prince Albert, Saskatchewan. At the age of seven I moved to Edmonton, Alberta, where my father went to university to become a teacher. He got a job in central Alberta in a small town called Ponoka with a population around five thousand. I grew up there until I went to university in Edmonton at the University of Alberta.

How did you first become interested in the markets?

I was a latecomer to the market. I actually had no involvement in investing until I got a job in the investment industry. In university, I got my Bachelor of Commerce degree with a major in finance and ended up with the top marks in the faculty, and so I won the Financial Executive Institute silver medal.

Congratulations.

Thank you. At the awards ceremony, one of my university professors asked if I had a job yet, which I had not lined up. He said, "I have an opportunity for you," and introduced me to someone by the name of Robert Kamp from Alberta Treasury at the time, which is now called AIMCo. They offered me summertime employment in the investment management division. From there it became a full-time job and that was my first interaction with investing.

What exactly did you do in the investment management division?

I was on the U.S. equity side. The U.S. equity portfolio manager liked my work so much that he went through the paperwork to get me hired as an analyst. I immediately began my CFA studies in '83.

Where else did your career take you from there?

Basically, I've only had three jobs. From Alberta Treasury I had an interim stint at the Principal Group, which was a trust company that did not survive. In the mid-eighties it went belly-up. I was there for just over two years. After that, I was invited back to Alberta Treasury and worked there until 1996. Then I accepted a job at Mawer Investment Management. One of the factors that I'm most proud of is if you look at 15 years ending December 31, 2014, my fund has the highest return out of any mutual fund in Canada.

You've had a great run heading up the Mawer New Canada Fund. What is your investment process?

My process follows the same procedures as we use for all equity classes at Mawer Investment Management. We focus on companies that can generate a return on invested capital greater than their cost of capital over time. Companies that create cash flow that in turn generate "wealth," as we call it. We then look at their management to determine how they've generated that high return on invested capital to ensure that they'll continue to do that going forward. However, if management does not pass that hurdle, then we don't go any further. Its needs to be a wealth-creating company with a competent management team. If they are, then we answer the question, "What is it worth?"

To try to figure out what it's worth, we use the discounted cash flow model. In fact, we have set up our own discounted cash flow models in order to determine intrinsic value. Those models go out 15 years. For the first five years, we use explicit assumptions. The next 10 years we use implicit assumptions that fade the company to steady state. And then at the end of the 15-year period we value this steady state company based on the dividend discount model. This gives us a single-point estimate of the intrinsic value of the company. But we know that this single-point estimate will be wrong. So we use Monte Carlo Analysis. With the push of a button, we create hundreds of iterations of potential future values for the company as we let the inputs in our model vary over set parameters. This gives us a fair value range for the company. You do that for hundreds of companies to get an idea of relative value in the marketplace.

Return on invested capital, or ROIC, is net income divided by the product of book value and long-term debt, is that correct?

That's very close. It's actually net operating profit after tax divided by all the capital that is in the company, which is both, you're correct, the equity and debt in the company.

Is ROIC the most heavily weighted metric that you use?

It is a qualifier. In other words, for a company to go into the portfolio it has to generate return on invested capital that's greater than its internal cost of capital. Now, in order for a company to do that it has to have external and internal competitive advantages. That's really what we're looking at in a company. Basically, external means that it has advantageous positioning against Porter's five forces, whereas internal means that the company has a competent management team that can help correctly allocate capital.

How do you determine internal cost of capital?

To determine a company's cost of capital you first establish the risk-free rate, which is basically the Government of Canada's long-bond curve going through the various maturities from one year out to fifteen years. Currently, that risk-free rate is somewhere around 2%. Then you subtract the risk-free rate from market rate, which is the average rate at which the equity market will return — let's say 6%. That product is the market risk premium. Finally, you add the risk-free rate to the market risk premium to get the required rate of return on capital. Anyways, the input numbers should vary from company to company depending on the amount of risk the company has taken on.

CALCULATING THE INTERNAL COST OF CAPITAL

FORMULA

$$R_c = r_f + (r_m - r_f)$$

EXAMPLE

$$8\% = 2\% + (8\% - 2\%)$$

WHERE

- R_c = required rate of return on capital
- r_f = risk-free rate
- r_m = market rate
- $r_m - r_f$ = market risk premium

As long as ROIC is higher than that internal cost of capital, the stock will be a candidate for your fund. In the above example, the company's ROIC must be greater than 8%. After that, you overlay the discounted cash flow model, the dividend discount model, and the Monte Carlo methods in your analysis?

Yes, it is somewhat of a soft skill. There's various questions that we have created that help us identify good and bad management. Management has to allocate capital, grow revenue, control cost, and control risk — four jobs. We can look at their track record, their attitude, and their understanding of those jobs. Also, look for management that really understands how the company makes money and also understands its competitive advantages. Basically, we want management teams that can grow the company's competitive advantages, not dilute them, and go into new enterprises. We want them to be able to tell us what those competitive advantages are and know that they're going to emphasize those as we go forward.

You must visit management then.

So since I've been here at Mawer Investment Management, which is coming up on 18 years, we've never invested in a company without first talking to management. Management is so important. They're the ones that reinvest the cash flows of the company and create value going forward. If they're not using that cash flow wisely, putting it to low return or inefficient uses, then they can destroy capital so quickly.

I do see striking similarities between your investment process and that of Jason Donville. However, you employ ROIC while Jason employs ROE — which metric is more important?

ROIC. But they're both important. ROE is the return on the common equity; that's very important. But ROIC takes into account the fact that companies can use debt and it also gives an idea of the overall return of the business rather than the equity. For example, there's two companies that are identical, except one uses 50% debt in capitalization while the other uses no debt in capitalization. The one that uses debt has a higher ROE because they're using low-cost debt in their capital. The other one with no leverage has a lower ROE but the businesses are the same. In my case, I'd be looking at two companies of equal ROIC and be able to differentiate the capital structure. Mr.

Donville, who is a smarter man than me, looks at ROE, but he's also aware of leverage. However, he looks "after the fact," once the debt has been removed from the equation.

Which stocks are usually included in your stock universe?

The first thing you must realize is that Canada is essentially a small-cap market. There are very few large-cap companies in Canada. There's hundreds of different definitions of "small-cap" but one that's used globally is $3 billion U.S. market cap or less. That seems to be a popular one. If we bring that definition to Canada there's hundreds of companies, give or take. Of course, it varies day to day and year to year.

We've actually been using the BMO small-cap index, which has been the small-cap index in Canada for years, although it's losing its pull because it's an un-investable index. No one can actually create derivatives on it because the companies are too illiquid. But it's still the one that's used. Up until about September of 2013, we used the definition that "small-cap" is companies in Canada with a market cap of $500 million or less. We had used that definition for 20 years. However, a $500 million market cap in 2013 is far smaller than, relatively speaking, a $500 million market cap company pre-inflation 20 years earlier.

Canada is a small-cap market? What's the small-cap range that you use now?

Picture Canada as a pyramid. At the top of the pyramid are the biggest companies, but there's very few of them. By the time you get to the base of the pyramid, the number of companies across the base is huge. In our universe, one limitation is that the company has to be small enough to be small-cap but also has to be big enough for us to spend our time and do our due diligence on to get a reasonably sized position. When I started here, our low-end size was $50 million market cap. Now it's obviously moved up. I'll still look at companies under $100 million market cap, but really $100 million market cap companies are about as small as I'd consider for the portfolio. Just because it takes so much time and effort to go through the due diligence if you can't get a big position in the company because it's too small. Currently, I look at companies from $100 million market cap up to about $1.5 billion market cap. And there's approximately four hundred of those small-cap stocks in the market today.

Do you automatically screen out certain sectors from your small-cap stock universe before moving onto the ROIC, various models, and management analysis?

No. We try to go in unbiased. What we're looking for is a company in any industry that can earn high return on its invested capital relative to its cost of capital. Remember, the cost of capital is determined by the risk of the company. The higher the risk, the higher the cost of capital. We keep our screens open and just look for any company because quite often there's companies in many industries that fit our filter. Now, one sector that we have not had exposure to in many years, almost a decade, is gold. Gold companies simply do not have the characteristics that we are looking for in a wealth-creating business. Very few gold companies have a high ROIC because they take on so much debt. Also, very few of them have competitive advantages, either internal or external, or even management that are good allocators of capital. Small-cap asset class is a risky asset class. There's a lot of risk here. Investing is a loser's game; what we try to do is put probabilities in our favour by sticking to our process, which means valuing companies based on their ability to generate wealth.

You've said that part of your strategy is to pick companies that can be resilient under all macro-economic scenarios. Are commodity sectors inherently risky because they lack pricing power? Their revenues are dictated by market prices.

Correct. As a generalization, they are riskier. They are price takers. They sell a commodity. Commodity means undifferentiated product. So, yes, they lack that pricing power. Now, having said that, there can be good and bad oil companies, gold companies, or mining companies. There can be commodity companies that do have competitive advantages. Additionally, they have better land, better resources, and so on. You cannot rule them out completely. The problem is that at the company level some make it through our screens. But then at the stock level very few of them meet our DCF [discounted cash flow] analysis. We cannot get a sufficient return given the level of risk that we're undertaking for us to consider gold companies.

Over 10 years ago, you determined that the small-cap technology sector in

Canada was undervalued. Which indicators told you that technology was undervalued?

During the tech bubble, 1999 to 2000, all investors were taking money out of other industries to put it in tech because tech was "the way of the future." At that time, we underperformed the market simply because we did not see the value in tech. I would say that we tend to be conservative. That said, you have to apply margin of safety in your models. However, at that time, none of the valuations made sense relative to other sectors in the market. During the tech bubble we probably had 1 to 2% tech weight in our New Canada Fund. There was just no opportunity for us to create alpha or to buy wealth-creating companies at good prices. Since then, the opposite happened. After the tech bubble, investors started to disassociate themselves from technology, and then started to look elsewhere in the market. And thus there was quite an opportunity in the tech sector about 10 years ago and even till today. However, we're closer to the end of that phenomenon that we've ever been. Though there's still an opportunity to buy high-quality companies that have strong competitive advantages, and good growth profiles, at very reasonable prices.

Can you share an example?

The one that I'll single out because it's been one of my best performers over the last decade has been Constellation Software. We bought Constellation Software at its IPO; it was a very illiquid stock. It was technically held by a couple of large institutions but we did what we at Mawer call "crocodile investing," which is when we are very patient, wait for a block to come at a price, and then buy it. And then we go back to waiting in the weeds with only our eyes and our snout showing through. We wait another couple of months until we bite again. It took us close to four years to get a full position in Constellation Software. But since then it's gone up over 20-fold. We loved its business model. We loved its competitive advantages. It was one of the best management teams in Canada and the valuation was highly attractive.

Constellation Software was highly illiquid when it IPO'd. In hindsight, I can agree that the company's performance is phenomenal. But at that time, how did you know the stock would multiply 20 times?

We loved the business model and we understood the business model. Constellation is a vertical market software provider. It provides software for a specific industry. They had a customer turnover of less than 5%. So 5% turnover meant they were keeping their customers for 20 years. They had locked-in clients and they were buying additional companies at a 25% or above return on capital. They were doing that over and over again. They were getting into industries where they controlled the niche, where they had majority market share, and they were up against the mom-and-pops that couldn't reinvest. When you actually looked at their competitive advantages over customers, over suppliers, over competitors, over new entrants, over existing rivals, all of the external checkmarks were checked off. Management understood how to create value by allocating capital to create more capital. Everything lined up, but I didn't have to pay any premium to get into it.

But aside from the qualities of the company, how did you know to get in early?

Now, my advantage is managing small-cap, so I get to see companies when they're small, whereas a lot of managers won't invest in a company until they're a certain size. By the time they grow to a certain size, the run may be done. Recently, I was at a round-table event and doing a media interview for the *National Post*. I was talking about the fact that one of my picks was Constellation Software. Another small-cap manager said, "Yeah, I looked at that. I thought it was interesting, but there's no liquidity so I've moved on." His idea of investing was different than mine. He couldn't get in. He couldn't get a block, so he moved on. Whereas I said, "I like this company. It'll take me four years to build a position, but I'm willing to do it because I like it."

What if a company's ROIC is above its cost of capital, but its P/E multiple is simply too high, signalling over-valuation? Would you pass on that stock?

That's a very good question. I'll answer it first of all by saying that we have a long-term perspective. We're not looking at today's P/E; we're looking at its internal rate of return. When you conduct a discounted cash flow analysis on a company, you figure out what cash flows it will generate into the future. As stocks go up in price, and the potential return falls, we actually look at de-emphasizing them in our portfolio. We always look at the potential return relative to the risk of all the stocks in the portfolio and we will work to emphasize those that have the best opportunity to provide the highest return on a risk-adjusted basis. So as tech stocks move up and become more expensive, we will start to trim them and invest in whatever other sectors look more attractive. My job as a fund manager is to be fully invested in small-caps at all times. So I am trying to generate an absolute return for my clients, while being aware at all times of relative returns.

With the resource sector having gone through a bear market starting in 2011, do you foresee that in 10 years' time you might be saying, "I determined that the resource sector was undervalued, and that's where our huge gain came from in the 2015 to 2025 period"?

I don't know if it will be the case. It's a potential. I want to talk a bit about mining versus oil and gas. Mines tend to be very large, and to cost hundreds of millions or billions of dollars for infrastructure. Small-cap companies in Canada very rarely have world-class deposits. You know, the competitive advantage that we're looking for on a global basis is harder to get from small-cap mining in Ontario, Quebec, or Saskatchewan than possibly an oil and gas company. Within oil and gas, the land with a well costs $1 million to $10 million. Indeed, you can still affordably own a world-class well, versus a mine, which costs $100 million to several billion dollars. So there's a bigger hurdle within the mining industry in Canada than there is in the oil and gas industry. As such, our exposure to mining companies in Canada is a lot lower than it is to E&Ps — energy and production companies. Having said that, we have very little exposure to even oil production and oil and gas creation companies in the portfolio. But we have sizeable exposure to the energy sector. Most of that is in the energy service side, where companies can have strong competitive advantages.

How many stocks do you hold on average in the New Canada Fund?

We hold on average 40 to 60 stocks. Currently, we hold 50 different companies. To get there, what we consider a full position is a 3% weight. So, in other words, in order to create a diversified portfolio, we assume we need about 33 companies. If you have 3% weight in each one of them and a little bit of cash, you have a very good starting portfolio. The problem with small-caps is that while we hold some smaller-cap companies with a large percentage of ownership in the actual company, it can still represent a very small weight in our fund. Because of that, I can have more companies in the portfolio. So 40 positions, more or less, is around a realistic minimum. About 60 and your efforts start to get diluted; you start to get over-diversified. Forty to sixty stocks is what we can work with in the New Canada Fund.

Do you increase weight when you have higher conviction in particular stocks?

Yes, so a theoretical full position is 3% weight. But we also have what we call "confidence weight," when we have a higher degree of confidence that any company will do well. We can extend a full weight up to six percent. 6% is the maximum we will hold in any individual company in the portfolio. When a company gets to 6% weight, we will trim it and we've done that many times in many different stocks.

Which positions reached 6% weight in your fund?

In the past there have been many. Constellation Software, for example. The most recent one that comes to mind is Home Capital Group.

With some experts and politicians saying that the Canadian real estate market is "over-heating," have you started trimming your position in Home Capital Group?

No. We have not.

Can you explain why not?

We are for the most part bottom-up investors. Stocks go in the portfolio because it makes sense from a bottom-up point of view. After the great recession, competition for non-prime mortgages in Canada went from about 11 major players down to two: Home Capital and Equitable Group.

So, after consolidation in the non-prime mortgage market, each player was left with higher market share. That's why you're not as concerned with the macro housing view?

Right. But it wasn't consolidation. It was the fact that there were companies that used securitization to fund their mortgage lending and then went out of business. They were usually subsidiaries of U.S. companies, and those U.S. companies didn't do well, so the subsidiaries disappeared.

Jeff Mo co-manages the New Canada Fund with you. What's your work dynamic together?

I've had three main people work with me in small-caps at Mawer. My first analyst was a fellow by the name of Jim Hall. He started with me in '97. In the year 2000 he went on to look after our Canadian Equity

Fund, which is our large-cap fund, and he's since moved on to become our chief investment officer and our chairman. The second analyst, Paul Moroz, was with me about three years when we started up the Mawer Global Small-Cap Fund and Paul was put in charge of that. So he's become portfolio manager and he's now the deputy chief investment officer at the firm.

The third analyst, Jeff Mo, is also a high-performing individual. And yes — he's young. He's 28, but we made him co-manager because he's smarter than me and is able to understand what it takes to be successful. So we work very well together. I have final decision rights but I hold those lightly. We go through a process we call "Challenge and Dissent." Basically, he will take devil's advocate position and ask, "What could go wrong? What are the risks? Why would we not do that? What are we missing?" Between the two of us, we get a more well-rounded idea because no one holds the complete truth by themselves.

That almost sounds like the dynamic between Buffett and Munger. Many of your analysts have risen through the ranks: do you attribute that to your ability to hire the best investment analysts or rather to your ability to train them into them into the best investment analysts?

It's a combination. I believe we have one of the best investment cultures in a research team in Canada. It's just a wonderful place to work when you have differing opinions and when you hold those opinions lightly because no one has a monopoly on the truth. Other people's opinions are just as valid. You can talk about them without affecting a person's feelings; there's no emotion involved here. But we also find it important to have a single decision maker. Committees do not work. You need to have somebody with the ultimate responsibility to make a decision. But before I'll make any decision, Jeff knows that he will be heard. I will listen. I will actually listen to everything he says, internalize it, work it in, and it will ultimately have an influence and bearing on my decision. I think one way to look at it, too, is ego. In this industry there's a lot of ego. I'm too afraid of failure to have a big ego. I think my ego is pretty small. Anyway, if I'm not listening to what others have to say, I'm going to just make mistakes.

Is it true that over the long term, small-caps will outperform large-caps?

Yeah, so while I was writing my CFA, which I did in '83 to '85, I read an article that explained why small-caps always outperform large-caps. Now, having said that, if you look over the last 15 to 20 years, small-caps in Canada have underperformed large-caps. So actually it's more like in the last decade that the trend has turned. But over the last decade the poor performances pull down the 15- and 20-year numbers, so to speak. I believe that there are opportunities in the small-cap area that exceed those in the large-cap area, offset by higher risk. The small-cap area is fraught with danger. Investing is a loser's game and if you do not have a sufficiently well thought out process in order to mitigate and to control your risks, you will surely fail. But if you do it right, there are enough market inefficiencies in the small-cap market that you can outperform large-caps over the long term.

How can an investor manage and control risks with small-caps in their portfolio?

Understand that small-caps are largely a loser's game. There's a lot of promises that are not kept, and there's a lot of dreams that are unfulfilled. We focus on companies with what we call a "complete business model." So not a company that's coming up with something that has yet to be produced or with a promise of the next cure. Companies that have actually shown that they can do it, with their infrastructure in place, and their whole business model functional. I think it's very important in small-caps to control the risk. Every single small-cap company has a dream, but most of those dreams will never be attained. But if we focus on the companies that have built the business, that are actually generating revenues, that are actually producing cash flows, that are actually generating return, then there's a lot of opportunity in the small-cap market. Part of the reason for high risk in small-caps is because of liquidity, or lack thereof. Generally, small-cap stocks tend to trade at lower multiples than large-caps. But liquidity is less of a risk to a long-term investor as the small company grows, which is another reason why successful small-cap companies should outperform their equivalent large-cap peers: they lose their liquidity discount over time.

So you accept the inevitability that not all small-caps will work out?

Growing up, I was very mathematically oriented and was also a perfectionist. In all of my classes I always went for 100%. But in this industry there's no such thing as perfection. All you can do is put probabilities in your favour. That's my message. By following a great process, and being true to that process through all markets, and all economic conditions, that will help you. We've just found a way to put probabilities in our favour and that's what you have to do in the market.

What are "favourable probabilities" for you?

I'm trying to prevent 30% declines. So nothing goes into the portfolio unless there's a reason for that individual stock; we've done the due diligence on that. However, as you say, things will not always work out. But if you do your work and you go through the process in every single decision you make, and follow the process, then you will put probabilities in your favour and you will win.

There you have it: ROIC — return on invested capital. That's another important metric that you should overlay on your security selection process. But remember, Martin favours companies with ROIC greater than their internal cost of capital. Those ROIC achievers are what Martin calls "wealth creators." Martin also applies additional analysis to his security selection in the New Canada Fund; namely, the Dividend Discount Model (DDM), Discounted Cash Flow model (DCF), and Monte Carlo Analysis. Those models and analyses are too technical to discuss in detail within this book, though I do encourage any readers who are interested to conduct further independent research online. The formulas are included below for both the Dividend Discount Model (DDM) and the Discounted Cash Flow model (DCF) for enterprising investors:

DIVIDEND DISCOUNT MODEL (DDM)
Value of a stock = Next Year's Dividend per Share / (Discount Rate – Dividend Growth Rate)
Discount Rate = required rate of return

DISCOUNTED CASH FLOW MODEL (DCF)
$DCF = Cash\ Flow_{Yr1} / (1 + discount\ rate)1 + Cash\ Flow_{Yr2} / (1 + discount\ rate)2 \ldots$

Start your education on advanced valuation formulas by going online and looking up the material from Aswath Damodaran, a professor of corporate finance and valuation at New York University's Stern School of Business. I am eager to follow the career trajectory of Martin's co-manager, Jeff Mo. I have a feeling that Mr. Mo is a Market Master in the making and that Martin can at least take some of the credit for his inevitable success. Finally, the Mawer New Canada Fund is currently closed to new money and new investors. Martin is quoted as saying, "We continued to grow to a point where we said we can't take on any more money. It just gets incrementally hard with each additional dollar brought into the mandate to do the best that we can for clients."

MASTER KEYS
MARTIN FERGUSON

1) "We focus on companies that can generate a return on invested capital greater than their cost of capital over time. Companies that create cash flow that in turn generate wealth."

2) "ROIC takes into account the fact that companies can use debt and it also gives an idea of the overall return of the business rather than the equity."

3) "Cost of capital is determined by the risk of the company. The higher the risk, the higher the cost of capital."

4) "We have set up our own discounted cash flow models in order to determine intrinsic value. Those models go out 15 years."

5) "We're not looking at today's P/E; we're looking at its internal rate of return. When you conduct a discounted cash flow analysis on a company, you figure out what cash flows it will generate into the future."

6) "Management has to allocate capital, grow revenue, control cost, and control risk — four jobs."

7) "If [management is] not using that cash flow wisely, putting it to low return or inefficient uses, then they can destroy capital so quickly."

8) "The first thing you must realize is that Canada essentially is a small-cap market. There are very few large-cap companies in Canada."

9) "I look at companies from $100 million market cap up to about $1.5 billion market cap. And there's approximately four hundred of those small-cap stocks in the market today."

10) "Investing is a loser's game; what we try to do is put probabilities in our favour by sticking to our process, which means valuing companies based on their ability to generate wealth. In this industry there's no such thing as perfection."

11) "As a generalization, [commodity companies] are riskier. They are price takers. They sell a commodity. Commodity means undifferentiated product. So, yes, they lack that pricing power."

12) "A lot of managers won't invest in a company until they're a certain size. By the time they grow to a certain size, the run may be done."

13) "We will work to emphasize those [stocks] that have the best opportunity to provide the highest return on a risk-adjusted basis. [But] as stocks go up in price, and the potential return falls, we actually look at de-emphasizing them in our portfolio [and] invest in whatever other sectors look more attractive."

14) "We hold on average 40 to 60 stocks. To get there, what we consider a full position is a 3% weight. So in other words, in order to create a diversified portfolio, we assume we need about 33 companies."

15) "We also have what we call 'confidence weight,' when we have a higher degree of confidence that any company will do well."

16) "I believe that there are opportunities in the small-cap area that exceed those in the large-cap area, offset by higher risk."

17) "If we focus on the companies that have built the business, that are actually generating revenues, that are actually producing cash flows, that are actually generating return, then there's a lot of opportunity in the small-cap market."

RYAZ SHARIFF
THE CYCLICAL COMMODITY INVESTOR

Ryaz Shariff journeys through jungles in far-off countries in search of valuable assets. Does that pique your interest? As you'll learn from our interview, Ryaz is something of an Indiana Jones in the investment world. Some may say that Ryaz is too hands-on in his running of Primevest Capital, but his fund, Primevestfund, has not only survived the prolonged commodities bear market and recent oil price collapse, but has managed to beat the market since 2005, with a 10% compound annual return.

Being a commodity investor in 2015 is a very lonely proposition. The commodity bear market that started in 2011 has yet to abate, and commodity-era darlings such as Sprott Asset Management have struggled. Ryaz, though, has managed to stay much more versatile. Aside from investing within his core expertise, which is the junior and mid-size mining market, he mandates that his fund remain flexible, which is to say that he adjusts Primevestfund's investment strategy to reflect the prevailing market conditions. This means taking advantage of non-resource special situations, including large-cap mergers as well as employing short-selling in down markets. Today, over one-third of the fund is in the non-resource sector.

While Ryaz insists that common investors cannot achieve comparable success in the junior and mid-size resource market because they lack "deep domain expertise," there have always been instances of average-joe stock-pickers who make outsized returns from resource booms. One such example is a family friend of mine, Robert Hirschberg, the owner of a sports apparel company who resides in Toronto. Robert parlayed $20,000 into $15,000,000 by speculating in junior mining stocks throughout the 2002–2007 commodity bull market in Canada. While this anecdotal evidence should bring you some hope, I caution that one should wait until the commodity cycle turns up before investing in this sector or else risk outsized losses. A (grizzly) bear market can be mean. As Ryaz explains in his most recent fund letter, "As we continue to experience one of the longest resource bear markets in history, we have maintained a disciplined focus on building further expertise within the sector, so when the fund flows return, as is now already becoming evident in small ways, we will be the premier hedge fund in the country to benefit."

I am not as well-versed in the resource sector as I invest in the non-resource sector of the market. Thankfully, Ryaz was both gracious and accommodating. Our interview was over the telephone, with me in Toronto and Ryaz in Vancouver. Ryaz's responses were short and to the point.

PRE-INTERVIEW LESSONS

BEAR MARKET: a prolonged declining market.

BLACK SWAN: an occurrence that is extremely hard to predict. Term coined by Nassim Taleb.

COMMODITIES: companies that sell commodities (e.g., Teck Resources) or the commodity itself (e.g., copper).

CYCLICAL: subject to and highly influenced by uncontrollable economic changes, prices, or other developments. Can apply to companies or sectors. For example, oil producers' profit is determined by the price of oil, which is not within their control.

FOREIGN EXCHANGE (FX) TRADING: trading in and out of currencies, which are traded on the FX market.

INEFFICIENT: not incorporating all available information into the prices in the market. "Inefficient" is a term generally used by investors who do not believe in the Efficient Market Theory (EMT). For example, one may feel a decline in the price of a stock was unwarranted given the available information at the time.

LEVERAGE: when an investor uses margin (i.e., loan) to increase his/her bet on an investment to amplify their returns. Can also refer to companies that use considerable debt for expansion, acquisition, or any other form of investment.

SHORTING OR SHORT-SELLING: a practice whereby some investors borrow a stock and sell it, with the anticipation that they can later buy it back at a lower price.

Where did you grow up in Canada?

I was actually born in East Africa, in Tanzania: a little town called Bukoba. However, we emigrated to Canada when the Idi Amin ideology in Uganda proliferated through other East African countries. We were basically refugees due to our political situation. At the age of five I moved to Vancouver.

How did you first get interested in the markets?

I think it was probably in my early high school days. My math professor was also an investor and so I invested some funds alongside him. That's how I invested in my first growth stock. And then I subsequently read a book by Peter Lynch, *One Up on Wall Street,* which was a guiding influence for me.

What was that first growth stock?

It was a Vancouver Stock Exchange–listed aquaculture operation.

And how did that stock perform?

I think I doubled my money in a matter of a year.

From that experience, I assume that you continued to invest throughout high school.

Yes — sure did.

Did you stick with commodity plays?

Yes, but really more in early-stage growth opportunities.

Did you ever lose along the way?

Of course, but the first big loser I had was actually in my early currency trading days.

What happened? Were you over-leveraged?

No, it was technical-based trading and trying to speculate on macro events, which was obviously foolhardy.

Which currency trade resulted in the loss?

The British pound.

Were you short the pound?

Yes, I was making multiple short-term trades on the British pound.

What was your thesis for being on that side of the trade?

Interest rate cycles occurring in the early nineties. The British pound took a big drop and that's when George Soros had made his famous short call on the British pound.

Soros "broke the Bank of England." Where did you start off in the industry?

My formal education is in mathematics with the expectation to practise actuarial sciences. I was introduced to the pension fund management business because of my studies at Simon Fraser University and because my uncle was a very prominent actuary in town. He introduced me to a couple of pension fund managers, but it was a very difficult business to crack into, so I actually got my start in the retail brokerage business with a bank-owned firm. I used to write investment policy statements for clients when nobody even knew what an IPS was. I picked my own stocks and bonds and used mutual funds for international exposure. Back then I would argue that the Solomon Smith Barney analyst was incorrect in their assessment of McDonald's and why one should buy Wendy's instead.

As time went on I became more entrepreneurial and started to realize that the former type of analysis without access to management wasn't adding much value. That was my "aha" moment and the world opened up to me in terms of earlier-stage growth investing. One of my clients at the time got involved in building an infrastructure operation in Brazil. I committed to allocate some capital to his company but, when I went back to my bank-owned firm, they said that from a compliance standpoint, I couldn't do so. Eighteen months later, Bell Canada bought out two-thirds of that early-stage company to control management at a four-fold valuation than the original investment. That experience opened my eyes and motivated me to get involved with inefficiently priced opportunities with management teams that we can get access to.

I've heard that you constantly look for inefficiencies in the small-cap market and special situations in the large-cap market.

Generally speaking, most of the names that you find inefficiencies in are ones that the market hasn't followed or that have been orphaned for some reason. You can find inefficiencies because these companies are under the radar and don't have sponsorship from brokerage houses. Typically, when you find these assets, you get to know management, and then you get to understand the growth prospects. When we get involved with these stories, we want to know that they will get institutional investor appeal at some point in time within a 12-month period.

Ultimately, what ends up happening is that you're investing in these companies early in their capital market strategy and before they get to premium values as the market recognizes their high growth profiles. Identifying the under-followed small-cap businesses is the first part of the treasure hunt; thereafter, you must figure out what catalysts will drive multiple expansion.

How do you separate the dogs from the ones that will actually grow?

Management is the critical element in any of these businesses. We'd rather invest in exceptional management teams than in ordinary ones. Time and time again, we observe that businesses always have hiccups, but management teams that are exceptional entrepreneurs always figure a way around those issues to create value, whereas poor management teams may have the best product but can still mess it up.

But how do you determine a small-cap's value then when there's no earnings yet?

Ultimately, you've got to forecast what the future earnings will look like. . . . I want to step back because while we do invest in these special situation opportunities, our real core focus historically has been on the resource sector.

Okay, so in the resource sector, what criteria do you use to gauge whether those early-stage companies can actually grow their multiples?

Typically we like to invest in advanced-stage resource development assets where we can utilize our technical expertise and our unique strategy. Here we can evaluate the base economic value of these assets and invest alongside exceptional management teams that have the ability to further increase the economic value through expansion of the resource and/or optimization of the asset.

Eventually, if management creates value from efficient capital allocation, the asset becomes attractive for larger companies with depleting asset bases to consolidate, at premium values. There's a limited group of investors that truly understand this space, hence the inefficient opportunity. This type of investing can be very volatile but there's no better risk-to-reward relationship if you can get it right.

Given the volatile commodity down-cycle that we're in, have you shifted your strategy?

It's always tough to forecast what's going to happen with commodity prices and that's also why we don't try to forecast commodity prices themselves but rather use long-term consensus estimates to model into these opportunities. These development assets aren't exposed to day-to-day swings of the commodity as they are not in production. Though, the movement in the commodities, of course, has sentiment impacts on their perceived value in the short term.

In terms of revisions, what we've done is allocate a portion of our portfolio outside of resources because that's where the opportunities have been. There's been a lack of capital and funds flow into the resource sector as we've endured a four-year bear market in the metals complex. Commodities are generally the focus in the late stage of economic cycles. When the metals cycle eventually turns, you tend to see multi-fold returns, so we want to be positioned with world-class entrepreneurial teams today even though it will be volatile for an undetermined time frame.

So what's your current portfolio allocation? You mentioned that you're still exposed to metals because they're undervalued, but what else?

Historically, the large majority of our assets are allocated to varying degrees between mining and oil and gas. Today we're at our largest exposure to non-resources, bordering on a third of our assets.

Is that 30% non-resource exposure primarily in non-cyclical consumer stocks?

It's everything from non-bank financials to technology and health care.

What will it take for you to re-allocate again? Do you need to see the commodity cycle turn up?

Well, yes. However, when things do turn, there will be a lot of appreciation that will be captured before everyone realizes that a turn has occurred. So, it's a balancing act. Today we have been making small allocations to management teams with long track records of starting companies at the bottom of cycles with potentially world-class assets. Rather than forecasting when the cycle will turn around, I'm happy owning companies where we have close relationships with management. They're doing all the right things, they're highly vested, and they don't run the risk of going belly-up. We're not really looking to forecast when the cycle turns because I don't believe anyone can.

In summary, we invest alongside exceptional management teams with high-quality assets that are financially sound. For example, one of our top holdings for probably about six or seven years is an oil company based in Colombia. We got involved with the company when it was at zero production. Today it's the only E&P company — exploration and production — that I have seen that actually has no debt, that can maintain their production of 26,000 barrels per day without going into debt at current low oil prices, and when oil prices move upward, it will become a go-to name.

Regardless of the commodity cycle, you want to own high-quality assets.

Absolutely. It's always easy in hindsight to forecast cycles, but the velocity of money in today's world is so fast that you can't really figure out the bottom of cycles, the top of cycles, and the turn of cycles.

This most recent decline in the oil market seems to have been propelled by a double whammy: an increase in U.S. shale oil supply and a decline in demand from China.

The issue is that we don't have a lot of visibility. It's very difficult to figure out exactly where the oil price is going to go. So the only way you can really give yourself a chance of success is to have a long-term horizon. Today within the oil market, and particularly in shale oil production, it's very difficult to quantify the costs. The question is whether you're looking at half-cycle costs or full-cycle costs. Half-cycle costs is basically operating costs, whereas full-cycle costs also include infrastructure, land, and any other associated expenditures to go from discovery to production.

In addition to that, you have large decline rates in shale oil production in the range of 75% from the time you put the well on production to a year later. It's tough to figure out where in that curve you are on a global level. Having said that, technology has improved so much that it has contributed to greater efficiencies in operations. Even if oil prices recover quickly, a large amount of new wells could be economically drilled reasonably quickly again. However, I think that in the short term, higher prices will be elusive as there's enough oil in the U.S. to meet supply.

Do you agree then that the cure for low oil prices is low prices? There's less incentive for rigs to pump oil. Supplies will thus deplete, but then under-supply will drive prices up again.

That's generally how commodity markets work. But it's very different in oil and gas than in mining due to the time lag. For example, mining requires very heavy front-end expenses and capital before you can generate a return on that mine. Moreover, the time frame for a world-class project to go from a discovery to production is approaching a decade. In the interim, you're spending a lot of money without receiving any revenue from it. The capital decisions in mining are made so far in advance that you're forecasting that these assets are going to be economically rewarding for a long period of time, even generations.

Sentiment has a lot to do with decision-making abilities when it comes to capital allocation in the mining sector. This is why we see such long cycles and violent cycles within the mining space. The actual cycle works like this: demand exceeds supply; capital is approved to develop supply; commodity prices increase in value till new supply comes on-line; supply exceeds demand; commodity prices decrease; non-profitable supply comes off-line and then we wait for demand to exceed supply again. Demand growth continues over a long-term basis because of the urbanization of large populations on a worldwide basis, but the supply side declines when you take away large expenditures to develop mines in a low-price environment. You basically put supply on hold and it takes some time to bring additional supply on again. Frankly, we're at that transition point today. I think we're going to see a copper deficit this year as supply is coming off-line or at least the growth of supply is coming off.

Your argument is that while long-term demand for commodities continues to increase, we experience anomalies, or downturns, in the long-term cycle, because of supply spikes.

Right. That's exactly right. While demand will be volatile in the short term, the long-term demand will be reasonably sustainable. On the supply side, we will continue to see a lot of volatility based on where commodity prices settle as there's such long-term capital allocation decisions that go alongside the cycle. Today it's a difficult environment to justify building a multi-billion-dollar copper mine. Remember, developing these metals mines takes a long time, particularly because of political and environmental factors that have become more stringent in the last number of years.

Do you worry about political instability? Is that a major risk in your portfolio?
Political instability is always a risk that you worry about. However, sometimes that's where I find the inefficient opportunities. If you can get involved when you see political change occurring within a resource market then there are usually significant returns to be made, especially if you can bring in somebody with local knowledge and understand how management is approaching the political change.

Hypothetically, if the Congo installed a new government that's open to development, you would initiate positions in the development companies operating in the Congo?
Sure. We were involved in the Congo 15 years ago. We were involved with Colombia when they opened their doors to foreign investment in the resource sector. Canadian oil and gas companies were among the chief beneficiaries when the Colombian government committed to pursue policies that would open up and reward entrepreneurs for utilizing their expertise to develop Colombian natural resources. Of course, the Colombian government and the people of Colombia significantly benefitted from the tax base, jobs, and standard of living increase. Arguably, today we may be seeing a similar kind of situation in Ecuadorian mining. Two of the most successful resource entrepreneurs that we do business with are entering Ecuador at the same time on different opportunities. Sometimes it doesn't work, but these prospects can be seized opportunistically as most investors don't want to even consider it. It's usually not easy work in the early-growth resource space but the potential returns can easily justify the trailblazing.

How would a retail investor acquire this information? For example, keep up to date with which governments are becoming more friendly for mining activities and oil and gas, for instance?
It's tough for a retail investor to get in at the early part of the curve unless they're spending most of their time focused on research and analysis, as well as travelling to those countries or having access to the management teams that are having the discussions, meetings, and conferences with various government entities within the countries. For example,

I'm having lunch with the CEO of a company that just acquired a mineral deposit in a country that has been *persona non grata* in the investment community. We're expecting some major political changes that will potentially result in a significant reduction in perceived geopolitical risk. That political risk change in itself could result in a multi-fold value creation event for that company over the next few years.

Besides the political change catalyst, how else can investors catch a turn in the mining sector or specifically in a mining company?

The two most important ingredients to look at are the demand/supply fundamentals and institutional fund flows. We do rigorous work in the fundamentals of the commodities markets and this is the basis of our preparedness for when the systemic changes occur. Although there's always a time delay. The resource markets are generally a small market so when institutional funds flow into the sector it can have dramatic effects. When we meet with resource equity analysts, the first questions we ask are, "What questions are the generalist institutional inventors asking you and what's their sentiment like?" Once they are looking to dip their toe in the water, that could be a signal to watch the market.

Do you employ people with technical expertise who can evaluate an asset, like a mine?

Absolutely. We retain those guys. I also travel the world and into the jungles of South America and Africa to get first-hand knowledge of select resources. As a retail investor, perusing articles and news portals is not going to get you a holistic perspective, because you never know the legitimacy and the credibility of what you're reading sometimes. You need to talk to people, and you need to be in the actual places to do that. A news article is not going to give you any sort of edge.

There must be regulated technical reports issued by management that investors can use?

Certainly, there are public disclosure requirements for public companies that require disclosure of technical and economic data. So a retail investor does have access to feasibility studies, scoping studies, and so on. Also, an independent engineering review would be able to provide a framework for value. But this takes a lot of scavenging and some technical expertise to understand the material. There are also a number of analysts in the investment world that provide assessments.

Let's shift gears to gold. In 2007, you said that you were bearish on the U.S. dollar and thus bullish on gold. You proceeded to say that you were buying into gold companies. And then from 2007 to 2012, gold went from $600 to $1,800: that's a three-fold increase.

I have to be careful about this because I never make macro forecasts. Because I don't believe that anyone can with consistency and accuracy. The interview that you are referring to was a more specific call. We were involved with a gold company that was expanding a gold asset in West Africa, particularly Ghana and Mauritania, and I had been travelling into the jungles of West Africa. There was a general sentiment of bearishness in the U.S. dollar at that time. It hit home for me when I got into a cab in Ghana and tried to offer U.S. dollars, but the driver wouldn't accept it. He wanted Ghanaian cedis, which is the domestic currency. This was a revelation to me because when I grew up in East Africa, the U.S. dollar had always been the preferred currency. I thought, "If this is happening at the grassroots here, then maybe this is something to pay attention to." It wasn't that I was necessarily bullish on gold. Rather, we had invested in a gold asset and at long-term consensus the price of gold was on an upward trajectory. That particular asset was worth $350 million when I invested in it. After two and a half years we sold out of our position in a takeover bid for $7.2 billion.

That's a huge return. Did the cab driver have foresight into the U.S. dollar's imminent decline?

I guess he must have been short [laughs]. Seriously, though, it was just the general sentiment that was occurring throughout the world at that time.

Unlike that cab driver, in your fund, you have up to 25% opportunity to short-sell any positions.

We always have a hedge in place: the ability to short positions. That usually represents 20 to 30% of the fund. Our limit is actually a net negative 25% so we can actually go 125% short. We never reach that limit though because we're a long-biased fund. We do short stocks on an opportunistic basis but really it's used to insulate some portion of the systematic risk within the portfolio.

What have been your biggest wins over the five years?

We've had a number of five- and ten-baggers but we've also had a number of losers. We've been involved in some companies for a decade. In one case, we've held a company through six spinoffs from our original investment. It continued to create value. Anyway, we've had some great wins and they tend to be accentuated by the cyclicality of the sector. We make good calls from both a fundamental value and macro event basis. Further, we've generated returns in our portfolio, over and above the benchmark, because we take very concentrated positions.

You operated various business for many years. Has that experience given you an edge in the markets?

For a period of eight years, I actually operated everything from manufacturing to wireless telecommunications technology to aviation to wind farm development. I've been on 70-metre towers and wind turbine towers, have negotiated import/export financing transactions, and have developed a couple of hundred megawatt wind farms in southern Alberta. I've had a lot of hands-on experience, which has allowed me to become a better analyst of businesses.

So that experience must give you an edge in the non-resource segment of the market, too.

When investing on the non-resource side, our criteria are generally the same. First, we look for fundamental under-valuation of the business. Second, we look for significant growth prospects in the enterprise. With resource investments, not only do we want the principal asset undervalued, we also like to see additional "blue sky" in another asset or business line that we get for free. Third, we look for businesses that have institutional investor appetite within a short period of time (12 to 18 months). Even if we get involved with a smaller illiquid situation that meets our investment criteria then we ultimately want to get liquidity and multiple expansion as their investor audience expands.

Again, it's all about treasure hunting. Find those under-followed, undervalued, and inefficient publicly traded companies that over time can build their businesses to realize value in a broad context.

When you say that you like to see additional "blue sky" in another asset or business does that mean that the market is inefficiently pricing some companies?

Correct. You could use breakup analysis. There's sometimes other assets that are hidden. Well, maybe not necessarily hidden in the company, but either it's just not focused on by the company or it's waiting for some catalyst before management allocates resources to it again. That asset may become interesting and have some sort of value down the road.

And how do you measure growth prospects?

In non-resource companies, it's usually revenue growth with corresponding earnings growth over time. However, in resource companies, we focus on pre-production assets, so they don't need to have revenues. There's on-going expenditures to develop the asset base which should eventually show a feasible economic value to continue to develop the asset into a productive asset that generates cash flows. An important concept to understand is that in the resource business, a company's productive asset is always in decline by the very fact that it usually constantly extracts minerals out of the ground. That's the major difference between the resource business and many other businesses. One of the major challenges of a large company that's pressured to grow is the replacement of that declining asset base.

So, naturally there's acquisition activity in the commodity markets because of the need to replace assets over time. Most resources are finite.

Yes, again, we look at those companies that do not necessarily produce anything and those that will likely get bought out as a result of larger companies that require or demand those types of asset bases to continue their growth.

Consolidation in the industry?

Absolutely.

But is there any opportunity on the other side of that transaction — large resource stocks?

We don't buy into large-cap resource companies.

Your fund page said that there's some large-cap, but it's essentially 100% small-cap.

It's not 100% small-cap. What ends up happening is that we get involved in stories that are small- or mid-cap that ultimately grow. For example, I told you about that gold asset that we got involved in when it was worth $350 million. And then two and a half years later it was worth $7.2 billion. Thus, it became a large-cap. We continued to own that stock as our top holding when it was worth $5 billion, $6 billion, and then ultimately $7 billion. Large mining companies are difficult to analyze because they have so many assets. We typically like single-asset companies. Some people argue that those small single-asset companies are riskier, but I could argue that they're less risky because we understand those deposits better than a larger company that has 20 different deposits.

What was that company that you held until it reached $7-billion market cap?
Redback Mining.

Okay. What's your take on the TSX Venture Exchange? It's been pretty much dead for the past eight years or so and recently it's hit recession-era lows. Is this an entry point?
That's a tough call. The Venture Exchange is predominantly composed of resource companies, and mostly early-stage resource stock, which are highly cyclical. It's hard to call the bottom. If you look at the history of the Venture Exchange, you'll see immense upticks and immense downticks. However, this down-cycle has been particularly long.

Do you invest entirely in Canadian companies, or do you invest in other companies abroad?
The majority of the companies that we invest in are Canadian-based companies. For clarity, the assets that these companies manage may be anywhere in the world, but the management teams are Canadian-based where we conveniently have access to management. We do invest, or historically have invested, in the Australian market, which has very similar characteristics to the Canadian market.

So, I'll ask you again before the interview comes to a close: how can the average investor get an edge and be successful in the resource markets?
Well, the key factor is that the investor has to have sufficient evidence to be able to bet on management. Have you read any of my commentaries?

No, I have not.
Okay, you should. There's one from June 30, 2014, in which I state that there are four different things to keep in mind when investing in resource assets: number one, regular contact and relationships with management who are world-class entrepreneurs with track records. Number two, assets require in-depth understanding resulting in a narrow investor base initially. Number three, access to capital and management group

that is highly invested. And number four, companies that can grow large enough to garner widespread institutional investor interest.

Anything else that you'd like to add?

I think if you read some of these commentaries, they will give you a good feel for how I think and what we're looking at at any given time in the market. It will take you a good hour if you want to read everything. Start from the beginning and don't stop reading until the end. What's interesting is that when we started this hedge fund 10 years ago, we probably had about two dozen peers. Today, all but a couple have survived. I think we're getting close to the bottom of this cycle and recently we have seen a large amount of capital formation that's gone into private equity funds focused in the resources space, for the first time ever of this magnitude. The next few years could garner some pretty significant rates of return in the resource space in Canada. But again, with volatility in the short term.

Perhaps soon will we see a resumption of the commodity cycle?

We've been in a four-year bear market. Bear markets tend to have violent moves both up and down. We're obviously closer to the bottom, if not past the bottom, than we are to the top. I think we're going to see this turnaround. When it happens, it could be a violent move. Maybe one like we've never seen before, as there are potentially large pools of capital to be injected in an area that is reasonably small.

A black swan event?

No. In hindsight it'll look obvious for all of the fundamental reasons. The valuation parameters of these businesses are extremely low, and there's been a lot of money that's been raised — tens of billions of dollars — by private equity firms to invest in a sector that they don't necessarily have the appropriate expertise to properly invest. As a result, they'll have to probably chase the market as the pressure rises to deploy capital.

Is there a lot of money to be made in the resource markets?

There's been a number of billionaires created in the last cycle that we know personally. And many more multi-millionaires and hundreds of millionaires. So yes, if it's done correctly, you've got the right time frame, and you can put up with the volatility.

It was no understatement when Ryaz said that he's one of the last men standing in the commodity hedge fund segment in Canada. The four-year commodity bear market and recent oil crash has devastated commodity investors. But Ryaz has an edge: vast connections with able management and travelling to faraway countries and through jungles (à la Indiana Jones, as I mentioned before) to assess resource companies before he invests. While I assume that the common investor doesn't actually have this edge in the commodity market, Ryaz did reaffirm, via a follow-up email, how one can uncover the best commodity companies for when the commodity cycle turns up.

> The investment philosophy in our bottom-up strategy has remained steadfast with the following criteria as core principles in security selection:
>
> 1. Management teams with successful track records and with whom we can build long-standing relationships and remain in regular contact;
> 2. Assets that require in-depth understanding resulting in a narrow investor base initially;
> 3. Companies with access to capital and a management group that is highly vested;
> 4. Companies that can grow large enough to garner widespread institutional investor interest with corresponding multiple expansion.

I would also add to the above list the concept of asset replacement as a core principle to security selection in the resource market. Ryaz made it clear that the opportunities for high stock returns are most plentiful in those junior or small- to mid-size resource companies that offer the asset replacement potential that larger companies need in periods of production ramp up once the cycle turns.

1) "We'd rather invest in exceptional management teams than in ordinary ones. Businesses always have hiccups, but management teams that are exceptional entrepreneurs always figure a way around those issues to create value."

2) "Most of the names that you find inefficiencies in are ones that the market hasn't followed or that have been orphaned for some reason."

3) "Identifying the under-followed small-cap businesses is the first part of the treasure hunt; thereafter, you must figure out what catalysts will drive multiple expansion."

4) "If management creates value from efficient capital allocation, the asset becomes attractive for larger companies with depleting asset bases to consolidate, at premium values. One of the major challenges of a large company that's pressured to grow is the replacement of that declining asset base."

5) "This type of investing [in advanced-stage resource development assets] can be very volatile but there's no better risk-to-reward relationship if you can get it right."

6) "We don't try to forecast commodity prices themselves but rather use long-term consensus estimates to model into these opportunities."

7) "Commodities are generally the focus in the late stage of economic cycles. When the metals cycle eventually turns, you tend to see multi-fold returns."

8) "We're not really looking to forecast when the cycle turns because I don't believe anyone can. The velocity of money in today's world is so fast that you can't really figure out the bottom of cycles, the top of cycles, and the turn of cycles."

9) "[The ideal energy and production company] has no debt, can maintain their production without going into debt at current low oil prices, and when oil prices move upward, it becomes a go-to name."

10) "The actual cycle works like this: demand exceeds supply; capital is approved to develop supply; commodity prices increase in value till new supply comes on-line; supply exceeds demand; commodity prices decrease; non-profitable supply comes off-line and then we wait for demand to exceed supply again."

11) "While demand will be volatile in the short term, the long-term demand will be reasonably sustainable."

12) "If you can get involved when you see political change occurring within a resource market, then there are usually significant returns to be made."

13) "The two most important ingredients to look at are the demand/supply fundamentals and institutional fund flows."

14) "The resource markets are generally a small market so when institutional funds flow into the sector it can have dramatic effects."

15) "We always have a hedge in place: the ability to short positions. It's used to insulate some portion of the systematic risk within the portfolio."

16) "We've had some great wins and they tend to be accentuated by the cyclicality of the sector."

17) "With resource investments, not only do we want the principal asset undervalued, we also like to see additional 'blue sky' in another asset or business line that we get for free."

18) "Some people argue that those small, single-asset companies are riskier, but I could argue that they're less risky because we understand those deposits better than a larger company that has 20 different deposits."

19) "If you look at the history of the Venture Exchange, you'll see immense upticks and immense downticks. . . . Bear markets tend to have violent moves both up and down."

PETER HODSON
GROWTH AT ANY COST

Peter Hodson finally hung up his hat in 2011 after wrangling up tremendous returns in the Sprott Growth Fund. "It was a high-risk, small-cap growth fund, like a cowboy fund," he says. After a disagreement with Eric Sprott over the fund, followed by a 62% drop in 2008, Peter finally decided it was time to ride out into the sunset. During the resource bull run from 2002 to 2007, Sprott Asset Management was a high-flying firm. As Peter quipped, his experience at Sprott Asset Management could be a book on its own.

Today, Peter Hodson is CEO of 5i Research Inc., an independent research network that provides conflict-free advice to individual investors. The five Is stand for integrity, independence, individuals, investments, and insight. "We're just trying to use our experience to help people," as Peter puts it. Through 5i Research, investors can get access to many easy-to-understand research reports, written for the average investor, with a simple rating system from F to A-plus. Additionally, the company offers over 28,000 questions that have been answered by Peter, as well as three model portfolios to follow. And it seems that Peter got trigger-happy again, because he recently announced the introduction of the Growth Portfolio model, in addition to the Income and Balanced-Equity models. Once a cowboy, always a cowboy.

Peter's still got a good shooting hand, judging by his ability to pick off new high-flying stocks in today's market. For example, Peter picked Amaya Gaming before many investors even knew it existed on the exchange. It was April of 2013 when Peter said, "Three very good acquisitions have set Amaya up for excellent growth, and it is well-positioned to benefit from legalization of online gaming. Revenue growth will be big this year, and the company is becoming profitable. It is well-managed, has excellent shareholder support, and is a relatively unique name in Canada." Following that recommendation, Amaya went on to post a whopping 500% gain through 2015.

It will be interesting to follow Peter's new growth stock picks. The Growth Portfolio holds 22 securities and is initially biased toward the technology and health care sectors, two areas that Peter expects will remain strong in the near term. As Peter explains, "these are also usually the more growth-oriented sectors." Peter is also the owner of *Canadian MoneySaver*, a fully independent financial magazine, published since 1981, which is chock-full of quality investment features written by Canadian experts in the industry.

Peter and I arranged to meet for the interview at Coffee Culture in uptown Waterloo. Memories of my University of Waterloo days flooded over me as I drove down King Street. When I arrived, I ordered an iced coffee, secured a table, and waited for Peter. When he entered the coffee shop wearing a tan leather jacket, black shirt, and jeans, it felt almost like a scene from a cowboy flick, the lead walking in through the swinging saloon doors seeking either a drink or a showdown. Our conversation was as entertaining as it was insightful, although no one was thrown through a saloon window. Peter is a funny guy who has a fun and compelling way of presenting his stories on the market.

PRE-INTERVIEW LESSONS

DILUTION: when management issues large equity offerings, increases the amount of shares outstanding, and effectively diminishes the existing shareholders' share values.

OVERBOUGHT: having a price that has been pushed unjustifiably high by demand, some assets may become overbought and then be driven to unsustainably high price levels, after which they may come down to more historically sustainable levels.

OVERSOLD: having a price that has been pushed unjustifiably low, some assets may become oversold and then be driven to unsustainably low price levels, after which they may rise back up to more historically sustainable levels.

PORTFOLIO: a collection of assets in which investors or portfolio managers have invested.

PUT OPTION: a contract that gives you the right, but not the obligation, to sell a stock at a specified price within a certain time frame.

YIELD: the income derived from either the coupon on a bond or the dividend on a stock.

Where did you grow up in Canada?

I bounced around a bit. I was born in Calgary. We spent a couple years there and then we moved to Winnipeg for 11 years. That got me used to the Canadian winters. And then we moved to Ottawa, and then Toronto. So four spots.

And you live in Kitchener now?

I'm in Kitchener. I came to Kitchener for a job at Mutual Life, which is now Sun Life. I haven't left Kitchener since.

How did you first get interested in the markets?

It's not that long of a story, but I have to go way back, about 40 years. I had a paper route in Ottawa, delivering about 70 papers. I was 12 years old, and eventually saved $300. My cousin was a stockbroker; she told me about this company called Mitel Corporation, which is an Ottawa company. So I invested all my $300 into Mitel Corporation. A year later it was worth $1,700. I thought, "This is so much better than carrying newspapers around Ottawa." I thought I had discovered some sort of magic potion.

So I sold the Mitel stock, took the $1,700, and then decided to invest in Vulcan Packaging. I don't know if it was Star Trek related or whatever, but they had a gas tank that didn't explode, and for some reason, being a 13-year-old boy, I thought that was good *[laughs]*. I probably should have bought the one that did explode. Six months later Vulcan Packaging was worth $400. And so I've spent the past 40 years trying to figure out what exactly happened there *[laughs]*. That got me interested. My dad was a computer science professor so I did a lot of computer stuff along the way. I started off in computers in university, and after a year decided, "This is not for me."

You changed programs after a year?

Yeah, I just couldn't take it anymore *[laughs]*. And then I bought a couple of stocks in university. But, you know, being a student I had no money. Especially after my disastrous Vulcan Packaging experience. So I really didn't start buying much until around age 23. As they say, the best lesson is losing money, so I learned some really good lessons there *[laughs]*.

You turned $300 into $1,700 with Mitel and then reversed that back down to $400 with Vulcan Packaging. After that experience, did you solidify what your investment strategy would be?

Not really. I had learned a lot about the market and I ended up actually getting an economics degree. So I knew the macro side. I had read enough about the Peter Lynches of the world to sort of try to "buy what you know." That seemed to work out more or less pretty well. But I hadn't developed any sort of strategy at all.

What was your first job out of university?

I had a couple of jobs that I quit and then I biked across Canada. It's a long story. The first real job was at a company called McLeod Young Weir, which is now part of ScotiaMcLeod. I was a money market guy. I wasn't a money market trader, I was sort of on the administrative side and it was a frustrating job because all of the people making money and having the exciting jobs were above me. I'm sure some of your other interviewees have told you this, but if you're good at the administrative side, you're never going to make the jump to become the trader guy. It sounded like an exciting job. I was looking after billions of dollars in collateral and people were borrowing money against it. I had an intercom on my desk that talked directly to the traders. So if you're on the phone with me, one of the traders would say, "Peter, could we do 50 million?" I would go, "Yeah, we can do 50 million." And it sounded like I was a swinger *[laughs]*. But I was just a paper pusher. So I did that for probably about six or seven months.

One of the things I learned in the business, and this is kind of contradictory to a lot of things I've read about other businesses, is that there's absolutely no loyalty in the investment industry. Basically, someone comes along and offers you a better job, and you just leave for that better job. Because eventually you're going to end up back to where you started; one company will buy another. So I got offered a job at a discount brokerage. It was very clear to me I was never going to become a money market trader, just because nobody ever made that leap. I got a job at a discount brokerage in 1986, which was just after the deregulations. Prior to that, commissions were fixed and everything was fixed. So when I started, they just threw that out the window and said, "Do whatever you want, and charge whatever you want." That was really kind of cool because there were only seven or eight people working there. And so I got to do everything: trading, handling client services, and opening accounts. We weren't allowed to give advice, because it was a discount brokerage. However, it was pre-internet; people would phone in, and part of my job would be to give people the quote for Bell Canada, for example. "Thirty dollars." Next phone call. "Forty dollars." But it was great because it gave me exposure to every single aspect of the business. One of the best things about it was that I was on the trading desk during the crash of '87. And that taught me more about investing and psychology than any experience I could have ever read or done.

Can you describe that experience?

Absolutely. The market had been kind of weak beforehand, but that day started off bad. It didn't really start accelerating until maybe 12 o'clock, and then it just basically plummeted. You're sort of sitting there trying to figure out what's going on. And again, this was pre-internet, so you don't really have the news flow that you might have had if it happened today. The story that sticks to my mind the most was when a client phoned in and was having a rational discussion with me about what was going on. Again, I couldn't tell him what to do, but I asked, "How old are you?" The guy was young, had a job, wasn't worried about losing his job, and hadn't borrowed money. He had basically done everything right but was worried about what he was hearing on the news. So he decided that, "Whatever, I'm young; I'm going to recover. The market goes up and down, nothing to worry about." Right when I was talking to him, a Bell Canada operator interrupted the line and said "Peter, I have an emergency phone call for you." And the next thing I know I had two clients on the same call. This new guy said, "Sell everything! Sell everything! Sell everything!" Literally, just like out of the movies, "Sell! Sell! Sell!" Then the guy I was talking to before said, "I was here first; sell mine first." And I was thinking, "Are you serious?"

The original caller immediately changed his sentiment about the markets. Herd mentality.

Yeah, he could feel the panic in the other guy's voice, and he literally said, "I was here first. Stop talking to the other guy." That experience gave me the best picture of the complete irrationality of investors and of herd mentality. That was a very good lesson for me. I had just discovered options about a month before that, and was selling uncovered put options. I remember selling puts on Cineplex Odeon. I presume you know about put options; I was getting the obligation to buy Cineplex at $13 or $14, and was getting 15 cents for that. I considered that free money. Someone was making me free money.

I assume that strategy worked because you were in an up market.
Otherwise, you'd end up taking ownership in many big blocks of stock.

Exactly. So I'd done that for a couple of months but wasn't making a lot of money at the time. Every month some foolish person would give me $200 or $300 on these Cineplex options and I thought, "What an idiot for giving me your money" *[laughs]*. And so the day everything crashed, Cineplex went to $3 and —

You were forced to buy those shares rather than collect the "insurance"
money.

I forced the purchase at $12 or $13, I can't remember the exact price, but I knew it was really bad *[laughs]*. I got this margin call, and my boss asked, "What's going on?" So I had to borrow. I was 23 at the time, and borrowing off my credit cards, like everything I could get. I covered it all and I managed to not panic. It all worked out in the end, and I didn't actually lose any money on that trade because Cineplex paid dividends so I started selling call options against it. Because the market was crazy, the premiums on the call options just went way up because of the volatility. I actually ended up making money over the next year on that stock. So that was bad because it gave me a bit of a bulletproof kind of mentality, because it could have been really quite bad *[laughs]*.

Did you continue to trade options after that roller coaster of an experience?

A little bit. It was a good lesson on volatility. An option that would have given me 20 cents the month before would give me two dollars that month, or three dollars for the same amount of net risk. So suddenly you get 25% a month to take that risk, so yeah, it worked out okay.

Did any of your clients enrich themselves through options?

In that period of time I saw a lot of clients do *really* stupid things. There was this one client who had effectively predicted the '87 crash and so bought puts for about three months prior to the crash. He had a fair amount of money, like a hundred thousand dollars, and he would buy 80 thousand dollars' worth of puts. Well, during the week of the crash, his account was probably worth about two or three million dollars. But he got greedy and he kept buying puts.

He must've got wiped out because the ensuing '87 market rebound was swift and ultimately continued on as a long-term bull market.

Yeah. All the volatilities went up; he just basically blew his brains out. He went from a hundred thousand to two million to a hundred thousand or less in a couple of months.

Any more lessons learned from your early experiences?

Yeah, both on the greed side and the fear side as I saw everybody do the exact wrong things for the exact wrong reasons. I saw greedy people get killed, and I saw fearful people get killed.

What about your most successful clients? Any common traits?

Really, the best ones were buying over time. The second-best ones did nothing. That "do nothing" lesson was huge for me, especially when I became a fund manager. The tendency to do something because you're getting paid is really high. While there's no rule that says you need to do something, it's hard because if you're charging your clients a fee, and your boss comes in and asks, "What are you doing?" and you say, "Nothing," that doesn't go over that well. But really, one of the best things is not to do anything.

So after that I got a job at Dominion Bond Rating Service on the credit side. I had taken my CFA, and by that time the discount brokerage industry had changed a lot. It got much bigger and the company I was at went from seven people to a hundred people. It was fun and all the people were great but I didn't have experience in the analytical side of stocks. So I got a job as a credit guy and it sounds kind of weird, because I didn't really care about bonds, but I wanted to be a better analyst. That was partly a money motive, too. They were offering me more money, it was more prestigious, and so on. But the opportunity was really much better than I thought, because when I went to DBRS there were only 10 people working there. And DBRS just got sold last year for $500 million — it did so well. I was there just as things were taking off. They had no room for me, so I sat in the hallway at a desk right outside of the boss's office.

This was in 1991, and 1991 was the real estate crash in Canada.

When my boss would come flying out of his office looking for the first sucker he could see, and I was conveniently right outside of the office. Literally, there was a real estate company going bankrupt every week that DBRS was responsible for. So he gave me Bramalea. Bramalea had just gone bankrupt. He'd say, "Peter, deal with this." And so suddenly I've got to deal with this $5-billion company that's gone bankrupt. But it was great because it wasn't my fault. Bramalea was probably rated pretty high but suddenly everybody lost their money. But nobody could blame me. I was there to put out the fire. It was awesome. I got to deal with all of these problems and I learned how companies go bankrupt, and what can happen when there's a shift in economic tides. Also, we would meet with the president of Canadian Pacific Railway that was issuing 40-year bonds. He'd outline a 40-year strategy because they had to be able to pay their bonds back in 40 years. That was fabulous, because here you are with the president of one of the biggest companies in Canada, telling you what they're going to do for the next 40 years.

Whereas if you join a company's quarterly earnings call, the president might just forecast the next couple of months, until the next earnings call.

Exactly. So that was the big-picture thinking that I picked up at DBRS. So say CPR wanted to buy a company. They would come to DBRS and explain what they were doing and say they were going to borrow a billion dollars to do it, and that they would be comfortable with that change in debt. They would walk you through the cash flow and the assumptions and how much money they were going to save and where they were going to cut costs and extract synergies. It was great because from a corporate point of view, the lesson I picked up from there was that corporations think differently than investors. As a corporation, you don't really care what the stock's doing right now.

Let's fast forward to your role at Sprott Asset Management. You ran the Growth Fund. What were some of your more memorable experiences there?

Sure. I can talk about Timminco. While it ended *really* badly, it was *really* good for a long period of time. We made a lot of money off of it. So Timminco had a new technique to develop metallurgical silicon, and it just came out of nowhere. As an aside, one of my best techniques to finding a great stock is to just look at new highs. When you see a new high, ask yourself, "Why is that a new high and what's the deal with that?" So we found Timminco and did some research; it was really cheap. Then they announced a big contract but the stock didn't move, and so we started to buy the crap out of it. And then they announced a deal where one of their customers pre-funded them to develop solar energy. Now suddenly a big customer just gave them $25 million to develop solar energy. So the stock just took on a life of its own. We owned 16% or 17% of the stock. When it blew up eventually, two years later, I had already sold a lot of stock, because it went *really* well for me. Unfortunately, Sprott itself got associated with it, and when it blew up it was kind of ugly. But from a fund point of view it was awesome. We started buying it at $1 or $2, and we probably pushed it up to $5, and then it went up to $35 in two years.

Can you elaborate on how you analyze companies once you see its stock make higher highs?

There's fundamentals. With Timminco, they were reporting better sales, but not better earnings. The solar sector was hot, so they were in the right sector, which is also pretty important sometimes. Sometimes it doesn't even matter how good of a company you are: if you're in the right sector, you're automatically hot. Also, I've probably made more money from this philosophy than anything else: you have to take a stock from $2 and go to $4, and then be willing to buy more of it at $4 than you bought at $2. I did that all of the time and the reason I did that was because generally there's been a shift in the business fundamentals, so it's not as risky at $4 as it is at $2.

Most people say, "Well, that's crazy, it's doubled." But you see, at $4 it's a larger company. It's more likely to get investors interested in it. And you get this whole multiple expansion as the company grows. So there's this *really* sweet section of companies that go from $50 million to $100 million in value. At $100 million, people care. At $50 million, they don't care, but it's exactly the same company. So you can get into a situation where you can be the one that pushes it from $50 million to $100 million. You can talk about it on TV, and you can mention it. At Sprott especially, we were going to all the brokers and the advisors and we would talk about our favourite stocks. It's a bit of a self-serving game obviously, but then they would go out and buy the stock and talk to their clients, too. So suddenly it goes from $50 million to $100 million, and nothing's changed; it's the same company. And then it goes to $500 million just because everybody's looking at it now.

Any other big winners?

One that worked out even better but was less famous was a company called Diedrich Coffee. Diedrich Coffee makes those little K-cup pods. No one had heard of Green Mountain or Keurig at that time. Green Mountain was doing *okay*. People were saying, "Oh, there's this new coffee thing going on," but it hadn't hit the mainstream yet. So we saw Diedrich Coffee report earnings, and again we looked at all the new highs. It hit a new high at $2.50, a 65% return in a week. And so we got our analysts on it. The earnings were rock-solid. We looked at the growth rate; it was 100%, but the stock was only eight or nine times earnings, because it was small-cap. It was about $50 million market cap. And so we thought, "Maybe it goes to $6?" Again, we just started buying it like crazy. You had to take that leap of faith and convince yourself that you're right.

I assume that there was then further multiple expansion?

Exactly. So we probably pushed it to $6 because it was a small company. Then they came out with another quarter and it was even better than before. It went to $10, and we're like, "Oh, this is pretty good." Then it goes to $15. And then it goes to $20. We're like, "We found it at $2." This happened really quickly because what had happened was Green Mountain started to win hotel contracts. I was in a hotel in Montreal, making a presentation to investors. I woke up in the morning and there's a Keurig machine there. It was called something else at the time, but it had the little pods. I didn't really care about the coffee at the time, but then I thought, "The room attendant doesn't have to come in and clean up the basket of coffee grinds. There's not a mess. This is going to be crazy."

I remember talking about it at this speech in Montreal, because we owned it at the time. "It's in my hotel room." I said *[laughs]*. I said, "I bet you it will be in every hotel room in the world in a couple of years." Sure enough, it's everywhere now. Anyway, Green Mountain at the time was doing really well, so Diedrich was starting to carry through, because they were one of the big manufacturers of the pods. And then a company bid for Diedrich called Pete's Coffee, and then Green Mountain counter-bid, and then Pete's bid again; they increased their price like seven times. Diedrich was eventually taken out by Green Mountain at $34, and this was just within two years. So somebody got it at $1, we saw it at $2, pushed it to $6, and then two years later, Green Mountain takes it out at $34.

What was the weight of Diedrich in your portfolio by the time it got bought out?

This was part of the problem. We probably started at a 1% or 2% position. But it was also during a time when money was just pouring into Sprott. So it was a situation where even though the stock doubled, the weighting didn't double because there was all this money coming into the fund to dilute the position.

Sprott was the "golden boy" at that time. You and the whole firm, for that matter.

Yep, and money was just pouring in. Literally, we had no salespeople, and so one of my jobs was to get salespeople, so the money could come in faster. We were bringing in $50 million a day with no salespeople. Because we had gone up 60% one year, then 80%. So it was crazy.

How did you achieve such high returns in the portfolio?

I think you'll find this interesting. This is where Eric Sprott's stock-picking ability is second to none. We didn't have that many analysts, but we would all sit around the table at eight o'clock in the morning every day, and basically, if an analyst pitched a story to Eric, and said, "Oh, I've got this stock, you know, BlackBerry. And I think it could go up 50%," he'd respond, "I don't care. Unless it's going up 200%, I don't care." We had a whole portfolio of 200%, 300% potentials, and of course they're not all going to work; some are going to flame out badly. So we needed the big giant ones to make up for the ones that went to zero.

It was a really frustrating time for the analysts. Some of them would come from more conservative shops where 10% returns would be awesome. They would do all this work on a company and say, "I think it's got 70% upside" but then nobody would buy the stock [*laughs*]. It was hilarious. So they were all trained to look for the giant winners. Every once in a while they would show up. I don't know if you are aware of the Taser story. We bought Taser at $2, and then ended up with 12% of the company — a big position. The executives from Taser would come in to try to score points with Eric by volunteering to get tazed right in the boardroom *[laughs]*. This is long before the lawsuits and stuff like that. But Taser went from $3 to $70.

So the good analysts were able to bring stocks to those board meetings that could potentially go up 200 to 300%. Would they constantly scan the Venture Exchange and Russell?

Yeah, everything.

Just North American small-caps?

Yeah, for non-resources it was North American, but for resources they would go around the world.

What common traits did the stocks have that eventually shot to the moon?

There was a lot of thematic stuff going on. "If *this* happens, this is the company that's going to own it." Or "If the world goes *this* way, that's the company we want to own in that category." But then you'd get these other companies that were off the radar screen, that were doing well and sometimes it was a self-fulfilling prophecy. You could find a pretty good company and tell everybody in the world about it, and it generally got some notice. Again, you have to make sure it's good at the get-go.

Would you add any stocks to the portfolio that didn't have earnings just yet, but you saw that revenue was expanding and so perhaps soon you'd start seeing earnings roll in?

Eric more so than me. Eric would buy companies and not expect them to make any money for five years. I was still small-cap, but I was larger small-cap. I was far more likely to pay $4 for something once it works than $1 on the hope that it works.

I see. So you want to see that the market has validated a stock.

Like Timminco. I didn't know anything about solar other than what I read. But when the largest solar company in the world gives them $25 million I had more confidence that there's at least something going on.

After a stock such as Timminco experiences aggressive multiple expansion over a short period of time, how do you know when to get out?

For me it's more of a portfolio decision. One of my mantras is not to sell too early. You know, you're never going to get a Google or an Apple, or any 50-bagger, if you sell too early. So I just take a look from a portfolio perspective, and ask myself, "How much am I betting my portfolio on this stock?" If you get one stock that goes way up you can just keep selling into the strength and selling as much as possible while still maintaining the exposure that you're comfortable with. Generally 6% or 7% weighting is my worry point. It depends on the company. I try not to time the market or anything like that. I have no idea which way the market's going to go, but you could lose a lot just in one stock. Anyway, I assume every stock I own could drop 50% tomorrow. It's very different than personally managing money because your bonus as a portfolio manager is such a big part of your compensation. If one stock screws up, it hurts. If your fund is 3% ahead of the index but then suddenly it matches the index, the difference to your compensation is huge. So you do take a different look at the portfolio in terms of your exposure, which is one of the problems with mutual funds because they all try to be extra conservative and all kind of do the same thing. But that's another topic.

What was it like at Sprott Asset Management during the financial crisis?

[Laughs] That could be a whole other book. I think the biggest problem was 2008. Obviously a lot of people had a problem in 2008. But from our early point of view there was a theme that the financial system was in trouble. GM was going to go bankrupt. Fannie Mae was going to go bankrupt. Countrywide Credit was going to go bankrupt. We had talked about all this for years. And then it all happened exactly as we predicted. But we just did *okay*. The way I equate it is that we had every single answer on the test right, but the teacher gave us a C. The reason is because in that time of crisis the only thing anyone wanted was U.S. dollars. So our gold positions didn't go up as much because they're priced in U.S. dollars and U.S. dollars surged. Additionally, the gold stocks didn't go up very much because they were stocks and nobody wanted stocks.

And then there was the Fed. The Fed changed all the rules. They stopped short-selling. They started buying all the lousy assets. They changed the margin rules. They changed the banking system, insurance deposits, and so on. At that time, we were playing poker with someone who could change all the rules: the Fed. They have an unlimited amount of money, because they can print money and you can't. So why would you sit at the table with these guys? *[laughs]*. We should have gone up 100% to 200% that year based on how the firm was positioned. When we didn't, a lot of the advisors said, "Well, you didn't make any money.

You were totally right, but you didn't make any money." So now if they thought that the money's going to shift the other way, they wouldn't need us as much. We'd gone public in 2008; our stock was at $10 and had gone down to $2, so it just didn't reflect well. Sort of a combination of factors. I'll take a lot of the blame because we started hiring salespeople. Then the market turned and we had all these mouths to feed but the money wasn't coming in anymore.

Your inflection point was a couple of years after the crash. You're quoted as saying that you "grew tired worrying about conflicts." What did you mean?

Yeah. To put this in perspective, I did really well at Sprott and I loved it. But I got to a point where I didn't need the job. So once I didn't need the job, I thought, "What am I actually doing here?" I was selling a fund and got paid on assets and performance. I got paid more money if I got more money into the fund. It was a high-risk, small-cap growth fund, like a cowboy fund. We could do anything we wanted. But I thought, "Is that really right to try to get as much money into that kind of fund?" If I'm talking to you and you're supposed to be conservative, you shouldn't be buying my fund. But I'll get paid more if you do." So I had a bit of an issue with that. But two other things threw me off. One was that we got paid on performance. We had *very* big performance incentives. So if I was having a bad year, I was incentivized to roll the dice, because I wasn't going to get a bonus at that point. I could gamble, for lack of a better phrase, and actually get a big nice bonus. But then the big awakening was when I looked at how I was doing in my personal portfolio, and it was so much better than my fund. I thought, "This is going to look really bad if somebody finds out." The reason was I didn't frequently trade in my personal portfolio. I didn't gamble. I didn't put on my cowboy hat, and have to worry about redemptions and withdrawals and stuff like that. I bought way more conservative dividend-type securities. And it was embarrassing. My Growth Fund was doing okay, but wasn't doing as well as years past. And of course then there's the fees. I thought that was dumb. Also, I was having a big feud with Eric at the time. Anyway, once I didn't need the salary I didn't like it as much as before.

After leaving Sprott you started 5i Research. Why that name: 5i?

It's really just five Is. Integrity: the fact that we don't trade stocks we talk about. Independence: we're not associated with a banker, or broker, whatever. Individuals: we're focused on individuals. Investments, and Insight. We're just trying to use our experience to help people.

Can you explain the rating system that you use at 5i?

Again, this is partly born out of my frustration with the industry. We would get all these reports from all these really smart analysts. They wanted to keep their jobs. So they would come out with these inoffensive terms: "market perform," "neutral," and "equal weight." I've read this stuff for 20 years, and I still have no idea what any of it means. Market perform? What do I do with that? Equal weight? Why do I care about weights when I'm not following an index? It was just kind of dumb. A couple of people would say "sell" and their bosses would yell at them, because nobody traded on a sell. A sell recommendation didn't bring out all the short-sellers to your firm to sell. So I'm a so-called professional who could barely understand what these guys were telling me to do. Anyway, my rating system: A is better than B. C is better than D. So that's what started it.

What's behind that rating system? How would a company achieve an A-plus?

We haven't given out any A-pluses yet. We've given a couple of As, though. We're trying to rate through a market cycle. So to get an A you need to be a management team that doesn't screw up. You must be reliable. You need to have a balance sheet that's not at risk. You need to be able to make money in a recession. So when the economy rolls over, somebody who bought an A-rated stock should not be losing money. This is where it gets a little trickier. The stock can still go down, but we don't want the fundamentals to deteriorate. So there's a lot of stocks that went down in 2008 but they still made profits and still paid dividends and even increased their dividends. So we're trying to basically say if it's an A-rated stock, you can own it for 10 years, and not even care. The market will go up, the market will go down, the stock will go up, the stock will go down, but through it all, it's a fundamentally secure investment that's not priced ridiculously high and that's not one you have to worry about. That would be the A category.

The B category would be a lesser degree of that. Maybe they have more debt or maybe it's growth by acquisition so they have to continue to make deals and if they stop deals they stop growing, or maybe management doesn't own as much stock as we like or maybe it's more expensive or maybe they don't raise their dividend or maybe they issued too much stock to grow. All kinds of factors.

C-plus is a buy with a caveat. Either it is debt or iffy management or it is cyclical. A lot of our cyclical companies will go in C-plus, where it's not a bad company but if the price of gold goes down, you're going to lose money. There's nothing you can do about it. Then we have a whole lot in the C rating, which are companies that have screwed up. Don't buy them. If they get cheap enough they'll probably go to C-plus, but they're probably never going to be your As because we don't like management, we don't like their business, we don't like their strategy, et cetera, et cetera, et cetera.

And then we've actually come out with a couple of F ratings just to prove a point. "This is a stupid company, don't buy it, stay away from it." Though our customers ask, "Why do you waste your time?" We say, "We want to educate you about *why* it's a bad company."

Your rating system shows that you're completely impartial. You dole out Fs.

Yeah.

Do you just cover small-cap stocks?

Keep in mind we've only been around for three years. Generally, small- to mid-cap. We can't really add a lot of value covering Sun Life or any other large-cap. It's well followed by Bay Street, so it doesn't really do that much for us. We have a couple of large-caps that we cover, but it's generally mid-cap, non-resource. Again, we prefer companies that are in control of their own destiny and not the greatest oil company in the world losing everybody's money when oil declines. We try to avoid that by focusing on economic cyclicality. To get a new company rated by us we want to make sure that they're going to withstand the next financial crisis. And I always come back to a couple of examples here. There's Home Capital Group, which we follow. Home Capital is a mortgage company, and as you know the financial crisis was started by alternative lending to people who could not get money from the banks. It sounds like the worst possible thing to own in the financial crisis of 2008. But they increased their earnings and their dividends in that time. Sure, their stock got killed, but from a fundamental point of view they made more money and paid more dividends during that time. That's what we're looking for. Oh, and, off topic, but we just can't stand it when companies issue stock.

You don't like dilution?

Some companies treat their stock like a printing press. Home Capital has not issued stock since '08. But there's another one, Constellation Software, that I know Donville would have talked about. They haven't issued stock in 10 years. Probably more than that, but that's just as far back as we go. And the company value has gone from $200 million to $5 billion without issuing a single piece of paper. To us, that's brilliant, as opposed to companies that set their watch and say, "Oh, it's time to raise $100 million." The reason I like to mention that is because the ones that do those financings like clockwork are always talked about. They have 10 analysts on them.

During the financial crisis, even though Home Capital's fundamentals were strengthening, the stock was being hit. Does that show that the market is actually inefficient?

Yeah. I don't want to say that it's always inefficient, but in a situation like that, based on my career, that was pretty unique. Because that was the first time I actually thought the financial world could end. I don't know how widely reported this is, but the Bank of England was going to shut down the entire English banking system. They said they were three hours from doing it. One of the banks, I think Bank of Scotland, was going under, and if they couldn't solve that problem, they were just going to shut everything down. And that just would have dominoed everywhere.

That would have been catastrophic.

It would have been really bad. But generally the headlines are worse than the reality, and the propensity to panic is more than what you should do. But of course it's all about the uncertainty. Nobody knows when the bottom is going to hit in those situations. People are selling because it's down. Every time I saw one of my stocks go down, I would basically ask myself, "Why are people selling? Are people selling because of earnings? Are they selling because they're worried about the market? Or are they selling because it's down?" And it's almost always the last point. They can't take it anymore. But there's some legitimate portfolio reasons as well. So say you've got a 5% position and it gets cut in half.

Now it's 2.5%. Say it gets cut in half again, so you have a 1.25% position that's pissed you off — it's the first thing to go. It's like you say, "Stupid stock," and you get rid of it. That's not a real reason to sell. It's just a portfolio reason to sell. When I was a fund manager, I'd do that all the time. "Ah, whatever, loser company; I'll just get rid of it," I would say. Once you've made that mental decision you don't care what the price is and you just don't want to look at it again.

Exactly. But then you can allocate that money somewhere else.

Yeah. But that happens on a retail individual basis as well. They just can't take it anymore. It's the efficiency question. I think in periods of time there's massive inefficiency. Over a longer period of time it's more efficient, though.

You also run a couple of portfolios through 5i.

Three.

Can you elaborate on those three portfolios?

Quite honestly, when we started, I didn't know how successful we'd be. It was a way to stay active and get a free Bloomberg. But it turned into a business. People started saying, "I like your reports, but what should I buy?" Remember, we don't give out individual advice, so I can't tell you to buy *this*, *this*, and *this*. I can say we like *this*, *this*, and *this*, but you're on your own. So we obviously try to put in our higher-rated companies.

But we also diversified by sector. We wanted to diversify a bit by market cap as well. We had to add a couple of companies that we didn't cover just to balance it out, and it's worked out *really* well, partly because we've chosen stocks conservatively. We don't want anybody losing a lot of money. We barely make any changes ever, because if we've chosen right, we shouldn't make any changes. We've avoided the problem areas like gold and resources and stuff like that. Again, not because we were smart and knew that oil was going to go down, but because we just don't like companies that have to deal with that.

The Balanced Portfolio has done really well. The Income Portfolio has only been out for a year. And the Growth Portfolio's only been out for a month, but everybody seems to be happy with it. I think what we're going to do is to focus people on the longer term. We had a very successful company in the Growth Portfolio. It made a new acquisition so the stock went up 20%. But when people asked, "Should I sell?" I would say, "You've owned it for two weeks. No! You don't sell after two weeks" *[laughs]*. Then some of our subscribers said, "I only want the five best stocks," to which I replied, "That's not a portfolio; there's 22. One of them is probably going to go to zero." We teach people to do the right thing.

Let's talk about your Growth Portfolio. It's got 22 holdings. Your focus is on technology and health care stocks — why is that?

The health care sector is a little bit more interesting than technology. So the Canadian health care sector was a basketcase for 20 years. When I was a portfolio manager, basically every health care stock that I bought would go down because a lot of Canadian health care companies would get tax credits to do trials in Canada. They shouldn't have even been public yet, yet they were getting all of this tax money, generally from the Quebec government. They'd go public, get all these tax benefits, and then they'd go to Europe to do the clinical trials. But often the FDA doesn't give a crap about Europe. All of these small trials would go well; the signs would look good. Then the FDA would reject it because the trials were not done properly, or the trial sites weren't approved, or the trial wasn't big enough. The FDA does whatever they want. So this $100 million company would go down to $15 million because they didn't have a drug anymore, and it was just the worst thing ever. The health care sector in Canada shouldn't have even been a sector; it was nothing.

It's like encouraging D-minus high school students to go to university, to then just watch them burn out and flunk out.

Exactly. So then things started. The large pharmaceutical companies needed to refill their pipeline, so they just started buying everything in sight. This is where Valeant started buying everything in sight. Then all of these little new companies started coming in, and it was almost like investors wanted more market exposure to health care. Resources were useless, so investors needed another sector. Everything worked out well in the sense that Catamaran was taken over, Valeant went from $20 to $250, and Concordia Heathcare, which we looked at when it was $6 in 2014, was popular. Anyways, we just think that health care is an interesting sector. It's one of those things where it's more of a theme than anything else. On the technology side it's really just about growth. We don't know how long the U.S. technology sector is going to continue to grow. Canada's technology sector is not really growing that much. But some of the technology companies are growing 25% annually.

Is the U.S. technology sector becoming overbought?

We don't think so. Apple is a great example. Apple at one point two years ago was only at 10 times earnings.

Maybe the resource sector will come back soon. Could that be the next hot theme?

This is where it's kind of liberating from a 5i point of view. If I was a mutual fund manager, I probably would be buying resources, because when they turn I could have a fund that goes up 50% and I could make a ton of money. But at 5i I don't get a bonus if that fund does well, so I'd rather play it safe.

You're just focused on good companies, right?

Yeah, there's no incentive for me to shoot the lights out. It's almost negative incentive because if that portfolio sucks, my customers aren't going to be happy. It's shifted a little bit from, "What's in it for me?" to "What's the right thing to do?" But on the tech side, if you're in early on a theme, then it works well for you. This is where being older helps. In 2000 and 1999 and 1998, even if you exclude the craziness of dot-com, technology stocks had always traded at these huge multiples, like 25 times earnings because they're all sitting on cash, they're all growing fast, and they all have ridiculously high margins with a software company it's about 95% margins. Then post-2008, tech stocks all went down again to 11 to 12 times earnings. It just didn't make any sense. You were guaranteed to make money if you had enough time to wait for normal market multiples to function.

What about Microsoft? Its stock reached a peak in 2000, which it has yet to reach again.

It depends. But it is different with the smaller companies. It's harder for Microsoft to grow at a fast rate, whereas it's easier for the little guys to grow.

Any additional tips for investors?

Everybody wants some of your money. Every single thing that you can buy, someone might make money off of it. You have to keep that in mind at all times. And it's true: every single thing that's out there, somebody wants a piece of it. I won't tell you which boss said this, but one of my bosses once said, "Why don't we have all of their money?" We did a study and found out that we managed only 10% of our clients' money. But he said, "Well, why don't we have all of it?" So just keep that in mind.

The other thing is selling too early. There's always a reason to sell. If you look for the negatives you'll find them. You can't buy a stock unless someone is negative on the other side. So just put yourself into a position to ask yourself, "Why am I selling?" But more so, ask yourself why the other guy's buying it from you. Are they buying it because they think it's going up? If yes, then maybe you should rethink your position. That's where the target price of the business comes in. Some analysts say, "Sell at $40." Well, what do they know? This is where being old like me is awesome. They'll tell you to "sell CPR at $40." And you'll think, "Okay, five years ago, you told me to sell it at $10, so what's up with that?" This is where Bloomberg comes into play, because it goes back 30 years. Once I saw an analyst recommend to sell Netflix with a $10 target four years ago. But then three years ago that same analyst had a buy recommendation with a $400 target. So in a year and half they've gone from sell at $10 to buy at $400. You will never *ever* get the big scorer if you sell too early.

The other point would be that companies that grow their dividends are vastly superior to companies with high-dividend yields. Don't get sucked into the 8% yield. Buy the 1% yield that's going to go to 2%, 3%, 4%, 5%. Don't panic. There's always going to be a reason to freak out and go to cash. You don't have to do that. If you consistently invest then it really doesn't matter if the market goes up or down. At the end of 10 years you'll have a good average price. You're not going to get the top and you're not going to get the bottom, but you'll have a good average price across the way. Also, this is a little bit counter-intuitive to my "don't sell too early" advice, but if you have a loser company — not a "stock" because sometimes stocks will go down — don't hang onto it. If I had a dollar for every person who said, "I'll sell when it breaks even," I'd be a bazillionaire. Breaking even is a bad investment strategy.

Peter Hodson's insights into growth stocks were eye-opening, especially the experience he shared about working at Sprott Asset Management as portfolio manager for the Growth Fund. It was interesting to learn of the extremely high expectations there for returns on stocks, when 50% gains were not good enough. While that is a bygone era (or maybe not — time will tell), Peter still has plenty of advice to share on how to pick growth stocks. I recently stumbled upon a blog post that Peter wrote entitled "How to Pick the Next Big Winner." In it, he builds upon the growth investment philosophy that he explained during the interview, as well as additional elements that come into play.

HOW TO PICK THE NEXT BIG WINNER

Investors who missed Amaya's gain (up 1,650% since mid-2010) often ask themselves, how do I find the next one? That is a difficult task, but here are five lessons we have learned from Amaya's meteoric rise. Maybe these lessons can apply to other potential big winners.

PLAY THE LONG GAME

Amaya's shares in early April dropped sharply after it missed quarterly earnings estimates. Investors sold the shares down to $5.81. Those investors, too focused on one quarter, missed out on tripling their money in less than three months. Lesson learned: good companies focus on the long term. If a company is still growing (as Amaya was in April), don't panic and sell because of the results during just one 90-day period.

MANAGEMENT IS KEY

David Baazov, Amaya's chief executive, owns 24.6 million shares of his company. He has sold very little. He and his team had a plan to grow into the gaming market, and have stayed focused on it. The team knows its market and — perhaps more importantly — the regulatory process.

Amaya first made progress and learned from its gaming businesses in emerging markets, and then used that expertise to break into North America. Now, it has global ambitions.

FINANCING GROWTH IS CRITICAL

Some investors really took notice of Amaya in 2012 when it managed to do an equity financing of $104 million at a premium to its share price. At the time, it was still trading on the Venture Exchange, and the huge deal showed the company knew how to sell its story to investors and had serious backing from underwriters. In its most recent massive deal, Amaya secured huge preferred share and common equity commitments up front to ensure it could make a cash bid for Rational.

A GOOD ACQUIRER IS A GOOD ACQUIRER

Prior to the recent deal, Amaya acquired several companies, including Chartwell Technologies, Cryptologic, and then (the much bigger) Cadillac Jack. Each acquisition added strategic products and customers, and each created lots of shareholder value. Investors are hoping the new acquisition does the same, only on a much bigger scale.

KEEP AN EYE ON THE BLUE SKY

Amaya, because of its ability to navigate the gaming regulatory landscape, was seen as one company that would massively benefit if the U.S. online gaming market opened up. Investors bought into the future, and were able to envision potentially huge revenue and earnings down the road. This made Amaya shares seem expensive at many points during the company's existence. But these investors have been rewarded. Amaya is now present in three U.S. states and recently indicated it hopes to knock off the other states "one by one."

1) "The best lesson is losing money, so I learned some really good lessons."

2) "I saw everybody do the exact wrong things for the exact wrong reasons. I saw greedy people get killed, and I saw fearful people get killed."

3) "That 'do nothing' lesson was huge for me, especially when I became a fund manager. The tendency to do something because you're getting paid is really high."

4) "Corporations think differently than investors. As a corporation, you don't really care what the stock's doing right now."

5) "Sometimes it doesn't even matter how good of a company you are; if you're in the right sector, you're automatically hot."

6) "I've probably made more money from this philosophy than anything else: you have to take a stock from $2 and go to $4, and then be willing to buy more of it at $4 than you bought at $2."

7) "There's this really sweet section of companies that go from $50 million to $100 million in value. At $100 million, people care. At $50 million, they don't care, but it's exactly the same company."

8) "You have to take that leap of faith and convince yourself that you're right."

9) "We had a whole portfolio of 200%, 300% potentials, and of course they're not all going to work; some are going to flame out badly. So we needed the big giant ones to make up for the ones that went to zero."

10) "One of my mantras is not to sell too early. You know, you're never going to get a Google or an Apple, or any 50-bagger, if you sell too early."

11) "I assume every stock I own could drop 50% tomorrow."

12) "If it's an A-rated stock, you can own it for 10 years, and not even care. The market will go up, the market will go down, the stock will go up, the stock will go down, but through it all, it's a fundamentally secure investment that's not priced ridiculously high and that's not one you have to worry about."

13) "Every time I saw one of my stocks go down I would basically ask myself, 'Why are people selling? Are people selling because of earnings? Are they selling because they're worried about the market? Or are they selling because it's down?'"

14) "I think in periods of time there's massive inefficiency. Over a longer period of time it's more efficient though."

15) "We barely make any changes ever, because if we've chosen right, we shouldn't make any changes."

16) "On the tech side, if you're in early on a theme, then it works well for you. [But] it's harder for Microsoft to grow at a fast rate, whereas it's easier for the little guys to grow."

17) "Put yourself into a position to ask yourself, 'Why am I selling?' But more so, ask yourself why the other guy's buying it from you. Are they buying it because they think it's going up? If yes, then maybe you should rethink your position."

18) "Companies that grow their dividends are vastly superior to companies with high-dividend yields. Don't get sucked into the 8% yield. Buy the 1% yield that's going to go to 2%, 3%, 4%, 5%."

19) "If you consistently invest then it really doesn't matter if the market goes up or down. At the end of 10 years you'll have a good average price."

20) "If I had a dollar for every person who said, 'I'll sell when it breaks even,' I'd be a bazillionaire. Breaking even is a bad investment strategy."

21) "One of my best techniques to finding a great stock is to just look at new highs. When you see a new high, ask yourself, 'Why is that a new high and what's the deal with that?'"

PART III

FUNDAMENTAL
(A MIX OF VALUE AND GROWTH)

Fundamental investors use a mix of value investing and growth investing principles to inform their investment decisions. While fundamental investors select their securities based on a company's fundamentals (for example their assets, cash flow, net income, and so on), they are at the same time mindful of value and growth. These investment paradigms are not mutually exclusive from a fundamental investor's perspective. The benefit of fundamental investing is that the stocks in a fundamental investor's portfolio are usually not grossly undervalued (value stocks) or overvalued (growth stocks), but somewhere in between. That's not to say that fundamental investors don't occasionally seek out mispricings in stock prices or opportunities in high-growth companies, but those are the exceptions rather than the rule. The risk inherent in fundamental investing is if a fundamental investor sways in the market, and switches regularly between growth and value as market conditions evolve. They must be decidedly fundamental, in that they don't invest in value stocks or growth stocks, but quality stocks that meet both criteria.

DEREK FOSTER
THE IDIOT MILLIONAIRE

Derek Foster is an "idiot." He saved, then invested, and then quit the rat race at age 34. He spent his twenties backpacking across Europe, Australia, and New Zealand, and lived a number of years in Asia. Who does that? He should be broke, living paycheque to paycheque, and working a dead-end job until he's 65. Instead, he's independently wealthy, having amassed around a million dollars in investable assets.

While Derek has branded himself as the "Idiot Millionaire," he's anything but — Derek is very, very smart. He uses the "idiot" angle to inspire the average Joe or Jane Canadian to achieve their own financial independence. And he sells a lot of books in the process. *Stop Working: Here's How You Can!* propelled Derek into Canadian financial folklore. I was enthralled by Derek's path to financial freedom, and have read most of his six books. Today, he touts buying strong dividend-paying companies. But dividends alone won't propel you to the million-dollar mark. There's more to it, and it's all revealed in my conversation with Derek.

The truth is that Derek Foster was a prudent saver who made some great calls in the market, from leveraging up on a cigarette company, piling into income trusts, taking advantage of the Canadian/U.S. dollar parity, and selling puts. He made these great calls by taking what the market gave. My favourite line from our interview comes when Derek describes his advantage in the market: "It's not foresight. I'm opportunistic. The opportunity was there and I took it while I could." One can glean Derek's investment mantra in his words — he isn't a value investor or a growth investor or a macro investor. Derek is a market "taker." Derek himself would tell you that anyone can use his "simple investment strategy that any six-year-old can follow." But as you'll soon learn, there's a higher learning curve to beating the market. Here's how a sophisticated investor amassed around a million dollars in the market by 34.

PRE-INTERVIEW LESSONS

BOTTOM: the point at which a stock or the stock market has reached a low but then turns back up.

INCOME TRUST: Canadian companies that paid out earnings to unit holders before taxes. Up until 2006, when the taxation structure changed for income trusts, investors could buy income trusts on a securities exchange and benefit from high yields.

LEADERS: those stocks that are in the top quartile of their market, industry, or peer group whether in reality or only in investors' perceptions.

LEVERAGE: when an investor uses margin (i.e., loan) to increase his/her bet on an investment in order to potentially amplify returns. Can also refer to companies that use considerable debt for expansion, acquisition, or any other forms of investment.

LONG: when an investor buys a stock in the anticipation that its value will rise.

METRIC: a figure or standard that investors use as a basis for a decision.

Where did you grow up in Canada?

Ottawa.

When and how did you first get interested in the market?

When I was really young, seven or eight years old. My parents divorced pretty early, and so I would visit my aunt and uncle on my mom's side. One night they cracked open Monopoly and we started to play; I was just hooked. What absorbed me was the fact that I could make money by investing on the board. Everybody knows Monopoly; you buy houses, hotels, railroads, and then collect money. It just made so much more sense than just passing Go on the board; in real life, just waiting for your salary every two weeks. So Monopoly got me interested in the whole idea of investing to get ahead. That planted the seed. And then when I was 12 or 13, I asked my mom for a book about buying stocks. So she bought me a very simple book on how to buy stocks. I read it and it explained that companies need to raise capital, yadda yadda. I found that quite interesting. And then when I was 18 or 19 I read *The Wealthy Barber*, and that brought it all together: regular investing over time can add up to a lot of money. Those were the three things that began me on my journey.

What were the first couple of stocks that you bought early on?

The very first stock I bought was Wendy's *[laughs]*. And I did not know anything about investing at that time. I just liked Wendy's hamburgers so I bought some shares of their stock but I don't think it went all that well. Shortly thereafter I was working for RadioShack, which is now called the Source in Canada. In the U.S., I think they're about to go bankrupt. But anyhow, I was working for the company and about a year before I was working there the shares had traded as high as I think $60 a share. But by the time that I started they were down at $24 a share. I thought RadioShack was cheap, so I took my life savings and bought shares. That's when I was about 18 or 19. Within a year I ended up losing half my money *[laughs]*. That was my first major experience in stocks.

What did those early experiences teach you? Did they shape how you would invest afterwards?

Oh, at first it scared me out of stocks. I figured it was all a rigged game and that I shouldn't bother investing in stocks. I ran over to mutual funds because that's generally what the herd was doing at that point in time. In the early nineties everybody was buying mutual funds. I was reading the newspaper one day and there was a journalist there saying, "Had you invested in mutual funds you would have *x* dollars, but if instead you would have invested with this Warren Buffett guy you would have had 20 times that amount." That piqued my interest so I started reading about Warren Buffett. It was a lot harder to get information then than it is now because it was pre-internet days. Also, I read a couple of books by Peter Lynch: *One Up on Wall Street* and *Beating the Street*. Those books were really helpful.

When did you divest out of those mutual funds and then re-enter the stock market?

It would be the early nineties. I might have been 21 years old. I felt that I could perform as well as the mutual fund managers and avoid the 2.5% MERs (Management Expense Ratios), which really bite into your returns over time. I gave an example of that in *The Lazy Investor*.

You performed better than those mutual fund managers. It was at age 34 that you achieved financial independence.

Yeah, I'm retired now. But I've got to start that off by saying I'm a pretty simple guy. I'm not really all that interested in doodads and gizmos and whatever. As long as I have three meals a day and don't fight to live, I'm pretty happy. In my early twenties after graduating university I backpacked around Europe, Australia, and New Zealand. I was living out of a backpack for a couple of years but was pretty happy. That reinforced the idea that you don't need a lot of stuff to enjoy life. When I was aiming for retirement I felt that I didn't need an unusually high income in order to leave the rat race. The other benefit that I had at that time was income trusts. You see, at that time in the late nineties, everybody was fixated on dot-com stocks because the internet was becoming huge. And because I didn't follow that trend, I was able to buy income trusts that were giving me 12 and 13 and 14% yields *[laughs]*. It's hard to believe. So you didn't really need a lot of money to create cash flow that would cover your retirement. When I crunched the numbers and looked at how the income tax acted I realized that I really don't need all that much.

So you avoided the tech boom and instead invested in high-yield income trusts.

I didn't understand technology stocks. I'm not that bright [*laughs*]. I didn't get it. So I never did invest in technology stocks.

How did you amass so much money by age 34?

I don't remember specifics but it wasn't difficult. This is going back to the early 2000s. We had a paid-off house in Ottawa, which we bought at a fairly good price. We were also living in Wasaga Beach at the time in a house with a little bit of debt on it but not much. And then I had my stock portfolio.

Which stocks helped to catapult your portfolio?

Again, I want to emphasize the fact that I wasn't really a big spender. I did things that I felt were fun. I scuba-dived on the Great Barrier Reef but I didn't buy stuff. I was a very avid saver. I saved a high percentage of my income throughout my life. In the early nineties any idiot with a dartboard could throw darts at a newspaper and pick stocks and make money. I made a ton of money when the tobacco companies were being sued. In the U.S., this is going back in time, but they had lost a lawsuit and the tobacco stocks just got hammered. But you had to look at that loss closely. I actually read a book about the size of the Yellow Pages at the time about the history of the tobacco industry in the United States going back about 150 years. It was really quite interesting.

What was so interesting?

One of the interesting things that I found was that, with the exception of tech, the market leader usually stays the market leader for many years. For example, in the eighties, Pepsi took a run at Coca-Cola and essentially said, "Hey, we're doing the Pepsi Challenge and we're gaining on Coke." But Pepsi never replaced Coca-Cola as the dominant market share leader. The same can be said for GM. It's only been recently that Toyota's surpassed them, but for years and years and years no one ever passed GM. So the market leaders were usually always the market leaders.

The only notable exception to that was in the cigarette industry. The market leaders at the time were Camel and Winston, which were owned by R.J. Reynolds. Marlboro was a bit player. I think it was the fourth- or fifth-biggest cigarette company at that time. And then in the early seventies, Marlboro came out with the Marlboro Man, and it took off. Marlboro was rapidly gaining market share, until they surpassed the market share of R.J. Reynolds in the early eighties. This was an interesting opportunity because if you look at the U.S. cigarette market, the Surgeon General's warning was instated pretty late. For example, if you buy a pack of cigarettes it says something along the lines of "This stuff's going to kill you; it's bad for your health," yadda yadda. Anyway, the fact that it's printed right on the package really diminishes a tobacco company's liability. Because if anybody sues the tobacco industry, saying, "Hey, your product harmed my health," the lawyers just need to point to the package and say, "Look, it says so right here, Surgeon General's warning — smoking is bad for your health." That label came out in the early to mid-sixties.

The interesting thing is that Philip Morris of Marlboro was actually a smallish player at that time, and only became bigger later. So the unique situation was their liability was somewhat less because a lot of their increased market share came after the Surgeon General's warnings came out. It was interesting thing, if you see what I mean. Their liability in comparison to their market share was much less than the other tobacco companies. Generally what happens is that people start smoking at a young age and they remain loyal to their brand and smoke it for years. So the fact that Marlboro had gained market share over the last 20 years or so meant that their customer base was a lot younger. So that means that going forward, Philip Morris had brighter prospects than some of the other cigarettes that had legacy brands. Those brands were dying, if you looked at their demographic makeup. So anyhow, I also read that for every five cents a tobacco company raises their prices, they generate an extra billion dollar of revenue. Also, governments didn't want to kill cigarettes because they were generating billions of dollars of tax revenue.

So with that informational edge on Philip Morris's Marlboro brand, how did you make the investment play in the market?

Philip Morris was so beaten up. So when I was about 26 years old I put my entire net worth of $60,000 into Philip Morris and actually margined to the maximum. Basically Philip Morris's stock more than doubled within six months. When I walked out of that trade I had $150,000. That was a huge boost within a six-month time period to my net worth. I wouldn't do it again, but all the stars were aligned when you looked at the industry and the fact that the company was beaten up. There was this unique situation where a company that had traditionally been a weaker player suddenly became a dominant player and they were gaining market share and expanding globally. They were selling a product that once people started using they basically never stopped. And their volume was increasing. Today, even though the cigarette industry's volume is going down 1 to 2% a year, it doesn't matter because the prices increase 5 to 6% a year, so they're actually making more money.

Where did you allocate your gains?

I traded more. Actually, I hate that term, trade, because I'm still a buy and hold investor, but I did sell my positions a lot more back then than I do now. I've evolved over time. I've learned over time. I'm not the same person I was 10 or 15 years ago. Once I got that money from the Philip Morris trade, I bought some blue-chip U.S. stocks, and then the Canadian dollar began to go down. It got down in the 60 cent range. So I sold the U.S. stocks at that time. I made this huge gain just because of the currency move. You have to take what the market gives you.

What happened next?

Then in 2003 I bought Canadian oil sands shares. They were about $8 a share split adjusted. At one point it had gotten up to $55 a share, and then after the financial crisis it went down below $20 a share. I sold at that time. If I was really smart I would have sold at around $55 a share, but I wasn't that smart. However, it was still a good gain because it paid phenomenal dividends for six or seven years, and I still got two and a half times my money when I cashed out. That is not the kind of company I would buy today because I do not think that the Canadian oil sands, for example, have a moat. I have evolved and I've become much more stringent in looking for companies that do have the competitive advantage so I don't worry so much.

At that time, how many stocks did you have in your portfolio?

I don't recall, but I don't think my portfolio's ever gotten above 25 stocks. Usually that's where it tops out.

At that time, you were still working and collecting a paycheque. What percentage of your paycheque were you investing into the stock market?

A huge amount. At that time I was teaching English in Korea and I was given an apartment that was provided for me. I met my wife at that time, too. We weren't married yet, so we would go out now and again, but other than that I needed nothing. I wasn't buying things. Probably about 70% of my paycheque I guess was being saved.

And fast forward to age 34; because of that saving discipline, combined with your strong market performance, you were able to live off your dividends.

Yeah. Again, our lifestyle is not extravagant. I provide for my family — wife and six kids — basically in perpetuity off my dividends. In fact, because I'm relying on the dividends alone, most companies increase their dividends over time, so in actuality my standard of living increases slightly every year in perpetuity.

Do you employ any other investing methods today to generate additional income?

I have sold put options on companies I want to buy. Also, I have sold a couple of covered calls on companies that I'm thinking of dumping. But that's really not germane to my whole approach — less than 1% of my portfolio. Basically I'm a guy that looks for companies with some sort of long-term competitive advantage. Companies that can increase earnings and increase dividends regularly over time. I hold them and get cash dividend cheques in return.

Can you explain the process of selling put options?

Basically, if I'm looking in the market and I find a company that fits my criteria, has a long history of paying dividends, and has some sort of competitive advantage, I may not have the money on me, or I might not want it at the current price. So if it's ABC company, and it's selling for $50 a share, and I want to buy it for $45 a share, what I'll do is sell a put option, let's say six months out. And I'll get paid a dollar premium for doing that because I've basically promised to buy it any time in the next six months. Then I basically just sit and wait. At the end of six months there's only one of two possible outcomes. Either the stock reaches $45 or below, at which point I'm forced to buy it at $45. If it doesn't reach $45, I get to keep the $1 premium and I'm done. I essentially make money for nothing.

What is your process for picking long stocks?

There's many different ways. For me, first and foremost, it's the quality of the company. Some people look at charts — not me. I don't understand charts. I'm not a technical analysis guy at all. Some people are deep-value investors — they're looking for a whole lot of assets on the cheap. That's not me either. Again, I look for quality. I look for a company that I feel has a sustainable competitive advantage. Generally speaking, as Warren Buffett has talked about in the past, I look for a moat: a reason that the company can continue to make obscene profits for years into the future. Unfortunately, there's not many of those companies out there. In the world, there's probably a hundred or even less than that. I don't know the exact number. Once I've identified those kinds of companies, I look for some sort of short-term fixable problem, so I can buy it at a good price. The example of Philip Morris — they were being sued. Or when four or five years ago the Canadian dollar was trading at par so it was a good time to go into the U.S. market, so I bought a lot of U.S. companies that I'd been looking at, and because the market had gone down, were trading at reasonable prices. Ultimately, the first thing I look at is the quality of the company, and then after that I look for a good price.

Once I find that stock, ideally I want to hold that stock forever. If the stock and the dividend keep going up, I'm getting an interest-free loan in essence as long as I don't sell the stock. Ideally, I don't want to be triggering capital gains very often if I can avoid it. Obviously there's times when maybe my analysis is wrong; I chose the wrong stock, I made a mistake, or something changed with the company. For example, 20 years ago Kodak might have been a wonderful company that had a huge moat. But then technology changed and Kodak wasn't nearly as good a company anymore. That would be a situation where the landscape shifted. Ideally it's as simple as that; I want to buy good-quality, dividend-paying stocks, hold on, and just collect the dividends.

Do you use standard metrics to analyze companies?

No. In the sandbox that I'm playing in, you don't need to be all that clever because these are pretty well-known companies. Stocks are almost like wine — they get better with age. Oftentimes, you're looking for businesses that have been in business for decades or ideally even over a century. That makes my job a lot easier. However, I do use some metrics. Return on equity. Low levels of debt — however, some companies can be an exception if they have stable cash flows.

Anyways, valuations are usually company-specific. It depends on the company because the valuation of certain companies might be higher or lower than the valuation of other companies.

Can you list some of the stocks that you hold now in your portfolio?

Right now my portfolio is heavily weighted towards the U.S. market. 85 to 90% of my portfolio is in U.S. stocks. Again, I'm just taking what the market has given me over the last few years. Because oil was high, and our Canadian dollar was flirting with parity for the last five years, it seemed like a good idea to buy some more U.S. stocks. I like Canadian companies, but the depth and breadth of the U.S. market is just so much bigger. It's not rocket science or anything. Coca-Cola, Colgate, Procter & Gamble, Pepsi, Walmart, UPS — these are *very* stable, steady companies. My Canadian-held companies are TD Bank, Scotiabank, Bell Canada . . . you get the idea.

Would you call that foresight, buying into the U.S. market when the Canadian dollar was strong? You must have known that the Canadian dollar would drop below parity again.

It wasn't necessarily foresight. It's just what the market's giving you. In my lifetime, with the exception of the last few years, the only other time the Canadian dollar traded on par for a prolonged period was back when I was in diapers — in the early seventies. So this doesn't happen very often. It's not foresight. I'm opportunistic. The opportunity was there and I took it while I could.

I heard that in 2008 or 2009 you divested all or a majority of your portfolio.

Yes, it is true. Why? Because I guess I'm an idiot sometimes. I had a dose of overconfidence at that point in time. At the time the market was going down quite a bit so I thought that I could time the market. I exited my positions, sold put options, and collected the premiums for a couple of months. That was lucrative but not as lucrative obviously as holding stocks. But then the market rebounded and started going up, and so that wasn't very good for me given my sold put options. At that time I would have liked to buy the traditional Canadian blue-chip stocks, like the Big Five banks, because they were super cheap. I totally missed that boat. Fortunately for me, when the market hit, I didn't sell out at the market low, and that's one of the misleading things in some of the articles written about me. I sold about a month and a half before the market low during the financial crisis. It had gone down another 20% after I sold out, so I sort of made a good move.

How did you recover?

Within a few months, I realized, uh-oh, that was a mistake. I missed out on buying a lot of the Canadian companies at their super-low prices because the market rebounded so strongly. But the one thing that did happen, and that a lot of people forget, is that when the market reached its low the Canadian dollar dipped below 80 cents. That's because when the crash hit, everybody bailed and went into U.S. treasuries, which boosted the U.S. dollar, which made the Canadian dollar go below 80 cents. Anyway, within a few months it was back trading close to parity. So it was actually cheaper for Canadian investors to buy U.S. stocks after the initial rebound, six or eight months after the market low, rather than exactly at the market low, because the dollar had rebounded so strongly. Again, that's part of the reason that I was led to the U.S. companies — because we had a strong dollar. The U.S. market was still pretty beaten up so it offered an opportunity for me to buy into the U.S. companies that I own today.

You turned a potentially missed opportunity into an actual opportunity.

It turned out *really* well for me.

Can someone today achieve what you did at the early age of 34?

No, probably not. Now, other people might have higher incomes — that would obviously help. But there are many factors going against people today. One, the markets are not cheap. Two, income trusts are not as common. They weren't outlawed, but tax rules all changed. Three, baby boomers have all scrambled into anything that has any yield, effectively suppressing yields, so it's really hard to get the same yield now as I got back then. A big part of my platform was the fact that I was able to buy income trusts at the 10 to 14% range. You'd be really hard-pressed to find any security even remotely close to that that has any sort of safety attached with it.

So there's no way? That's demoralizing.

Well, the advantage that young people today do have, and I'm a huge advocate of, are the tax-free savings accounts (TFSA), which weren't around when I was young. So you can put in, you know, $100 bucks a week or whatever, and that's all tax-free. That's a huge benefit.

However, to retire at age 34 is pretty hard. Age 44 I think is definitely within reach for a lot of people. It depends on the math and everything of course.

What investments are ideal for the TFSA?

Generally, I would stick to the stable earnings and dividend growth companies. There could be opportunities in certain companies that perhaps don't pay much of a dividend or don't pay any dividend, but are *really* growing. I'm not saying to invest in growth stocks. I hate that term. However, there's definitely an element of risk there. Definitely not utilities. Nothing offers good yield right now because everybody's chasing yields all the way down. Cheap today would be integrated oils because the price of oil's so cheap. The Canadian banks have come off a bit — those might be reasonable. It's harder to get into the U.S. market right now because our dollar's below 80 cents. I'm just trying to be as realistic as I can be, because for me right now it's pretty easy. I have my portfolio, and it's fossilized there. I don't really do much with it. Because there's tax implications if I do.

Which stocks have a lot of growth in them for the next five-plus years?

Recently I bought a company that I wouldn't have bought five years ago because I needed dividends. I don't need dividends anymore. Panera Bread. They had some short-term earnings misses because they're investing a lot of money in implementing Panera 2.0, which is a computer ordering system. It will make ordering so much easier for customers. I look at Panera and I see an upscale Subway. I'm sure they wouldn't want to be termed that way, but it's more upscale fast-casual. I think we're trending towards that because the baby boomers' kids have left the house and they'll dig a little deeper in their pockets for higher quality. There's currently about 1,800 Panera locations. Peter Lynch went and bought Panera when they had just 80 locations. I'm not that smart. If you look there's something like 25,000 Subways across North America. So if you think Panera's maxed out at 1,800 locations, you'd be wrong. I think they have room for 6,000 locations at least. Anyway, I was an idiot because when I moved to Vancouver in 1996 I bought shares in Starbucks and within a week or two weeks they went up 20% and I sold them for that 20% gain. That's nothing. I sold them for a 20% gain and now they're up 20-fold.

Do you play turnarounds?

No, I don't. Prem Watsa bought a ton of BlackBerry, and that's just not the kind of sandbox that I'm comfortable playing in. He might make a ton of money on that turnaround, but it's not the type of thing that I could do. Again, I'm a follower of Buffett in the sense that I stick to my circle of confidence. Because I'm not that bright, my circle's fairly small, but that's okay as long as I stick within that circle. BlackBerry's way out of my circle of confidence — I don't even own a cell phone. So what do I know? *[laughs]*

What would you say to your critics who have said that over time you veered from your investment strategy? For example, the complete capitulation in 2008. Most expected you to be the "buy and hold"-type investor.

That's a good question. I don't think I really have veered from my investment strategy. I don't think I've ever put myself out there as the genius investor. I explained to you earlier why selling out of the market in 2008 turned out all right for me. Would I do that again? No, I don't think so. When I first started I looked for yields because my goal was not to maximize my wealth. My goal was to stop working. Now I've stopped working. And my portfolio is substantially bigger.

Again, I'm not interested in investing in companies that have 50 to 80% payout ratios. I'm not interested in milking all those earnings and taking them as income, paying tax, and then reinvesting a portion. I'm a simple guy and I don't have high tastes. I don't need all the income that my portfolio throws off. So over the last few years I've shifted more into companies that don't pay a dividend. For example, I own shares in Berkshire Hathaway, which doesn't pay a dividend. I own shares of Markel, which is a mini–Berkshire Hathaway, and which doesn't pay dividends. I own shares of Panera Bread, which doesn't pay dividends. Another example: I bought shares in Visa, and the dividend yield was puny. It was less than 1% when I bought it. Now Visa is rocketing higher. The stock has tripled or quadrupled since I bought it, and the dividends are up as well. So you know, yield on cost basis, these are becoming about like 2 to 4% yielders. That growth is great because they're only paying out less than 20% of their earnings in dividends. The other 80% is being reinvested into the business, whether they're expanding, or opening into new markets, buying back their shares. That's still enriching me. And that's the secret to why the rich get richer — the second million, and then the third million, and then the fourth million all get easier and easier and easier. Only a fool, somebody who's *really* stupid, would not change when the circumstances change, if you follow what I'm saying. My strategy's changed over time and I've shifted more towards companies that have lower payout ratios but higher growth.

Anything else you'd like to add?

Yeah. That I'm not a genius. I'm not that smart of a guy. I'm just disciplined and I stick with it. I don't think that you have to be that smart. Sure, I'm knowledgeable in the markets but you don't have to be a genius to invest in the markets, that's the thing. You just have to be disciplined and regularly save and invest. It's not that you have to be that bright, you just have to be persistent, that's it.

Derek Foster is a market taker. He capitalizes on the opportunities that the market practically "hands him," as he would say. For example, Derek captured a big win by investing in new market leader Philip Morris upon a shift in smoking regulation in the U.S. Separately, Derek expounds on the importance of dividend growth over dividend yield. We've witnessed high-dividend yields slashed throughout this current market environment as companies shore up capital for operations. This was especially true in the energy sector following the oil crash. Finally, while Derek does confess that it might be more challenging today to amass a million dollars through the market by age 34, you never really know, as the market may give you opportunities in the future that you can't envision now.

DEREK FOSTER'S BOOKS
- *Stop Working: Here's How You Can*
- *The Lazy Investor*
- *Money for Nothing*
- *Stop Working Too*
- *The Idiot Millionaire*
- *The Worried Boomer*

1) "With the exception of tech, the market leader usually stays the market leader for many years."

2) "Even though the cigarette industry's volume is going down 1 to 2% a year, it doesn't matter because the prices increase 5 to 6% a year, so they're actually making more money."

3) "I was a very avid saver. I saved a high percentage of my income throughout my life. Probably about 70% of my paycheque."

4) "You have to take what the market gives you."

5) "I look for quality. I look for a company that I feel has a sustainable competitive advantage . . . And then after that I look for a good price . . . Once I find that stock, ideally I want to hold that stock forever."

6) "I don't think my portfolio's ever gotten above 25 stocks. Usually that's where it tops out."

7) "Most companies increase their dividends over time, so in actuality my standard of living increases slightly every year in perpetuity."

8) "I have sold put options on companies I want to buy. Also, I have sold a couple of covered calls on companies that I'm thinking of dumping."

9) "I look for a moat: a reason that the company can continue to make obscene profits for years into the future. Unfortunately, there's not many of those companies out there. In the world, there's probably a hundred or even less than that."

10) "Stocks are almost like wine — they get better with age. Oftentimes, you're looking for businesses that have been in business for decades or ideally even over a century."

11) "It's not foresight. I'm opportunistic. The opportunity was there [buying U.S. stocks with the CAD at parity] and I took it while I could."

12) "The advantage that young people today do have, and I'm a huge advocate of, are the Tax-Free Savings Accounts (TFSA), which weren't around when I was young."

13) "Baby boomers' kids have left the house and they'll dig a little deeper in their pockets for higher quality."

14) "I stick to my circle of confidence. Because I'm not that bright, my circle's fairly small, but that's okay as long as I stick within that circle."

15) "That's the secret to why the rich get richer — the second million, and then the third million, and then the fourth million all get easier and easier and easier."

16) "Only a fool, somebody who's *really* stupid, would not change when the circumstances change."

CHARLES MARLEAU
THE YOUNG BLOOD

Charles Marleau was born into the investment world. His father, a prominent capital markets pioneer, groomed him to be a financial whiz kid. When he was 25, Charles started the Palos Management hedge fund with his father. Since its inception in 2001, the Palos Income Fund has beaten the TSX benchmark 11.51% versus 7.69%. In 2014, it was a second-place winner in three categories of the 2014 Canadian Hedge Fund Awards: Best One-Year Return, Best Five-Year Return, and Best Five-Year Sharpe Ratio. The fund's objective is to deliver trading-enhanced returns, in order to outperform the TSX, but with less risk. It achieves this objective through investing in a core portfolio of select Canadian high-grade and under-valued dividend-paying stocks, preferred stocks, bonds, and convertible bonds. Charles seeks to enhance the returns in his fund by opportunistically engaging in merger arbitrage, pair trades, statistical pair trades, and selling covered calls.

I must have caught Charles in the middle of an important trade, as he hurried our telephone conversation. His advice, therefore, was short but sweet.

PRE-INTERVIEW LESSONS

CASH FLOW: the amount of cash generated by a company's business operations.

CORRECTION: a short-term 10% decline in the markets (not as severe a drop as a bust, bubble, or bear market).

CORRELATION: when two things move in a similar fashion. For example, the price of oil and the Canadian dollar are correlated, such that when the oil price goes up, the Canadian dollar usually also goes up.

DE-LEVERAGE: when a company or person starts to pay down their debt in a motivated fashion.

INDEX: a particular set of stocks that are chosen to represent a particular market or a portion of it. The Dow Jones Industrial Average is an example. An index is usually used as a benchmark to measure one's performance.

MEAN REVERSION: when market asset prices, which fluctuate around an intrinsic value or price, come back to that intrinsic value.

PAIR TRADING: when investors take both a long position and a short position in a pair of highly correlated assets that are usually in the same peer or industry group.

VOLATILITY: the degree of variation in asset prices over a period of time.

Where were you born in Canada?

Montreal.

How did you first get interested in the markets?

I was pretty much born into it. My father was one of the pioneers in the capital markets. So around the table we always spoke about finance.

Can you tell me more about your father, Hubert Marleau?

My father started his career at Nesbitt, and after Nesbitt he went to Lévesque Beaubien. After that, he was instrumental as a senior executive at Beaubien International Bank. Then he started his own brokerage firm called Marleau Lemire. I got into business with him after he sold Marleau Lemire. We decided to start Palos Management, so that's how it all began.

So the investment business is in your blood.

Yes, finance, the economy, everything.

What were the first couple of investments that you remember taking on in your early years?

I was quite young. I was still at McGill University. My first couple of stocks were in the tech bubble so I definitely learned about the market pretty quickly when there was such a rise and such a downfall.

Did that era shape you? What kind of investor are you now?

I don't consider myself a value investor or consider myself a growth investor. What I'm really after is companies that can generate a tremendous amount of cash and grow that cash flow year after year.

Okay, let's fast forward to the founding of Palos Management. How old were you?

I was about 25 years old.

Was it tough starting out so young?

I had a very good guru — my father. As I said, we started the company together in 2001. He taught me the ropes from the macro side to the micro side of investing.

What is the investment strategy at Palos Management?

Our strategy has always been to invest in companies that generate a lot of cash. The quality of cash that's being generated depends on their products and on the services that they provide.

The Palos Income Fund LP has outperformed the TSX since its inception in 2001. And it's diverged upwards since 2008. Why has it outperformed?

One area where we're different from other funds is that we care more because our own money is invested in the fund. One of our principles at Palos Management is to always own close to 16% of the assets in the fund. So there is no question that we have the motivation and work ethic to make the fund work. Our ultimate goal has been to always outperform the market with lower volatility — less risk. How we do this is obviously not by mirror-imaging the index, but by really trying to think outside of the box. The index is broken up into industries. Our goal on the macro side is to identify which industry in the index will outperform in upcoming years. For example, after the financial crisis, the automobile industry basically fell apart, and we saw that as an opportunity to invest, as the average vehicle age had risen very high. We're still overweight in the auto sector and continue to find the best companies possible that generate the most cash. That's how we outperform the market year over year. In addition to that, we employ a trading strategy that manages additional systematic risk or market risk in the portfolio.

You front-load your fund with industries from the index that have the highest future return potential. I see that your fund is 60% weighted in financials, energy, and consumer discretionary. Why?

It's important to know that the financial companies that we are currently invested in are mostly participating in the U.S. economy, not the Canadian economy. In the energy space, we're on the exploration and production (E&P) side over the services side. We still see a massive deficit in energy infrastructure, such as pipelines, gas facilities, and so on. And the other aspect would be water treatment companies in the energy space. We think that there's a very big opportunity as water cuts increase year over year organically.

You own a position by the name of Whitecap Resources. I looked at its performance and was surprised to see how well it held up through the commodity bear and even the oil crash.

When we're looking at investing in companies such as Whitecap Resources, we're looking at how much cash they can generate. But we also make sure that the company can sustainably pay that dividend or distribution. They must have a very strong balance sheet. And

Whitecap Resources is a leader in Canadian E&P, with the strongest balance sheet in the industry. Other companies that have sold off more aggressively will likely bounce higher; however, we always want to play it safe. Whitecap Resources may not have the same rebound, but it can actually benefit from making a creative acquisition, because it's better positioned, has a better balance sheet, and it's safer.

So you won't be bottom-feeding for any distressed oil stocks at this point.

When you're investing in any E&P companies, you're not investing in the company for oil. You're investing in the company because you're investing in that company alone.

Can you expand on some of the additional trading strategies that you employ in the fund?

One of the strategies is pair trading, in which we invest in a company that we believe will outperform another company. The reason that we like this strategy is because we're removing the market risk or systematic risk. How do we find these opportunities? Well, we look for companies that have very similar products, and then determine which one we want to own, and which one we're going to short. However, we don't just look at fundamentals to determine our long/short strategy. We also look at a six-month and a twelve-month correlation. Two companies trade in parallel to each other if you have a correlation of 0.90 and above. But at times, a company that we fundamentally like sells off aggressively. We'll accumulate that company and then short the other company that has weaker fundamentals. The company that we go long on should revert back to its average in the correlation.

Could you give an actual example of this long/short pair trade strategy?

Yes, for example, we're looking at Boardwalk REIT [real estate investment trust] and Canadian Apartments REIT. Boardwalk is usually traded at a premium. However, it has a bit more exposure to Western Canada, so it got really punished during the oil crash in 2014. This is the first time that Boardwalk REIT is trading at a discount to its net value. So we're buying Boardwalk. We know that fundamentally we want to own Boardwalk. We go long. Then we'll look for a similar company to sell, which in this scenario is Canadian Apartments REIT. It's currently trading at a premium to its peers. It has lower growth because it operates in rent-controlled provinces. We go short. Of course, we also conduct a six-month correlation of Boardwalk REIT against Canadian Apartment REIT before we lock in the long/short positions.

So a pair trade ensures that you are always hedging your bets, by offsetting a long position on a stock with a short position on another stock in the same industry?

Yes. And the ideal situation is that the long appreciates and the short declines.

Can you discuss some of the best event-driven trades that you've made?

Yes, after the financial crisis, with the U.S. housing market recovery. We looked at how to expose ourselves to single-family homes all over the U.S. and we did this with a company called Tricon. We also invested in lumber stocks because we felt that housing was going to pick up, which it is, it's just maybe a little slower than we had anticipated. That will be a big theme for our portfolio.

What will be the catalyst for those lumber stocks?

The major catalyst will be when the single-family-home housing starts moving in the right direction. However, we didn't want to play the housing market in Canada for many reasons. We think Canadian single homes are probably overpriced.

The other big theme would be, again, the automobile industry. With higher automobile demand there's a massive trend taking place where OEMs [original equipment manufacturers] are outsourcing more. We looked at companies like Linamar, Monterey, Sun Ray, Magna — anything that was associated with the car. We're very underweight Canadian banks. We don't want to be long Canadian banks for many reasons right now, one being that growth is going to be very difficult in the next couple of years. We know that Canadians' servicing of debt is at an all-time high, so we do believe that the banks on the lending side are going to have a very tough time.

Ray Dalio focuses on debt cycles, and he might say that Canada has just started a de-leveraging cycle, where Canadians have started to pay down their debt. That affects the economy through lower growth.

Well, I haven't seen the data yet, but I think Canadians are still well indebted. They do have an asset, which is a house. However, if the housing market corrects by 10 to 15%, their assets may not be large enough against their liabilities. So yes, I believe that the housing market is pricey. Canadians, as you know, have their wealth in two places: in their houses, and in their RRSP accounts. After that, there is really no other disposable cash or investments.

What criteria do you use to evaluate a company?

Specifically, we look at how much cash they generate, historical performance, and earning power in the good times and the bad times.

Can you expand on that concept of earning power?

For example, when you look at Magna — what was the earning power of that company ten years ago, what was the earning power five years ago, what was the earning power last year? The reason we look at historicals is because we can see how the company reacted in different cycles. We try to buy our stocks at intrinsic value.

How do you calculate a company's intrinsic value?

We do it through free cash flow.

The discounted cash flow model then?

Right, exactly.

Any other criteria?

The other aspect that is very important for us is that we meet management so that we have an understanding of what management wants to do, and where management is going with the company. For us, that is extremely important. We like to see the whites of their eyes. You know, at times we even go and see their facilities to make sure we understand what we're investing in. When we're writing a large ticket, we're writing a *large ticket*. And we are always open to meeting new managers, especially when they're competitors, to understand what they're doing that's different.

Now on to the sell side. You've developed a "reverse engineering model" to determine when to sell out of a position.

Exiting a position is probably one of the harder disciplines. Say, for example, that Magna is trading at $66. We will look back at historicals to see what that price is implying about margins, earning power, and so on. Because we've looked at the company for over 10 years, we have a good idea of its historical standard deviation, meaning whether the current price is expensive or cheap compared to the past. Or if Magna's trading at $75, is it implying an evaluation that's unsustainably high? If we make the decision that it may not be sustainable at this price, the first thing that we'll do is place a covered call for 25% of the position at $75, and receive a premium. Then we will reassess the company — maybe there's something that's fundamentally changing, such as new management or a new growth opportunity in the company. You need to understand what is going on at the management level so that you can adapt to those changes. We will immediately set up a call with management.

When you say "unsustainable stock," does that mean that the stock price is diverging from the underlying fundamentals?

Yes, I'm just saying the fundamentals are unsustainable.

So the earnings aren't increasing at the same rate, and thus the P/E multiple is increasing to all-time highs.

Yes, "unsustainable" is just a fancy way of saying it.

I understand that you're busy. But is there anything else you'd like to add?

My most important tip in investing is that you should not invest in equity for just three months. You're investing for the long term to create wealth. To manage wealth takes time and patience. The only aspect that you can control is basically looking at the companies' fundamentals, understanding management, and making sure that the companies have strong balance sheets. I think at times that people basically look at these stock tickers and make very irrational decisions, rather than looking at the fundamentals and the company's DNA.

In his investment newsletter, Charles explains his security selection criteria and outlines six primary financial ratios.

> In selecting equity investments for the fund, the manager focuses on companies that, in its judgment, provide good value. The manager believes that good-value companies are likely to experience capital appreciation and/or increases in distributions to investors, and that these companies tend to have significant potential for growth of cash flow, increases of dividend distribution, and stock buy-backs. In making the

determination of what companies' stock present good value, the manager typically focuses on a variety of financial ratios and metrics that provide relative points of reference that are transferable across companies and industries. The manager primarily considers six financial ratios: earnings yield spread, debt versus EBITDA [earnings before interest, taxes, depreciation, and amortization], cash per share, return on equity, price to earnings (P/E ratio), and free cash flow yield.

EARNINGS YIELD

The earnings yield is the earnings per share for the most recent period (typically 12 months) divided by the current market price per share. The earnings yield (which is the inverse of the P/E ratio) shows the percentage of each dollar invested in the stock that was earned by the company. The manager considers the differential between the earnings yield compared to the stock price versus the U.S. Treasury Bond yield, sometimes called the earnings yield spread. A wide earnings yield spread represents good value, particularly as compared to bonds, and therefore presents a buying opportunity for the manager.

DEBT TO EBITDA

The manager also considers a company's debt as a percentage of its earnings before interest, taxes, depreciation, and amortization, or EBITDA. A low ratio indicates that the company is able to repay its debt and/or to take on additional debt, thus allowing it to finance expansion of operations or share buy-backs. Conversely, a high debt/EBITDA ratio suggests that a firm may not be able to repay debt and interest as it comes due, which could potentially lead to a restructuring and/or bankruptcy of the company.

CASH PER UNIT

Cash per unit (sometimes known as free cash flow per share) is determined by dividing free cash flow by the total number of units outstanding. It is a measure of a company's financial flexibility. More free cash flow allows a company to engage in a variety of transactions, such as repaying debt, paying and increasing dividends, buying back stock and facilitating the growth of the business. The amount of free cash flow per unit can also be used to give a preliminary prediction concerning future share prices. For example, when a firm's unit price is low and free cash flow is on the rise, the manager believes that this is a positive indicator that earnings and share value will soon increase, because a high cash flow per share value means that earnings per share could potentially be high as well.

RETURN ON EQUITY

Return on equity (sometimes known as return on net worth) is the amount of net income returned as a percentage of unitholders' equity. Return on equity measures a corporation's profitability by revealing how much profit a company generates with the money unitholders have invested in common stock (preferred stock is generally excluded, as are the dividends paid on that stock). Net income is for the full fiscal year (before dividends paid to common stock holders but after dividends to preferred stock). Unitholder's equity does not include preferred shares. The manager uses return on equity to compare the profitability of a company to that of other firms in the same industry. If a given company's return on equity is particularly high compared to its peers, then the company may present good value and therefore may be a good buying opportunity.

PRICE TO EARNINGS

Price to earnings, or P/E, is one of the most commonly used financial ratios. In general, a high P/E suggests that the market is expecting higher earnings growth in the future compared to companies with a lower P/E. However, a high P/E ratio may also imply that a company is overvalued. The manager focuses on companies with low P/E ratios because a low P/E ratio implies that a significant component of the company's stock price is comprised of earnings, rather than market expectations for future growth. The manager also recognizes that it is impossible to base a decision on the P/E ratio alone. The denominator (earnings) is based on an accounting measure of earnings that is susceptible to forms of manipulation, making the quality of the P/E only as good as the quality of the underlying earnings number.

FREE CASH FLOW YIELD

The free cash flow yield is a measure of the free cash flow per unit a company is expected to earn against its market price per unit. As compared to the price to earnings ratio, the free cash flow yield is a more standardized measure that eliminates many of the problems involved in evaluating the quality of the earnings as reported by a company. Because free cash flow takes into account capital expenditures and other on-going costs a business incurs to keep itself running, the manager believes that the free cash flow yield is a more accurate representation of the returns shareholders receive from owning a business compared to the price to earnings ratio.

─────────────────── **MASTER KEYS** ───────────────────
CHARLES MARLEAU

1) "What I'm really after is companies that can generate a tremendous amount of cash and grow that cash flow year after year."

2) "Our ultimate goal has been to always outperform the market with lower volatility — less risk."

3) "The index is broken up into industries. Our goal on the macro side is to identify which industry in the index will outperform in upcoming years."

4) "We also make sure that the company can sustainably pay that dividend or distribution. They must have a very strong balance sheet."

5) "One of the strategies is pair trading . . . we look for companies that have very similar products, and then determine which one we want to own, and which one we're going to short. We're removing the market risk or systematic risk."

6) "At times, a company that we fundamentally like sells off aggressively. We'll accumulate that company and then short the other company that has weaker fundamentals. The company that we go long on should revert back to its average in the correlation."

7) "Canadians, as you know, have their wealth in two places: in their houses, and in their RRSP accounts. After that there is really no other disposable cash or investments."

8) "[For evaluation] we look at how much cash they generate, historical performance, and earning power in the good times and the bad times."

9) "Exiting a position is probably one of the harder disciplines. We have a good idea of [companies'] historical standard deviation, meaning whether the current price is expensive or cheap compared to the past."

10) "You should not invest in equity for just three months. You're investing for the long term to create wealth. People basically look at these stock tickers and make very irrational decisions, rather than looking at the fundamentals and the company's DNA."

PAUL HARRIS, BILL HARRIS, AND PAUL GARDNER
THE THREE AMIGOS

Avenue Investment Management's office is situated on a quaint street in downtown Toronto. It feels tucked away, but the office is only a five-minute walk away from the hustle and bustle of the financial district on Bay Street. The "Three Amigos" who run Avenue Investment Management — Paul Harris, Bill Harris, and Paul Gardner — seem to have so much fun working together that I almost imagine them tap-dancing to work every morning. Their office exudes a general sense of happiness, with bright, open spaces, light brick walls, and long wooden floors. Their main meeting room's wide windows allow the sun to shine through. It was in that meeting room that all Three Amigos came together to answer my questions, and share both their individual and collective experiences in the market.

This is the only multiple-interviewee format in the book. At times, I felt like a referee, guiding the conversation, switching between talkers, and handing out penalties to any of the three who started to dominate the conversation. This interactive format worked, however, as each of the three investors had lots of great information to share. All Three Amigos are masters in their own right, but overlay their niche knowledge with one another to make final investment decisions. This process works a bit like the sounding board that exists between Warren Buffett and Charlie Munger at Berkshire Hathaway, in which both partners reach an investment decision after a constructive process. Paul Harris focuses on financial institutions, technology, and telecom. Bill Harris's areas are resources, utilities, and infrastructure. Paul Gardiner covers bonds, real estate, utilities, and telecom.

While their mandate is to double portfolios' values every 10 years, which implies a 7.3% annual compound rate of return, their flagship Avenue Equity Portfolio has exceeded that mandate by *tripling* over a 10-year period. Paul, Paul, and Bill are as much focused on risk management as they are on their upside returns. As we discussed in the interview, the Three Amigos managed to save their portfolios from a complete crash before the financial crisis in 2008 that decimated banks around the world. They witnessed weakness in the global financial sector and then quickly took action to eliminate that risk from their portfolios.

Paul Harris was actually my first point of contact at Avenue Asset Management. After years of watching BNN's *Market Call*, I've come to respect Paul's no-nonsense advice to callers. Also, his fashion sense and swagger rival those of Norman Levine, who you'll hear from later (but a winner is just too close to call). Paul usually wears a colourful bow tie with a brightly coloured shirt and thick-framed circular glasses to accentuate his face. And his buttery smooth voice makes listening to Paul talk about the markets comforting and reassuring, especially during a period of market turmoil. Unfortunately, family man Paul Harris had to step out halfway through the interview to pick up his daughter, but later supplemented the transcription with additional comments. As well, Paul Gardner was slightly late to the interview, so his answers don't appear in the first few questions. I was so involved in this conversation that I lost track of time as our conversation went late into the morning.

To clear things up before we get started, Paul Harris and Bill Harris are not related; their identical last names are simply a matter of coincidence — just as it is a coincidence that the other two are named Paul. Perhaps they were fated to be a team.

PRE-INTERVIEW LESSONS

DOWNSIDE: the amount of risk, and possible weakness, inherent in an investment.

MOVING AVERAGE: a trend line that is based on the average of past prices, notably 50-day and 200-day averages, that some investors use to compare to current market prices.

REAL ESTATE INVESTMENT TRUST (REIT): an investable fund that contains real estate or mortgage investments. The Canadian government's taxation changes (2006) did not affect this form of income trust.

SECTOR: an area of the stock market, such as technology, telecom, or consumer staples.

SUPPORT: a lower price level in a stock chart that makes it difficult for a stock price to break under to re-price itself to previous lows.

Where did you guys grow up in Canada?

PAUL HARRIS: I actually grew up in India. And like a lot of Indians, when we emigrated to Canada we moved to the Bramalea-Brampton area. And so that's where I grew up in Canada. I went to the University of Toronto for my post-secondary education.

BILL HARRIS: I grew up here. I'm part of one of those unusual families who have been living within five streets since 1860. So I'm the fifth generation; my son is sixth-generation.

Would that be downtown Toronto? Also, where did you go for school?

BILL: Yeah, five blocks from downtown Toronto. I did classics and philosophy in university. My dad told me to go to university and "learn how to think." It sounded like a nice idea but afterwards it was really hard to get a job with a classics degree unless I opted to stay in the classics department. So, I enrolled in statistics and accounting at night school as well as wrote the CFA. After that, I had to actually further qualify myself to get a job. We get asked pretty regularly, "How do you get a job in this industry?" There's no way to know. There's no simple way to say, "You do *this* and then you qualify for a job." It's really hard to get a job in this industry. People do it all the time, but everybody will have a completely different story.

Interesting. So, Paul, what did you study at U of T?

PAUL HARRIS: I studied history and economic history. So, similar to Bill, I didn't really study finance or anything like that. When I wanted to get into the industry, I had to go back and retrain myself in some ways. But when I finally got into the industry it was very different because mutual funds had just started to take off in Canada. There was a lot of opportunity and a lot of growth in the investment industry. Whereas nowadays, there's just not a lot of growth, so those opportunities are slim. That's the bigger problem with people trying to get in. There's just not a great number of job opportunities like there were in the eighties and early nineties when there was a tremendous amount of growth in the area.

Peter Lynch had a similar educational background as both of you — history and classical studies. Does that background allow you to apply unique frameworks to the markets?

PAUL HARRIS: I think it makes you a good investor. But it doesn't make it easy to get a job *[everyone laughs]*. Okay, I just heard Paul come in through the front of the office. I'll quickly tell you his introduction. Paul Gardner grew up in Windsor, and then went from there to York University, where he studied economics. Thereafter, he was in the first group of people to start work at TD Waterhouse Green Line.

BILL: Green Line. Green Line was an amazing breeding ground . . .

PAUL HARRIS: So then he went to Treasury, and that's where I met him. We worked at TD Treasury together. Then I left to go to [TD] Asset Management and he also left to go to Asset Management. And then funnily enough with Bill and me, we have the same last name, but obviously people know we're not related in any way. But I started at TD Asset Management in January and he started like three months later in the same group. I knew Paul from TD Treasury and he came over and basically took my job from the fixed-income side when I was at TD Asset Management and I moved to the equity side at TD Asset Management. So we all have known each other for a long time.

*[Paul Gardner enters the meeting room and
after introductions, we get him up to speed.]*

So we've established your early lives. But how did you first get interested in the markets?

PAUL GARDNER: My parents were older. Not that that has anything to do with it, but we tended to watch the seven p.m. news as part of their routine. I do remember this specific moment where ABC News featured a story on the London Stock Exchange's trading pit. There was a bunch of commotion with brokers screaming at each other. But I thought, "That looks really interesting." At that point, I realized that that seemed like a great place to be. So I researched it more and learned the difference between institutional trading at the banks and trading in the pit, where it's more old-style.

I was weird in that I knew exactly what I wanted to do when I was 22. In university, I passed my securities course, got the CFA shortly after that, and then started my career upon graduation. I wanted to be a trader in my twenties, but then in my thirties I actually wanted to be a portfolio manager for a large firm. And then in my forties I wanted to start my own firm with a couple of people. So, there was never any doubt in my mind as to what I wanted to do.

What about you, Paul? How did you first get interested in the markets?

PAUL HARRIS: It was just by luck *[laughs]*. I didn't really have any idea that I wanted to do any of this stuff. After I finished university, I worked at Canada Trust in a branch, and then in the loans department. My manager liked me, but also said, "It doesn't seem that you're interested in this." I admitted that I wasn't interested in that work. So she said, "Stay here until you find something." Later on, I read an article in the *Globe and Mail* about this Canadian who worked for a Japanese company in the foreign exchange department. And so I thought, "Oh, this seems very interesting." After that, I went and researched foreign exchange, and then eventually got my first job with the Bank of America in their foreign exchange department. Thereafter, I went to TD Securities to work in foreign exchange. And that's where I met Paul — he was a trader for the U.S. dollar and Japanese yen and I worked on the corporate side in foreign exchange. Finally, I ended up working in the fixed-income department of TD Asset Management, running a bunch of relatively small funds but in a very rapidly growing business. I got lucky and fell into a bunch of things, you know, and opportunities sort of came up in my way. I wouldn't say that I had Paul's plan.

PAUL GARDNER: Just as an add-on, before you get to Bill, all of our careers coincided with the "big bang." In 1986, markets were all de-regulated, and banks and brokers were allowed to survive and thrive. There was a tremendous amount of opportunity there. Nothing like it is today. Literally, if you just got in the door, there was this tidal wave pushing you through the company. As long as you played the game you could get into almost any area that you wanted to get into. Of course, you had to have aptitude and skill, but it was such a growth area. Incredible growth.

It's not like that now in the banks.

PAUL GARDNER: Oh, it's the complete opposite. I'm talking a 360-degree turn. It's so different.

Finally, Bill, how did you first get interested in the markets?

BILL: Both my dad and my grandfather worked in the financial industry. Neither of them talked about it, but I remember one of the conversations

I had with my grandfather, where he told me, "Don't do it." And his point, which I always thought was really interesting, was that he found the industry to be really stressful. This was when he was 86 and close to death. He just said, "My friends are accountants; we were members of the same golf course and ate the same food." I think he got unbelievably stressed over financial markets going up and down his entire life. That, I thought, sounded really exciting. [Others laugh] At that time, I was doing graphic design out of university. But then my dad told me to go out and take a summer student job at Dominion Securities. Over lunch he said, "Here's your career path: to get this kind of job, you've got to get your CFA, work for 10 years, and then you might be a money manager." He laid it out for me. It took some time but it all happened.

How was Avenue Investment Management founded?

PAUL HARRIS: I was sitting at a café on Avenue Road in NYC one day. That's the reason why "Avenue" is in our firm name. Anyways, I was having a cup of coffee, and bumped into Paul's wife. She asked, "What are you doing?" I said, "Nothing." And then she said, "Well, my husband's doing nothing as well, so why don't you call him?" Paul had just recently left TD Asset Management, so we got together and I said to Paul, "I'm not really interested in working for a large firm anymore. I want to start my own company." He felt the same way. So that was the genesis for the company starting up. And because I knew Bill for many years, when he got in touch with me and asked, "What are you doing?" I told him our plan to start a business to manage money. Bill told me that he wanted to join, too. But that final decision was made within six months.

BILL: I have two subtleties, because you can make it a little more dramatic. Paul Harris was working in the World Trade Centre. The ninety-first floor. The way I spin it is that he got a free ticket. Anyway, from my point of view, I thought it was a great idea. For me, knowing these two guys, and managing money together, was only going to happen to me once in my life. However, it took me a year to convince my wife that it was a good idea [others laugh].

She finally bought in.

BILL: I'm not sure. No, just lately she bought in [laughs].

PAUL HARRIS: What's unique about the firm is that we're not just like everyone else. When guys start these kinds of firms they tend to have just an equity focus. We actually also manage debt here. Paul Gardner worked in one of the largest bond funds in Canada and is an expert on corporate debt and high-yield debt analysis. So we started a firm that's not about just managing equity. We have different experiences that we've brought to the table that push us together to make it work a lot better.

I am aware that there's division of labour. Paul Harris, you cover financial institutions, tech, and telecom. Paul Gardner, you cover bonds, real estate, utilities, and telecom. And Bill, you cover resource, utilities, and infrastructure.

PAUL GARDNER: Part of our success is having all of the stars aligned. If we were all equity heads, it would be hard to succeed because we'd have to look at different investment frames. It was by sheer coincidence that the three of us, although we come from the same discipline, have different expertise. For instance, one of our critical advantages is that we understand the capital structure of any company. Also, we're agnostic as to whether we own equity or debt. That liberates us if we can find in the debt markets an equity-like return that is far safer. It's a weird thing in the institutional world where there's a separation between the equity team and the bond team. They're rarely mixed together. That was mostly due to personalities and ego. One group thought that they were smarter than the other. And that also happened in the trade rooms. You would just spend most of the time dissing each other. We take those shackles off. Many times, I'll go to Bill and say, "There's this distressed oil and gas bond," and then we'll cross-reference all of our abilities to make an informed investment decision. I'll look at it from the structure of the bond side — the indentures and the covenants — and he will look at the overall company and its management.

So, what's the key advantage to your multi-disciplinary approach?

PAUL GARDNER: Once you're in the bond world, you can achieve a 10% to 12% rate of return. All you need to determine is whether a company is going to go bankrupt. That's all. The upside is very easy. And also, this is another frame, but another reason for Avenue's success is that we asked ourselves early on, "Can we succeed by not failing?" That's a different mentality than asking, "How do we not fail?" I can deal with success in a minute, but I always obsess about failure.

It's important to understand the downside risk.

PAUL GARDNER: It's all about the downside for me.

What other risk management controls do you have in place?

BILL: So, picture the TSX as a pie. The trick is to determine the most consistent companies in the TSX. For example, we don't cover biotech. We own one biotech right now — the most consistent company in biotech — but we would say, historically, that those companies don't traditionally make money, and we don't own things that don't make money. So we would immediately take the TSX and wipe things off and then just have a handful of companies. So if you ask, "Which are the best banks?" we could quickly respond, "Consistently the best banks in Canada are TD and RBC." We own those banks. And if TD and RBC are the best banks today, they probably were the best banks five years ago. They've got a culture that will probably sustain them five years from now, too. If you want to know the lowest-cost heavy oil producers, I can tell you that, too. We find that really good companies don't change that much over time. In other words, we cover everything that needs to be covered.

So you control downside risk by automatically removing unfavourable sectors, such as biotech. Also, by investing in consistent leaders in each industry. And also by conducting full due diligence on all of your investments.

PAUL HARRIS: It's not absolute, but it's a general rule. If we need to have some exposure to a sector, then we try to find the best in class and just immunize our risk. It would be nice if over the last year we were triple our weight in biotech, because of course that's been a great sector, but it's not in our DNA.

Is Valeant Pharmaceutical in your portfolios?

PAUL GARDNER: No. We did own Valeant a long time ago in the world of Biovail. But —

BILL: Biovail got restructured. It started to fail when we owned it and so it was tough because there was massive volatility while it was being restructured. What tends to be a lot easier for us is to identify historically great companies, with great numbers, that we can we buy at a decent price.

Do you guys every butt heads?

BILL: The financial crisis was really intense because we actually had 10 minutes to think at all times. We were trying to win by not losing. In this money management business, if our clients can get consistent rates of return that compound at 7% or 8% returns, then it's a good business.

That makes sense — your objective is to double the portfolio every 10 years with minimal downside risk, so would that imply 7% annual compounded returns?

BILL: 7.3%. If you try to compound consistently at 10% or 12%, you will end up hitting air pockets. The problem is that you take up more risk and thus increased probability that you get no return. 40% of people might achieve their return objective, but then 40% of people actually lose. That's why we invest in stocks and bonds that compound at 8%, and then just lock in to dramatically lower the risk. For the first 10 years since inception we've been at 25% less volatility than the TSX, and 30% less volatility than the S&P 500. Most of our clients aren't going to understand that, but they feel it. Everybody feels that the portfolio really doesn't move around all that much. It keeps people in the game. We have a 30-year time horizon, but it's very hard to get clients to think that way. So, there's mechanisms to ensure the consistency of the portfolio. You can double your money, then double it again, and double that again. But you need to give yourself the highest probability that it actually happens.

What else makes you guys different than other funds?

PAUL HARRIS: The idea is to be a devil's advocate. I don't know all the details about the oil business, but I know enough to ask Bill, "Does it meet these qualifications for our portfolio?" and then understand the risk to the portfolio. "Are we overweight in small-caps?" That never happens but you get the point. If we make a mistake — we're going to make lots of mistakes — we don't have to sit in a committee or worry about these guys saying, "Well, that was a dumb idea." But on the other side, I'm not going to automatically say, "That's a great idea, I'm going to continue owning it."

If we make a mistake, we can sell it. But there's not this intense pressure that you'd feel if you were at a big institution. We're never in the position where we recommend a stock, add it to portfolios, and then three days later, say, "Oh my god, I just said the wrong thing, I didn't analyze it properly, I'm going to look like an idiot." In any institution, your job would be at risk. That doesn't happen here, partly because we all own the company, but partly because we know we're going to make mistakes, so let's just leave it at that. Sometimes you miss stuff. You thought you got it right but you didn't, but then you just drive on. I think that there's the tendency in a smaller firm to be able to do those things and to not be worried about your job or not be worried that "Oh, I'm going to look like an idiot in front of my colleagues." So you can have a much more robust conversation, you can understand the risk profile a lot better, and if you make a mistake, you just drive on.

PAUL GARDNER: Not having the politics really helps. It frees your mind. There's no politics in this firm. We don't have to position ourselves, other than maybe our egos if we get an investment wrong. Again, we just win by not losing. That's how we survived the financial crisis, by being smart enough to acknowledge our mistakes.

Can you elaborate on how you actually survived the financial crisis?

BILL: Going into 2008, you had air pockets, like I've alluded to before. If you looked at Cameco, Potash, or Teck Cominco, the commodities were dramatically above their long-term price averages. 2007 was actually our worst year. Stocks were really expensive. Back then, only four new stocks went into our portfolio. We massively underperformed the TSX that year. The TSX's performance in 2007 was due to only a handful of companies, one being Potash, which we didn't own, because we just though its price was ludicrous. Alcan got taken over by Rio Tinto. And 12 months later, Alcan almost bankrupted Rio Tinto.

So, you survived the financial crisis by avoiding overvalued stocks?

BILL: Yes, which is why leading up to the financial crisis, we underperformed the market. We said, "This feels horrible." But we know good businesses and we know good valuation, so we couldn't justify owning overvalued stocks. Goldman Sachs is a great investment bank, but my god it was expensive in 2007. And then in 2008, the markets really looked like they were rolling over. Through the summer, it looked like it could end really badly. So I think it was the first week back in September that I came into the office and printed off the charts of the markets and all of our stocks. I was freaking out.

PAUL HARRIS: We had 80 graphs printed out. At that time, we owned Citibank, Merrill Lynch, Bank of Scotland, and some others.

Those were some of the financial stocks that eventually exploded on the market.

BILL: The problem was that they were trading at 10 times earnings. We asked, "Is there a potential air pocket in any one of those stocks if a collapse happens?" Anyway, by 9:35 a.m., bam, bam, bam, they all got hit, and we sold out. We were 45% in cash after that.

How did you finally sell out of those financial stocks?

BILL: We just drew a line 10% under the current prices but once prices fell below that line, and broke technical support, we sold out.

Was that technical support the 200-day moving average?

BILL: No, it was not.

PAUL GARDNER: We were selling Merrill Lynch at roughly $58. And then we sold Citigroup in the sixties. And Royal Bank of Scotland was 25 pounds when we sold it. But all of these stocks eventually declined 90%, or went bankrupt, like Merrill Lynch.

You obviously protected capital. 10% versus 90% loss.

PAUL GARDNER: Yeah, we protected our capital, but we lost money. We lost only about 10%.

BILL: It was horrible going through September and October, but we turned around very quickly because we bought high-yield bonds. You could buy high-yield bonds that yielded 10% to 12%. That was great. But also, if the bond recovered, we could actually make 50% to 60% return over six months if we got the timing right. Those bonds sold off during the crisis, and so we thought, "We're not going back into the stock market just yet." We spent two months picking up all of these high-yield bonds. The stock market didn't bottom until March. But gold bottomed in October. I was walking around in Fort McMurray visiting some companies when Paul phoned me and said, "Niko's at 30 bucks." We always said that if Niko ever dropped from 60 to 30 bucks that we'd buy it.

Other than that commitment, did you have a thesis to buy into gold at that time?

BILL: We always have exposure to a certain sector.

Certainly, QE, mass money circulation, and inflation fears helped to propel the gold bull.

BILL: That was much later. Stocks all bottomed: gold bottomed in

October, oil bottomed in November, financials bottomed in March. So you had to buy all of your oils in November. All our gold investments were done in October, and all our oil investments were done by the end of November, and we were fully 100% invested by March.

In that period, there was a broad decline across all asset classes and sectors. But most recently, there's been a sharp but concentrated decline in oil and gas. Would you discriminately buy oil and gas companies now just because their prices have all been cut by 50%?

BILL: I did this analysis again last night. When oil's at $100 or $110 Canadian, it's great to own an oil company, because they're making all this money. But marginal cost of production is still $80. If the price of oil's trading below its long-term cost of production, you should own less of it.

One runs the risk of buying into an oil and gas company that could very well go bankrupt.

PAUL GARDNER: Yeah, for example in the darkest days of the financial crisis, there was an 80% chance that Teck Cominco would have gone bankrupt. What happens with any company is that if they get the capital structure wrong, then their debt overwhelms their business and that's when they can go into bankruptcy.

Is that why you primarily bought bonds rather than stocks during the financial crisis?

PAUL GARDNER: If you buy a bond at a discount, there's an end to the story. It's called par. Conversely, stocks are indefinite. They can stay there forever. A bond has to have an end. You should know your rate of return, and then at the end of the game you end up at maturity.

As long as there's no default on a bond, you know the return that you'll receive by maturity.

PAUL GARDNER: Mm-hm.

BILL: Just make sure it doesn't default. Promise me it's not going to default.

PAUL GARDNER: So GMAC is a great example. We held GMAC through the whole crisis. GMAC is the financial arm of General Motors Canada. GMAC was trading at 50 cents on the dollar. They were going into receivership. But, you see, GMAC Canada guarantees the bonds. If that fails, GMAC USA will back the bond. I would call the CFO every week during the crisis, asking, "Are you still there? Are you still operating?" He said, "Well, unlike in the U.S., in Canada we're not really being hit." The GMAC bonds eventually matured. I got my 12% and skated on, which is like winning by not losing. I also got a 15% rate of return from GMAC bonds.

Can you share other experiences where you generated high rates of return from bonds?

PAUL GARDNER: So, I came into the office after hearing that Buffett made a $10-billion capital infusion into Goldman Sachs, General Electric, and Bank of America. He bought warrants and got 10%. I thought, "Wow, I wish we could do that." So, I came up with a strategy where we could do something that was just as good and probably even better than Buffett's strategy. You see, 30-year GE financial bonds were trading at a discount of 70 cents on the dollar, so you'd get a 10% to 12% rate of return. GE was getting crushed; its stock price high was $70, but it was now trading at $14. Instead of saying, "Well, I hope it all works out, let's buy GE stock at $14," we actually bought the GE financial bonds, at 70 cents on the dollar. I conducted all of the analysis and there was enough capital there that assured me I would get paid out. So, Buffett made the capital infusion in GE, but because they had to issue so many shares, the stock got diluted and didn't move again for five or six years. However, when the company recovered, my bond went from 70 cents to $1. We earned a 30% rate of return in a year and a half, and it was a far safer way of entering GE in the crisis. We were higher on the capital structure, and interestingly ahead of Warren Buffett.

The other example is with Bell. So as you know, Ontario Teachers' Pension Plan attempted a leveraged buy-out of Bell. As a result, Bell's 10-year bonds went from par down to 80 cents. We knew that they were going to get downgraded by the credit agencies below investment grade, so that's why of course it got hit. However, we bought the bond because first of all we'd earn a 10% to 12% rate of return. Second, the Ontario Teachers' Pension Plan would not buy Bell and risk going into bankruptcy. The OTPP was a back-stop in a sense. So we thought, "Why don't we just buy the bonds, and collect a decent rate of return?" The risk to Bell equity holders was that the deal could have blown up. I never counted on that, but it was a free option in the sense that if the deal got cancelled, the stock would go down by 40%, but the bond would go back up by 25%. KP&G came out with a solvency test and literally said, "The deal's too levered." After that ruling came out, the deal fell apart, but our bonds immediately went from 80 cents to one dollar.

Whereas some investors took on an equity risk arbitrage position in Bell, perhaps also with leverage to collect bigger potential gains, but then got stomped on when the deal fell apart.

PAUL GARDNER: See, buying the bond was a better way to play it.

BILL: It was either that the deal goes through, or it doesn't go through; it was a coin toss. Paul laid it all out, and said, "Scenario A, we win, and Scenario B, we win."

PAUL HARRIS: That's exactly what we're looking for. I don't know why you would ever lever up.

PAUL GARDNER: Yeah, we don't lever up. Anyway, during the financial crisis, all of our bonds were up 40%. But the stock market also turned, and in '09 was up about 30%. We were up 30%, too. So, in that scenario we generally tend to overperform on the downside and underperform on the upside. During market collapses, we go out and find these special situation bonds that can go up and can crush the volatility, so that we can still get equity-like returns. Those are mechanisms that we execute once or twice a year that help us dampen the volatility, but also give us some consistent rates of return.

BILL: We can get the same rate of return with less volatility. But if somebody gives you an index and says, "Beat this index," that creates different behaviour, and then you cannot do this strategy.

There's constant pressure in this industry to beat the index.

PAUL HARRIS: Yeah, you need to get out of those beat-the-index shackles. For example, at one point, Nortel was 30% of the index. Many in the industry would have deliberated whether to be underweight, 20% or 10% exposed to Nortel. Anyway, when we started at Avenue we spent the summer just looking at annual reports. We did it in alphabetical order, so Nortel was pretty close to Leon's Furniture. Leon's Furniture's annual report was 18 pages, whereas Nortel's was an *inch and a half*. After the first hour of reading through Nortel's annual report, we both looked at each other and said, "I don't know what the hell any of this means," and threw the report in the garbage, agreeing to never own Nortel.

BILL: Yeah, Nortel was trading at a hundred times earnings. It was supposed to make $1 in earnings, and then go to $1.20 in earnings. It was growing at 20%. But then it became known that Nortel had serious accounting irregularities. The whole thing was absurd. Generally, people in the industry had so much professional career anxiety over Nortel that they spent hours talking about it when there was nothing to talk about.

Nobody back then would dare say, "We should have zero exposure to Nortel"?

PAUL GARDNER: No one, because you'd lose your job. In today's institutional meetings, they're probably having a five-minute conversation about Valeant Pharmaceuticals and saying "We cannot *not* be invested in Valeant." You can imagine that they're obsessed with Valeant and the reason is that institutions are measured on relative performance. They might get fired if they don't have some exposure to those big movers.

PAUL HARRIS: Yeah, you know, stats, an index, and all these other things really hamper the ability to invest properly in the market. For example, Buffett in reality doesn't just sit in his office and think about the S&P 500. He thinks about the companies he buys, and he thinks about investing in those companies. That's why he can make a decision so quickly, because he's not thinking about the relative performance of S&P 500 all the time. We don't care about the index. What we care about is getting you this rate of return between 8% and 10% with the least amount of risk. If we can do that for you, I'm doubling your money every eight to ten years.

Let's put it all together now. Can you summarize your investment strategy?

BILL: Firstly, how do I not lose? How do I not blow up? The first thing we say is that, "We'll own good companies." But what does that mean? Well, that means that you're not going into every sector. Balance sheets need to be conservatively financed. Companies should be in profitable markets. Managements need to actually be good at what they do. Shoppers Drug Mart was a great example. It was kicking out $700 million of cash flow. They were growing at a hundred stores a year, and then they suddenly put up a flag and said, "We don't need to grow anymore." Then, nine months later, it got bought by Loblaws. However, there's no Johnson & Johnson in Canada. So we have to go outside of Canada for certain opportunities. There's great banks in

Canada. Great real estate in Canada. Great resources in Canada. Great pipelines in Canada. We don't have to go outside of Canada often.

Secondly, we ask, should I buy it today? Well, that's actually kind of expensive. I probably shouldn't buy it today. For example, Agnico Eagle was trading at $55, but I wanted to buy it at $30. It finally reached $30 and so I said, "Well, I guess we're buying it." It was at fair valuation.

How do you determine fair valuation?

PAUL GARDNER: Free cash flow yield is what we really focus on.

BILL: Yeah. Most companies give you a 3% to 5% free cash flow yield, which does not beat an average corporate bond. You need 8% to 12% free cash flow yield, and you can get that if you're super patient. RBC right now has a 9% free cash flow yield. But people look at RBC now and they say, "I hate the banks and real estate in Canada. If you don't pay your mortgage in Canada the banks take your house" *[laughs]*. Anyway, you want to invest in companies that can either maintain the rate of return or enhance their rate of return when they reinvest their earnings.

PAUL HARRIS: However, be cognizant of companies that enhance their rates of return through acquisition strategies or financial engineering. It seems that it's just better to keep reinvesting in your business. Because some companies go outside of their expertise, and then there's execution risk. We would wave a yellow flag there. For example, Canadian Pacific Railway owned the Blue Jays, real estate, restaurants, and hotels at one point in time. That seemed great but then look at what eventually happened to the stock.

So, misallocation of earnings can dilute or even significantly impact future free cash flow.

PAUL GARDNER: Right.

BILL: But then occasionally there are conglomerates such as Brookfield that's got an incredible culture of asset management and asset allocation. You'll find great diversified businesses like Brookfield, but for the most part, you want to invest in clearly defined businesses.

PAUL HARRIS: The macro level's about management. There's chronic repeatable behaviour. Bad people and bad managers keep doing bad things. Good people and good managers generally keep doing good things. It's a very simple concept.

Do you sometimes invest in companies based solely on their management?

PAUL GARDNER: Well, Bill has, but I haven't.

BILL: Yeah. For example, 70% of Leon's Furniture is owned by the Leon family. So, there's 25 to 28 aunts and uncles who own this stock, and Mr. Leon's only job is to get them their dividend. If he doesn't get them their dividend, then talk about shareholder pressure. It's family pressure. The other good management team is at Boardwalk REIT, where the two brothers own a large stake in the company. They don't pay themselves a salary at all. Zero. They only make money from Boardwalk REIT's distribution. They own 25% of the company and it's worth $1 billion. You can find a handful of these unbelievable companies where management is completely on side with you. There's no dilution factors, and there's no guy skimming 10% here and there. But you have to go out of your way to find those companies. There's not that many of them. It's nice to know that when you invest in those stocks, you're 100% aligned with the owners and management.

I'm curious; what do you when you invest in a stock but then it reverses, say –20%?

BILL: That's what recently happened to Timber Creek. Once it drops, you can add to it once, from a disciplined point of view. You've got to make sure that it is going the right way in the long run. You should draw a line under the price, and say, "We'll give it *this* much time at *this* price." You have to be very vigilant. Are you confident enough that you'd buy the whole company today at *this* price? Can you own it for 30 years? Is this that good of a business? Anyway, if the fundamentals start going wrong, the nice thing about public markets is that you have the advantage to sell a bad investment.

What about when the income trust taxation structure was overhauled in 2006 and those income trusts subsequently reversed course?

BILL: That was our best day.

PAUL HARRIS: That was our best day ever.

Really?

PAUL GARDNER: We never were in love with the income trust market. We had a couple here and there, but as time ticked by we saw the writing on the wall. Even publicly we said, "The income trust market's going to be yanked." The government put a halt to income trusts as soon as Bell started turning itself into an income trust.

BILL: Management was going to chop Bell into five pieces, and Royal Bank of Canada into four pieces. That's a nice idea for pensions but you can't run an economy with little bits.

PAUL HARRIS: We saw the writing on the wall. We went all dividend payers and no income trusts.

It seems that income trusts were simply vehicles that spit out monthly distributions, rather than companies that reinvested earnings for growth.

BILL: Yeah.

PAUL GARDNER: And that made sense for pipelines, real estate, and for very stable businesses. But they moved the line; that's the trouble with investment bankers. They moved the line away from stable businesses. For example, they spun Yellow Pages into an income trust.

BILL: At that time, there was a big income trust investor in Canada. All he ran was "trust of trusts." His head was just beet-red when the government folded income trusts. Paul went on BNN the next morning, and they asked him, "What do you think of this?" Paul replied, "It's the right thing to do." Anyway, that big income trust investor's business was destroyed.

A trust of trusts?

PAUL: It was a terrible thing; a lot of people got hurt. There are very naïve investors out there, and they got it bad. Even today we see a lot of fixed-income "fund of funds." The only fixed income in my opinion is bonds. That's the only type of fixed income.

Income trusts were too good to be true then. Those huge monthly distributions couldn't last forever.

PAU GARDNER: No.

Anything else to add?

BILL: I do. How many managers do you think have a 10-year record in the mutual fund industry?

Probably only 5%.

BILL: Only 200 out of 3,000 have a 10-year record, based on a CFA study. We've been running this business for 12 years. I went into this because the investment business is what drives me. We've all committed to managing money at least until we're 65. Maybe if we still have our wits about us, we can keep going a little longer. Anyways, the point of the article was that the 200 guys with a 10-year record stayed in the business, not because they beat market, but because they just didn't blow up. So how you win in the stock market is by not blowing up; that's the point. Make sure you never blow up on anything, and just be as consistent as possible.

Also, you have to start with a strategy. People get all excited about their investments and get to a point where they don't know why they are investing anymore. So your real work is to come up with a very tight strategy, then stick to it. And you can be wrong. Actually, you're going to be wrong sometimes. That's the humbling part about this business. If you're a relatively smart person, then how are you going to deal with being wrong most of the time? It all comes back to the strategy. What we've found is that the smart people in this industry, because it attracts a lot of them, do really poorly. They'd be great investment bankers, forcing people to do things they don't want to do, but that doesn't mean that they'd be good at compounding money. I consider myself to be of average intelligence, but have a strategy that I stick to that keeps me balanced. The smartest guy in the room is not the guy who makes the most money. The smartest guy is the one who is just super consistent, has a strategy, sticks to it, and is humble enough to say, "I got that wrong," but then actually adjusts to it. That's how we work together. If you think that you're super smart, the stock market is not a good place for you.

PAUL GARDNER: The one thing you must accept is that the world doesn't end tomorrow. Funny enough, the human race keeps on adapting, and that's why we're at the top of the evolutionary scale, because we kept reacting and changing. If you look at '08 and '09 you would have thought that the world ended, but moments later, it was the bottom of the market. So you can't go to that extreme; you can't be in-out, in-out of the market. What would Warren Buffett do in this situation? Because he's the only one who from 1952 to 2015 actually compounded his money consistently while always being in the market.

BILL: Still around 18% annual compound rate.

PAUL HARRIS: Yeah. He never assumed that the world was going to end. He didn't say, "I'm in" then "I'm out" the next day. He just says, "I do know that Coca-Cola's going to be around."

BILL: Peter Lynch said to just spend two minutes on economics a year and then get on with your life. You really don't need to know much more than that. The stock market and the economy are not correlated. They're not. Your portfolio might act completely differently to what's going on in the economy. If the economy was growing at 5%, what would happen? The central bank would increase interest rates, and the stock market would go down. So the last thing we want is the economy to do well from a stock market point of view. We love this 2% growth economy because rates and wages don't go up.

Debt is cheap and labour is cheap. The cost base is extremely low for companies now.

PAUL GARDNER: This is the best time to be investing.

BILL: Ever.

PAUL HARRIS: Ever.

BILL: They're the highest markets ever in history.

PAUL: So you have labour all over the place. You have no trade barriers anymore. You have low interest rates. You have a fluid capital market. You have global growth; albeit not the greatest, but it's not supposed to feel that great. It's probably the best time ever to invest. Also, don't grab onto any conspiracy theories. It just doesn't work in today's society. No one's that smart to coordinate central planning and, for example, buy U.S. treasuries to cover the fact that they're hiding all this debt. The market's pretty efficient. Also, stop acting like a stockholder and start thinking like you're the owner of a company. I'm sure you get that repeated a lot, but it's an important mentality. If you owned a thriving company, you wouldn't buy it and then sell it the next day based on short-term market prices. When you own shares in a company, you're technically an owner of that company.

BILL: Yeah. For example, Royal Bank of Canada — I don't care where it goes for 10 years. Because I've got a $75 stock with a $3 dividend, times 10 years, that's $30 worth of dividends. Additionally, RBC's going to be worth more than that in 10 years with capital appreciation. You need to isolate everything else. If China has a financial disruption, that's bad for everybody. Everything goes down 50% in a day, but that doesn't change whether you continue to shop at Loblaws.

There's always tail risk in the market.

BILL: Yeah, as far as you can predict them. We have a 20% insurance policy inside the portfolio at any one time. So it's always a drag on performance, but then we have the ability to react at whatever that black swan event is, because we're going to get impacted by events in different markets at different times.

Is that insurance policy through buying puts?

BILL: No, it's just a cash system.

PAUL: That's cash and it's bonds. It's not a fair one-to-one relationship, but if I own bonds and stocks collapse by 40%, the bonds will, say, go down by 10%, and that's a cushion because I can always sell the bonds and buy something else really cheap. We don't give up that much by being 20% bonds and cash because those high-yield components give us income while we're sitting there.

BILL: In institutions, you're allowed between 1% and 2% cash. If you go more cash than that, you have to explain yourself *[all laugh]*.

It's true: Paul, Paul, and Bill have lots to be happy about. Avenue Asset Management recently achieved top equity portfolio rankings in a survey of 88 Canadian investment firms. This has helped spur their growth in assets under management, which has ballooned to $350 million. Avenue Asset Management has been ranked by Pavilion Advisory Group as:

TOP 3% — Higher Returns (Annualized Return)

TOP 4% — Lower Volatility (Standard Deviation)

TOP 4% — Higher Risk-Adjusted Returns (Sharpe Ratio)

TOP 4% — Value Added from Active Management (Information Ratio)

TOP 4% — Relative Performance to Passive Strategy (Jensen's Alpha)

TOP 1% — More Up Quarters and Fewer Down Quarters (Annualized Return)

1st Quartile Manager over 1 yr., 2 yr., 3 yr., 4 yr., 5 yr., 7 yr., 8 yr. (Annualized Return Periods)

Obviously, those results came as no surprise to me. More so than the other Market Masters, Paul, Paul, and Bill instilled in me the importance of risk management in my portfolio. Bill Harris said it best: "We're trying to win by not losing." The following from their website is additional insight from the Three Amigos on the virtues of risk management.

LOWER RISK EQUITIES = MORE RELIABLE RETURNS OVER TIME.

HOW DO WE LOWER RISK?

We start by focusing our research on quality companies or assets. The businesses we invest in need to be profitable, consistent, and well run, with a conservative level of debt. However, there are occasionally special situations where we find undervalued assets or businesses that are in the process of being fixed up.

DON'T OVERPAY FOR THE INVESTMENT

We have a disciplined approach to valuation. When we find a quality investment and it isn't trading at a fair price, we simply don't buy it. At Avenue, investing is about patience and knowing that a successful investment starts with buying it at a fair price.

BUILD IN A MARGIN OF SAFETY

A margin of safety is built-in insurance against uncertainty in the market, at every level of the investment process. We run our own in-depth analyses and research to keep you safe.

MANUAL STOP-LOSS

If any investment falls by 20%, our discipline requires us to conduct a full review of the fundamentals of the business and decide whether to keep or exit the investment.

Also, be sure to check out Avenue Investment Management's fund letters. With every quarterly performance letter, Paul, Paul, and Bill include a market or company case study, which I found were all very insightful. The more you learn, the more you earn.

It was mentioned during our interview that family-owned companies are top candidates for the Three Amigos' portfolios. The University of St. Gallen's Center for Family Business in Switzerland conducts an annual study, the Global Family Business Index, that ranks the world's five hundred largest family-controlled firms by revenue. The study concluded that "of the world's five hundred biggest family-owned or -controlled firms, 20 are Canadian."

CANADA RANK	GLOBAL RANK	COMPANY	FAMILY
1	37	GEORGE WESTON LTD.	WESTON FAMILY
2	43	POWER CORP. OF CANADA	DEMARAIS FAMILY
3	54	HUSKY ENERGY	LI FAMILY
4	66	EMPIRE CO. LTD.	SOBEY FAMILY
5	74	BOMBARDIER INC.	BOMBARDIER FAMILY
6	114	THOMSON REUTERS	THOMSON FAMILY
7	118	ROGERS COMMUNICATIONS INC.	ROGERS FAMILY
8	125	CANADIAN TIRE CORP.	BILLES FAMILY
9	169	SAPUTO INC.	SAPUTO FAMILY
10	207	JIM PATTISON GROUP INC.	PATTISON FAMILY
11	259	MCCAIN FOODS GROUP INC.	MCCAIN FAMILY
12	269	KRUGER INC.	KRUGER FAMILY
13	272	SHAW COMMUNICATIONS INC.	SHAW FAMILY
14	308	JAMES RICHARDSON & SONS LTD.	RICHARDSON FAMILY
15	309	ATCO LTD.	SOUTHERN FAMILY
16	322	QUEBECOR INC.	PÉLADEAU FAMILY
17	353	CASCADES INC.	LEMAIRE FAMILY
18	371	SAMUEL, SON & CO. LTD.	SAMUEL FAMILY
19	475	THE JEAN COUTU GROUP INC.	COUTU FAMILY
20	491	ELLISDON HOLDINGS INC.	SMITH FAMILY

Source: Global Family Business Index. Center for Family Business, University of St. Gallen, Switzerland. 2015.

1) "Part of our success is having all of the stars aligned. If we were all equity heads, it would be hard to succeed because we'd have to look at different investment frames."

2) "One of our critical advantages is that we understand the capital structure of any company. What happens with any company is that if they get the capital structure wrong, then their debt overwhelms their business and that's when they can go into bankruptcy."

3) "Once you're in the bond world, you can achieve a 10% to 12% rate of return. All you need to determine is whether a company is going to go bankrupt. That's all. The upside is very easy."

4) "We just win by not losing. That's how we survived the financial crisis."

5) "Picture the TSX as a pie. The trick is to determine the most consistent companies in the TSX. We don't own things that don't make money."

6) "Really good companies don't change that much over time. [We] identify historically great companies, with great numbers, that we can we buy at a decent price."

7) "If we need to have some exposure to a sector, then we try to find the best in class and just immunize our risk."

8) "If you try to compound consistently at 10% or 12%, you will end up hitting air pockets. The problem is that you take up more risk and thus increased probability that you get no return."

9) "We have a 30-year time horizon. You can double your money, then double it again, and double that again. But you need to give yourself the highest probability that it actually happens."

10) "We know we're going to make mistakes, so let's just leave it at that. . . . If we make a mistake, we can sell."

11) "If you buy a bond at a discount, there's an end to the story. It's called par. Conversely, stocks are indefinite. They can stay there forever. A bond has to have an end. You should know your rate of return, and then at the end of the game you end up at maturity."

12) "We generally tend to overperform on the downside and underperform on the upside. During market collapses, we go out and find these special situation bonds that can go up and can crush the volatility."

13) "We don't care about the index. What we care about is getting you this rate of return between 8% and 10% with the least amount of risk."

14) "[Generally], balance sheets need to be conservatively financed. Companies should be in profitable markets. Managements need to actually be good at what they do."

15) "You need 8% to 12% free cash flow yield, and you can get that if you're super patient."

16) "You want to invest in companies that can either maintain the rate of return or enhance their rate of return when they reinvest their earnings. However, be cognizant of companies that enhance their rates of return through acquisition strategies or financial engineering."

17) "Bad people and bad managers keep doing bad things. Good people and good managers generally keep doing good things. It's a very simple concept."

18) "You should draw a line under the price, and say, 'We'll give it *this* much time at *this* price.' You have to be very vigilant. If the fundamentals start going wrong, the nice thing about public markets is that you have the advantage to sell a bad investment."

19) "People get all excited about their investments and get to a point where they don't know why they are investing anymore. So your real work is to come up with a very tight strategy, then stick to it."

20) "The one thing you must accept is that the world doesn't end tomorrow. If you look at '08 and '09 you would have thought that the world ended, but moments later, it was the bottom of the market."

21) "The stock market and the economy are not correlated. They're not. Your portfolio might act completely differently to what's going on in the economy."

22) "If you owned a thriving company, you wouldn't buy it and then sell it the next day based on short-term market prices. When you own shares in a company, you're technically an owner of that company."

23) "We have a 20% insurance policy [i.e., cash] inside the portfolio at any one time. So it's always a drag on performance, but then we have the ability to react at whatever that black swan event is, because we're going to get impacted by events in different markets at different times."

24) "It's nice to know that when you invest in those stocks [companies with an ownership stake] you're 100% aligned with the owners and management."

KIKI DELANEY
THE TRAILBLAZER

I was referred to Kiki Delaney through someone I met after my interview with Gaelen Morphet. "Alex, come meet Robin," said Gaelen to an employee passing by our interview room at the Empire Life offices. "Alex is one of the brightest stars at the firm." Alex, a relatively junior employee, glowed at the praise. After all, Gaelen is a senior executive. Alex is around the same age as me and we found that we shared the same perspective on the market. So, we decided to meet some weeks later for coffee at Aroma Café in downtown Toronto.

Alex was excited to hear about this book. After reading my list of Market Masters to him I asked Alex, "Am I missing anyone?" to which he said, "Yeah," and offered a couple of names. Upon further research there on my smartphone, one individual he had mentioned resonated with me: Kiki Delaney. How had I missed Catherine "Kiki" Delaney? Her firm, Delaney Capital Management, boasts $2 billion in assets under management, with a track record that spans more than 20 years. So, my next email, which I hammered out as soon as my meeting with Alex ended, was a direct request to Kiki: "Would you like to be featured in *Market*

Masters? It would be an honour to have you be a part of the project." I was delighted, and grateful to her and to Alex, when Kiki said yes.

In the meeting room for our interview, a statue of a defiant bull stood tall over a defensive bear. That statue was especially appropriate since negative news seemed to be hitting the global markets on a daily basis in the first half of 2015 — Greece, China, Oil, the Fed, and so on. I stared at that statue and thought, "Will the bull be too weak to continue to assert its market dominance? Will the bull market finally succumb to the tail risks?" I would soon get reassurance from Kiki that those factors should not matter, that investors must continually find value in the market regardless of whether the bull or the bear reigns supreme.

An important concept that Kiki conveyed is to invest in relative value. For example, while the broader market, industry, or peer group can be overvalued, a particular stock within any of those domains can still be fairly valued or undervalued. Sometimes, the market and stocks within that market are mutually exclusive, in that returns of the market are not always perfectly correlated with all of its constituents. For instance, today, while the broader market can be down, some of your stocks may in fact be up. And that inverse correlation, among other factors, could be because those stocks were relatively cheaper than the broader market at the time, and did not join the market sell-off. Separately, Kiki shares her opinion on which is the more challenging asset class to manage in a portfolio: equity (stocks) or debt (bonds).

Kiki succeeded early on in an industry that was even more male-dominated than it is now. As a young adult, she moved to Toronto, where there were more opportunities, not just for women, but in general in the job market. Kiki got her start at Merrill Lynch before moving to Guardian Capital, where she managed equity and fixed-income portfolios. Prior to founding Delaney Capital Management (DCM), Kiki was a partner, executive vice-president, and portfolio manager at Gluskin Sheff + Associates. Interestingly, Martin Braun, whom I also interviewed, filled Kiki's role as Canadian equity manager at Gluskin Sheff.

With the success of DCM, Kiki became one of the most powerful women on Bay Street. In addition to DCM, Kiki is chancellor of OCAD University, a member of the board of trustees for the Hospital for

Sick Children, chair of the investment and pension committee at the Hospital for Sick Children, and a member of the Leadership Council of the Perimeter Institute for Theoretical Physics. And she was appointed a member of the Order of Canada in 2006. The Governor General of Canada wrote this of her: "After a steady rise through major investment houses, she launched her own investment counselling firm, one of the first women in Canada to do so." Kiki Delaney is a trailblazer.

PRE-INTERVIEW LESSONS

BOTTOM-UP: a style of investing where an investor starts his or her selection process by analyzing individual companies, e.g., by their financial statements. The opposite would be a top-down style.

BUY-BACK: when a company buys its own shares to then terminate / cancel them. This action reduces the number of common shares outstanding.

CRITERIA: the collective standards that investors apply to their stock selection decisions. For example, a criterion might be an ROA (return on assets ratio) greater or equal to 10%.

OUT OF FAVOUR: assets that have lost support or are currently experiencing lack of support from the investment community. This usually happens after a bear market (e.g., commodities are out of favour in 2015).

You were born in Winnipeg. Why did you move to Toronto?

When I graduated from university there were almost no women in the investment business other than in administrative roles. This was the early 1970s. The opportunities in Winnipeg were quite limited. They were not great in Toronto either. But I got a job as a research assistant in Toronto.

How did you first get interested in the markets?

My father was in the investment business. He was a currency trader in Holland prior to the war, and moved to New York and then Winnipeg to start his own brokerage firm. So I basically grew up immersed in the market. It's interesting though because neither of my two brothers went into the investment business. I literally grew up on it.

The markets must have been talked about at the dinner table.

My dad had his own business so he lived and breathed the stock market. His success or failure was all related to the market and his business. I always joke that I could probably go back to when I was six years old and know what markets were doing just by recalling his mood and the conversation.

Can you elaborate on your first job as a research analyst?

I worked for MGF Management, a mutual fund company that was taken over by Guardian Capital Group about six months after I joined. So I worked at Guardian for 13 years, first as an analytical assistant, then an analyst, and finally as a portfolio manager.

From Guardian Capital you transitioned to Gluskin Sheff, became a partner there, and then founded Delaney Capital Management in 1992. What were some of the best calls you've made over your storied career?

Some of the best calls I have made involve avoiding disasters. For instance, we did not have a position in Nortel. We also avoided the Bre-X catastrophe. Bre-X was a major scandal. We had a lot of pressure to own both of those securities, but Bre-X didn't pass the "smell test," and Nortel, in our opinion, was way too expensive. So we avoided both of them. When I look back at our performance after the tech bubble of the late 1990s, our performance was greatly enhanced by avoiding the Nortel demise.

Bre-X is very much the same story as the more recent Sino Forest blow-up. There's a connection.

A connection in that it was fraud.

Exactly. But how can investors avoid blow-ups? Can you describe the "smell test"?

It's really tough. Both companies' assets were in faraway jurisdictions where the rule of law is not a factor. It was difficult to validate the legitimacy of their assets. In the end, both "stories" lacked credibility. They did not pass the smell test.

You've managed both fixed-income and equity portfolios. What's the more challenging asset class to manage?

I would say fixed-income.

Why?

It is easier to pick great companies than to make the macro calls required to manage fixed-income portfolios.

What have been your biggest wins?

Our biggest win is Constellation Software, which is up 25 times.

What was your reason for buying Constellation Software?

It was inexpensive. We bought it when it went public. It is a software company that operates in mission critical verticals. Plus, they had good growth prospects, largely through acquisitions. It has surpassed any of our expectations. The chief executive officer has done a brilliant job and has made fantastic acquisitions. Another strong performer has been Alimentation Couche-Tard which is up about 10 times from our original purchase. Also, CNR was bought when it went public in the mid-1990s and we have continued to hold it. More recently, we bought Concordia Healthcare when it went public.

Can you describe your investment process that leads to these big winners?

We are bottom-up investors. We are very company-specific and we are value investors. When we look at a company we compare it to others in the same industry and buy the company that is statistically the cheapest. We want companies that are cheap, but also are well managed, have a strong growth profile, have a good product, and where there is the catalyst for change to unlock value. One of the problems with being a value investor is that it is very easy to fall into a value trap where you buy a stock that is statistically cheap and it

remains inexpensive for a long time. To counter that, we look for catalysts for change.

What are those catalysts?

Catalysts can vary. It can be an outlook for a commodity. For example,
the price of oil has fallen by over 50%. If you believe that it is going to
move up substantially from these levels then that might be a catalyst.
A catalyst can also be a management change, a new product, an acquisition, or a de-leveraging of the balance sheet. There are all kinds of
potential catalysts for change.

You mention that you're a value investor but your biggest winners were
bought at or near their market debuts. Wouldn't those be described as
speculative growth stocks?

We want to get in early. But we look at both the company's valuation
and its growth rate.

How can regular investors get in early?

It's not all that easy to do that. You have to read broadly and follow
the flow of new issues. It is difficult for someone with a day job to try
to find these gems.

So an investor may be able to find gems by constantly monitoring IPOs.
Let's go back to value — I've heard that you seek "relative value." Can you
explain that concept?

Relative value could mean relative to its peers or relative to its historical pricing. That's generally what we mean. Or it could be relative to
the growth rate.

You've also said that you rarely buy the darling in any industry. Instead,
you focus on out-of-favour companies or industries. How do you define "out
of favour"?

Well, let me back up. Let's go back to the late 1990s and the massive
decline in the NASDAQ. We didn't buy technology stocks because we
couldn't rationalize the pricing in that sector. But after that massive
decline, valuations were more appealing to us. At that time, not only
did we buy technology stocks, but also the darlings in the industry. It's
really a matter of pricing.

What were some of the darlings that you bought when the NASDAQ
crashed in 2000?

Cognos, which was later bought by IBM. When we bought Cognos, it was very attractively priced. The problem with being a value investor is that growth companies are often just too expensive.

But in talking to some of the other investors, I've found that they've come to accept the probability that for the most part, 40 to 60% of their stocks will be winners, and the rest will be losers. Why discriminate?

I am not sure about those numbers, but certainly every investor has his or her share of losers.

When you spot an out-of-favour industry, would you just pick one darling stock, or would you pick a handful of stocks?

It really depends. If the industry fundamentals are strong and the valuations are appealing, then it makes sense to buy more than one company in the sector.

Do you ever take positions in ETFs then that cover entire out-of-favour industries?

Not often. We will buy ETFs for very small accounts and over the short term will buy them to offset a tax loss.

You only invest in North American equities, but you focus on companies that are globally positioned. Why would you invest indirectly rather than directly in global growth?

We do fundamental research in house. Our portfolio managers and analysts spend the bulk of their time reading all the materials available on a company, researching the competition, creating spreadsheets, and meeting with management teams. Our style is very research-driven. We have seven people in our investment department. It is hard to cover the global universe with seven people. We decided early on to focus on North America and when we want global exposure we look at Canadian and U.S. companies that have that exposure.

Which global markets do you want exposure to through the North American equities?

Europe. The economies in Europe appear to be improving because of the weak euro and falling oil prices. Companies like CGI, Alimentation Couche-Tard, or WSP all have strong exposure to Europe.

WSP Global, the infrastructure firm?

Yes. Excellent company. And it, too, has very big exposure there.

Is it more challenging to find and invest in multinational Canadian companies?

No. Actually, that's an interesting question. A lot of people look at the Canadian market and say, "I don't like the Canadian market. It's resource-oriented. Also, I don't like the Canadian dollar, so I'm going to go somewhere else." The reality is that the Canadian market is two-sided. You have on the one hand resource names, and then on the other hand, you have everything else. So the resource companies today might make up 30% of the Canadian market, but there's also a lot of world-class international companies. Funnily, a lot of them reside in Quebec.

I've noticed that, too — Quebec is full of well-run, shareholder-friendly international companies.

I know; it's really quite interesting. When you look at CGI, Alimentation Couche-Tard, and WSP Global, that is certainly the case.

What's your theory as to why that is?

I don't know. Though I do think that Quebec companies get positive reinforcement. In many cases, the Caisse de dépôt takes a fairly substantial position in underwriting companies to help them expand through very large acquisitions. I think that's helpful. It is absolutely correct that there are some fantastic companies based in Quebec that are very international in scope. But beyond that I'm not sure.

Do you also look at whether a founder or CEO has a stake in their business?

I think it's really important. Not stocks options, though.

What about stock buy-backs? It seems that stocks accelerate in this market as soon as buy-backs are announced.

I'm not a huge fan. I think companies should buy their stock back when it is fundamentally cheap. Not every month, or every year. I find it troubling that companies have nothing better to do with their cash. Many investors prefer dividends. I have a constant running argument with one of my partners on this topic. He is a big fan of buy-backs, but I prefer dividends.

What's your partner's argument for stock buy-backs?

It positively impacts earnings per share.

I see that you also invest in both small-cap and mid-cap companies; what's the percentage allocation across both segments?

It varies. It varies according to our view of the market and the opportunities available in the small- and mid-cap market. It would typically be 5 to 10% of the portfolio. It could be larger. Our philosophy is to invest initially no more than 1% in a small-cap company. If it works, it's probably *really* going to work, and it'll be very beneficial. But if it doesn't work, it will hurt the portfolio to the extent of its 1% exposure.

Do you employ different investment criteria in small-cap or mid-cap stocks than you would in a large-cap stock?

I would like there to be greater growth potential to offset the increased risk.

But primarily your philosophy is to be a long-term investor rather than a short-term trader.

That's correct.

What's your holding period?

Our typical holding period is about four years, though there are many positions in the portfolios that have been owned for a much longer period of time. We want to buy a company that is fundamentally undervalued with significant potential for capital growth. As long as a company continues to represent good value and has decent capital gain potential, we will continue to hold it.

What's your opinion on investing based on themes?

We believe that if you can find a relatively undiscovered theme and marry it with a well-managed and undervalued company, you will probably have a winning combination. The problem is that it is hard to find undiscovered themes.

What are some of those undiscovered themes?

Commodity stocks.

Because it's a scarce resource?

Yes. Another theme that has been very successful recently is companies that make significant and highly accretive acquisitions. This has worked really well in a low-interest environment.

But when rates do eventually go up and debt becomes more expensive, do you think that acquisitive companies will fade?

I think it will depend on how expensive the companies are and whether or not they are accretive. If you buy something cheap enough, it may still be accretive.

Speaking of debt, what criteria do you use to invest in corporate bonds?

We invest in triple-B or better. We invest in bonds with a term of 10 years or less in order to avoid the volatility inherent in longer-term bonds.

Do you apply equity-centric criteria to corporate bonds, such as whether the company generates sufficient cash flow to service debt payments?

For the most part we buy corporate bonds as opposed to provincial bonds. So clearly you have to do a credit analysis.

Do you think that there's an inverse correlation between debt yield and the equity market? Such that when bond yields are low, the stock market's higher, and when yields are high, the stock market's lower? Essentially, the opportunity cost that's been priced into both asset classes.

Declining interest rates are positive. Once interest rates start to go up, they do hit a point where they shut off the economy and that clearly is not good for the stock market.

Some would argue that we'll face a significant correction once rates do start to go up.

Well, the question is how much will interest rates go up? I believe we are in a prolonged period of slow growth. As a result, we do not see a major uptick in interest rates.

What's your advice for investors?

You have to read as much as you can. And you have to be as informed as you can be. My son, who is in the real estate business, has read more books on the stock market than most people I know. And he has become incredibly well informed through that process. That's what you want to do. You don't want to buy cocktail tips. It doesn't work.

And in this information age, everything is at your fingertips.

Today, there is the opportunity to access all kinds of information. If you look back 30 years ago, this kind of information was not readily available.

What resources did you use back then to access information?

I don't want to sound like a complete dinosaur, but when I started out, if you wanted to invest in a company, you would call the company. And they would put the annual report in the mail. A week later it would arrive. It is amazing to think about it. Today, if you want an annual report you either go to a company website or you go to SEDAR and instantly you have the report.

Has that made markets more efficient? Information is readily available to the masses.

No. I don't think so.

You don't believe in the Efficient Market Theory?

It is hard to be a stock-picker and believe in the Efficient Market Theory.

But within the 20-plus years that you've run the firm, have there been periods where it's much easier to find value in the market?

Sure.

Can you elaborate?

Well, it's more difficult to find value today. But that's talking about absolute value. Certainly, when you look at companies on the S&P 500 or TSX today, and you look at their valuations, they are higher than they've been for a number of years. But then interest rates are lower. So I don't believe you can just look at these valuations in a vacuum. Though it's wonderful to look backwards. Obviously, in 2009 there were great opportunities because so many companies had been beaten up.

What about in 1987?

I was a portfolio manager at Gluskin Sheff. It was unbelievable to watch.

What was it like in the office then? How did people react?

Stunned would be the response. Because nobody had seen anything like that.

Was there selling going on or was that crash seen as a buying opportunity?

The decline was so fast. It is hard to imagine within a short time that you had one of the great buying opportunities all time.

Through the market's ups and downs, you've built DCM into a firm with $2 billion in assets under management. How did you do that? What were the key principles for its success?

I wanted to create an environment where clients are treated with the utmost respect and where employees really want to come to work.

Who makes a good research analyst?

People with drive, passion, and curiosity.

Kiki mentioned that there's something special about Quebec. The Caisse de dépôt et placement du Québec takes fairly substantial positions in the underwriting for Quebec companies' acquisitions in order to help them expand worldwide into new markets. I completely agree with Kiki's sentiment that "it is absolutely correct that there are some fantastic companies based in Quebec." Many of the most successful stocks in my portfolio, based on annual rates of returns, are Quebec-based companies: Alimentation Couche-Tard, Dollarama, Canadian National Railway, CGI, Lassonde Industries, and Savaria, to name just a few. What I find is that not only do Quebec-based companies benefit from the Caisse de dépôt's financial support in global expansion, but they also contain some of the best and most shareholder-friendly management teams in Canada. Below I've listed a segment of the publicly traded Quebec-based companies on the market. Interestingly, you'll find that these companies are incredibly well diversified, somewhat like the U.S.'s market.

COMPANY	SECTOR
5N PLUS INC.	BASIC MATERIALS
AIR CANADA	TRANSPORTATION
ALIMENTATION COUCHE-TARD INC.	SERVICES
AMAYA INC.	TECHNOLOGY
ASTRAL MEDIA INC.	SERVICES
BCE INC.	SERVICES
CAE INC.	TECHNOLOGY
CANADIAN NATIONAL RAILWAY COMPANY	TRANSPORTATION
CASCADES INC.	BASIC MATERIALS
CGI TECHNOLOGIES AND SOLUTIONS INC.	TECHNOLOGY
D-BOX TECHNOLOGIES INC.	CONSUMER CYCLICAL
DAVIDS TEA INC.	SERVICES
DOLLARAMA INC.	SERVICES
DOREL INDUSTRIES INC.	CONSUMER CYCLICAL
GDI INTEGRATED FACILITY SERVICES INC.	FINANCIAL
GILDAN ACTIVEWEAR INC.	CONSUMER CYCLICAL
GOODFELLOW INC.	CAPITAL GOODS
INTERTAPE POLYMER GROUP	BASIC MATERIALS

KNIGHT THERAPEUTICS INC.	SERVICES
LASSONDE INDUSTRIES INC.	CONSUMER NON-CYCLICAL
LAURENTIAN BANK OF CANADA	FINANCIAL
LE GROUPE JEAN COUTU PJC INC.	SERVICES
LOGISTEC CORPORATION	TRANSPORTATION
METRO INC.	SERVICES
MTY FOOD GROUP INC.	SERVICES
NEW LOOK VISION GROUP INC.	SERVICES
QUEBECOR INC.	SERVICES
RICHELIEU HARDWARE LTD.	CONSUMER NON-CYCLICAL
RONA INC.	SERVICES
SAPUTO INC.	CONSUMER NON-CYCLICAL
SAVARIA CORPORATION	CAPITAL GOODS
STELLA-JONES INC.	BASIC MATERIALS
STINGRAY DIGITAL GROUP INC.	CONSUMER CYCLICAL
SUPREMEX INC.	CONSUMER NON-CYCLICAL
TEMBEC INC.	BASIC MATERIALS
TRANSAT AT INC.	SERVICES
TRANSCONTINENTAL INC.	SERVICES
TRANSFORCE INC.	TRANSPORTATION
UNI-SELECT INC.	CONSUMER CYCLICAL
VALEANT PHARMACEUTICALS INTERNATIONAL INC.	HEALTH CARE
WSP GLOBAL INC.	CAPITAL GOODS

MASTER KEYS

KIKI DELANEY

1) "Some of the best calls I have made involve avoiding disasters."

2) "It is easier to pick great companies than to make the macro calls required to manage fixed-income portfolios."

3) "When we look at a company we compare it to others in the same industry and buy the company that is statistically the cheapest. . . . We want companies that are cheap but also are well managed, have a strong

growth profile, have a good product, and where there is the catalyst for change to unlock value."

4) "If the industry fundamentals are strong and the valuations are appealing, then it makes sense to buy more than one company in the sector."

5) "We look for catalysts for change . . . a catalyst can be a management change, a new product, an acquisition, or a de-leveraging of the balance sheet."

6) "The reality is that the Canadian market is two-sided. You have on the one hand resource names, and then on the other hand, you have everything else."

7) "[On the TSX] there's also a lot of world-class international companies. Funnily, a lot of them reside in Quebec . . . Quebec companies get positive reinforcement. In many cases, the Caisse de dépôt takes a fairly substantial position in underwriting companies to help them expand through very large acquisitions."

8) "I think companies should buy their stock back when it is fundamentally cheap. Not every month, or every year. I find it troubling that companies have nothing better to do with their cash."

9) "[We] invest initially no more than 1% in a small-cap company. If it works, it's probably really going to work, and it'll be very beneficial. But if it doesn't work, it will hurt the portfolio to the extent of its 1% exposure."

10) "As long as a company continues to represent good value and has decent capital gain potential, we will continue to hold it."

11) "If you can find a relatively undiscovered theme and marry it with a well-managed and undervalued company, you will probably have a winning combination . . . [for example] companies that make significant and highly accretive acquisitions. This has worked really well in a low-interest environment."

12) "Declining interest rates are positive. Once interest rates start to go up, they do hit a point where they shut off the economy and that clearly is not good for the stock market."

13) "You have to read as much as you can. And you have to be as informed as you can be. You don't want to buy cocktail tips. It doesn't work."

NORMAN LEVINE
THE OPPORTUNIST

Norman Levine has been around the block. Over his 39 years in the investment industry, he survived the inflationary era in the 1970s, Black Monday
in 1987, the technology boom and bust in 2000, the global financial crisis
in 2008, and the euro crisis in 2011. Up on Norman's office wall is an old
framed photo of a Bloomberg terminal screen that shows the carnage
that occurred on that Bloody Monday, where the Dow Jones Industrial
Average dropped 22.61% and the TSX dropped 11.32%. It was an angst-
filled, record-breaking day. By the end of October, the TSX had fallen further to post a 22.5% decline. I asked Norman how he reacted on Bloody
Monday and over the remainder of that October. His response should be
carefully studied, as there's no doubt that you will experience similar flash
crashes in your time as an investor.

It seems that an uncertain market is a profitable market for Norman.
You'll find through numerous examples in the interview — BCE,
European stocks, U.S. financials, CCL Industries — that he is an opportunist. Norman sees opportunity before it is obvious to the common
investor and captures not only the early leg up but then another string of
gains when institutions and retail investors pile into his holdings. Norman

swoops in like a hawk as soon as he sees some short-term negative event impact stocks or when he finds stocks that are overlooked and improperly priced. His experience also teaches us that simply buying mispriced stocks will not earn investment glory. One also needs to foresee and then anticipate a catalyst that will propel those stocks out of their low points or holding patterns. Norman is an expert at a challenging skill: finding opportunity.

Every time I see Norman, he's wearing a new suit with a coordinating tie or bow tie and cufflinks. His closet must be the size of my one-bedroom condo. Norman tells me, "It's important to dress well in this business. It really does make a difference." He sprinkles in some Yiddish when he explains that his "dad used to dress like a *shmatte*." I can't help but glance around his office; there's so much history packed within Norman's four walls, not to mention a mini putter machine on the floor, which most likely serves as a relaxing escape from a tough day in the market. I was drawn into Norman's storytelling as we spoke. Norman has that classic old-style swagger, combined with a hard gaze when he locks onto your eyes. Norman is a remarkable figure in the Canadian markets — it's hard to fathom that he was *fired* from his first job as a broker. It just goes to show that you never know what the future holds.

PRE-INTERVIEW LESSONS

BLUE-CHIP STOCKS: stocks that contain certain characteristics that denote stability: large size, long history, reliable products or services, dividend increases, solid reputation or brand perception, and so on. Blue-chip stocks can be concentrated in banks, utilities, and telecom. An example would be Bell Canada.

FUNDAMENTALS: figures such as assets, cash flow, and net income, usually derived from a company's financial statement and used by investors to determine the worth of a company.

OPPORTUNISTIC INVESTORS: investors who scan the market in search of opportunities that they can capitalize on. For example, an opportunist would be able to buy assets at cheaper prices after a 10% correction.

PROCESS: the set of customized ascending or descending steps that most investors follow to select investments for their portfolio.

SCUTTLEBUTT: the practice by which investors ask questions of company directors or any other sources to build their knowledge in that company. The term was popularized by Philip Fisher.

Where did you grow up in Canada?

Toronto.

How did you first get interested in the markets?

I first got interested in the markets when I was 13 years old. I'm Jewish and I had a bar mitzvah. Two uncles of mine gave me shares for my bar mitzvah present.

What were those shares?

One of them was a company called Columbia Cellulose, which was in B.C. It eventually got bought, many years later after many ups and downs, by a company with the acronym of BCRIC. Eventually I made money. The other company was called Wellington Financial, which was owned and run by a guy named Sinclair Stevens. Sinclair was a self-made financial whiz kid on Bay Street at the time, having built an investment empire allegedly worth $130 million. Anyway, the company had tons of controversy; it went bust.

You hung on to both?

I tendered the one to BCRIC, and the other one I hung on to until it went bust.

What early lessons did you learn from that bust experience?

Well, they're not the first stocks I ever bought for myself. The first stock I ever bought for myself was in high school — Crush International. Crush, as I'm sure you know, is a soft drink. Orange Crush. I sold it at the all-time high it ever had *[laughs]*.

This was the seventies?

I'm an old guy, so I was in high school. I graduated in '70 so it was probably in the late sixties.

Why did you invest in Crush International?

I was a consumer *[laughs]*, and I liked the product. It caught my attention.

Since then they've been gobbled up by Dr Pepper.

Well, Jimmy Pattison bought it, and then he sold it to Procter and Gamble. P&G sold it to Cadbury Schweppes, and then I think they spun it off within the Dr Pepper Snapple Group.

Would you buy into a soda pop company today?

[Laughs] I no longer drink soft drinks, but we own PepsiCo. However, we own it more for the snack food business than the beverage business.

There's some talk that PepsiCo will spin off parts of its business.

It's possible. There's arguments on both sides.

You obtained your BA from York University. Were you investing on the side?

I did. In Yorkdale Mall there used to be a brokerage firm, Dougherty Roadhouse, that had an office on the outside of the mall, facing the 401 highway. I dealt there for a while. And then I switched to Richardson Securities on Adelaide, and dealt with a broker there by the name of Peter Oliver. Peter Oliver is the Oliver and Bonacini Oliver. He was a retail broker then. He partnered with a guy named Morris Keston and they set up their commodities brokerage firm. You see, Morris was a meteorologist. They figured that they would be able to trade agricultural commodities based on weather forecasts.

Did that work out for Oliver?

He's in the restaurant business now [laughs].

[Laughs] Good story. Did you trade commodities?

I never traded commodities, but I became a licenced commodity broker.

There was a commodities boom in that period.

Yeah. Because there was inflation. Commodities do well in an inflationary environment.

Where did you land after York University?

After York I got my first job and that was as a retail broker.

Merrill Lynch?

Yes. My father happened to be talking to a cousin of mine, David Stalberg, who was a retail broker for Merrill Lynch in Detroit. He was at the time their biggest producing retail broker.

And you got the job?

David said, "Have him meet me; I can get him a job at Merrill Lynch." I drove down to Detroit and talked with him, and next thing I know I get a call from Merrill Lynch in Canada — back then it was called Merrill Lynch Royal Securities. They had bought Royal Securities. I was brought in for an interview and they offered me more than the other guys did to become a retail broker. I took political science and psychology in school. But I took the Canadian securities course while I was in university.

How was your experience at Merrill Lynch?

One, it was a true branch plant. The president was an American and it was all directed from the U.S. Two, I was 21 years old, and didn't know anybody or anything. Third, I got my licence in October of '73 just as the Six-Day War finished in Israel and the Arab oil embargo raged on. The markets only went down every day. A big day of volume in Toronto was half a million shares. A big day in New York was five million shares. There were no options markets that you could trade in Canada. Interest rates kept going up the whole time. And here I am, a kid, not knowing anybody or anything. It was impossible to do business.

Volatile environment.

Every day, I would ask myself, "Why call this client today when tomorrow it's going to be cheaper?"

You must have felt conflicted.

Yes. But the bottom line was, it was a disaster for me. I was not meant to be a retail broker. And I wasn't meant to be one in that situation. At Merrill Lynch they send you down to New York for a few months for their training program. They had a whole school there, they probably still do, where they teach you about markets and you have to pass various tests. But more time is spent on teaching you how to sell, which I learned was the case again when I worked at Nesbitt Burns. Brokers are salesmen. They're not investors. People think they are; they are not. They are salesmen that just happen to luck out and be in the investment business, which pays more than any other business. They could have been car salesmen, or shoe salesmen, or whatever. They happen to be in that business, though.

Did you eventually quit?

So I started with Merrill Lynch in May of '73 and in November I got my licence. The following August I was walked into the boss's office and he said, "You're not generating enough commissions, we can't carry you anymore." At the time, this was the end of the world.

You were young and full of optimism.

I was 22.

How did that shape you, and how quickly did you bounce back?

Well, I didn't know what I wanted to do and so I went on various interviews, but in the end I decided I should get an MBA. However, I discovered it was too late to get into Canadian universities in September
because I hadn't written the GMAT and it was too late to write it.
So I chose Syracuse University in the U.S., which, until I got there in
January of '75, I had no idea that it was in the snow belt *[laughs]*.

You were hoping to escape the Canadian winters?

Right. So I got my MBA there. I started looking for a job from Syracuse.
I wasn't interested in staying in the U.S., and they weren't recruiting
Canadians. And no Canadian companies were going to Syracuse to
recruit.

You were caught in the middle.

Yes, so I would send out letters and come home on weekends for a
few days or on spring break or whatever it was and do interviews.
One of the interviews I went to was in Oakville at Ford Canada. I
had an interview with the VP of finance there, a fellow by the name
of Hymie Schwartz, which is interesting on its own because, in my
opinion, Henry Ford was a huge anti-Semite.

Did you get the job?

I show up at the interview, and Hymie's got his feet up on his desk and
he's reading *Barron's*. He puts it down, and he says, "I see you used to
be in the investment business." I go, "Yeah." He responds, "It's in your
blood, that's not going to change, you don't want a job here, let's go
have lunch" *[laughs]*. And he was right.

Straight-up guy. He knew your passion was in the investment business.

Right. But retail brokerage wasn't it. I didn't know the world of finance
and investing then. So I started sending out resumés to financial firms.
And I ended up getting hired by Crown Life Insurance, which no
longer exists in that form. It got bought eventually by Canada Life,
which then got bought by London Life, which then got bought by
Great-West Life. Anyway, I got hired in May of '76 in the investment
department at Crown Life. The fellow who hired me was a fellow by
the name of J.J. Woolverton, who's an officer at Guardian Capital now.
He still hasn't retired yet. He hired me because of Syracuse. "I'm an

American from upstate New York, and I went to Syracuse, too." That was a research job in their investment department covering Canadian and U.S. stocks. So that was my first job on the buy side: my first *real* investment job.

You loathed the sales side. So you must have been very happy to get that new job.

And I really want you to talk about that in your book because most investors don't understand that. Investment counsellors have a fiduciary duty. Brokers do not. We have to put clients into what's best for them. Brokers only have to put them into what's called "suitable" investments for them. Not best for them, but best for the broker. And brokers are no longer given much training in selecting individual securities. The huge push is to put clients into fee-based accounts and let somebody else manage it. They are salesmen, collectors of assets. Most people do not understand that. I told you, brokers are salesmen who happen to be in the investment business. Investment counsellors, such as us, are investors who'd rather not have to go out and sell and meet with clients and all that. But we have to eat.

Which stocks did you cover at Crown Life?

I covered the Hudson's Bay Company. It was an independent company at the time. It was one of the stocks I had recommended and that we eventually bought and owned. There ended up being a takeover battle for it between the Weston family and the Thomson family.

Did you foresee its takeover potential before recommending the Bay?

Oh hell no. We bought it just because we liked the fundamentals. There was no such thing back then as the internet or cross-border shopping or any of that stuff.

How did you research companies at that time?

It used to be really different back then. It was much more difficult. You had to pore through books and annual reports. You had to do real reports *[laughs]*. Now, you can fake it out there. The *Financial Post* used to put out a book on common stocks. They still do it on bonds and preferred shares, though.

Which criteria did you use to analyze the Bay's fundamentals?

I can't recall. The interesting thing is that there ended up being a takeover fight for it, and in the end the Thomson family won. We thought that was a big win until my big boss John Burton, who was the treasurer of the company, took credit at the board level. That just pissed me off.

Rightfully so; it was your recommendation.

Yeah. So that was one interesting thing that went on there. Another interesting thing was that I had my first brush with the Securities and Exchange Commission back then. One of the stocks we owned was a company called Babcock and Wilcox, which made boilers for buildings, among other things. There ended up being a takeover battle for that company, too, between United Technologies and a company called J. Ray McDermott.

Who won that takeover battle?

At the time, United Technologies was run by this guy, Harry Gray, who had a big personality. The other company, J. Ray McDermott, was based in New Orleans, and was more an oil service type company. At one time Harry Gray called me to try to get us to tender our shares to them, which I thought was pretty neat. At around the same time, the management of J. Ray McDermott came up to Toronto and had a meeting at what's now the Hilton. It used to be called the Hotel Toronto back then. In that meeting, the president of J. Ray McDermott said stuff about the takeover that was pretty confidential. He shouldn't have disclosed any of it. One day later we got a phone call from the SEC wanting to find out what exactly the president of J. Ray McDermott disclosed in that meeting. We weren't guilty of anything, though. I was just there, but of course had to get the company's lawyers involved. It was scary — I was a kid. But that was my first and only brush with the SEC.

And the winner?

In the end, J. Ray McDermott bought Babcock and Wilcox.

Where did you go after Crown Life?

Canada Trust. Running money at Canada Trust was a combination of Canada Trust money, pension fund money, estates, and trusts. It was a big bureaucracy. Every stock you bought had to be on an approved list. If you wanted to get in on the approved list there was red tape to do so. You could never be timely on something new.

That's unfortunate.

Yeah. And back then they would not allow us to own anything on NASDAQ. It was viewed as being too risky.

What was the market like in this point of history?

In the summer of '82, Henry Kaufman, who was the chief economist at Solomon Brothers at the time, made a pronouncement that interest rates had peaked and were coming down. Subsequently, the stock market took off, interest rates came down, and that was the beginning of a big bull market.

What was the actual sentiment back then, though? I recall the famous Businessweek article —

"Equities Are Dead." Or "The Death of Equities."

Exactly. So was that the common sentiment?

Business Week is known for having, or was known at the time for having, front-page headlines that were entirely poorly timed.

Do you invest against the crowd, against common sentiment?

We are, being value investors, somewhat contrarian. So, yes, we do that.

How long was the bull market that started in 1982?

It went straight up until '87. That's when we had the crash. But then it went straight up again until the tech boom and then the tech bust in 2000.

You must have naturally benefited from that bull market.

I was managing a small-cap pool pension fund. Pension funds would buy units in that fund. And the first year I ran it, it was the number one pension fund in Canada, performance-wise. I loved it. Small-cap stocks were a lot of fun to invest in.

Why small-caps?

In the Canadian market, they had been ignored, and there were great values in that space.

What were the multiples?

They were tiny. When I first got in the business, multiples were single-digit. Because interest rates were so high and there was this thing called the Rule of Nineteen or the Rule of Twenty. Inflation plus P/E multiples used to have to equal 20, or 19, whatever it was. Wall Street has this stuff all the time. It's way too simplistic but they fawn over it. So multiples were *really* low back then.

If you were investing in the ignored small-caps space, what were others investing in?

Everyone else was investing in large-caps.

What is your investing process?

Well, remember, back then we didn't have the internet, so I had to read a lot. You would read lots of brokerage reports, newspapers, and magazines to get your ideas. You'd have to meet with management. In small-cap stocks, meeting management is absolutely critical.

Is meeting management still critical today?

Even today it's critical.

Philip Fisher referred to that as "scuttlebutt."

Yes, in smaller companies, meeting management is critical. Especially entrepreneurial companies. And I learned to do facility tours, too. Go and see their physical plants. Because I had more than one instance where there was nothing there. It was a façade. Or, there was one company called Lumonics based up near Ottawa that had a huge multiple because it was a laser company. Anyway, I went up there to see them and some other companies for plant tours. Lumonics turned out to be a machine tool company that happened to use lasers in what they did. I couldn't sell that stock fast enough.

Was it easier to get an edge in the markets back then because information wasn't as readily available to the masses as it is today?

You had to find this stuff on your own. That's why going to see companies, talking to people, was much more important.

What do you think about the Efficient Market Theory?

That's what they teach you in school, but it's crap. The market is hugely inefficient.

How so?

If the markets were efficient, you wouldn't have the volatility. At all. There's emotions. I can't remember names of books, but I read many books on human behaviour and investing. It's so critical to understand how people think when they invest. They're not efficient at all.

How did you react during the mass crash in '87?

In '87, I was at an investment counselling firm called E.J. McConnell and Associates. In October of '87, on the day of the crash, I was in Montreal visiting one of our clients, a printers' union. I had lunch planned with one of the analysts, Marty Kaufman, who was the retail analyst at Nesbitt Thomson in Montreal. I met with the union but it was a very difficult meeting because you're aware that things were not okay. After that visit, I went across to Nesbitt Thomson's offices, and we watched the tape. We just had our jaws drop watching the tape. That's where I was that day, in Nesbitt Thomson's boardroom, watching that.

Did you exit positions the next day?

I went back to the office the next day, or that night, and obviously we had a meeting as to what's going on. One of the guys in our office said, "We have to sell everything we own because they're going to ratchet this market down." Thank goodness we didn't listen to him.

You would have realized all those losses if you'd listened to him.

Yes. So we didn't do that.

Was it a buying opportunity then?

It was a huge buying opportunity. But we didn't realize yet at the time that it was a huge buying opportunity. Unfortunately, the CEO panicked. We were specialists in Canadian and U.S. small- and mid-cap stocks. What happens when there's a major crash in the markets is that the interest in small- and mid-caps goes away. Anyway, the CEO panicked and said, "We have to shift our focus to large-caps, because small- and mid-caps are going nowhere when the recovery comes, but large-cap stocks will go somewhere." He was worried about not picking up performance. That was a huge mistake that ultimately ended up hurting the business a lot.

That's unfortunate. The small- and mid-cap stocks resumed their marvellous run. Do you invest in small-caps today?

No. That's not what our clients hire us for. We are for the most part mid- and large-caps. We do have some small-caps, but for the most part, no.

Small-caps can be extremely volatile. On the topic of volatility, you recently stated that the commodity super cycle has come to an end.

Yeah.

Why is that your conviction?

Commodity markets move in decade and even multi-decade cycles. Recently, there was a huge cycle that ended, but we're only about four years into commodities being out of favour. To me, it's far too early to buy into commodities again now. Nothing goes straight up and straight down in the market. You get these rallies and people get sucked into them. I would rather lose some opportunity on the way up than lose capital on the way down. So I would rather see commodities *stop* going down, probably tread water for a long time, or even form a V, and then buy them when they're starting to go up again. Also, commodity stocks are not value stocks. And they never will be.

They're not value stocks? Is that because their business is dictated by market prices?

Yeah. They are actually stocks that you would buy on momentum and off the charts as opposed to buy based on value. So they can be great value today, which will show up in 10 years, but I don't care. I've got lots of time to go back to them.

What is the makeup of the equities that you actually buy?

We're global in what we buy. We're value investors, and we tend to be contrarians. You know, this is not always, but we look to buy things that are out of favour that have good balance sheets. But, for whatever reason, they also happen to be out of favour because of some bad headlines, a temporary bad quarter or two, and so on.

Can you elaborate? What are your other criteria?

If it has lots of debt, we're not interested. We want good balance sheets. We want to be confident in management. We don't buy industries, and we don't buy countries; we buy stocks. And we look all over the world for them.

Where do you see the most value now?

The most value now is not in North America. The U.S. market's at an all-time high because of free money. Valuations are quite stretched. We hold U.S. stocks, but we can't find any new ones to buy now. Recently, we doubled our position in U.S. banks because we found that the financial sector is the only area that we find attractive in the U.S. right now.

I would imagine that the eventual increase in rates will boost revenues at U.S. banks. When U.S. market valuations are stretched, where in the world do you invest?

So in Canada, because our market at any given time is 70% to 75% resources, financials, and materials, it's hard to buy in Canada when resources are out of favour, especially when you find other countries' financials more attractive than yours. Canadian financials, especially the banks, were the best part to be in for like 10 years. But we don't think they are anymore. We only own one. We own one Canadian bank and we own two non-banks.

Which Canadian Bank?

We own Scotiabank, because it has the smallest footprint in Canada. Most of its assets relative to the other banks are outside of Canada in Central and South America and in Asia.

With Euro QE [quantitative easing] happening for the next three-plus years, are you allocating money into European stocks?

We were early buying in Europe. And we're still in Europe. The markets are attractive there but the currency's been killing your European investments. Especially if you look at it through U.S. dollars. In Canadian dollars not as much though because we've gone down, but the euro's gone down more. But you have to look at currencies as well here. Japan was a great market to be in as long as you didn't have to translate it back to dollars. As soon as you did, all the gains were gone. One of the areas we're actually looking at right now is Swiss companies. We already own one or two Swiss companies, but we're looking at another one. Its currency's been doing better. We've got some Asian assets, too. We're not there yet, but we think that soon will be a time to start looking in Latin America. We go where people don't want to go. And being value investors means, by definition, you're going to be early. And you're going to be wrong for a while. Sometimes longer than you think.

When did you enter into the European markets?

We went into Europe when nobody wanted Europe. When Europe was falling apart and the first time Greece was speculated to leave. We went in there, and we bought multinational companies based in northern Europe. The problems were in southern Europe. Most of the northern European multinational companies assets are outside of Europe. But the market didn't differentiate that. "You're in Europe, eh? I don't want you." We made a lot of money doing that.

Great foresight. I assume you'll hold on to those European stocks.

Yeah, we're not looking at selling any of our European stocks right now.

Russia seems to be going through the same turmoil as Europe was in 2011. Would you invest there now?

We never invested directly in Russia. But in the past we've invested in companies that have large Russian holdings. PepsiCo has a big Russian holding. Carlsberg, which we don't hold anymore, had its biggest market in Russia due to an acquisition they made there. So, no, we've never invested directly in Russia. Also, we've never invested directly in China, or in India, but that's subject to change in the future. Basically, their security markets are not mature and do not have the safety standards of markets we like to invest in. If I go buy Chinese companies, we'll buy ones that are listed in Hong Kong.

You're worried about the lack of market checks and controls.

Right. Whereas Hong Kong is a legitimate, well-governed market. Corporate governance is very important.

From what I've heard, it sounds like you first identify undervalued markets in the world and then second, invest in those securities, either directly or indirectly.

No. We look at companies. We never buy countries. We've never woken up one morning and said we've got to buy Germany or we've got to buy China or whatever. We buy companies.

So you're a bottom-up, fundamental investor. Can you walk me through your framework with an actual example?

The best call we ever made was BCE. If you remember, a number of years ago the Ontario Teachers' Pension Fund was buying it until they weren't anymore. The day that the Ontario Teachers' Pension Fund announced the takeover was off, we bought BCE stock when it plummeted in the market. Our thought process was that OTP was offering to pay too much for BCE and so the value was going to come *way* down after the takeover inevitably fell apart. To us, BCE was great value but everybody was bailing out because the takeover was off. But nothing changed with BCE. It was the same company except now nobody was taking it over. Anyway, we bought BCE when it was in free fall and it's been a fabulous investment for us since. The dividend keeps going up. The yield on the original investment is huge.

On the other hand, have you bought into a mispriced stock that didn't work out?

Oh, that happens all the time. I don't know if the other guys have told you, but if you're a genius in our business, you're right 60% of the time. So you're wrong 40% if you're extraordinary.

That's why it's important to have a diversified portfolio.

You got it. That's why you've got to have a diversified portfolio. Because you're going to be wrong a lot.

How many stocks should one own in their portfolio to be diversified?

Institutions usually own 40 to 45 stocks. When I worked for Ted McConnell we owned 30 stocks. For retail investors, I would suggest around 20 stocks. And they should be diversified. Too many people don't diversify. Investors out in Alberta only want to own energy stocks. I would have big fights with them over that, because their portfolios weren't diversified.

It seems that you don't buy cyclical stocks at all then.

Yeah. There's lots of people that I run into that only own Canadian banks. And their idea of diversification is owning five or six of them. That's their diversification. I would say, "You're not diversifying at all," then they would say, "But they've been so great." Yeah, but one day maybe they won't be. Look at the U.S. banks and what happened to them in '07 and '08; nobody thought that would happen until it did.

Citigroup, a "blue-chip" stock, got clobbered.

Oh, yes. Citi has done a one for ten consolidation. It's just a $10 stock.

Would you buy into Citigroup now?

No, no, it's a different company than it was then, with different management. We don't own any "money-centre banks." We only own regional banks right now.

What are the biggest holdings in your portfolio? Are there commonalities across the stocks?

Our biggest holdings tend to happen because either you've bought a whole lot of it compared to other stuff, or it's gone up a whole lot.

Do you add on to your winners, though?

Sometimes. We recently did that in two U.S. bank stocks. We doubled our positions. But our biggest position is a company that most of your readers won't know. It's a big successful Canadian multinational company called CCL Industries.

I'm kicking myself for not investing in that company.

It is a 10-bagger for us.

Why did you buy into CCL Industries? How did you have the conviction back then?

It was a value stock. The dividend would grow regularly. It had good management and a good balance sheet, and it was restructuring itself. It started off as a maker of private label goods. CCL was Connecticut Chemicals, or something like that, and they would make aerosol products for companies and stick their names on it.

It was a sleepy stock though. There wasn't much movement in its price.

Yeah, sleepy stock. But then they got more into the label business and that's when they started to grow.

That was a catalyst for growth. If you buy into value stocks, do you want there to be a catalyst?

Yes. If you own a value stock that doesn't have a catalyst, it might go down and out. There's a thing called the value trap. If there is no catalyst to change the company, it's always going to be a value stock, and that's the trap. People get sucked in to that all the time, saying, "Well, the stock is cheap." That's not a good reason to buy it. What's going to change it from being cheap is the question, not is it cheap?

Is it from your experience that you understand what the catalysts are across different industries and businesses?

Well, you look for it and sometimes you're wrong. As I said, you're wrong 40% of the time if you're really good. But you try to identify a catalyst. So the catalyst here was that CCL Industries went into growth mode. They identified that the pressure-sensitive-label business was that growth product.

What about buying stocks after they've had a run-up? Will you pay more for great companies?

We have. But we won't pay too *high* a multiple.

When have you broken that rule, though? Paid a much higher multiple for a stock?

I don't think we own anything currently where we've broken that rule. No, these are all companies we've identified as really good value at reasonable prices.

So back to the value equation: how do you determine whether a stock has a margin of safety?

That's a difficult thing to answer, and there's not just one answer for it. But you're trying to say you're buying this stock that people aren't paying a lot for, so if something goes wrong it's not going to get hurt a lot because nobody's bid it up. When somebody's bid a stock to what we call "priced to perfection," nothing stays with perfect forever. The bigger you are, the harder you fall. That's what happens. If you buy something that's already down and out, yeah, you may get hit a bit temporarily, but then it usually just comes back, unless it's a value trap, of course.

How important is risk management?

We may be in the investment business, but we're really in the trust business. Our clients trust us to protect their capital. Earning money is really nice and a lot of people are fixated on return, but smart investors are more interested in protecting their capital, and then a return on that.

So what annual rates of return do you target?

We don't have any target whatsoever. You can't have a target; a lot of people get hurt by targets. If somebody asked me, "What are you going to return for me this year or next year or the next five years?" I'll respond, "I haven't got a clue."

Historically, what has been your biggest blow-out year?

The biggest blow-out year was when I was managing money at Nesbitt Burns. It was probably in '99, when my portfolio was up 48%.

What were the contributing factors to that 48% return?

I had some technology stocks, but the portfolio wasn't full of technology stocks. I was a value investor, actually. Back then I was more of a GARP investor — growth at a reasonable price. Small difference to value, but there is a difference. I still remember, in the early part of 2000, brokers calling me up, "Oh you had such a phenomenal year last year, I'm putting my clients into your fund." But I was saying, "That was last year. Don't expect that again." Some people don't understand the market — they chase performance. You shouldn't do that. If you're an investor, and you're paying 48% more than you would have a year ago, how stupid is that?

Human nature — chase the hot trend. Did you foresee that that bubble was going to pop? What was the sentiment like in 1999?

Things were crazy. Back then I used to short stocks in my own portfolio. I don't do it anymore. I made some good money doing that, and I lost some good money doing that.

Which stocks did you short?

A couple that really taught me my lesson back then. One was a semiconductor stock, and I can't remember the name, but it was trying to be a competitor to Intel in the microprocessor market. I thought that was crazy. I think I shorted it at about 20 bucks, and then it went up to 80 bucks, before coming back and eventually going to zero.

The market can be highly irrational in the short term.

It just went crazy. And if you shorted stock you would need to put up more money to cover that position that's going up. A lot of times, you'd just throw up your hands and give up. I don't short stocks anymore, but it taught me that just because something is overvalued doesn't mean it's going to soon drop. If you want to short stocks, wait until they're going down. Follow the trend going down.

Did you ever trade options?

I would dabble with options when I worked at Canada Trust; they had me writing options against the company's portfolio, just to gain extra income. I don't do that anymore either.

Do you think that rates will go up anytime soon?

Maybe, because everybody's been wrong up to now.

What actions does an investor need to take once the U.S. Fed raises interest rates now or any time in the future?

Well, there's a saying: "Never fight the Fed." And generally that's true. If the Fed says that they want to send interest rates down and keep them down, don't bet against them. The opposite is also true.

How do interest rates affect the stock market?

Interest rates have been declining since 1982. Therefore, most people only know a declining interest rate environment. They have no idea what happens when interest rates go up. When I first got in the business, interest rates only went up. And that was accompanied by high inflation, too, which we don't have anymore. Now they're worried about deflation. In a high interest rate environment, P/E multiples get compressed and lots of people put money into fixed income because they can earn x% and not have to worry about it. When interest rates are close to zero, as they are now, fixed income becomes very unattractive. We have our lowest allocation to fixed income that we've ever had here, because it's so unattractive. So what that's done is driven all kinds of money into the stock market. Because people are searching for returns, and searching for yield. So that's why we believe the U.S.

stock market is so overvalued because all that money is going in there searching for yield and searching for returns because they can't get it in fixed income. Once interest rates start going up, money starts to leave the stock market and heads into fixed income.

What areas should you be investing in the stock market when rates go up? Or should you just pull out completely?

You want to own financials, because they benefit when interest rates go up. You want to own companies that have real growth. You get hurt in companies that people have only bought to get the income. So utilities, for example, will suffer, because money will start going out of them into actual fixed-income products.

That makes sense. Any more advice, Norman, before we wrap up?

Don't fall in love with what you own. Most investors fall in love with what they own. It's a stock. It doesn't know you own it. It doesn't care that you own it. Don't be afraid to sell something because of the capital gains tax. You're in the business of making money. Paying taxes along the way is part of the game. Many times there've been instances where investors didn't want to sell something because of the capital gains tax, and a great example of that was BCE back in 2000. I was working at Nesbitt Burns at the time, and telling the brokers, "You should get your clients to sell BCE because it's pregnant with Nortel." Back then, the value of Nortel was more than the telephone company, BCE. "How could I sell that? Look at the capital gains we're going to have to pay." Well, in the end, there were no capital gains. And every one of those clients today would tell you, "I would have gladly paid the capital gain." So don't fall in love with stocks. Be prepared to change your mind.

The best sale I ever made was in Philip Morris, the tobacco company. I was working at E.J. McConnell at the time, and we had bought a position in Philip Morris. Two days after we bought it, we got a visit from an analyst who was the tobacco analyst at a company that doesn't exist anymore called Kidder, Peabody and Company. He came in and his story was that the tobacco business was about to go through a dramatic change, that generics were eating up more and more of the tobacco business and making companies like Philip Morris vulnerable. He thought something had to give, and would not own the stock. We had bought the stock two or three days earlier. The next day we met and said, "We've got to get out of this thing." The next day was Marlboro Friday, as it's called, where Philip Morris cut the price of Marlboro dramatically and Philip Morris dropped 25% almost immediately.

It's important then to keep an open mind. You can stick to your thesis but risk losing it all.

Yeah, and the other thing to keep in mind is don't trade. Unless it's absolutely necessary. Buy good stuff and keep owning it as long as it's good stuff and the company's doing well. I've been here 11 years, and we hold stocks here that we had when I got here. There hasn't been a reason to sell them. These stocks continue to do well, and, more important, the dividends continue to grow. And we have stocks that have gone up multiple times, and the yield on which you originally bought has gone up multiple times as well. It's fabulous.

Norman Levine is an incredibly observant investor who constantly prowls the market for opportunities in areas that are overlooked by most others. For example, buying multinational companies based in northern Europe when other investors were staying away from the continent as a whole. Here is Norman's overarching investment strategy, as summarized on the Portfolio Management website:

> We are long-term stewards of capital, not traders. Thinking long-term allows us to purchase stocks for sale at value prices due to temporary issues but where we believe a reversion to prior operating levels is probable. We look for catalysts that will allow this thesis to occur and buy low before the often myopic market is able to see it. Our focus on the long-term prospects of a company allows us to put the short-term news flow into the background and focus on more meaningful long-term trends.
>
> In addition to solid Canadian and U.S. assets we have found that non–North American exposure offers significant

return and diversification opportunities. Our clients benefit from a global value orientation which increases industry diversification and provides exposure to areas of the world that have either faster growth prospects or alternatively where there is a great amount of pessimism embedded in stock prices. We have substantial and tenured expertise in international investing.

In assessing individual companies and their management, we are guided by four key principles:

- We think like enterprising businesspeople, not risk-taking speculators.
- We focus on the valuation of individual companies instead of macro-economic events.
- We look for long-term investment growth and stability rather than short-term fads.
- We make decisions based on thorough assessments.

MASTER KEYS
NORMAN LEVINE

1) "If the markets were efficient, you wouldn't have the volatility. There's emotions. It's so critical to understand how people think when they invest. They're not efficient at all."

2) "Commodity markets move in decade and even multi-decade cycles."

3) "Nothing goes straight up and straight down in the market. You get these rallies and people get sucked into them. I would rather lose some opportunity on the way up than lose capital on the way down."

4) "I would rather see commodities stop going down, probably tread water for a long time, or even form a V, and then buy them when they're starting to go up again."

5) "Commodity stocks are not value stocks. And they never will be."

6) "We don't buy industries, and we don't buy countries, we buy stocks. And we look all over the world for them."

7) "We've never invested directly in China, [Russia,] or in India, but that's subject to change in the future. Basically, their security markets are not mature and do not have the safety standards of markets we like to invest in."

8) "If you're a genius in our business, you're right 60% of the time. So you're wrong 40% if you're extraordinary. That's why you've got to have a diversified portfolio. Because you're going to be wrong a lot."

9) "For retail investors, I would suggest around 20 stocks. And they should be diversified. Too many people don't diversify."

10) "We don't own any [U.S.] 'money-centre banks.' We only own regional banks."

11) "If you own a value stock that doesn't have a catalyst, it might go down and out . . . It's always going to be a value stock, and that's the trap. People get sucked in to that all the time, saying, 'Well, the stock is cheap.'"

12) "A lot of people are fixated on return, but smart investors are more interested in protecting their capital, and then a return on that."

13) "You can't have a target [price]; a lot of people get hurt by targets. If somebody asked me, 'What are you going to return for me this year or next year or the next five years?' I'll respond, 'I haven't got a clue.'"

14) "If you want to short stocks, wait until they're going down. Follow the trend going down."

15) "'Never fight the Fed.' And generally that's true. If the Fed says that they want to send interest rates down and keep them down, don't bet against them. The opposite is also true."

16) "Most people only know a declining interest rate environment. They

have no idea what happens when interest rates go up. Once interest rates start going up, money starts to leave the stock market and heads into fixed income."

17) "Don't fall in love with what you own. Most investors fall in love with what they own. It's a stock. It doesn't know you own it. It doesn't care that you own it. Don't be afraid to sell something because of the capital gains tax."

PART IV

MACRO
(TOP-DOWN)

Macro or top-down investors generally base their decisions on current or future economic events. They start their selection process by analyzing asset classes, themes, markets, sectors, and industries, before (if at all) moving on to analyzing individual companies. Macro investors may very well pick a basket of stocks that fit their top-down profile or macro prediction. For example, if an investor predicts that water will be a scarce and profitable resource in the future, then he or she will invest in stocks that operate in that sector currently. Because of this, macro investors are generally different in their approach than bottom-up investors (value investors, growth investors, or fundamental investors). The inherent risk in top-down investing is in the case that one's macro prediction does not materialize (perhaps water utilities do not become a very profitable business). In that example, the associated positions that were invested in to initially capitalize on that macro prediction do not achieve the expected returns for the investor.

DAVID BURROWS
THEMATIC INVESTING

Is that a bird? Is that a plane? No, that's David Burrows in his helicopter, flying high in the sky, scouring for opportunities in the markets. David may not actually be in the sky, but he is not a bottom-up investor. Which means, in this case, that he doesn't care as much about individual securities as he does about entire countries, markets, and sectors. At Barometer Capital, David and his team continuously scan and rank over 63,000 global securities in more than 41 industry sectors with their quantitative analytics machine. David mainly invests in ETFs (exchange-traded funds) based on where he identifies opportunities. Barometer Capital was co-founded by David Burrows in 2001, and today remains an independent partner-owned firm. The firm has $3 billion in assets under management. And David tells me during our interview that Barometer Capital's equity strategy has earned on average 15% annually over 25 years.

David would fit in well with the Manhattan hedge fund manager crowd. He has a crew-cut, dresses very sharply, and talks as if he was top of his class at Toastmasters. He's also a good teacher, using his MacBook to show me a set of macro charts to walk me through his investment model. I was intrigued by the "breadth model." As David explained, expanding market breadth signals an increasing amount of investors, money, and volume, into the market. Logic dictates that the more potential investors that there are in the market, among other factors, the greater the upward pressure on prices. David follows shifts of capital into asset classes, then themes, then sectors, and then individual securities. Those shifts of capital cause that breadth expansion (more volume), which then triggers multiple expansion (higher prices). In other words, for David, the trend is his friend.

There was a pause in our interview when Greg Guichon, chairman of Barometer Capital, poked his head into the room and asked to talk privately with David. While I waited for David to return, I glanced outside the meeting room and into the open office and that's when I grasped the ingenuity of the Barometer Capital floor space, which is a mini–trading floor. All 10 employees had dual monitors set up with Bloomberg on one screen and MS Office on the other. BNN was playing on a large TV screen hanging over the office space. The BNN host had started to talk about the continued slide in oil prices when David returned to the meeting room to continue our conversation.

PRE-INTERVIEW LESSONS

ACCUMULATION DISTRIBUTION: an indicator that gauges supply and demand based on volume activity.

BREADTH EXPANSION: when there are more buyers of stocks than sellers, or when there is an increase in volume activity in the market that influences stock prices (e.g., greater demand).

CAPITAL: the capital in a business (financial assets, property, machinery, etc.) or the investible cash an investor has to make investments in the market.

EMERGING MARKETS: less developed markets in non-G7 countries (e.g., Pakistan) that may or may not have the same standards of regulatory control.

MULTIPLE EXPANSION: when prices of assets expand at a multiple of x, which may or may not be aligned to its internal rate of return or its earnings growth. Markets determine multiple (or price) expansion.

ON-BALANCE VOLUME (OBV): an indicator that measures volume flow to predict stock price changes. Developed by Joseph Granville.

POINT-AND-FIGURE CHART: a chart composed of significant and non-significant price movements.

STOP-LOSS ORDER: an automated order to sell a stock at a designated price below its purchase price. Used to limit downside risk should a stock decline.

TOP-DOWN: a style of investing where an investor starts his or her selection process by analyzing markets, sectors, and industries, before (if at all) moving on to individual companies.

VOLUME: the amount of shares traded in a market in any given stock.

Where did you grow up in Canada?

I grew up in the Kingsway area of western Toronto.

How did you first get interested in the markets?

There were a couple of family friends who were in the investment business, and I had early conversations with them. I was one of the lucky people who sort of knew from an early age where I wanted to go and what I wanted to do. Nobody in my family has ever been in the investment business, but it was something that caught my attention.

How old were you?

I started being interested in the stock market when I was 12 or 13 years old. I followed stocks in the newspaper and learned what it was that made their prices go up and down.

Do you recall the first stocks that you followed or bought?

One of the first companies that I ever invested in was Transmount Pipelines. Pipeline stocks did particularly well when I was young.

So Transmount Pipelines must have worked out for you.

Yeah, I made some money in it. And, interestingly, I had some money from my grandparents that they had put away for me, and so I used that money for the second investment I made, which was in a global mutual fund. What was interesting to me was that it was more of a big-picture investment, and an investment in a theme. Thematic investing has stayed a passion of mine since I was a kid — trying to take advantage of big shifts that take place in the market.

You look at markets from a macro level — top-down rather than bottom-up.

That's right. So in our firm I come at things from a big-picture view, to try to identify key themes that are at play in the market.

How do you play themes in the market?

Let's take a step back. What moves share prices? One factor of course is at the company level. But 80% of returns come from the impact of capital inflows — breadth expansion (more volume) — into an asset class. That's when multiple expansion (higher prices) or re-valuation starts. And then within that asset class you can find themes, sectors, and securities that start to become re-valued versus their historical valuation.

To summarize, you can capitalize on multiple expansion in three areas. First, get to the right asset class. Second, find the right themes and sectors within that asset class. And third, find securities within that universe where companies are changing for the better. My focus is on the 80% of the return that comes from getting into the right neighbourhood.

So your main focus is to follow flows of capital in the market.

Yes. For example, between 2000 and 2012, resources and emerging markets were the beneficiaries of the boom that took place in China. As a result, money was slowly leaving the U.S. stock market that had been in favour through the nineties, and heading over to hard assets in the emerging markets. Now, I would make the case that since 2012, those flows have been reversing course. Further, capital flows have been slowly coming out of bonds, emerging markets, and commodities, and then going into consumer-led developed economies. Low inflation and falling commodity prices are great for a consumer economy. Of course, when that got accelerated by the move in oil prices downward over the last six months, the huge beneficiary is the consumer. The U.S. market is the biggest beneficiary as it's the biggest consumer-led economy on the planet. So sectors like consumer discretionary, consumer cyclical, health care, and technology have been winners there. Another example is with QE in Europe. It will continue to keep inflation down, because it makes capital free. There's lots of capacity in the system, and that is a big win for consumers around the world. So, a combination of loose monetary conditions, but more importantly plentiful energy, is likely to be a driver for years in front of consumer-led economies.

How did you capitalize on that period from 2000 to 2012?

Because our investors are more North American–centric, we focused on areas that do well in a period where stocks in general were not in a secular bull market. So between 2000 and 2012, the earning multiples that stocks traded at in the U.S. and in Canada contracted all throughout that period, as money left for other areas, specifically emerging markets. In 2000, we used more buckets across multiple asset classes, looking for securities that paid you something. And, most importantly, we were looking for re-valuation at the asset class level, at the sector level, and at the security level. We looked at a bunch of different yield-generating asset classes and focused on sectors or themes where something was changing for the better and then tried to find securities with rising streams of cash flow. So not only securities that paid out dividends, but where their ability to pay those dividends was improving over time. That was our focus in that period of time.

So it sounds like you didn't follow the capital inflows into emerging markets in 2000. What specific positions did you take on then?

Well, in the early days we were focused on the concept of the income trust, which many people thought was a really negative structure. Interestingly, when you commit to paying your investors, it makes management more prudent. For example, before making an acquisition, analyzing whether it will help increase shareholder payouts over time. So in the early 2000s we focused on income trusts and dividend payers. As the legislation changed, and income trusts converted to corporations, the appetite for yield had been established in Canada. We believed that the more unpredictable the stock market became, the more attractive a predictable stream of revenue or dividends would become to investors. And so just how multiples on stocks expanded all the way through the nineties, multiples for dividend payers expanded all the way through the 2000s.

Remember, we're always looking for the asset class that is being revalued. In early 2000, nobody cared about yield. High-yield securities traded at the lowest multiples then. By 2011 to '12, the best-performing stocks were yield generators, and they traded at the highest multiples. It's now flipped. Capital flows are always moving, and so we move on to the next opportunity, too.

I've noticed that multiples in utilities have expanded to high levels. I believe Enbridge is trading at 60-plus P/E.

Right. So, the thing to keep in mind is that probably our best trade over the last few years was being relatively early on investing in the energy infrastructure companies in the beginning of the boom in energy production. What happened was not only were they predictable, but the volume growth led to significant dividend growth and multiple expansion and that group was a prolific group to be focused on over about a five-year period.

Starting in 2012, you realigned to the U.S. to take advantage of this new

*paradigm in the markets. Which other consumer-led economies are you
taking positions in?*

Our biggest focus is in the U.S. Again, we believe that we are in the relatively early days of a secular bull market for developed and consumer-
led economies, and specifically in the U.S. So that is our biggest focus.

*In the U.S., which themes or sectors have the most re-valuation or multiple
expansion opportunity?*

Health care, because it's driven by consumer and by demographics.
And it's a highly predictable industry. There's been a lot of change in
that industry. It was an industry that was out of favour for 12 years,
though it's the biggest industry in the U.S. What made it less attractive
in the early part of the 2000s was that health care had become a lower-
growth industry, and thus less exciting. You know, here we are 15 years
later, and biotech companies are no longer speculative securities that
might have one compound that they are trying to get approved. These
are multi-product and multi–cash flow stream businesses with relatively higher growth rates that are sustainable businesses.

Would you bucket China into consumer-led economies?

No. China's boom has come to an end for now. We believe that it's in
a slow transition from an economy driven by fixed investment, which
made up 50% of their GDP last year, to a consumer-led economy.
But that can't happen overnight. Every million dollars of GDP that
you produce in a service economy like Canada's requires a lot fewer
jobs than in an economy that's driven by fixed investment. So that
is a painful transition to make. There's no country on the face of
the earth that has ever had 50% of its GDP come from fixed investments, like bridges, tunnels, and railroads. And China's 7 or 8% GDP
growth is largely fuelled by one-time items. Once those projects are
built, they're built. It's not like you build a McDonald's that sells hamburgers forever. So we believe that China was re-valued during the
period 2000 through 2012. And all the countries that supplied China,
like Latin American countries, other Asian countries, and essentially
all of the commodities producers, were favourably re-valued through
that period. But now they face significant headwind as China invariably will slow at around a time that the highest production came in

from all those countries. So supply and demand is out of whack and will take a long time to come back into play.

So avoid China.

Yeah. The problem right now is that China's cutting interest rates to try to stimulate demand. If there's too much capacity to begin with it doesn't matter how cheap money can get. As we've seen around the world, QE has pushed money into the system but the velocity of money just isn't there. So if you've got too much capacity and there's no demand for additional debt, then that debt just replaces old debt that's come due. It's hard to see how it really stimulates. Anyway, the big issue that investors succumb to is that they have a tendency to look at what has worked in their recent past, which is their recent experience, and then try to figure out how to make money in it again. Just like in 2003, two years into the tech bust, people tried to pick bottoms in tech stocks. It would take 10 years before tech stocks really got going again. And although the boom in commodities ended in 2012, and the emerging markets boom ended in 2012, the question we get asked all the time is, "When is it time to buy commodities, when is it time to buy in emerging markets, when is it time to buy in China?" It probably will not be the right time for many years.

If the commodity super cycle really has ended, would it be a mistake to bottom-feed now?

Way too early. I started appearing on BNN in 2001. When I talked about investing in agriculture companies like Monsanto and John Deere, people's eyes would glaze over and they'd say, "Yeah but when's it time to buy Cisco?" So right now we tell people they should be buying Disney and Home Depot, and they say, "Yeah, yeah, yeah, but when should I buy Suncor?" Or "When should I buy gold?" The reality is that there will be short trading rallies in those securities, but that's it. You won't get secular re-valuation for a long period of time. However, by the time commodities get to another big boom, there will have been both restructuring and rationalization, which is what will create the shortage that will give those companies pricing power again.

Do you use a standard investment system or process?

We have a process that we use that helps to identify secular themes. Let me build a simple premise. As you go through a down-cycle in the market, everything doesn't start selling off on day one. The weaklings sell off in the beginning. But as the sell-off picks up steam, more securities are impacted, until late in the decline where almost nothing's performing well in the market. That's when people hate that universe of securities. They're under-owned, and they're unloved. But then when the most aggressive folks start to re-allocate to that asset class, theme, or sector, they don't want to buy "Moose Pasture Mines"; they want to buy the securities that they're most confident in. So often in the beginning, the leading securities will perform well, and as the theme picks up steam, more securities participate, until late in the advance where almost everything's performing well. So in a healthy market, breadth expansion, or market participation, pushes prices higher. It just means there's more money flowing into that universe.

Remember, the leading securities are not the ones that get hit in the beginning of a downturn. It's the weaklings. So while the leaders carry an index on to make new highs, fewer securities participate in the advance. That doesn't tell you that they're all about to get creamed, but it tells you that there's not enough money flowing into that area. At that point, it's a red light. Stop making any new investments in that universe. In our case, tighten up the stop-losses on the positions you have in that universe, and to the extent you get stopped out don't try to pick a bottom. Let the breadth narrow as long as it narrows. It could be years. We use a breadth model, which helps us to find asset classes, and themes, and sectors that have come to a point where almost nothing's performing well. Invariably, they're unloved; there's one or two companies doing better than the rest. And so when we start to see an expansion in breadth, or volume, that simply means money's starting to get put to work in that universe. At that point, we take a close look and try to understand why.

You employ a wait-and-see approach.

You don't need to be first. You can wait until multiple expansion begins before you invest in that area. I use something called point-and-figure price charts. They're quantitative in nature. Higher highs and higher lows — that's an uptrend, and lower highs and lower lows — that's a downtrend. Each one gets a single vote. Then we break the world up into pockets; equities, 16 geographic regions, and 41 global sector silos. And we track every day the percentage of stocks that are in long-term price advances.

[David had a point-and-figure chart on hand
for our interview, which he goes on to explain.]

So this is the chart for global consumer stocks. As it stands today, about 54% of those stocks are long-term positive. The aggregate price advance in this consumer stocks group is in acceleration, which means that money's working its way into these equities. There's no bear market in history that took place while breadth expansion was taking place.

Where did you learn how to read point-and-figure charts?

I learned point-and-figure charts from a company called Chart Craft that was doing this in the 1950s. Also, there's an excellent book written by a fellow named Tom Dorsey, who writes about point-and-figure charting. But point-and-figure charting was invented by Charles Dow back in the early part of the twentieth century. His view was that information wasn't well disseminated. Information gets out there whether you get it or not. However, one should want to understand when the balance of power is changing. So I can tell you that as long as breadth is expanding, we don't worry about the market. Again, there's no bear market in history that happened while breadth was expanding.

Do you also use accumulation distribution and on-balance volume (OBV) to determine the magnitude of breadth expansion?

You could, but it's not the same. Both indicators work off a similar principle, but I don't think that they're as quantitatively driven as point-and-figure charts. Point-and-figure charts are more informative. I can go back to the 1950s and see that there's no significant bull market that ever ended before 70 or 80% of stocks participated in an advance. In the NYSE, today, we're sitting at only about 60% participation. Indeed, there's more breadth expansion, and as a result multiple expansion, to come. I look at the global universe in our system, and take each of the major countries and markets and plot them on a bell curve based on the percentage of stocks that are doing well. If any area is green it means that there's breadth expansion in that area. For the past 18 months, largely the countries that have shown expansion are consumer-led developed markets. The areas in pink are emerging markets, or largely commodity markets. Our industry's built largely by people who start as analysts, who spend the first 10 years working for a brokerage firm telling people why they're right and why the market's wrong. And then they ultimately become portfolio managers and see that as their job: to be the smart one. We believe ultimately the market gets it right. So forget about what you think should happen; let's use tools to understand what will happen.

The trend is your friend.

Ultimately, yes, but the breadth models will have us enter sectors while they're out of consensus. Breadth is very narrow before a momentum investor would ever enter the area. However, at some point we do become more momentum-driven, until breadth starts to break, and even then the leaders will still have good momentum.

On your website, it mentions that you order securities from "good to great." Is there some fundamental analysis to your process, too?

So we run this top-down model that looks at asset classes and sectors globally to try to identify where money is getting put to work. And then from the bottom up we look at about 60,000 securities daily. We have a combination of about 20 factors that we look for in the income statement, in the balance sheet, and in price behaviour. If we can find that combination of factors, and it's fundamental and technical in nature, it's highly likely that something's changing for the better. This is just *Moneyball* for investing. We're looking for a combination of factors that historically have pointed to something changing for the better.

What are the top fundamental factors out of the total 20 factors?

Cash flow growth, margin expansion, earnings revisions, those types of pieces of data. Along with positive price behaviour. So if the fundamental picture is doing *this* but the price behaviour is *that*, it's not of interest. We want both — one confirming the other. The price should be doing what you would expect it to do, given what you think you know. Again, we apply this screen daily on a global universe of securities, and every day a few securities come out of these tests. We are not ever looking for a "broken getting fixed" security. We are looking for a "good getting better" security.

Are "broken getting fixed" securities oftentimes value traps?

They can be value traps. The biggest mistake people in our industry make is that they think, "I'm right, and the market's wrong." No matter how smart you are, sooner or later you will get put in the ditch with that mentality. So that's why we look for factors in securities that point to something changing for the better, and price behaviour doing what we would expect it to do given what we think we know.

The year after he wrote the seminal book on value investing **The Intelligent Investor,** *Benjamin Graham said that pure value investing doesn't work like it used to. What's your take on that?*

It may well work for the right kind of investor. I'm going to make a point here. From the very beginning our focus was earning money for families and individuals. Families and individuals are emotional by nature. And while rationally they may believe in being a long-term investor, they have a very short attention span and only so much patience. You may wind up getting a value investment dead right, but if it takes too long for it to work they may have fired you along the way. That's why our strategy is aimed at our clients.

Private investors have three expectations. First, in a decent market, they expect you to find a way to make money. If the market rallies tomorrow, they expect to participate. And it's not for us to say what's right or wrong, rather, what's working. Second, they expect that when market leadership changes, we recognize it early and deal with it. So as new leadership emerges and old leadership recedes, you have to be able to effectively configure your holdings. So for us, when we start to see deterioration in breadth, or volume, whether or not the fundamental data's still great, it's time for us to start to reduce our weight. When breadth starts to expand in a group that's been universally hated, it's not for us to say they're wrong. We better take a look at what there is in that universe that we could participate in. Third, they expect us to preserve capital. This is the most important thing. The biggest fear a private investor has is losing the money they spent their life building.

What controls do you have in place to preserve capital?

If nothing's working in the market, we have an ability to be on the side-lines or out of big parts of the market. Most importantly, be a good seller. To explain, we run stops on all of our positions. We will never say, "The market's wrong, and we were right." If something stops working, and it hits our stock, we're gone. The biggest mistake investors tend to make is by saying, "No, no, no, this is a big company, I'm going to be patient, it's going to come back, it was expensive, now it's cheap, I'm going to buy more." You should have the ability to play defense.

Also, being very style-specific is very troublesome because private investors often find their way to a manager with a very specific style or expertise after it's worked well for three or four years, just in time for it to stop working. With our breadth models, the world is open to us. We are nimble, which is also a component of our risk management strategy. There's nothing we can't invest in. Where we see breadth expansion, we will start with small positions. We'll stay there as long as there's breadth expansion. It doesn't matter if it's growth or value or in Canada or the U.S., or in large companies or mid-size companies or specific themes; it's about being agnostic to all of that. Our security selection process is very quantitatively driven, and we have a due diligence process that we complete.

You are obviously a firm believer in the Efficient Market Theory.

In a bull market, investors say, "Earnings are growing at 6%, so how can the market be going up 15%? That's irrational." Well, that's multiple expansion. There's nothing irrational about that. Let me just grab my computer.

> *[David leaves the meeting room to get his MacBook*
> *from his office and projects a presentation to better*
> *explain the concept of multiple expansion.]*

At some point in every secular bull market, prices wind up, stocks become overpriced, and then the market goes through years of sideways choppy markets as money slowly leaves the asset class in favour of other greener pastures. So in 2000 the market rolled over. The tech boom comes to an end. NASDAQ's trading at a hundred times earnings. And for the next 12 years, money slowly leaves the U.S. stock market in favour of China, commodities, and emerging markets. The problem is that investors are told that "buy and hold" is how you make money. It's very hard to change their spots. Instead, you must follow the market's movements.

If you're not buying and holding stocks, then aren't you timing the market? That could be dangerous.

Somewhat; we'll start with partial positions in companies that are meeting our business tests in groups that are experiencing expansion in breadth, and will continue to add and build exposure so long as breadth is expanding in that group. The hard part in a bull market is to stay with the stuff that's working well for you. Conversely, in a bear market, the hard thing to do is to be a good seller. An then once you end up in a bull market, everyone's scared because of the previous bear market; they want to take profits off the table as soon as things start to work. You want to stay in a position so long as the multiple grows and as long as the earnings grow. There's lots of analysts that will say at some point, "It's higher on valuation" because the multiple was higher than it was three years ago. In a bull market, multiples can expand for years. Sooner or later, though, breadth starts to deteriorate and while it may not be evident in an index, fewer securities will carry the index higher. That means you've got to stop putting on new positions, but rather tighten up on your stocks.

With your breadth model, were you able to avoid the financial crisis?

Well, I can tell you exactly. A year before the crisis — 2007 — the breadth model for global financials, led by the European banks, started to deteriorate. Financials became *persona non grata* for us in the fall of 2007. We had no idea what was coming but we started getting stopped out at that point. So we stopped buying financials in 2007. In the spring of 2008, the breadth model for the NYSE and for the leadership group at the time, which was energy, both rolled over. By the end of June, our equity portfolios were 25% cash. As breadth deteriorated through that summer, our cash reserves increased to 35%. 45% cash by August. 75% cash by September. Again, we had no idea what was coming other than that breadth in the market just kept deteriorating.

From September 30 to November 30, the S&P 500 went down 38%, and continued to decline until March of 2009. But then, finally, in the third week of March, breadth started to expand. So when Greg and I had our next morning meeting, I said, "Let's put money to work again." He looked at me, and for the second time in my career as partners, he said, "Well, that's a career decision" *[laughs]*. That's how it felt at the time. If I was wrong, our clients were going hate us.

Specifically, which positions did you take on when market breadth started to expand?

Bank bonds and bank-preferred shares. Those were our initial positions.

The equity model turned positive in March of 2009. And it was across a bunch of different sectors. That led us back into equities. The first groups to turn up were REITs, telcos, utilities, and pipelines — highly predictable, low-economic-sensitivity, yield-generating securities. And that theme stayed in place until 2012. Then in 2012 we got the first sign that interest rates might go higher at some point. From there, the markets rotated from what I'll call interest rate proxies to more economically sensitive groups. And that moved us into some of these other groups including energy, but then energy rolled in the fall of 2014, and that's when technology and consumer discretionary took over.

Investors can employ a similar strategy with ETFs, correct?

Yeah. So, we run a tactically managed basket of ETFs across asset classes and sectors. Long/short. ETFs are a great tool for that because you can get 80% of the attribution of what drives a return just by buying the right ones. You still have to know when to enter and exit though. We then fill in underlying positions with our security selection process.

What is the key to Barometer Capital's success?

We tend to have quite a low correlation to an index, which makes us attractive. We've had less than 50% of the volatility of the market. If you sliced our returns into rolling five-year periods, there hasn't been a five-year period where we weren't at or ahead of a benchmark.

But there must have been a time when your breadth model was wrong?

I would say the biggest weakness became apparent in 2011 and 2012. During that period, you may remember that we went through a period of 14 months where there were nine advances and declines of between 10 and 20%.

Okay, so the breadth model is not as effective in times of extreme and short-term volatility.

In any transition there's a period of higher volatility where the buyers and sellers battle it out until one side wins and you either transition higher or lower. In that period — 2011 and 2012 — you may remember the discussion was "risk on, risk off." With "risk on," everything moves downward together as a school of fish, highly correlated. It was because that period of 14 months was probably the greatest period of central bank intervention in the history of the market. The macro factors would push things lower and then the central banks would throw firepower at the market and push it back the other way. And this was happening over two- and three-week periods. So if your process is to identify key themes, and then run stop-losses underneath, we just kept getting stopped out of positions.

Is it normal for the market to experience periods of extreme volatility?

We went all the way back to the 1920s. My recollection before we did the study was that these things happen over two- and three-month periods at transition points but then they resolve themselves, which is not a big deal. There was no period in a hundred years where you got that kind of outsized volatility over as long a period.

Paul Tudor Jones conducts similar back-studies to inform him of what the market will do.

I think that he's very bright. There's a couple of fellows who I think add a lot of value. George Soros is an incredibly smart guy, and he also looks for big shifts in capital flows, and ultimately believes that once the market is in gear it's very hard to dislodge it. That's why he won that big bet against the Bank of England. He's probably the most successful macro investor of all time. Then, on the security selection side, we've always been big fans of William O'Neil, who was one of the early Quants and believed in the idea of multiple expansion, at the security selection level. I think investment managers never know what will happen, but they need to know what *can* happen. Investors for the most part look at the world through a lens that includes their most recent experience. And it will almost never be the same thing that happens next as what has just happened *[laughs]*.

Like what Wayne Gretzky said: "Don't look to where the puck is, but where it's going to be."

That's exactly right. We spent 12 years telling our clients secular bear markets are very challenging. You have to generate yield. You have to be a really good seller. And you have to be prepared to be active. And I said, "At some point we will re-enter a secular bull market, but at that time you will hate the stock market. We need to get you there with your capital and your confidence intact so that you'll allow us to take advantage of it early on, not at the end of a secular bull market." If you look at the eighties and nineties, the big money didn't pile into the stock market until the late nineties, 15 years into a bull market. And so we believe that 2012 marked the beginning of a secular bull market that will likely go on for another 12 or 13 years.

When did you start up Barometer Capital?

We started our firm here in 1991. It was in a bull market. At that time, we launched the equity strategy. The equity strategy has earned 15% annually over 25 years.

Any other insights?

I would highlight the concept that one should understand what is happening. Don't try to justify what you *think* should happen. For us, having a rules-based process that is very much about measuring what is happening, and then making sure our portfolios make sense given what we know, and the way the market's behaving, is really important. The mistake that people make is that they rationalize. You can't ever afford to rationalize. There's no room in investing for being emotional. You have to be able to change your view given new information. People like to fight that. Our most important job as a manager, really, sounds simple, is that we're an inventory manager. Our job is to make sure we get the best inventory we could have, and the most important job of an inventory manager is to know when something isn't attractive to mark it down to get rid of, so the third piece is a really disciplined selling strategy. As you go through a decline one might not sell off until late in the decline, almost nothing's working.

This statement from David resonated with me: "You make money in stocks from two things. One is earnings growth and then the other is what multiple investors ultimately pay from that earnings growth." You need both things to come together in order to realize any sustainable returns from your stocks. There are always flukes, whereby stocks with no earnings, and no earnings growth, are bid up by investors. But, as we know, fads die hard. The other exception seems to be Amazon. Investors will bid up Amazon's stock price based on its revenue growth alone, as Amazon's net margins are extremely thin and for years struggled to eke out any profit at all. Earnings growth seems to be a nice-to-have, but not a must-have to send Amazon's stock price up. Perhaps into the future Amazon's net margin will expand considerably, nullifying this example.

Also, David's selling strategy may be the most systematic out of all the Market Masters. For each position, he sets up a stop-loss that will trigger at a pre-determined sell price, below the initial purchase price. In the event that the security price falls below its stop loss, a sale is triggered, which ultimately limits his downside without the need for manual intervention. David said, "This strategy is designed to eliminate rationalization and emotion from the sell decision. The point is to ensure small losses don't become big losses, and to realize full value for the key positions that drive returns." He explains further on the Barometer Capital website:

THE BAROMETER SELLING STRATEGY WORKS LIKE THIS:
- Clearly define an exit price — below purchase — that triggers a sale if the price falls below an acceptable price level
- Regularly reset stop alerts not lower than before — in that if prices rise as expected, alerts are ratcheted higher to continuously limit the downside
- Consistently use, and adhere to, stop-loss alerts

The most common investment mistakes have very little to do with what people buy, but almost everything to do with what they don't sell.

--- **MASTER KEYS** ---
DAVID BURROWS

1) "What moves share prices? One factor of course is at the company level. But 80% of returns come from the impact of capital inflows — breadth expansion (more volume) — into an asset class. That's when multiple expansion (higher prices) or re-valuation starts."

2) "You can capitalize on multiple expansion in three areas. First, get to

the right asset class. Second, find the right themes and sectors within that asset class. And third, find securities within that universe where companies are changing for the better."

3) "My focus is on the 80% of the return that comes from getting into the right neighbourhood."

4) "Capital flows are always moving, and so we move on to the next opportunity, too."

5) "The big issue that investors succumb to is that they have a tendency to look at what has worked in their recent past, which is their recent experience, and then try to figure out how to make money in it again."

6) "As you go through a down-cycle in the market, everything doesn't start selling off on day one. The weaklings sell off in the beginning. But as the sell-off picks up steam, more securities are impacted, until late in the decline where almost nothing's performing well in the market."

7) "When the most aggressive folks start to re-allocate to that asset class, theme, or sector, they don't want to buy 'Moose Pasture Mines'; they want to buy the securities that they're most confident in."

8) "You don't need to be first. You can wait until multiple expansion begins before you invest in that area."

9) "I use something called point-and-figure price charts. They're quantitative in nature. Higher highs and higher lows — that's an uptrend, and lower highs and lower lows — that's a downtrend."

10) "There's no bear market in history that happened while breadth was expanding."

11) "I can go back to the 1950s and see that there's no significant bull market that ever ended before 70 or 80% of stocks participated in an advance. In the NYSE, today, we're sitting at only about 60% participation."

12) "We believe ultimately the market gets it right. So forget about what you think should happen . . . No matter how smart you are, sooner or later you will get put in the ditch."

13) "If the fundamental picture is doing *this* but the price behaviour is *that*, it's not of interest. We want both — one confirming the other."

14) "We are not ever looking for a 'broken getting fixed' security. We are looking for a 'good getting better' security."

15) "When we start to see deterioration in breadth, or volume, whether or not the fundamental data's still great, it's time for us to start to reduce our weight."

16) "We run stops on all of our positions. If something stops working, and it hits our stock, we're gone."

17) "In a bull market, investors say, 'Earnings are growing at 6%, so how can the market be going up 15%? That's irrational.' Well, that's multiple expansion. You want to stay in a position so long as the multiple grows and as long as the earnings grow."

18) "Once you end up in a bull market, everyone's scared because of the previous bear market; they want to take profits off the table as soon as things start to work."

19) "In any transition there's a period of higher volatility where the buyers and sellers battle it out until one side wins and you either transition higher or lower."

20) "One should understand what is happening. Don't try to justify what you think should happen."

21) "Our job is to make sure we get the best inventory we could have, and the most important job of an inventory manager is to know when something isn't attractive to mark it down."

PETER BRIEGER
THE HISTORIAN

Peter Brieger would tell you that it's *time in the market* and not *market timing* that matters most for investment success. He has a long-term investment horizon. Peter holds high-quality stocks as long as they deliver ample returns. This is the reason why Peter has a sweet spot for income-producing securities that provide a consistent dividend stream. With 50 years in the industry, it's hard to fathom just how many dividend cheques Peter has received for himself and on behalf of his clients. In addition to dividends, there's capital appreciation. The Canadian stock market has gone from $800 to $15,000 in that time period. Imagine buying into the market at $800, and then selling out at $1,000, on the belief that after a 25% return, markets were "too lofty." That's the major downfall of timing the market. Not only can you miss prolonged run-ups in the market, but significant short-term advances, too. Based on my analysis in *Lessons from the Successful Investor*, the S&P 500, from 1871 to 2009, delivered positive returns 72% of the time, while negative returns only 28% of the time. That means that for every ten-year time horizon, you can expect seven years of positive returns and just three years of negative returns in the market. These findings can be extrapolated to the TSX, as the returns in Canadian and U.S. stocks are similar. From 1934 to 2014, compound annual returns on Canadian stocks were 9.8% while 11.11% on American stocks. And, importantly, over that 80-year period, an investment in Canadian stocks has grown 1,597-fold despite 13 recessions, double-digit interest rates, and several world crises.

Peter has worked in the top financial centres in the world — Toronto, London, and New York — as a research analyst, then market strategist, and then portfolio manager. He started GlobeInvest in 1988, with the mandate to ·invest in high-quality businesses that benefit from global operations, in which he requires that 50% or more in revenues come from non–North American markets. Now, Peter finds himself at a crossroads. While his passion remains the market, investing, and making money for his clients, he recently sold his firm, GlobeInvest, to Christine Poole. Peter jokes before the interview starts that he'll "stick around as long as Christine still needs me." But if I was a betting man, I'd wager that Peter would come in to the office whether or not he was being paid. As a result of the sheer amount of time he's had in the market, the seventies-ish Peter *is* the market. He's an asset.

On interview day, I walked into Peter's spacious office to find him slouching comfortably in a giant red leather chair behind his enormous wooden desk, clearly in his element. I saw a cane leaning on the desk to his right. A poster to my right caught my eye, a photo of an old bi-plane that had crashed into a tree. A caption read *Money management and aviation are in themselves not inherently dangerous. But to an even greater degree than the sea, they are terribly unforgiving of any carelessness, incapacity, or neglect.* Before we started our conversation, Peter riffled through and organized several stacks of paperwork on his desk, preparing the material that he would later use in the interview to explain his investment process. In his distinctive, growly voice, Peter went on to share with me some of the most crucially significant milestones in not just Canada's market history, but that of the world. I felt like a student. And Peter Brieger was the master teacher.

PRE-INTERVIEW LESSONS

CAPITAL EXPENDITURE (CAPEX): improvements, projects, or new investments undertaken by management.

COMPOUND RETURNS: the process by which money builds on itself over time in an exponential fashion. For example, $100 grows at 10% to $110 in year one. But then in year two, $110 becomes $121 at the same 10% return.

CONSUMER PRICE INDEX: a measurement of the change in the cost of living for consumers.

MARKET TIMING: when investors frequently buy or sell investments based on events that occur within a short period or at a specific time (e.g., a stock price crosses over the 200-day moving average).

Where did you grow up in Canada?

In Toronto.

Downtown Toronto?

Yes, I have always been a downtown brat.

How did you first get interested in the markets?

There were two reasons. The first was that in the summer of 1955 I got a summer job as a lowly rookie assisting some geologists who were conducting magnetometer surveys on several mining properties near Val d'Or, Quebec. One of my jobs was to transcribe the survey numbers onto a grid map. As the shares of the company whose site we were surveying were listed on the TSX, it was fun to see the impact of those numbers on the share price. However, the main reason I became interested in the markets was a reflection of the times. Life was pre-ordained. At university, you met your wife, married after graduation, had the requisite number of children, and started to work for a major company, which you expected to be with possibly for life. For example, working for P&G, learning how to flog cake mixes and toothpaste. Being very independent-minded and even then an out-of-the-box thinker, I wanted something I thought would be more interesting. I thought the investment business would provide that.

Did you immediately start up your own firm?

No, but after university and after about 10 years in the business I started dreaming about it. Upon graduation from the Richard Ivey School of Business at Western, my first position was as an analyst-in-training. The opening salary for an honours business graduate in June 1962 was three thousand dollars a year. It was a struggle, but nevertheless, from day one my expectations about the investment business were fully met. Initially as an analyst I talked to interesting people at the corporate level. I wasn't allowed to interface with individual investors until I had been in the business about 10 years. But during the first 10 years I wondered if I could do better than the way things were being done.

What was the market like in the fifties and sixties?

After the Korean War, which ended in 1952, there was the fear of a recession or possibly a depression. Eisenhower was in the White House.

During the fifties, economic growth was sluggish. While corporate profits rose from 1952 to the mid-fifties, by the end of the decade they were back to 1952 levels. But because inflation was relatively stable, the market's price earnings ratio had expanded from seven times in '52 to twenty-two times by the end of the decade. That proved to be the high point until the dot-com period. In the early sixties with JFK's election there were great hopes for an economic recovery. But fate played a cruel hand and we all know the mess that LBJ's "Guns and Butter" policies got us into. That said, the stock markets in Canada and the U.S. did quite well until 1970.

What were some of your early wins in that era?

What traditionally happened when you started as an analyst is that the research bosses gave you the simple industries and companies to follow. For example, soft drink companies, retail chains, food chains, and beer companies. My big win was a result of going out to look at companies which banded small independent grocery stores into the IGA chains. One of those companies was Oshawa Wholesale. In my view it was the best of the bunch and investors did very well.

So you pick the market leaders in an industry?

Essentially. Once I had decided that I liked an industry, I focused on the leaders.

Going back to where we left off, what about the seventies?

Inflation started to ramp up in 1974 when the price of oil took off. Inflation exploded until Paul Volker took a firm stand in 1980 and broke its back. Until 1974, I didn't think about it, but my parents' worries about inflation were always with me. They were of German extraction and had lived there during the Weimar Inflation. My father, who was a struggling young professor, was paid twice a day — at nine a.m. and again at noon. His mother met him at the pay office, took the German marks, and ran out to buy something. Had she waited even an hour or so the mark's decline in purchasing power made the pay worth far less. After I started in the investment business full time, they would always ask, "What is inflation doing?"

What's the sentiment like in the market today? Fear of inflation or deflation?

The unwarranted sentiment today relates to the fear of deflation. While the reported Consumer Price Index (CPI) in the U.S. has been low, more recently, as of July of 2015, 80% of the components showed a 2.14% rate. However, once the negative impact of the recent decline in energy prices passes, it will cease to be a drag. Then I expect CPI to be in the 2.0% to 2.5% range later this year and next. I look for a fairly stable inflation rate going forward. I don't want to bore you with history; however, in my view the fear of deflation or even disinflation is misplaced. If you look back to 1870 and the period from then until the start of World War I, it was a period of virtually no inflation and economies showed positive growth. That period has been referred to historically as the Gilded Age. I think we're back to that same type of environment today because of a reverse of what happened in the early seventies. As mentioned, oil prices skyrocketed and changed the world as we then knew it. It took years for the economy, corporate managements, and consumers to adjust to the shock. Today, some 41 years later, we have the same thing happening but in reverse. Now what do I mean by that? Thanks to fracking and the development of other non-conventional sources, I think we could be entering a long period of relatively stable energy prices. The short-, medium-, and long-term benefits could be substantial for world economies and stock markets.

What others indicators, besides CPI, do you periodically review to inform your investment decisions?

There is a host of factors. Aside from any macro-economic inflation or disinflation indicators, I focus on micro-economic factors. Those would include a review of a company's past earnings growth rate, estimated future growth rate, actual and relative price earnings ratios — to itself and the main markets in which the shares trade — and current and forward ratios relative to the market and its outlook. I also look at the level of and the rate of change in interest rates and most importantly the shape of the yield curve. Nothing will kill an economy and stock market faster than a flat or inverted yield curve because they are usually the forerunner of a recession. There are many others, but at GlobeInvest we are deep-value buyers and an industry's and company's fundamentals are the most important in the investment decision process.

You said that we are entering a new gilded age. How does an investor capitalize on this new era?

There are two sources of investment returns: income and capital gains. Traditionally, investors chose bonds and preferred shares for the income component. But that has changed. On a macro market basis one has to evaluate the long-term outlook for bonds versus equities. Given the current levels of interest rates and yields on bonds compared to the yields on many equities, equities are the clear winner. We have recently completed a huge bull market in bonds and now that bond yields are likely to rise, bond prices will decline, reducing any nominal returns and even potentially creating losses.

Given the likelihood of some equities' future earnings and dividend growth and the decline in bonds' real returns because of inflation and the potential for losses, which would you rather own today, Johnson & Johnson or a 10-year U.S. Treasury? On a global macro-economic basis, if you take a look at world demographics, we like emerging markets long-term. Why? Because, with the exception of China and a few others, the emerging economies have the same demographic trends we had in North America in the fifties and sixties. We were all young, starting families, and buying houses. But now in North America we're a generation of older people, and that will have a major impact on North American economic dynamics. In my view the main driver of world economic growth will come from outside North America. One can gain exposure by investing in major international companies that have at least 50% of their business in emerging markets.

Procter & Gamble?

Our clients own similar companies but they also own global industrial companies.

So you invest in North American companies that have a higher-than-50% exposure to emerging markets, but not directly in companies that operate in emerging markets.

That's correct. We think that investing directly in the shares of a company which is located in emerging markets is one risk too many for most of GlobeInvest's clients.

Before you get into your investment strategy, can you share more experiences from your extensive involvement in the markets?

Okay. So, the first craze that I experienced was in the sixties with what was referred to as the "Nifty Fifty." They were stocks whose growth extended as far as the eye could see. The masses felt that they could buy them regardless of their price earnings ratios and could hold them forever. They collapsed in 1970 mainly because their reported results no longer supported their outrageous price earnings ratios.

What about the impact that the formation of the Organization of the Petroleum Exporting Countries (OPEC) had on markets? Did that rock the market, too?

By way of a confession, had I been smarter I would have caught on to OPEC's game earlier. I had been transferred to London, England, in late 1969. My then–bank manager at Royal Bank of Canada told me, "You've got to get down to Riyadh in Saudi Arabia — there's a lot of stuff going on." I spoke with someone else who had just returned. He said he didn't meet any sheiks but did meet lots of retired members of the Texas Railroad Commission. The TRC was the model on which OPEC was built. By '73, '74, the Saudis and other cartel members had done their homework on demand/supply factors. The price of oil skyrocketed from about $3 to $3.50 a barrel to about $39.50 in 1980. The world changed completely. I mean everything one had learned in school and subsequently had no more relevance to economies and markets after that.

This history lessons is fascinating. Can you share more?

The next trend in the seventies involved what I will call "hidden inflation beneficiaries." These were companies whose assets were reported on a depreciated historical book value basis and not replacement value. If a company wanted to expand, it was cheaper for it to buy a listed company than to expand through capex [capital expenditures]. So everyone ran out to buy companies which had those undervalued assets. In the eighties, markets had to adjust to Paul Volker's successful battle against inflation. Also markets had really not done much for a long time and investors were discouraged. Then we had the "flash crash" in 1987, which further spooked investors. However, by then Japan's stock market became the flavour of the month until it, too, became extraordinarily overvalued and collapsed. It went into a long-term funk until several years ago. Then came the dot-com frenzy and eventual collapse from 2000 to 2003. Then came the U.S. housing bubble and the markets' eventual collapse in '07– '08. And now, as of late July 2015, it will be interesting to see just how the share buy-back and M&A [mergers and acquisitions] activity, both of which have shrunk the available supply of stocks substantially, turn out.

Okay, thanks for all of those history lessons. Now, what's your investment strategy?

GlobeInvest's and my strategy is to purchase fundamentally sound stocks at prices we think represent long-term value to our clients. For some stocks, current and future dividend growth is important. I believe it was Professor Jeremy Siegel of the Wharton School who pointed out that long-term stock returns were between 6% and 8% but half of that return came from dividends and their growth. So dividends are important. But they are not always necessary. When I see a company with superior growth prospects, I like to see it use its capital to fund future growth rather than paying dividends.

But with your macro lens, do you also overlay themes in your security selection process?

We do pick themes. The anticipated emerging market growth is clearly a theme. My biggest theme now is water. I think water's the next oil, and fortunately we've had good luck with water companies that have been taken over. We are looking at five right now but they are a bit too pricey for us because to some extent they're tied into U.S. capital spending. The rise in the U.S. dollar has impacted the growth in capex but I think that the growth in U.S. capex will resume sooner than later.

What other themes do you have your eye on?

I think that it's pretty obvious that if you believe the emerging market story, their populations will demand a higher standard of living, especially with better quality foods. So we review fertilizer, seed, and agriculture equipment stocks. Also, given the world's geopolitical situation we should be sharpening our pencils on defense stocks. Another theme that I think is unfolding is the renaissance of U.S. manufacturing, a future bright spot for U.S. markets, through the increased use of 3D printing and robotics. Another question we have for some management is, "To what extent can you replace some of your manufacturing process with the 3D and/or the use of robots?" I think one or both are going to revolutionize North American manufacturing.

What does your investment decision-making process finally come down to before you actually add a position to the portfolio?

I want to point out the merits of conducting one's own research. While we think there's some great research on Bay Street and Wall Street, where possible we try to go to talk to companies before we invest in them. We do not look for inside information. We simply want to hear directly from a company's management what their plans are.

How do you gauge management and assess their plans?

First I look at the person's body language, their tonality, and the level of eye contact when responding to my questions. I always send a list of questions beforehand and assess how they answer them. You get an impression not available from reading a research report.

What are some standard questions that you ask management?

"If we were having this conversation five years from now, what are some of the things that you'd be doing that you aren't doing today and what are you doing now that you might not be doing then? How are you going to reach your objectives in terms of strategic planning, existing management talent, and finances? What is the worst nightmare that keeps you awake at night?"

Sometimes the answers are nonsense and sometimes they make sense. That to me is invaluable in making the investment decision.

Do you believe the Efficient Market Theory, though? The idea that all of your additional independent research, including interviews with management, are already readily available and priced into the stock?

Not in the least. The basic truth is that if you give 10 different money managers the same information, you may see 10 different reactions.

To identify inefficiencies in securities, can you simply compare a company's book value to its market capitalization?

I don't. I've been criticized for that. I think book value matters less, though. It's what the assets produce that actually matters.

So how exactly do you identify mispricings in the market?

That's a tough one. In one set of circumstances it may involve a company we like but haven't bought because the price was too high or we own and want to buy more but haven't for the same reason. If the price takes a hit, we quickly determine whether that hit was a one-off or something more serious. If it is the former, we buy. If we think it is the latter, we don't buy. A recent example involves SNC-Lavalin. It is a truism that when something in a company's operations goes wrong there seldom is a *single* bedbug or cockroach in the story. In

SNC's case, several opined that following the initial weakness because of corporate misbehaviour, one should buy the stock. I chose not to.

There were more bedbugs to be found in SNC's sheets [laughs].

Exactly *[laughs]*.

Is it harder now to find value in the market today?

Yes, it is. Mainly because of interest rate levels and the shrinkage in the supply of stocks, values have become extended. There is a variety of ways of measuring value. For example, one states that the appropriate multiple is 20 minus the rate of inflation. As some see inflation continuing at close to zero, they say stock market multiples can expand to close to 20 times. I take a different view. Based on my expectation that inflation (the U.S. CPI) could reach 2.5% next year, the best multiple on forward earnings one can expect is 17.5 times relative to 16.8 today. In my view going forward, earnings' growth must be what powers markets upward. The same is true for many individual equities.

Has high-frequency trading changed the game, making it more difficult to find and invest in value in the market?

Yes, people's time horizons have drastically shrunk. They want instant gratification through returns. That's not investing — it is sheer speculation. A slow and steady approach such as our value approach is GlobeInvest's style. "Slow and steady wins the day." If you think of our themes and you think of their duration, water is not the next three-month, six-month, or one-year story — it's a twenty- to thirty-year story. Feeding the population in emerging markets is the same. The pipeline business in Canada is a 30-year story. We do not trade frequently. I'll give you an example. Some years ago we started buying a pipeline at $7, and we bought it all the way up to the current price. People still ask, "Why do you still hold it?" Because for many clients the yield at book is double-digit. If I was to sell, it would be difficult to find a comparable return, especially if the stock was held outside a registered account and the sale proceeds were subject to capital gains tax.

Do you think that it's the new generation today that seeks instant gratification in the market?

I think there's some segment of market players who will always be looking for instant returns. After a while they will hopefully learn that the long-term view is the best view. Another story I tell to young people who are concerned about how to start an investment program is about the "gift of time" or really the magic of compounding returns. For example, if when a young person in his or her twenties starts investing and puts aside $100 a month for 40 years, the total investment will have turned into $48,000. If he or she waits 20 years and then starts investing $200 a month for 20 years he or she will have invested the same $48,000. But the dollar value of their account would be, even after saving the same $48,000, a third of the former, assuming a 6% average annual compound return. The spread widens the higher the long-term total return.

Do you think that being a successful investor in the market is innate or rather learned through experience?

I think it's a little of both, but more learned. Staying with a discipline is key. From time to time it may seem not to be working, but assuming it has been well thought out, it will serve you well in the long run. I think people could observe, learn from their mistakes, and hopefully become successful investors.

What do you read on a daily basis to stay current on the markets?

The morning starts off with the *Wall Street Journal*, the *Financial Times of London*, the *Globe and Mail*, the *National Post*, the *Washington Post*, and, on the weekends, *Barron's*.

What are some other sources that you use to base your investment decisions?

Yardeni Research. Ed Yardeni, whom I have known for 40 years, is in my view one of the finest economists and strategists alive. Don Coxe, whom I have known for about the same time, has had a major influence on my long-term investment thinking. Robert Krembil, a co-founder of the Trimark Funds, also had a major impact on my approach to security selection. For geopolitical information, Stratfor is first-class. They give you information and interpretations you don't always get in the regular news.

Who are some of the people who have had a major influence on your investment thinking?

There are far too many to list here but of those whom I knew personally, Russell J. Morrison, a name whom many today would remember, played a key role in mentoring me in my early years in the business. Jim Moltz, a partner at an old-line NYSE form, and C.J. Lawrence (Ed Yardeni's former boss) also played a key role, including stressing the importance of historical perspective. Of those of my vintage, certainly Ed and Don mentioned above and Gary Shilling of A. Gary Shilling & Co. Inc., and Robert Krembil played important parts in my investment thinking.

What are some of the books you've read that stand the test of time?

Once again, there are too many to list, but a few stand out mainly because they provided historical perspective. The first is *A History of Interest Rates* by Sidney Homer, the dean of bond market history. It takes you back to 1800 BC and, while it may sound dull, I found it absolutely fascinating. Equally fascinating is *The Great Wave: Price Revolutions and the Rhythm of History* by David Hackett Fischer. It describes in great detail the role of inflation from 1180 up to today. Another is *The Rise of Financial Capital: Integration of Capital Markets During the Age of Reason* by Larry Neal. It describes the increasing integration of London and Amsterdam securities from 1700 to 1800 and includes vignettes about certain misbehaviours which show that misbehaviour is certainly not a modern invention. Finally, for a perspective on equities, *Stocks for the Long Run* by Professor Jeremy J. Siegel will add to any reader's perspective.

Anything else to add before we wrap up?

Block out the random noise. We all get too much information. Learn what information you really need to make your investment decisions. Take a look at long-term themes that make sense. Finally, stay with your discipline.

Peter focused in on a multitude of trends — past, present, and future — that influence the market. In my opinion, the most impactful trend that he mentioned is that of significant future demographic changes around the world. Peter officially calls this favourable demographic trend the "Seismic Shift," a change that will involve the population bases in many developing nations, larger and younger when compared to those in developed nations, and their faster projected growth rates. In these developing nations this change has and will lead to a dramatic increase in their middle classes and industrial bases. These areas are expected to be the main drivers of world growth for the next several decades. And as

Peter said, "One can gain exposure [to this seismic shift] by investing in major international companies that have at least 50% of their business in emerging markets."

MASTER KEYS

PETER BRIEGER

1) "Once I've decided that I like an industry, I focus on the leaders."

2) "Aside from any macro-economic inflation or disinflation indicators, I focus on micro-economic factors."

3) "I . . . look at . . . the shape of the yield curve. Nothing will kill an economy and stock market faster than a flat or inverted yield curve because they are usually the forerunner of a recession."

4) "There are two sources of investment returns: income and capital gains."

5) "On a global macro-economic basis, if you take a look at the world demographics, we like emerging markets long-term. Why? Because, with the exception of China and a few others, the emerging economies have the same demographic trends we had in North America in the fifties and sixties."

6) "One can gain exposure by investing in major international companies that have at least 50% of their business in emerging markets."

7) "I believe it was Professor Jeremy Siegel of the Wharton School who pointed out that long-term stock returns were between 6% and 8% but half of that return came from dividends and their growth."

8) "My biggest theme now is water. I think water's the next oil, and fortunately we've had good luck with water companies that have been taken over. [However], water is not the next three-month, six-month, or one-year story — it's a twenty- to thirty-year story."

---

9) "If you believe the emerging market story, their populations will demand a higher standard of living, especially with better quality foods. So we review fertilizer, seed, and agriculture equipment stocks."

10) "The basic truth is that if you give 10 different money managers the same information, you may see 10 different reactions."

11) "I think book value matters less. . . . It's what the assets produce that actually matters."

12) "If the price takes a hit, we quickly determine whether that hit was a one-off or something more serious. If it is the former, we buy. If we think it is the latter, we don't buy."

13) "Earnings' growth must be what powers markets upward."

14) "People's time horizons have drastically shrunk. They want instant gratification through returns. That's not investing — it is sheer speculation. 'Slow and steady wins the day.'"

15) "Staying with a discipline is key. From time to time it may seem not to be working but, assuming it has been well thought out, it will serve you well in the long run."

PART V SYSTEMATIC (OR TECHNICAL)

Systematic or technical investors invest in positions based largely on a quantitative, rules-driven, technical system that limits any manual qualitative analysis. While the investors we've already heard from — value, growth, fundamental, and macro (top-down) — would likely agree that investing is an art, systematic or technical investors would argue that it's a science. Success for these investors is the extent to which one can remove human intervention, and possible erroneous decisions, in the selection of securities in the market. At the core of these investors' systems is a strong risk management foundation.

BILL CARRIGAN
GETTING TECHNICAL

"I'll be the old guy with the black jacket on," said Bill Carrigan the day before we met at the Grimsby food court for our interview. In hindsight, the Grimsby food court was not the ideal location for our interview — it was small, noisy, and busy. So, before the interview got started, I asked Bill to raise his voice and talk as close to the recorder as he could throughout our conversation. He complied, but not until he got a cold-cut sandwich from Mr. Sub, and a double double from Tim Hortons, both of which he ate and drank through the first half of the interview. I didn't mind the munching or the noisy atmosphere, though. This was pure, unadulterated Bill Carrigan, the "straight shooter." He was honest, brash, and, above all, chock-full of bang-on observations about the market. I was able to watch some of Bill's astute predictions from our interview play out in the stock market over the next couple of months. I was awe-struck. Bill is a genius — although, to the people around us in the food court, Bill probably came across as just an old guy with a black jacket on.

Bill is very pessimistic about both the markets and the investment industry, questioning the way in which they operate. To illustrate, his Twitter bio reads, "With 30 years' experience in the investment industry I have learned to never get sucked into a compelling story — leave it for the Investment Sheep. Baahhh humbug." During our interview, he expounded upon the compelling story of the month: Patient Home Monitoring (PHM). Sarcastically he said, "We're all going to be rich, we're all going to make a fortune. Nobody's going to lose buying that stock." I guess that's the opinion of Bill's Investment Sheep. Clearly, PHM ranks high on Bill's shitstorm meter.

If it doesn't become obvious during the interview, Bill is also a fan of the immensely popular Canadian mockumentary TV show *Trailer Park Boys*, where the character Jim Lahey often uses "shitstorm" in reference to any dire situation fuelled by Ricky, Julian, or Bubbles, the trailer park's hellions. Truth be told, I was against any form of technical investing in my early days of investing. Today, while I don't use technical investing to *ultimately* inform my final stock selection, it does help me *validate* my investment decisions. I leverage technical analysis to assess a stock's relative strength, as well as monitor its moving-day averages, and support or resistance levels. Bill has lots more technical indicators to share, many of which could very well become key inputs into your stock selection process. What's especially intriguing about his technical investing framework is that he combines technical indicators to uncover future takeover plays.

Bill was a technical sub-advisor to Stonebrooke Asset Management Ltd., which manages the Hybrid Investment Program under the Elite Wealth Strategies for Union Securities Ltd. During his time there, Bill made five astute technical selections that were eventually the subject of takeover bids: Gerdau Ameristeel, El Paso Corp., Biovail Corp., Viterra Inc., and ShawCor Ltd. He has been writing a business column on technical investing in the *Toronto Star* since 1997, and continues writing the *Getting Technical Market Newsletter*, which he founded in December 1998.

PRE-INTERVIEW LESSONS

CHARTIST: an investor who engages in "charting," primarily using stock charts and technical indicators to inform his or her decisions on stocks (e.g., choosing to invest in stocks with positive trend lines).

CONSOLIDATION: companies within a sector (e.g., health care) that merge to create a smaller number of larger companies or volume that builds at or around a particular price point in a stock and determines its technical support.

MOMENTUM: price movements, either upward or downward, that continue, establishing a trend.

RESISTANCE: an overhead price level in a stock chart that makes it difficult for a stock price to break through to make new highs or re-price itself to previous highs.

ROLL-UP: a highly acquisitive company that acquires companies, integrates them into their parent company, and then makes them accretive, often within a very short period of time, to the bottom line. Can also be referred to as a platform company.

SUPPORT: a lower price level in a stock chart that makes it difficult for a stock price to break under to re-price itself to previous lows.

TREND LINE: a line drawn on a chart to show the general price direction.

Where did you grow up in Canada?

I grew up in Toronto.

Whereabouts in Toronto?

East York.

How did you first get interested in the markets?

I bought my first shares when I was a teenager — Thomson Newspapers.

What was your thesis to buy Thomson Newspapers?

Well, I had two choices. This is back in the early sixties. I could buy Thomson Newspapers, or RCA, which was making colour TV sets. The advisor recommended RCA, because of the TV boom. But I looked at the charts, and I found one was going down and the other was going up. So I bought the one that was going up, which was Thomson Newspapers.

You didn't care about fundamentals?

No, either they're going up or going down. That's all I cared about.

Your focus then was purely momentum.

Here's an example where one stock, RCA, had a compelling story. Thomson Newspapers was not a compelling story. It was kind of a dull story. But the compelling story stock was going down. The boring story was going up.

Your Twitter handle is @InvestmentSheep. Do you believe that, generally, investors buy into compelling stories, and usually when it is too late? When the story ends, those stocks crash.

Usually when the compelling story gets very compelling, the stock has pretty well peaked. But when the stock starts to peak and go down, the story gets even more compelling. There's a compelling story out there now — one stock based in Vancouver that everybody has to own. It's mentioned about 10 times a day.

Which stock is that?

Patient Home Monitoring.

Yes, I've heard of that company.

Everybody has to own that stock. So, "We're all going to be rich, we're all going to make a fortune. Nobody's going to lose buying that stock." Well, you know, I've heard and seen that all before.

Is the story that it will ride the baby boomer wave?

Yeah, basically. So, it's in the medical field. Medical is a hot sector now. The demographics are right because it's taking care of old people. People are obviously getting older. Well, there's a lot of companies running the same type of business but, according to this company, they're going to buy them all out. So it's just going to go to the moon and everybody's going to be rich and live happily ever after.

You've seen these hot stocks before. The people buying into them must make you cringe.

Do you ever watch *Trailer Park Boys*?

Yes, I've watched all the episodes.

Okay, in my opinion, very soon over at Patient Home Monitoring the "shit hawk" is going to start flying over the stock. Unfortunately there's a lot of guys that actually own the stock. So there could be a real mess. But let's see what happens. If it takes six months to unfold, we'll find out. It will be interesting to watch because I've seen these things before.

Going back to your early days, did you go to university or college?

I went to Ryerson.

Did you continue to buy stocks after your win with Thomson Newspapers?

Pretty much. Although I have a musical background, too. Believe it or not, there is a relationship, because the technical analysis of the stock market requires a bit of math. And music requires a lot of math. So actually musicians are pretty good mathematicians. I spent most of my time while I was at Ryerson watching Ronnie Hawkins. So I used to cut classes a lot because I was watching Ronnie Hawkins and The Band.

Upon graduation you worked for a company called MarketFax Info Services. You helped them develop their charting software for technical analysis, correct?

This was before the internet. So we were connecting PCs via Bell networks that you could dial up. We had a server in downtown Toronto. It cost us about $35,000 and it filled up about half a room. It was ridiculous. However, the internet was coming, and basically another guy in New York saw this coming, too, and started doing the same thing. His name is Bloomberg. So the rest is history.

I assume that charting wasn't as popular back then as it is now.

It was popular, but it was hard to do. Because without the internet you just had to draw your own charts, or you had to buy books. And the books would come out about twice a month.

So you were always lagging the market.

You were lagging the market. You had to fill it in.

After MarketFax Info Services was beaten in the market by Bloomberg, you moved to Southam Communications.

Yeah, I did. We were broadcasting quotes there. You've heard of the radio station Q107?

Q107, yes.

Well, FM is a band and there's space above and below the band. So we used to put the stock quotes in there. So if you had a PC with a low antenna you could pick up stock quotes by tuning in to the radio station Q107.

That's interesting.

Yeah, so that worked for a while, but again, the internet was coming. We just didn't think it would be coming that fast and change everything so quickly.

From there, you became a weekly columnist for the Toronto Star *on technical analysis, and also started up the* Getting Technical Market Letter.

That's right.

Also, you worked at Union Securities, where your mandate was to find five stocks that would eventually be subject to takeover bids. How do you go about identifying takeover candidates through technical analysis?

I have two criteria. That they have a long base, and the stock is sort of out of favour. That would rule out stocks like Patient Home Monitoring. So you just pick a stock that's out of favour and has a long base. And the idea is if you buy into a long base and it's a decent stock, and it's overlooked, the worst thing that can happen to you is *nothing*.

Long base, meaning that the stock's been consolidating? It's been flat for a period of time?

Yeah. Vetera was a classic case. No one was interested in the stock — it was just going sideways. So I thought, "Well, the market's going to wake up to this." So we bought in.

Aside from looking for long bases and out-of-favour stocks, I heard that you also use accumulation distribution and on-balance volume (OBV) technical indicators.

You've done your homework there *[laughs]*. Yeah, I like to find the accumulation distribution. You're basically following the money. Smart money. There's always somebody smarter than you. Somebody's going to find out about a stock before you will. If a stock's going sideways, but the accumulation distribution lines are still slightly rising, that tells me that there's smart money buying the stock. What happens is that people are accumulating a position. The up-days have higher volume than the down-days. And these lines show that. So you'll have quiet days where the volume shrinks, then you'll have two or three up-days where the volume increases, and then the buyers back away and let the stock settle down. It touches down the low bottom. Then they come back in, push the stock back up, and the volume starts increasing. If you see these accumulation distribution lines start to rise, that's kind of your clue.

So you monitor volume, not price.

Yeah, and there's always somebody that's working harder than you are. You can't look at every stock. So somebody's out there doing their homework.

You bought into the languishing Biovail before it became Valeant. Now Valeant is a mega-stock that has just eclipsed RBC in market capitalization, making it the biggest stock on the TSX. How did you catch that opportunity through technical analysis?

It was pretty well hated because of Biovail's founder and CEO, Melnyk. He wasn't a very popular guy. At Union Securities, I was co-managing the portfolio with a fundamental guy. I was the technical guy. You might not know this — I got my CIM designation because I wanted to know how these fundamental guys think, so that when they're talking to me I know where they're coming from. Anyway, I said to the fundamental guy, "The chart for Biovail looks good; there's smart money buying this stock; it's got accumulation. What do you think?" So the fundamental guy looks at it and says, "Well, the fundamentals and the balance sheet looks okay. I can't see that we're going to get hurt." My thesis was that somebody's buying Biovail but it's out of favour. This was in the early days before the health care hysteria really got going in the market. So we got into it around $14. Anyway, we sold the stock in the $30s. Not because of the technical reasons. It's because the fundamental guy said,

"It's too high at $38, it's too expensive. The valuation is out of whack." So the lesson here is, never sell a stock just because it's "expensive." Because, oftentimes, expensive stocks simply get more expensive. The stocks that are cheap, they just keep getting cheaper. So the fundamental guy was to me a real pain in the neck. He was always selling too soon.

Did you ever buy back into Biovail?

No, we never bought it back. Bought it at $14 and sold it at $38.

Selling Biovail at $38 was definitely a misguided decision. Through its transformation into Valeant, it's gone on to become a $300 stock.

The same guy went and bought RIM before RIM changed its name.

So that would be your example of cheap stocks that get cheaper.

He started buying RIM at $70. Bought more at $50.

He was forced to average down, because if he didn't, his cost base would have been high.

It was getting cheaper, so he kept buying it. I kept saying to him, "You know you can't have this thing sitting in clients' statements month after month losing money. People just aren't going to tolerate it; they're going to think there's something wrong with you." He finally sold out of BlackBerry at $19, after averaging down all the way from the $70s. And it's never seen $19 since. This was years ago.

Does technical analysis still tell you that BlackBerry is not a buy?

That's right. Even though the company probably has a turnaround plan. It's trying to build a base. But the on-balance volume (OBV) isn't showing me that I should buy it, so I don't see any reason to buy it yet.

How did the technical versus fundamental dynamic work at Union Securities between you and your partner? Was is sustainable?

I always touched base with the fundamental guy. I just wanted to know if there's a horror story, something in the closet I did not know about the company, because technically they looked good. The fundamental guy would basically say that if the fundamentals of the company were neutral, then he'd be in.

I also heard that you identify the leading stock sectors as measured by a weekly and/or monthly rotation table. Can you describe those rotation tables and how you construct them?

Well, it's basically a combination of momentum and relative analysis. Relative analysis is, how does something perform compared to something else? So when you construct the table, you're ranking momentum — which is first, second, third, fourth, you know — in sectors. But you're also ranking them on how they're doing versus themselves. So how they're doing versus somebody else, and how are they doing versus themselves.

Can you elaborate?

You can have a sector go to number one. First rank gives it momentum. And then it can stay at number one but the momentum can become weaker. So the number one is still number one versus everybody else, but number one can be getting weaker relative to itself. So the tables are two-dimensional. I go first dimension, and then second dimension.

How often do you produce rotation tables?

I use a spreadsheet for that, but there's another method I use, which is done by the software.

Which software do you use?

There's two. There's Metastock, and then there's Supercharts, which is an older software package which runs only in XP, and will not run on the 64-bit systems. Which means that I'm forced to keep two XP machines — I'm always running them.

Supercharts must be your preferred program then.

That's right. So I have to use XP for a while yet until I catch on to Metastock.

Do those rotation tables — whether in spreadsheets or programs — give you buy signals?

Well, I'm working with a BMO set of funds. I set up a basket of 10 exchange-traded funds on a global basis, and compare. Essentially, I'm conducting a relative analysis test against a benchmark. So right now we're using the TSX as a benchmark. That's why we're doing a relative study versus, let's say the European ETF or the Japanese ETF. I want to know how Japan is doing versus the TSX.

If you were to see a convergence of the Japanese and U.S. indexes, would that be a buy signal for the Japanese index?

Yep.

What would be a sell signal?

A divergence. If you're an investor for the long term, use the 26-week low.

The 26-week low?

The lowest week of 26 weeks. Basically anything in a bear market should make a new low within a six-month window of 26 weeks. To me that's the definition of a bear. So if you have a market that trades down, makes a correction, and then doesn't take that low within six months, then it's not a bear.

So, rather, it would be a buy signal if it doesn't break that support?

Yes. But if it does break it, it's a sell signal. Though if you're a short-term trader you would use 10-week low.

If a stock has strong momentum, but an excessively high P/E multiple, would you not buy it?

Meaningless. As a matter of fact, when I see a fundamental guy saying it's expensive I think he's full of crap. When I hear them say it's cheap, "cheap" means it's cheap for a reason.

What can go wrong though near the end of a momentum stock's run?

The problem comes from the money manager who focuses on thin-trading stocks. Half of the activity of the stock can often be his money, so the stock's rise can be a self-fulfilling prophecy. He's the one driving the stock higher. But then eventually it comes time to sell. And when everybody wants to sell, who's left to buy? So some of these stocks that are being promoted are relatively thin trades. So you have to be careful.

Sounds like Patient Home Monitoring.

See, the problem with fundamentals is that the fundamental analyst isn't going to know anything about jewellery stores by going to the annual meeting. He needs to have actually worked in a jewellery store to under-stand the real story. Take a stock like Auto Canada, which everybody loved for a while. When I was in Ryerson, to pay my tuition I worked at a GM dealer selling cars. Also, I worked as an apprentice mechanic. So I was at the back end of a dealer and at the front of it. I knew how com-plicated a dealership is: you've got new cars coming in, you're dealing with trade-ins, you're dealing with mechanics, you're dealing with the union, you're dealing with sales and marketing, you're dealing with the workers' compensation. You've got so much going on, so the only people who can run a dealership is the owner who is an entrepreneur. And why would a dealership ever go up for sale? It's because the owner can't take it anymore and wants to get out. So he's going to unload it to AutoCanada. Well, good luck with that.

Growth through acquisition or "roll-ups" seems to be a source of extreme returns in the market.

That's right.

Is that fuelled by cheap debt?

So, there's a choice: "Should we look for gold in Chile?" or "Should we come up with a roll-up story on health care? Let's go the health care route." When gold gets hot and the other stuff falls apart, then five years from now it'll be, "Let's do gold in Chile."

Should an investor interested in using technical analysis start with stocks or ETFs?

Do stocks. However, you'll find that stocks tend to move in herds. So for example the group of stocks that have started to attract money right now is the mining stocks. Something's going on. There's accumulation going on. The trick is, if you think there's money going into the group, you want to be there early. However, if there's an exchange-traded fund that covers the group, you'd be better off to buy the exchange-traded fund.

But if you buy into the right stocks at the right time, you should realize higher returns than ETFs?

Yeah, if you pick the right stocks at the right time, like health care. Or these mining stocks. If you buy one stock, you could hit it big. But the trick is to buy a basket. For example, for junior mining stocks there's no ETF. So you need to buy a basket of them. So if you buy five, two are going to up, one will go broke, and two will go down, you know?

It's a probability game. As long as your winners outpace the losers.

Right. But if you can get an index fund that covers the group of stocks, then do that. Otherwise you've got to stock pick.

What are some other common technical indicators?

The most popular right now is the moving average convergence divergence (MACD). But when you're looking at a MACD buy signal, there's about 20 million other people looking at the same signal. I want to know what these 20 million other people are thinking, because they're not all going to be right. So it's going to be a false signal. Basically, I like to deduce the signals that are not popular. Very corny and old-fashioned signals. The most old-fashioned signal is a trend line. It's hardly ever used today.

A trend line?

Just look at the chart and look at the trend line. Is it going up or going down? All a technician wants to know is, is it going up, is it going down, and will it stop doing that?

So the 200-day and 50-day moving averages?

Yeah. As an aside, the most popular tools now are the golden cross and the death cross. Well honestly, they're just a lot of crap. If you traded on the cross — between the 200-day and 50-day moving averages — you'd break even, because the cross always carries out halfway through the move. So I never use the cross. What I use is the difference — when the 50-day moving average gets too far above or too far below the 200-day moving average, that's all I care about. I don't care about the cross.

When the 50-day moving average goes higher than the 200-day moving average, what does that indicate and how do you play the stock at that point?

That means that the stock is overbought. You don't want to acquire up there. So you let the 50-day average calm down a bit; either it'll touch or go below or go too far below, one or the other. But overall, you still have to watch the overall trend.

I've seen you use a chart where you compare USD to the crude oil price. You demonstrated that there's an inverse correlation between the two. Further, you highlighted that because this relationship recently changed, crude found its bottom.

Okay so you're looking at say the 15-year chart of crude versus the U.S. dollar. They're monthly closes. We don't care about weekly closes or daily closes. Okay, so what's going on now? So I want to see divergence. If the U.S. dollar makes the new high versus an older high, and if crude is inverse, crude should make a new low versus the old low. The last major highs and lows with crude and the dollar were the '08 financial crisis. The U.S. dollar made a high during the financial crisis, and crude made a low during the financial crisis. However, right now the U.S. dollar has reached above the financial crisis high. So if they're operating inversely, crude should have gone below the financial crisis low.

But crude did not make those lower lows.

Yeah. So crude is saying, "We're not going to do it this time." That's a positive divergence, telling me there is a bottom in oil prices. I'm not saying how long it's going to be, but I am saying it's a bottom. So you're not going to see crude at 30 bucks.

Whereas the fundamental analyst would look at geopolitical issues to speculate on the price of oil.

"There's nowhere to put it, people are going to be putting it in their basements, they have nowhere to hide it" *[laughs]*.

That's not common sense. Purely speculative.

It's ridiculous.

I've heard you make mention of trading based on dominant themes. Can you explain?

Well, you have to look at the history of dominant themes. One of the rules of the dominant theme is that it persists for a generation or more and it also has to be investible. Because besides being able to identify it, most dominant themes are recognized after the fact. The first modern dominant theme is the railroad. When Charles Dow invented the first average, it was not the industrial average, it was the transportation average. So it was a basket of railroads that you could buy. The next dominant theme after that was the automobile. For example, you could buy automobile stocks, such as Ford or GM. Then we had dominant theme of war. The Second World War. Auto production stopped. The Big Three started making tanks and trucks and so on. Then after the war the auto makers started making cars and we started making highways. Okay, that was quite an investable dominant theme, because out of that, you got mass urban sprawl — suburbs. Fast-food restaurants, drive-in theatres, shopping malls, and so on.

What are the next dominant themes?

So aerospace is a dominant theme, and health care certainly is. Health care is getting a little bit out of control right now, but still it's going to go until it pops. Dominant themes can pop and return in different forms. In the late eighties I saw the internet coming, but I really didn't realize it was *coming* to that extent. And then the dot-com bubble of 2000 popped, but technology has still gone on.

Did you capitalize on the internet dominant theme?

Early, yeah. Some of the stocks I bought at $2, sold them at $8 or $10, and then they went to $100. It was just ridiculous. However, that first internet dominant theme was mainly restricted to the English-speaking countries. Now, the technology boom we've got is a global event. The internet is being rolled out all around the world.

What will end the next technology bubble?

Well, everybody has a smartphone. Eventually, when the whole world owns a smartphone, who's left to buy a smartphone? That bubble will burst. It'll turn into a commodity.

How do you identify dominant themes, and invest in them, before they start?

You have to try to see things early. It's hard. For example, the defense stocks. When you look at the dot-com bubble and the crash, defense stocks did very well thereafter.

So, the War on Terror that had started in 2001 was the dominant theme. Once could have invested in that theme as early as the September 11 terrorist attack on America.

Yes.

Do you trade options?

No, I don't.

Why don't you?

Back in the late seventies, I liked a stock and I wanted to buy call options on it. But then a very wise man told me, "Young man, if you like the stock, just buy the stock." When you buy options, you need to get three things right. When you buy stocks, you only need to get one thing right: invest in it, and it'll go up. If you buy an option, you need to decide which way's it going to go, when it's going to do that, and to what extent it's going to do that. So, you need to get the direction, the time, and the magnitude right. Why have three problems when you can only have one? Just buy the stock.

What have been some of your biggest winners?

The biggest success I had was when I picked a basket of Toronto stocks in the early 2000s that were beneficiaries of global growth. Magna, CGI, and so on.

Great foresight.

Yeah. We had some consumer stocks in that basket, too, but that's an obvious story now. Consumerism is long in the tooth. So I'd be very cautious.

Why are you cautious on the consumer theme?

The Dow Jones Industrial Average — they've recently added Apple to it. S&P states that Apple is a technology stock, but that's a lot of crap. Apple's a vertically integrated consumer stock. It's a sales machine for Mr. Consumer and Mrs. Consumer and Teenager Consumer. "Buy the crap that we make in China and we're going to deliver it to you." The Dow Jones has become an index full with "buy crap made somewhere else" companies.

If Mr. Dow were alive today, would he include those companies in the index?

He'd roll over in his grave.

Why?

The Dow Jones Industrial Average is supposed to contain industrials. So industrials meaning companies like General Electric. There's only about six actual industrials in the average right now. When Charles Dow put the index together, that's when all the stuff was made in the U.S.

So the Dow Jones Industrial Index does not reflect the real production of the U.S. economy?

The U.S. economy now is composed of people buying and selling crap to each other that's made somewhere else. That's the U.S. economy. It's a joke. I can't go into a Walmart store and find anything made in North America. There might be shoes there, or the odd jacket, but basically Walmart is like China Export Inc. They should just change the name.

How can one study up on technical trading?

Pring wrote a book called *Technical Analysis Explained*. That's probably the most reasonable book. And also, if you get a chance, learn how to do point-and-figure.

David Burrows also uses point-and-figure charts to inform his investment decisions.

You have to, because point-and-figures are reversal charts — you can see where and when something reverses. Very reliable, but hardly anybody uses them. So when you have a tool that works that hardly anybody else uses, then use that tool.

Why don't many people use point-and-figure charts?

It's old. It's been around so long. Young people don't want to look at old stuff. Who wants to look at an indicator that their grandfather used?

Good point. I assume that if you want an edge in the market today, you would look at indicators or information that other people generally wouldn't look at.

Right. So you look at the popular ones and what they're using, and then you look at the ones they're not using. You make your decision from there.

Any more advice?

The biggest mistake investors make is getting sucked in by a compelling story. And, again, compelling stories get more compelling as the stock starts to fall apart. I was just looking at a stock that I got involved with about five or six years ago. It was a good story. The company was called Hip International. Anyway, the stock started to break down but the story got even better; the press releases got more frequent. Usually when a stock is going up you'll see one press release a week. And then when things start to go bad you get almost one press release every day. Those press releases will say wonderful things that are going to happen. So you've got to be careful of that stuff. When the press release machine really starts to crank, you've got to be really careful.

When I was at the Money Show in October 2014, you demonstrated an intriguing correlation between the most negative newspaper headlines on the financial crisis and the market bottom at that time. That seemed to have been the ideal time to buy stocks.

The financial press is looking for headlines or news that people are going to be interested in reading. They really like to focus on a crisis. Usually the crisis occurs at the end of a move, not at the beginning. So the financial crisis actually started coming in '07 when the housing stock started to top out. And then when Lehman went bust, it was pretty well over. But the *Globe and Mail* had a picture of these giant U.S. banks being swallowed by a sinkhole. Goldman Sachs hit bottom right then and there. If you had bought Goldman Sachs, that was the low. That was October '08. And the rest of the market bottomed pretty much after that.

Good point — "Usually the crisis occurs at the end of a move." What's next, then?

I think health care and biotech are going to pop. Look at Concordia Healthcare.

Yeah — it's all over the news now.

So, these roll-ups have these tremendous growth acquisition stories. But they're using their stock prices as currency. Eventually these stories come to an end. Now I'm not saying the end's going to come in the next month, or this week, but eventually the bubble will pop. I would say that the bubble is probably going to be in biotechnology because a lot of them still are not making any money.

Bill and I chatted about various unrelated topics as well, but he sprinkled in some important stock market insight not found in our transcribed conversation that I deemed important enough to include here:

- "Don't react if the stock price has broken up or down; wait for a couple of days so it validates the move."
- "Don't go against the market trend."
- "Key reversals should be validated against fundamentals."

Also, while Bill uses subscription software to run technical scans and display charts, there is free online software that you can use to perform the same functions: StockCharts.com. On StockCharts, you can run daily scans on indicators such as new 52-week highs and strong volume gainers. Additionally, you can apply a multitude of technical indicators on each individual security under your analysis. For example, you can pull up RBC's chart, and overlay on-balance volume (OBV), accumulation distribution, and 50- and 200-day moving averages, spanning a period of one to five years. Personally, I like to run daily scans on trending strong volume gainers, to follow the "smart money," as Bill said, into new positions, before any stake is publicly announced or known to the masses.

Bill expounded on two other important concepts: dominant themes and rotation tables. Below are Bill's direct explanations of both concepts as well as his recommended reading list, from the Getting Technical website:

> In the long run you're better off seeking out the dominant theme and staying with it for as long as it takes to unfold. The dominant theme is a group of related stocks that emerges from obscurity during a crisis to assume a leadership role for several years. Investors who identify the dominant theme early can buy and hold their way to investment greatness. The last modern dominant theme was the "new economy" technology boom of the 1980s and 1990s. In that 20-year period the tech-laden NASDAQ advanced non-stop over 3000%, grinding out an annualized return of over 20%.
>
> Our approach is to identify the leading stock sectors as measured by our weekly and monthly rotation tables. We then scan the sector components for stocks with the strongest relative performance. Stock sectors group stocks by asset class, e.g., consumer, technology, or materials. Sector selection takes advantage of natural sector rotation as measured by our weekly and monthly rotation tables. Sector selection can also include global asset classes such as Japan, Hong Kong, Eastern Europe, or Mexico. Exchange-traded funds are used whenever available.

RECOMMENDED READING ON TECHNICAL ANALYSIS

1. *Technical Analysis of the Futures Markets*
2. *Technical Analysis Explained*
3. *Elliott Wave Principle*
4. "Comparative Study" in *The Encyclopedia of Technical Market Indicators*

You can also find some of technical investing's most notable technical indicators in the glossary section of Bill Carrigan's Getting Technical.

1) "Usually when the compelling story gets very compelling, the stock has pretty well peaked. . . . The biggest mistake investors make is getting sucked in by a compelling story."

2) "If you buy into a long base [i.e., consolidation] and it's a decent stock, and it's overlooked, the worst thing that can happen to you is nothing."

3) "If a stock's going sideways, but the accumulation distribution lines are still slightly rising, that tells me that there's smart money buying the stock."

4) "Never sell a stock just because it's 'expensive.' Because, oftentimes, expensive stocks simply get more expensive."

5) "The stocks that are cheap, they just keep getting cheaper. 'Cheap' means it's cheap for a reason."

6) "Basically anything in a bear market should make a new low within a six-month window of twenty-six weeks. To me that's the definition of a bear. So if you have a market that trades down, makes a correction, and then doesn't take that low within six months, then it's not a bear."

7) "Half of the activity of the stock can often be [the money manager's] money, so the stock's rise can be a self-fulfilling prophecy. He's the one driving the stock higher. But then eventually it comes time to sell. And when everybody wants to sell, who's left to buy?"

8) "If you think there's money going into the group [of stocks], you want to be there early. However, if there's an exchange-traded fund that covers the group, you'd be better off to buy the exchange-traded fund."

9) "I like to deduce the signals that are not popular. Very corny and old-fashioned signals. The most old-fashioned signal is a trend line. It's

hardly ever used today. . . . Is it going up or going down? All a technician wants to know is, is it going up, is it going down?"

10) "I never use the [death] cross. What I use is the difference — when the 50-day moving average gets too far above or too far below the 200-day moving average, that's all I care about."

11) "One of the rules of the dominant theme is that it persists for a generation or more and it also has to be investible. [Also], dominant themes can pop and return in different forms."

12) "When you buy options, you need to get three things right: which way's it going to go [direction], when it's going to do that [time], and to what extent it's going to do that [magnitude]."

13) "Point-and-figures are . . . very reliable, but hardly anybody uses them. So when you have a tool that works that hardly anybody else uses, then use that tool."

14) "Usually when a stock is going up, you'll see one press release a week. And then when things start to go bad, you get almost one press release every day. When the press release machine really starts to crank, you've got to be really careful."

15) "The financial press is looking for headlines or news that people are going to be interested in reading. They really like to focus on a crisis. Usually the crisis occurs at the end of a move, not at the beginning."

16) "Roll-ups have these tremendous growth acquisition stories. But they're using their stock prices as currency. Eventually these stories come to an end."

JASON MANN
THE QUANT MOMENTUM INVESTOR

Jason Mann is all about momentum. At EdgeHill Partners, Jason runs the flagship EHP Advantage Fund. That fund has delivered a 23% compound annual return since its inception. How does Jason deliver such high returns? He employs a quant-based, rules-driven system for stock selection. Additionally, he follows a strictly balanced long/short policy, and maintains 400 to 500 highly liquid positions in the fund at any given time. Through the EHP Advantage Fund, Jason buys undervalued, rising, stable stocks and shorts overvalued, declining, volatile stocks. He actively gears down risk in declining markets and rotates toward more defensive stocks and strategies to preserve capital. Impressively, Jason geared down before the oil crash impacted Canadian markets. In the EHP Advantage Fund's fact sheet, there's a chart that shows a clear divergence starting in August 2014 between the fund and the TSX, whereby the former rose while the latter plunged.

Jason's idea of "gearing down" means taking very specific steps: reducing net exposure, rotating to more defensive strategies, and reducing beta to zero. This gear-down concept demonstrates that while Jason is full speed ahead in rising and stable markets, he knows when, how, and where to take a detour when there's a crash up ahead. Jason says, "We aim to participate in bull markets and sit out of bear markets." All investors should understand and implement risk management in their trading or investing practice, since protecting capital is just as important, or some might argue more important, than growing capital in the market.

In addition to the core long/short investment strategy employed at EdgeHill Partners, Jason also shared with me the other strategies he used while he was a managing director, co-head of the Absolute Return/Arbitrage Group at Scotia Capital. The Absolute Return Group is responsible for developing and delivering cross-platform alpha-generating ideas for the hedge fund community.

PRE-INTERVIEW LESSONS

ALGORITHM: algorithmic trading or "algos" is used by larger institutions to decide the pricing, timing, and quantity of stock orders.

BETA: measures volatility and correlation of a stock, in comparison to the stock market.

BOUGHT DEAL: financing in which investment bank(s) commit to buy a new equity offering from the company, at a designated price, on a set date.

DRAWDOWN: a loss incurred by an investment between its high and low over a given period of time.

LIQUIDITY: how easily an investment can be converted to cash, at or around market prices.

QUANTITATIVE OR RULES-DRIVEN: employing algorithms to capture gains in the market, as in quant-based trading or investing strategies.

VIX: ticker symbol for the CBOE Volatility Index, which is the measure of the volatility of SAP 500 index options. Can also be referred to as the "fear index."

Where did you grow up in Canada?

I was born in Hamilton and I grew up in Dundas.

When did you first get interested in the markets?

I recall making my first investment when I was either 12 or 13 years old. I had a decent paper route that was inside an apartment building with 100 customers. Whether it was raining or snowing, I could do my route in 20 minutes. One Christmas I remember getting $500 in tips from my clients. Also, my father was a stockbroker at one point in his life, as well as a mutual fund investor, and I remember telling him, "Okay, I've got this $500; I want to invest it in mutual funds." I also recall that was around 1987; the crash of '87 was shortly after and my investment went down 20 or 30%. I asked my father, "What are we going to do about all of this?" and he said, "Absolutely nothing." This is what equity investment can sometimes be about — you need to take a long-term time frame and don't worry about it. You're 13, and you've got 60 years of investing life ahead of you.

At what point did you shift from mutual funds to stocks?

I was more of a traditional buy-and-hold index or mutual type investor up until university. I did a business degree at Laurier University. But at that time, I was actually more interested in marketing, sales, and technology — that side of the business world. It wasn't until I was running my own business, which was an internet company that we raised money for in 2000, that we actually had some cash flow and an ability to invest, that we started buying individual stocks.

What was that internet company?

It was a company called Brainhunter.com and it facilitated a direct relationship from employer to candidate with a software tool.

And how did you finance Brainhunter.com?

We financed it. So just prior to that, when I came out of school, I worked at a company called Procom, which was an IT contracting firm. I left Procom to start Brainhunter. It was basically an online version of Procom, in terms of the model. We raised $12 million with TD Bank. TD led the financing with a group of private investors and venture capital firms.

What was the outcome of Brainhunter.com?

It was a great learning experience. We raised the money in August of 2000, so basically at the end of the technology boom, and frankly it had already started to go bust. We sold the company for $4 million a couple of years later. It was a great learning experience, but not a particularly profitable one for us or our investors. Ultimately, Workopolis, which is owned by the *Globe and Mail*, bought a piece of it for $10 million later on. But at that point I had left the company. However, the experience taught me about the true workings of a business — cash flow statements, balance sheets, income statements — which you can really only understand after you actually run a business or can really dig into one. And it was through that experience and that willingness to change careers.

And then eventually at Scotiabank you worked your way up to managing director and co-head of the Absolute Return Arbitrage Group. Can you describe the alpha-generating ideas that you employed there?

Sure, so we ran a portion of the banks' proprietary money. And our group also covered hedge fund clients. So we would analyze, trade ideas, recommend them to hedge fund clients, help them execute, and we would also put those trades on ourselves. The prop desk is a funny place because you've got one client: the bank. You'll never get fully paid for knocking it out of the park, but you'll absolutely get fired for losing money, so there is a strange risk/reward profile. You're focused on the risk first, and then you figure out what you can make given the risk you're willing to take. That's not that different from running a fund, so it's a good training ground for that. In terms of the trades, we did a lot of merger arbitration or what's also called risk arbitrage. While we employed strategies there that had a high probability of a small gain, we could lever up to magnify the gain.

Though, today, the spreads have narrowed on risk arbitrage.

Yeah, sort of. When I was at Scotiabank from 2003 to 2010, the spreads were tighter by that point. Risk arbitrage spreads are a function of interest rates; the higher interest rates are, the higher the cost of capital and therefore the higher the demand of return on a risk arbitrage spread. In the late nineties, there was so much money chasing the dot-com stocks that risk arbitrage spreads annualized at 20% were being completely ignored in favour of a dot-com stock that could go up 20% every day. So there was a lack of buyers and that created an opportunity. Now, with interest rates near zero, risk arbitrage spreads for a high-quality merger deal could be 4, 5, or 6% annualized. That's a pretty low rate of return. Frankly, we don't use it in our fund, because the absolute rate of return is too low. We'd have to lever it up to get a return that's high enough for us. Risk arbitrage is a strategy where you're picking up pennies in front of a steam roller in the first place. And adding a lot of leverage to that is a surefire way to get yourself hurt.

Regardless, what's been one of your biggest wins from risk arbitrage?

Probably our largest absolute dollar win was the Fording Coal merger with Teck Cominco. Teck Cominco was buying Fording Coal right in the middle of the '08 crisis. When it happened there were a lot of arbitrage players using a lot of leverage, but at that point in time, banks were pulling in leverage and effectively margin-calling clients. There was one particular client in Canada, with a very large position on Fording Coal, who had their bank pull their lines. They had to unwind that risk arbitrage position. The spread opened to extremely wide levels. The deal itself was questionable and was done right at the top of the market with a lot of debt, so it almost bankrupted Teck Cominco. It was a challenged deal in the first place. You had the sense that if Teck Cominco could have gotten out of the deal, they would have, so that means that you're going to have a wider risk arbitrage spread. That, coupled with the fact that you had this margin call seller blowing out the spread at any price, created a huge opportunity. We had a large position on our books, and then the bank itself actually entered into a special agreement with Teck Cominco to acquire more shares of Fording Coal to help them close the transaction. Anyways, it was a good trade to start, which then started losing a lot of money, and then became a great trade, because it was someone else's risk mismanagement that was to our benefit.

You didn't succumb to pressure to also unwind from that trade?

Well, we didn't know that that client was unwinding from Fording Coal. All we saw was the spread widening so then we started to dig around to figure out why. The initial concern of course was that the deal was blowing up and that it wasn't going to close. Anyway, anytime you have a position going against you, it's like I said before, you'll absolutely get fired if you lose too much money. So there's always pressure to contain that risk. But we eventually determined that the deal was solid. We were speaking to the bankers that were financing the deal: the debt was going to be there, Teck Cominco clearly wanted to close the transaction, and the pressure was really being driven by a forced seller. That gave you the conviction to actually add to the position.

Would you also enter risk arbitrage positions based on rumoured deals?

No, that would be a category called pre-arbitrage, which really isn't a category at all. You could call it event-driven — that's probably a kinder way to say it. It wouldn't really be our style. We were looking to play announced deals of high quality for a high probability of a small gain because we had access to a lot of capital and could effectively leverage that trade to get a decent absolute return. It's the kind of thing that you could do on a prop desk when you have a high degree of confidence; you can't really do it in a fund because it's a capital pig. You ruin your rate of return. It is not going to be great unless you really lever that up. There are potentially better uses for that capital.

So, with risk arbitrage spreads now at 3 to 5%, what strategies do you focus on in your current funds?

The way we run money here is quantitative, or systematic, or rules-driven. We effectively evaluate stocks based on their attributes, as opposed to what an analyst thinks, what the street's saying, what the story is, or what management's telling us. The attributes we look for are value, price momentum, and low volatility. To put it another way, we want to buy the best combination of cheap, rising, and stable stocks.

How do you determine value?

Value for me is returns-driven. It's not based on price to book. We use a combination of price to cash flow, return on equity, earnings beats and misses, interest coverage, and balance sheet leverage. Most important though is to determine the price of a company relative to its historical ability to generate cash. That's what we care about when we measure value. So we're not using forward estimates. Forward estimates are just that — an estimate, just a collection of guesses — whereas backwards looking is a factual representation of what a company has been able to do. Value works because the market becomes overly pessimistic about a formerly good company's ability to ever regain its footing and generate cash flows. Most of the time, on average, that's not true. And a stock gets overly discounted relative to the ability of that company to recover.

Do you immediately buy into a company that's fallen out of favour?

We don't. Value's a great discounting mechanism and it's a great source of future returns, but value is not a great timing mechanism. So you can buy way too early. I always say, "What do you call a stock that's down 90%? A stock that was down 80% and then got cut in half." You can buy something at an 80% discount and still take a lot of pain waiting for that value to play out.

So you wait for a catalyst, or price momentum, before you buy in.

That's right.

Otherwise, the stock could drop further or go sideways for years.

It can go sideways for years, or it can go much lower than you could have ever imagined. We want the combination of value and the rising trend. So with a rising trend, you can measure momentum both on an absolute basis where the stock itself is moving higher, or you can measure it on a relative basis where the stock is moving higher relative to everything else. We do both. The stock itself doesn't have to be moving higher, if everything else is moving lower, relatively speaking. We take shorts on the other side. So relative valuation and relative momentum matters as much to us as absolute value and absolute momentum. Because we are both long and short, we can benefit from both sides of that trade.

Why do out-of-favour stocks reverse their trend?

It can be a number of reasons. It can be the bottoming process. Momentum just tells you about the money flows. So if a stock is sideways, it's because, most likely, an entire raft of investors has given up on it. There are new buyers to propel it higher, and yet there are new sellers to take it lower. And so it just literally trades sideways typically with lower and lower volume. What often happens is that there's an event like the company reports earnings that aren't quite as bad as everyone expected, or that the sector starts to go back into favour. The energy sector is a good example right now. Energy has been extremely out of favour for months — really a number of years — but it's finally just starting to get back into favour, so that in itself can push an entire sector up. Or there's literally one or two large sellers left that get cleaned up, and there's no one left to sell, and the pressure is to the upside. Momentum feeds on itself. Think about the manager who manages $100 million, but then receives another $100 million. What do they typically do? They go buy the same stocks they already own. So momentum is a self-fulfilling prophecy, and once a stock gets moving in one direction, it has a tendency to move in that direction for a period of time. It's funds flow–driven.

Do you use any technical indicators to identify money flow?

Momentum is what I call a technical indicator. So we're not technicians in the classical sense of trend lines and trend patterns. We really try to keep it simple. The classic definition of momentum is 12-month rolling returns. I ask, "What has this stock done over the last 12 months, relative to all the other stocks in the index?" In Canada, momentum tends to move a little faster, so three- to six-month momentum is actually more effective. It has to do with the fact that Canada is a resource-heavy market, and resources tend to have slightly faster cycles. So, we'll literally measure three- to six-month momentum and score a stock relative to how well it's done on that measure, relative to all the other stocks, and we want to buy the stocks that have the best price momentum and the cheapest valuation.

Do you use a proprietary algorithm that systematically selects stocks based on your criteria: cheap, rising, and stable?

Proprietary makes it sounds like we invented the wheel. Valuation and price momentum are two very commonly used, commonly understood, and well researched behavioural anomalies. So we haven't invented anything, but we are very systematic and very rules-driven in terms of how we apply it. As it relates to the Select Fund, we go one step further. Once we've screened out stocks from a universe of say 300 stocks in Canada, we use our screening process to identify the best candidates for picking longs and the best candidates for picking shorts, based on their value and momentum characteristics.

What's that 300-stock universe based on?

Liquidity. We'll take the 300 most liquid stocks in Canada and start there. We'll say, "These 60 ranked the best based on value, momentum, and volatility, and these 60 stocks ranked the worst." We'll go one step further and overlay a qualitative perceptive on that stock. We dig into those 60 companies to select a portfolio of 25 stocks. And that's ultimately how we run the Select Fund. Twenty-five of our best longs, and twenty-five of our worst shorts. We run it in a structure where we are approximately 130/30. So a little bit of leverage is used to add shorts in order to reduce the overall risk, and that gives us the portfolio.

Can you elaborate on the criteria for those 25 worst shorts?

It's exactly the opposite of our criteria for longs. So we want the worst combination of value, momentum, and volatility. Each of those factors historically have led to poor future returns. Who would ever *buy* overvalued, declining, volatile stocks? However, there's a huge behavioural bias to buy those stocks. They have lottery ticket–like payoffs. So there is a behavioural bias to trade relatively liquid, small-cap, volatile stocks that can go up or down 10% a day. These are the stocks people like to trade. Although people can make money doing that, holding those stocks in a buy-and-hold-type environment is ruinous to returns on a long-term basis. You can get periodic great returns, and long-term terrible returns.

So you don't trade low-volume stocks at all.

Well, even if they're liquid, stocks that are overvalued, declining on a momentum basis, and volatile historically have been a terrible place to put money. And stocks that are the opposite of that — rising, stable, and cheap — have been a great place to put money. In the short term, just about anything can happen, in terms of the noise, but in the medium to long run, investing using those simple parameters will keep you on the right side of your stocks.

What are your annual target rates of return?

The Advantage Fund targets 10 to 12% with 10% drawdown. The Select Fund targets 15%-plus returns with drawdown in the 15% range. When I talk drawdown, that again goes back to that prop desk mentality of risk management. We don't really target returns, we target a drawdown or a volatility characteristic. With the Advantage Fund, for example, we don't want to endure peak to trough drawdowns or pullbacks that are more than 10%. For that fund, 10% is our pain threshold. That's when our clients would start to throw in their towel, make bad decisions, and sell at the bottom.

Does that mean you have stop-losses on every position in the Advantage Fund at a 10% loss?

We don't do it quite like that. 10% is a target, so it doesn't mean that we can't have worse drawdowns. It just means that we take an amount of risk where the expected volatility and drawdown is going to be in the 10% range. We actually back-test our theories. It's nice to say that we think buying cheap, rising, stable stocks is a good strategy, but it's another thing to actually go test that and run it back 20 years to make sure that we're actually correct. So we can back-test everything we do, which gives us a level of comfort on how much risk we're taking and what our drawdowns are going to be. I say "a level of comfort" because the future will never look exactly like the past. But because we're operating with repeatable human behavioural biases in terms of the market participants, you have a market that rhymes. Markets may not repeat themselves exactly, but they absolutely rhyme. That's why we've got an expected downside of around 10%.

You're operating with repeatable human behavioural biases in the market. Your partner, Ian Fairbrother, has a BA in psychology. How has he influenced EdgeHill's investment framework?

Ian absolutely uses behavioural finance in his work. Ian is the portfolio manager, and the stock-picker on the Select Fund, and will actually dig into the individual companies. But I would say whether it's a formal rules-based approach or just his instinct, he absolutely understands those behavioural biases and takes advantages of them. I would say that virtually all investors who are successful over the long run are either very good at instinctively understanding what their own behavioural biases are and what behavioural biases are out there to take advantage of, or they've built a set of rules and processes to constrain their actions, their risks, and their own behavioural biases. Ideally they have both qualities, but I don't know any successful people that run money who aren't ultimately very process-driven, whether those rules are written out and followed in that manner, or whether they're instinctually followed. But it's critical to have a set process and that you understand risk management.

How did the partnership between you and Ian come about?

Ian and I worked at Scotiabank. Our third partner, Brad White, was really the catalyst for the firm. Brad was our client. Post-'08 it was clear that the prop desk environment wasn't going to look the same for the next 10 years as it did the prior 10. We were looking to start a hedge fund, and Brad was as well, so it was a perfect match.

We've talked about your systematic trading strategies, but what about the opportunistic trading strategies — can you describe them?

Sure. For us, it's harder to talk about specific stock examples, but I'll give you two types of things we do as part of our opportunistic strategy. First, we play bought deals. A bought deal is when a company issues stock to the secondary market at a discount to its trading price.

Would Bombardier be a recent example of a bought deal?

Yes. Bombardier did that bought deal recently at quite a good discount. That's a deal we played. It was moderately profitable.

Can you explain how you actually play a bought deal?

So, bought deals are done at a discount. And if that bought deal is liquid, oversubscribed, and borrowable — meaning that we can borrow to hedge our risk — then it's of interest to us. Bought deals that are oversubscribed are usually priced too low, meaning there's a high probability of a small gain. So we will play every bought deal that's liquid, oversubscribed, and borrowable, and we will hold them for two hours to two days. It's a purely opportunistic strategy. We look to capture small mispricings, hedge our risk, and use that capital for the next trade.

Do all investors have access to these bought deals?

They do through their brokers. The challenge is that it's difficult to get access to the good bought deals unless you're participating all the time or generating trading commissions for the banks.

Where would one get information on these bought deals before they're actually released to the market?

You don't get any information before bought deals are released to the market. Basically a deal comes to market, along with a press release, and then we take a look at it to see if we're interested.

How can you tell if a bought deal is oversubscribed?

The only way to figure that out is to talk to the book runners to try to understand how much demand there is for the bought deal. We have a set of rules that we follow, but there's always an element of art to it.

What's the other example of an opportunistic trade?

Mean reversion, or liquidity provision. So, for example, our Advantage Fund holds 400 to 500 positions at any given time. 250 longs and 250 shorts. We get a good look at a large part of the market, both in the U.S. and in Canada. In the fall of 2014, we went short energy stocks. We didn't have a call on the price of crude oil going from $110 to $40, but we had a call on stocks that were overvalued, declining, and volatile.

So, the energy sector was finally experiencing mean reversion after years of overperformance?

Correct. The price momentum in the summer of 2014 started to decline. Volatility started to pick up. So on two of our three measures, energy stocks started to become a sector that we didn't want to hold. Given that we initiated an energy short position, and those stocks moved down 10 to 20% in some cases, there was an opportunity created for us. You see, in the very short run, markets tend to have a lot of noise, so even if the trend is down, there is short-term trading to provide liquidity. It's very much how we run our bought deal strategy. We play volatile stocks where there's a high probability of a small gain in a short period of time. We may discover that there's a very large energy stock that's moved down 15% on really no news. It's down due to panic selling. That's an opportunity for us to take a small short position for a couple of days to make a further 10% return and then be out.

Are you going to ride that energy short down for a prolonged period?

We are. Day-traders, scalpers, and traders effectively do that as part of their strategy, too. We'll use it around the edges to add value to our existing portfolio.

Two sectors today make up the majority of your long positions: materials and manufacturing. Why is that?

It's always the same process. We don't have any biases for whatever sector we're in. We just look for cheap, rising, and stable stocks. We will often become correlated with global macro trends not by going and seeking out those trends and trying to predict them, but by virtue of us trying to pick stocks that are, again, cheap, rising, and stable.

You validate those global macro trends through investing in momentum.

We participate in those trends. For example, a global macro trend that led us into industrials, or manufacturing, was the rising U.S. dollar.

For a Canadian firm, a rising U.S. dollar and, inversely, a declining Canadian dollar, is beneficial. We don't have a call on the dollar, though. As for materials, our system deemed them to be value stocks post the oil crash carnage in the fall of 2014. Materials stocks became quite cheap, relative to their historical ability to generate cash. In the spring of 2015, those materials stocks started rising again. Now they have positive price momentum and they're cheap. That pushes us into that sector. Again, not because we have a call on the base metals, or because we have a call on inflation, although both of those things might be happening in the world, but because we have a call on the individual stocks that are scoring well in our system.

Are you only exposed to North American markets?

Right now we are just in North America, so about 50/50 U.S. and Canada.

When markets are in severe gear-down mode, what do you do?

We do three things. We'll gear down our risk, meaning raising cash on the sidelines; we'll add shorts; and we will also rotate to more defensive strategies. In our Advantage Fund, for example, we have a credit strategy that's long high-yield debt. In a risk-off market, we will switch to U.S. treasuries. U.S. treasuries tend to rise in a bear market, assuming yields aren't rising. They can be uncorrelated with a stock portfolio. So that's a way of decreasing the portfolio's risk, simply by shifting one asset class.

How do you know if markets are gearing down?

We use really three very simple indicators to determine the risk/reward of the market. First, we look at the trend of the market. A market that is moving below its 50-, 100-, and 200-day moving averages is a warning sign for us. Second, we look at volatility; the VIX going from a stable state to a rising state indicates an increase in volatility. Third, we look at the spreads between high-yield debt and treasuries. If spreads widen, then that's an alarm bell. Those three things help us to determine if the risk/reward of being exposed to the market isn't as good as it was before. If it isn't, we'll take risk off the table. The whole point is to try to manage our drawdown. We don't want to get "fired." We don't like to lose money. We don't like drawdowns. There's a certain amount of drawdown we're willing to take to achieve our returns, but beyond that we don't want to take losses. And that's part of the process.

Have you endured big losses at any time throughout your career?

Yeah. Sure, numerous times.

Can you elaborate?

In many ways, you earn your investing knowledge the hard way. But I can't think of any one single loss that stands out as being a massive lesson. There are literally too many losses to count. Any investor can make a lot of money with a 40% win rate. I can be right only 40% of the time if I manage my risk well and I let my profits run. In other words, a 40% win rate can be a phenomenally good strategy if your winners are two times as big as your losers.

You accept that win/lose probability in the market.

That's right. You have to understand that you're going to take losses, and lots of them. I'm always comfortable taking a loss when I've followed the process and discipline. The existence of probability is part of the reason why we run money systematically. It's to avoid breaking a rule, letting our emotions get to us, buying too much of something, not selling when we should have, failing to take a capital gains loss, doubling down, and so on. All of those things are rule breakers. Personally, I track every single trade I make in a spreadsheet and put a reason for why I bought it or why I sold it, and record whether it was a win or loss, and how big. Over time, you start to learn from your mistakes. You can only get punched in the face so many times before you realize, "I guess I can just stop getting punched in the face by not doing that."

What mistakes do you tend to see retail investors make in the market?

Fear and greed. They are the dominant behavioural biases. Also, not taking losses is a mistake. But people hate taking losses. If you've ever told yourself, "I'm underwater on that stock; it was meant to be a short-term trade but now it's going to be a long-term investment until I break even," that one sentence described just about every bad behavioural bias you can make as an investor. You've got loss aversion. You're anchored to some artificial price that you created. You likely had greed when you bought it. Now, you've got fear. You ignored your risk control process. Everything that you could do wrong you've captured in that one trade. And all those mistakes are made repeatedly in the market. Also, investing in momentum in and of itself is another mistake. Sure, you can make a lot of money by just trading momentum stocks and staying with trends.

But it's a dangerous strategy because you don't have the back-stop of valuation most of the time. So you'd better have rules that make sure you cut your losses quickly, because losses from momentum stocks can be massive and unrecoverable as opposed to a loss on a truly good company trading at a deep discount. With a good company, your loss may be large in the short run, but you often still own a good business. Conversely, with a growth stock or a momentum stock, you might not own a piece of anything, other than a piece of paper once momentum abates and you're forced to take a loss.

To avoid massive losses on growth or momentum stocks, do you have a P/E ceiling that you won't go over?

No, because we care as much about relative value as we do absolute value. We don't have a cap on absolute valuation as long as we can find stocks that are more overvalued to short. But we're always mindful of absolute valuation in the overall market because it can indicate future volatility stocks that are highly valued have a long way to fall before they get into a category where value investors step in and apply a floor to the price of the stock. With any period where the overall market gets to a high valuation, you effectively have to tighten up your risk controls.

Anything else to add?

No, I think you covered it all. But to be clear, the way I run money means that I'm not as concerned about individual stocks. Everyone else wants a story when it comes to a stock because that in itself is another behavioural bias. It's imparting some emotionality or personal experience into a stock. Stocks aren't your friends or your family. You don't have to stick with them. We definitely view stocks in aggregate, which is why we hold 400 to 500 stocks in our Advantage Fund. We clearly aren't digging into each individual stock and holding them because we really like management or really like the story. We own stocks in aggregate to capture inefficiencies in the market. Unfortunately, I don't have a lot of good stories on individual stocks. It's not how we run money, and it's not how we manage risk.

Who influenced your investment philosophy?

Influences for me would be Cliff Asness of AQR Capital Management, and any of the more quantitative, rules-driven type investors. Also, the commodity traders — guys like Paul Tudor Jones. What we do is as similar to commodity trading as it is to fundamental investing. We try to blend both of those characteristics.

Have you watched that rare early documentary on Paul Tudor Jones?

Yeah, I have an unlicenced copy. It's hard to get.

Yes, it is hard to get. I recall that Jones and his chief economist at the time overlaid the 1920s bull run chart to the 1980s chart, and from that he was able to call the impending crash.

Well, like I said, markets rhyme. Bubbles have similar characteristics. You can determine those characteristics and then build a set of rules to profit from future bubbles.

Paul traded in many different international markets. Have you and your partners considered expanding your exposure?

The models that we use to valuate stocks work equally well internationally. But it's slightly more complicated to trade. Frankly, we have a lot of capacity in North America. But as we outgrow North America, and hopefully that will be the case, we'll absolutely trade internationally. However, we can get the return and risk profile we want from North American markets, so we focus on where we think we have an edge.

Speaking with Jason made it clear that you can't win it all. "For any investor, you can make a lot of money with a 40% win rate. I can be right 40% of the time if I manage my risk well and let my profits run. In other words, I let my good trades continue, and I cut my losses quickly. A 40% win rate can be a phenomenally good strategy if your wins are two times as big as your losses." Jason also noted that investors should keep their fear and greed in check in the market. Of course, it's ideal to act with rational intention in the market every single time.

Finally, Jason named two quant hedge fund managers that I suggest you look up and read more about: Cliff Asness and Paul Tudor Jones. I also watched the rare documentary about Paul Tudor Jones, *Trader*, which was filmed about one year before the major market crash in 1987. On film, Paul Tudor Jones said, in his southern U.S. drawl, "There will be some type of a decline, without a question, in the next 10, 20 months. And it will be earth-shaking; it will be saber-rattling." Sure enough, on October 19, 1987, the U.S. market crashed. It posted a 508-point (20%-plus) decline within hours. Paul placed a short on the market and netted $100 million in profits on October 19, 1987. As a parallel, during the energy bear market and before the eventual oil crash (2014), Jason took on a Tudor-esque bet. He explained, "We were long energy stocks, but by the summertime we were neutral because of their price momentum and volatility characteristics. But then by September, October, 2014, we were short energy stocks." Jason goes on to explain that he continues to ride down his energy short positions, as there's still weakness in that market sector. Given that it's now August 2015, and the energy sector has dived down further since then, I'm certain that Jason has continued to profit immensely from his energy short positions. Remember Jason's mantra: "Buy undervalued, rising, stable stocks and short overvalued, declining, volatile stocks."

MASTER KEYS

JASON MANN

1) "The way we run money here is quantitative, or systematic, or rules-driven."

2) "We want to buy the best combination of cheap, rising, and stable stocks."

3) "Most important though is to determine the price of a company relative to its historical ability to generate cash. That's what we care about when we measure value."

4) "Forward estimates are just that — an estimate, just a collection of guesses — whereas backwards looking is a factual representation of what a company has been able to do."

5) "Value works because the market becomes overly pessimistic about a formerly good company's ability to ever regain its footing and generate cash flows."

6) "'What do you call a stock that's down 90%? A stock that was down 80% and then got cut in half.' You can buy something at an 80% discount and still take a lot of pain waiting for that value to play out."

7) "Because we are both long and short, we can benefit from both sides of that trade."

8) "Momentum feeds on itself. Think about the manager who manages $100 million, but then receives another $100 million. What do they typically do? They go buy the same stocks they already own."

9) "The classic definition of momentum is 12-month rolling returns. I ask, 'What has this stock done over the last 12 months, relative to all the other stocks in the index?'"

10) "[We'll] score a stock relative to how well it's done on that measure, relative to all the other stocks, and we want to buy the stocks that have the best price momentum and the cheapest valuation."

11) "Who would *ever* buy overvalued, declining, volatile stocks? However, there's a huge behavioural bias to buy those stocks. They have lottery ticket–like payoffs."

12) "There is a behavioural bias to trade relatively liquid, small-cap, volatile stocks that can go up or down 10% a day. Holding those stocks in a buy-and-hold-type environment is ruinous to returns on a long-term basis. You can get periodic great returns, and long-term terrible returns."

13) "We take an amount of risk where the expected volatility and drawdown is going to be in the 10% range."

14) "Because we're operating with repeatable human behavioural biases in terms of the market participants, you have a market that rhymes."

15) "Virtually all investors who are successful over the long run are either very good at instinctively understanding what their own behavioural

biases are and what the behavioural biases are out there to take advantage of, or they've built a set of rules and processes to constrain their actions, their risks, and their own behavioural biases."

16) "A bought deal is when a company issues stock to the secondary market at a discount to its trading price. Bought deals are done at a discount. And if that bought deal is liquid, oversubscribed, and borrowable — meaning that we can borrow to hedge our risk — then it's of interest to us."

17) "We play volatile stocks where there's a high probability of a small gain in a short period of time."

18) "A market that is moving below its 50-, 100-, and 200-day moving average is a warning sign for us."

19) "The VIX going from a stable state to a rising state indicates an increase in volatility."

20) "The existence of probability is part of the reason why we run money systematically. It's to avoid breaking a rule, letting our emotions get to us, buying too much of something, not selling when we should have, failing to take a capital gains loss, doubling down, and so on."

21) "Stocks that are highly valued have a long way to fall before they get into a category where value investors step in and apply a floor."

SOM SEIF
THE INDEX INVESTOR

Som Seif is the Steve Jobs of the Canadian investment industry. At the age of 27, Som started building Claymore Investments Inc. using a laptop in his living room. Once he had built the company, Som was able to capture 15% of the ETF [exchange-traded funds] market by 2012, and by that time, Claymore Investments had grown into a powerhouse in Canada, with $7 billion in assets before it was sold to BlackRock. Claymore Investments was first to bring fundamental indexing ETFs to Canada. In an earlier interview conducted by Craig Saunders for the *Globe and Mail*, Som said, "The industry [exchange-traded funds] was one where I felt there was a lot of room for innovation and improvement. The idea was to create a better investment management business focused on the client with cheaper, low-cost, intelligent solutions."

Unlike Steve Jobs, Som was not ousted from Claymore Investments. Rather, Som stepped down after Claymore Investments was sold to BlackRock. Almost immediately, he started to dream about a new company: Purpose Investments. Som started Purpose Investments Inc. in 2013 to sell ETFs to institutional and retail investors. As I write this, Purpose Investments has already accumulated something close to $1 billion in assets. By contrast, it took him four years to raise $1 billion at Claymore. Som doesn't think small — he plans to top Claymore Investment's $7-billion assets under management in due time. He supports that goal with the firm belief that systematic, disciplined, rules-based investment strategies will outperform active management over the long term. That's food for thought for any existing or aspiring stock-pickers.

Exchange-traded funds (ETFs) have grown in popularity year after year, not only in Canada, but around the world. I sometimes employ ETFs to play major themes in the market or to form critical foundations in my portfolio, for example with XIU, which consists of Canada's 60 largest corporations based on market capitalization. Regardless of whether or not you are interested in passive investment through ETFs, I do believe that you will be intrigued by Purpose Investment's high-conviction Best Ideas Fund. The Purpose Best Ideas Fund invests in just 25 major North American stocks held by some of the world's most renowned investment managers: Carl Icahn, George Soros, Warren Buffett, Nelson Peltz, and David Einhorn, to name only a few. Aside from the other strategies that you can employ through ETFs in your portfolio, Som will walk you through how he constructs the Best Ideas Fund on a quarterly basis. And from that knowledge you can make your own Best Ideas portfolio.

While I waited to meet Som, I scanned my surroundings in the large meeting room at Purpose Investments' headquarters in Toronto. A job interview was going on in the next meeting room. Traders were tapping away on their keyboards after market hours. Outside the window, I could see Google Canada's offices, brightly coloured outdoor furniture scattered over the patio. Inside the meeting room was an old ticker-tape machine. When Som arrived, he brought his trademark strong and confident presence with him.

PRE-INTERVIEW LESSONS

EXCHANGE-TRADED FUND (ETF): an investment fund that holds a basket of stocks, bonds, or other securities. ETFs trade on the stock market.
PASSIVE INVESTING: an investment approach that usually equates to less portfolio turnover.

Where did you grow up in Canada?

I was actually born in England. My parents are Iranian and we moved to Canada when I was three. I grew up in beautiful Unionville, Ontario. Look, my family are immigrants. We didn't come from anything. We didn't have any money. My dad came here with hope and his Ph.D. and saw Canada as a country that was welcoming to immigrants but more importantly was a society that was expanding as opposed to shrinking. If you look at countries like the U.K. and some other parts of the world, they aren't evolving societies. They're already evolved. Whereas Canada is always evolving.

Anyways, we came here, our parents made a life for themselves, and worked their tails off. My dad worked his whole life under one corporation until his retirement. In my first year of working I made as much money as he made in his best year. He was quite amazing. I came from a family that was extremely loving and supportive but had massive amounts of pressure on me to perform.

Given your success at such a young age, have you ever been falsely accused of not achieving it on your own?

No, most people know me. I've never had a "friend" in a company. I didn't have someone to help me skate along. What I had was my own efforts and my own desires and my own goals and that's what got me to where I am. I made it.

You studied engineering. That's not a typical major in the financial industry. So, how did you first get interested in the markets?

I studied engineering because I wanted to be an architect. I loved creative thinking. I loved designs. I loved building things. I loved the idea of creating something that you actually could see and touch and make an impact that way. The reason that I decided not to become an architect was because of the lack of money one could earn in the industry. Coming from my background, money was a very important driver for me throughout life. All through elementary school, junior high school, high school, and university, I was dreaming of driving wonderful cars and flying extravagant planes; all the great grandeur that comes with money. But that that didn't align with becoming an architect. After a couple of months, I thought, "I'm not going to go from engineering to go do my architecture degree, so what's my next love?" Business. I didn't know much about the markets at that time, though. Anyway, I got a really wonderful opportunity to go work at RBC in the investment banking division of corporate finance. I was a young pup. That actually gave me a really intriguing interest in the market. So, from that point on, I started paying attention to what was going on in the markets.

Was it through RBC that you met the contact from Claymore in the U.S. who would eventually ask you to build the Claymore ETF business in Canada?

Yeah. So here is actually how it all happened. I was advising a bunch of different asset management companies in North America, Canada, and the U.S. One of them was a really unique group of guys in Chicago: a startup called Claymore Group. One day I said to them, "You should build your business in Canada." I didn't think of it from a personal gain perspective though. Eventually, I helped them think through the analysis of that decision and then one day they called me up and said, "Som, we would love it if you would build it for us." That was the start of it all. One month later I resigned from RBC and started Claymore Investments Canada. That was the end of 2004. I started the firm and built it up. At first it was just me, and then I hired an assistant, and then got an office space a couple months later. But until that time I basically built the business with a laptop in the living room of my house. It was pretty amazing. I thought there was going to be a lot more depth into what the partnership would be, but in the end it was just an unbelievable opportunity.

Claymore Investments Canada was eventually sold to BlackRock.

We sold it in March 2012. And we announced the deal in January 2012, which was exactly seven years after I built it up. It was a great exit personally. It was the fastest-growing asset management company in Canada. We built it on a foundation of all the things we were thinking about.

Shortly after the sale, you started up another ETF company: Purpose Investments. Are you the sole owner of Purpose Investments?

When I started Purpose Investments I decided to start it myself. I did not take anyone else's capital to start it up. I funded it, and today, I control the company in all the elements of the business. The only other people who co-own the company are my partners, who are people in the company that have participated and have received equity in Purpose Investments.

What is the investment philosophy behind Purpose Investments?

So I've always been a big believer that when it comes to investment management there's strong factors in the market that will ultimately, over time, continuously create opportunity and returns. And so I've always been a big believer that fundamental investing can add value but at the same time you always have to be thoughtful about how you execute. I'm a big believer in blending the best of what active money managers do with passive investment discipline. That would be systematic, rules-based, disciplined, and transparent. That is very powerful. Honestly, I don't believe that most people have skill in the market. Skill is what most people have a shortage in. There's no question that there are people out there who have skill but they are few and far between. Granted, I don't think that I necessarily have more skill than anyone else. Therefore, I've created an advantage for people through my ETFs. Great investment discipline, strategies, and then just charge less for it. That's what makes me successful. As simple as that.

Now, at Claymore Investments, that too was the foundation of our business. If you look back at our business model and the results of the products, we had some of the best-performing funds in the country. Even today, one of the things I am most proud about is what we did for Canadian investors. The products we delivered were phenomenal. We had some of the best-performing top core-tile funds in the country. Most investment managers are just riding the waves of the market: up and down. One of the things that I spend a lot of time thinking about post–2008 financial crisis is this idea of behavioural economics: the elements of psychology that go into the markets. It became really ingrained into me, this idea that we're not here to beat markets. We're here to meet investors' liabilities and goals. That's it.

So your goal is to meet an investor's expectations rather than to be or beat the market.

Yes. So that's exactly the problem. Most investment products now state, "If the market returns are x, I'm either going to give you better performance, or I'm going to give you the market." Index funds are just the market. And my view is that that's not what clients want. What clients want is for a fund to meet their goals. Behavioural finance tells us that clients are emotional. However, while the most important thing to winning in the market is to actually stay committed to it, that's the hardest thing for people to actually do. Generally, people make bad decisions. They will buy at the highs and they will sell at the lows; those are very expensive decisions. We also realize that the number one priority that investors should have is to compound wealth. And, in fact, the best way to compound wealth is to avoid loss. You don't make better compounded returns when the market is up 15% and you're up 16%. You make better returns when the markets are down 15% and you're not down anywhere close to 15%.

Risk management plays a big part in actually meeting an investor's expectations.

This is it. And to me, this is the difference between what Purpose is and what Claymore was. That's what we're focused on now, which is not only giving phenomenal investment strategies and keeping costs low, but also focusing on risk management. Thinking about how we make money for clients through different types of cycles and not being insecure with the idea that if the markets are up 20%, we don't have to beat the market. But, again, what I truly do need to answer is that when the markets are down 20%, our ETFs do not come close to that type of return.

In the actual Purpose Investment ETFs, how do you construct a portfolio and then apply risk management controls that preserve capital?

Everything is systematic. Everything is rules-based. We use empirical research on what works. For example, we think that when you pick stocks that you should look at that process in quality and relative value terms. So we're a value company. We think that companies that are cheap will ultimately outperform companies that are expensive. That's a factor that over time is very important to us. "Relative value terms" means that if stocks in general get expensive, we're not going to be out of the market. We're still going to be looking for the cheapest companies on a relative basis to the rest of the market. But, importantly, we marry that with quality. Companies that are high-quality will ultimately out-perform companies that are low-quality. When we put those two things together, relative value and quality, you have a very powerful foundation for picking securities. Now, in the event that low-quality and expensive companies rally, we're okay with underperforming the market during that time. We're giving that up and we're happy to do that.

Interestingly, another factor that we use in risk management is momentum. Momentum is driven by the behaviours in the market. What momentum tells us with strong evidence is that markets tend to overshoot their fair value on the high end and undershoot their fair value on the low end. So, we use momentum to actually signal to us when markets are strong and when markets are weak. When markets are strong, we want to take on risk. When markets are weak, we want to take risk off the table. We use the momentum signals to basically tell us when we want more or less market exposure.

What are some of those actual signals that you use to inform you on the strength or weakness of the market?

So, very simply, we use a total of 10 moving average trend signals on the underlying markets that we follow. And those 10 moving averages range from the short-term 10-day moving average all the way up to the long-term 52-week moving average. If the price of a benchmark that we're following is above all of those moving averages, it means markets are robust, and they're positive, and so we want to be long. Conversely, if all 10 are negative, in that the actual price is below all 10 moving averages, it means the market momentum is negative and so we want to be out of the markets. But in the event that the price is above just three of those moving-day averages, we want to have 30% exposure. If the price is above eight moving-day averages we want to have 80% exposure to the market.

So, do you actually shift capital in and out of the market based on momentum?

Yeah, but we don't trade every day. The more often you trade, the more likely you are to actually make mistakes. We rebalance our portfolios every two weeks on the hedge decisions. We don't rebalance it every day. What we're trying to capture is the medium- and long-term trend that's truly happening in the market and react to those environments.

I was intrigued by the Purpose Best Ideas Fund. There are only about 25 holdings in that fund at any given time. Can you explain the fund?

The Best Ideas Fund is all about following the best money managers in the world. We've selected a very specific group of money managers who have, over not just the short term but over the long term, proven to consistently add value. More importantly, they have a unique fundamental approach themselves. Most are deep fundamental value money managers while the others are activists. Guys like Bill Ackman, Warren Buffett, George Soros, Carl Icahn, and so on. Some of the best money managers in the world. What we're doing is investing in the most concentrated bets that these guys have in their hedge funds. That's it.

Interesting. You're riding the coattails of the highest-performing investors.

Yeah. There's really fantastic research out of the University of Pennsylvania that measured whether active managers beat passive investors. Well, that's the stupidest study in the world because the average person can't afford the active manager's fees. Although, I do believe that the active manager can add value over time. The research looked at portfolios to see whether an active manager could actually pick 5, 10, 20 stocks that they could actually add value on. Did they pick best ideas? Well, what U of P was able to find was that there was strong evidence that a manager could pick five stocks that were going to beat the market. With a little bit less evidence they could pick 10 stocks. But once you get past 10 stocks, they couldn't beat the market. Then they held the most overweight positions in all of their portfolio against the benchmarks to see if these were the best ideas. In conclusion, U of P had strong evidence that active managers could beat the market with their highest-weighted holdings. So what does this tell you? It tells you that good active money managers can usually pick a good couple of stocks, but the problem is that most mandates would never allow them to just hold five stocks so they have to dilute it with 60 or 80 other stocks. Unfortunately, by the end of the day, they perform just like the market.

So the Best Ideas Fund only invests in their concentrated holdings? For example, the top stocks by percentage of total holdings that Bill Ackman holds in his hedge fund would go into the Best Ideas Fund.

It's as simple as that. We take the best, most high-conviction positions that these guys hold in their hedge funds, and then take all the rest of the noise out and agree, "We're betting on that," and that's it.

Is there someone in your company that tracks these money managers?

Yes, we receive 13F filings every quarter. Basically, after the Friday that they're released, we balance the Best Ideas Fund on the Monday and Tuesday. The key to this is that the money managers list does not include short-term traders; they are all long-term investors. So when they buy, they're buying billions of dollars of the stock and they're going in for many quarters and they're investing for three to five years or longer. So for us it's wonderful. We can lag by months without missing out on returns.

Do you include any "best ideas" positions from Canadian money managers?

No, because this is from the filing disclosures, it's all U.S.-based.

Okay, with big-time money managers fuelling your stock picks, surely the Best Ideas Fund must be beating the market.

Since we launched, we have outperformed the S&P 500 by 8% in less than a year.

What are the other high-performing ETFs at Purpose Investments?

Our dividend fund has beat the next best dividend strategies in Canada and the U.S. by about 6% since we launched it. Our hedged equity fund — a long/short strategy — has beaten the majority of long/short equity money managers in this country. I would say it's beat 90% of them.

Do you think that ETFs will someday replace mutual funds?

No. I think ETFs are mutual funds and it's the silliest notion to ever think that ETFs are different. ETFs are just a delivery mechanism. Mutual funds trade on the exchange. The problem is that people have bucketed ETFs as "low-cost passive" and mutual funds as "high-cost active." However, I do think that ETFs are going to become more a part of overall portfolio construction and therefore a larger part of the market. But mutual funds are not going away. In fact, mutual funds are a very powerful pooling structure for mass investors. What I do think has changed though is that high-cost money management is getting smaller. The greater share of wallet and portfolio and asset flow will go to lower-cost and lower-fee money managers. Whether that be index funds or active managers with a lower fee.

Is there more competition now than there was when you first started up Claymore ETFs?

Oh, yes. There's nine players now instead of just Claymore and iShares at the time. And so there's competition but they're still relatively small. The ETF industry is only $80 billion in Canada. On the other hand, the mutual fund industry is $1 trillion. The total aggregate liquid investment space in Canada is $4 trillion. ETFs are irrelevant. I don't wake up every day thinking that the ETF market is significant in size.

How can an investor employ ETFs in their portfolio?

So here's my honest opinion. I think that investors need to make a decision: are you a speculator or are you an investor? I believe that most people should not be speculators or traders. Some people will be good traders but that's the same probability of the person who goes to the blackjack table and basically wins right away. People should ultimately decide that they're long-term investors. You don't become rich investing in the markets; you augment your wealth. What you get rich from, and this is one of my fundamental beliefs, is human capital, and what you do personally to make your money. Whether you make $50,000, $100,000, $200,000 or more, that's how you make money. You put your net savings into the markets and build portfolios that are hugely diversified, and over time you'd produce 7 to 8% annualized returns.

Which three Purpose Investments ETFs would you recommend for a well-rounded portfolio?

Just three? Wow. If it was just three I would hold our monthly income fund, our hedged equity fund, and our market neutral fund. Those three ETFs would build you the ultimate broad diversified portfolio. I would probably allocate about 75% of the capital into the monthly income fund, 10% into the hedged equity fund, and then 15% into our market neutral fund. That will give you a really wonderful portfolio. You're going to have your equity long-dividend strategy portfolio, bond allocation, and real asset for inflationary protection.

Can you further explain what a market neutral strategy achieves?

The principle of market neutrality is to make absolute returns independent of the market. So the idea is if equity markets are up or down that you're still able to generate long-term returns that are positive. It has three underlying assets: equities, currencies, and commodities. Basically, we're going long equities, and long currencies, and short commodities, and short currencies. It's very powerful but it's just risk management. The idea is to avoid losses and to win over time making very small fractions through market cycles.

Interesting. Are you short any currencies?

We went short a week and a half ago on the Canadian dollar. And we've also been short the euro since its slide against the U.S. dollar.

What about on the commodity side?

On the commodity side it's short Brent Crude but long in copper. But we rebalance the portfolio every month and systematically select positions based on curve structure and momentum.

How many positions are usually within each ETF?

Anywhere from 25 for our Best Ideas Fund, which is a more concentrated portfolio, to our hedge equity, which is 70 stocks. But we don't believe in buying a thousand stocks and just holding them.

What is your outlook on the Canadian markets for the long term?

I think that Canada is a sector bet. It's been a sector bet for many years both in the positives and the negatives. It's in these environments, unfortunately, where we see the energy market roll over like it has in the last six months, that investors recognize Canada's cyclical nature. It's hard to forecast what the Canadian market will look like in the future without forecasting what we think energy is going to look like. Commodities are going to be under pressure for a while because we're in a low-inflation environment. In fact, you could call it a deflationary environment. There's no real fundamental drive for the assets right now and that's going to be a negative for Canada. There's not going to be a quick fix to this problem. People are saying, "Oh, we're going to have a transfer from the west to the east. Manufacturing will cover the losses since the Canadian dollar has come off well." Guess what? When you let go of something for so long, and for the greater part of a decade, the economy says, "Screw manufacturing, we're not going to be a manufacturing hub." You just can't turn the lights on and say, "Okay, now we're going to be a great manufacturing exporter." The challenge is that Canada's got a lot of time and work to go in order to recover manufacturing capacity. That might take two or three years before we actually start to see some evidence of improvement. Again, real evidence, to offset the losses in the west.

Now, the biggest benefit that Canada faces is that our biggest trading partner, the U.S., is actually on very strong footing at the moment. The U.S., despite all of the noise and all the crap that's gone on in the last couple of years, actually looks like it's improving quite nicely. So that's a very positive thing for Canada especially when the Canadian dollar is at 80 cents to the U.S. dollar. Because if America starts to improve, and starts to become more aggressive, Canada is going to become a continued exporter for that. Canada will be a cheap partner for the U.S. in terms of production and we'll see the benefits. If they're growing, then we're going to grow right alongside them and that's our hedge right now.

So a potential strategy could be to take on positions in Canadian companies that trade with the U.S.?

Yes. Canadian companies that make the majority of their revenue in U.S. dollars is no question. On the flip side of that, U.S. multinational companies that have greater than 50% of their revenues coming from outside of the U.S. are being hurt from a strong U.S. currency.

This next question might be of interest to any readers with an engineering or science background. How has an engineering foundation helped you in the markets?

It's everything I do. Engineering to me has been one of the great foundations that I have and the reason is because I'm a math guy and a black-and-white thinker in many ways when it comes to the markets. I try to cut out noise. What I think engineers do very well is come up with an answer for everything. That's the belief system: there's a solution to the problem and the best way to get to the solution is to cut out noise and get to the problem. So what I've done in this business, what's made me a strong investor and made me successful, has been the idea that you can apply systematic thinking, discipline, all the rest of it, to what we do to make money over time. And it's all about mathematics in my opinion. It's about probabilities of success. You may have multiple solutions to the problem but the reality is that you want to get to the solution but you also want to have the highest probability of success. Minimize your tail risks. Minimize your outcome risks that you're wrong. We do that here by having really phenomenal investment strategies based on research that we know adds value. What I've found in my professional career in building Claymore and now building Purpose is that if you keep doing those things really well and you stick to the disciplines, your cream will rise to the top. You know, I laugh a little about it, but it's so consistent. Money managers have a hard time being persistent. And what we do is stick to persistence.

Is your plan to build Purpose into another acquisition target or to stick with it?

No, no, I'm building Purpose Investments to create a very strong long-term asset management company that I want to own forever. I say that quite honestly. I sold Claymore Investments, but I didn't want to sell it, to be honest. I sold it because I had a financial partner that wanted to exit. I would have loved to have owned Claymore for another 30 more years. With Purpose Investments, I own it, I control it, and I want to build this into a meaningful and impactful company in the country.

Do you have any closing comments?

I'm a big believer that there are four things that investors need to do and this will make up to 99% of your long-term outcome and success if you do these four things consistently. First is that you've got to invest. You've got to make a commitment to it. If you haven't done that already, take your next paycheque and make a budget and allocate a meaningful portion of your income to savings. Second is to focus on diversified portfolios: don't put all your money in one stock, or all in energy stocks; build a well-diversified portfolio. Third, make sure that that diversified portfolio is low-fee. I'm not talking about buying the lowest-cost product. Buy products that make sense and have good strategies but also have low fees. And fourth, two times a year, rebalance your portfolio. Go back, rebalance to your target weights, and keep doing that for 30 years and keep adding money every year to your portfolio. You will wake up when you're 50 years old and you will be the happiest person in the world. I promise you that investors will be rewarded for doing those things. Once you do all that, you focus on building human capital. Focus on yourself. Invest in yourself. Don't invest in trying to beat the markets. Invest in yourself, because that's where you make your real opportunities as an individual and that's how you make real wealth.

After the interview, Som recommended that readers research and possibly use the Piotorski Score in their investment selection process. He said that he personally employs the Piotorski Score to help him avoid any value traps in the market. The Piotorski Score, a nine-point scoring system to determine the value of stocks, is beyond the scope of this book, but a wealth of information about the system is available online.

I found the concept behind the Best Ideas Fund brilliant. You can easily create a portfolio, or segment a subset of your portfolio, with holdings from hedge fund managers around the world who regularly report their holdings through 13F filings. Here is more information about the makeup of the fund, as described on Purpose Investment's website.

> The world's best portfolio managers tend to only manage money for an elite group of investors. Their reputation and history of success allow them to charge investors high fees and require large minimum investment amounts, putting their funds and investment ideas out of reach of all but a few very wealthy investors. The Purpose Best Ideas Fund takes these fund managers' top investments and puts them into one fund [with 25 total holdings] that is accessible to all investors, at a low fee, and without a mandatory minimum investment. The fund is built by looking at the portfolios of a predefined set of top-tier investment managers and selecting the securities that have been most thoroughly researched and that have highest concentration across the manager's holdings.

--- **MASTER KEYS** ---
SOM SEIF

1) "While the most important thing to winning in the market is to actually stay committed to it, that's the hardest thing for people to actually do . . . they will buy at the highs and they will sell at the lows."

2) "The best way to compound wealth is to avoid loss. You make better returns when the markets are down 15% and you're not down anywhere close to 15%."

3) "Companies that are high-quality will ultimately outperform companies that are low-quality."

4) "When markets are strong, we want to take on risk. When markets are

weak, we want to take risk off the table. We use the momentum signals to basically tell us when we want more or less market exposure."

5) "We don't trade every day. The more often you trade, the more likely you are to actually make mistakes."

6) "What we're doing [in the Best Ideas Fund] is investing in the most concentrated bets that these guys have in their hedge funds. That's it."

7) "I think that investors need to make a decision: are you a speculator or are you an investor? I believe that most people should not be speculators or traders."

8) "You don't become rich investing in the markets; you augment your wealth."

9) "The principle of market neutrality is to make absolute returns independent of the market. So the idea is if equity markets are up or down that you're still able to generate long-term returns that are positive."

10) "What I think engineers do very well is come up with an answer for everything. That's the belief system: there's a solution to the problem and the best way to get to the solution is to cut out noise and get to the problem."

11) "What I've done in this business, what's made me a strong investor and made me successful, has been the idea that you can apply systematic thinking, discipline, all the rest of it, to what we do to make money over time."

12) "It's all about mathematics in my opinion. It's about probabilities of success. . . . You want to get to the solution but you also want to have the highest probability of success. Minimize your tail risks."

CAMERON WINSER
MULTI-DISCIPLINARY APPROACH

When my interview with Lorne Zeiler had concluded, he said, "You should really talk to Cameron; he's the head of equities at TriDelta Financial. Your readers should be aware of his strategic shift into momentum." This piqued my interest, as a strategic shift in 2015 could likely extend to the next couple of years. An investor should understand why, when, and how to make shifts in their portfolio. You wouldn't want to be the owner of a flat or declining portfolio, and watch other areas of the market go up.

Before I contacted Cameron, I conducted some research. Sure enough, the *Financial Post* had featured him, confirming Lorne's recommendation: "Winser has shifted into a momentum strategy. [Momentum] has been out of favour for a while, but multiple expansion has happened. Now the markets are actually going to reward earnings and companies that can continue to show positive momentum."[2] This shift in strategy to momentum in a low-growth environment makes sense given the major headwinds affecting the market, notably a slowdown in the commodities

---

2 *National Post*, a division of Postmedia Network Inc.
http://www.financialpost.com/m/wp/blog.html?b=business.financialpost.com
//investing/buy-sell/slowing-asia-momentum-strategy-fuel-managers-strategies

sector, which has continued its bear market decline since 2011. You will need to look very closely at the market for those quality momentum opportunities, as they are few and far between in 2015.

We conducted this interview by phone while Cameron was driving home from work. Surprisingly, though, our discussion was fluid and on point. While driving through a residential area Cameron articulated — safely using his hands-free Bluetooth mobile device — a clear three-step process to add stocks to a portfolio that fit his momentum mandate. Some of you may also appreciate Cameron's seemingly unorthodox educational background; he studied psychology at York University. While Cameron wasn't able to draw a direct correlation between his psychology education and the markets, saying "I've never come up with anything definitive," this example shows that one can learn investing outside of a traditional educational framework. You don't need a finance, math, or specialized degree. You do need, among other things, experience through time in the markets, combined with successful strategies and an insatiable drive to master the markets. Many of the world's top investors do not have those previously mentioned degrees. Do your own research and you'll find *B.A.* sprinkled throughout the various biography pages of famous investors, money managers, and hedge fund managers. Even Warren Buffett earned a B.A. in economics, and then was turned down for enrollment by the Harvard Business School. Here are some other notable examples of the world's top investors who hold ("only") a B.A. degree:

- Bill Gross (B.A. in psychology)
- George Soros (B.A. in philosophy)
- Carl Icahn (B.A. in philosophy)
- Peter Lynch (B.A. in history, psychology, classics, and philosophy)
- James O'Shaughnessy (B.A. in economics)

PRE-INTERVIEW LESSONS

QUALITATIVE: measuring variables such as brand, products, services, and management to assess a business before an investment is made.
QUANTITATIVE: measuring variables such as financial ratios and technical indicators to assess a business before an investment is made.

RELATIVE STRENGTH: the comparison of the performance of a stock, or any other investment, to the performance of its industry, peer group, or market to gauge its comparable strength. For example, Bank A's 15% gain might seem good until one compares it to the banking industry's overall 20% gain.

Where were you born in Canada?

Grimsby.

How did you first get interested in the markets?

I got interested in first-year university. A friend of mine had been involved in the markets. It's a little shadowy now, but he knew some "promoters," we'll call them, back then, and got involved in a couple of micro-cap stocks. In talking with him I got interested in the markets, and continued to do some of my own investing during first-year university. I took the Canadian securities course shortly after that.

Do you remember some of those early micro-cap stocks?

Oh, man. There's one, but I wish I could recall its name. It was an entertainment stock; the company made a drag-racing simulator. So basically it was like a miniature version of a drag-racing car that you would sit in and then a parachute would pop out.

What were the returns?

Oh, I have no idea. It would be just a pure guess.

Did you establish a set stock-picking strategy in those early days?

It was pretty primitive throughout university.

You're a psychology grad. Have you applied a psychological framework to the markets to gain an edge over other investors?

Yeah, but I can't come up with anything specific. I've thought about this stuff myself. I remember taking an environmental psychology class in university. I learned that there are certain things that subconsciously cue the mind, and I've never come up with anything definitive.

What are the funds that you manage at TriDelta?

I'm basically in charge of the equities. With that we've got a number of different models. One is called the core model, which is for people who are looking for a more growth-focused type of strategy. The other one's called the pension model, and it's essentially for people seeking less volatility and a higher dividend payout, more or less. Finally, there's the pooled fund, and that's divided between Edward Jong and myself. Edward has the fixed-income side, and I've got the equity side. The equity side is divided into two different strategies. There's the U.S. strategy, which is an indexing with an options overlay. And then there's the quantitative technical fundamental strategy. I join all of those disciplines together and look for stocks that cover all three fronts.

How do you actually join all three disciplines — quantitative, technical, and fundamental — together in your framework?

First, I use the quantitative scrutiny to basically shrink the stock universe. In North America, there's well over two and a half thousand stocks that are available. So somehow you need to come up with a way of shrinking that two and a half thousand down to a list that's a little more manageable.

What metrics do you use to filter down that stock universe?

Well, that depends on the mandate. Though there are some basic metrics. For example, estimate revisions. We look for companies that have had their estimate revisions go higher. Another basic metric is simply stable earnings growth. Also, we look at dividend growth, especially if dividend income is our mandate. Finally, we look for earnings surprises, where management is able to beat analysts' earnings consensus on a consistent basis. Although you can look at that earnings surprise metric in one of two ways. Either management is able to manage the street's expectations very well or they're actually just able to execute very well. A lot of the time it's a combination of both factors.

What's the difference between earnings revisions and earnings surprises?

Revisions generally come in before earnings are released. For instance, if in between quarterly reports the earnings estimate gets bumped up throughout the period, that would be a revision. Surprises happen when the street expects that, for example, the company will report earnings of 25 cents but then they actually report earnings of 30 cents.

What data sources do you use to tracks that earnings information?

There's a number of different sources we can pull that off of. Bloomberg is one source. There's another system called CPMS which has a lot of fundamental data that you can screen through.

Once you've narrowed down the stock universe, it's on to technical analysis, right?

Yeah. Basically, you reduce the universe from 2,600, for example, to a hundred stocks. Then you use the technical analysis to flip through a bunch of the stocks to see which ones appear technically stronger, which could be based on relative strength to their benchmark or index.

Would you use the Relative Strength Index (RSI) technical indicator to measure a stock's relative strength?

Well, there's two different RSIs. One is "RSI," which is an indicator that measures on an individual day where a stock closes within its range. So if the RSI is drifting higher, that's telling you that it's consistently closing in the upper half of its daily range. The relative strength that I'm talking about is comparing a stock's returns versus an index. For example, look at the Royal Bank of Canada versus the TSX. If the trend line is going down, then RBC has been consistently underperforming the TSX. If the trend line is going up, then RBC has been consistently outperforming the TSX. Some stocks go through cycles when they underperform for a while. But then when you overlay a moving average, you can sometimes pick stocks up at the point in which sentiment has changed for the better. People can discount a stock but then all of a sudden it can start to gain favour in the market again. Even better would be to compare RBC to the TSX financials index. Basically, with relative strength analysis, you can see which stocks are in favour or not in favour, and you can also catch them at turning points. Finally, you can gauge your relative performance. For instance, if Royal Bank is up 10%, but the financial sector is up 30%, then you picked a significant underperformer.

You're consistently seeking alpha from the market. Investing in stocks that achieve higher returns than the index or a comparable group.

Obviously that's everyone's goal. Relative strength is a signal that I use to pick out stocks that consistently achieve higher returns, because generally speaking stocks don't always do that. They're going to go through cycles of favour and out-of-favour relative to something else. It's also important to figure out even when you've got a good stock with good fundamentals, that it quantitatively ranks very well, and that you can then find some potential inflection points on a regular chart to buy it. To illustrate, I look at a tree and think, "That's a pretty big tree, but you know, relative to other trees, it's actually tiny." You need to look around you and figure out how a stock is doing relative to peers.

How long a period do you look at for relative strength analysis?

Generally, what I look at is a weekly chart that goes back about three years. On the sell side, a stock will start to underperform relative to its peer group before you see a complete price underperformance. To explain, before a stock actually starts to sell off, it first exhibits weakness relative to its peers. That's an early warning signal.

Let's hypothetically say that a couple of stocks pass that technical analysis test in that they show relative strength over three years. What's next?

I look at both support levels and overhead resistance on the chart. Further, I focus in on trend lines that have been breached on the chart.

Did you also look for stocks that are breaking out of their patterns?

There's the cup and handle formation, which is big with a number of people. I don't know if you're familiar with that guy who wrote *How to Make Money in Stocks* —

O'Neil?

Yeah, William O'Neil, exactly. He's big on the cup and handle formation.

Can you explain the cup and handle formation and why it's important?

Generally, you would have a bit of a run-up, then consolidation, and then a sell-off. So the run-up makes the edge of the cup, the consolidation makes the top of the cup, and then the sell-off makes the handle, which marks the point before its takeoff. From there, if the stock breaches the consolidation point, then that can signal a decent move higher.

Have other patterns delivered predictable moves?

Coming down to a support level is generally one of the things I'll try to weigh more on as opposed to some type of wedge pattern or anything like that.

So would you buy on a support level because you know you have a greater margin of safety? There's less downside risk once there's that support.

Exactly. There's more volume around that area, which means that there's investors who have been in there willing to support it before. Additionally, there's investors who look to bargain shop. They'll say, "Well, if it gets back down here I'll buy some." Through charts you can try to get into the mind of the other investors in the market.

What behaviours do your winners actually exhibit on their charts?

The stocks that turn. They've had a decent period of outperformance, and then a period of underperformance. For example, it outperformed for about a year and then basically underperformed for the last three months. But then you finally start to see a ramp up again and it resumes its course of outperformance.

I see. So you capture the return on the upside of the cycle?

Yeah.

Why do you think technical analysis works? The fact that you can read a chart to validate a future move upwards or downwards.

I don't know. I've thought about that, too. Is a chart just psychology? Is there some type of psychological bent in there where people say, "Wow, it's oversold by this indicator, so I'm going to step in and buy it?" For that to be true you'd have to have a lot of people in the market using technical analysis for it to be a self-fulfilling event. But I have a feeling that technical analysis and charting are the primary drivers in a lot of stocks. In and around the fringes it can move us here or there on a day, especially on some of the mega-cap stocks, where more people might be watching with a close eye. Whereas some of the smaller-cap stocks might have only a handful of investors looking at charts. They might move it up for a day or two but they're not going to create a sustained move unless there's some real money from the bigger guys behind the stock.

Let's move onto the final stage of your process, which would be fundamental analysis.

Exactly. So now that you've whittled the list down even more, you can start going through and reading some analyst research. Generally, the analyst research is the easiest to read and to understand. We're in a smaller firm, so we rely more on the analysts. But to be clear, I don't rely on the buy or sell recommendations of the analysts but the summarized information that they provide to me. From that research, we glean performance drivers, quality of management, and potential catalysts for a sustained stock move.

Do you also seek validation from hedge fund managers?

I ignore the hedge fund world here. But when I was back at Scotiabank there was a little more time and so I'd actually go through and peruse the hedge funds' holdings.

So after all three phases you would add the final candidate stocks to your funds?

Yeah. But sometimes you need to be selective. That being said, additionally, you can overlay sector analysis to determine whether at any point in time you want to buy financial or industrial stocks, for example.

So there's a macro overlay, too.

Yeah. When I was at Scotiabank I employed a similar but different process to formulate a view of the general market. I created a grid system and applied various inputs to it. For example, I applied the VIX to inform me on volatility in the markets. Also, I applied a service called Lawrie that shed light on whether the market was going up because a lot of people were buying stocks or because not as many people were selling stocks. Buying pressure versus selling pressure. In all, I tried to put together all of the pieces of that jigsaw puzzle to get a pretty decent picture of the factors that could affect the market. But I knew that I'd never complete the full puzzle.

Over time, have you noticed commonalities in stocks in your funds?

No. It's everything. In the grand scheme of things I let the market tell me what to do. I do not try to dictate to the market what to do. I do more listening than talking to get a feel for what the markets are doing and where they're going. You know, a lot of people have pegged themselves to a style. They say, "I'm a value investor" or "I'm a growth investor." I've pegged myself as style-agnostic. I'll go through, look at, and apply any and all of the different investment methods. Though, to support my decision, I will back-test strategies over a 10- to 15-year time period on each sector. Back at Scotiabank, I picked a couple of strategies that worked really well in a bull market, and picked a couple of strategies that worked really well in a bear market.

What strategies worked well in a bull market?

It depends. A bull market in energy is going to favour different variables than a bull market in technology. Generally, the strategies were all over the place. Well, I shouldn't say all over the place, but different models worked better for different sectors over different time periods and during different market environments. When I was at Scotiabank in 2009, the technology models informed us to move to a dividend model for stability. We rotated the technology portfolio to a large-cap dividend payout portfolio. That portfolio rotation led to a significant amount of outperformance. There's a hundred different ways to skin a cat in this game. Everybody's going to come up with their own thing that works.

What strategies worked well in bear markets?

Obviously, the best investment in a bear market is cash. But you need to be in tune with the environment and ask, "Where are the most overvalued assets? Where's the pain trade?" I remember that in 2007 and 2008 the biggest hedge funds in the industry employed quant-based strategies. If 10 new hedge funds started up, nine of them were quant funds. And most of those quant hedge funds were collectively self-fulfilling entities, as they all used similar variables in the market to trade and to invest in stocks. Throughout that period, I thought, "This is going to end ugly." Once the correction began, you wouldn't want to own the stocks that had historically done well by quant metrics. A lot of the stocks held in quant hedge funds were overbought and over-owned at that time.

Do you judge valuation based on current multiples or future multiples?

There's multiple ways to look at the earnings multiple. For example, there's the 80 times current earnings multiple on Valeant. Well, that's based on Valeant's trailing earnings. Some people would say that using trailing earnings in a valuation is like trying to drive a car while looking in the rear-view mirror. Basically, most analysts out there would say that Valeant's actually trading at 20 times its forward earnings. Use the forward P/E rather than current P/E.

While we're talking about Valeant, they reported "surprise earnings" this week. That would factor into your model, right?

Exactly. Valeant ranks high. Its growth is quite astounding. Indeed, the management group has done a fantastic job. You know, they employ a roll-up strategy, whereby basically the acquisitions they make are immediately accretive to their earnings. That in turn bumps up their valuation. Valeant management buys stocks at 10 times earnings and rolls them up into their company so that they're then valued at 20 times earnings. That's alchemy right there. They're looking at achieving 30% earnings growth this year, and then another 40% earnings growth next year. So again, if these guys continue to execute, acquire, and then roll up the companies, they're going to do a fantastic job.

Can you share some of your most successful calls that you've made?

Most recently one of our really big winners was Magna. We picked up Magna back in 2011. Quantitatively, it looked good. And technically, too. It started to turn up after some underperformance because of the Eurozone crisis where they have a decent amount of market exposure. Plus, they were still coming out of the doldrums of the North American car market. Other winners are Bank of America and Wells Fargo. We were able to invest in those banks fairly close to their lows after the financial crisis. They've been a phenomenal success. From a technical standpoint, I was able to go through and pick off those stocks on their turning points based on their relative strength. To elaborate, Bank of America and Wells Fargo started to outperform both their sector and the index.

So, again, catching the turning point is essential to your overall strategy.

Yeah. But you also had to understand the fundamental viewpoint. Take Citigroup. It was a company that through the crisis shut off assets and thus basically shut off future earnings potential. But both Wells Fargo and Bank of America were able to go on and acquire more businesses during that period. For example, Bank of America's acquisition of Merrill Lynch. I figured that once the economy started to turn around, both of those stocks would start to fire on all cylinders. Their earnings multiples would be higher than what they were prior to the crash. Whereas, because of their divestures, Citigroup's future earnings would be a fraction of what they were prior to the crash.

What about the bets that didn't work out? Stocks that passed all of the tests but didn't perform as planned?

One of the most important things to do after bad bets is to cut your losses relatively early on. I'm not exactly a big proponent of doubling down — the stock goes against you, so you buy more. Generally, you should buy at an inflection point where the stock can go higher. But you shouldn't exactly pick the lows, because you need to have some assurance that it will turn around the way that you would assume it would.

You listen to the market.

Exactly. I would much rather try to buy strength rather than buy weakness, and sell weakness rather than buy it.

Anything that we missed that you want to talk about?

Find a discipline. Stick to it. Also, this will sound a little bit odd, but steal. Look around and try to find a bunch of great ideas and see if there's a way that you can combine them into fitting your own strategy. There's a million ways to skin a cat, and there's ways to create something that feels natural to you. You'll get someone who loves action, and then they'll go and try to be a deep-value long-term investor. Well, that's going to drive them squirrelly. They'll just be itching to try to do something and they're going to end up sabotaging their investment. You must realize what your own personality is, and if you need to be more active, there's an active strategy that you can find and follow that will keep you entertained and hopefully make you some money. If you're more of a "sit back and don't want a whole lot of action" person, there's another methodology and strategy that you can follow.

Cameron joins three disciplines together to form his security analysis process: quantitative, technical, and fundamental. He wants to ensure that he can make arguments along all three fronts to validate attractive opportunities in the market. I've synthesized Cameron's three-step process for you below.

QUANTITATIVE

Use quantitative scrutiny to shrink your stock universe. Preferred metrics in a stock scan or filter include:
- Positive estimate revisions
- Positive earnings surprises
- Earnings growth
- Dividend growth

TECHNICAL

RELATIVE STRENGTH
Analyze relative strength in stocks to see which ones are technically stronger relative to their peer group, industry, index, or any other benchmark. You want to invest in the stocks that are currently in favour. Cameron offered an analogy to explain relative strength: "You look at a tree and think, 'That's a pretty big tree,' but relative to other trees, it might actually be tiny." Cameron

will analyze a chart by looking back about three years. On the sell side, a stock will start underperforming relative to its group before it experiences a complete price underperformance. That's an early warning signal.

SUPPORT AND RESISTANCE LEVELS

Look for trend lines that have been breached that can form new support (upward pressure) or resistance (downward pressure). Generally, stocks that come down to support levels are at a good entry point to invest, as support levels can validate a long-term move higher. Also, there's more margin of safety. Cameron explains, "There's more volume around that area [support]. People who were willing to support it before will look to bargain shop once it gets back down to that level."

REVERSION TO MEAN

When asked, "What behaviours do your winners actually exhibit on their charts?" Cameron replied, "The stocks that are turning. The ones that have had a decent time of outperformance, then a period of underperformance, [and then a resumption of the uptrend]."

CUP AND HANDLE FORMATION (OPTIONAL)

Generally, look for a bit of a run-up, then consolidation, and then a sell-off. So the run-up makes the edge of the cup, the consolidation makes the top of the cup, and then the sell-off makes the handle, which marks the point before its takeoff. From there, if the stock breaches the consolidation point, then that can signal a decent move higher.

FUNDAMENTAL

Cameron leverages analyst research — for example, margins, forecasts, management effectiveness — for the final fundamental stage of his security selection process. He finds that analyst research is more efficient than conducting his own. Also, as part of this stage, Cameron would overlay sector analysis to finally determine the stocks to add to his portfolio.

1) "We look for companies that have had their estimate revisions go higher."

2) "We look for earnings surprises, where management is able to beat analysts' earnings consensus on a consistent basis. Either management is able to manage the street's expectations very well or they're actually just able to execute very well."

3) "[We] flip through a bunch of the stocks to see which ones appear technically stronger, which could be based on relative strength to their benchmark or index."

4) "'RSI' . . . is an indicator that measures on an individual day where a stock closes within its range. So if the RSI is drifting higher, that's telling you that it's consistently closing in the upper half of its daily range."

5) "Some stocks go through cycles when they underperform for a while. But then when you overlay a moving average, you can sometimes pick stocks up at the point in which sentiment has changed for the better."

6) "If Royal Bank is up 10%, but the financial sector is up 30%, then you picked a significant underperformer."

7) "You need to look around you and figure out how a stock is doing relative to peers. Before a stock actually starts to sell off, it first exhibits weakness relative to its peers. That's an early warning signal."

8) "I look at both support levels and overhead resistance on the chart. Further, I focus in on trend lines that have been breached on the chart."

9) "There's investors who look to bargain shop. They'll say, 'Well, if it gets back down here I'll buy some.' Through charts you can try to get into the mind of the other investors in the market."

10) "Technical analysis and charting are the primary drivers in a lot of stocks."

11) "You can overlay sector analysis to determine whether at any point in time you want to buy financial or industrial stocks, for example."

12) "I tried to put together all of the pieces of that jigsaw puzzle to get a pretty decent picture of the factors that could affect the market. But I know that I'd never complete the full puzzle."

13) "In the grand scheme of things I let the market tell me what to do. I do not try to dictate to the market what to do. I do more listening than talking."

14) "A lot of people have pegged themselves to a style. They say, 'I'm a value investor' or 'I'm a growth investor.' I've pegged myself as style-agnostic. I'll go through, look at, and apply any and all of the different investment methods."

15) "Some people would say that using trailing earnings in a valuation is like trying to drive a car while looking in the rear-view mirror. Use the forward P/E rather than current P/E."

16) "One of the most important things to do after bad bets is to cut your losses relatively early on."

17) "Generally, you should buy at an inflection point where the stock can go higher. But you shouldn't exactly pick the lows, because you need to have some assurance that it will turn around the way that you would assume it would."

18) "Look around and try to find a bunch of great ideas and see if there's a way that you can combine them into fitting your own strategy."

PART VI OTHER STYLES

In this section I have included those investors who do not fall into any of the groups we've explored so far — value, growth, fundamental, macro (top-down), or systematic (technical). These investors have a style all their own.

BILL ACKMAN
THE ACTIVIST INVESTOR
(WITH A CANADIAN LOVE AFFAIR)

I know what you're thinking: "Bill Ackman doesn't belong in this book; he isn't Canadian." In my mind, though, Bill is almost an honorary Canadian, since he's been heavily involved in the Canadian market through three large and notable plays: Wendy's/Tim Hortons, Canadian Pacific Railway, and Valeant. While each of those Canadian investment plays is unique, they all underscore Bill's multi-faceted activist methodology at Pershing Square Capital Management. The first, Wendy's/Tim Hortons, was a breakup play. The second, Canadian Pacific Railway, was a turnaround play. The third, Valeant, is a growth or "platform" play.

Bill capitalized on all three of his Canadian investments, which is why in my first email to him, I asked, "Do you have a love affair with Canadian companies?" Honestly, I didn't expect to hear back from the man who heads Pershing Square Capital Management, with close to $20 billion in assets under management. Bill's one of the most high-profile hedge fund managers in the world, and it seemed unlikely he would take time to talk to a kid from Toronto rather than U.S. media outlets like CNBC or Bloomberg. Not to mention I had emailed Bill during a period in which his Herbalife short had attracted the attention of the media, the FBI, and the SEC. He must have been busy. But since my mantra is "Don't fail to try. Try to fail," I went for it. Just two minutes after I sent Bill my "Canadian love affair" email to ask if he would be willing to be interviewed, he responded: "Sure."

As I prepared for the interview, I started to think that while Bill's Canadian investments are excellent market case studies, the way in which he invests and then realizes value in companies is out of reach to most, if not all, common investors. Bill is an activist investor with deep pockets and strong influence. He can and does push the board of directors and management at companies to make changes that will positively affect operations, and as a result, raise stock prices. Take Canadian Pacific Railway, for example. Yvan Allaire, executive chair of the board of directors for IGOPP, the Institute for Governance of Private and Public Organizations, summed up Bill's CP play quite eloquently in the *Financial Post*: "In 2011, Pershing Square Capital Management, an activist hedge fund founded by William (Bill) Ackman, acquired some 14.2% of Canadian Pacific Railway's outstanding shares and proceeded to require several changes in the management and governance of the company. The CP board resisted fiercely his entreaties. A memorable proxy fight ensued, which was won by Pershing and resulted in a new CEO, new board members, and a new strategy for CP. Results of this palace revolution were, in share price terms at least, remarkable — astounding, actually. From September 2011 to December 31, 2014, CP's stock jumped from less than $49 to north of $220, a compounded annual rate of return of 62% (including dividends)." The average investor won't be able to accomplish something of that magnitude. So, I asked Bill how an investor with limited resources could replicate the activist approach, to which he replied, "You can ride the coattails of shareholder activists." Investors can indirectly employ the activist approach, by directly buying the stocks that successful activist investors hold in their portfolios, along the lines of Som Seif's Best Ideas Fund. In fact, Som includes Bill Ackman's highest-conviction positions in that fund.

Bill is a busy man, and he occasionally had to pause our telephone interview (Bill's office is in Manhattan), to address people as they came into his office. However, Bill is a talented enough multitasker that he was able to hold the thread of the conversation while carrying out his business. He was archetypal Bill Ackman: confident, articulate, and to the point — everything I had come to expect about Bill from his television appearances. I highly recommend that you watch the CNBC clip "Billionaire Showdown: Bill Ackman vs. Carl Icahn," to get a better picture of Bill's attitude, demeanour, and train of thought.

PRE-INTERVIEW LESSONS

ACTIVIST INVESTOR: an investor who takes a stake in a business to make changes at board, management, and operation levels to improve shareholder return.

BOARD OF DIRECTORS: a group of directors elected by the shareholders of a company.

How did you first get interested in the markets?

I was vaguely interested as a kid. It wasn't until I went to work in the real estate business after I graduated from college that I became interested in the markets. I followed the stock market to a certain extent in college but did not make my first investment until I went to business school.

What was that first investment in business school?

It was Wells Fargo Corporation.

What was your thesis for Wells Fargo at the time?

Basically, I had worked in the real estate investment banking business for two years prior to going to Harvard Business School. When I went to HBS I opened a brokerage account, and I thought I would learn about the investment business by investing in the market. The only thing I knew from a career point of view was real estate, and to some extent banking, because I had worked in real estate helping to arrange financing for real estate ownership investors. So I chose Wells Fargo because bank stocks had gotten obliterated, and because people believed the banks weren't solvent because of their real estate exposure. Additionally, I knew that Wells Fargo was very conservative in the way that they lent money. And the core earnings of the banks were very profitable once they worked through some losses. Even then, a worst case scenario wasn't going to be more than a year's worth of earnings, and then they could go back to being very profitable again. I paid a very low price for Wells Fargo based on where the stock had gone.

Did you decide on an investment philosophy early on? I'm certain you've read The Intelligent Investor *by Graham, but did you consider yourself a value investor? Has that evolved?*

The first investment book I read was Ben Graham's *The Intelligent Investor*. It was recommended to me by a guy I met at a cocktail party who was a friend of my dad's. He was a good investor. That was the beginning of my value investing education.

At Harvard you obtained your bachelor of arts degree as well as your MBA. And then you started up Gotham Partners. You've previously said that "raising money early on was like blind dating." Can you elaborate?

We were calling up people, most of whom we didn't know particularly well, endeavouring to get a meeting and pitching them on investing with us. Remember, we were two guys fresh out of Harvard Business School with no experience and no track record. That's difficult.

Was it at Gotham Partners that you solidified your activist investment strategy? Essentially, invest in companies and then directly help improve them?

It just sort of happened by accident. I was a passive investor, and then I saw an opportunity for a company to do something that would create more value, and that made me into a shareholder activist, which wasn't planned.

What was the most memorable investment for you — the one that created the most value for your clients at Gotham?

Well, the most memorable and the one where I created the most value are probably different things. But one of the most interesting investments was a company called Rockefeller Center Properties, which I invested in beginning in 1994. It was a very high-profile asset, and with a relatively small amount of money we became the biggest shareholder in an entity that held the equity in the mortgage on the Rockefeller Center.

But eventually Goldman Sachs also saw the mispricing in Rockefeller Center Properties and started buying a stake in it.

Yeah. We ended up competing to provide financing to the company with backing from the Rockefeller family. But ultimately they chose Goldman Sachs over our transaction.

Fast forward to Pershing Square Capital Management. With $20 billion assets under management, you run one of the highest profile and most successful activist hedge funds in the world today. Which companies fit your criteria for investment?

The things we own *[laughs]*.

But are these consumer franchises? Have they been around for a while? Large-cap?

For us the most important thing is what we call "business quality." We're looking for a simple, predictable free cash flow generative dominant company. You know, a business that Warren Buffett would describe as having a moat around it. The moat is usually created by brands, unique assets, long-term contracts, market position, or perhaps some combination of all of these factors.

Do you also look for companies that are ripe for turnaround where their full value is not entirely reflected in the market?

We've done a couple of real turnarounds, but in most cases it's about optimizing a business as opposed to completely transforming it. The most difficult transformation we ever attempted was unsuccessful, which was the JCPenney investment. But with most of our investments we're investing in a great business that has perhaps gotten a bloated cost structure, or that has not thought about its business correctly and maybe over-invested in parts of the business or has not allocated capital correctly, or perhaps has lost focus and owns assets it should sell.

You seem to have a love affair with Canadian companies. Through Pershing Square, you've invested in Wendy's, Canadian Pacific Railway, and now Valeant. Did you buy into Wendy's solely for the Tim Hortons asset?

We bought into Wendy's because it was undervalued. Basically, if you netted out the value of Tim Hortons you were paying negative for Wendy's. The market was focused on Wendy's declining business, weak same-store sells, rising beef commodity prices, and mismanagement. Instead, we were focused on Tim Hortons, which was an unbelievable franchise.

Have you ever had a coffee from Tim Hortons?

No.

So it was purely a financial transaction. Why do mispriced assets, like Wendy's in that example, exist on the market? Does that mean that the market is inefficient?

You know, there's some degree of complexity. The company in that case was called Wendy's. Tim Hortons had a very different kind of business model, as they were a pure franchise restaurant company, whereas Wendy's owned a lot of its own stores. And the consolidated financial statements were difficult but not incredibly complicated to figure out. However, I think some of the profitability of Tim Hortons was masked by the weakness of Wendy's. In a market, most stocks are based on people's estimates of next year's earnings: analysts' estimates. If there's one business making $2 billion and another business, or another subsidiary, losing $1 billion, people will look at it and say, "Oh, it's got $1 billion of earnings." But that's not the right way to think about it.

So you looked at the breakup value of Wendy's. You saw that Tim Hortons was a gem within Wendy's corporate entity. You invested in Wendy's and then influenced the board to spin off Tim Hortons. Was the board hesitant to spin off Tim's?

Yes.

Why?

I think that most CEOs prefer to run a bigger business. If you take a more skeptical view, CEO compensation tends to be correlated with the size of the company that you're running, so you get to be paid more if you're running a bigger business. You can also justify a bigger airplane *[laughs]*, you know. Incentives drive human behaviour.

Tim Hortons IPO was a huge success. But then recently, Burger King bought out Tim Hortons. Did you have a hand in that as well? You had a stake in Burger King Worldwide.

Yes.

Okay, makes sense — I just put the puzzle pieces together.

Well, to clarify, I encouraged them to take a look at Tim Hortons, but they did all the work.

Where do you see Tim Hortons in the next 10 years? Will worldwide expansion work?

Yes.

Let's move on to Canada Pacific Railway. To me, this was a pure turnaround play. Why did you take a stake in Canadian Pacific Railway?

It was the worst-run railroad in North America. It had constantly disappointed its shareholders. The stock was cheap as is, and for good reason. So we got Hunter Harrison to work with us for several months to teach us the industry. He convinced us that the problems at CP Railway were not structural and that he could fix them. So it was with the best railroad CEO in the world — Hunter Harrison — and a cheap stock price that we thought we could create enormous value at CP Railway.

What were some of the things that Hunter implemented straightaway, to turn around CP?

Well, we just let Hunter loose. We didn't tell him what to do. He had done this two or three times before. So we stayed out of his way, I guess I would say.

Aside from installing able management to turn around a company, what other elements are required to make a turnaround work?

The key things are, one, finding a good target. A good target is a great business that's undervalued because of under-management. Two, figuring out and finding the right person to run the company. And then a big part of the execution, which is three, is getting ourselves in a position where we can install that management and have meaningful influence going forward over the company. That can mean negotiating representation on a board, it can mean running a proxy contest like in CP Railway at the time.

Buffett has said that the railroads are a good indicator for the economy as a whole.

Sure.

From what CP is telling you now, do you think that the next five years will be okay for the Canadian economy?

Well, I wouldn't use the success of the Canadian Pacific Railway to conclude that the economy's going to do better. The success of Canadian Pacific Railway, and the vast majority of the increase in its share price, is driven by the improvement of the profitability of the railroad, the improved efficiency of the railroad, the improved asset utilization of the railroad, and by making the railroad more efficient. For example, reducing delivery times from Toronto to Vancouver so that CP is more competitive with other alternatives. As a result of being more competitive with other alternatives, CP started winning more business, which is helping to drive the revenues of the company. So CP Railway is a bit of an outlier. Though I would say that I would agree with Buffett, assuming that the railroads are being run well. You know, as it transports goods to retail stores and commodities to factories or consumers. Otherwise, it's obviously a pretty good indicator of demand in the economy.

Now onto the third Canadian company — Valeant Pharmaceuticals. What opportunity did you see at Valeant?

Valeant is an exceptionally well-run, extremely cost-disciplined, brilliantly structured company run by a management team that has a strategy that we think makes enormous sense in a sector where there are very few companies that operate that way.

So, this was a case where good management was already there. Their acquisition strategy's been incredibly aggressive. Shareholders have definitely been cheering that on. But how long do you think that Valeant's aggressive acquisition drive will sustain the stock's high multiples?

The stock doesn't trade at a high multiple. What we think of are its core earnings. There's a lot of accounting complexity because they've done a large number of acquisitions. We think if they don't even do another deal then they still have a very profitable business. But there are a large number of opportunities that can be done in the pharma space.

So you're looking for multiple expansion over the years. Valeant's CEO has been quoted as saying that he wants to be in the top five pharma group in the world.

I think there's a decent chance it becomes the largest pharma company in the world. But we don't focus on scale, and neither does the CEO. He focuses on per share value.

Looking back at all of your Canadian investments, is it simply a coincidence that you've found opportunities in Canadian companies? Or does this indicate that there's better opportunity in the Canadian market than in the U.S. for asset mispricings, turnarounds, and so on?

It's just that we tend to focus on North America because it's close to home. The language is English, and the law in Canada is similar to the U.S. We've had a very favourable experience in Canada in pretty much everything we've done.

I wonder why that is. How do you select your investments in Canada?

We need to focus on big companies, because we're actually closer to $20 billion in assets today. And so we only want to do things that will move the needle, and as a result we tend to focus on bigger things.

How to you keep up to date on Canadian companies? Do you employ Canadians who understand how these companies operate before you invest in them?

No. Well, do we employ Canadians? Yes, one of my traders just walked in — he's Canadian. We've got an analyst who's Canadian. But I don't think you need to be Canadian to understand Canadian companies. But we do employ Canadians, for sure.

What criteria need to be met before you take on your next position?

High-quality business, fair price, and cheap, if we can, very cheap, and if we can make changes that fix the company.

Do you set a target return that you want to achieve in each investment?

No. Not a target return on a one-year basis. We focus on what's the worth, what can we make it worth, and how long it is going to take. I would say we have a view of a few years out of what it's worth, not a year out.

Can you disclose some of the other Canadian investments that you were considering investing in but didn't?

We don't do that.

Are you aware of any of the activist investors in Canada?

I don't follow them that closely, to be honest.

There's a fellow named Prem Watsa.

Yeah, I certainly know who he is.

Do you believe in his turnaround strategy at BlackBerry? He's invested in BlackBerry and installed a very able CEO, John Chen.

You know, I've never looked at BlackBerry.

How does an investor who does not have the means to influence management identify a turnaround opportunity in the market, invest in it, and generate good returns?

Well, you can ride the coattails of shareholder activists. You know, pick your favourite activists, and do your research on their securities under management. If you like the situation, you can buy the stock and let the activist do all the work. And you'll have more liquidity and you don't have to pay fees, so that's a pretty good strategy. You can't necessarily buy at the activists' price, but once they announce the investment you can invest in it alongside them. And oftentimes stocks don't go straight up, so there's an opportunity to buy it again at a cheaper price.

Who would you follow in the market?

I think Value Act has done a good job. I think Triton has done a good job. I think Dan Loeb had some good success. You know, the usual suspects, I would say.

Are there some sectors in the market that are more challenging to turn around?

We've avoided businesses that are hard for us to predict with a high degree of confidence.

I would imagine that would be retail and technology.

Yeah, we've not been particularly successful in retail in recent years. We were earlier in the history of Pershing Square, but not later, or now.

What final advice do you have for investors?

You know, I would really encourage people to invest in the highest-quality businesses that they can identify in the market. Make sure you buy them at attractive prices. And hold them for the long term. I think that's the lowest-risk, highest-reward strategy.

Amazingly, Bill Ackman's Pershing Square Capital Management has continually beaten the market since it was established in 2004, with compound annual returns of 23% versus the S&P 500's 8% return.

In the 2014 Pershing Square Holdings annual report, Bill succinctly outlined his activist investment approach:

> Find a great business where there is an opportunity for management, operational, and/or governance improvements. Build a large stake at an attractive price. Work with management and the board to make necessary changes. Seek board representation for members of the Pershing Square team or affiliated or independent representatives that we identify. [However], we do not believe it is necessary for us to have a board seat in these commitments if we are confident that the existing board already has appropriate shareholder representation, and a management team with exceptional operating and capital allocation discipline. Restaurant Brands, which is controlled by 3G, is a good such example. While the bulk of our capital is invested in Pershing Square 2.0–like commitments, we are still open to shorter-term commitments if the opportunity for profit relative to risk is large enough. Once we are in a position of influence and own a high-quality business run by able management who manages the business well and allocates free cash flow intelligently,

absent excessive over-valuation or a substantially better use of capital, there are few good reasons to sell. It is essential though that these commitments have all of the above: high business quality, managerial and operating talent, and intelligent capital allocation for them to continue to generate high rates of return over the long term.

Bill goes on to explain his core security selection principles:

> We generally invest in higher-quality businesses with dominant and defensive market positions that generate predictable free cash flow streams and that have modestly or negatively leveraged (cash in excess of debt) balance sheets. We buy these businesses at deep discounts to our estimate of intrinsic value, giving us a margin of safety against a permanent impairment of capital. I say "generally" again here because we do make exceptions in certain limited circumstances; that is, we may buy a more leveraged or lower-quality business if we believe the price paid sufficiently discounts the risk.

Lately it seems that Bill has concentrated more on "platform value" than "activism" to generate the greatest returns in his hedge fund. But perhaps that is simply an instance rather than a trend. During his presentation at the Sohn 2015 conference, Bill said, "Businesses managed by superior operators that execute value-enhancing acquisitions and shareholder-focused capital allocation have substantial platform value." Valeant is an example of a platform company.

After the interview, I wondered what Bill Ackman's next Canadian investment plays could be. That night, I drafted and then sent an email with the subject line "Canadian ideas" to Bill Ackman, listing the securities below. I wonder if any of these stocks will show up on a future Pershing Square Capital Management 13F report.

POSSIBLE BREAKUP / SPINOFF PLAYS
- Rogers Communications
- Bombardier

POSSIBLE TURNAROUND / OPTIMIZATION OPPORTUNITIES
- Thomson Reuters
- TransCanada Corporation
- Suncor Energy

IMMEDIATE PLATFORM VALUE
- Magna International
- Brookfield Asset Management
- CGI Group
- Alimentation Couche-Tard
- Sun Life Financial

MASTER KEYS
BILL ACKMAN

1) "I was a passive investor, and then I saw an opportunity for a company to do something that would create more value, and that made me into a shareholder activist, which wasn't planned."

2) "For us the most important thing is what we call 'business quality.' We're looking for a simple, predictable free cash flow generative dominant company."

3) "The moat is usually created by brands, unique assets, long-term contracts, market position, or perhaps some combination of all of these factors."

4) "We've done a couple of real turnarounds, but in most cases it's about optimizing a business as opposed to completely transforming it."

5) "With most of our investments we're investing in a great business that has perhaps gotten a bloated cost structure, or that has not thought about its business correctly and maybe over-invested in parts of the business or has not allocated capital correctly, or perhaps has lost focus and owns assets it should sell."

6) "In a market, most stocks are based on people's estimates of next year's earnings: analysts' estimates."

7) "If there's one business making $2 billion and another business, or another subsidiary, losing $1 billion, people will look at it and say, 'Oh, it's got $1 billion of earnings.' But that's not the right way to think about it."

8) "If you take a more skeptical view, CEO compensation tends to be correlated with the size of the company that you're running, so you get to be paid more if you're running a bigger business. You can also justify a bigger airplane."

9) "[Turnaround strategy:] The key things are, one, finding a good target. A good target is a great business that's undervalued because of under-management. Two, figuring out and finding the right person to run the company. And then a big part of the execution, which is three, is getting ourselves in a position where we can install that management and have meaningful influence going forward over the company."

10) "We've had a very favourable experience in Canada in pretty much everything we've done."

11) "You can't necessarily buy at the activists' price, but once they announce the investment you can invest in it alongside them. And oftentimes stocks don't go straight up, so there's an opportunity to buy it again at a cheaper price."

12) "We've avoided businesses that are hard for us to predict with a high degree of confidence."

13) "I would really encourage people to invest in the highest-quality businesses that they can identify in the market. Make sure you buy them at attractive prices. And hold them for the long term."

LORNE ZEILER
BEHAVIOURAL INVESTING

"This is your brain on drugs." A study from Laurence Tancredri, entitled "Hardwired Behaviour, What Neuroscience Reveals about Morality," showed that "there is a resemblance between the brain of someone predicting a financial gain and that of a drug abuser. A dopamine 'buzz' is created by the cue, which prompts us to be more aggressive with our money. When acting on the cue fails to produce a reward, the dopamine level still increases dramatically, leaving us in a profound funk. The result: you overreact and prematurely remove your money from the market. If enough people did that, the market would inevitably drop precipitously."

Lorne Zeiler, vice-president and associate portfolio manager at TriDelta Financial, would also argue that your behavioural drive often dictates your investment decisions. That's why Lorne travels the country to educate people about their own brains. Don't do drugs, kids. Seriously, though, this is how Lorne opens his presentation, "What You Don't Know Can Be Harmful to Your Investment Returns": "Have you wondered why your investment returns have been below your expectations? Why others seem to be able to take advantage of buying opportunities, while you sit on the sidelines? Have you sold stocks that seem to continue to go up, while holding on to securities that continue to go down in value? This is because emotion often has a much greater impact on investment decisions than most people realize." You'll also learn from Lorne why women make better investors than men. Pretty controversial.

PRE-INTERVIEW LESSONS

BEHAVIOURAL FINANCE: the study of how human behaviour affects our thoughts, decisions, and effectively, our performance in the markets.

CAPITULATION: the point at which investors "give up" in the market. Usually this occurs at the tail end of a huge market decline or bear market. The investor erroneously sells low.

DURATION MANAGEMENT: measure of the sensitivity of a fixed-income investment to a change in interest rates.

HEDGE: to offset risk in one investment by investing in another (e.g., one can hedge a decline in the U.S. dollar currency with an investment in gold, since it is seen as a store of value).

See the conclusion on Lorne Zeiler for behavioural finance defined terms and concepts.

To start off, where did you grow up in Canada?

Toronto.

How did you first get interested in the markets?

I took my CSC back in 1994. I did that after completing my undergraduate degree, which was at McGill in political science. I also did a minor in economics and found the economics side much more interesting than the politics side. I started working for Scotiabank in the nineties and I graduated with my MBA then, too. As you know, the mid-nineties were an extremely exciting time in the market, and that's when I really got interested in how companies were being valued. Basically, the risk/reward didn't seem to be logically valued in the marketplace.

Can you elaborate on the risk/reward paradigm in the mid-nineties?

As an example, when I was taking my CFA, a number of my presenters highlighted the fact that people had all these expectations on Amazon and these other technology companies, yet you could be buying their debt and getting 15%-plus returns. So if it's such a great company, you shouldn't be able to make that kind of return on their debt, because the higher coupon you're getting on their debt, the greater likelihood there is of a default on that type of company.

Was that a leading indicator for a market top in the late nineties?

In fairness, there's probably so many indicators when you go back to the nineties. And more so than in 2008 because in the nineties you had a change of rules which I'm still amazed went through. The government allowed pro forma financial statements. Companies that were literally not making any money but rather losing money and were just focused on market share. In fairness, there are companies today, like Twitter, in which you can still see the value, but it isn't earning money. In the nineties, there was no proprietary value. There were no barriers for entry for someone else to do the exact same thing. Regardless, there was a doubling of the market between '98 and 2000. That was illogical. But as you probably realize, just because it's illogical doesn't mean it can't continue to move up. And the market can get more illogical before it comes back to reality.

During that period of "irrational exuberance," what types of investments did you take on?

I'll tell you one story in particular, which worked out really well for me. In the late nineties I had just moved out. Expenses were still fairly high versus everything else, and I remember in order to get my engagement ring for my now-wife, I had to sell something from my equity portfolio. The stock that made the most sense to sell, because in fairness I didn't understand the valuation well enough, was BCE, which at the time had a huge position in Nortel. Now, mind you, had I sold it six months later I would have been much richer, but I ended up selling off my entire position in BCE to afford the engagement ring. Back then I was primarily focused on Canadian equities in my own portfolio. If you had managed to focus on value in the late nineties, which wasn't being rewarded, and you actually got clients to stick with you while the market was moving crazily, you actually did quite well from 2000 to 2003. You had opportunities to buy some utility companies, banks, insurers, and so on.

Why did this particular market shift, or re-valuation, happen?

When I was in school in '95 through '97, there was a complete philosophy change in terms of what was rewarded in the market, versus today. So in '96, '97, and '95, the philosophy was that a good management team should not be returning money to shareholders. Top-quality management teams should be reinvesting in their business and be able to generate more income from that reinvestment. And then I think because of what happened, and also you've had a major demographic shift, and more focus was on getting dividends returned to you instead. There were also companies like BCE that continuously could have done so much better for their shareholders had they been returning money. In Canada, we had the unique experiences with income trusts, which was a vehicle to return money to shareholders from mature businesses. Anyways, it was really interesting in the late nineties. Those were the companies that were rewarded, where the management team was taking the money, re-deploying it internally, and theoretically generating a higher ROE with the internal investments than an investor could have gotten from simply receiving dividends.

Interesting. Earlier you mentioned that "It can get more illogical before it comes back to reality." You sold BCE six months early; it continued its run-up. Why do markets become irrational?

So markets can become irrational for a variety of reasons. The media is definitely one reason. What the media wants is people with opinions, which means both sides of the coin, but extreme. They don't want people in the media saying, "Things are typical, expect 8% returns, here's your balanced portfolio," because that's not exciting. And people like to follow those ideas. Part of the value that we're seeing in the market today is offset from the very low returns we're getting from fixed income. That is driving more people to the market because you've got the possibility of buying stocks paying 3%, 4%, maybe even 5% dividends versus getting 1.3% now on a Canadian 10-year bond. People are saying, "I can get dividends and capital gain stocks," but forgetting there's also an opportunity for capital loss.

However, there can be so many reasons why people move markets to irrational levels. In the late nineties it really was sort of a philosophy of "This time is different; the internet's changing the world," which it did, but not from a valuation perspective. There was obviously a very cozy relationship going on at that time between the analyst community and the banks, which were jockeying prices. There were a lot of things that were happening. But the best description I've ever heard is when John Maynard Keynes termed it "the animal spirits." When the animal spirits are there, people get excited, and rationality doesn't necessarily meet up. Keynes is also the one who came up with the saying "Markets can stay irrational a lot longer than you can stay liquid," because he himself actually declared bankruptcy. He made a fortune later on in the market, but he actually declared bankruptcy from his early stock picks.

There's an opportunity cost in the markets: stocks versus bonds. What happens when interest rates start rising from our extreme lows? Will there be a rotation out of stocks and into bonds?

So actually one of the ways we've made a significant return is that we've been expecting what's called a "yield curve flattening." A lot of people don't follow the fixed-income market. But I don't think rates are going to go up very quickly. And in fact, the biggest error that a lot of people have made is to think, "Well, you know, 2.6% or 2.5% is a ridiculously low interest rate on a 10-year bond and therefore rates have nowhere to go but up," without looking at the global market. If Germany's paying 0.5% on their debt, and Japan's paying incredibly low rates on their debt, it's likely that you're going to get a double benefit of the U.S. currency going up, and U.S. bond yields going down because you're going to have global flows of funds come into the U.S. from those lower debt–yielding countries, among others. However, if yields were to rise and go back to what people consider to be a normalized rate, then, yes, it would be damaging to the stock market. In particular, I think those people who've been buying stocks as an income substitute, would start switching back to bonds.

So yields will continue to stay flat?

We're also of the belief that the U.S. is going to raise interest rates later than people expect, and it's going to be on a slower pace than people expect. And we've been holding that view for a long time and it's gone right into the overall investments.

Let's move on. You follow behavioural finance, and also teach it.

Yeah.

One of your course presentations is online: "What You Don't Know Can Be Harmful to Your Investment Returns." The first claim you make is that "investment returns are lower than expectations."

So a couple of things. Retail investor returns have historically been a lot lower than average for a variety of reasons. Retail investors tend to come into the market after it's already moved up. They tend to then hold on with the expectation that when things are turning negative, they can ride it out and things will be fine. There's an emotional cycle that people go through in the market. They get to a point of what's called "capitulation," where they just can't take it anymore regardless of what values are and regardless of what books they've read, or what studies they've done. They just say, "I can't take it," and they exit the market. So that's one reason why a typical retail investor does poorly: they're buying unfortunately high, they're selling unfortunately low, and they're exiting and entering the market at the wrong point.

Also, people are of the expectation that if markets have returned 9% a year, markets are going to continue to return 9% a year. This is called "recency bias." I'm a believer, and this is from a number of other authors that I've read, that a good way to look at where you think the next 10 years will be in terms of current returns is what your current valuation is and what the factors are. So if you look at today — inflation's lower than usual, growth rates are lower than usual — partly that's demographics, and valuations are slightly higher than usual. The offset to that obviously is we've got interest rates at significantly less than usual, which would put people into the equity market. I would expect [, though,] that during the next 10 years we [will] start to get to more normalized rates. You're going to get positive returns from equities, but they're going to be lower than historical average.

Is the emotional cycle that you alluded to fundamentally based on fear and greed?

Yes.

Why are retail investors prone to sell at the bottom and buy at the top?

Most people who are retail investors don't necessarily take the time, nor do they necessarily enjoy conducting the due diligence on a company. One of the things I highlight at the beginning of my courses is that when you're buying stocks, what you're actually doing is buying a fractional ownership in a company. A lot of people forget that. They think of the equity market as a casino, and they forget that what they're buying is an actual company, and the value of that company really should be based on its future prospects, future cash flows, future dividends, and future market share. That's what a fundamental analyst is trying to figure out. They may be wrong on some of their assumptions, but that's the basis of their assumptions. Most retail investors don't do that, and don't think that way. They just think of the market as a whole. So that's the first reason of why I think they sell at the bottom or buy at the top: valuation is not even a thought in their mind. Second, there are a number of biases people have where they tend to follow the herd. It is actually very difficult emotionally to go against the herd, even if all of your logic is there, even if you've done all your research, and even if you're very confident in your conviction.

On a personal basis, I started to re-enter the market in late October, early November 2008 because to me it was obvious that the financial system was being protected. Governments were doing whatever was necessary to step in, and in particular if you looked at high-yield debt, there were enormous opportunities where you could buy companies for less than liquidation value. I invested in a lot of structured products and I found opportunities in that side on split shares, particularly on the preferred side. But, as you probably know, I basically was right for about a month and a half, and then the market turned and went down, before it moved up again in March 2009. And that's a very difficult thing to live through. Now, with that example, I was only managing personal money and family money and friends' money, so it's easier to deal with them, but if it had been a book of clients it would have been very difficult to work through.

Did you stick with your positions when the markets turned down again in December 2008?

I did take some profits in December on some stocks, but it was more because I wanted to move into additional positions. Again, because I had a background on structured products, there were actually unbelievable opportunities. Not only could you buy cheap assets, but you could buy cheap assets that were trading at discounts. A way to get very good returns would be to go much higher up on the capital structure. So as I mentioned, with high-yield debt you could have bought the Canadian banks' tier one capital notes yielding 13% back then. And all you had to figure out was that you didn't think the Canadian banks were going to go under.

Let's revisit the emotional cycle in the markets.

Okay. So as a retail investor, you see what's on the media, and the media tends to be all bad news, or all good news. So it's very difficult to take a contrarian point of view. The other thing is that there are lots of elements going on in the market as well. Also, as individuals, we like to consider that we're going to be right; that's called hindsight bias. For example, we make a mistake and then go back and say, "Well, I've learned from it, I won't make that mistake again," even though we will. And there's confirmation bias, which is when you've taken a position and then look for other people who've got the same view without looking for people with different views, because you want to be confirmed that you're right. One of the first comments I get from individuals is, "Oh, it's great that you talk about such and such stock, because I own it, too." People want that confirmation.

Finally, numerous studies have been conducted that demonstrate that we as individuals are predisposed to be risk-averse. They've actually found that emotionally we view a loss as twice as powerful as a gain. So a sell-off period can have a serious impact on your thought process. It's also been found that during periods of volatility, the body naturally produces from stress more cortisol levels, which also makes us more risk-averse. There's a number of things happening that really, for the average individual, make it very difficult if they're investing on their own, to try to stay through a market, and to try to get in on a bottom.

How can an investor control their emotion and be rational? For example, buy at the bottom of the market?

First of all, you never know a bottom until after it's gone up from the bottom. That's the first thing. There are some very good technical indicators and Cameron Windsor, who's head of equities, has some particularly good ones he'll share with you. We look at relative strength to try to identify where stocks are moving. In 2008, from my understanding, and I'm not a technical person, there were a number of technical signals showing an impending sell-off. Those are helpful, but again you're never going to figure out when a bottom has occurred and say, "Okay, all is clear; time to get back in now." I'd say at that stage you take a lot of risk/reward.

Let's go back to the example of those Canadian banks. You could have gone into some very good quality investment-grade-rated corporate bonds, and effectively capitalized on yield to maturities in and around 10%. However, the one asset class that did very well then was U.S. bonds. Because the U.S. was the biggest currency in the world, and the safest currency in the world, and that's where people put their money. However, in 2008, when Lehman went down, we could have had a situation worse than the Great Depression. And there was no potential bottom in sight because that was a potential for a complete collapse of the financial system. Again, the big thing that changed for me is when I saw all of the action by governments around the world. They weren't going to let a collapse happen. Ben Bernake among others wanted to protect the financial system. The U.S. government effectively safeguarded deposits. They were doing so many things to basically demonstrate that they were going to safeguard the banks after what happened with Lehman, that they weren't going to let another big bank fail, and that they were also going to be putting money into the economy. On the Canadian bank side, there were a lot of initiatives that people aren't aware of that the Canadian government did to shore up and protect the Canadian banks. So it's tough to say how an individual protects themselves in that environment, but I think you've got to separate the news a little bit from reality and figure out what it all means. When QE passed, that meant a significant amount of financial stability for the markets.

Would you argue that because investors generally have so many emotional and behavioural deficiencies, the markets are largely inefficient?

If you ever want to read somebody who's done really good work on market efficiency, check out Howard Mark. He's one of the founders of Oaktree Capital. So, one of the issues with the Efficient Market Theory is that it states that the market reacts to information immediately. But that doesn't mean it reacts *properly*. It means that the market is able to digest information that is sent out and it's able to make a decision on it. So, probably Lehman's the best example. When the Lehman bankruptcy occurred, the market actually moved up for about 50 minutes, and then it fell off a cliff. Both are reactions to information that came out, which was that the government wasn't going to save Lehman. One of the reasons that I like the fixed-income market is that it tends to be more institutional, and so it tends to react more logically to events going on. As a result, we think the fixed-income market is more efficient than the stock market.

Why do some investors continue to hold on to stocks that are falling?

Okay, so there's been a lot of studies on the winners and losers. Basically the idea is that we are inherently risk-averse. People are supposed to look at the potential return for the future on an investment. Instead, they often look at what they paid for that investment, which is called "reference dependence" or "anchoring."

Let's say an investor bought two stocks and they're exactly the same. You buy them at $10. One has made a move from $10 to $13. The other has made a move from $10 to $7. This example is without any analysis of the underlying fundamentals of the company by the way. If that stock, which went from $10 to $13, now drops from $13 to $12, there's going to be a lot of investors that inherently are going to say, "I've paid $10, I've made two dollars on the stock, and so I'm going to sell this stock," because they're able to now say to themselves, "I made a good selection, I've made money, I've got a $2 gain." They become more risk-averse in that scenario. In the other scenario, where the investor paid $10, but it's now down to $7, they become risk-seeking because they say to themselves, "Well, I paid ten, it's worth seven, I've already lost money. If I lose more money, what's the big deal?" They don't want to admit to themselves that they've made a mistake, and so they actually will now start riding that stock further and further and further down. Fortunately, studies have shown that in general winners outperform your losers. Stocks that have generally done well are often going to continue to do well but there are a lot of people who will continue to hold onto that losing position, because they don't want to admit that loss. I'm sure if you spoke to people they'd have stories about BlackBerry, Nortel, and loads of similar stocks.

Are stop-losses the answer?

We have a very strong sell discipline within our portfolio. So we do a lot of quantitative selection and if our screens show it's a sell, unless there's a fundamental reason not to sell it, then our natural decision is to sell. Also, if for example a dividend payout is cut or eliminated, that would be a natural reason to sell the stock unless there's something logical about why management did it and we would expect the dividend to come back, which usually isn't the case. A dividend cut is usually a sign of something else going on and the best thing to do is to take the loss and move on. If you see a negative quarter of earnings or an actual loss, that's usually a reason to sell, but there might be rationale behind it. There could be a fine, there could be something else going on with the company, which might be a reason to override that philosophy, but generally I think that you'll find with probably most people you speak with, along with very good stock selectors, the hardest thing is the sell because oftentimes it means admitting a mistake, and that's one of the reasons we do conduct a lot of screens. Screens help to make the sell decisions easier for us.

I see. But sometimes I would imagine you override your quantitative sell screens?

Rarely. Usually if the screens are telling us to sell, we will sell. But we do have the ability to make the call. Typically, it might only be one or two stocks in a portfolio at most that we could decide to keep. One stock that I remember we did make a call on was Manulife. Manulife had a quarterly loss but we determined that it was a one-time item, and felt that Manulife at that price was still worth holding and we'd continue to hold. I think we ended up selling it for about $3 or $4 a share higher, but I'm not sure of the exact price. Again, it's a very rare exception. Also, we held for example Barrick Gold in the portfolio. When it failed on a couple of those tests the decision was to sell it. It was a position we bought for clients. Every client had a loss on it, and it's not an easy conversation to talk to clients about losses, but every client had a loss on it. The logic to buy it had changed. And when the logic to buy changes, you have to sell.

Did you completely sell out of Barrick Gold before it declined further? I believe it went right down to $12 a share at some point.

Oh, yeah. We sold out. I'd have to look back at the two levels, but between our two portfolios we sold it at two different levels because we have two different types of clients. I think one sell was in the high thirties, and the other one would have been in the low thirties or high twenties. But a loss is still a loss. The sell discipline is very key. *Very key.*

Have your quantitative sell screens ever sold you out of a position prematurely? For example, it sells a stock after a 10% decline, but then that stock reverses upwards 100%.

Oh sure, there have been. But with all those you've got to chalk them up as "You win more often than you lose," and continue on. By the way, that also means when you look back, if something fundamentally has changed about the company, then that might also be a reason for you to buy back the stock. And we've done that before. We've sold the company and bought it back because there had been some fundamental changes. We actually sold a couple of airlines on the individual accounts, but bought them back in our pooled funds, because we saw a fundamental shift happening on oil prices and load factors, and both worked out very well for clients. But those trends happened over a period of months before we went back in. But when we bought back in, it was at a higher level than when we sold; it just made sense at that time.

What is your overarching investment philosophy?

There's a low correlation in general between equity and fixed income, and if equity markets are dropping, hopefully your fixed-income portfolio is going up.

Can you explain your thought process on hedging with fixed income?

Most equity managers use fixed income simply as a hedge. As a result, they tend to buy a portfolio of bonds that is very similar to the bond index. Conversely, we think that there's actually lots of opportunities to add incremental value on the fixed-income side. We try to be very active with fixed income. So I'd say that's one key difference in our hedging philosophy. In fairness, we're not as nimble to move in and out of positions within the separately managed accounts because there's gains, losses, and trading costs, but on our pooled fund, there is that opportunity. There's a number of ways in fixed income that you can make a return. One notable way is through what's called duration management.

Can you elaborate on duration management?

There's two things that affect what's called the duration. One is the coupon. The other is the maturity date, which is the most important factor in a bond. The biggest one. For simplicity, we'll just focus on the maturity date. If you are a believer that bond yields are going to drop — for example, quantitative easing is ramping up or people have expectations that rates are going to rise when they're not — then the greater return potential can generally be achieved by owning a longer-dated bond. Because if a bond has a 20-year maturity, and it goes from a yield of 3.5% to 3%, you're actually going to be making a return in and around 8%.

It's an inverse correlation — if yields down, prices go up. If yields go up, prices go down. But you also take on interest rate risk the longer the maturity of the bond.

There's definitely risk involved in these decisions, but again, we're trying to be active and we're trying to make these decisions based on global fund flows. What's been really unique in the last year is that everyone's said, "Rates are so low, they're going to go up." People missed what was happening in Europe and Japan. And we actually are still of the view, even with how low rates are today, that you could see U.S. rates drop even further. Because on a relative value basis, it's roughly 0.3% on a German 10-year bond, and 1.9% on a U.S. 10-year bond, both of which are ridiculously low. But you take the idea of being able to borrow at 0.3% to buy at 1.9% — it's a massive difference. And if people have been doing that in Europe, and they have — it's called "carry trade" — then they've been making significant gains because currency gains have also compounded those returns. Look at the Canadian bond: we're paying 1.3%, but again, the U.S. is paying 1.9%, and we think that there's a greater likelihood of the U.S. dollar rising further in this environment. We're actually relatively neutral to the market now, because we're at 1.9% debt. If we go back to 2.1% or 2.2%, we'd probably change that philosophy. You can choose whether you want high-yield, where you can pick up 6.5% yields, and where the credit quality's also good. One of the bonds we own is Bombardier. With Bombardier, you're getting a 7 and a 7.5% yield.

Isn't Bombardier in dire straits? Their dire sitatuion is certainly reflected in its high debt yield. So, do you ever worry that a company such as Bombardier will default on its bond?

We've actually owned Bombardier debt for a while, so we're probably flat to slightly up, including the coupon. But I just can't ever see the Quebec government letting Bombardier — their national champion — fail. Now, that's not to say that the stock can't be very volatile in the interim and not to say the bond couldn't be a bit volatile, too, but Bombardier has taken action on their balance sheet in order to keep their current credit quality and credit rating sustainable. So there's distressed debt like that that you can buy on the high-yield side. With corporate bonds, there's something called "the spread" — that's how much additional yield you make from owning a corporate bond versus a similar-maturity-date government bond. We think corporate bond yields are above their historical average yields so we have a portfolio that's heavily invested by weight in corporate investment-grade bonds.

Let's move on to equities. What's your equity strategy?

So, we have two main equity strategies. The first strategy is for conservative clients: a portfolio that generates income through dividend growth in Canada and the U.S. The main reason for owning U.S. stocks is that the Canadian market just isn't sufficient. There's virtually no health care sector, for example. The second strategy is for more risk-tolerant clients: a blend of half dividend stocks and half growth-oriented stocks. But the growth stocks are still good solid businesses. The growth philosophy combines elements of momentum investing. We'll look for companies where the P/E ratios may look high, but if you look at forecast earnings two or three years out, then the forward P/E can actually be quite low based on the growth rate. Also, technical screening is a very big part of determining those portfolios, which Cameron will elaborate on for you.

The Canadian market isn't sufficient?

Yes. We feel that U.S. really gives you a lot more global exposure. However, we do have some exposure internationally through ETFs, which is what we employ if we think that there's markets that are offering better opportunities than in the U.S. Particularly, by valuation perspective, I think one of the most interesting markets is the emerging markets. But they're also potentially more risky in the near term.

What criteria do you use to forecast a company's future prospects?

We do rely on a lot of third-party reports for that type of information. It's hard in the sense that you've got to really forecast what's going to happen within the overall industry, too. So, what you're asking is really about fundamental analysis. We do that, but a lot of what we'd do is technical screening. For example, we're 5% weighted in energy right now because that's what the technical inputs are telling us to do. We've had low exposure to energy as far back as the summer of 2014, and that includes in our pooled fund, too. That's before the oil crash. So we definitely rely on technical screening, and let that become the driver for the overall stock selection process for the portfolio. Because of our technical system, we're not as worried about managing overall sector allocation and how much we necessarily vary from the sectors.

Finally, and this is a loaded question, you've previously said that females make better investors than males. Why would that be?

It's all about overconfidence. Men tend to trade more. And men tend to be more overconfident in their abilities. If someone started investing in 2011, made a number of trades, and made money in all those trades, they would start thinking that they're a great trader without realizing that they've been in a buoyant rising market. So what tends to happen is you get a lot more trading by men than women. Women tend to be more conservative. These are massive generalizations. But they tend to have plans in place, they tend to work with a professional, and they tend to stick with the plan. As a result, they watch their portfolio less, which often results in a better overall return than men.

Are there any other insights that you would like to add?

So I'd say that people should figure out if investing in the markets is something that they'd enjoy doing. If this is not something that you'd enjoy doing, then I'd say come up with a strategy that is low-cost, index-based, or find a professional manager. I think if unless you truly, truly enjoy it — unless you feel that you truly can separate the emotion out and then also build the plan, and stay on the plan — I'd highly suggest index investing.

It's true — what you don't know can be harmful to your investment returns. My discussion with Lorne almost felt like a therapy session, as I have personally succumbed to many, if not all, of the negative behavioural tendencies that he shared with me. I've summarized those behavioural tendencies below.

BEHAVIOURAL INVESTING 101

BUY HIGH; SELL LOW: investors tend to come into the market after it's already moved up (buy high). Investors then later get to a point of what's called capitulation (sell low), after a market decline, where they just can't take it anymore regardless of actual valuations. They enter and exit the market at the worst possible times.

CONFIRMATION BIAS: when you've taken a position and then look for other people who have the same views, because you want to confirm that you are right.

HINDSIGHT BIAS: the inclination, after an event has occurred in the market, to see the event as having been predictable, even if there was little or no objective basis for predicting it (for example, a black swan event).

RECENCY BIAS: investors have the expectation that if markets have returned 9% a year, that they are going to continue to return 9% a year indefinitely.

REFERENCE DEPENDENCE OR ANCHORING: the common human tendency to rely too heavily on the first piece of information offered when making decisions. Individuals use an initial piece of information to make subsequent judgments.

RISK AVERSION: individuals are predisposed to be risk-averse. We emotionally view a loss as twice as impactful as a gain. So a market sell-off can greatly influence one's thought process.

STRESS: studies have found that during periods of market volatility, the body naturally produces more cortisol levels to combat stress, which also makes us more risk-averse.

Another notable Canadian investor, David Dreman, has written some fantastic books on behavioural finance:

- *Psychology and the Stock Market: Investment Strategy Beyond Random Walk*
- *Contrarian Investment Strategy: The Psychology of Stock Market Success*
- *The New Contrarian Investment Strategy*
- *Contrarian Investment Strategies: The Next Generation*
- *Contrarian Investment Strategies: The Psychological Edge*

Other Notable Psychology / Behavioural Investing Books:

- *Extraordinary Popular Delusions & the Madness of Crowds* by Charles Mackay
- *Irrational Exuberance* by Robert J. Shiller
- *Your Money and Your Brain: How the New Science of Neuroeconomics Can Help Make You Rich* by Jason Zweig
- *Inside the Investor's Brain: The Power of Mind over Money* by Richard L. Peterson
- *How We Know What Isn't So* by Thomas Gilovich
- *Thinking, Fast and Slow* by Daniel Kahneman

─────────────── **MASTER KEYS** ───────────────
LORNE ZEILER

1) "Just because it's illogical doesn't mean it can't continue to move up. And the market can get more illogical before it comes back to reality."

2) "The best description I've ever heard is when John Maynard Keynes termed it 'the animal spirits.' When the animal spirits are there, people get excited, and rationality doesn't necessarily meet up."

3) "Retail investors tend to come into the market after it's already moved up [and] tend to then hold on with the expectation that when things are turning negative, they can ride it out and things will be fine."

4) "There's an emotional cycle that people go through in the market. They get to a point of what's called 'capitulation,' where they just can't take it anymore."

5) "People are of the expectation that if markets have returned 9% a year, markets are going to continue to return 9% a year. This is called 'recency bias.'"

6) "When you're buying stocks, what you're actually doing is buying a fractional ownership in a company. A lot of people forget that."

7) "The value of that company really should be based on its future prospects, future cash flows, future dividends, and future market share."

8) "It is actually very difficult emotionally to go against the herd, even if all of your logic is there, even if you've done all your research, and even if you're very confident in your conviction."

9) "A sell-off period can have a serious impact on your thought process."

10) "You never know a bottom until after it's gone up from the bottom."

11) "One of the issues with the Efficient Market Theory is that it states that the market reacts to information immediately. But that doesn't mean it reacts properly."

12) "I like the fixed-income market in that it tends to be more institutional, and so it tends to react more logically to events going on."

13) "Studies have shown that in general winners outperform your losers. Stocks that have generally done well are often going to continue to do well but there are a lot of people who will continue to hold onto that losing position, because they don't want to admit that loss."

14) "Unless there's a fundamental reason why not to sell it, then our natural decision is to sell . . . the sell discipline is very key."

15) "If something fundamentally has changed about the company, then that might also be a reason for you to buy back the stock."

16) "There's a low correlation in general between equity and fixed income, in that if equity markets are dropping hopefully your fixed-income portfolio is going up."

17) "If you are a believer that bond yields are going to drop — for example, quantitative easing is ramping up or people have expectations that rates are going to rise when they're not — then the greater return potential can generally be achieved by owning a longer-dated bond."

18) "With corporate bonds there's something called 'the spread' — that's how much additional yield you make from owning a corporate bond versus a similar-maturity-date government bond."

19) "The main reason for owning U.S. stocks is that the Canadian market just isn't sufficient."

20) "Men tend to trade more. And men tend to be more overconfident in their abilities. Women tend to be more conservative. As a result, they watch their portfolio less, which often results in a better overall return than men."

RANDY CASS
ROBO-INVESTING

Randy Cass's booming voice fills a room. Randy likens himself to Jim Cramer, the host of CNBC's *Mad Money*. I disagree with that comparison — Cramer is obnoxious on *Mad Money*, whereas Randy Cass is dynamic but well spoken. Randy became a household name, at least among Canadian business watchers, when he co-anchored the show *Market Sense* on BNN with Catherine Murray. The show was a success. While both anchors were highly adept in the financial markets, their personalities were almost complete opposites, with an effect like the dynamic between Kevin O'Leary and Amanda Lang from the long-running CBC show *The Lang & O'Leary Exchange*. Randy Cass's tenure on *Market Sense* wasn't as long-running as Catherine's, though, as he departed the show after three years, in 2012, to focus his energy on Nest Wealth, a robo-advisor company.

Nest Wealth provides investors access to low-cost, high-quality managed investment accounts at the click of a mouse. This is how Nest Wealth works: first they get to know you and your financial goals, second they invest your money in low-cost ETFs, and then third, they monitor and rebalance your portfolios. The philosophy that drives their investment accounts is based on the Efficient Market Theory (EMT) and the idea that passive investing beats active investing. With the exception of Som Seif, who actually develops ETFs that track the market, Randy is the only other individual featured in this book who actually stands by EMT, which was popularized by Burton Malkiel in his book *A Random Walk Down Wall Street*. This is what Randy has to say on the topic: "Studies demonstrate that over the long term, passive investing — building a portfolio to perform like the market instead of trying to beat it — does better than active management. Over the last five years in Canada, nearly 80% of actively managed Canadian Equity Funds failed to perform as well as the S&P/ TSX Composite." Compelling data like this makes Nest Wealth's mandate to "be the market" instead of "beat the market" a viable option for investors. The active managers in this book have for the most part beaten the market, but the evidence is clear: the majority of managers won't grow your money faster than the market.

All portfolios in Nest Wealth are built on three rules by David Swensen, the chief investment officer of Yale University, as available on the Nest Wealth website:

1. The investor should maintain a portfolio allocated to six core asset classes and be diversified. (These include domestic equities, emerging market equities, international equities, government fixed income, real-return bonds, and real estate.)
2. The investor should rebalance the portfolio on a regular basis.
3. The investor should, in the absence of a confident market-beating strategy, invest in low-cost index funds and ETFs.

During the interview, Randy explained that he had suffered a bout of disillusionment, as we all do in some form, upon first entering the workforce. He started as an articling intern at a law firm, but saw that the career path to becoming a partner was fraught with stress and that the long days wouldn't magically vanish once he "made it." One Sunday morning, he was working across from a senior partner, and he realized that he would still be working Sundays at a law firm no matter how much success he had. The difference between Randy and the average person is that Randy actually made a crucial change in his life to redirect his path. He actually wrote to Jim Cramer, got his surprisingly astute advice, and then from then on, blazed a path through the investment industry.

Prior to founding Nest Wealth, Randy managed quantitative portfolios at the Ontario Teachers' Pension Plan and institutional assets at Orchard Asset Management. Randy's last startup, First Coverage, developed a proprietary technology-based system that measures the effectiveness of information given by the sell side to institutional investing clients. It won multiple awards as a top startup, including a financial services Morningstar award for best use of technology in Canada. First Coverage expanded into the United States and the U.K. and was ultimately sold to a U.K. company in 2011.

The interview with Randy is informative, though I've removed parts of some responses in which Randy sounded too much like a salesman for Nest Wealth to keep the information balanced. What you'll glean, instead, is the effectiveness of Randy's entrepreneurial drive and a strong foundation in the markets, as well as the merits of the Efficient Market Theory. As a bonus, Randy shares his experiences with FX trading — a job that he can laugh about now.

PRE-INTERVIEW LESSONS

EFFICIENT MARKET THEORY (EMT): the belief that markets constantly incorporate all available information into the prices in the market, and that the markets are therefore efficient.

FOREIGN EXCHANGE (FX) TRADING: trading in and out of currencies, which are traded on the FX market.

Where did you grow up?

I was born in Toronto, and I've lived here all my life. Actually, I went away for university as far as London, Ontario, to go to the University of Western Ontario. I don't have any regrets. However, I would have loved to have lived somewhere else for a while. I think it would have been great for the family, for the kids, and for me. But no, I've been Toronto-born since day one.

If you were to rewind, where would you go to study or to live abroad?

Live abroad and study are different. My wife and I had an amazing trip to Australia — Sydney, Melbourne, and the Great Barrier Reef — before we started a family. I always thought it would be great to go back there. I was amazed at the Asian influence. You always think of Australia as a sunnier, warmer Canada, but it was amazing that when you got there the influences in everything from food to culture to sports seemed to come from Asia as opposed to North America. So that would have been the easiest place to slide into, but even going somewhere in Europe where we don't speak the language and learning how to adapt to a new culture would be interesting. I have three boys now and having them learn new languages and habits and customs makes me want to go.

How did you first get interested in the markets?

By figuring out that I didn't want to be a lawyer.

Why did you want to become a lawyer in the first place?

I grew up in the days of *L.A. Law*, which was one of the most popular shows on TV. It seemed like a glamorous profession. My mom was a lawyer, and I've always had the ability to speak well and to say things in a way that seem convincing to the listener. It seemed natural that a lawyer is what's meant for me and so I went and I summered at a law firm in downtown Toronto and got hired back as an articling student. You're expected to work there for years on the weekend, but it was my first weekend and it was a Sunday and I was doing due diligence on a deal. "Due diligence" means looking for pages that were misnumbered, or typos, or grammar. I had no "value add" at that point. At the same time on that Sunday morning, on the other side of the table, was one of the senior partners of the firm. And his value add was clearly much more extensive than mine, but he was still there.

Your life flashed before your eyes.

[*Snaps fingers*] Like that. So I excused myself, went into my closet, which is what they called my office at the time, picked up the phone, and called my girlfriend, who is now my wife. We had already been going out for an inordinately long amount of time, like eight years, so she thought, "He's finally got a job, we're going to move on and get married soon." I called her and said, "I don't want to be a lawyer. I just saw my future and I don't want that to be my future." She said, "Well, all right, so what do you want to do?" and I said, "I don't know, but I know this isn't it." And so then, with free time to fill because I decided I didn't want to get hired back as an articling student, I started falling in love with stocks. I started a stock club at the law firm. It just became a given that my transition was going to be from law to the financial services.

But how did your passion for finance, stocks, and the markets come about?

I am a competitive person by nature. It was an industry that could present you with a winner and a loser on a daily, monthly, quarterly, annual basis — that got me interested. There was no ambiguity about it. At the time, it appeared to be a battle of who's the smartest, who's got the best ideas, who can pick up on something that others don't see. It just seemed to appeal to my competitive nature.

What was your bridge from law to financial services? I believe that you started at TD Securities as an FX derivatives trader, correct?

You've done your research. So I figured if you want to get into any industry, the best thing to do is to set yourself up in a position where people are coming to recruit you. It's funny actually, because this is a story that I haven't thought of in a long time. I figured the way to enter the industry was to go do an MBA program and then have everybody come and recruit me upon graduation. I was good in school. I knew I'd have good marks and there would be a recruiting process. I remember in the late nineties, there was a guy who wrote an article that I read in a magazine about how to get into the industry and his name was Jim Cramer. I emailed him and I said, "I applied to the MBA program at Ivey, I got in, this is what I'm doing, this is the career I'm leaving, this is the industry I'm getting into. What do you think of this as a research project?" He emailed me back and said, "I don't care, but whatever you do, get your foot in the door because this is the greatest industry in the world." And back then he was nothing compared to what he is today. He was a hedge fund man and he was doing well. I looked at that email and I thought, "Well, all right, the way to get my foot in the door then is to get accepted into the MBA program and then complete it." So that was the pact: set myself up so that those that you want to meet with are going to come to you and the MBA was the way to achieve that.

I assume that you were recruited by TD Securities through the MBA program, then. What were some of the currencies that you traded?

I was recruited into a one-year program at TD. They rotated you around four different areas and then you got offered a job, cross your fingers, at the desk that you wanted and that became your career. And so currency derivatives was the second desk of the rotation that I sat on and it was the one that both seemed most exciting and made the most sense. Conversely, stocks require extensive fundamental research and bonds require an entire mathematical quagmire that one might not want to get into.

However, FX moved on miniscule basis points over seconds and you could tell very quickly whether you were up or down. If you wanted a scorecard, this was the most merciless scorecard out there because it also seemed random. Events would happen and currencies would fluctuate but there wasn't always a sense of fundamental rhyme or reason under them. I was the young guy on the FX desk. I took a full-time position with the FX derivatives team and we would facilitate trades for others and then also try to make a profit in our books. I would show up at five in the morning to take the handoff from the Asian desk, because the FX is 24 hours a day. It's not like equity markets where they close at set times around the world. The U.S. dollar is trading 24 hours a day, the Canadian dollar, even though it's less likely, is trading 24 hours a day, too. So I would take the handoff from the Asian desk and when I left I would usually have a trade on against the yen or some other currency. I remember we would leave stop-losses on because we couldn't let a currency trade run without any risk management because we would lever, and so you could get your head handed to you otherwise. Currency trading was all about picking up nickels and nickels and nickels and nickels on every transaction. You don't want to be giving up dollars because you forgot to leave a stop-loss.

How levered were some of these currency trades?

I can't recall. Everything was within the risk parameters though. But you just knew you were picking up pennies and you were giving up dollars if you didn't have good risk management on these trades. I remember that we would get called whenever we got stopped out of a trade. Anyways, the phone was on my wife's side of the bed and it would ring at like three in the morning three days out of the week and say, "You've been stopped out." My wife would pick up and hand the phone to me but I would just hang up. She'd ask, "Stopped out again?" and I'd respond, "Yeah." It seemed like that was not a sustainable lifestyle.

Currency must have been top of mind 24 hours a day.

And while it gave me the "scorecard" that I was interested in, it seemed like it lacked a bit of the long game. No one can tell you today, except in rare exceptions, where currency's going to be the next month or three months or six months. You weren't living for anything more. And even if you were right, the odds of getting stopped out before you were right three months down the road were high. So FX didn't seem to have the mental stimulation that I was looking for. Again, it had the scorecard, but it lacked long-term thinking. After that epiphany, I got the opportunity to go up to Ontario Teachers' Pension Plan.

What was it like at OTPP?

"Teachers" was an informative part of my process. I was there for almost five years. I came into the quant program there as an analyst, then became associate, and then was promoted to portfolio manager there under probably the best mentor I've ever had in the business. A guy named Morgan McKay. Morgan McKay was the exact type of boss that you always hope steps into everybody's career at some point. Encouraging and understanding, he gave you enough rope to hang yourself and then when he found the swinging rope he wanted to understand how you got there so you didn't get there again. He's a guy that I have nothing but the fondest of words for. In the U.S., those guys come out of MIT with Ph.D.'s, computer science and engineering degrees, and into quantitative-based algorithmic-type trading. In Canada, that part of the industry is a lot less robust. It's there for the people who want to learn and be trained in that way. Morgan's group would handle areas like the index fund and algorithmic trading. It opened my eyes to an entirely new world. I thought, "Oh wow! There's a logic to why I can justify that Coke and Pepsi are trading out of whack, or there's a reason that yield doesn't line up with all the other yields in the marketplace, or there's math underlying *this*." That aspect really appealed to me.

In his group, I started to bring out new strategies like risk arbitrage, statistical arbitrage, mean reversion, and pairs trading. And then we ended up creating a portfolio that used income trusts and hedged them using similar duration of bonds on the other side, which was the first time that this was done. Math was opening up all these ways to invest in a methodical fashion that made it seem *that* much more tangible. It was the first thing that connected with me. The people at OTPP were smart, the conversations were lively, and the resources were vast because you were at Teachers. It was long before the time where there were activist hedge funds or multi-billion-dollar money managers in Canada. Teachers was where flow happened. I was learning about how to trade those strategies, how to create them, incorporate them, and it was that education that stuck with me. I thought, "All right, there's probably a market for this in Canada outside of Teachers, let's set this up."

What were some of the most successful quant strategies that you employed at Teachers?

A lot of them. Risk arbitrage was a very successful strategy. Pairs trading was a successful strategy. Index arbitrage was a *very* successful strategy, too. It was strategies based on smart people having good information, good technology, and the tools to execute on the information. When my company, Orchard Asset Management, started up, we launched a pairs mean reversion strategy. However, the most successful fund at Orchard Asset Management was a closed-end fund that employed an arbitrage strategy. We built an entire system that captured the differences in value between closed-end funds and the underlying assets the closed-end funds had within it, as well the Net Asset

Value, which could be redeemed for once a year or once a quarter. We were the first out of the gate with that and the technology was great and the strategy was successful.

Orchard Asset Management was created by you to capitalize on the untapped market for multi-strategy money management at the time.

Yeah, so at Orchard we started thinking, "How do we create more strategies that can be based on quants and algos and formulas that make sense to us?" We always thought sentiment was a powerful driver in the marketplace, but it had never really been captured in a systematic fashion. So we built software that created for the first time a portal that allowed information from the sell side of the street to be captured by the buy side of the street and formalize it so a user could say, "All right, among the people that cover me, there's increase of sentiment on auto manufacturers and a decrease of sentiment on gold." This was a real time measure of not only what they were trading but what they were actually thinking and talking about at the time. The software ended up spinning off into its own company called First Coverage that built what's called an alpha capture system, which is now a portal that exists between the buy side and the sell side and allows information to be exchanged on a permission basis.

That's phenomenal. What have been some of your biggest wins?

I think my best trades are from back at Ontario Teachers because that's when we traded the largest dollar sizes. We always thought, "How much did I make on that trade?" We were playing with tens and hundreds of millions of dollars back then. I remember we had set up a risk arbitrage portfolio, which is a portfolio solely to take positions on announced deals on the anticipation that they're going to close. We spoke before of how with FX trading you pick up nickels instead of dollars and you don't want to give up dollar bills; well, risk arbitrage was exactly the same. So the way it typically works is that Company A will announce that they're buying Company B and say, "We're buying it for $20." Then Company B will all of a sudden go from $12 to $19.25. And everybody will ask, "Why doesn't it go right to 20 bucks?" That's because of two things. The first being the value of time; how long is it going to take for me to get my 20 bucks? Everybody discounts it back maybe six months. They're not going to pay $20 for $20 today if it's not going to close for another six months. And the second being, what's the chance the deal doesn't close? There's always a chance that regulatory approval or one of the terms doesn't get fulfilled or someone walks away. There's deal risk. So that will explain the spread, too. You're not going to argue over time value. You might say, "It's going to take six months to close" and I might say, "It's going to take nine months," but that's not the real issue. The real issue is the risk to the deal closing. And so the first issue at Teachers with the risk arbitrage portfolio was that because it was so large at the time we couldn't invest in any deals that Teachers was already involved in. In many cases, we were conflicted right away. The portfolio was hard-pressed to find actual meaningful positions you could take.

But then in 2002 PayPal had just gone public. It was a darling stock that had lived through the tech bubble massacre. It was to be taken out by what had seemed like another *real* company, eBay, and yet the market didn't believe that this was going to happen. I had the legal background and I had the trading background and I would sit there looking at these documents: the terms and conditions and the regulatory concerns. Also, I would talk to colleagues and ask, "Why is this spread so wide? Why are people saying that it's risky when it's not?" I just couldn't figure it out. At that point, you just have to believe that maybe you're right and everyone else is not. And so we invested in a meaningful way into that PayPal risk arbitrage position. That was an incredible experience. If you know a lot about a particular area at some point, you can't keep doubting yourself. So that was the lesson I learned from that one. Do your research because the market is usually telling you something. In that case the research was, "I think this deal is going to close. I think other people are gun-shy from the fact that it's two tech companies and that the tech crash just recently happened. They want nothing to do with tech."

Interesting; that deal was soon after the technology bust in 2000.

Oh, yeah. People had lost 80% of their portfolios. They just wanted nothing to do with tech. A Canadian stock that everybody I think recalls from then was Nortel. Nortel was the perfect example of investors' incorrect belief that they always had to value things based on the dollar point in which they invested in them. If I buy Nortel at $100, "There's no way I'm getting out until it goes back up to 100." And, "If it was worth $100 then, it's got to be worth $100 now." Nortel was such a meaningful part of the exchange and such a meaningful part of everybody's portfolio. It went from $100 to $80 to $60 to $40 to $20. It just was so hard to let go of Nortel. It was like cutting off a limb or saying goodbye to a family member. The lesson learned was that everything doesn't always have to come back. We see that in Canada's many tech companies over the last decade and a bit. Many companies, not just tech. Stocks don't have to come back. Markets can materially shift for a variety of reasons and the lesson there was that if you're going to play that game, if you're going to try to fundamentally out-think everybody, you can't be captive to whatever your old thought process was. It has to continually adjust with what's new and what's current.

That's a good lesson. So, switching gears, you recently started up a company called Nest Wealth. Why Nest Wealth, and why now?

So I've been in this industry for about 15 years now and I think I've seen a lot of different aspects of it. I've seen it from the institutional side, I've seen it from the hedge front side, I've seen it from the technology side, and I've also seen it from the retail investor's side. Why Nest Wealth and why now is because I think Canadian retail investors are stuck between a rock and a hard spot. The average Canadian who defaults into mutual funds right now is going to be paying 2.5% for an equities portfolio according to Morningstar and that could end up destroying 40%-plus of the potential wealth that that person could have earned. And we sit here and our country talks about the fact that we need to save more and we have a problem with a whole generation that's not going to be ready for retirement. The most meaningful material thing we can do to fix this is to come up with a solution that provides you with a portfolio managed by an institution in a sophisticated and professional manner. Most importantly, we are no longer going to take away 40 to 50% of your potential wealth. You now get to keep 95% of it.

Some have termed this movement "robo-advisors." But how is money actually being managed?

I believe that there are decades of objective research that back this up and everything I've seen within the industry backs this up as well. It's incredibly hard, next to impossible, to actually beat the market on a consistent basis. Moreover, it becomes ridiculously hard when you're paying someone else 2.5% to do it on your behalf. So, build a passive, low-cost, and optimized portfolio that sits on the efficient frontier that's customized specifically for you. It's made up exclusively of low-cost ETFs from blue-chip providers.

I would assume that Vanguard ETFs and BlackRock iShares are placed in the portfolios?

Yes, most of the ETFs we use are Vanguard and iShares. We believe that with ETFs it's not about performance, but whether it does what it says it's going to do. Does it mimic what it says it's going to mimic? Does it have good liquidity? Does it have low fees? Does it have minimized tracking error? These are all the things we look for and all the things we consider when selecting the best-in-class ETFs. Then we build a portfolio based on David Swensen's suggestions. He came out with a book and said, "These are the six or seven asset funds that you need to own." As a result, we thought, "All right, we're Canadian so we need to have Canadian equity exposure in there. But outside of that, we'll add U.S. equities; global equities; long-term, short-term, medium-term real-return bonds; and a little real estate exposure." That's it. That's all you need. What Canadian investor needs more than that?

Can you comment on high-frequency trading (HFT) and how you see that impacting the market today and in the next five to ten years?

Well, I'm going to go out on a limb here and say it's had the most dramatic impact on the market to date. As a result, we're going to see solutions coming to market that might minimize the impact HFT has going forward or at least marginally reduce it. It's not just high-frequency trading. Trading in and of itself right now is a technology arms race. It's about who can get their hold in the market the fastest. It's about who can co-locate their server the closest to the exchange. It's about who can build something that can do billions upon billions of procedures faster than the other guy's computers. And when it comes to the market, the retail investor doesn't stand a chance. I know people who will say, "Oh it doesn't matter, they're taking small cuts of pennies on each transaction." But of course it matters! This is billions upon billions of dollars. Every time the retail investor trades, they are moving their money from their own pocket to the pocket of the industry. And there's just no way to compete against it. There are buildings being hulled out, reinforced with steel floors, next to European exchanges where servers are being put up just so there's no one on the floor except servers. They're co-located next to the exchange so that the information can get there faster than the next guy's information. How are you going to compete against that? So you layer that on top of the fact that passive beats active. It's hard to come out ahead when you trade.

So if Benjamin Graham were still alive today, would he have completely dropped his value investing approach? It seems as though margins of safety have been cut due to highly efficient traders and trading systems.

I've never said it's impossible for someone to add value, or generate alphas as they're called in the industry. I think there are very smart people who do exceptional things on a semi-frequent basis. Benjamin Graham would probably still be Benjamin Graham, but the odds of becoming that person as a retail investor are stacked against you today. That's why over five years 90%-plus of funds will underperform the benchmark. If you stretch it out to 10 years, it becomes almost a certainty that you underperform the benchmark. And when you look at all the studies, there's a reason that every legal document has to say, "Past performance not indicative of future performance." It's a fact. There's no study and there's no body of knowledge that can show there is consistency of returns from one year to the next. Yes, there's going to be a Warren Buffett and, yes, there's going to be the guy who did it 10 years in a row. But that's why they're "the guys," because out of thousands of fund managers, they're the one or two who did it. If we had a thousand people sitting with us right now, I could have them stand up and flip coins and guarantee that one of them is going to get 10 heads in a row. This multi-trillion-dollar industry in North America is built on the notion that everyone is a winner. "Invest in us because we're the black swan." That's not the case in 99% of instances. So if you're going to try to do this, you need to understand that the odds of you being the guy who can consistently outperform the market doesn't compensate you for the risk that you're going to take to actually try it. And if you're going to do it, the best way to do this, in our opinion, is to control what can be controlled. Risk management.

Did you leave BNN? Your show was great.

BNN asked if I could give them more air time at a time when I was actually looking to do less because Nest Wealth was beginning to take off. It was a very tough decision, because BNN gave me the ability to reach Canadians that were interested in the markets. But it wasn't about picking a stock, telling them, "You have to buy this." It was about making sense of the market. It was a great way to get that message out. I got a ton of positive feedback walking down the streets. But I knew that Nest Wealth was an opportunity to do that in a much more meaningful and material way. If I can give you an option that's going to put an additional $300,000 in your account when you retire because you didn't have to pay high fees, that's what I need to do with my life right now. I need to roll out of bed and I need to make that dream work. Look, I loved being up on BNN. I imagine I'll be back on in the future. But for now, Nest Wealth is my mission.

Any more advice?

If you have no money, set up a fund for emergencies. A rainy day fund. That's your first $10,000 — anything less than that is not an investment. That's money you might need while in debt. Start there. Like everybody says, "If you have ridiculous debt on all your credit cards, and you're paying double-digit interest, get that down. That's a guaranteed return that you can't get anywhere on the market." Once you've taken care of those two things, then you can start thinking about the market. And here's my advice to 99% of the people out there: life's busy, and life's wonderful. There's a thousand things you can do rather than worry about what stock you should be buying. Understand that this market can remain irrational vastly longer than you can afford it to be irrational. Come to the conclusion today that what you need is just a professionally managed, diversified portfolio that doesn't try to hit a home run, but gives you an average return. No home runs, no upset stomachs. Just be the market, be properly diversified, minimize your fees, and focus on the rest of your life.

Randy's insights into the shadows of high-frequency trading (HFT) were alarming, if not discouraging: the idea of trading as a "technology arms race." It's daunting to imagine that you are up against computers in the market. Man versus machine is a troubling image. Randy goes on to say that because of technological change and great accessibility, "The retail investor doesn't stand a chance." I'll disagree with Randy, and say that retail investors still do stand a chance. In the battle of man versus machine, it's plausible that man can outperform high-frequency trading systems with astute security selection that may fly under the radar of the mainframe servers that power HFT.

MASTER KEYS

RANDY CASS

1) "We would leave stop-losses on [FX trades] because we couldn't let a currency trade run without any risk management because we would lever, and so you could get your head handed to you otherwise."

2) "Currency trading was all about picking up nickels and nickels and nickels and nickels on every transaction."

3) "If you were right, the odds of getting stopped out before you were right three months down the road were high. So FX didn't seem to have the mental stimulation that I was looking for."

4) "The most successful fund at Orchard Asset Management was a closed-end fund that employed an arbitrage strategy. We built an entire system that captured the differences in value between closed-end funds and the underlying assets the closed-end funds had within it."

5) "If you know a lot about a particular area, at some point you can't keep doubting yourself."

6) "[Stocks don't] always have to come back. We see that in Canada's many tech companies over the last decade."

7) "Markets can materially shift for a variety of reasons and the lesson there was that if you're going to play that game, if you're going to try to fundamentally out-think everybody, you can't be captive to whatever your old thought process was."

8) "It's incredibly hard, next to impossible, to actually beat the market on a consistent basis."

9) "We believe that with ETFs it's not about performance, but whether it does what it says it's going to do. Does it mimic what it says it's going to mimic? Does it have good liquidity? Does it have low fees? Does it have minimized tracking error?"

10) "Trading in and of itself right now is a technology arms race. It's about who can get their hold in the market the fastest. It's about who can co-locate their server the closest to the exchange. It's about who can build something that can do billions upon billions of procedures faster than the other guy's computers."

11) "Passive beats active. It's hard to come out ahead when you trade."

12) "There are very smart people who do exceptional things on a semi-frequent basis."

13) "Benjamin Graham would probably still be Benjamin Graham, but the odds of becoming that person as a retail investor are stacked against you today."

14) "Over five years 90%-plus of funds will underperform the benchmark. If you stretch it out to 10 years it becomes an almost certainty that you underperform the benchmark."

15) "When you look at all the studies, there's a reason that every legal document has to say, 'Past performance not indicative of future performance.' It's a fact."

16) "If we had a thousand people sitting with us right now, I could have them stand up and flip coins and guarantee that one of them is going to get 10 heads in a row. If you're going to try and do this [i.e., invest in the markets], you need to understand that the odds of you being the guy who can consistently outperform the market doesn't compensate you for the risk that you're going to take to actually try it."

ROSS GRANT
BEAT THE TSX ("BTSX")

Ross Grant has just inherited the "Beat the TSX" model. *Lucky guy*. After 28 years of beating the TSX, David Stanley, Ph.D. and long-time contributing editor to the *Canadian MoneySaver*, is retiring from his post and passing the torch to Grant, who followed the model for years and achieved financial independence early in life. This is a significant milestone, since Beat the TSX has proven itself to be a successful investment model, albeit an extremely boring one. Boring because the concept is simple and the application easy for any investor to create wealth in the market. In this case, boring = good.

At a Toronto Money Show presentation, David Stanley explained the history of where and how Beat the TSX originated:

> In 1991 Michael O'Higgins wrote a book called *Beating the Dow*. His "Dogs of the Dow" uses an emotion-free method to select high-dividend stocks. From 1974 till 2012 (38 years) BTD has averaged 11.7% vs. 9.1% for the S&P 500 index, an increase of 29%. O'Higgins's book became an instant investment classic and served to get me interested in dividend

investing. After I took early retirement in 1995 I looked at the stock price and total return data for the TSE 35 blue-chip index. I was struck by how much the total return index with its reinvested dividends had outperformed share price appreciation. I adapted the structured decision-making process of BTD to the TSE and wrote my first "Beating the TSE" column in 1996.

In the presentation, David Stanley explained how to implement the Beat the TSX strategy: "The list of S&P/TSX 60 stocks is ordered from high to low by dividend yield, the top 10 stocks are then ordered from low to high price. Stocks are purchased in equal dollar amounts and held for one year or more. Investors build up a portfolio of high-quality stocks purchased at a reasonable cost. No secret sauce, hocus pocus, animal spirits, etc."

BTSX is both a contrarian and passive strategy: buying into those high-dividend yields implies that those stocks have declined in the market in the current year, and will theoretically revert to their means since they are Canada's largest and most prominent companies by market capitalization. The BTSX strategy has racked up high annual compound returns, and yes, it has actually beaten the market. Over its 20-year history, BTSX has achieved a 12.26% compound annual return versus the index's 9.83%. BTSX beat the index by 25%. However, as David explains in his final column for *Canadian Money*, "BTSX: The Last Hurrah," this data only reflects the annual average total return. "The strong point of the BTSX system is the influence of compounded reinvested dividends. Those results are much more convincing: $1,000 invested in both the BTSX portfolio and the total return index (benchmark) would now be worth $18,056 for our portfolio versus $10,409 for the index."

Ross Grant will carry on the BTSX tradition going forward and report its progress. Peter Hodson, owner and editor of *Canadian MoneySaver*, said to Ross in the editorial piece for David Stanley's final issue: "Ross, you have some big shoes to fill. But since David hand-picked you for the task, we are sure you will do just fine." Peter may well be right: at 22, Ross calculated what it would take to retire early, and 21 years later, he reached his goal of financial independence at age 43.

Beat the TSX is a strategy that you can easily employ. But before you do, Ross has some additional refinements to the BTSX model that you should follow.

PRE-INTERVIEW LESSONS

BLUE-CHIP STOCKS: stocks that contain certain characteristics that denote stability: large size, long history, reliable products or services, dividend increases, solid reputation or brand perception, and so on. Blue-chip stocks can be concentrated in banks, utilities, and telecom. An example would be Bell Canada.

TSX 60: a stock index that contains 60 large publicly traded Canadian companies from the S&P TSX index. This index is the primary source for the BTSX model.

When did you first get interested in the markets?

Probably when I was about 14.

Before you started your financial independence journey, did you already trade stocks?

I actually didn't buy my first mutual fund until I was about 22, but at a younger age I was researching and looking into investing. I really didn't know how to go about investing. My parents didn't invest in the stock market and there weren't many people I knew who were investing in the market. I was intrigued by it, but just didn't know enough about it.

So where did you learn about investing?

I started seriously learning about investing after I graduated university. I just started to read books at that point. Obviously we didn't have the internet so the pace of learning was a little slower than it would be today. My education continued from there.

Can you name some of those books?

Unfortunately, I don't remember the name of one of the first books I read. But it really got me started. It was a part of a self-study course that my aunt had purchased for herself that was quite expensive. She passed along the books to me as she got them. I think she received one book a month. That course provided a nice overview of different financial investment options that were available.

Where did your drive come from? Was it when you were 22 that you mapped out your financial independence journey?

Yes. It was when I was 22 that I laid out a financial plan, but the drive came a lot earlier. When I was about seven I put some money, 25 bucks, into my first bank account and earned interest on it. Money was hard to come by as a kid. My main source of income was my allowance. I started off getting a dime every two weeks. It eventually went up to a quarter but then got discontinued when it hit about $2 and I was a teenager. Anyway, when I got this interest from this bank account without having to work, I thought "Wow, that's cool!" So the concept of having my money work for me was picked up at a young age. As I mentioned in my book, when I started working, I was really mismatched with my first job. I didn't like it too much. One day I came home and thought, "How long would a person really have to work?" *[Laughs]* How much would I have to save to not have to work? So I spent a couple of hours on an Excel program and just did some calculations and I thought, "Gee, this is possible." So it sort of went from there.

Interesting. So the key motivating factor was that you didn't want to work for an employer your whole life. You wanted to quit the rat race earlier, right?

Yes, that is correct. Some people might hear that story and say, "Oh, the poor guy was in the wrong job." They would be correct. I consequently got a new job a couple of months later, and then after that other jobs that I did eventually love. But it was that first job that got me wondering what it would take to not have to work at all.

How much money did you start with at the age of 22?

I had nothing. Well, sorry, to clarify that, I had saved up enough money to buy myself a brand new car. So, when I graduated I bought my car with cash. I've always paid cash for my cars, and my parents have always paid cash for their cars. After I purchased the car, I had nothing *[laughs]*. So I started saving from there.

So you started from scratch. Can you explain your financial independence model?

It's nothing complex. It's probably the most basic Excel file calculations you can do. I did also create the "What If Retirement Planner," which is just a more user-friendly version of the same spreadsheet. The spreadsheet shows my savings each year and their growth. In parallel to that there was a column that indicated what I needed to live on, which grew at the rate of inflation. It's kind of a cat and mouse game. The amount you need to live on every year grows, but what you set aside hopefully grows faster. So eventually at some point in the future you get to the point where you can take out 4% a year to live on, and still have some money left when you die many years later.

Did you save a percentage of your paycheque every month? What was your savings rate?

Here is how I got started. When I graduated I had to figure out how I was going to buy a house. When you buy a house you need a down payment, and in order to get a down payment, you need to know how much cash you can save per month. So I made a budget and what was left over at the end of my budget was my savings. All of that savings was put aside. It was a very dynamic process. You get a pay raise, the amount goes up, which then you can save. But then your rent goes up, so the amount you can save goes down by a little bit *[laughs]*. So you make a guess and determine how much you can actually save per year.

I assume that you also overlaid the average annual return that you could achieve from investments. What was your average compound rate of return at that time?

My whole life I've used 8% as my estimated return, with inflation at 3%.

So you're left with 5% return?

Yeah. And it was like a game, because the fun part of it would be for me to sit down in front of the computer and say, "Okay, I think can retire when I'm 65" *[laughs]*. And then you get a pay raise that can dramatically affect what you save. As long as you keep your expenses under control, your savings could begin to grow far faster than the rate of inflation. And if you can also get a greater return than 8%, then all of a sudden your savings grow quicker. Next year you run the numbers and it shows that now you can retire at 60 due to your improved financial situation.

To achieve financial independence, did you need to accumulate $1 million?

I don't remember what the numbers were in the first models, as that is a long time ago. Inflation's effect over time on these old numbers makes it less meaningful to look back on them now. I really was just trying to calculate what it would take to maintain my lifestyle, which would require an annual withdrawal rate of 4%. So if you had a million dollars you could take out $40,000 per year, and you'd have a relatively high probability of not out-living your nest egg. So for every $40,000 that you want in income, you would need $1 million in your nest egg.

That must have been a daunting task when you first started accumulating savings. $1 million.

You are correct. When you first start, the main growth in your nest egg is due to the annual savings you contribute. If in the first year you save $5,000 and then add another $5,000 then in next year you will have $10,000 plus a bit of growth due to the investment return. In my case the majority of my nest egg growth came from the contributions and not much from the returns. This balance changes as the nest egg grows in size relative to the annual contributions. My point is that the growth rate in the initial years has much less impact than the size of your contributions.

What was your investment strategy?

Well, I started out with mutual funds and eventually moved to index funds and then individual stocks.

Can you elaborate on that evolution?

Mutual funds and then exchange-traded index funds. And along the way, I added stocks where I'd think, "Oh yeah, Royal Bank seems good, let's throw that in there." But it's really been in the last 20 years where I've completely moved into the Beat the TSX strategy: only dividend-paying stocks. I have been quite happy with those results. My 14-year average annual return for Beat the TSX stocks is 12.6%. The simplicity of the process is really what attracted me to it.

Were there any clear winners from the past 20 years that helped push you closer and faster to your goal of financial independence?

The clear winner was switching to the dividend-paying stocks. The key aspect of these stocks is the steady and often growing income stream. This helped me solve a problem that I had from the beginning. I knew that I needed a nest egg of a particular size, but never really knew what I was going to do with it. Once I realized these companies paid an average of 4% or more in dividends, and I knew I needed 4% to live on, I had found the answer to that problem *[laughs]*. "I'll just live off the dividend income." The management of the portfolio, in relation to the income generation problem, became very simple. It was one of those "a-ha" moments, when you say, "Oh yes. That's the answer!"

But if you were to go into your portfolio now, what would be the top five dividend stocks that you own by performance since inception? Cumulative gains from the time that you invested.

That would be difficult to answer. I do have my index funds, like XIU, which I started to collect 20 years ago and have never had a reason to sell. So those are high up on the list. With the Beat the TSX strategy you look at the list of stocks you have every January 1 and decide what has to leave because it's been doing well *[laughs]*, and which ones you have to add. So there's quite a bit of a turnover during a 10- or 20-year period of time.

Can you summarize the Beat the TSX strategy and why it's so effective?

So every January 1, or December 31, you look at the closing prices of the stocks in the index. The index we're trying to beat is Standard & Poor's TSX 60, so there's 60 stocks in it. You rank those 60 stocks by their dividend yield. You put the highest-dividend-yielding stocks at the top and sort them down to the lowest at the bottom. Then you remove the previous income trusts as you find that most of them are all energy stocks. They're not as stable as your blue-chip companies. You take the top 10 that remain and you invest 10% in each of those 10 stocks. You let them sit there for a year and do it again the next December 31. The one element that I added to Beat the TSX, which David didn't have in there, was that if any company cuts its divided, I sell it and buy the next one that's down on the list at that point in time. Fortunately that doesn't happen too often, but it's happened a few times. I've learned from my pain.

So you restrict the selection of your TSX stocks to the TSX 60. You immediately remove the energy sector as well as the old income trusts, which have recently converted to corporations.

Yeah. I wouldn't say remove the energy sector, but remove the previous income trusts. But, yeah, they happen to be energy companies.

And then you sort by dividend yield, and you'd invest let's say $10,000 in each of the top 10 yielding stocks in the TSX 60 that year.

Right.

Why does the Beat the TSX strategy work?

I feel that there's two aspects that make the BTSX strategy work really well. One is that you limit yourself to big blue-chip companies, which are relatively stable. They pay out a chunk of their cash that they earn to the investors. It ties into that blue-chip idea that they are stable enough that they can give a lot of money out. The second aspect of this strategy that supports its success is that there can be some significant capital gains generated in the group of 10 stocks that are purchased. Where they get the extra boost often comes from the stocks that are in the seventh, eighth, ninth, tenth positions. Very often they are the new ones to the list. They're blue-chip companies that have had a rough time. Those stocks may be unpopular, so the stock price is down, but it's still paying the same dividend. Its higher yield has moved it up from maybe the eighteenth position, for example, to the seventh position on the list.

In essence what you're doing is that you're buying low. You're saying, "Here is this company that's probably not too bad, and we should buy some of it." A lot of the capital gains from Beat the TSX often come from stocks that are in the lower positions, and a higher percentage of your dividend yield comes from positions one, two, and three. The BTSX process guides you to buy low and put these new stocks in your portfolio. As well you may have a stock that was in the seventh position last year, and it's recovered in price and everybody loves it now. Its price has gone up but they haven't been able to keep their dividend increases up with the fast-rising stock price. This stock may move down in the list to spot number 18, so you need to sell it. But you don't want to sell it because you love it. It has done so well for you *[laughs]*. And if you were left to your own accord you would keep it, and you would not buy the brand new one that came into spot seven.

I see. So it's not so much that you're capturing the dividend yield every year, but rather buying into "value" in a systematic way.

Yes.

In that case, why couldn't one instead buy into the same TSX 60 universe, but limit the stock selection to the top 10 with the lowest price to earnings multiples?

You might be able to do that with success *[laughs]*. I bet you there are some different combinations you could use that would yield positive results, but you would have to do your own back-testing to determine if it was going to work. I think you could probably beat any index using a similar strategy. This is just the one that we happen to focus on. The one other thing I must mention too is that one of the key elements of this being successful is the fact that these stocks pay dividends. With my goal of getting an 8% return every year to meet my model projections, the dividends really help to support that 8% goal. If I'm being given 4% in dividends, it is just like "money in the bank," I call it *[laughs]*. I'm already halfway to my annual goal, assuming the company is paying its dividends during the year. All I really need to do is scrape a 4% capital gain out of the rest of the year on average, and I'm going to get to my goal.

BTSX has performed better than 8% annual returns. I've read that Beat the TSX has trumped all comparable mutual funds and ETFs over the years. It beat the TSX index 70% of the time for the past 27 years, and it beat it 80% of the time for the past 6 years. David Stanley said that the best sectors to invest in, regardless of the model, are telecoms, utilities, real estate, and financials. He calls it TURF. So why would these be the best sectors to invest in?

Back to a lot of what I said before. They're blue-chip, stable, and established. Plus they pay consistent returns, and grow dividend payments over time. It's great getting a dividend stream every year from a stock. But imagine if the next year you're getting an increase of 10% on the dividend. If you were getting a dividend of 4% and then it increased by 10%, it is like you are making a 4.4% yield on your initial investment. This is in addition to any capital gain you may have. This type of increase is not unusual for some of these stocks.

You mentioned that you've refined the BTSX model in that if a company cuts its dividend you would immediately replace it. Is that something that will be made official in the BTSX model going forward?

I guess that since I'm supplying the data and writing their articles, I'm trying to inform people as best I can to help them preserve their capital.

Are there any other refinements that you've personally made to the model over the years?

The only other one, very minor, is that I changed the start and end date. David had his start and end date in May. That just happened to be when he started his data collection many years ago. When I started my data collection I switched over to January 1, because I could then easily compare my annual returns to other annually tracked indexes.

Over the next five, ten, fifteen years, do you predict that the BTSX model can repeat the success it's had? On average about 12% annual returns every year.

So one of my philosophies that I live by is that no one knows the future. But we all desperately want to know what's going to happen in the future. That's why the horoscope business is so good. So much of the financial information that you hear is, "This stock is going to do this and going to do that." So I honestly don't know how BTSX is going to do. History has shown that it's done well in the past 28 years. There are years and chunks of years where it doesn't do as well. I could have two or three years in a row where it will underperform the index. But as David has shown, and I've seen, over the long run it appears to be doing well. So I'm hoping for good average returns in the future.

What would be the risks of blindly following the BTSX model? David Stanley talked about the Nortel effect one year.

Yes, that is correct. What happened with the Nortel effect and how it affected us was that Nortel brought the index up quite significantly. So much so that just by investing in your blue-chip companies there's no way you could have kept up to that rise in the index and beat it. A very similar thing happened when the energy stock boom happened. There were a number of years when you just couldn't keep up with the index. I mean you had a great absolute return for BTSX and you had your income coming in, but relative to the index, it didn't keep up. So far what I've seen with the BTSX stocks is that their variability is less than the index, which is something that, as an investor who's been investing for income, I would certainly be looking for and appreciate.

Would you still recommend the Beat the TSX model to people starting out today who want to achieve their financial independence?

I think BTSX is a great stepping stone for those folks who want to spread their wings beyond mutual funds and get more actively involved in their portfolio. I think it forms a good process from which to build a person's wealth. It is a very simple process to follow. It should be used as a benchmark for people to measure other investment strategies against for its simplicity and its long-term average results. I think you can see from the results and the simplicity that this is a really good package deal.

But is it too simple? Have you ever worried about buying a dog stock that scored high on the model?

Yes; actually, I'm glad you asked me that question. Because there was another element that I did add to BTSX and which I wrote about in the book, which is that I have to be able to sleep at night *[laughs]*. So every new addition to the list I research and then ask, why is it on the list? What are its problems? What are some fundamentals about the company that seem to be okay? Is there good cash flow? I'll research all new additions because often there are companies that I'm not familiar with. I think there was only one company that I couldn't get comfortable with. That happened about a year or so before they went bankrupt, and I didn't buy the stock because I wasn't comfortable with a number of aspects of it. That was the right call to have made. I always say to investors that you need to be comfortable with any stock you buy. Just because it's on the BTSX list doesn't mean you blindly buy it. You need to ask, do I really want to own this? I've talked to some investors who follow the BTSX list and they say, "You know what, I didn't like number seven, so I bought number eleven instead." You know you're picking from a list of high-dividend-paying Canadian blue-chip companies. You will probably do all right.

What does "blue-chip" mean to you?

Blue-chip means a well-established company that is paying consistent dividends, and they've been consistent dividend payers over time. They also regularly increase their dividends. And they are well diversified in their product line. You know, you pick up some of these annual reports from the banks and they state that it's the 184th annual report or some other large number. You think, "There must be something about this business that works very well. With the banks, people need money, and they are in the business of providing it. The Canadian banks have been good blue-chip stocks to own.

You were 43 years old when you achieved financial independence and quit your job.

Yes, that's right.

Why don't more Canadians do that? What's holding them back from leaving the rat race, gaining financial independence, and doing what they love?

I think you could write a whole book on that because that question has stumped me. Not knowing the answer to that question was actually one of my biggest problems early on. When I was 22, I sat down at the computer and thought, "I think it is possible to retire early. My computer program says this will work." Obviously I was missing a lot of knowledge about how to do it but on paper it looked like it would work. But I wasn't reading about anyone who was doing something like that, or even trying to achieve it. I thought, "Well, maybe I've got something wrong here." And then finally I was approaching 43 and knew that it was going to work. Now that I have been retired now for eight years, I can say it does work. That's actually why I wrote the book. Also, I want my kids to know about this strategy. However, I think a lot of people should have this as a known lifestyle option if they want to do it. So anyways, "Why don't other Canadians do it?" I wonder if they don't know that it's possible. I know it is a long-term plan and it took me over 20 years to achieve. It's not a get-rich-quick scheme by any means, and you've got to have a lot of discipline.

If you look back, what were the keys to actually meeting your goal?

That's a good question. First, the most important step was having a plan. Second, starting early. Third, getting above-average market returns. Fourth, minimizing taxes through RRSPs and the dividend income tax credit. And now we have the Tax-Free Savings Account, which is an incredible tool. Educating myself on the world of investing was important as well. Doing this I discovered that if I could live off 4% or less of my income, that I should be okay. But that's something I only found out in the last 10 years. That is the kind of information I would like somebody to know when they're 22. If I knew all this stuff when I was 22, I would have achieved my goal a little sooner than 43.

You've recently taken over from David Stanley on that long-running Beat the TSX or BTSX strategy that's featured in **Canadian MoneySaver.** *I'm curious, how did that passing of the torch from Mr. Stanley to you come about?*

Well, about 18 years ago, I started reading David's articles. I thought, "This sounds quite interesting." But at that point I'd read lots of articles so I kept reading his articles for five more years before investing in it. But over those years I started to accumulate some of those stocks that were on his list anyway. Then 14 years ago I decided to really put some money into it and try it out for myself. When I started out, I put $2,500 in each of the 10 stocks. The results seemed fairly good after a year, so I put some more money in and then put some more and more. I thought it was working really well for me. When I retired, I decided to write the book and I realized I was going to be referencing a lot of David's material. So I thought I should contact David and see if he was okay with me referencing his work in my book. I contacted him and he said, "No problem." He invited me to make a presentation for his share club, and after the meeting he said that he enjoyed listening to me speak and that I sounded just like him *[laughs]*. A few days later he called me up and said he was ready to retire from doing what he was doing, which was Beat the TSX, and asked me if I would take it over from him. I was honoured that he would consider me and of course I accepted the challenge.

Anything else to add on BTSX or other advice that you'd like to share?

One of the things I lay out in my book is that buying index exchange-traded funds is better than mutual funds, because you don't have the MER that's dragging down the return. If you graduate from mutual funds to the exchange rate funds, you would be doing well. A lot of mutual funds have great difficulty, on average, even on a five-year basis, of equalling the return of the index. The first step is for the investor to realize if they go with the index, on average, they are going to be much better off than with the mutual funds. BTSX just tries to push you up one step on the investment ladder above exchange-traded funds. David's work shows that you can get an extra 2 to 2.5% extra every year, on average, over a long period of time and I'm finding that I have the same results.

As Ross explains, the BTSX system is powerful, consistent, and sustainable. The small selection of BTSX high-dividend stocks outperformed by quite a wide margin the total return average of the top 20 Canadian balanced funds for both 5 years and 10 years. In fact, BTSX topped 19 out of the 20 mutual funds in 5-year returns and all 7 of them in 10-year returns. What follows comes from David Stanley's Toronto Money Show presentation.

ADVANTAGES OF THE BTSX SYSTEM
- No broker or financial advisor, but it can beat the TSX
- No mutual funds, MERs, or market timing
- No time-consuming research
- Low-risk, less stress, independence, passive
- Acquiring high-yielding Canadian blue-chip stocks at reasonable cost that you hold for a long time

DISADVANTAGES OF THE BTSX SYSTEM
- No one to blame but yourself
- Dividend cuts, tax code changes
- Index itself — Laidlaw (– 94%) 1999

Given the parameters of the BTSX model, I've created the table below of the 10 highest-yielding stocks (high to low) from the master list (TSX/60) to form my very own BTSX portfolio as of September 18, 2015. I have not included any former trusts in this table. The average dividend yield is 4.84%. I would hold this portfolio of stocks until next year, September 18, 2016, when I would complete the exercise over again — invest in the ten highest-yielding stocks . . . and repeat.

COMPANY NAME	DIVIDEND YIELD
BCE	4.82
NATIONAL BANK OF CANADA	4.74
BANK OF NOVA SCOTIA	4.73
CANADIAN IMPERIAL BANK OF COMMERCE	4.69
BANK OF MONTREAL	4.61
SHAW COMMUNICATIONS	4.6
POWER CORPORATION OF CANADA	4.46
ROYAL BANK OF CANADA	4.27
ROGERS COMMUNICATIONS	4.26
TELUS	3.99
AVERAGE YIELD	4.52

MASTER KEYS
ROSS GRANT

1) "The amount you need to live on every year grows, but what you set aside hopefully grows faster."

2) "Eventually at some point in the future you get to the point where you can take out 4% a year to live on, and still have some money left when you die many years later."

3) "So for every $40,000 that you want in income, you would need $1 million in your nest egg."

4) "When you first start, the main growth in your nest egg is due to the annual savings you contribute . . . this balance changes as the nest egg grows in size relative to the annual contributions."

5) "My 14-year average annual return for Beat the TSX stocks is 12.6%. The simplicity of the process is really what attracted me to it."

6) "The key aspect of these [BTSX] stocks is the steady and often growing income stream."

7) "Blue-chip means a well-established company that is paying consistent dividends, and they've been consistent dividend payers over time. They also regularly increase their dividends. And they are well diversified in their product line."

8) "So every January 1, or December 31, you look at the closing prices of the stocks in the index. The index we're trying to beat is Standard & Poor's TSX 60, so there's 60 stocks in it. You rank those 60 stocks by their dividend yield. You put the highest-dividend-yielding stocks at the top and sort them down to the lowest at the bottom. Then you remove the previous income trusts as you find that most of them are all energy stocks. They're not as stable as your blue-chip companies. You take the top 10 that remain and you invest 10% in each of those 10 stocks. You let them sit there for a year and do it again the next December 31."

9) "I feel that there's two aspects that make the BTSX strategy work really well. One is that you limit yourself to big blue-chip companies, which are relatively stable, [and two] there can be some significant capital gains generated in the group of 10 stocks that are purchased."

10) "A lot of the capital gains from Beat the TSX often come from stocks that are in the lower positions, and a higher percentage of your dividend yield comes from positions one, two, and three."

11) "If I'm being given 4% in dividends, it is just like 'money in the bank.'"

12) "If you were getting a dividend of 4% and then it increased by 10% it is like you are making a 4.4% yield on your initial investment."

13) "What I've seen with the BTSX stocks is that their variability is less than the index, which is something that, as an investor who's been investing for income, I would certainly be looking for and appreciate."

14) "'Why don't other Canadians do it?' [i.e., early financial independence] I wonder if they don't know that it's possible. I know it is a long-term plan and it took me over 20 years to achieve. It's not a get-rich-quick scheme by any means, and you've got to have a lot of discipline."

15) "First, the most important step was having a plan. Second, starting early. Third, getting above-average market returns. Fourth, minimizing taxes through RRSPs and the dividend income tax credit. And now we have the Tax-Free Savings Account, which is an incredible tool."

16) "Buying index exchange-traded funds is better than mutual funds, because you don't have the MER that's dragging down the return."

▲

FINAL WORDS

▼

The Market Masters project was an enlightening journey. I met some incredible investors and learned from their own words their investment philosophies, strategies, and processes, as well as their successes, challenges, and outlooks in the market. Now that you have finished reading *Market Masters*, you can take some or all of the Market Masters' proven investing strategies and apply them in the market to make your winnings more plentiful, predictable, and profitable. The ability to apply these strategies to the market should stand the test of time — and remain relevant one year, five years, ten years, and twenty-plus years into the future. That promise to you — timeless strategies — is the outcome I set out to achieve in each and every interview.

Market Masters is like a cookbook of investing strategies. Choose a combination of the ingredients that work best for you, whether those be value, growth, fundamental, macro (top-down), systematic (technical), investing styles, or something entirely different. Take your time. There's no need to rush. Keep learning, make mistakes, build your portfolio, enjoy your successes, and grow in the market. Who knows? Maybe you will be the next Market Master.

What I hope you also gleaned from this book is that the Canadian market can play a crucial role in your investment success. Here are the facts: Canadian stocks have exceeded the returns of international stocks, bonds, and T-Bills, from 1934 to 2014. And we're not very far behind the U.S. market's compound annual return of 11.1% versus Canada's 9.8% over that same 80-year period. An investment in Canadian stocks has grown 1,597-fold despite 13 recessions, double-digit interest rates, and several world crises.

Investing in the markets can be incredibly fun. From research to analysis to purchase, I love picking stocks. I was fortunate to have the opportunity to play in the market at a young age. I've been saving, investing, and building my portfolio since the age of 18. Now, at 28, I've amassed a relatively sizeable stock portfolio of $225,000. There may be readers who scoff at that number — "my portfolio is much bigger" — but my disclosure is intended to be inspirational to those budding investors. You can start with little funds and at a young age.

Let me be clear: one does not have to have an IQ of 170 to be successful in the markets or to build a sizeable portfolio. Making money in the markets is simply a calculated game. The objective, if you want to excel at that game: beat the market. To help you beat the market, in addition to the Market Masters' proven strategies, I've put together a list of concepts that all of the Markets Masters share, which in my view, explains how they can continuously beat the market. You should emulate them if you wish to do the same.

HOW THE MARKET MASTERS CONTINUOUSLY BEAT THE MARKET

- **DISCIPLINE:** they stick to their market paradigm (e.g., value or growth or both).
- **FLEXIBILITY:** they employ additional strategies (within their paradigm) to supplement returns.
- **LOVE:** investing in the markets is their passion.
- **EXPERIENCE:** they have been investing for a long time and learn from their mistakes.
- **RISK MANAGEMENT:** they limit any and all downside risk to avoid capital destruction.
- **BEHAVIOUR:** emotions are always in check — they don't ebb and flow with the market's gyrations.

- **INDEPENDENCE:** they formulate their own theses based on logical reasoning and analysis.
- **REACH:** many also invest indirectly (through Canadian and other multinationals) in global markets to capitalize on unique opportunities.
- **RESEARCH:** they are voracious readers and consumers of market data.
- **OBSERVANCE:** they leverage their awareness of themes or business to profit in the market.
- **PROBABILITY:** they accept that they will have many losers, and bigger winners.
- **CONVICTION:** their research into each investment is substantial and they allocate more capital to "sure bets" to amplify their returns.
- **PROCESS:** they follow a highly refined and proven approach to investing in the market.

▲

COLLECTION OF MASTER KEYS

▼

The following is a collection of the Master Keys, organized and then summarized by topic rather than by Market Master, as they were within the chapters. They represent the most important things that I learned from the Market Masters. The collection follows a top-down flow, and it starts with you — the investor. Let's get started.

YOU — THE INVESTOR

FEAR, GREED, AND LOATHING IN THE MARKET. CONTROL YOUR EMOTIONS.

We're all human. And we all exhibit uniquely human traits, especially when it comes to emotions. Success in the markets, however, is largely determined by our ability to control emotion. Emotions have the potential to ruin your portfolio. You must be a rational thinker if you want to be a successful investor. If you are not rational, start to build that temperament now. Understand that we will naturally seesaw between greed and fear in the market. It's an emotional and draining cycle. "The human condition is subject to cycles of both greed and excess optimism, or fear and excess pessimism," as Jeff Stacey said. Stocks drop — we become fearful and sell. Stocks rise — we become greedy and buy. There is no doubt that's a money-losing strategy. Remember what your father told you, or at least what my father told me: "Buy low, sell high." You can't get much more rational than that.

> BENJ GALLANDER: *"'Buy when there's blood in the streets.' If everything or virtually everything has been beaten up, you've then got a much better chance in the market. During tough times, people get scared and, well, that's the wrong time to run out of the market."*

You must "understand how you feel when your stock goes down 20% and what your reaction will be," as Gaelen Morphet said. If you haven't done so already, put a little money in the markets, and observe how you react to even minor price movements. The final step is to actually take control of your emotion. How? By establishing guiding principles. As Jason Mann said, "[Successful investors] build a set of rules and processes to constrain their actions, and their own behavioural biases." For example, I don't become fearful during a decline and sell out, or "capitulate" after my portfolio is down 50%. I only sell securities when their underlying fundamentals have also fallen. But that's my rule, my style. There are other styles that may call for a sell-off after a 10% drop, regardless of the business fundamentals. "Your style of investing has to fit your personality type," as Jason Donville said.

DISCIPLINE. DECIDE ON ONE (OR MORE) PROVEN LONG-TERM STRATEGIES AND STICK TO THEM IN MARKET UPS AND DOWNS.

Once you have picked your investment styles (growth, value, and so on) and implemented rules to control your emotions, you need to build discipline in the markets. This isn't a walk in the park. If you want to be successful, you need to be professional. Your mandate should be to implement proven strategies in the market to grow your wealth. Don't stray from that objective. Follow Som Seif's advice: "Investing success, like any other discipline or profession, is achieved through the rudimentary core knowledge that you need to know. It's in the application: how you think, your discipline, and whether you can you stick with that discipline."

BILL HARRIS: *"People get all excited about their investments and get to a point where they don't know why they are investing anymore. So your real work is to come up with a very tight strategy then stick to it."*

PASSION. PRACTICE MAKES PERFECT.

I won't go into great detail why passion is important. Being amazing at anything takes passion. I'm not, for example, passionate about sports. So, I'm a terrible athlete (and a lousy fan). Passion fuels practice, which builds experience, which predicates excellence. Clearly, if you are not interested in money, investing, or building wealth, you will not excel in the markets, since you won't care enough to learn to grow to succeed.

KNOWLEDGE IS POWER. BUILD AND THEN LEVERAGE YOUR EDGE.

All of the Market Masters have an insatiable drive to read in order to empower themselves on a daily basis in the markets. Understand the facts. "Don't invest on the basis of a tip. Do your own research. Even if someone tells you that you should go buy some shares, don't just go 'Okay!' and buy some shares," as Martin Braun said. I've read somewhere around 150 to 200 books on personal finance, investing, and the markets, combined with 10 to 25 articles per day, but I'm still thirsty to learn more. The market is a living, breathing entity. Your investing success will be highly correlated to your information store, which needs to be constantly up to date. Read books, magazines, newspapers, annual reports, analyst research, and so on to become more informed on the markets, or you will be quickly eaten up by those who are more informed than you.

FRANCIS CHOU: *"When you read about great men and women of the past, it is like having a conversation about world affairs in your living room. It is not only educational but it builds perspective about life and business in general."*

Additionally, become more aware. Observe your surroundings. Jeff Stacey said, "You have to get out and you have to travel and you have to see what people are eating, what they are drinking, what they are smoking, what they are wearing, and so on." When you're at the mall, ask yourself, where are people shopping? What bags are they holding? Where are the longest lineups? When I worked at Best Buy during my high school years, I noticed that iPods sold out on a daily basis and inventory would have to be constantly replenished by the store manager. I didn't think much of Apple back then, but obviously people were swarming that breakthrough product, the iPod, in droves. I would have made a lot of money had I invested in Apple based on that observation. So, keep an open mind — read, observe, reflect, and then apply your theses to the market.

> **MARTIN BRAUN:** *"Try to get as close to the business as possible. Maybe it's a consumer-oriented business and as a consumer you can check it out and see if it makes any sense to you as a consumer."*

If that's all too overwhelming, you can adopt Derek Foster's philosophy: "I stick to my circle of confidence. Because I'm not that bright, my circle's fairly small, but that's okay as long as I stick within that circle." There's nothing wrong with sticking to your circle of competence. Knowing a few things really well is better than knowing many things not very well.

EXPERIENCE VERSUS NATURE. EXPERIENCE WILL DETERMINE YOUR INVESTING SUCCESS.

I'm firmly of the belief, and I'm confident most Market Masters would agree, that experience rather than nature has the greatest influence on investing success. We aren't born ultimate traders who conquer the world. Martin Braun likened the market to a casino, and jokingly said, "You might get lucky the first time or the second time, but you'll get wiped out by the third time. It's like a guy who goes to Vegas and gets 'hot.' Day one at the table he cleans up. Day two he breaks even. Day three he gives it all back to the house plus some." We build experience through the markets that enhances our winnings, but most importantly increases the probability, as a result of becoming ever wiser, that we will win. However, not all of us *will* win. Some will try and fail. Others will simply fail to try. The ones who do make it will persist and perfect their craft. It's all about experience and time in the market. As Gaelen Morphet said, "To be a good investor you must go through some very difficult times where you really do question your abilities and your resolve." Be persistent — don't quit. Quitters never win and winners never quit.

Through experience, hopefully sooner rather than later, you can perfect your investment strategy. Francis Chou would encourage you to hone your stock valuation skills: "Investments are most profitable when the selection process is most businesslike. Therefore, you must have the skill level to evaluate a business."

SAVINGS RATE. START SAVING AND INVESTING EARLY IN LIFE TO COMPOUND YOUR WEALTH.

It all starts with cash. Earn, save, invest, and then repeat. Derek Foster revealed his savings system: "I was a very avid saver. I saved a high percentage of my income throughout my life. Probably about 70%." I'm not going to suggest that you consistently save an exact percentage of your paycheque. That's restrictive, as our earnings and situations throughout life do fluctuate — changing jobs, starting a family, supporting our parents. However, remember that early on, "the main growth in your nest egg is due to the annual savings you contribute," as the other super saver Ross Grant told us.

Both Derek and Ross started saving and investing early in life. Eventually, those investments started to snowball, thanks to compound returns. And then money practically started working for them. Now, their main source of income in early retirement is dividend income. "For every $40,000 that you want in [dividend] income, you would need $1 million in your nest egg," said Ross Grant. Personally, I don't keep track of my savings — I just save. It's innate. It's a force of habit. (Though some may call it a bad habit, especially my girlfriend if we go to Wendy's one night rather than a hip restaurant, because I'd rather save and invest the differential.)

> **DEREK FOSTER:** *"That's the secret to why the rich get richer — the second million, and then the third million, and then the fourth million all get easier and easier and easier."*

GO AGAINST THE HERD. BE AN INDEPENDENT THINKER.

Going against the herd is tough. Not only are we naturally emotional, but we are incredibly social, too. We usually just want to get along with everybody and live in an inclusive environment. That's why we formed tribes, cities, countries, and civilizations. Weren't we taught to believe that there's "safety in numbers," and that "two heads are better than one"? The point is that in the market, large numbers of people can be wrong at the same time. You must think independently and then take your own actions regardless of what others say, do, or feel. Benj Gallander's mandate is to go against the herd in the market to capitalize on any collective malfunctions in mass thought, such as when he bought into airline stocks following 9/11. Most of the other Market Masters also capitalize on their understanding of herd mentality. Barry Schwartz, for example, said, "Do you know the famous story about Joseph Kennedy? When he heard the shoe-shine boy or the cabbie give him investment advice, he knew that it was time to sell or short everything." This story shows that herd mentality goes both ways. The masses can rush into the market as quickly as they rush out. When they rush in, that can be a late warning sign of a market top. As Michael Sprung explained, "When you see that retail investors are all rushing in and that people are lining up to buy something, that's usually a good time to sell out." Ultimately, I do not recommend that you simply trade opposite of the herd. Sometimes, and some would argue, most of the time, the herd is right. Do remember to think independently. Question what you see in the market. Take a step back and reflect once in a while. "You have to go against the grain. You have to do your own independent work, your own analysis, and you stand on the merits of your own judgments," as Francis Chou said.

> BILL CARRIGAN: *"Usually when the compelling story gets very compelling, the stock has pretty well peaked . . . the biggest mistake investors make is getting sucked in by a compelling story."*

MISTAKES COST MONEY. LEARN FROM THEM AND MOVE ON, NEVER TO REPEAT THEM.

Let's be clear: you will make mistakes in the market. What's important is that you learn from those mistakes and never repeat them. Most of the Market Masters openly talked about their mistakes in the markets over the years, as those experiences have taught them many valuable lessons. Peter Hodson admitted, "The best lesson is losing money, so I learned some really good lessons." If you fall off your bike and scrape your knee, you can apply a Band-Aid and a few days later your wound will heal. In the markets, though, if you repeatedly make the same mistakes, akin to falling of your bike, you will permanently lose money — that hurts. Benj Gallander also explained, "It's important to say, 'Okay, maybe I was wrong' and 'I have to get out of this position, take my loss, and move on.' If you can lose 20% instead of 50% or 100%, that's huge." I would rather scrape my knee (take a 20% loss) than break my leg (a 50% to 100% loss).

BARRY SCHWARTZ: *"We've gotten smarter over time. When you stick your fingers in the tiger's cage, you get bit. So you don't do it again. You know, the cat doesn't go sit on the hot stove. It learns its lesson and moves on."*

THE MARKET

MULTI-STRATEGIES IN THE MARKET INCREASE
AND ENHANCE YOUR WINNINGS.

The market is a dynamic place. There are many different opportunities to make money. As a result, you can supplement your basic long equity strategy with other repeatable low-risk strategies. It was clear that the most heavily employed "multi-strategy" or "alternative strategy" that we learned from some of the Market Masters was risk arbitrage (mergers and acquisition, or M&A). Now, the spreads on M&A risk arbitrage are not as high as they were in the past, perhaps because of heightened aware-ness or high-frequency trading that squeezes the spreads. Martin Braun explained, "Every time a company announced it was being acquired it would go into that database and we'd just go trolling, looking for the best spreads with the least risk. . . . It didn't take me very long to figure out that I didn't just have to trade on announced deals. I could also trade rumoured deals or theoretical deals."

When Company A announces its purchase of Company B for x amount, Company B's stock price will rise close to but not exactly at the announced x amount. That's because there's still the risk that the deal won't actually close, combined with the existence of Time Value of Money or, in other words, opportunity cost. What one can then do is pur-chase stock in Company B, wait until the deal finally closes, and collect the spread. That's risk arbitrage. It sounds simple but, again, you need to assess the probability of the deal actually closing as it was announced to the public. Jeff Stacey enters into a wider range of multi-strategy plays, in what he calls event-driven transactions. "Event-driven transactions are the pursuit of profits from announced corporate events. So that's liquidations, mergers, acquisitions, recapitalizations, tender offers, anything where you can say, 'Okay, if this event happens we're going to make *this* amount of money in *this* amount of time.'"

BULL VERSUS BEAR. BE AWARE OF THE BATTLE THAT RAGES ON THAT DETERMINES THE DIRECTION OF THE MARKET.

Bulls and bears have become symbols of the market. Bulls represent optimism; bears, pessimism. I liked how David Burrows so eloquently explained the dynamic between bulls and bears and how their battle establishes direction in the market: "In any transition, there's a period of higher volatility where the buyers and sellers battle it out until one side wins and you either transition higher or lower." Luckily for investors, bull markets last longer and extend gains higher, overshadowing the bear markets that precede them. However, what I've witnessed, especially after the financial crisis of 2008, is that bear markets can leave investors with a sluggish hangover. In other words, after a bear market, investors can take a while to once again participate in the market to perpetuate the resumption of a bull uptrend. "Once you end up in a bull market, everyone's scared because of the previous bear market; they want to take profits off the table as soon as things start to work," as David explained.

But, as David Burrows points out, "There's no bear market in history that took place while breadth expansion was taking place. . . . I can go back to the 1950s and see that there's no significant bull market that ever ended before 70% or 80% of stocks participated in an advance. In the NYSE, today, we're sitting at only about 60% participation." If David is right, while we have experienced wild gyrations in the market in 2015, the expansion in volume indicates that markets will continue to rise, at least until that 70 to 80% threshold. This same analysis can be applied to markets in the future, too. Bill Carrigan offered more insight on how to tell whether one is in a bear market: "Basically anything in a bear market should make a new low within a six-month window of 26 weeks. To me that's the definition of a bear. So if you have a market that trades down, makes a correction, and then doesn't take that low within six months, then it's not a bear." To monitor bull and bear markets as told by Bill Carrigan, you can pull up the TSX or S&P 500 charts on StockCharts.com and track those technical levels. While the symbolism behind the battle between bull and the bear offers insight into directionality in the market, I don't put much weight into it in my portfolio. I buy quality stocks that can either defend themselves or continue to rally through bear markets, and can move even higher through bull markets.

MARKET CAPITALIZATION: SMALL-, MID-, AND LARGE-CAPS. KNOW THE SEGMENTS OF THE MARKET IN WHICH YOU INVEST.

Market capitalization refers to the size of a company on the exchange. As a simple calculation, market capitalization = stock price × common shares outstanding. There are four segments of market capitalization (subject to change due to inflation):

- Small-cap: $50 million–$2 billion
- Mid-cap: $2 billion–$10 billion
- Large-cap: $10 billion–$150 billion
- Mega-cap: $150 billion or more

As retail investors, we have an advantage in the small-cap space. Barry Schwartz explained, "It is easier [for retail investors] to buy some smaller-cap companies. The billion-dollar-or-less stocks that a company like ours can't get access to anymore because we have gotten too big and would own too much of the stock." But while the small-cap space is off limits for many large money managers, the mid-cap space is not. Jason Donville argued that "in Canada, the mid-cap segment is probably the most inefficient part of the market." In other words, there's money to be made in the mid-cap space. Personally, I like to invest more in mid-cap companies than I do in small-cap companies. The mid-cap companies have established themselves; they've gone from good to great, whereas the small-cap companies are less predictable. They can go from good to nothing. That's why it's important to understand the risk/reward concept in investing your capital in the market.

> **MARTIN FERGUSON:** *"I believe that there are opportunities in the small-cap area that exceed those in the large-cap area, offset by higher risk."*

But as Martin Ferguson explained, "Canada essentially is a small-cap market. There are very few large-cap companies in Canada." Martin said he looks at "companies from $100-million market cap up to about $1.5-billion market cap. And there's approximately four hundred of those small-cap stocks in the market today." However, as we know, Martin Ferguson is the small-cap king, so he can more readily pick winners within the small-cap space. But now you can, too — return on invested capital (ROIC) over internal cost of capital, among other criteria, is the starting point. I would suggest employing Kiki Delaney's approach to allocating small-cap companies to your portfolio: "[We] invest initially no more than 1% in a small-cap company. If it works, it's probably really going to work, and it'll be very beneficial. But if it doesn't work, it will hurt the portfolio to the extent of its 1% exposure." This way, you can limit your downside. As for large-caps and mega-caps you should not expect as much movement over time (five-plus years), considering the law of large numbers. Though, these stocks can serve as natural hedges in your portfolio as they tend to move with the market (smaller beta), without as wide gyrations up and down as small-caps and mid-caps often experience. As some will agree, "slow and steady wins the race." It's important to mention that while my classification of large-cap and mega-cap stocks as "slower movers" is true in the long run, that isn't necessarily the case in the short run. Looking at the four largest Canadian stocks, as of October, 2015, one may be struck by their volatility and wide moves in the market. Here is the difference between those stocks' 52-week highs and lows: RBC (23%), TD (21%), Valeant (113%), and BNS (34%). I would attribute those wide differences to the correctionary market condition we are coming out of in Canada at the moment. What's important is that you understand the segments of the market in which you invest, as they exhibit different characteristics.

CANADA VERSUS GLOBAL REACH. STRIVE FOR
GLOBAL EXPOSURE IN YOUR PORTFOLIO.

The majority of my portfolio is in Canadian equities. But these also tend to be companies that have significant business operations around the world. Many investors turn a blind eye to Canada, opting instead to invest in U.S. multinationals, which arguably offer more global breadth and diversification. As Kiki Delaney explained, though, "[On the TSX], there's also a lot of world-class international companies. Funnily, a lot of them reside in Quebec . . . Quebec companies get positive reinforcement. In many cases, the Caisse de dépôt takes a fairly substantial position in underwriting companies to help them expand through very large acquisitions." I, too, have found that many quality Canadian companies reside in Quebec. I've made a lot of money through those Quebec-based companies — WSP Global, Canadian National Railway, Alimentation Couche-Tard, and CGI, to name a few. However, the reality for most investors is that "the Canadian market is two-sided. You have on the one hand resource names, and then on the other hand, you have everything else," as Kiki explained.

But one should not feel the need to be patriotic in the markets. Again, there's no room for emotion. The U.S. and Europe are obviously wonderfully large markets. As Peter Brieger explained, "One can gain [global] exposure by investing in major international companies that have at least 50% of their business in emerging markets." Most importantly, that exposure through western companies is safe, whereas direct investment in developing regions or countries can be risky. As Norman Levine said, "We've never invested directly in China, [Russia,] or in India, but that's subject to change in the future. Basically, their security markets are not mature and do not have the safety standards of markets we like to invest in."

Market preference can be rather subjective. While American Bill Ackman said, "We've had a very favourable experience in Canada in pretty much everything we've done," Canadian Lorne Zeiler said, "The main reason for owning U.S. stocks is that the Canadian market just isn't sufficient." You be the judge. What we have learned is that achieving global exposure in your portfolio is crucial, if only through western multinational companies, to limit your risk. While most investors will invest in U.S. multinationals to indirectly enter international markets, there exist Canadian multinationals that can provide international exposure, too.

RIDE THE COATTAILS. INVEST ALONGSIDE PROMINENT INVESTORS.

A friend of mine has profited immensely from "riding the coattails" in the market, emulating prominent investors like the Market Masters in this book and buying the same stocks that they take positions in. For example, when Bill Ackman publicly revealed his stake in Mondelez, my friend bought into Mondelez, too. The logic behind "riding the coattails" is to follow the smart money. Prominent money managers have deep pockets, and — for example in Bill Ackman's case — can actually optimize the companies that they invest in and push stock prices up. Som Seif created a fund that invests in the highest-conviction positions among the most notable investors in the world. "What we're doing [in the Best Ideas Fund] is investing in the most concentrated bets that these guys have in their hedge funds. That's it," Som Seif explained.

Bill Ackman added, "You can't necessarily buy at the activists' [or prominent investors'] price, but once they announce the investment you can invest in it alongside them. And oftentimes stocks don't go straight up, so there's an opportunity to buy it again at a cheaper price." Regardless, the drawback, if you are to solely ride the coattails, is that the common investor gets delayed information; you must wait until the next 13F filing. You only learn about the position *after* the prominent investor is already in at a much lower price, and rarely learn when he sells out or, at best, learn much later. That is why you should ride the coattails of those longer term investors who stay invested in a stake for full value realization. Alternatively, as Cameron Winser told us, you can simply learn from prominent investors, such as himself, and apply their proven strategies to better your results in the market. "Look around and try to find a bunch of great ideas and see if there's a way that you can combine them into fitting your own strategy."

BREADTH. FOLLOW THE VOLUME.

The ultimate philosophical question, which one can ponder for years and still not come up with an answer, is "What is the meaning of life?" The equivalent ultimate question, albeit not as complex, in the markets is "What moves stock prices higher?" While this book won't offer an answer to the meaning of life, it does help solve for the key technical variable that drives stock prices: volume. The stock market operates on free-market supply and demand principles. Economics 101.

> DAVID BURROWS: *"80% of returns come from the impact of capital inflows — breadth expansion (more volume) — into an asset class. That's when multiple expansion (higher prices) or re-valuation starts."*

But how does one follow the volume? You can use a technical indicator: accumulation distribution. As Bill Carrigan explained, "If a stock's going sideways, but the accumulation distribution lines are still slightly rising, that tells me that there's smart money buying the stock." I like accumulation distribution because you can get in early on a stock, usually small-cap to mid-cap, before it starts to move up. You can also heed Benj Gallander's advice regarding the price at which money managers will start to accumulate stocks. "If I'm buying a stock under $5, there's a lot of institutions and funds that won't even buy it under $10. It's only once it hits those higher levels that they can buy in. In simple economics of supply and demand, all of a sudden there's more demand but supply doesn't change; it's constant. And that pushes the stock up further." So, once a stock price hits that $10 threshold, and pushes higher, that could indicate that money managers have started to build a stake, if previously they were unable to do so, even if it was a great company.

You can follow the volume for currently rising stocks, too. For example, pay close attention to the average volume versus daily volume. If a stock's daily volume consistently exceeds its average volume, then there's incremental volume gains pushing the stock higher. You can access the "Predefined Scans" for free on StockCharts.com; these list the "Strong Volume Gainers" on a daily basis. Finally, remember that Jason Mann explained volume can be self-fulfilling, in that money managers continue to accumulate the stocks that they already own. So, one can research the top stocks held by money managers, and follow the money that way, too, similar to riding the coattails. "Momentum feeds upon itself. Think about the manager who manages $100 million, but then receives another $100 million. What do they typically do? They go buy the same stocks they already own."

THEMES. YOU CAN CAPTURE BROAD GAINS IN
THE MARKET FROM THEMATIC SHIFTS.

Thematic investing is a top-down process. The theme that you support (for example demographics) will determine what you invest in (for example health care). You aren't restricted to just one theme alone, as there may be a multitude of themes that can make you money. Kiki Delaney explained, "If you can find a relatively undiscovered theme and marry it with a well-managed and undervalued company, you will probably have a winning combination . . . [For example,] companies that make significant and highly accretive acquisitions. This has worked really well in a low-interest environment." There, Kiki's theme was acquisitive companies in a low-rate environment, as their cost to acquire accretive companies is lower due to cheap debt.

Sometimes, though, people can wind up chasing themes or "hot stocks." For example, the technology theme is full of potential. Though, I do feel that too many investors try to pick the next Facebook, and that can be a destructive practice. Conversely, Peter Hodson explained, "On the tech side, if you're in early on a theme, then it works well for you. It's harder for Microsoft to grow at a fast rate, whereas it's easier for the little guys to grow." In order to successfully invest in a theme that will grow and generate outsized returns, you need to develop a specialized competency in that sector. That's why I like Bill Carrigan's concept of "dominant themes." Rather than focus on and invest in a minor theme, which could very well be a fad, Bill recommends that you invest in a dominant theme, which usually has more beneficiaries and spans a longer period. "One of the rules of the dominant theme is that it persists for a generation or more and it also has to be investible. [Also,] dominant themes can pop and return in different forms." If you choose to invest in a theme, whether that be minor or dominant, I suggest investing in an exchange-traded fund (ETF) rather than your own basket of stocks. The ETF will contain more stocks that fit your theme, at a lesser cost.

DAVID VERSUS GOLIATH. KNOW WHO YOU ARE UP AGAINST.

The market is a place where large investors like banks, pension funds, insurance companies, and hedge funds participate alongside retail investors like me and you. It's very much a case of David and Goliath. How can David — us — compete in the market, let alone survive, is the question. As Bill Carrigan explained, "Large investors can control the market simply through their buying activity." In the short term, that can seduce oblivious retail investors into a stock, theme, or broader market until the rally ends, and the little guys lose money en masse. "Half of the activity of the stock can often be his [a money manager's] money, so the stock's rise can be a self-fulfilling prophecy. He's the one driving the stock higher. But then eventually it comes time to sell. And when everybody wants to sell, who's left to buy?"

Large investors, such as pension funds, can employ high-frequency trading (HFT) platforms that exploit minuscule pricing inefficiencies in the market. Obviously, retail investors don't have access to those expensive HFT platforms, let alone know how to use them. We must cope with these machines trading both with and against us in the market. As Randy Cass explained, "Trading in and of itself right now is a technology arms race. It's about who can get their hold in the market the fastest. It's about who can co-locate their server the closest to the exchange. It's about who can build something that can do billions upon billions of procedures faster than the other guy's computers." This wasn't meant to discourage you. It's to inform you of the players, and the activity, that make up the market. Because, remember, when you make a trade, you are not the only one participating. There's a buyer or seller on the other side. Peter Hodson said, "Ask yourself, 'Why am I selling?' But more so, ask yourself why the other guy's buying it from you. Are they buying it because they think it's going up? If [the answer is] yes, then maybe you should rethink your position."

DON'T FIGHT THE FED (OR CENTRAL BANK). FIGHT YOUR OWN BATTLES. OWN GOOD ASSETS.

We're at the cusp of great change in Fed policy. While readers of this book will primarily be Canadian and invest on the TSX, there's no denying that the U.S. Federal Bank's policies do influence Canada and the world over. For the past seven years, the U.S., and many of the developed economies of the world, including Canada, have been in a low-interest environment. Right now in 2015, overnight rates are in fact extremely low. Canada's is 0.5%. But the U.S. is hinting at every Fed meeting that it will raise rates. What that can do to an economy is analogous to turning off "money taps," effectively removing money supply from the market, which could send asset prices lower. Norman Levine warned us, "Most people only know a declining interest rate environment. They have no idea what happens when interest rates go up. Once interest rates start going up, money starts to leave the stock market and heads into fixed income." That is worrisome. I don't know a high interest rate environment — I was in diapers through the high-rate period of the eighties. While higher rates could very well put a damper on the market, others would say that rates, or the economy, do not influence the markets to such a high degree. For example, Bill Harris argued, "The stock market and the economy are not correlated. Your portfolio might act completely differently to what's going on in the economy." This would mean that the economy and the market are mutually exclusive. They can coexist but not influence each other in a perfect correlation. As said before, that's why I simply invest in high-quality companies that can weather recessions and thrive to a greater extent in economic booms. It's a win-win. So, if you can't beat 'em (the Fed), don't fight 'em. Fight your own battles. Own good assets.

MARKET EFFICIENCY. THE SIDE YOU TAKE WILL ULTIMATELY DETERMINE THE STRATEGIES YOU EMPLOY IN THE MARKET.

There's a divide among investors: those who believe the market is efficient versus those who believe it's inefficient. This debate has been going on for years with no end in sight. It's similar to the divide in religion. You can try to convince a devout Christian that the law of evolution is right and creationism is wrong but he'll continue to hold firm to his creationist beliefs. Likewise, it's virtually impossible for a devout Christian to change a non-Christian's beliefs on the law of evolution. In the Efficient Market Theory (EMT) camp are those investors — mostly technical, systematic growth investors — who believe that all available information is priced into the market at any given time and that market prices are correct. Whereas those who oppose EMT — mostly value investors — believe that while information is available, the participants in the market — investors — don't all apply it correctly at any given time to inform their actions. I've provided both sides of the coin, with arguments for and against the Efficient Market Theory. Which side you choose will ultimately determine the strategies you employ, as well as your overall investment philosophy.

EMT

DAVID BURROWS: *"We believe ultimately the market gets it right. So forget about what you think should happen. No matter how smart you are, sooner or later you will get put in the ditch with that mentality. One should understand what is happening. Don't try to justify what you think should happen."*

NON-EMT

BENJ GALLANDER: *"How can a market be perfectly efficient when it drops 22.4% in a day? It's impossible. Human psychology is a major driver of how people react. And that's what creates so much of the pendulum effect that goes too far, which allows me to make money, both in the times of euphoria and the times of depression. People do not react in many cases rationally."*

We learned that the majority of the Market Masters firmly believe that the market is inefficient, that both individual stocks and the market are subject to fear and greed, which can provide opportunities for investors.

RELATIVE VALUE. YOU CAN STILL INVEST EVEN WHEN YOU THINK THE MARKET IS OVERVALUED.

Relative value is a crucial concept to know when you are investing in a strong market. It's where you think, "Stocks are just so . . . overvalued." Rather than pricing yourself completely out of the market, you can focus on investing in relative value. Kiki Delaney said, "When we look at a company, we compare it to others in the same industry and buy the company that is statistically the cheapest." Of course, she also makes sure that she buys a quality company. But the point is that you don't have to completely put investing on pause during "overvalued" markets, because it's likely that not all stocks within the market will be overvalued at any given time. In addition, Gaelen Morphet reinforced the benefit of investing in relative value: "If you're always building wealth with a portfolio that's less expensive than the market, when the market rolls over, you'll have that margin of safety that other investors do not have." This shows that relative value can act as a risk management control, too — margin of safety.

SENTIMENT. THE NADIR OF SENTIMENT CAN OFTEN INDICATE A BOTTOM IN THE MARKET.

It's important to remember that the mood of the market fluctuates on a daily, monthly, and yearly basis. I actually consider the market to be a living and breathing thing. You will never know what the mood of the market will be tomorrow. It might be cranky. Or it might be joyous. Don't exit the market, though, because you don't understand, or can't handle, its ups and downs. There's usually no logic to its daily moves. In the short run, sentiment will shake the market, but in the long run, valuation will shape the market. Not surprisingly, the media plays a heavy hand in shaking the market as well. As Martin Braun explained, "I think that, generally speaking, the research and the commentary from media is very bad. You generally don't want to do what they tell you to do." I remember going to see Bill Carrigan talk about investing at a workshop. He held up a newspaper, and said something along the lines of "When this newspaper printed this issue in the winter of 2009, its headline suggested that the world was going to end. Doomsday!" He then went onto to say that two months after that issue, both the economy and stock market started to come off their bottoms and experienced a buoyant rise. The moral of that story: the nadir of sentiment can often indicate a bottom in the market.

PORTFOLIO

PRUNING. MAXIMIZE YOUR WINNERS AND MINIMIZE YOUR LOSERS.

One of the most important but challenging things to do is to let your winners run and cut your losers short. It's difficult because many of us don't implement guidelines that help us maximize winners and minimize losers. I've organized key lessons from some Market Markets that will tell you how to prune your portfolio and optimize returns.

MAXIMIZE YOUR WINNERS

MARTIN FERGUSON: *"We will work to emphasize those [stocks] that have the best opportunity to provide the highest return on a risk-adjusted basis."*

PETER HODSON: *"I've probably made more money from this philosophy than anything else: you have to take a stock from $2 and go to $4, and then be willing to buy more of it at $4 than you bought at $2."*

BILL CARRIGAN: *"Never sell a stock just because it's 'expensive.' Because, oftentimes, expensive stocks simply get more expensive."*

MINIMIZE YOUR LOSERS

MARTIN FERGUSON: *"As stocks go up in price, and the potential return falls,* *we actually look at de-emphasizing them in our portfolio [and] invest in whatever other sectors look more attractive."*

BENJ GALLANDER: *"When we buy I set an initial sell target, which is something I don't believe I did in the early days. That grounds me now."*

BENJ GALLANDER: *"I only average down once on any stock."*

Pruning your portfolio amplifies returns because you are constantly allocating capital to those opportunities that are most favourable at any given time. It's based on the premise of opportunity cost, where one is always cognizant of the loss of potential gain from other alternatives when one alternative is chosen. In other words, you should make decisions in your portfolio that will provide the biggest potential for gain.

DIVERSIFICATION. DIVERSIFY YOUR PORTFOLIO — HOLD BETWEEN 13 AND 30 STOCKS.

In any university-level finance class, at least in mine, you are taught that the point of maximum benefit from diversification is around 13 stocks in your portfolio. Any number below 13 heightens portfolio risk, making you vulnerable to volatility, and any number above 13 doesn't significantly decrease portfolio risk. I've found that investors, especially those further into their investing career, hold too many stocks in their portfolio. Holding too many stocks can dilute your return potential, such that you *become* the market or the index, and track its returns rather than beat them. The question is, do you want to *be* or *beat* the market? Benj Gallander pointed out, "If you're buying 60, or 100, or 200 stocks through funds, you're overly diversifying. If you overly diversify, you cut your returns automatically. I've usually held 15 to 25 stocks in my own portfolio. I don't want to exceed 25 stocks." From the various other conversations on diversification, most Market Masters hold a similar number of stocks in their portfolio. Martin Ferguson said, "We assume we need about 33 companies [to create a diversified portfolio]." Derek Foster said, "I don't think my portfolio's ever gotten above 25 stocks." And Norman Levine said, "I would suggest around 20 stocks. And they should be diversified." While there isn't a definitive range, holding 13–30 stocks seems ideal, as you benefit from diversification with lower volatility in your portfolio, but also don't over-diversify and diminish your portfolio's total return.

CONVICTION. MAGNIFY YOUR RETURN POTENTIAL WITH CONCENTRATED BETS.

You can take on *some* high-conviction positions in your diversified portfolio or you can construct a completely high-conviction portfolio. The latter does open you up to more risk, which is why I suggest the former — taking on *some* high-conviction positions. You do that by allocating more capital to stocks that you understand to a higher degree, stocks that you believe have more upside than other positions in your portfolio. Martin Ferguson explained, "We also have what we call 'confidence weight,' when we have a higher degree of confidence [or conviction] that any company will do well." Martin will double his average allocation weight in a stock — from 3% to 6%. Martin Braun, by contrast, operates a completely high-conviction portfolio. "I invest in a handful of businesses, not a whole bunch of them, and get to know them really well. 'Just put a few eggs in the basket but watch the basket *very* closely.'" Martin explained further, "Once you've learned so much about that business, don't put just a couple bucks in — *put a lot of bucks in.* If one of those stocks goes off the rails, then you'll be one of the first ones to realize that it's coming off the rails, and push it out the door before everyone else." However, take heed of Jason Donville's words of wisdom when he said, "If you're a good stock-picker, concentration works in your favour, and if you're not, you should own an ETF instead."

OPTIONALITY: STOCKS THAT ARE PREGNANT WITH POSSIBILITY CAN BIRTH BIG RETURNS.

Below I've included an excerpt from my conversation with Martin Braun, who revealed a concept that can achieve outsized returns in the market:

> Optionality is a buzzword for "pregnant with possibility." It's a fancy way of saying "upside." So there's a lot of cheap optionality embedded in stocks. In other words, you're not paying for *this* happening, and you're not paying for *that* happening; you're paying maybe a little teeny bit for a third thing

and maybe a little bit more for a fourth thing happening to the stock. If any of those four things were to happen, you'd make good money because the market's not really paying for them. Any one of them. But if all four of them kicked in, oh my god! That's what I mean by optionality. The optionality is the part of the equation that the market has not paid for. What the market has already paid for is the risk: the disappointment the market might face when it realizes that what it's been paying for isn't going to happen.

Recently, I've invested in Tweed Marijuana, a small-cap stock. Investing in Tweed was out of character for me, as I've committed myself to only invest in companies with superb long-term track records. However, Tweed serves a once-illegal market: marijuana smokers. I believe that Tweed is "pregnant with possibility" (optionality). If any or all of these following factors play out for Tweed, I think it will be a big winner: a) become the leader in consumer marijuana; b) generate high profit; c) consolidate most of the micro-marijuana companies; d) benefit from increased de-criminalization or legalization of marijuana in Canada; e) potentially get bought out in the future by a multinational company (I'm thinking of cigarette companies that may want to enter this market). If those options don't play out, though, Tweed will go up in smoke. Consider this an experiment in optionality.

STYLE. EMBRACE (OR AT LEAST EXPERIMENT WITH) ALL OF THE INVESTING STYLES.

While there exist many unique investing styles, as we have already discussed — value, growth, fundamental, top-down, technical — I've found throughout my investing career that to be truly successful in the market, one should embrace (or at least experiment with) all of the various styles in the stock selection process. Cameron Winser underscored this idea when he said, "A lot of people have pegged themselves to a style. They say, 'I'm a value investor' or 'I'm a growth investor.' I've pegged myself as style-agnostic. I'll go through, look at, and apply any and all of the different investment methods."

My own rationale as to why you should be a "renaissance investor" who draws on a variety of investing strategies is that you will miss opportunities in the market if you only look at securities though one lens. For example, if you are solely a value investor, you will miss or willfully ignore the stock that makes a technical breakout on its way to a new 52-week high. Similarly, if you are solely a growth investor, you will miss the moment you can buy the quality stock for less than its intrinsic value after it crashes due to short-term negative sentiment. Martin Braun commented on the ability to be flexible: "A good hedge fund manager is not limited by those little boxes where you need to play within a specific sandbox. You can do whatever the spirit moves you." Remember, I learned this lesson the hard way for many years as a staunch, and unsuccessful, value investor. Be open. Choose and implement the styles that achieve the greatest returns for you in the market.

VALUE TRAPS. CHEAP STOCKS CAN GET CHEAPER. THERE MUST BE A CATALYST.

Value traps are the great enemy of value investors. Mark my words: every self-described value investor has been unknowingly lured into a value trap. Boulders fall hard on their already beaten-up stock, pushing it deeper into the abyss. At that point, the value investor becomes disillusioned and swears to never again be lured into a value trap. Martin Braun, the reformed value investor, revealed his distaste for value stocks and value traps: "I've learned that being a value investor is very often a bad idea because a lot of value stocks are value traps; they lure you into the position because they're 'cheap.' But in actual fact they're cheap for a reason."

There are ways to knowingly avoid or narrowly escape value traps. Michael Sprung instructed, "Look for those companies that have deteriorating leverage or margins relative to their competitors — that's usually a sign that a value trap is going to develop." In Michael Sprung's chapter, I used RIM as an example, and showed their string of rapidly fading margins, a result of Apple's and Samsung's entry into the smartphone space. RIM was a value trap. It looked cheap at the time but, as Bill Carrigan said, "The stocks that are cheap, they just keep getting cheaper." That's not to say that all value stocks are value traps. But before you buy into a value stock, you should consider whether there is a catalyst that will eventually reverse it out of its slump. Kiki Delaney said, "We look for catalysts for change . . . a catalyst can be a management change, a new product, an acquisition, or a de-leveraging of the balance sheet."

INVESTING IN VALUE. DON'T MAKE IT YOUR ENTIRE MANTRA.

If the section above on value traps didn't scare you, then you are either a successful value investor or committed to learning more on how to effectively invest in value. A relatively small portion of my portfolio is designated to value stocks because, in my view, the ideal value opportunities are few and far between. Although, the value stocks that have worked out for me (such as my purchase of Starbucks in 2008) have *really* worked out. Starbucks is up 800% since I invested in its 2008 nadir, a time when concern was high that people would tighten their belts and spend less on premium coffee. In hindsight, that sentiment was wholly misguided, as Starbucks continues to expand worldwide and delight the millions of people who drink their coffee, tea, and cold beverages and eat their pastries and sandwiches. Below I've pulled together some key advice on value investing from some of the Market Masters:

BARRY SCHWARTZ: *"Bad things happen to good companies, but that provides you with opportunities. If they're profitable companies, they can get through it, and sentiment may revert."*

MICHAEL SPRUNG: *"The whole key to value investing is to buy often when stocks are unpopular, when people do not recognize the inherent value in those companies."*

MICHAEL SPRUNG: *"There's always the question of whether you are too early or too late [investing in a value stock], but as long as we are fairly convinced that a company has the wherewithal and good management to be a survivor, we don't mind being too early."*

GAELEN MORPHET: *"I follow the theory that all companies have an intrinsic value, and that stock prices fluctuate around that intrinsic value. I look for companies that build their intrinsic value over time."*

GAELEN MORPHET: *"I compare the intrinsic value to the current stock price, and record the difference. I want stocks that are trading below their long-term or intrinsic value."*

While value investing can work for you, I encourage investors to take a more holistic approach to the markets and marry the various investing disciplines to maximize the opportunities that you capture, invest in, and profit from in the market. As Martin Braun pointed out, "Growth is the key driver in the markets. [But] it's the combination or synthesis of all three — growth, value, and catalysts — that create, for me, the investment thesis that I'm looking for."

HOLDING PERIOD. STAY INVESTED TO BUILD WEALTH OVER THE LONG RUN.

The Market Masters I spoke with are not traders. They are investors: some for the long run and others for the short term. The majority of them believe that it's time in the market and not market timing that is the key to achieving sustainable returns. Some people, though, expect to profit in the markets on day one or shortly thereafter. As Peter Brieger explained, "People's time horizons have drastically shrunk. They want instant gratification through returns. That's not investing; it is sheer speculation. 'Slow and steady wins the day.'" Hopefully, an investor will quickly realize that generating winnings in the market requires not only effective investment strategies, but also an ample holding period for those strategies to reach fruition. Gaelen Morphet said, "You need to stay invested to build wealth over time. If you trade in and out of the market, you'll miss the best moves. You need to buy high-quality companies and let them appreciate in value over time."

Statistically, the number of up-years in the market outnumber the number of down-years, seven to three. What I firmly believe and follow, and what is one of Peter Hodson's key mantras, is that you will miss the big baggers if you sell out too early. "One of my mantras is not to sell too early. You know, you're never going to get a Google or an Apple, or any 50-bagger, if you sell too early." This also ties into Gaelen's rationale. Derek Foster added, "I look for quality. I look for a company that I feel has a sustainable competitive advantage. . . . And then after that I look for a good price. . . . Once I find that stock, ideally I want to hold that stock forever." However, also know when to sell. The flip side to the "buy and hold" argument is that nothing goes up forever, or at least to the extent that it did at the earlier rate of return. Benj Gallander said, "Nothing goes up forever. There's no stock that does that. These stocks that go up for a long time, like Apple, are a complete exception. I'm not a believer in 'buy and hold.'"

LONG AND SHORT. CAPTURE RETURNS ON BOTH SIDES OF THE MARKET.

Operating a portfolio that goes long and short on positions has a key advantage; namely, as Jason Mann explained, "because we are both long and short, we can benefit from both sides of that trade." Take caution, though, as taking on short positions can lead to more pain than taking on long positions. Norman Levine said, "If you shorted stock you would need to put up more money to cover that position that's going up. A lot of times, you'd just throw up your hands and give up. I don't short stocks anymore, but it taught me that just because something is overvalued doesn't mean it's going to soon drop. If you want to short stocks, wait until they're going down. Follow the trend going down." I do not short stocks in my own portfolio, as I have found too many wonderful long opportunities: stocks that build wealth on an annual basis. But that doesn't mean that you won't be able to capture returns on both side of the market: long and short.

PASSIVE VERSUS ACTIVE.

As in the broader investment community, the Market Masters I interviewed have differing opinions on whether one should be passive or active in the markets. Both approaches have their merits and will largely depend on your personality, commitment, and previous experience in the market, but I do believe that being active is better than being passive. Active needs to beat passive, if one is ever to beat the market. Below, I've outlined the differing thoughts on both active and passive investing.

ACTIVE

MARTIN BRAUN: *"In the mid- to late nineties and then after the crash, I couldn't just sit there and say, 'This is what I do and I can't do anything different.' Something works for a while and then it doesn't work. Then it works again, and then it doesn't. We adapt."*

DEREK FOSTER: *"Only a fool, somebody who's really stupid, would not change when the circumstances change."*

PASSIVE
RANDY CASS:
"Passive beats active. It's hard to come out ahead when you trade."

"There are very smart people who do exceptional things on a semi-frequent basis."

"Over five years, 90%-plus of funds will underperform the benchmark. If you stretch it out to 10 years it becomes an almost certainty that you underperform the benchmark."

Others may share this feeling with me: investing is fun. If I can actively beat the market then I will continue to select stocks for my portfolio, as the journey is as fun as the destination. Passive, in my opinion, is boring — pick a mutual fund, wait, cash out in 50 years, and realize that your real return was eaten away by a high MER (management expense ratio). If passive investing was my recommendation, I would not have written this book. Active investors are those who want to take greater control of their financial destiny.

VIOLENT VOLATILITY. YOU CAN CAPITALIZE ON REVERSION TO THE MEAN.
The market can be violent and volatile over short periods. You can choose to capitalize on short windows of volatility, through reversion to the mean. But, first, access the indicator that measures volatility: the VIX. As Jason Mann explained, "The VIX going from a stable state to a rising state indicates an increase in volatility. We play volatile stocks where there's a high probability of a small gain in a short period of time."

Now, how does one play volatile stocks? Mean reversion. Charles Marleau said, "At times, a company that we fundamentally like sells off aggressively. We'll accumulate that company and then short the other company that has weaker fundamentals. The company that we go long on should revert back to its average in the correlation." Here's a word of caution: unless you plan to be a professional investor, I do not recommend that you place trades in and out of the market during a volatile market. Not only can you quickly lose your money, but it can also be a hazard to your health. As Jason Mann said, "The expected volatility and drawdown is going to be in the 10% range [in the markets in any given period]." Through the period of writing and compiling this book — from January to September 2015 — the markets have been incredibly volatile. This is normal, though, at certain points in a market's run, as it adjusts to new rates, earnings growth, and so on — conditions that exist today but not forever. Remember, nothing in the markets is forever — especially not volatility. Buckle up and enjoy the ride.

RISK MANAGEMENT. IMPLEMENT CONTROLS TO LIMIT YOUR DOWNSIDE.
While much of what we've covered is on the upside potential in the markets, one should understand and implement controls that protect on the potential downside, too. As Martin Braun said, "I always think about the risk first. If I can deal with the risk side then I find that the return side tends to take care of itself." Picture it like this: You've invested $100,000 into the market. That $100,000 is your principle. You should do everything in your control to protect that initial investment. Before you take on a position, ask yourself, "How much can I lose?"

> **FRANCIS CHOU:** *"Whenever the majority of investors are purchasing securities at prices that implicitly assume that everything is perfect with the world, an economic dislocation or other shock always seems to appear out of the blue. And when that happens, investors learn, once again, that they ignore risk at their peril."*

Unfortunately, the vast majority of investment books, not to mention actual investors in the market, ignore risk management. And that's why I feel it's wise to delve deeper into risk management, based on the lessons from the Market Masters:

AVOIDANCE (PREVENTATIVE)
KIKI DELANEY: *"Some of the best calls I have made involve avoiding disasters."*

JASON MANN: *"We run money systematically. It's to avoid breaking a rule, letting our emotions get to us, buying too much of something, not selling when we should have, failing to take a capital gains loss, doubling down, and so on."*

QUICK EXIT
BILL HARRIS: *"You should draw a line under the price and say, 'We'll give it this much time at this price.' You have to be very vigilant. If the fundamentals start going wrong, the nice thing about public markets is that you have the advantage to sell a bad investment."*

DAVID BURROWS: *"We run stops on all of our positions. If something stops working, and it hits our stop, we're gone."*

FLEXIBILITY
DAVID BURROWS: *"When we start to see deterioration in breadth, or volume, whether or not the fundamental data's still great, it's time for us to start to reduce our weight."*

SOM SEIF: *"When markets are strong, we want to take on risk. When markets are weak, we want to take risk off the table. We use the momentum signals to basically tell us when we want more or less market exposure."*

OPTIONS PROTECTION
JASON DONVILLE: *"Our biggest tool for risk mitigation right now though is put options on the TSX. That's an insurance policy. That won't protect me from a 30% correction but it should protect me from a 10% correction."*

CASH CUSHION
BILL HARRIS: *"We have a 20% insurance policy [i.e., cash] inside the portfolio at any one time. So it's always a drag on performance, but then we have the ability to react at whatever that black swan event is, because we're going to get impacted by events in different markets at different times."*

BEN GALLANDER: *"I always have cash on the sidelines. It's good to have for rainy days."*

TIME

BILL HARRIS: *"We have a 30-year time horizon. You can double your money, then double it again, and double that again. But you need to give yourself the highest probability that it actually happens."*

PROBABILITY. ACCEPT THAT YOU CAN'T BE PERFECT IN THE MARKET.

It's inevitable: regardless of how effective your risk management controls are, some of the holdings in your portfolio will take a hit from time to time; either permanent capital loss or short-term damage. But don't let this truism get you down. All of the Market Masters have faced challenges in the market throughout their career, and some losses to prove it. After all, they're human. As Michael Sprung (and others) said, a lot of investing is winning the loser's game. "You just try to make fewer mistakes than your competitors. And as long as your winners outweigh your losers, you're doing well." Martin Braun added, "I figure my upside is at least three to one of my downside. That's all you want to do when you put together a portfolio: make sure the ratio of the upside to the downside is in your favour." Interestingly, Martin Ferguson, a high achiever throughout school who always strived for the best possible grades, quickly realized that no one but god himself could post a perfect track record in the market. It's impossible. "In this industry, there's no such thing as perfection." In fact, "if you're a genius in our business, you're right 60% of the time," as Norman Levine said. So, that means that if your portfolio consists of 40% losers and 60% winners in any given year, that's okay, as long as your winners outsize and surpass your losers in the long run.

STOCKS

PRICE-TO-EARNINGS RATIO (P/E).
IT'S JUST ONE METRIC IN YOUR TOOLBELT.

For many investors, the famous P/E (price to earnings) indicator is the first, and sometimes only, indicator that is referenced to glean a stock's valuation. However, P/E, which is calculated by dividing a stock's price by its current earnings, is a lagging indicator. Why? P/E only accounts for the current valuation of a stock. It does not take into account the future potential in a stock's valuation. That is why I like to use the forward P/E to valuate a stock, as it takes into account future earnings. Forward P/E is calculated by dividing a stock's price by its forecasted earnings: next year's earnings. Imagine passing up on a stock because you decide that 20 P/E is too high while, unbeknownst to you, the forward P/E is 13 because of high earnings forecasts that are likely to materialize, and that are supported not only by analysts but by the company's management team in their forward guidance estimates. Cameron Winser explained, "Some people would say that using trailing earnings in a valuation is like trying to drive a car while looking in the rear-view mirror. Use the forward P/E rather than current P/E." Martin Ferguson added, "We're not looking at today's P/E; we're looking at its internal rate of return. When you conduct a discounted cash flow analysis on a company, you figure out what cash flows it will generate into the future." But, it is also true that to base an investment decision on P/E, or forward P/E, alone, is much too simplistic. You must use the other financial metrics, combined with P/E, to best serve your security selection. And while I prefer forward P/E over P/E, only about one-third of all stocks will have a forward earnings estimate available.

BOOK VALUE. A COMPANY'S WORTH ON ITS
BALANCE SHEET IS NOT THE TELL-ALL.

Book value, or book value per share, can be a treacherous metric if one doesn't look further into what actually underlies book value on a case by case basis. As Francis Chou explained, "Most investors invest in terms of premium or discount to book value. That is a serious mistake. Let's say the year was 2006. You examine the loan portfolio [of a bank] and see all the junk there. As a result, you wouldn't touch a U.S. bank with a barge pole." So, while a 0.5 book value per share may at first lead you to believe that a stock is undervalued, you need to understand that there may exist no value at all and that the market is adequately pricing the company at 0.5 book value, or else it would be higher. But then Francis goes on to explain, for the book value that is not merely a mirage, "I'm trying to buy 80 cents for 40 cents." Also, a company that has posted growth in *good* book value over a long period of time can be an indicator of a sustainable business. As Jason Donville said, "Measuring growth in terms of . . . book value per share is a better methodological way than measuring growth in terms of earnings per share."

There's another, simple way, to valuate a company. Ask yourself, "If I were to buy this company, how much would I pay?" as Francis Chou said. Is that figure, the price *you* would pay for the whole company, higher or lower than its market capitalization? If higher, then consider an investment in that stock, regardless of whether it's above or below the book value. Because, book value, the company's worth on its balance sheet (Assets less Liabilities), is not the tell all of a company's worth.

COMPETITIVELY ADVANTAGED LEADERS.
LEADING RETURNS IN THE MARKET.

It's a rewarding practice to invest in leaders, whether that be anywhere in the market or in a select industry. Leaders usually benefit from less competition, higher margins, and enduring brands, all of which deliver seemingly guaranteed streams of clients, profits, and returns. And as Derek Foster said, "the market leader usually stays the market leader for many years." Leaders possess what's called "competitive advantage" or a "moat," two interchangeable terms used by the Market Masters throughout. What constitutes a competitive advantage or moat? Bill Ackman explained, "The moat is usually created by brands, unique assets, long-term contracts, market position, or perhaps some combination of all of these factors." Derek Foster said, "I look for a moat: a reason that the company can continue to make obscene profits for years into the future. Unfortunately, there's not many of those companies out there. In the world there's probably a hundred or even less than that." There are few leaders. For the most part, you must go to the TSX 60 (in Canada), the Dow 30 (in the U.S.), and the Stoxx 50 (in Europe) to find them. But you should widen your scope to the entire market to capture all leaders. While leaders are generally those large-cap or mid-cap companies, they can also be found in the small-cap or mid-cap segment of the market. For example, in Canada, Tweed, Spin Master Toys, and Shopify benefit from virtually no competition, making them leaders in consumer marijuana, children's toys, and e-commerce solutions. In addition, you can profit immensely with these smaller leaders as they grow on the market, and potentially reach large-cap status. It's important to understand, though, that when an acknowledged leader, bid up to a high price, becomes a large-cap, it will likely deliver lower appreciation in the future. So, you shouldn't limit your portfolio to the largest stocks with the biggest moats, except if you buy some at a time when there are significant uncertainties and doubts about the company, or earnings have taken a dip, and the price is off.

PROFIT. COMPANIES YOU INVEST IN SHOULD ACTUALLY BE PROFITABLE.

What I find most troubling, because it's so common, is that most new investors invest sometimes in stocks that are not generating positive net income. Those stocks, notoriously most common in the technology and biotech sectors, have never generated profit, and likely *never will*. All I need to do is show those new investors the income statement, point them to the net income line, and watch them gasp as they discover that their "hot" concept company is in the red; it's not making any money at all. First and foremost, the stocks you invest in should actually be profitable, or at least, will soon be profitable. Their income statements should be in the black. As Peter Brieger said, "Earnings' growth . . . powers markets upward."

> **BARRY SCHWARTZ (REITERATING A MANTRA TOLD BY DAVID BASKIN):** *"We don't buy Nortel for our clients because it's not profitable. We stick to profitable companies."*

DEBT. AVOID COMPANIES WITH TOO MUCH BAGGAGE.

Just like in your own finances, companies that have too much debt on their balance sheets will struggle, if not now, then further down the road, if their ability to service that debt suffers. Benj Gallander said, "I've learned that debt is a killer in many situations, so if you can invest in companies that have very nominal or no debt, that helps companies survive during the hard times." For example, Barrick Gold, during this commodity bear market, has had to aggressively de-leverage its balance sheet from under-performing assets in order to bolster its cash reserves and pay down debt. Why? Not only to ride out the current low gold price environment, but also to be on firm footing when the cycle resumes, so that it can grow again. That's why I use the debt-to-equity ratio (D/E) to assess a company's debt level, and to determine when there's an unsustainable amount of debt on its balance sheet. D/E that is greater than 1 is not sustainable in my opinion. An investor should avoid too much debt, and invest only in companies with nominal or no debt. An ideal company should be able to finance expansion of operations through their free cash flow, rather than through debt, as financing costs can cut into returns.

BREAKUP VALUE. SOMETIMES THE PARTS CAN BE GREATER THAN THE SUM.

Like human relationships, not all companies stay whole forever. Perhaps it just so happens that their parts are greater than their sum. While breaking up is hard to do, it is sometimes for the better. As Bill Ackman explained, "If there's one business making $2 billion and another business, or another subsidiary, losing $1 billion, people will look at it and say, 'Oh, it's got $1 billion dollars of earnings.' But that's not the right way to think about it." If you can identify that a company's parts are greater than its sum, you may have caught on to a future spinoff opportunity, such as Tim Hortons spinoff from Wendy's, which finally unlocked significant value for Tim Hortons, and its sole shareholders. As its own separate entity on the stock exchange, Tim Hortons flourished with expanded ownership and increased support from institutions and analysts. You can also capitalize long into the post-breakup. For example, spinoffs will often outperform their parent companies on the exchange, in the long run, years after the break-up, and even outperform the market.

OPERATIONAL EFFICIENCY. INVEST IN HIGH ROE AND ROIC ACHIEVERS.

Operational efficiency is a company's ability to "either maintain . . . or enhance their rate of return when they reinvest their earnings," as Bill Harris said. In my view, and that of many of the Market Masters, both return on equity (ROE) and return on invested capital (ROIC) are the best financial ratios to measure operational efficiency. The two Market Masters that immediately come to mind for both financial ratios are Jason Donville (ROE) and Martin Ferguson (ROIC).

> ### JASON DONVILLE ON RETURN ON EQUITY (ROE):
> *"First we look for companies with ROE greater or equal to 20%. Second, we look for companies in that high-ROE group that are sustainable based on the competitiveness of their products."*

"Return on equity can be broken down into three pieces through DuPont analysis. You've got good ROE and bad ROE. We want to make sure that the ROE is good ROE."

"You can fake good ROE in one year. But to achieve high ROE seven years in a row is tough. When I see a company that has achieved an ROE of 23, 22, 23, 24, 23, 22, over the past seven years, without even knowing what industry they're in, I go, 'Wow! There's something in place here.'"

MARTIN FERGUSON ON RETURN ON INVESTED CAPITAL (ROIC):
"We focus on companies that can generate a return on invested capital greater than their cost of capital over time. Companies that create cash flow that in turn generate wealth."

"Cost of capital is determined by the risk of the company. The higher the risk, the higher the cost of capital."

Investing in only those companies with seven-year ROEs of 20% and above has proven an incredibly effective and successful practice for Jason Donville. By contrast, when asked which was the best measure of operational efficiency, Martin Ferguson said, "ROIC," because, "ROIC takes into account the fact that companies can use debt and it also gives an idea of the overall return of the business rather than the equity." Paul Harris echoed that sentiment, when they warned to "be cognizant of companies that enhance their rates of return through acquisition strategies or financial engineering." Though, to be clear, Jason Donville is wholly aware of debt, as he alludes to the use of DuPont analysis to further explore the makeup of ROE.

FREE CASH FLOW IS KING. CASH SHOULD BE INVESTED TO ENHANCE VALUE FOR SHAREHOLDERS.
Remember, strong free cash flow is a telling indicator of a company's financial performance. Free cash flow is operating cash flow less capital expenditures, representing the cash a company generates after incurring the capital expenditure to maintain or expand its asset base. Most importantly, free cash flow allows a company to capitalize on opportunities that

enhance value for its shareholders; for example, accretive acquisitions that increase both the top and bottom lines.

As you recall, one of the biggest proponents of free cash flow out of all the Market Masters was Barry Schwartz. When I read through Barry's transcript well after the interview, I counted how many times he said "free cash flow." It appeared in the interview 23 times. It was like that other time I counted another F-word in the movie *Scarface*.

Barry is absolutely right. Strong free cash flow is crucial.

"When companies generate free cash flow, and a high amount of free cash flow, good things happen. If you shoot a bazooka, you're going to blow something up. It's the same effect with free cash flow. I've never made a bad decision by buying into a company paying 8% or 9% free cash flow yield or higher." To calculate free cash flow yield, divide a company's free cash flow by its market capitalization (free cash flow yield = free cash flow / market capitalization). Others shared Barry's sentiment on the importance of free cash flow. Bill Harris said, "You need 8% to 12% free cash flow yield, and you can get that if you're super patient." Charles Marleau added, "What I'm really after is companies that can generate a tremendous amount of cash and grow that cash flow year after year." Unfortunately, there can be a pitfall to having so much free cash flow: some companies do not use their cash wisely. "If [management is] not using that cash flow wisely, putting it to low return or inefficient uses, then they can destroy capital so quickly," said Martin Ferguson. This then takes us into our next section, which emphasizes the need for good management.

ABLE MANAGEMENT AND GOOD CAPITAL ALLOCATION. DEMAND SMART DEPLOYMENT OF CAPITAL THAT COMPOUNDS RETURNS.

Able management and good capital allocation are one and the same. Able managers must by definition be good capital allocators, which means they deliver excellent returns for shareholders on a long-term compounded basis. So, before you invest in a company, remember to assess the efficacy of its management team. As Paul Harris pointed out, "Bad people and bad managers keep doing bad things. Good people and good managers generally keep doing good things. It's a very simple concept." Jason Donville added, "I'm buying awesome companies and just hoping that they'll be awesome forever. I get to hang out with the really great CEOs all the time as opposed to having argumentative discussions with mediocre CEOs who aren't doing a very good job running their companies."

The following are other insights from the Market Masters to help you invest in only those companies with the most able management teams who possess the best capital allocation skills.

JEFF STACEY: *"Read the letter to shareholders in the annual report. Is management talking to you like an owner, or does it seem like it's written by some PR person who really doesn't know what the business is about?"*

FRANCIS CHOU: *"I don't want to chase businesses where management is making decisions that don't make economic sense."*

MARTIN BRAUN: *"It takes a certain skill to be able to execute. It's one thing to say, 'I'm going to do this,' and it's another to actually do it. The stocks that I didn't make money on or I lost money on was because I misjudged management."*

JASON DONVILLE: *"Most of the companies we own have people running them that are very good capital allocators. Because if you can keep your ROE over 20% year after year, you almost by definition are a good allocator."*

RYAZ SHARIFF: *"We'd rather invest in exceptional management teams than in ordinary ones. Businesses always have hiccups but management teams that are exceptional entrepreneurs always figure a way around those issues to create value."*

MARTIN FERGUSON: *"Management has to allocate capital, grow revenue, control cost, and control risk: four jobs."*

While management doesn't necessarily need to have a stake in the businesses they run, I have found that the most successful companies in my portfolio are run by high-ownership management. Whether they are family businesses or not, there's an added self-interest in those management teams who own a stake in the company, as their performance, and smart capital allocation, can further enrich them through their shares rising in the market. Bill Harris said, "It's nice to know that when you invest in those stocks you're 100% aligned with the owners and management."

PRICING POWER. RAISING PRICES TO INCREASE PROFITS IS A PRIVILEGE.

Companies that have pricing power are those that often also enjoy an enduring competitive advantage; if they didn't, they would very quickly price themselves out of the market. Take for example Tim Hortons, which is now owned by Restaurant Brands International. When Tim Hortons raises its coffee price by 10 cents, do Tim's coffee drinkers go across the street to a different coffee shop? No. Do they reduce their coffee consumption? No. The value in that loyalty is that a company such as Tim Hortons can increase profits year after year by simply raising their coffee prices. Tim Hortons can also implement cost efficiencies or increase volume to maximize profit, but the ability to increase prices without an adverse impact to the company is indicative of a competitively advantaged company. In economic terms, that resiliency of demand in relation to pricing is what's referred to as inelastic demand.

> **BARRY SCHWARTZ:** *"If you have control over your pricing, too, then you can either benefit when input costs go down or when prices go up. Warren Buffett said something along the lines of, 'If you have to have a meeting before you go out and raise your prices 10%, that's not the type of business I want to be in.'"*

Resource companies, on the other hand, do not have pricing power. Those companies are "price takers," meaning they must sell their product at the market price, which is not determined by them. For example, before the recent oil crash (2014–2015), oil producers could pump oil out of the ground and then sell it for $110, which was the prevailing crude oil market price. But then after the oil crash, those same oil producers sold that same oil for $45 (as of September 2015). Imagine the hit to their bottom line. The costs to pump oil remained the same while the prices at which they could sell that oil dropped below break-even levels. As Martin Ferguson reaffirmed, "Commodity companies are riskier. They are price takers. They sell a commodity. Commodity means undifferentiated product. So, yes, they lack that pricing power."

SHARE BUY-BACKS. A COST-EFFECTIVE WAY
TO IMPROVE EARNINGS-PER-SHARE.

In a perfect world, a company would only buy back its shares (and then cancel them) if management decided that its shares were cheap on the market. Often companies will buy back shares at high share prices, which, it may be argued, is at a disadvantage to shareholders, because that money could have been used in other ways such as capital allocation or dividend increases. There's a prevailing reason, though, for buying back shares, even at higher prices on the market. When companies buy back shares they effectively decrease their total common share count. As a result, their earnings per share (EPS) rises, as the denominator (common shares outstanding) drops. So what? I've seen cases where companies release an annual financial statement and while their net income shows a decrease, their EPS shows an increase.

This is clever financial engineering, which is why you must delve into income statements to verify that the following has occurred in the company: a) an increase in net income *and* b) an increase in EPS. Share buy-backs are not inherently bad if management has the right intentions: buying back shares at reasonable prices, and not trying to significantly "dress up" financial results, as in the previous example. Especially in this low-rate, cheap-debt, low-growth environment, management may find that share buy-backs are cost-effective ways to slightly improve their financial statements, specifically their earnings per share, and to appease the investment community.

KIKI DELANEY: *"I think companies should buy their stock back when it is fundamentally cheap. Not every month, or every year. I find it troubling that companies have nothing better to do with their cash."*

INDUSTRIES. YOU CAN INVEST IN INDUSTRIES THAT ARE
BENEFICIARIES OF THE PREVAILING ECONOMY.

There are two ways to invest directly into specific industries on the market. Both with the goal to capitalize on prevailing economic conditions that will benefit those industries. You can employ a top-down approach where you invest in industry-centric ETFs or a basket of stocks. Or you can employ a bottom-up approach where you invest only in those leaders, or those likely top beneficiaries, within each industry. For example, in 2015, with a lower CAD/USD exchange, Canadian manufacturing exports are leading beneficiaries, as those goods are now cheaper to purchase from foreigners. I can either invest in a Canadian manufacturing ETF or basket of stocks (top-down), or I can hand-pick the industry leaders. Using insights from the Market Masters, we'll continue to explore each approach to investing in industries.

TOP-DOWN APPROACH TO INDUSTRIES

CHARLES MARLEAU: *"The index is broken up into industries. Our goal on the macro side is to identify which industry in the index will outperform in upcoming years."*

PETER HODSON: *"Sometimes it doesn't even matter how good of a company you are; if you're in the right sector, you're automatically hot."*

JASON DONVILLE: *"Think about the market as a baseball game. Let's say there's nine innings in the game. We're now six years into this bull market. You never know until it's over, but we're probably in the seventh or eighth or ninth inning of the baseball game. That's usually a bad time to own financials."*

BOTTOM-UP APPROACH TO INDUSTRIES

PAUL BRIEGER: *"Once I had decided that I liked an industry, I focused on the leaders."*

PAUL HARRIS, PAUL GARDNER, AND BILL HARRIS: *"If we need to have some exposure to a sector, then we try to find the best in class and just immunize our risk."*

KIKI DELANEY: *"If the industry fundamentals are strong and the valuations are appealing, then it makes sense to buy more than one company in the sector."*

ASSETS. WHAT A COMPANY OWNS SHOULD MAKE THEM MONEY.

All companies have assets, which should always be greater than their liabilities. Increasingly, though, less value is placed on tangible or physical assets in our modern economy. For example, Jeff Stacey explained, "The asset-light company is generating these recurring revenues. That's a classic example of a business that from a balance sheet point of view doesn't really have much in the way of assets, but it has enormous economic value." Think about asset-light companies inherent in our economy: technology, consumer, service, healthcare, consulting, and so on. Peter Brieger explains, "I think book value matters less. . . . It's more about what the assets produce that actually matters." The "old-age" economy companies, such as those in resources, suffer constant asset depletion rather than enjoy recuring income production. Ryaz Shariff said, "One of the major challenges of a large company that's pressured to grow is the replacement of that declining asset base. . . . If management creates value from efficient capital allocation, the asset becomes attractive for larger companies with depleting asset bases to consolidate, at premium values." I prefer to invest in more asset-light companies, where less value is derived from tangible or hard assets, and more emphasis is given to the higher return on a lower cost asset base inherent in a company like Dollarama.

DIVIDENDS: SIZE DOESN'T MATTER. GROWTH MATTERS.

Dividends are an essential component to the total return some investors generate in their portfolio. Total return = capital gains (when a stock goes up) + dividend income (what a company pays out). Peter Brieger demonstrated, "Long-term stock returns were between 6% and 8% but half of that return came from dividends and their growth." I want to warn you, however — don't chase yield. That is, don't invest in those companies with the highest yields on the broader market (although the BTSX model is okay, as TSX constituents are some of the most sustainable companies on the exchange). High-dividend yields (above 5%) on stocks, unless they're a REIT (Real Estate Investment Trust), are a warning sign to investors. The greater than 5% dividend yield can indicate a future dividend payout cut, that the company is in dire straits or a combination of both of those factors. As Charles Marleau adds, "We also make sure that the company can sustainably pay that dividend or distribution. They must have a very strong balance sheet."

I am a firm believer, as are many of the Market Masters, in investing in companies with low but growing dividend yields. Remember, size doesn't matter: growth matters. While a lower dividend yield (less than 5%) won't stuff your wallet with cash, you can be assured (if you have validated with management's actual actions) that those lower yielding companies are allocating capital back into the business to perpetuate future run-ups in the stock price — capital gains. Most people who have invested in very high-dividend-yield companies, including me in the early years, have been badly burned. When a company slashes its dividend, the stock price free-falls downward, too — sometimes never to return, as many investors will just invest in a stock for its high yield, and immediately dump it if the high yield vanishes.

> **DEREK FOSTER:** *"Companies that grow their dividends are vastly superior to companies with high-dividend yields. Don't get sucked into the 8% yield. Buy the 1% yield that's going to go to 2%, 3%, 4%, 5%."*

ANALYST EXPECTATIONS. THE MARKET PLACES A LOT OF WEIGHT INTO WHAT ANALYSTS SAY.

Consensus analyst expectations are a funny thing. They are often taken very seriously by the market. For example, if Company A's profits increase 45%, but a consensus of analysts expected a 50% increase, the stock can drop. Why? Because, even though the profit increase (45%) set a record for the company, it missed the street's 50% expectation by 5%. "When everybody's playing the same stocks and the expectations are there, it's difficult for companies to always meet investors' expectations, and that's where the volatility comes from. A great deal of investing is about meeting or exceeding expectations," Gaelen Morphet explained. This is why, as we've discussed, one should ignore short-term market volatility and instead focus on actual results and the long-term trajectory of companies (a 45% profit increase is excellent in my books). You could also choose to invest in companies with little or no analyst coverage. Those companies will most likely reside in the small- to mid-cap segment of the market. "There are always opportunities in companies that don't have analyst coverage or are neglected or are smaller ideas," as Barry Schwartz explained.

The reverse can also be true: earnings surprises. As Martin Braun explained, "If the market was paying for 75 cents and the company makes

90 cents, then 'Oh, the market's happy!' and the stock goes up.'" For the most part, you need to cope with the existence of analyst expectations in the market. They will be a permanent overhanging factor. "In a market, most stocks are based on people's estimates of next year's earnings; analysts' estimates," as Bill Ackman explained.

> CAMERON WINSER: *"We look for earnings surprises, where management is able to beat analysts' earnings consensus on a consistent basis. Either management is able to manage the street's expectations very well or they're actually just able to execute very well."*

MULTIPLE EXPANSION. THE MARKET APPLIES PREMIUMS TO STOCKS THAT CAN BE GREATER THAN THEIR INTERNAL RATES OF RETURN.

Value investors and growth investors will likely be at odds with regards to the concept of multiple expansion. But I do find that stocks will grow at a greater exponential rate than their internal rate of return. Why? The market applies premiums to stocks, and more so to quality or popular stocks. Beware, though, of the irrational multiple expansions where stocks, such as those with no earnings, are run up to lofty highs. That's simply the reality that you need to trade around to avoid excessive valuations. David Burrows said, "In a bull market, investors say, 'Earnings are growing at 6%, so how can the market be going up 15%? That's irrational.' Well that's multiple expansion. You want to stay in a position so long as the multiple grows and as long as the earnings grow."

TECHNICALITIES. USE TECHNICAL INDICATORS TO HELP VALIDATE YOUR STOCK SELECTION.

While Cameron Winser said, "Technical analysis and charting are the primary driver in a lot of stocks." I — like Cameron — believe that the stock selection process should include fundamental analysis, too. As I've said, stock selection is very much a multi-disciplinary practice. Understand these six technical indicators, but don't base your investment decisions solely on them.

PRICE MOMENTUM

> JASON MANN: *"The classic definition of momentum is 12-month rolling*

returns. I ask, 'What has this stock done over the last 12 months, relative to all the other stocks in the index?' . . . [We'll] score a stock relative to how well it's done on that measure. . . . We want to buy the stocks that have the best price momentum."

BILL CARRIGAN: *All a technician wants to know [on the trend line] is, is it going up [or] is it going down?"*

RELATIVE STRENGTH
CAMERON WINSER: *"[We] flip through a bunch of the stocks to see which ones appear technically stronger, which could be based on relative strength to their benchmark or index. . . . If Royal Bank is up 10%, but the financial sector is up 30%, then you picked a significant underperformer."*

NEW 52-WEEK HIGHS
PETER HODSON: *"One of my best techniques to finding a great stock is to just look at new highs. When you see a new high, ask yourself, 'Why is that a new high and what's the deal with that?'"*

BOTTOM-OUTS AND TURNAROUNDS
NORMAN LEVINE: *"I would rather see commodities stop going down, probably tread water for a long time, or even form a V, and then buy them when they're starting to go up again."*

DAVID BURROWS: *"I use something called point-and-figure price charts. They're quantitative in nature. Higher highs and higher lows — that's an uptrend, and lower highs and lower lows — that's a downtrend."*

CAMERON WINSER: *"I look at both support levels and overhead resistance on the chart. Further, I focus in on trend lines that have been breached on the chart."*

MOVING AVERAGES (REVERSION TO MEAN)
CAMERON WINSER: *"Some stocks go through cycles when they underperform for a while. But then when you overlay a moving average, you can sometimes pick stocks up at the point in which sentiment has changed for the better."*

ACCUMULATION DISTRIBUTION

BILL CARRIGAN: *"If a stock's going sideways, but the accumulation distribution lines are still slightly rising, that tells me that there's smart money buying the stock."*

▲

ACKNOWLEDGEMENTS

▼

Market Masters was a journey made possible by many people. I am grateful for everyone. Thank you.

All 28 Market Masters — thank you for agreeing to meet me for interviews and believing in my project. I learned so much from all of you. This project literally could not have been possible without your open and expert input on the markets.

Elena — you very quickly but accurately transcribed all of the interviews in this book. This was a very significant job: 150,000+ words.

Jack David and David Caron — you believed in me and in *Market Masters*, and took a leap of faith on a first-time published author to get *Market Masters* into the hands of investors across Canada.

Morad Moazami— your suggestions through the initial stages of the manuscript helped me to improve *Market Masters*, from the pre-interview lessons to the expansive conclusion (Collection of Master Keys).

Ellen Roseman — you believed in me and my self-published book, *Lessons from the Successful Investor*, in 2010, and that gave me the confidence years later in 2015 to write *Market Masters*.

John P. Reese — you took the time from your busy schedule to provide a succinct expert review of *Market Masters*. Your advice helped me to improve the validity and accuracy of my own investment ideas.

Catherine London — your eye for detail is much more acute than mine. During the copy edit process, you helped me strive for perfection in my writing. *Market Masters* is a smoother read because of you.

Michael Holmes — your sobering comments, especially about my overuse of waffle words, helped me tighten my writing throughout the book to make it a more enjoyable and less cumbersome read.

Crissy Calhoun, Rachel Ironstone, Erin Creasey, Sam Dobson, and Sarah Dunn at ECW Press — you all made sure that *Market Masters* successfully launched across Canada, getting the book in the hands of as many readers as possible.

APPENDIX

▲

MY INVESTMENT STORY

▼

I ran a paper route in my hometown of Mississauga by the time I was 12. That paper route grew, and so did my weekly paycheque. My mother recommended that I invest the proceeds of those paper route cheques into bonds, so I did, with every month's accumulated savings. After I progressed from that paper route job to other odd jobs throughout high school, my thirst grew for a higher return than my bonds' 4% interest. In my high school's grade 10 business class we learned about the stock market by picking just one stock out of the *Toronto Star*'s business section and tracking it through the semester. My stock pick: Forzani Group Ltd., a sports apparel company. Forzani Group (FGL) would languish throughout the semester around $18. Ultimately, I would end that stock-picking assignment with a zero-growth stock.

Later in high school, I became the branch manager of the Investors of Tomorrow group, and also participated in its country-wide competition. I went on to win that competition as the number-one stock-picker in the country by placing a large bet on Elan Corporation, a pharmaceutical stock that was severely beaten down after a fatality caused by its drug. Months later, Elan recovered, netting me close to a 300% return. Upon entering university, I cashed out my bonds, combined those proceeds with my savings, and then opened a brokerage account. I invested in just five stocks to start: Suncor, Petro-Canada, RIM, RBC, and Best Buy, but through university, and eventually through my career, my equity portfolio transformed based on my ever-evolving investment philosophy. That evolution as an investor was tumultuous at times, as I changed from high growth to deep-value to passive.

Finally, my investment philosophy settled into what I call "growth at a reasonable price through market-leading global consumer franchise companies," combined with investing in strong capital allocators, which I discovered by delving into companies' long-term return on equity (ROE), return on invested capital (ROIC), and profit margin track record. My portfolio has since generated 13% in annualized returns since inception (2005). In 2010, at the age of 23, I self-published my first book, *Lessons from the Successful Investor*, which chronicled all that I had learned from the stock market up until that time. That book went on to sell just over 3,500 copies: a satisfying return for a young author's first book.

Initially, downloads of the ebook trickled in. However, my value investing speaking appearance at the University of Toronto, coupled with select media coverage, catapulted *Lessons from the Successful Investor* to the top of major digital bookstores. At that point, downloads started to pour in, and I began to receive wonderful feedback from readers: aspiring investors around the world. A reader review from a gentleman based in Portland, Oregon, said, "I have the Ben Graham book but you have made it make sense." Benjamin Graham is the father of value investing, the author of *The Intelligent Investor*, and one of my investing idols. That review was a turning point for me. I started touring Canadian universities and spreading the 85 investing lessons from *Lessons from the Successful Investor*.

My personal objective, now that I have finished the *Market Masters* journey, is to beat the market, grow my capital, and then eventually achieve financial independence. By growing your capital in the markets you can pursue and achieve what you want. Isn't that the goal in life's journey? Choice.

ROBIN R. SPEZIALE

▲

FINANCIAL RATIOS

▼

STOCK VALUATION

- **Price/Earnings Ratio (P/E)** = *Stock Price / Earnings Per Share (EPS1)*
  - › Ideal Threshold: 5–30 P/E
- **Forward Price/Earnings Ratio (Forward P/E)** = *Stock Price / Expected Earnings per Share*
  - › Ideal Threshold: 5–20 Forward P/E
- **Price/Sales Ratio (P/S)** = *Stock Price / Sales per Share (SPS²)*
  - › Ideal Threshold: 0.5–5 P/S
- **Price/Cash Flow Ratio (P/CF)** = *Stock Price / Cash Flow per Share (CFPS³)*
  - › Ideal Threshold: 5–15 P/CF
- **Price/Book Ratio (P/B)** = *Stock Price / Book Value per Share (BVPS⁴)*
  - › Ideal Threshold: 0.5–3 P/B
- **Dividend Yield** = *Annual Dividend / Stock Price*
  - › Ideal Threshold: 0.5–5% Yield
- **Free Cash Flow Yield** = *Free Cash Flow per Share / Stock Price*
  - › Ideal Threshold: 5–10% FCF Yield

1. *EPS* = Net Income / Shares Outstanding
2. *SPS* = Revenue / Shares Outstanding
3. *CFPS* = Operating Cash Flow / Shares Outstanding
4. *BVPS* = Shareholders' Equity / Shares Outstanding

BUSINESS VALUATION

- **Return on Equity (ROE)** = *Net Income / Shareholders' Equity*
  - › Ideal Threshold: 15%–50% ROE
- **Return on Invested Capital (ROIC)** = *(Net Income – Dividends) / (Long-Term Debt + Shareholders' Equity)*
  - › Ideal Threshold: 10%–35% ROIC
- **Return on Assets (ROA)** = *Net Income / Total Assets*
  - › Ideal Threshold: 10%–35% ROA
- **Current Ratio** = *Current Assets / Current Liabilities*
  - › Ideal Threshold: 1.5–5 Current Ratio
- **Net Profit Margin** = *Net Income / Revenue*
  - › Ideal Threshold: 5%–30% Net Profit Margin
- **Debt/Equity Ratio (D/E)** = *Total Liabilities / Shareholders' Equity*
  - › Ideal Threshold: D/E 0–1

ADVANCED VALUATION

Internal Cost of Capital

$$R_c = r_f + (r_m - r_f)$$

Where:

- › R_c = required rate of return on capital | r_f = risk-free rate | r_m = market rate | $r_m - r_f$ = market risk premium

Dividend Discount Model (DDM)

Value of a stock = Next Year's Dividend per Share / (Discount Rate – Dividend Growth Rate)

Discount rate = required rate of return

Discounted Cash Flow Model (DCF)

DCF = Cash Flow$_{Yr1}$ / (1 + discount rate)1 + Cash Flow$_{Yr2}$ / (1 + discount rate)2 . . .

ONLINE RESOURCES

STOCK ANALYSIS
Google Finance
Morningstar
Finviz
StockCharts
TMX Money

NEWS
BNN
Bloomberg
Reuters
MarketWatch
Financial Times

RESEARCH
WhaleWisdom
Investopedia

FINANCIAL STATEMENTS
SEDAR
Companies' websites

OPINIONS
StockChase
StockHouse

▲

RECOMMENDED READING

▼

Buffettology, Mary Buffett and David Clark
Common Stocks and Uncommon Profits, Philip Fisher
The Essays of Warren Buffett, Lawrence A. Cunningham
The Intelligent Investor, Benjamin Graham
The Investment Zoo, Stephen Jarislowsky
Lessons from the Successful Investor, Robin R. Speziale
Market Wizards, Jack D. Schwager
The Money Masters, John Train
One Up on Wall Street, Peter Lynch
Poor Charlie's Almanack: The Wit and Wisdom of Charles T. Munger,
    Peter D. Kaufman
A Random Walk Down Wall Street, Burton Malkiel
The Richest Man in Babylon, George S. Clason
The Snowball, Alice Shroeder
Stocks for the Long Run, Jeremy Siegel
Super Stocks, Ken Fisher

▲

ABOUT THE AUTHOR

▼

Robin R. Speziale was born in Mississauga and now lives in downtown Toronto. His prime passion in life is investing in the markets, an ever-evolving, arguably "living" organism that challenges him like no other outlet or pursuit. Robin graduated from the University of Waterloo in 2010. Upon graduation, he self-published his first book, *Lessons From the Successful Investor*, which contains 85 important investment lessons that he learned throughout his own investment trials, tribulations, and winnings in the markets.

GET IN TOUCH

Robin would like to hear from you — whatever is on your mind. And maybe, if you're in or around Toronto, he can meet up with you for a coffee (or tea).

Email: r.speziale@gmail.com
Twitter: @robinspeziale
Website: RobinRSpeziale.com

GLOSSARY

A

ABSOLUTE RETURN: a measure of performance; does not compare to a benchmark such as the S&P TSX.

ACCUMULATION DISTRIBUTION: an indicator that gauges supply and demand based on volume activity.

ACQUISITION: when a company acquires the controlling interest in another company.

ACTIVE INVESTING: an investment approach that usually equates to more portfolio turnover. Opposite of "passive."

ACTIVIST INVESTOR: an investor who takes a stake in a business to make changes at board, management, and operation levels to improve shareholder return.

ALGORITHM: algorithmic trading or "algos" is used by larger institutions to decide the pricing, timing, and quantity of stock orders.

ALPHA: the amount by which an investor's performance exceeds his or her benchmark.

ANALYST: a financial professional who covers certain indexes, sectors, and/or stocks, and makes recommendations on those securities.

ANCHOR/ANCHORING: events or values known to investors. Investors sometimes base decisions on erroneous anchors because they are familiar.

ANNUAL REPORT: a financial account sent on an annual basis to shareholders.

ANNUAL RETURN: an account showing the performance of a company, stock, or portfolio, on an annual basis.

APPRECIATION: a stock price increase or an asset value increase.

ARBITRAGE: the various strategies used in the markets to exploit discrepancies in price (e.g., risk arbitrage).

ASSETS: what a firm or individual owns (e.g., buildings, inventory, and brands).

ASSET ALLOCATION: the percentage of capital that you invest into various asset classes (stocks, bonds, etc.). Your asset allocation is based on a variety of factors such as return objectives, risk tolerance, and income needs.

ATTRIBUTION ANALYSIS: breakdown to assess the investment efficiency or capability of a portfolio manager and his/her fund.

B

BAGGER: when an investor hits it out of the park on a stock. A "10-bagger" would mean that your stock increased 10-fold or 1000% since initial investment. The phrase was originally coined by Peter Lynch.

BALANCE SHEET: a component of the financial statement that shows a company's financials at a point in time (e.g., Q2 F2015: second quarter, 2015). Main sections are Assets, Liabilities, and Shareholders' Equity.

BARGAIN: a term usually used by value investors to denote a value stock.

BASKET: oftentimes used in reference to an ETF or similar strategy, where a group of stocks cover a specific theme (e.g., Eurozone net-exporters).

BEAR MARKET: a prolonged declining market.

BEHAVIOURAL FINANCE: the study of how human behaviour affects our thoughts, decisions, and, effectively, our performance in the markets.

BENCHMARK: a standard to which an investor compares his/her investment results. Usually a benchmark will be an index (e.g., the S&P TSX).

BENEFICIARIES: the countries, industries, or companies that will benefit from a certain economic climate (e.g., a lower Canadian dollar benefits Canada manufacturing).

BETA: measures volatility and correlation of a stock, in comparison to the stock market.

BLACK SWAN: an occurrence that is extremely hard to predict. Term coined by Nassim Taleb.

BLOCK: a large one-time transaction of stock, usually 10,000 shares or greater. Very large block trades indicate that an investor or institution is accumulating a stake in a company.

BLUE-CHIP STOCKS: stocks that contain certain characteristics that denote stability: large size, long history, reliable products or services, dividend increases, solid reputation or brand perception, and so on. Blue-chip stocks can be concentrated in banks, utilities, and telecom. An example would be Bell Canada.

BOARD OF DIRECTORS: a group of directors elected by the shareholders of a company.

BOND: a debt instrument with the promise to pay interest and to return the principal amount on a specified maturity date.

BOOK VALUE: the fundamental value of a company, as it appears on its balance sheet. Calculated by subtracting total liabilities from total assets.

BOOM: a huge, and usually irrational, run-up in the stock market (e.g., the nineties tech boom).

BOTTOM: the point at which a stock or the stock market has reached a low, but then turns back up.

BOTTOM-UP: a style of investing where an investor starts his or her selection process by analyzing individual companies, e.g., by their financial statements. The opposite would be a top-down style.

BOUGHT DEAL: financing in which investment bank(s) commit to buy a new equity offering from the company, at a designated price, on a set date.

BREADTH: volume in the market.

BREADTH EXPANSION: when there are more buyers of stocks than sellers, or when there is an increase in volume activity in the market that influences stock prices (e.g., greater demand).

BROKER OR BROKERAGE: an agent who handles the public's orders to buy and sell securities, commodities, or other property. A commission is generally charged for this service.

BUBBLE: an unsustainable event that usually occurs at the end of a "boom," marked by an equally huge, but opposite, move (a decline or "bubble burst") in the stock market that can wipe out previous gains (for example the 2000 tech bust).

BULL MARKET: a prolonged inclining market.

BUSINESS MOAT: the illustration of competitive advantage, which is usually created by strong brands, unique assets, long-term contracts, market position, or some combination of all of these factors.

BUY AND HOLD: a discipline in the market whereby an investor holds on to stocks, usually all of the stocks in his/her portfolio, regardless of the ups and downs in the market.

BUY-BACK: when a company buys its own shares to then terminate/cancel them. This action reduces the number of common shares outstanding.

C

CALLS: when an investor makes a prediction and then makes money on that prediction in the market (e.g., an investor predicts the Fed will increase rates, so he shorts bonds and then profits).

CALL OPTION: a contract that gives you the right, but not the obligation, to buy a stock at a specified price within a certain time frame.

CAPITAL: the capital in a business (financial assets, property, machinery, etc.) or the investible cash an investor has to make investments in the market.

CAPITAL ALLOCATION: when management makes investments in a company to improve operations, revenues, and expand product lines, or to make new acquisitions. Successful capital allocation requires an ample return on that investment (return on invested capital).

CAPITAL EXPENDITURE (CAPEX): improvements, projects, or new investments undertaken by management.

CAPITAL GAIN: the profit that investors realize when they sell a stock that is higher than its purchase price. Subject to taxation.

CAPITAL LOSS: the loss that investors realize when they sell a stock that is lower than its purchase price.

CAPITULATION: the point at which investors "give up" in the market. Usually this occurs at the tail end of a huge market decline or bear market. The investor erroneously sells low.

CASH: cash on hand in a company or cash that an investor has to make investments.

CASH FLOW: the amount of cash generated by a company's business operations.

CASH FLOW STATEMENT: a component of the financial statement that shows a company's cash flows from operating, investing, and financing activities.

CATALYST: an event that positively affects a value stock and sends the stock price higher (for example when a company finally reverses a decline in revenue or a management change).

CFA: Chartered Financial Analyst (an official accreditation).

CHARTIST: an investor who engages in "charting," primarily using stock charts and technical indicators to inform his or her decisions on stocks (e.g., choosing to invest in stocks with positive trend lines).

COMMODITIES: companies that sell commodities (e.g., Teck Resources) or the commodity itself (e.g., copper).

COMMON SHARE: a share that represents an actual stake in a company and that can be purchased at any point in time during market hours at the current bid/ask price on the exchange.

COMPETITIVE ADVANTAGE: a market advantage. Usually refers to companies that have such a powerful brand that customers buy their product on brand alone (e.g., Disney). Can also include companies that enjoy, for example, unusual pricing, service, or regulatory advantages.

COMPOUND RETURNS: the process by which money builds on itself over time in an exponential fashion. For example, $100 grows at 10% to $110 in year one. But then in year two, $110 becomes $121 at the same 10% return.

CONCENTRATION: when an investor or portfolio manager allocates a higher-than-usual percentage of capital to particular stocks, asset classes, or investments. Similar to "Conviction."

CONGLOMERATE: a large company that contains an expansive and diverse set of businesses (e.g., Berkshire Hathaway).

CONSERVATIVE INVESTING: an approach in which investors make safe investments in the market.

CONSOLIDATION: companies within a sector (e.g., health care) that merge to create a smaller number of larger companies or volume that builds at or around a particular price point in a stock and determines its technical support.

CONSTITUENTS: the securities, or any other investments, that make up an index (e.g., S&P TSX 60).

CONSUMER PRICE INDEX: a measurement of the change in the cost of living for consumers.

CONTRACTION: see "bear market."

CONTRARIAN: an investor who usually bets against the market or "the herd."

CONVICTION: when an investor has such a firm belief in a particular stock that he or she allocates more money to it than usual in anticipation that its returns will be more than those of other holdings in the portfolio.

CORRECTION: a short-term 10% decline in the markets (not as severe a drop as a bust, bubble, or bear market).

CORRELATION: when two things move in a similar fashion. For example, the price of oil and the Canadian dollar are correlated, such that when the oil price goes up, the Canadian dollar usually also goes up. See also "beta."

COUPON: the interest rate stated on a bond.

CRITERIA: the collective standards that investors apply to their stock selection decisions. For example, a criterion might be an ROA (return on assets ratio) greater or equal to 10%.

CURRENT ASSET: an asset that could be converted into cash within a 12-month period.

CURRENT LIABILITY: a liability that has to be paid within a 12-month period.

CYCLICAL: subject to and highly influenced by uncontrollable economic changes, prices, or other developments. Can apply to companies or sectors. For example, oil producers' profit is determined by the price of oil, which is not within their control. See also "commodities."

D

DARLINGS: stocks that are much loved by "the street" (e.g., Bay Street), either because of their positive price advances, attractive potential, or great management.

DAY-TRADERS: people who make it their daily business to trade stocks.

DEBT: an obligation to repay principal, plus interest, to a lender (for example a bank).

DEEP-VALUE INVESTORS: value investors who invest in extreme situations where companies have reached their nadir due to huge sell-offs that often occur because of deterioration in the actual business.

DEFAULT: when a company or person fails to or chooses not to repay their debt obligations and are unable to repay their debt obligations in the future.

DE-LEVERAGE: when a company or person starts to pay down their debt in a motivated fashion.

DEPRECIATION: stock price decreases or asset value decreases.

DERIVATIVE: a security with a price that is dependent upon or derived from one or more underlying assets.

DETERIORATION: a decline in a company's fundamental business, rather than a decline in its stock price, although both often occur together.

DE-VALUATION: when investors reassess a stock or asset, deem it less valuable, and then sell off.

DILUTION: when management issues large equity offerings, increases the amount of shares outstanding, and effectively diminishes the existing shareholders' share values.

DISCOUNT BROKERAGE: a firm that facilitates the purchase and sale of securities.

DISINFLATION: a slower rate of price inflation.

DIVERSIFICATION: the allocation of money into unique investments with the intent to reduce risk in your portfolio (e.g., to invest in stocks and bonds so that you are protected if bonds go down but stocks go up).

DIVIDEND: money distribution paid to company shareholders usually on a quarterly basis (every three months).

DIVIDEND DISCOUNT MODEL: the calculation by which investors determine the price of a stock by discounting dividends back to present value.

DIVIDEND TAX CREDIT: an income tax credit available to Canadian investors who earn dividend income.

DOLLAR-COST AVERAGING: when investors continue to put money into a stock while its price on the market declines, either to reduce the average purchase price (and limit their loss), and/or to buy more when it's cheaper, signifying a value stock opportunity.

DOWNGRADE: when a professional analyst negatively alters his recommendation on a stock (e.g., from "buy" to "hold").

DOWNSIDE: the amount of risk, and possible weakness, inherent in an investment.

DRAWDOWN: a loss incurred by an investment between its high and low over a given period of time. See also "bear market."

DURATION: a measure of the sensitivity of a fixed-income investment to a change in interest rates.

E

EARNINGS: the profit, after all costs are subtracted, that a company generates from its operations.

EARNINGS PER SHARE (EPS): net income divided by the amount of shares outstanding on a company's balance sheet.

EFFICIENT MARKET THEORY (EMT): the belief that markets constantly incorporate all available information into the prices in the market, and that the markets are therefore efficient.

EMERGING MARKETS: less developed markets in non-G7 countries (e.g., Pakistan) that may or may not have the same standards of regulatory control.

EQUITY: the net worth of a company. See also "book value."

EVENT-DRIVEN INVESTMENT: an investment prompted or triggered by unique situations that occur within a certain time frame (e.g., risk arbitrage).

EUPHORIA: when investors become emotionally driven and drive prices higher in the market.

EXCHANGE-TRADED FUND (ETF): an investment fund that holds a basket of stocks, bonds, or other securities. ETFs trade on the stock market.

F

FED: the U.S. Federal Reserve, the American central bank that sets monetary and fiscal policy (such as overnight rates and money supply) and moves to control factors such as inflation. Similar to the Central Bank of Canada.

FIXED INCOME: investments such as bonds and GICs that pay a fixed rate of interest to investors.

FINANCIAL RATIOS: calculations that investors make to delve deeper into company fundamentals (e.g., ROE ratio = Net Income / Shareholders' Equity).

FLOAT: the total number of shares in a company available for trading in the market.

FORECAST: a prediction of the future. For example, a prediction of a company's revenue in the next year.

FOREIGN EXCHANGE (FX) TRADING: trading in and out of currencies, which are traded on the FX market.

FORWARD P/E: measures the price that investors will pay today for a company's future earnings per share. Current stock price divided by future earnings per share projection.

FREE CASH FLOW: the money left over in a company on a regular reporting basis (quarterly, semi-annually, and annually), calculated by subtracting capital expenditures from operating cash flow.

FRONT-RUN: when a broker places a trade based on privileged information before a large client places a trade, in order to profit at the outset.

FUNDAMENTALS: figures such as assets, cash flow, and net income, usually derived from a company's financial statement and used by investors to determine the worth of a company.

FUNDAMENTAL ANALYSIS: the analysis done by investors based on figures usually derived from a company's financial statement (e.g., assets, cash flow, net income, etc.) to determine the worth of a company.

G

GROWTH: stocks that have higher-than-average return potential or positive financial changes to a company (e.g., revenue growth).

GROWTH INVESTOR: someone who invests in growth stocks.

GUIDANCE: projections offered by management on key business metrics or financial figures in the future.

H

HEDGE: to offset risk in one investment by investing in another (e.g., one can hedge a decline in the U.S. dollar currency with an investment in gold, since it is seen as a store of value).

HEDGE FUND: a fund that is not limited by the same restrictions placed on mutual funds. Usually employs a wide range of investing strategies (e.g., long/short, risk arbitrage, etc.).

HOLDINGS: the investments that make up a portfolio.

I

ILLIQUID: when a security or other asset cannot easily be sold or exchanged for cash on the market.

INCEPTION: the start date of an investment or fund. Performance reports usually post returns since inception to show results over a long period of time.

INCOME STATEMENT: a component of the financial statement that shows a company's financials over a period of time (e.g., Q2 F2014–Q2 F2015). Contains revenue, net income, earnings per share, etc.

INCOME TRUST: Canadian companies that paid out earnings to unit holders before taxes. Up until 2006, when the taxation structure changed for income trusts, investors could buy income trusts on a securities exchange and benefit from high yields.

INDEX: a particular set of stocks that are chosen to represent a particular market or a portion of it. The Dow Jones Industrial Average is an example.

An index is usually used as a benchmark to measure one's performance.

INDEX FUND: a mutual fund or ETF that strives to match the movements and returns of an index.

INDICATOR: macro-economic or technical company measurements that help inform investment decisions.

INEFFICIENT: not incorporating all available information into the prices in the market. "Inefficient" is a term generally used by investors who do not believe in the Efficient Market Theory (EMT). For example, one may feel a decline in the price of a stock was unwarranted given the available information at the time.

INFLATION: increase in the general price of goods and services in an economy. See also "consumer price index."

INFLECTION: the turning point in a company or stock price, either up or down, for better or worse.

INITIAL PUBLIC OFFERING (IPO): the first sale of a company's shares to the market.

INSIDER: management and/or senior officers in a company.

INSTITUTIONAL INVESTOR: institutions including pension funds, insurance companies, universities, and banks, among others, which pool money to purchase securities, property, and other investment assets.

INTANGIBLES: non-physical assets, such as brand, that cannot be easily or accurately quantified by accountants and can be subject to depreciation-based changes in perception alone in some cases, or write-downs on erroneous acquisitions (i.e., "Goodwill") from the past that did not realize an ample return.

INTEREST: payments made by a borrower to a lender.

INTEREST RATES: the overnight rate, which is determined and controlled by a central bank. Overnight rates influence the prime rates at banks, which are applied to any loans or lines of credit.

INTRINSIC VALUE: the actual worth of a business, which may or may not be different than its book value or market capitalization. Can be a highly subjective figure.

INVESTMENT: money that is invested into an asset to generate a return.

INVESTMENT COUNSEL: a firm or individual who gives investment advice on a fee schedule.

IRRATIONALITY: a general enthusiasm for a limited period in the markets that inflates asset prices to a level not supported by fundamentals. See also "euphoria."

L

LARGE-CAP STOCK: a public company that usually has a market capitalization over $10 billion.

LEADERS: those stocks that are in the top quartile of their market, industry, or peer group whether in reality or only in investors' perceptions.

LEVERAGE: when an investor uses margin (i.e., loan) to increase his/her bet on an investment, in order to amplify returns. Can also refer to companies that use considerable debt for expansion, acquisition, or any other form of investment.

LIABILITIES: what a firm or individual owes.

LIQUIDATION: when a company uses the proceeds from a sale of assets to pay any outstanding debt, or as part of the bankruptcy process.

LIQUIDITY: how easily an investment can be converted to cash, at or around market prices.

LONG: when an investor buys a stock in the anticipation that its value will rise.

LONG-TERM: a holding period for a stock usually greater than one year. See also "buy and hold."

LONG-TERM DEBT: debt that comes due after more than one year.

M

MANAGEMENT: the salaried team of individuals who manage a company. May or may not be the founders or family owners, and may or may not own a stake in the company.

MANAGEMENT EXPENSE RATIO: the rate an investor in a mutual fund will pay in fees to the mutual fund company.

MARGIN ACCOUNT: an investment account that allows investors to buy stocks on loan, with the obligation to pay back, or with the possibility to receive a "margin call" to cover lost credit if the investments decline past a point determined by the brokerage.

MARGIN OF SAFETY: the difference between a stock's market price and its intrinsic value.

MARKET: the place, whether physical or virtual, in which securities are bought and sold by a collection of market participants, which can include professionals and non-professionals.

MARKET CAPITALIZATION: companies can be categorized into various market cap tiers (small, mid, large, and mega) based on their size on the market. To calculate market capitalization, multiply the stock price by the number of outstanding shares.

MARKET ORDER: an order submitted to an exchange to buy or sell a stock at any given time.

MARKET PRICE: the price at which a stock, bond, or any other asset is currently trading on the exchange.

MARKET TIMING: when investors frequently buy or sell investments based on events that occur within a short period or at a specific time (e.g., a stock price crosses over the 200-day moving average).

MATURITY: the date at which a bond duration ends.

MEAN REVERSION: when market asset prices, which fluctuate around an intrinsic value or price, come back to that intrinsic value.

MEGA-CAP STOCK: a public company that usually has a market capitalization over $150 billion.

MERGER: when two companies agree to form one entity or corporation.

METRIC: a figure or standard that investors use as a basis for a decision. Similar to "indicator."

MID-CAP STOCK: a public company that usually has a market capitalization of between $2 billion and $10 billion.

MISPRICING: when investors, usually value investors, deem that a stock is being priced inaccurately on the market based on its underlying business fundamentals, or because of sentiment, or unusual events.

MODERN PORTFOLIO THEORY (MPT): a systematic approach to portfolio diversification based on asset class allocation (e.g., bonds, stocks, etc.), that seeks to maximize return for a given amount of risk in one's portfolio.

MOMENTUM: price movements, either upward or downward, that continue, establishing a trend.

MOVING AVERAGE: a trend line that is based on the average of past prices, notably 50-day and 200-day averages, that some investors use to compare to current market prices.

MULTIPLE: a metric that is used to estimate the value of a stock. See also "financial ratios."

MULTIPLE EXPANSION: when prices of assets expand at a multiple of x, which may or may not be aligned to its internal rate of return or its earnings growth. Markets determine multiple (or price) expansion.

MUTUAL FUND: a pool of money from a group of investors that is managed by a mutual fund manager. The manager makes investments in a mutual fund to grow that initial and subsequent capital.

N

NET ASSET VALUE: mutual fund holdings, less the fund's liabilities.

NON-CYCLICAL: not subject to or highly influenced by uncontrollable economic changes, prices, or other developments. Can apply to companies or sectors. Opposite of "cyclical."

NON-REGISTERED ACCOUNT: an investment account in which taxes are applied to capital gains and dividends.

O

ON-BALANCE VOLUME (OBV): an indicator that measures volume flow to predict stock price changes, developed by Joseph Granville. Similar to "accumulation distribution."

OPPORTUNISTIC INVESTORS: investors who scan the market in search of opportunities that they can capitalize on. For example, an opportunist would be able to buy assets at cheaper prices after a 10% correction.

OPTION: the right or obligation to buy or sell a security at a specific price, at a specific quantity, within a set period of time.

OPTIONALITY: asset returns that are not currently priced (or appreciated) in the market but that can occur in the future, if one or some factors (options) play out.

OUT OF FAVOUR: assets that have lost support or are currently experiencing lack of support from the investment community. This usually happens after a bear market (e.g., commodities are out of favour in 2015).

OUTPERFORMANCE: when stocks or funds outperform their own historical returns, index benchmarks, or any competitors in the same space.

OVERBOUGHT: having a price that has been pushed unjustifiably high by demand, some assets may become overbought and then be driven to unsustainably high price levels, after which they may come down to more historically sustainable levels.

OVERPRICED: assets that are priced significantly over their fair value or intrinsic value.

OVERSOLD: having a price that has been pushed unjustifiably low, some assets may become oversold and then be driven to unsustainably low price levels, after which they may rise back up to more historically sustainable levels.

OVERWEIGHTING: the decision to hold a higher-than-average portion of a portfolio in one sector or stock you believe will outperform. Similar to "concentration" and "conviction."

OVERVALUED: assets that are priced considerably over their fair value or intrinsic value.

OWNERSHIP: any sizeable owners in a public company (e.g., an investor with 11% stake).

P

PAIR TRADING: when investors take both a long position and a short position in a pair of highly correlated assets that are usually in the same peer or industry group.

PASSIVE INVESTING: an investment approach that usually equates to less portfolio turnover. Opposite of "active investing."

PAYOUT RATIO: the percentage of earnings that a company pays to shareholders in the form of dividends.

PERFORMANCE: the key determinant of the success of an investor or fund is its returns, either relative or absolute, in the markets, usually over one-year, three-year, five-year, ten-year, and since-inception periods.

PHILOSOPHY: an investor's overarching frame of thought or framework of ideas on which he/she bases his/her decisions on the market. Strategies, styles, and processes stem from a philosophy.

PICKING: generally, investors who believe that the market is not entirely efficient will pick individual securities in the market in the pursuit of generating greater gains than an index, ETF, or mutual fund.

POINT-AND-FIGURE CHART: a chart composed of significant and non-significant price movements.

PORTER FIVE FORCES: a framework containing five "micro environment forces" developed by Michael E. Porter to analyze the level of competition that a company faces within an industry. Those forces — threat of new entrants, bargaining power of suppliers, bargaining power of buyers, threat of substitutes, and industry rivalry — can affect a company's ability to earn a profit.

PORTFOLIO: a collection of assets in which investors or portfolio managers have invested.

PORTFOLIO MANAGER: a finance professional, who usually holds a CFA, who manages the investments in a portfolio.

POSITION: the type of investment that an investor makes in the market, which is usually either a long position (anticipating a price increase) or a short position (anticipating a price decrease).

P/E: price to earnings ratio. Measures the price that investors will pay for a company's earnings per share. Current stock price divided by its current earnings per share.

PROBABILITY: the likelihood that an investment will perform or not perform based on an investor's initial thesis. Probability can be applied at the market, portfolio, and stock level.

PROFIT: see "earnings."

PROCESS: the set of customized ascending or descending steps that most investors follow to select investments for their portfolio.

PUT OPTION: a contract that gives you the right, but not the obligation, to sell a stock at a specified price within a certain time frame.

Q

QUALITATIVE: measuring variables such as brand, products, services, and management to assess a business before an investment is made.

QUANTITATIVE: measuring variables such as financial ratios and technical indicators to assess a business before an investment is made.

QUANTITATIVE EASING (QE): when a central bank (e.g., U.S. Federal Reserve) creates new money to buy financial assets, most commonly bonds, in order to both influence higher private sector spending and to meet the designated inflation target during recessions or downturns in the economy

QUANTITATIVE OR RULES-DRIVEN: employing algorithms to capture gains in the market, as in quant-based trading or investing strategies.

QUOTE: the prevailing price of a share of a security, on the market.

R

RALLY: a rise in particular stocks and/or the market in a short period of time that may be the result of positive developments (e.g., a great earnings release), or coming off its lows after a decline.

RATE: the overnight rate, which is determined and controlled by a central bank. Overnight rates influence the prime rates at banks, which are applied to any loans or lines of credit.

REAL ESTATE INVESTMENT TRUST (REIT): an investable fund that contains real estate or mortgage investments. The Canadian government's taxation changes (2006) did not affect this form of income trust.

REAL RETURN: the return on an investment after one applies the rate of inflation. Calculated by subtracting inflation from the return on a stock. The real return if inflation is 2% and the return on a stock is 10% is 8%.

RECESSION: a significant decline in the economic activity of a country, region, or the world (global recession). Marked by two consecutive quarters (six months running total) of a decline in GDP.

REGISTERED ACCOUNT: any investment account that offers shelter from taxation on capital gains and/or dividend income. Examples include the RRSP and TFSA.

RELATIVE PERFORMANCE: performance compared to a benchmark. This is usually how professional money managers are evaluated. For example, a money manager's – 10% performance can be perceived well if his/her benchmark posted – 15% in the same year.

RELATIVE STRENGTH: the comparison of the performance of a stock, or any other investment, to the performance of its industry, peer group, or market to gauge its comparable strength. For example, Bank A's 15% gain might seem good until one compares it to the banking industry's overall 20% gain.

RESISTANCE: an overhead price level in a stock chart that makes it difficult for a stock price to break through to make new highs or re-price itself to previous highs.

RESOURCES: see "commodities."

RETAINED EARNINGS: a company's accumulated profits.

RETURN ON ASSETS (ROA): a measure that shows a company's ability to generate profits from their assets.

RETURN ON EQUITY (ROE): a measure that shows a company's ability to generate profits from their shareholders' equity (not including long-term debt).

RETURN ON INVESTED CAPITAL (ROIC): a measure of a company's ability to invest and use its money to generate incremental returns for its shareholders (including long-term debt).

RETURNS: the capital gains and/or dividends from stocks as well as the proceeds from any other investments.

RISK: the inherent possibility of downside or loss.

RISK ARBITRAGE (MERGER AND ACQUISITION): when an investor purchases stock in a company that is to be acquired in anticipation of a gain from the spread in the current market price and final purchase price once the deal finally closes.

RISK-FREE RATE: the return from a relatively conservative investment, such as a GIC.

RISK MANAGEMENT: when an investor implements controls in his or her trading or investing practice that protect the downside in order to preserve capital.

RISK PREMIUM: the return over and above the "risk-free rate," which an investor can achieve in the equity market.

RISK/REWARD RATIO: the inherent opportunity cost investors must be aware of in the markets. Generally, the greater the risk, the greater the reward and the lesser the risk, the lesser the reward.

ROLL-UP: a highly acquisitive company that acquires companies, integrates them into their parent company, and then makes them accretive, often within a very short period of time, to the bottom line. Can also be referred to as a platform company.

RULES-DRIVEN: quant-based trading or investing strategies that employ algorithms to capture gains in the market. See also "algorithm."

S

SCREENS: a piece of software, database, or service that investors can use in their security selection process to filter stocks based on their input criteria.

SCUTTLEBUTT: the practice by which investors ask questions of company directors or any other sources to build their knowledge in that company. The term was popularized by Philip Fisher.

SECTOR: an area of the stock market, such as technology, telecom, or consumer staples.

SECURITY: a financial instrument such as a stock, bond, or option.

SELF-FULFILLING: describes the phenomenon in which one's actions directly determine a given response in the market. For example, this may be true of a large investor who invests in small-cap illiquid stocks. His buying activity may push those stocks higher.

SENTIMENT: the common feeling or emotion that participants in the market share.

SHARES: see "common share."

SHAREHOLDER: a minority owner. An investor becomes a shareholder when he/she buys shares in any publicly traded company on the exchange.

SHAREHOLDERS' EQUITY: the assets that are attributed to a company's shareholders.

SHORTING OR SHORT-SELLING: a practice whereby some investors borrow a stock and sell it, with the anticipation that they can later buy it back at a lower price.

SHORT TERM: a holding period for a stock usually less than one year.

SMALL-CAP STOCK: a public company that usually has a market capitalization of between $50 million and $2 billion.

SPECULATION: an investment that has significant risk but also very large return potential.

SPINOFF: a divesture of a parent company's division or subsidiary to existing shareholders in the form of a new publicly traded company. For example, eBay's spinoff of PayPal in 2015.

STOCK: an actual stake in a company. Can be purchased at any point in time during market hours on an exchange at the current bid/ask price.

STOCK EXCHANGE: see "market."

STOP-LOSS ORDER: an automated order to sell a stock at a designated price below the purchase price. Used to limit downside risk should a stock decline in price.

STRIKE PRICE: the price at which an option holder can buy or sell a stock.

STYLES: various approaches to investing in the markets. These include value investing, growth investing, bottom-up investing, top-down investing, technical investing, and so on.

SUPPORT: a lower price level in a stock chart that makes it difficult for a stock price to break under to re-price itself to previous lows.

SYSTEMATIC: see "rules-driven."

T

TAKEOVER: see "acquisition."

TARGET: a company that is likely to be acquired by another company, usually larger than itself.

TECHNICAL ANALYSIS: see "chartist."

TICKER SYMBOL: a letter symbol that identifies a company on a stock exchange (e.g., Amazon = AMZN).

TOP-DOWN: a style of investing where an investor starts his or her selection process by analyzing markets, sectors, and industries, before (if at all) moving on to individual companies. The opposite would be "bottom-up."

TRADE: a securities transaction.

TREND LINE: a line drawn on a chart to show the general price direction.

TSX: the Toronto Stock Exchange.

TSX 60: a stock index that contains 60 large publicly traded Canadian companies from the S&P TSX index. This index is the primary source for the BTSX model.

TURNAROUND: the outcome in which a fledgling company improves itself to regain and sometimes even surpass its previous success. An example of a turnaround would be Apple in the late nineties to the early 2000s.

U

UNDERPERFORMANCE: when stocks or funds underperform their own historical returns, index benchmarks, or any competitors in the same space.

UNDERVALUED: how investors, usually value investors, refer to stocks that they perceive as trading below their intrinsic value on the market.

UPGRADE: when a professional analyst positively alters his or her recommendation on a stock (e.g., from "hold" to "buy").

V

VALUATION: the worth of a company or asset.

VALUE INVESTOR: an investor who buys "undervalued" stocks.

VALUE STOCKS: see "undervalued."

VALUE TRAP: a value stock that continues to get cheaper and fails to rebound. It lacks a catalyst.

VIX: ticker symbol for the CBOE Volatility Index, which is the measure of the volatility of SAP 500 index options. Can also be referred to as the "fear index."

VOLATILITY: the degree of variation in asset prices over a period of time.

VOLUME: the number of shares traded in a market in any given stock.

W

WATCH LIST: a list of stocks that an investor creates to monitor, and possibly invest in, in the future.

WEIGHTING: the percentage of capital that you allocate to each of your investments (stocks, bonds, etc.).

Y

YIELD: the income derived from either the coupon on a bond or the dividend on a stock.

YIELD CURVE: a representation of the relationship among yields of similar bonds of differing maturities.

INDEX

Page references that appear in italics indicate an entry that is defined in the glossary or in a pre-interview lesson. The use of t following a page number refers to a table.

▲

DISCLAIMER

▼

Robin Speziale is not a registered investment advisor, broker, or dealer. Readers are advised that the material contained herein should be used solely for informational purposes. This information is not investment advice or a recommendation or solicitation to buy or sell any securities. Robin Speziale does not propose to tell or suggest which investment securities readers should buy or sell. Readers should conduct their own research and due diligence and obtain professional advice before making investment decisions. Robin Speziale, anyone associated with Robin Speziale, or anyone interviewed in *Market Masters*, will not be liable for any loss or damage caused by information obtained in *Market Masters*. Readers are solely responsible for their own investment decisions. Investing involves risk, including loss of principal.

▲

NEXT MARKET MASTERS

▼

ARE YOU CANADA'S NEXT MARKET MASTER?

If you feel that you are the next Market Master in Canada, go to NextMarketMasters.com and submit your profile. All profiles will be displayed on NextMarketMasters.com for all to see. Additionally, a select group of the original Market Masters will form a judging panel to select the top 30 Next Market Masters, who will be featured in Robin Speziale's future book, *Next Market Masters*. Who knows . . . it could be you.

Submit your profile now — NextMarketMasters.com

CRITERIA:
- Do-it-yourself investor
- 18 years or older
- Resident of Canada
- Invest primarily in equities on the Toronto Stock Exchange (TSX)
- You have beaten the market, developed a system/strategy, or have a compelling story

At ECW Press, we want you to enjoy this book in whatever format you like, whenever you like. Leave your print book at home and take the eBook to go! Purchase the print edition and receive the eBook free. Just send an email to ebook@ecwpress.com and include:

- the book title
- the name of the store where you purchased it
- your receipt number
- your preference of file type: PDF or ePub?

A real person will respond to your email with your eBook attached. And thanks for supporting an independently owned Canadian publisher with your purchase!